Introduction to Teaching

Becoming a Professional

Second Edition

Donald Kauchak
University of Utah

Paul Eggen
University of North Florida

Upper Saddle River, New Jersey
Columbus, Ohio

Library of Congress Cataloging-in-Publication Data

Kauchak, Donald P.
Introduction to teaching : becoming a professional/Donald Kauchak, Paul Eggen.—
2nd ed.
p. cm.
ISBN 0-13-113771-9 (alk. paper)
1. Teachers. 2. Teaching—Vocational guidance. I. Eggen, Paul D. II.
Title.
LB1775.K37 2005
371.1'0023'73—dc22 200400985

Vice President and Executive Publisher: Jeffery W. Johnston
Executive Editor: Debra A. Stollenwerk
Development Editor: Kimberly J. Lundy
Editorial Assistant: Mary Morrill
Production Editor: Kris Roach
Production Coordination: Carlisle Publishers Services
Design Coordinator: Diane C. Lorenzo
Text Designer: Kristina D. Holmes
Cover Designer: Ali Mohrman
Cover Image: Superstock
Photo Coordinator: Valerie Schultz
Production Manager: Pamela D. Bennett
Director of Marketing: Ann Castel Davis
Marketing Manager: Darcy Betts Prybella
Marketing Coordinator: Tyra Poole

This book was set in Galliard by Carlisle Communications, Ltd. It was printed and bound by Courier Kendallville, Inc. The cover was printed by Phoenix Color Corp.

Photo Credits: Bruce Ayres/Getty Images Inc.—Stone Allstock, p. 480; Robert Brenner/PhotoEdit, p. 211; Michelle Bridwell/PhotoEdit, p. 360; Cleo Photography/PhotoEdit, p. 377; Gary Conner/PhotoEdit, p. 1; Corbis/Stock Market, p. 206 (left); Scott Cunningham/Merrill, pp. 21, 61, 106, 108, 115, 188, 213, 246, 248, 302, 371, 404, 418; Bob Daemmrich/Bob Daemmrich Photography, Inc., pp. 262, 278; Bob Daemmrich/The Image Works, pp. 24, 89, 451; Bob Daemmrich/Stock Boston, p. 93; John Dakers/Getty Images, Inc.—Photodisc, p. 206 (right); Mary Kate Denny/PhotoEdit, pp. 86, 310, 393; Amy Etra/PhotoEdit, p. 137; EyeWire Collection/Getty Images—Photodisc, p. 2; Tony Freeman/PhotoEdit, pp. 132, 416; Geostock/Getty Images, Inc.—Photodisc, p. 131; Getty Images, Inc.—Photodisc, p. 257 (top); Jeff Greenberg/The Image Works, p. 505; Jeff Greenberg/PhotoEdit, pp. 168, 191, 462; Charles Gupton/Corbis/Stock Market, p. 459; Will Hart/PhotoEdit, pp. 57, 151, 240, 333, 412, 474, 487; Richard Hutchings/PhotoEdit, p. 241; Richard Hutchings/Photo Researchers, Inc., p. 81; InFocus, Inc., p. 437; Zigy Kaluzny/Getty Images Inc.—Stone Allstock, p. 73; Bonnie Kamin/PhotoEdit, p. 146; Kathy Kirtland/Merrill, p. 498; Emma Lee/Getty Images, Inc.—Photodisc, p. 146; courtesy of the Library of Congress, pp. 160, 164, 172, 183; Anthony Magnacca/Merrill, pp. 16, 20, 22, 31, 42, 52, 58, 82, 202, 221, 223, 228, 282, 289, 290, 321, 322, 348, 357, 388, 396, 441, 473, 492, 499; Lawrence Migdale/Getty Images Inc.—Stone Allstock, p. 159; Modern Curriculum Press/Pearson Learning, p. 449; Michael Newman/PhotoEdit, pp. 10, 126, 149, 257 (bottom), 292, 314, 325, 347, 355, 427, 477, 494; PH School, p. 285; A. Ramey/PhotoEdit, p. 460; Mark Richards/PhotoEdit, pp. 101, 272, 369; Robin Sachs/PhotoEdit, p. 70; Schnepf/Getty Images, Inc.—Liaison, p. 375; Blair Seitz/Photo Researchers, p. 446; courtesy SYATP, p. 329; Don Tremain/Getty Images, Inc.—Photodisc, p. 142; Tom Watson/Merrill, pp. 6, 55, 255, 364; Ulrike Welsch/PhotoEdit, p. 236; Dana White/PhotoEdit, p. 176; Todd Yarrington/Merrill, pp. 7, 99, 484; Yellow Dog Productions/Getty Images Inc.—Image Bank, p. 33; David Young-Wolff/Getty Images Inc.—Stone Allstock, p. 140; David Young-Wolff/PhotoEdit, pp. 64, 219, 334, 422, 434.

Pearson Education Ltd.
Pearson Education Singapore Pte. Ltd
Pearson Education Canada, Ltd.
Pearson Education—Japan
Pearson Education Australia Pty. Limited
Pearson Education North Asia Ltd.
Pearson Educación de Mexico, S.A. de C.V.
Pearson Education Malaysia Pte. Ltd.

10 9 8 7 6 5 4 3 2
ISBN: 0-13-113771-9

Keys to Success on the Praxis™

This text is designed to help you succeed on the Praxis Principles of Learning and Teaching (PLT) exam. As of January 2003, thirty-five states use Praxis exams as part of their teacher licensing requirement. Among the Praxis exams are three Principles of Learning and Teaching (PLT) tests, one each for teachers seeking licensure for grades K–6, 5–9, and 7–12.

Each Principles of Learning and Teaching exam has two parts (Educational Testing Service, 2002). One consists of multiple-choice questions similar to those in the Test Bank and Companion Website interactive Practice Quizzes that accompany this text. The second part is based on cases, which you will be asked to read and analyze, similar to the ones at the beginning of each chapter in this text.

The two types of items in the case-based part of the Praxis Principles of Learning and Teaching exam are constructed-response and document-based questions. In the first type, you read a case study and are then asked to analyze it, responding to short-answer Constructed-Response Questions (Educational Testing Service, 2002). In the Document-Based Questions you evaluate student or teacher-prepared documents, such as student work, excerpts from student records, teachers' lesson plans, assignments, or assessments. We have designed this text to help you succeed on the Praxis Principles of Learning and Teaching exam by including case-based format questions at the end of each chapter and by providing feedback to the end-of-chapter questions on the Companion Website at **www.prenhall.com/kauchak**.

The PLT covers four broad content categories:

- Students as Learners (approximately 22% of total test)
  - Student Development and the Learning Process
  - Students as Diverse Learners
  - Student Motivation and the Learning Environment
- Instruction and Assessment (approximately 33% of total test)
  - Instructional Strategies
  - Planning Instruction
  - Assessment Strategies
- Communication Techniques (approximately 33% of total test)
  - Basic, effective verbal and nonverbal communication techniques
  - Effect of cultural and gender differences on communications in the classroom
  - Types of questions that can stimulate discussion in different ways for particular purposes
- Profession and Community (approximately 11% of total test)
  - The Reflective Practitioner
  - The Larger Community

The matrix on pages v to vi outlines the coverage of these topics in this text.

Preparing for the Exam

Plan ahead and acquaint yourself with the topics in the test. The ETS booklet *Tests at a Glance* (available online at www.ets.org/praxis or free by mail) includes detailed descriptions of topics covered in each of the four content categories. Study this booklet carefully and take the sample tests available on this website and in the print materials. Analyze the different kinds of questions asked and the feedback and criteria provided.

Using This Text to Succeed on the PLT

What strategies should you employ as you use the exercises in this text to prepare for the Praxis? Experts offer the following suggestions (Educational Testing Service, 2002):

- ***Read the test directions carefully.*** Make sure you understand the test formats, what is being asked of you, and the time restrictions for each section.
- ***Answer all parts of the question.*** For instance, if the questions ask you to identify five characteristics of professionalism that were demonstrated in a case, be sure that your response includes all five.
- ***Demonstrate an understanding of the theory or pedagogical concepts related to the question.*** As you analyze the case in writing, be sure to discuss key elements of the relevant concept or theory.
- ***Demonstrate a thorough understanding of the case.*** In your answers, be sure to discuss the case in general, as well as specific details within the case that relate to the question.
- ***Repeat key words from the question.*** This helps to focus your response and communicates to the reader that you are directly responding to essential elements of the question. For example, if asked to list three important elements of student diversity, write, "Three important elements of student diversity are a, b, and c."
- ***Support your answer with details.*** By specifically referring to the case and identifying the concepts that are being demonstrated, you will provide documentation for your answer.
- ***Before you write a response, organize and outline your thoughts so they clearly represent your best thinking.***

After you've written your own answers to the constructed-response and document-based questions that appear at the end of each chapter in this text, you can receive feedback by going to the *Praxis Practice* module for each chapter on the Companion website at www.prenhall.com/kauchak.

For additional help in preparing for the Praxis exams, you might want to purchase a copy of the *Principles of Learning and Teaching Study Guide* published by the Educational Testing Service. To find information for purchasing the study guide, go to the *Praxis Practice* module at www.prenhall.com/kauchak.

References

Educational Testing Service. (2002). *Tests at a glance: Praxis II subject assessments/Principles of Learning and Teaching.* Available online: www.ets.org/praxis/prxtest:html

Rogers, J., & Yang, P. (1996). Test wiseness: Its nature and application. *European Journal of Psychological Assessment, 12,* 247–259.

Correlation Matrix for the Praxis™ Principles of Learning and Teaching Exam

Knowledge Covered in the Praxis Principles of Learning and Teaching Exam	Chapter Topic Aligned with Knowledge Covered in the Praxis Principles of Learning and Teaching Exam	
	I. STUDENTS AS LEARNERS (APPROXIMATELY 22% OF TOTAL TEST)	
A. Student development and the learning process	**Ch. 2**	Creator of productive learning environments
	Ch. 7	Early childhood programs, elementary schools, high schools, junior highs, and middle schools
		What is an effective school?
	Ch. 10	The curriculum and the professional teacher
	Ch. 11	Personal characteristics of teachers
		Teaching strategies
		Cognitive views of learning
B. Students as diverse learners	**Ch. 3**	Cultural diversity
		Gender
		Ability differences
		Learning styles
		Students with exceptionalities
	Ch. 4	Changing student populations
		Students placed at-risk
C. Student motivation and the learning environment	**Ch. 2**	Caring professionals
		Creator of productive learning environments
	Ch. 3	Culturally responsive teaching
		Instructional responses to learning styles
	Ch. 4	Effective teachers for students placed at-risk
	Ch. 11	Personal teaching efficacy
		Caring
		Modeling and enthusiasm
		Teacher expectations
		Classroom organization
		Teacher questioning
		Effective feedback
		Classroom management
	II. INSTRUCTION AND ASSESSMENT (APPROXIMATELY 33% OF TOTAL TEST)	
A. Instructional strategies	**Ch. 3**	Culturally responsive teaching
		Instructional responses to learning styles
	Ch. 4	Effective teachers for students placed at-risk
	Ch. 6	Teacher decision making: Applying the traditional philosophies
	Ch. 11	Teacher questioning
		Effective presentation of subject matter
	Ch. 12	Using technology to support instruction
		Capitalizing on technology to teach problem solving and higher-level thinking skills
		Using the Internet in problem-based learning
B. Planning instruction	**Ch. 1**	Standards-based education
	Ch. 2	Creator of productive learning environments
	Ch. 3	Educational responses to cultural diversity
		Ability grouping and tracking: Schools' responses to differences in ability
		Changes in the way schools and teachers help students with exceptionalities
	Ch. 4	Effective teachers for students placed at-risk
	Ch. 6	Teacher decision making: Applying the traditional philosophies
	Ch. 10	The curriculum and the professional teacher
		State and district standards

Knowledge Covered in the Praxis Principles of Learning and Teaching Exam (*cont.*)	Chapter Topic Aligned with Knowledge Covered in the Praxis Principles of Learning and Teaching Exam (*cont.*)	
	Ch. 11	Goals and teacher thinking
		Instructional alignment and teacher thinking
	Ch. 12	Using technology to support instruction
		Capitalizing on technology to teach problem solving and higher-level thinking skills
	Ch. 13	Domain-specific knowledge in teaching
		Knowledge and decision making
C. Assessment strategies	**Ch. 1**	Standards-based education
	Ch. 2	Creator of productive learning environments
	Ch. 7	Frequent monitoring of student progress
	Ch. 10	State and district standards
	Ch. 11	Effective assessment
	Ch. 12	Classroom assessment
III. Communication Techniques (approximately 33% of total test)		
A. Effective verbal and nonverbal communication	**Ch. 2**	Ambassador to the public
		Collaborative colleague
	Ch. 3	Accommodating different cultural interaction patterns
		Instructional responses to learning styles
	Ch. 4	Effective teachers for students placed at-risk
	Ch. 11	Teacher expectations
		Communication
		Teacher questioning
	Ch. 12	The Internet as a communication tool
B. Cultural and gender differences in communication	**Ch. 3**	Accommodating different cultural interaction patterns
		Instructional responses to learning styles
	Ch. 4	Effective teachers for students placed at-risk
	Ch. 11	Teacher expectations
		Communication
		Teacher questioning
C. Stimulating discussion and responses in the classroom	**Ch. 2**	Creator of productive learning environments
	Ch. 3	Culturally responsive teaching
		Instructional responses to learning styles
	Ch. 4	Effective teachers for students placed at-risk
	Ch. 11	Teacher questioning
		Communication
		Effective feedback
IV. Profession and Community (approximately 11% of total test)		
A. The reflective practitioner	**Ch. 1**	Characteristics of professionalism
	Ch. 2	Learner and reflective practitioner
	Each Chapter	Decision making: Defining yourself as a professional
	Each Chapter	Personal journal reflection
B. The larger community	**Ch. 2**	Ambassador to the public
		Collaborative colleague
	Ch. 4	It takes a village: The community-based approach to working with children placed at-risk
	Ch. 7	Parental involvement
	Ch. 11	Communicating with students
	Ch. 12	Communicating with parents
	Ch. 13	Professional organizations

Preface

Introduction: A Case-Based Approach

Like the first edition, the second edition of this highly applied text introduces beginning education students to teaching and attempts to present an honest look at the real world of students, teachers, classrooms, and schools. The topics included in this book and the ways in which they're presented have been designed to answer the question, "What does this have to do with me and my future life as a teacher?"

To answer this question, we have developed case studies and features that highlight the issues and challenges important in teachers' everyday lives. Each chapter begins with a case study that provides a framework for the discussions that follow and helps readers understand how chapter topics relate to the real world of teaching. Additional cases and vignettes are used to further illustrate the content of the chapter to make it real and concrete. The case margin icon identifies where cases and vignettes are integrated with the topics in each chapter.

Text Themes

The book is organized around three themes—Professionalism, Reform, and Decision Making—which provide the threads that bind together the topics of the chapters.

Professionalism

Professionalism is the theme that ties together topics such as career selection, teacher working conditions, career-long development, teacher evaluation, and relationships with supervisors, peers, students, parents, and the community. The movement toward professionalism provides a tangible goal that can guide beginning teachers as they develop, and it has both short- and long-term potential for improving teaching. Professionalism also provides a framework for examining a number of important issues that developing teachers face, such as standards, accountability and testing, and merit pay. The *Online Portfolio Activities* at the end of each chapter are connected to INTASC standards. The activities are intended to encourage students to evaluate their own professional growth. The first portfolio activity in each chapter uses a *Personal Journal Reflection* to help the reader connect his or her ideas to issues raised in the chapter. The *Reflect on This* feature within each chapter connects the reader to realistic online cases that provide additional opportunities for professional growth through decision making.

Reform

Reform has always been a factor in our educational system. However, at no time in the past has reform had a more profound influence on education. Standards, accountability, and testing—for teachers and students—are being proposed as solutions to both educational and societal problems. No Child Left Behind, a sweeping federal reform initiative, has already changed schools and will continue to shape the profession for new teachers. The *Teaching in an Era of Reform* feature in each chapter frames a specific reform issue as it relates to chapter content and asks students to make a personal evaluation of its potential.

Decision Making

Decision making, which involves goal-oriented problem solving based on professional knowledge, is one of the central characteristics of teacher professionalism. This theme is introduced in Chapter 1 and integrated throughout the book. Each chapter concludes with *Decision Making: Defining Yourself as a Professional*, which asks readers to begin thinking about personal and professional decisions that will influence the kinds of teachers they will become.

New to This Edition

This edition of *Introduction to Teaching: Becoming a Professional* continues to focus on providing students with a realistic view of the teaching profession along with the knowledge and decision-making skills that will help shape them as professionals. To do this, we have updated and expanded coverage of current issues and practices, such as culturally relevant teaching, portfolio building, preparing for the Praxis test, and developing a personal teaching portfolio. These carefully selected additions and updates support the thrust of the second edition—to help students answer the question, "What does this have to do with me and my future life as a teacher?"

The content of this edition places a strong emphasis on professionalism by focusing on:

Professional Decision Making. This theme is introduced in Chapter 1 and reinforced in each chapter.

Reflection. This topic is also introduced in Chapter 1 and expanded upon in every chapter as a critical part of professional development.

Praxis: Comprehensive Teacher Testing. The Praxis guides in this edition are intended to help students be accountable for meeting professional standards.

No Child Left Behind. NCLB is examined in Chapter 1 and connected with other topics throughout the text.

Induction Programs. Characteristics of quality induction programs are analyzed for beginning teachers.

Action Research. This new topic is described and connected to teachers' career-long professional development.

Expanded Coverage of Classroom Management. Beginning teachers' primary challenge is described in terms of the realities of classroom life.

Merit Pay. The pros and cons of this reform effort are analyzed.

Privatization. The privatization movement is described in terms of its potential effects on students.

Expanded Coverage of School Choice. Recent developments in charter schools and vouchers are described and related to teachers and students.

Homeschooling. This growing national movement is analyzed in terms of strengths and potential pitfalls.

New features to this edition include:

Praxis Practice Exercises. Each chapter contains practice exercises with feedback on the text's Companion Website to prepare students for the Praxis Principles of Learning and Teaching exam.

Praxis and INTASC Correlation Guides. These guides connect chapter topics to the Praxis Principles of Learning and Teaching exam and the INTASC standards.

Keys to Success on the Praxis. This new feature provides helpful tips for students on how to succeed on the Praxis Principles of Learning and Teaching exam.

Decision Making: Defining Yourself as a Professional. This end-of-chapter feature emphasizes professional decision making and encourages readers to define themselves as professionals in terms of chapter content.

Classroom Windows DVD. Each text now comes with a DVD containing eight videos of real teachers in real classrooms. These are integrated in Chapters 1, 2, 6, 7, 10, 11, 12, and 13 and are also available on videocassettes for use by instructors in their classrooms.

Personal Reflection Portfolio Activities. These are found in each chapter, encouraging students to personally reflect upon chapter content through portfolio activities.

Features of the Text

The book is interactive, encouraging prospective teachers to make conscious decisions about the kind of teacher they want to become. To create this interactive environment, the text includes Theme Features, Field Experience Features, Video Features, and Pedagogical Features to enhance the content and aid prospective teachers in their journey toward becoming a professional.

Theme Features highlight the three themes around which the book is organized—Professionalism, Reform, and Decision Making—and present the content in an interactive way.

Exploring Diversity examines an issue related to each chapter's content for which the increasing diversity in today's students has important implications.

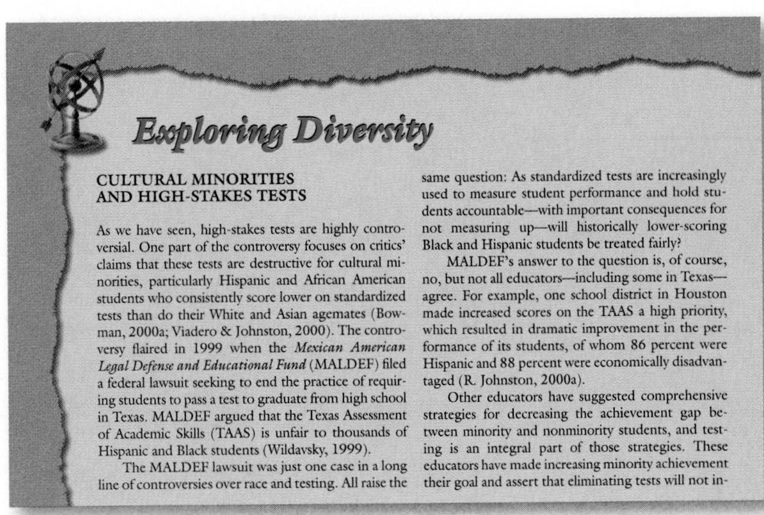

Exploring Diversity

CULTURAL MINORITIES AND HIGH-STAKES TESTS

As we have seen, high-stakes tests are highly controversial. One part of the controversy focuses on critics' claims that these tests are destructive for cultural minorities, particularly Hispanic and African American students who consistently score lower on standardized tests than do their White and Asian agemates (Bowman, 2000a; Viadero & Johnston, 2000). The controversy flaired in 1999 when the *Mexican American Legal Defense and Educational Fund* (MALDEF) filed a federal lawsuit seeking to end the practice of requiring students to pass a test to graduate from high school in Texas. MALDEF argued that the Texas Assessment of Academic Skills (TAAS) is unfair to thousands of Hispanic and Black students (Wildavsky, 1999).

The MALDEF lawsuit was just one case in a long line of controversies over race and testing. All raise the same question: As standardized tests are increasingly used to measure student performance and hold students accountable—with important consequences for not measuring up—will historically lower-scoring Black and Hispanic students be treated fairly?

MALDEF's answer to the question is, of course, no, but not all educators—including some in Texas—agree. For example, one school district in Houston made increased scores on the TAAS a high priority, which resulted in dramatic improvement in the performance of its students, of whom 86 percent were Hispanic and 88 percent were economically disadvantaged (R. Johnston, 2000a).

Other educators have suggested comprehensive strategies for decreasing the achievement gap between minority and nonminority students, and testing is an integral part of those strategies. These educators have made increasing minority achievement their goal and assert that eliminating tests will not in-

Teaching in an Era of Reform provides an in-depth analysis of a reform issue related to each chapter's content. At the end of this section, *You Take a Position* invites the reader to take a personal position with respect to the issue presented in the chapter.

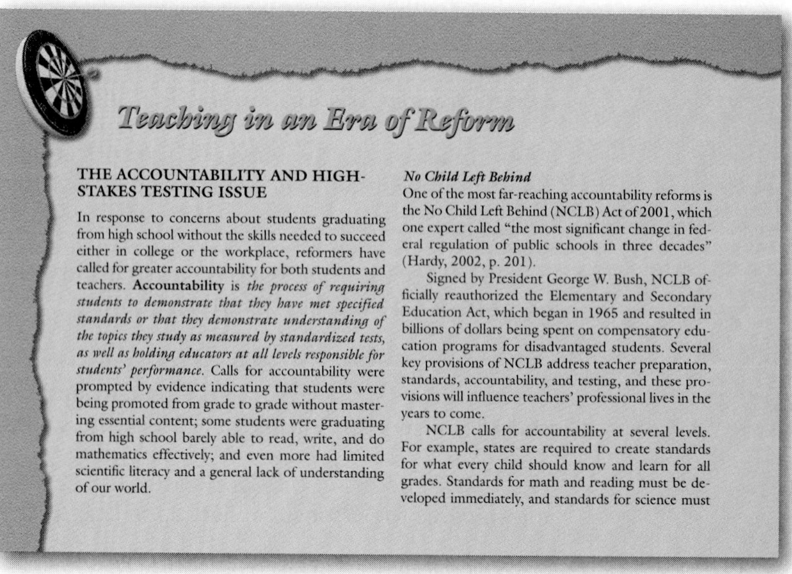
Teaching in an Era of Reform

THE ACCOUNTABILITY AND HIGH-STAKES TESTING ISSUE

In response to concerns about students graduating from high school without the skills needed to succeed either in college or the workplace, reformers have called for greater accountability for both students and teachers. **Accountability** is *the process of requiring students to demonstrate that they have met specified standards or that they demonstrate understanding of the topics they study as measured by standardized tests, as well as holding educators at all levels responsible for students' performance.* Calls for accountability were prompted by evidence indicating that students were being promoted from grade to grade without mastering essential content; some students were graduating from high school barely able to read, write, and do mathematics effectively; and even more had limited scientific literacy and a general lack of understanding of our world.

No Child Left Behind

One of the most far-reaching accountability reforms is the No Child Left Behind (NCLB) Act of 2001, which one expert called "the most significant change in federal regulation of public schools in three decades" (Hardy, 2002, p. 201).

Signed by President George W. Bush, NCLB officially reauthorized the Elementary and Secondary Education Act, which began in 1965 and resulted in billions of dollars being spent on compensatory education programs for disadvantaged students. Several key provisions of NCLB address teacher preparation, standards, accountability, and testing, and these provisions will influence teachers' professional lives in the years to come.

NCLB calls for accountability at several levels. For example, states are required to create standards for what every child should know and learn for all grades. Standards for math and reading must be developed immediately, and standards for science must

Reflect on This is an online activity that promotes professional reflection by presenting students with realistic dilemmas in the form of case studies that ask students to make professional decisions. Students can then compare their responses to feedback on the book's Companion Website.

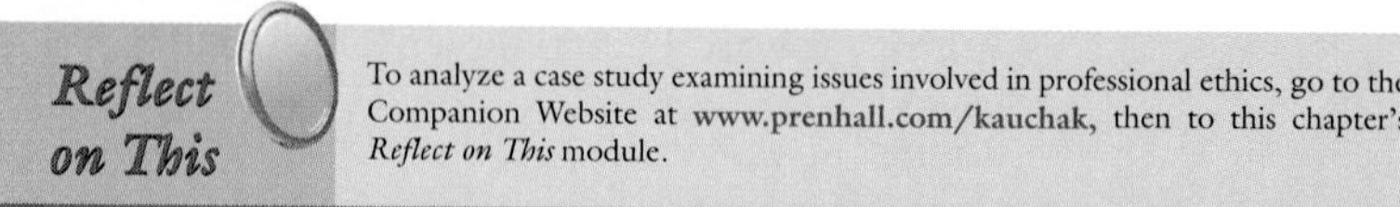
Reflect on This

To analyze a case study examining issues involved in professional ethics, go to the Companion Website at **www.prenhall.com/kauchak**, then to this chapter's *Reflect on This* module.

Decision Making: Defining Yourself as a Professional, a chapter-closing section, integrates chapter topics with implications for contemporary teachers.

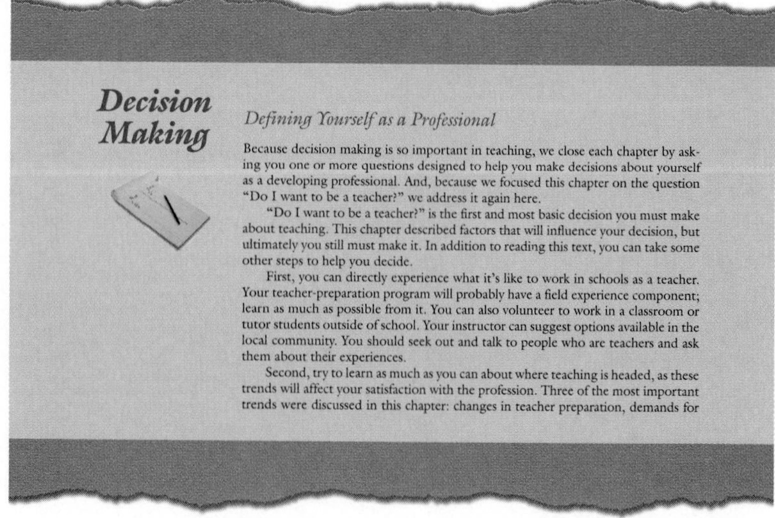
Decision Making

Defining Yourself as a Professional

Because decision making is so important in teaching, we close each chapter by asking you one or more questions designed to help you make decisions about yourself as a developing professional. And, because we focused this chapter on the question "Do I want to be a teacher?" we address it again here.

"Do I want to be a teacher?" is the first and most basic decision you must make about teaching. This chapter described factors that will influence your decision, but ultimately you still must make it. In addition to reading this text, you can take some other steps to help you decide.

First, you can directly experience what it's like to work in schools as a teacher. Your teacher-preparation program will probably have a field experience component; learn as much as possible from it. You can also volunteer to work in a classroom or tutor students outside of school. Your instructor can suggest options available in the local community. You should seek out and talk to people who are teachers and ask them about their experiences.

Second, try to learn as much as you can about where teaching is headed, as these trends will affect your satisfaction with the profession. Three of the most important trends were discussed in this chapter: changes in teacher preparation, demands for

Online Portfolio Activities, linked to INTASC standards, encourage students to begin constructing professional portfolio entries tied to each chapter's content. These involve students in a range of activities, including visiting the Web sites of professional organizations, beginning work on their philosophy of education, as well as connecting with local districts and state offices of education. The first portfolio activity in each chapter involves a *Personal Journal Reflection* that asks students to think about chapter content in terms of their own strengths and goals.

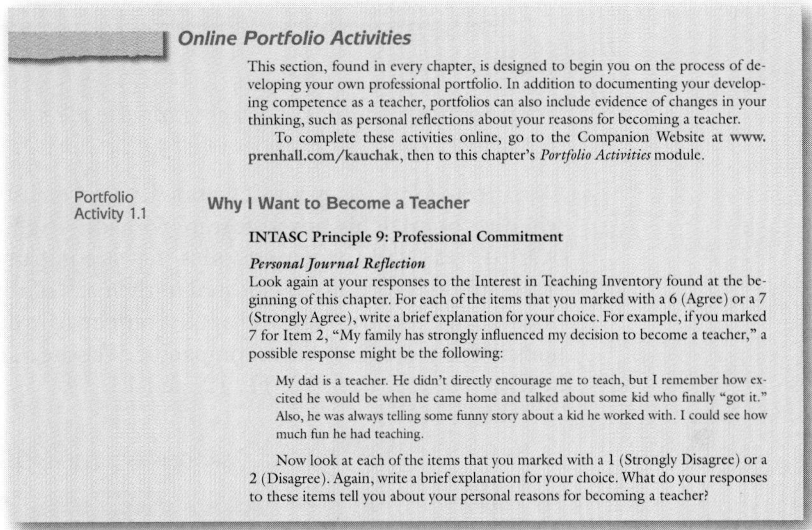

Online Portfolio Activities

This section, found in every chapter, is designed to begin you on the process of developing your own professional portfolio. In addition to documenting your developing competence as a teacher, portfolios can also include evidence of changes in your thinking, such as personal reflections about your reasons for becoming a teacher.

To complete these activities online, go to the Companion Website at www.prenhall.com/kauchak, then to this chapter's *Portfolio Activities* module.

Portfolio Activity 1.1

Why I Want to Become a Teacher

INTASC Principle 9: Professional Commitment

Personal Journal Reflection
Look again at your responses to the Interest in Teaching Inventory found at the beginning of this chapter. For each of the items that you marked with a 6 (Agree) or a 7 (Strongly Agree), write a brief explanation for your choice. For example, if you marked 7 for Item 2, "My family has strongly influenced my decision to become a teacher," a possible response might be the following:

> My dad is a teacher. He didn't directly encourage me to teach, but I remember how excited he would be when he came home and talked about some kid who finally "got it." Also, he was always telling some funny story about a kid he worked with. I could see how much fun he had teaching.

Now look at each of the items that you marked with a 1 (Strongly Disagree) or a 2 (Disagree). Again, write a brief explanation for your choice. What do your responses to these items tell you about your personal reasons for becoming a teacher?

Field Experience Features engage the student in real or virtual classroom experiences to enhance their understanding of chapter content.

Going into Schools, which appears at the end of each chapter, invites students to apply the information in the chapter to themselves and school settings. Using observations and interviews, students connect to the schools and classrooms in which they'll teach.

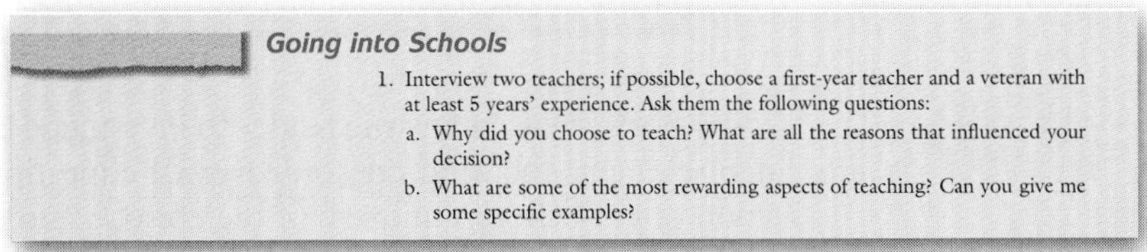

Going into Schools

1. Interview two teachers; if possible, choose a first-year teacher and a veteran with at least 5 years' experience. Ask them the following questions:
   a. Why did you choose to teach? What are all the reasons that influenced your decision?
   b. What are some of the most rewarding aspects of teaching? Can you give me some specific examples?

Classroom Observation Guides describe concrete suggestions for observing and analyzing classrooms. Found in Chapters 3, 6, 10, 11 and 12, these observational guides encourage students to apply chapter content to actual classrooms.

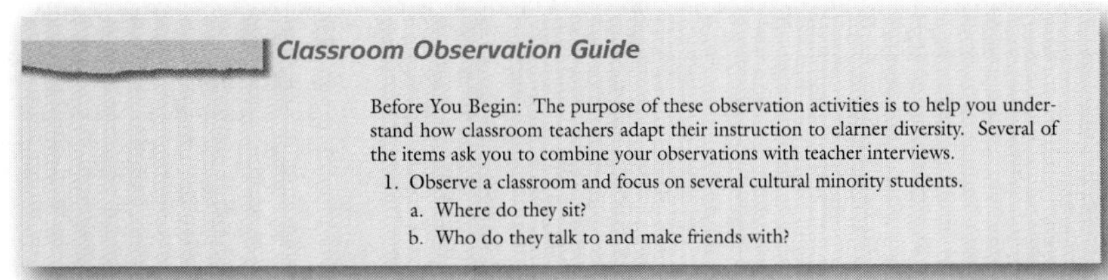

Classroom Observation Guide

Before You Begin: The purpose of these observation activities is to help you understand how classroom teachers adapt their instruction to elarner diversity. Several of the items ask you to combine your observations with teacher interviews.

1. Observe a classroom and focus on several cultural minority students.
   a. Where do they sit?
   b. Who do they talk to and make friends with?

Virtual Field Experience, an extension of the *Going into Schools* feature, allows students who do not have a formal field experience component as part of their course to explore issues and topics through the Internet. This feature can be found in the *Field Experience* module of each chapter on the Companion Website.

Virtual Field Experience

If you would like to participate in a Virtual Field Experience, go to the Companion Website at www.prenhall.com/kauchak, then to this chapter's *Field Experience* module.

Video Features, found in each chapter, use videos of real-world situations and issues to connect with concepts presented in the text.

Classroom Windows provides students with realistic glimpses of teachers working in real classrooms. This boxed feature contains a summary of the unscripted and unrehearsed, real-world video episodes that accompany the text. Students can view the video episodes on a DVD (located in the back of the text) and then respond to questions asking them to apply chapter content to what they've seen. Feedback for the questions is available on the Companion Website. *Classroom Windows* videos are found in Chapters 1, 2, 6, 7, 10, 11, 12, and 13.

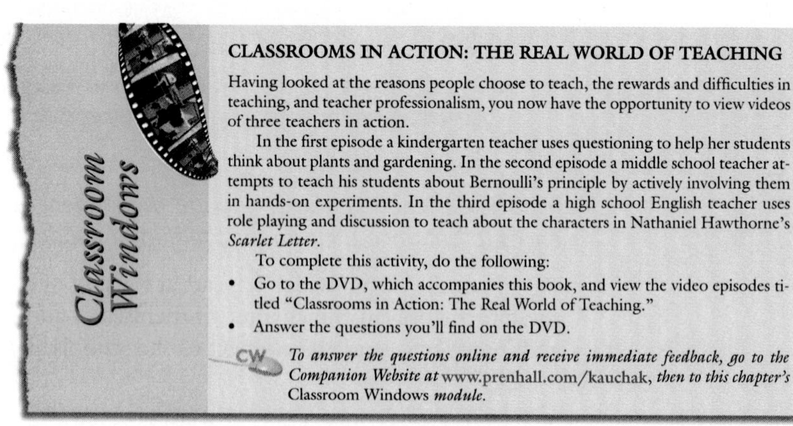
Classroom Windows

CLASSROOMS IN ACTION: THE REAL WORLD OF TEACHING

Having looked at the reasons people choose to teach, the rewards and difficulties in teaching, and teacher professionalism, you now have the opportunity to view videos of three teachers in action.

In the first episode a kindergarten teacher uses questioning to help her students think about plants and gardening. In the second episode a middle school teacher attempts to teach his students about Bernoulli's principle by actively involving them in hands-on experiments. In the third episode a high school English teacher uses role playing and discussion to teach about the characters in Nathaniel Hawthorne's *Scarlet Letter.*

To complete this activity, do the following:

- Go to the DVD, which accompanies this book, and view the video episodes titled "Classrooms in Action: The Real World of Teaching."
- Answer the questions you'll find on the DVD.

CW *To answer the questions online and receive immediate feedback, go to the Companion Website at* www.prenhall.com/kauchak, *then to this chapter's* Classroom Windows *module.*

Video Perspectives allow the reader to investigate chapter topics through ABC News video segments focusing on controversial educational issues. Each *Video Perspective* section offers a short summary of the episode and asks students to respond to questions relating to the video and chapter content. *Video Perspectives* are found in Chapters 3, 4, 5, 8, and 9.

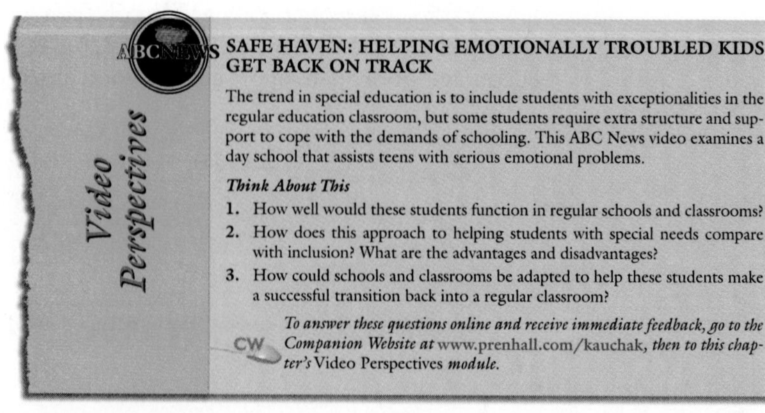
Video Perspectives

ABC NEWS

SAFE HAVEN: HELPING EMOTIONALLY TROUBLED KIDS GET BACK ON TRACK

The trend in special education is to include students with exceptionalities in the regular education classroom, but some students require extra structure and support to cope with the demands of schooling. This ABC News video examines a day school that assists teens with serious emotional problems.

Think About This

1. How well would these students function in regular schools and classrooms?
2. How does this approach to helping students with special needs compare with inclusion? What are the advantages and disadvantages?
3. How could schools and classrooms be adapted to help these students make a successful transition back into a regular classroom?

CW *To answer these questions online and receive immediate feedback, go to the Companion Website at* www.prenhall.com/kauchak, *then to this chapter's* Video Perspectives *module.*

Video Discussion Questions direct students to view video clips of educational leaders, such as Theodore Sizer and John Goodlad, answer discussion questions online, and receive immediate feedback through the text's Companion Website. These appear in Chapters 1, 2, 4, 7, 8, and 10.

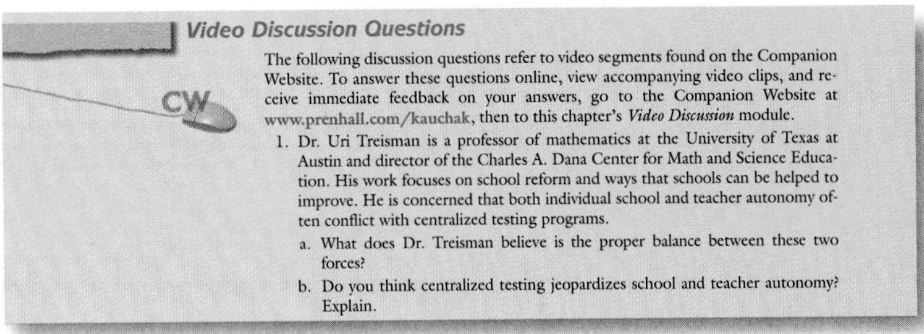

Pedagogical Features provide additional instructional support for students in their understanding of chapter content.

Chapter Introductions and Focus Questions introduce chapter content and identify major issues and questions.

Integrated Case Studies introduce each chapter and provide concrete frames of reference for the topics discussed in the chapter.

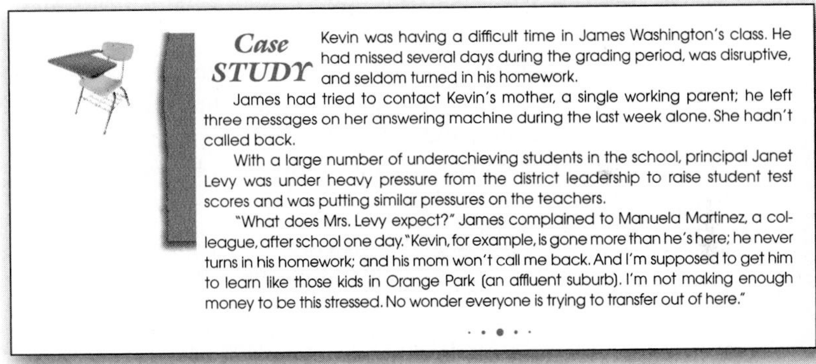

Increasing Understanding Questions, included in the margins of each chapter, encourage students to apply their understanding of the chapter topics to real-world situations. Students can answer these questions and receive immediate feedback on the Companion Website.

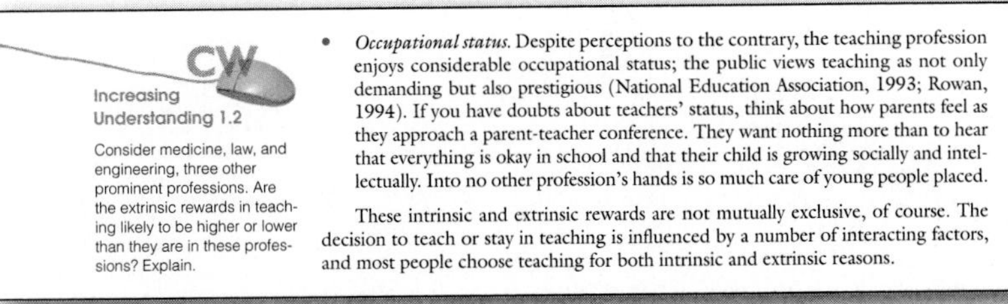

Chapter Summaries provide a concise recap of the major ideas discussed in each chapter.

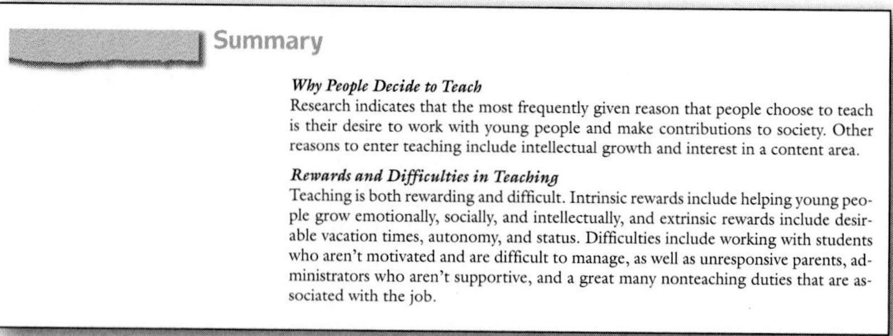
Summary

Why People Decide to Teach
Research indicates that the most frequently given reason that people choose to teach is their desire to work with young people and make contributions to society. Other reasons to enter teaching include intellectual growth and interest in a content area.

Rewards and Difficulties in Teaching
Teaching is both rewarding and difficult. Intrinsic rewards include helping young people grow emotionally, socially, and intellectually, and extrinsic rewards include desirable vacation times, autonomy, and status. Difficulties include working with students who aren't motivated and are difficult to manage, as well as unresponsive parents, administrators who aren't supportive, and a great many nonteaching duties that are associated with the job.

Important Concepts lists key concepts and identifies the page on which each concept is located and defined.

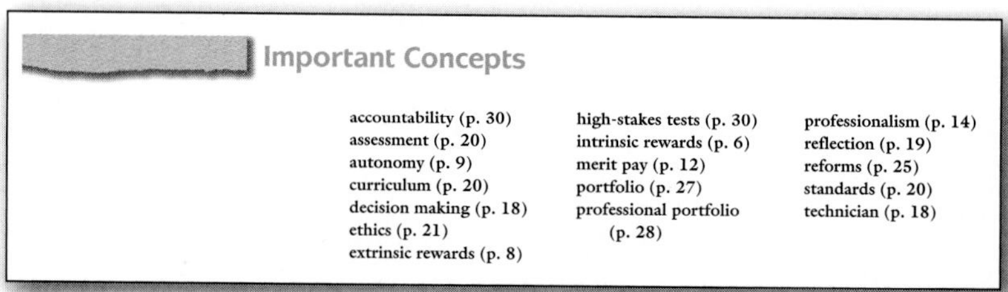
Important Concepts

accountability (p. 30)
assessment (p. 20)
autonomy (p. 9)
curriculum (p. 20)
decision making (p. 18)
ethics (p. 21)
extrinsic rewards (p. 8)
high-stakes tests (p. 30)
intrinsic rewards (p. 6)
merit pay (p. 12)
portfolio (p. 27)
professional portfolio (p. 28)
professionalism (p. 14)
reflection (p. 19)
reforms (p. 25)
standards (p. 20)
technician (p. 18)

Praxis Practice provides opportunities for students to assess their knowledge of chapter content in realistic case studies similar to those found in the Praxis Principles of Learning and Teaching exam. Students can take the exam and then receive immediate feedback on the Companion Website.

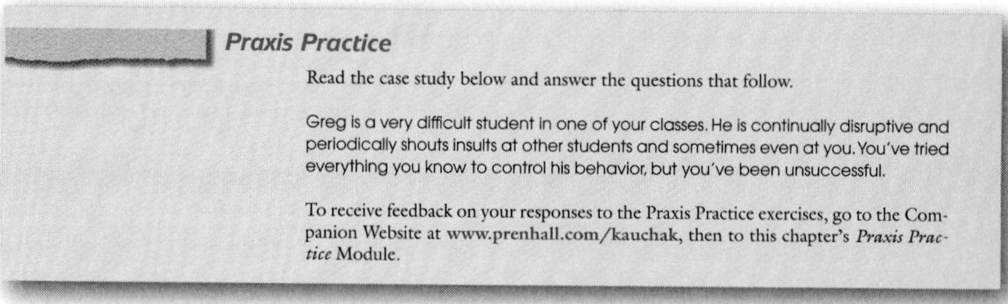
Praxis Practice

Read the case study below and answer the questions that follow.

Greg is a very difficult student in one of your classes. He is continually disruptive and periodically shouts insults at other students and sometimes even at you. You've tried everything you know to control his behavior, but you've been unsuccessful.

To receive feedback on your responses to the Praxis Practice exercises, go to the Companion Website at www.prenhall.com/kauchak, then to this chapter's *Praxis Practice* Module.

Discussion Questions provide opportunities for students to integrate and personalize the content in the chapters as they interact with their peers in discussion formats.

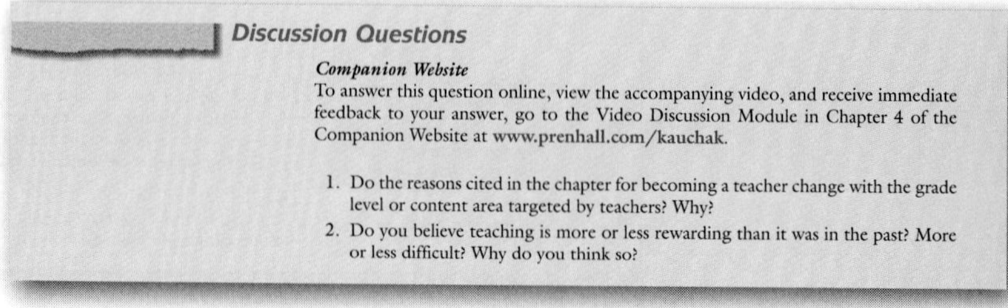
Discussion Questions

Companion Website
To answer this question online, view the accompanying video, and receive immediate feedback to your answer, go to the Video Discussion Module in Chapter 4 of the Companion Website at www.prenhall.com/kauchak.

1. Do the reasons cited in the chapter for becoming a teacher change with the grade level or content area targeted by teachers? Why?
2. Do you believe teaching is more or less rewarding than it was in the past? More or less difficult? Why do you think so?

Supplemental Materials for the Instructor

The text provides the following ancillary materials to assist instructors in their attempts to maximize learning for all students.

Instructor's Manual and Media Guide provides concrete suggestions to actively involve students in learning and to promote interactive teaching. This manual contains many aids for professors as they teach chapter topics and integrate the accompanying media to the fullest extent. The media guide allows the instructor to integrate themes of diversity and culturally relevant teaching into their course using real-life video cases and activities, providing examples, additional activities, and correlating chapter content with cases and content in the *Exploring Diversity: A Video Case Approach* package.

PowerPoint Slides and Acetate Transparencies allow instructors to present and elaborate on topics covered in the text. These transparencies are available on the Companion Website and as acetates.

Print and Computerized Test Banks give professors access to Multiple-Choice, Critical-Thinking, and Extended-Response questions for each chapter. These questions are available in hard copy and in Mac and PC formats.

Classroom Windows Case Videos, connected to Chapters 1, 2, 6, 7, 10, 11, 12, and 13, provide realistic looks at teachers in classrooms. These are available to students on a DVD (located in the back of every new copy of the second edition) and on videotape for instructors.

ABC News Video Library: Critical Issues in Education, Volume 2, features news segments from ABC programs such as *Nightline, 20/20,* and *Good Morning America*. The news clips are tied to chapter topics and can serve as the focal point for classroom discussions. These are available on videotapes and appear as *Video Perspectives* features in Chapters 3, 4, 5, 8, and 9.

Discussion Videos contain interviews with John Goodlad, Theodore Sizer, and Uri Treisman. These 15- to 20-minute interviews on videotape can be used to supplement shorter video clips found on the Companion Website or as stand-alone discussion starters. These appear in Chapters 1, 2, 4, 7, 8, and 10.

Web-Based Supplements for Students and Instructors

Companion Website (CW). The CW for this text, at www.prenhall. com/kauchak, is an online learning environment for both students and professors. The CW is organized by chapter and provides both instructor and students with a variety of meaningful resources to augment the content and features of the text.

For the Professor

Syllabus Manager™ is an online syllabus creation and management instrument with the following capabilities:

- Syllabus Manager™ provides you, the instructor, with a step-by-step process for creating and revising syllabi, with direct links into the Companion Website and other online content.
- Your completed syllabus is hosted on our servers, allowing convenient updates from any computer on the Internet. Changes you make to your syllabus are immediately available to your students at their next logon.
- Students may log on to your syllabus at any time. All they need to know is the Web address for the Companion Website and the password you've assigned to your syllabus.
- Clicking on a date, the student is shown the list of activities for that day's assignment. The activities for each assignment are linked directly to text content, saving time for students.
- Adding assignments consists of clicking on the desired due date, then filling in the details of the assignment.
- Links to other activities can be created easily. If the activity is online, a URL can be entered in the space provided, and it will be linked automatically in the final syllabus.

For the Student

The Companion Website provides students with resources and immediate feedback on exercises and other activities linked to the text. These activities, projects, and resources enhance and extend chapter content to real-world issues and concepts. Each chapter on the CW contains the following modules or sections:

Chapter Overview. An outline of key concepts and issues in the chapter.

Self-Assessment. Multiple-choice quizzes with automatic grading that provide immediate feedback for students.

Web Links. Links to World Wide Web sites that relate to and enhance chapter content.

Increasing Understanding. Margin questions that students can answer online and receive immediate feedback.

Reflect on This. Case studies and reflection questions that extend chapter content.

Exploring Diversity. Links to multicultural/diversity content and websites.

Praxis Practice. Answers to the case-based Praxis exercises.

Portfolio Activities. INTASC-linked projects that give students the opportunity to begin their professional portfolios.

Field Experience. Projects and activities that create a virtual field experience for students who do not have a formal field experience as part of the course.

Video Perspectives. Thought-provoking questions that correspond to the issue-based ABC News Video segments offered with the text (Chapters 3, 4, 5, 8, and 9).

Classroom Windows. Critical-thinking questions with immediate feedback that connect the video cases to chapter content (Chapters 1, 2, 6, 7, 10, 11, 12, and 13).

Video Discussion. Video clips with discussion questions (Chapters 1, 2, 4, 7, 8, and 10).

New York Times eThemes of the Times. Links to a collection of online articles related to topics in education, along with activities designed to enhance students' understanding of issues in education.

Teaching in an Era of Reform. Users can respond online to the "You Take a Position" section of this feature.

Message Board. A virtual bulletin board for posting or responding to questions or comments to/from a national audience.

Other Resources. Users also have access to PowerPoint transparencies, the INTASC standards as they are connected to chapter content and activities, and links to professional organizations.

OneKey Online Learning

OneKey is Prentice Hall's exclusive new resource for instructors and students. OneKey is an integrated online course management resource featuring everything students and instructors need for work in or outside of the classroom, available in the nationally hosted CourseCompass™ platform, as well as WebCT and Blackboard. For more information about OneKey online courses please contact your local Prentice Hall Representative.

Also Available

Exploring Diversity: A Video Case Approach, by Stephen D. Kroeger and Anne M. Bauer. This CD-ROM and accompanying booklet introduce students to culturally relevant teaching through real-life classroom footage and interviews with educators and students. The video cases depicted on the CD-ROM show real educators demonstrating and discussing principles of culturally responsive instruction. Two classrooms are highlighted, in which children from various cultures and socioeconomic groups are successfully engaged in the classroom community and in learning. Interview cases challenge students to consider their own assumptions and to look at the school environment in a new light. The CD-ROM allows students to view expert commentary, answer reflective questions, and build their own custom case studies. The accompanying text provides foundational knowledge and reflective activities to enhance the learning experience offered by the video cases. An *Instructor's Media Guide* to accompany this CD and text is available to instructors.

Exploring Diversity: A Video Case Approach is available as a package to adopters of *Introduction to Teaching: Becoming a Professional.* For additional information, contact your Prentice Hall sales representative.

Annotated Chapter Outline

Part 1: The Profession

Chapter 1: Why Become a Teacher?

Chapter 1 invites readers to consider their beliefs and reasons for wanting to become a teacher. In addition to describing the themes for the book, the chapter analyzes reasons for entering teaching and factors that influence those reasons. The chapter also introduces portfolios and describes how the book can promote success on the Praxis Principles of Learning and Teaching exam.

Chapter 2: The Teaching Profession

Chapter 2 examines the characteristics of the present teaching force and analyzes teaching using professionalism as a framework. The chapter also considers the complexities of teaching, the different roles teachers perform, and characteristics of the present teaching force.

Part 2: Students

Chapter 3: Learner Diversity: Differences in Today's Students

Learner diversity is described as both a challenge and an opportunity facing tomorrow's teachers. Differences in ability and background knowledge require curricular and instructional adaptations. Cultural diversity, including language differences as well as student exceptionalities, require educational adaptations. In addition, helping both boys and girls reach their full potential poses additional challenges.

Chapter 4: Changes in American Society: Their Influences on Today's Schools

The changing American family, shifts in demographic and socieconomic patterns, and other changes in society are analyzed, and their implications for teaching are discussed. Challenges facing modern youth, including alcohol and drug use, violence and bullying, suicide, child abuse, and increased sexuality, are discussed. Educational efforts to assist American youth in facing these changes and challenges are described in terms of community, school, and instruction.

Part 3: Foundations

Chapter 5: Education in the United States: Its Historical Roots

The history of education in the United States focuses on changing conceptions of teachers and teaching. Using historical changes in aims of education as a frame of reference, the chapter analyzes the evolving role of education in the United States.

Chapter 6: Educational Philosophy: The Intellectual Foundations of American Education

Chapter 6 describes the influence of different philosophical movements on schools and schooling. The traditional philosophies idealism, realism, pragmatism, and existentialism are discussed, along with their educational counterparts—perennialism, essentialism, progressivism, and postmodernism. Their implications for teaching are examined. The final section of the chapter helps developing teachers begin the process of developing their own philosophy of education.

Chapter 7: The Organization of American Schools

School aims, which were introduced in Chapter 4, are used to analyze different school organizational patterns. Developmental needs of learners and school responses are considered for the preschool, primary, middle, and high school levels. Research on effective schools is discussed, and its implications for teaching are analyzed.

Chapter 8: Governance and Finance: Regulating and Funding Schools

Chapter 8 describes the uniquely American configuration of school governance and finance. Constitutional law is used as a framework to analyze the interconnected forces influencing both the governance and financing of American education. Recent reforms, such as school choice in the form of charter schools and vouchers, are used to analyze governance and finance issues.

Chapter 9: School Law: Ethical and Legal Influences on Teaching

The chapter begins by examining how ethics and law influence professional decision making. The U.S. legal system is described as an overlapping and interconnected web of federal, state, and local influences. The concepts of rights and responsibilities are used to frame legal issues for both teachers and students.

Part 4: Teaching

Chapter 10: The School Curriculum

The aims of education are again used to frame the evolving American curriculum. The formal and informal curricula are described, and reform movements in education are placed within a historical context and used to analyze current curricular trends. Curriculum controversies are described using ideological struggles over the control of American education as a framework. Specific examples such as textbooks, banned books, and underrepresented minorities are used to illustrate these ideological conflicts.

Chapter 11: Instruction in American Classrooms

Promoting student development and learning is an essential role for teachers. The chapter begins by examining the effective teaching literature and continues with a historical look at two views of learning—behaviorism and cognitive psychology. Implications of the cognitive revolution in teaching are described with respect to learner-centered instruction, learner self-regulation, social influences on learning, and changing views of assessment.

Chapter 12: Technology in American Schools

The chapter begins with a brief history and overview of technology and teaching. Different ways that technology can influence learning are described and linked to different teaching functions. The chapter concludes with an examination of issues for the future and a look at how technology is changing teaching.

Part 5: Careers

Chapter 13: Developing as a Professional

This chapter examines lifelong teacher development from multiple perspectives. The chapter begins by discussing the types of knowledge teachers acquire in learning to teach. It continues by examining the characteristics of beginning teachers, including their beliefs, concerns, and experiences and how these will influence their development as professionals. It concludes with sections on succeeding in the first year of teaching and career-long professional development.

Brief Contents

Contents

Chapter 4

PART 3 *Foundations* 159

Chapter 5

Chapter 9

School Law: Ethical and Legal Influences on Teaching 310

PART 4 *Teaching* 347

Chapter 10

The School Curriculum 348

Chapter 11

Chapter 12

PART 5 *Careers* 473

Chapter 13

We would like to thank the reviewers who provided invaluable comments and suggestions. They are: Carolynn Akpan, *Pace University*; Harriett Arnold, *University of the Pacific*; Mary Lou Brotherson, *Nova Southeastern University*; Sandra L. DiGiaimo, *University of Scranton*; Katherine K. Gratto, *University of Florida*; Nancy Hoffman, *University of North Carolina, Wilmington*; Marcia N. Janson, *Penn State Erie, The Behrend College*; David H. Vawter, *Winthrop University*; Mack Welford, *Roanoke College*; and Lynne R. Yeamans, *Bridgewater State College.*

Note: Every effort has been made to provide accurate and current Internet information. However, the Internet is constantly changing, so it is inevitable that some Internet addresses in this textbook will change.

Special Features

Exploring Diversity

Classroom Windows

Video Perspectives

Reflect on This

Teaching in an Era of Reform

Video Libraries

Classroom Windows Video Cases DVD

Now included on a DVD located in the back of the text, these real-life, unrehearsed video cases present students with a glimpse into the world of professional teachers. *Classroom Windows* boxed features throughout the text connect the video episodes to chapter content. Activities and guided reflection questions enable students to explore topics and determine how these concepts and experiences relate to them as professionals.

Chapter 1 Classrooms in Action: The Real World of Teaching

This video segment looks at three teachers teaching at different levels.

Kindergarten. This interactive lesson shows a kindergarten teacher using questioning to explore the topic of planting a garden with a class of inner-city students.

Middle School. A seventh-grade science teacher wants his students to understand Bernoulli's principle, the physical law that explains why airplanes can fly. His teaching methods include reviewing concepts, demonstrating the principle, and then introducing the students to the term *Bernoulli's principle.*

High School. A high school English teacher is teaching her students about character development in Nathaniel Hawthorne's *The Scarlet Letter.* After briefly reviewing the book, she asks her students to break up into groups and assume the roles of two specific characters. Once the role playing is completed, the students are asked to come back as a class to discuss their reactions to the characters.

Chapter 2 Working with Parents: A Parent–Teacher Conference

This video touches on barriers to parental involvement as well as strategies for involving parents. In this episode a fifth-grade teacher conducts a conference with a parent of a student who is struggling in her class. The parent is somewhat defensive at different points in the conference, and the teacher attempts to simultaneously support and disarm the parent by grounding her discussion with specific facts about the student's performance.

Chapter 6 Examining Philosophies of Teaching

This video segment illustrates different philosophies of teaching by presenting two secondary social study lessons. One is at the high school level, and the other is at the junior high level.

The junior high students are introduced to different climate regions of the United States by doing a hands-on project involving small groups. The high school teacher provides his students with historic background knowledge of the Vietnam War by presenting an organized lecture, using outlines and maps to illustrate main points.

Chapter 7 Within-School Coordination: A Grade-Level Meeting

In this episode a fifth-grade teacher leads a grade-level meeting with her colleagues as they discuss various issues related to their duties as teachers in an elementary school.

Chapter 10 Math Curriculum in Elementary Schools

By using jelly beans, a second-grade teacher teaches graphing skills. These skills are then applied to other problem-solving situations.

Chapter 11 Learning About Balance Beams in Fourth Grade

A fourth-grade teacher wants her students to know how to solve math problems using a balance beam and weights. After breaking the class up into small groups, a balance beam and weights are given to each group. The teacher asks students to find different ways to balance the scales. The students are encouraged to use number sentences such as $8 \times 4 = 32 = (10 \times 3) + 2 = 32$ to explain their answers.

Chapter 12 Technology in Classrooms

The teacher in this video uses technology in a variety of ways to reinforce her students' developing understanding of graphing. In one segment, students call different pizza restaurants to find the price of pizza and then graph their results. In another, students watch a video clip of students racing through alternate routes on an obstacle course. They are then asked to time and graph the runners' results. In another, students use computers to graph the results of a student survey on students' soft drink preferences.

Chapter 13 Demonstrating Knowledge in Classrooms

The kinds of knowledge that expert teachers possess is displayed in four teaching segments with students at different ages. In the first segment a kindergarten teacher uses hands-on experiences to teach about properties of air. In the second, a seventh-grade teacher illustrates the concept of symmetry for his students. The third shows a chemistry teacher attempting to help her students understand Charles's law of gases. In the final episode a fifth-grade teacher brings in live examples to teach the concept *arthropod.*

Critical Issues in Education, Volume 2

An updated **ABC News/Prentice Hall Video Library,** ***Critical Issues in Education, Volume 2,*** is available on videotape to adopters of this text. *Video Perspectives* boxed features throughout the text connect the news segments to chapter content, and the accompanying activities provide students with the opportunity to explore and engage in discussion regarding current issues in education.

Chapter 3 Safe Haven: Helping Emotionally Troubled Kids Get Back on Track

The trend in special education is inclusion, but some students require extra structure and support to cope with the demands of schooling. This ABC News video examines a day school that assists teens with serious emotional problems.

Chapter 4 Action, Reaction, and Zero Tolerance

This ABC News video examines the effects of zero tolerance policies on schools and students. The news crew first visits an elementary school where an 8-year-old boy was expelled for playing "cowboys and Indians" with a paper gun. Next the video focuses on a high school in Virginia where the school mascot, a Spartan, is not allowed to wear a cardboard sword.

Chapter 5 God and Evolution in Kansas Classrooms

This ABC News video examines a recent controversy in Kansas in which the Kansas Board of Education decided to drop the teaching of evolution from the required coursework in the state's public schools. It features interviews with a candidate for the Board of Education, who questions this decision, as well as two experts on the topic.

Chapter 8 Home Room: One Last Chance

This ABC News video describes a unique kind of school, SEED Public Charter School, a public urban boarding school in Washington, DC. The news crew interviews the founders of the charter school, as well as teachers and students. These interviews provide insights into the promises and challenges of this innovation.

Chapter 9 Affirmative Action

This ABC News video examines the issues around the recent U.S. Supreme Court decision on affirmative action policies at the University of Michigan. The video features a short clip of President George W. Bush calling the University of Michigan policy a quota system and shows the president of the University of Michigan defending the school's policies.

Part 1

The Profession

Chapter 1

Why Become a Teacher?

Welcome. You're beginning a study of teaching, one of the most interesting, challenging, and noble professions that exists. No one, other than parents and other caregivers, has more potential for touching the personal, social, and intellectual lives of students than do caring and dedicated teachers.

This book is designed to help you answer two questions:

1. Do I want to be a teacher?
2. What kind of teacher do I want to become?

This chapter focuses on the first question, and our goal is to help you begin the process of answering it by posing some additional questions:

- Why do people decide to teach?
- What are some of the rewards in teaching?
- What are some of the difficulties in teaching?
- Is teaching a profession?
- How will educational reforms affect your life as a teacher?

This logo appears throughout the chapter to indicate where case studies are integrated with chapter content.

Case STUDY Before I became a teacher, I majored in Business Administration in college and worked for 10 and a half years in the banking industry. I held jobs as a receptionist, an accounting clerk, a customer support representative, and a staff auditor. My last job in business—staff auditor—was fun because I got to travel, meet new people, and periodically train other workers. Still, even it wasn't rewarding; I was just a number in a corporation, making money for some big company.

I've always wanted to make a difference, and I've always enjoyed working with young people. Then a couple years ago I read a book in which the author described the difference between a person's "job" and a person's "work." Your job is how you make money; your work is how you contribute to the world. It really crystalized everything for me. Business, for me, was a job, but I didn't really have any "work," and I longed for it.

In some ways, I think I always wanted to be a teacher. I remember all the way back to my fourth-grade teacher, Mrs. May. She was like my second mother because she was always so willing to help, and she seemed to care about me, just like my mother did at home. And I also remember my 10th grade history teacher, Mr. Fleming, who explained how important school was for us to develop and grow. We would complain that his tests were so hard, and he would laugh and tell us how good they were for us; he thought history was *so* important. You had to like it, because he loved it so much. All the kids talked about Mr. Fleming and his antics, like when he came into class in his coonskin cap and buckskin outfit when we studied America's westward expansion. And he asked questions that would make us think, like "Why does a city way out in Iowa have a French name like Des Moines?" I never fell asleep in his class. I still remember it, and it was years ago.

So, to make a long story short, I went back to school, and this time I did what I've always wanted to do. Of course it's tough some days. The kids are sometimes "off the wall," and I periodically feel like I'm drowning in paperwork, but when you see the light bulb go on for someone, it's all worth it. Now, my job and my work are the same thing. (Suzanne, middle school science teacher and recent entry into teaching)

• • ● • •

Many of you reading this book have characteristics similar to Suzanne's. You're intelligent and introspective, and you've had a number of life experiences. Perhaps you're married, have children, and your spouse is successfully employed in some other profession. You've thought a great deal about becoming a teacher, and you're clear about your reasons for wanting to teach.

Others of you are less certain. You're also intelligent, but you're still in the process of deciding what you want to do with your life. You enjoyed your school experiences, and most of your ideas about teaching are based on them. The idea of working with and helping young people is attractive, but you're not quite sure how you will do this.

That's okay. One of our goals in writing this text was to provide you with a close-up and in-depth look at teaching. Either way—if you've already made the decision to teach, or if you're still in the process of deciding—this book will help you understand what teaching is all about.

Do I Want to Be a Teacher?

To begin answering the question, "Do I want to be a teacher?" let's consider some different reasons people go into teaching. To examine your thinking, respond to the Interest in Teaching Inventory that follows.

Interest in Teaching Inventory

For each item, circle the number that best represents your thinking. Use the following scale as a guide.

1 = Strongly disagree
2 = Disagree
3 = Somewhat disagree
4 = Agree and disagree
5 = Somewhat agree
6 = Agree
7 = Strongly agree

	1	2	3	4	5	6	7
1. A major reason I'm considering becoming a teacher is job security.	1	2	3	4	5	6	7
2. My family has strongly influenced my decision to become a teacher.	1	2	3	4	5	6	7
3. Long summer vacations are very important to me as I consider teaching as a career.	1	2	3	4	5	6	7
4. I've never really considered any other occupation besides teaching.	1	2	3	4	5	6	7
5. A major reason I'm considering becoming a teacher is my desire to work with young people.	1	2	3	4	5	6	7
6. I'm thinking of becoming a teacher because I'd like to be of some value or significance to society.	1	2	3	4	5	6	7
7. A major reason I'm considering becoming a teacher is my own interest in a content or subject matter field.	1	2	3	4	5	6	7
8. A major reason I'm considering entering teaching is because of the influence of a former elementary or secondary teacher.	1	2	3	4	5	6	7
9. The opportunity for a lifetime of self-growth is a major reason I'm considering becoming a teacher.	1	2	3	4	5	6	7

Major: Elementary / Secondary (Circle one)
If secondary, what content area?_______________
Gender: Male / Female (Circle one)
Age:_______________

CW

Increasing Understanding 1.1

In Table 1.1 we see that the lowest average response on the Interest in Teaching Inventory is for Item 4, and the highest average responses are for Items 5 and 6. Are these consistent or inconsistent results? Explain.

To answer the Increasing Understanding questions online and receive immediate feedback, go to the Companion Website at **www.prenhall.com/kauchak**, then to this chapter's *Increasing Understanding* module. Type in your response, and then study the feedback.

We gave this same survey to several classes of students taking a course similar to the one you're now in, averaged their responses, and ranked them from most (1) to least (9) important reasons for becoming a teacher. Let's see how your responses compare to those of our students.

We see from Table 1.1 that the desire to work with young people (Item 5) and wanting to contribute to society (Item 6) were our students' two most important reasons for considering teaching. These reasons are consistent with Suzanne's thinking, as presented in the introduction to the chapter, and they're also consistent with polls of teachers conducted by the National Education Association over a nearly 25-year period (National Education Association, 1997).

Table 1.1 Responses to Interest in Teaching Inventory

Item	Item Focus	Average Response of Students	Survey Rank
1	Job security	4.3	6
2	Family influence	3.9	8
3	Summer vacations	4.0	7
4	Other careers not considered	2.6	9
5	Work with youth	6.4	1
6	Value to society	6.3	2
7	Content interest	5.4	4
8	Influence of teachers	5.0	5
9	Self-growth	5.5	3

A recent Public Agenda poll of new teachers found similar results (Wadsworth, 2001). It found that 86 percent of new teachers thought of teaching as "a true sense of calling," 75 percent considered teaching a lifelong choice, and 68 percent reported getting a lot of satisfaction out of teaching. In addition, an amazing 96 percent of beginning teachers reported that teaching was work they love to do.

Let's look a little more closely at the reasons people go into teaching and the kinds of things that keep them excited about their decision.

Rewards and Difficulties in Teaching

As with any occupation, people choose to teach because they think it will be rewarding. Rewards can be intrinsic or extrinsic.

Intrinsic Rewards

Intrinsic rewards *come from within oneself and are personally satisfying for emotional or intellectual reasons.* A number of people, such as Suzanne and the students in our survey, enter teaching because they seek the personal satisfaction that goes with believing they are making a contribution to the world. Intrinsic rewards for teachers fall into two broad categories—emotional and intellectual.

Emotional Rewards Let's look at different kinds of emotional rewards that teachers receive from their teaching. The following are true stories shared with us by teachers.

• • • • •

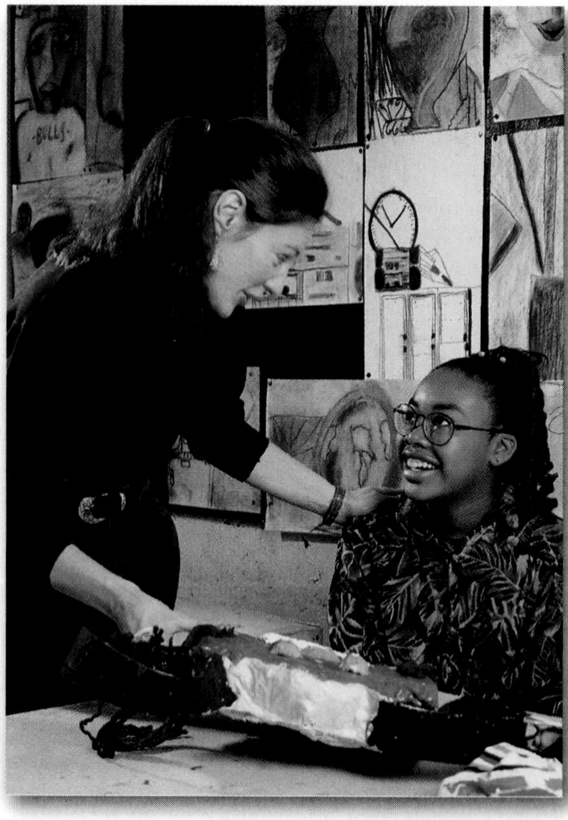

Kasia, 23, called her boyfriend, Jeff. It was "Teacher Appreciation Week" at her middle school, and she had just received a dozen roses from a group of her seventh-grade science students.

"I was always on them about whispering too," she excitedly told Jeff. "I maybe would have expected this from my fifth-period class, but never from this bunch.

"Let me read the note I got from them," she continued. She read

> Thank you for all that you've done for us and for all the wonderful things that you've teached [*sic*] us. You are truly an amazing teacher. Thank you again.
>
> Happy Teacher Appreciation Week,
>
> Sincerely, Alicia, Rosa, Shannon, Tina, Stephanie, Melissa, Jessica, and Becca

"That's wonderful," Jeff laughed. "Good thing you're not their English teacher."

"I know. I showed Isabel [the students' English teacher] the note, and she broke up. 'So much for grammar,' she said."

• • • • •

Judy, 42, a teacher in the same school, brought home the following note from a student's parents.

> Dear Mrs. Holmquist,
>
> Thank you very much for working so diligently with Michael this year. I think he now has a better understanding of the world. I hope he told you that he lived in Egypt for nearly 2 years. We have a large amount of Egyptian souvenirs should your class like to view them. Again, thanks for all of your work day after day.
>
> Sincerely,
>
> Shirley and Bob Wood

• • • • •

Teachers' interactions with their students provide a major source of intrinsic rewards.

Interactions with other teachers provide opportunities for intellectual stimulation and growth.

Miguel Rodriguez, 29, another middle school teacher, received the following note from one of his students.

Mr. Rodriguez,

I wanted to think of some creative way to thank you for being the best teacher I ever had. (But I couldn't ☺).

Even though all the geography skills I'll ever use in my life I learned in second grade, I just wanted to say thanks for teaching me how to really prepare for life in the years to come.

Every day I looked forward to coming to your class (and not just because of Mike [a boy in the class]). I always enjoyed your class, because there was a hidden message about life in there somewhere.

Your [*sic*] my very favorite teacher and you've taught me some of the best lessons in life I could ever learn. Thank you so much.

A grateful student,
Erica Jacobs

P.S. No, I didn't write this to raise my grade ☺.

• • ● • •

These notes and the flowers Kasia received symbolize some of the emotional rewards in teaching. Each teacher had an understandably satisfying emotional reaction to these tokens of appreciation. "They're what keep you going," Judy commented matter-of-factly while discussing her enjoyment of her work.

Sharon, a veteran first-grade teacher, also looks to emotional rewards in her teaching. "The beginning of the day gets me going," she said, smiling, when we asked her about her continued commitment to her career. "I stand at the door, and the children give me a hug, a high five, or a handshake when they come in the room. Even if the previous day was a bad one, all those little faces are enough to get me started all over again."

Sometimes students show their affection in strange ways.

• • ● • •

Kerrie, a first-year teacher, entered her classroom first thing in the morning on her birthday. Her students had arranged with the custodian to gain access to her room and had moved *all* the desks to the center of the room and had wrapped them with tape and toilet paper. How would you react?

Kerrie was delighted. "I called [the perpetrators] out of class and had them come down and [another teacher] took a picture of them standing out in the middle of it all. I left it here all day. I made them sit on the floor. It was really fun. It was really a fun day." (Bullough, 1989, p. 86)

• • ● • •

It helps to have a sense of humor when you teach. All teachers reap emotional rewards from their work with students, whether they are wide-eyed first graders, middle school students like Erica Jacobs, or high school juniors and seniors struggling to become adults.

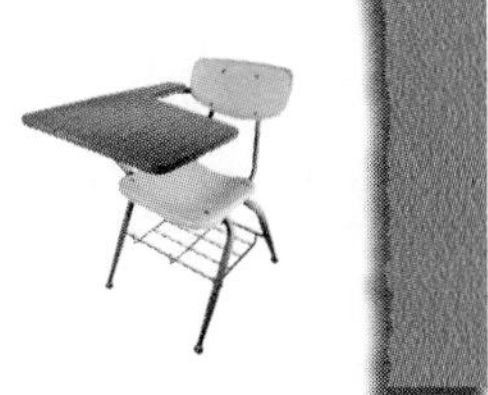

Case STUDY

David Ling, an eighth-grade physical science teacher, enthusiastically began his class: "Think about these questions and try to figure out what they have in common." He wrote the following on the board:

Why do we have seatbelts in our cars?

Why does an automatic washer have holes in the drum?

How does a dog shake the water off itself when it comes out of a pond?

The bemused students looked at the list, and after several seconds David continued, "Now, what have we been studying?"

"Inertia," Taneka responded after hesitating briefly.

"Exactly," David said, smiling. "So let's review for a minute. What is inertia? . . . Go ahead, Dana."

"The tendency . . . of something moving to keep on moving . . . straight."

"Or something not moving to remain still," Jamal added.

"Excellent, both of you," David said with a nod. "Now, a challenge. Let's answer the questions on the board using the idea of inertia."

With David's guidance the students concluded that if their cars suddenly stop, their bodies keep moving because of their inertia, and the seatbelt stops them, so they don't get hurt. They also decided that inertia separates water from clothes in the washer, because the water goes straight out through the holes in the drum, but the clothes are kept in it. Finally, they determined that as the dog shakes one way, and then stops, the water keeps moving, and the same thing happens when it shakes the other way. So the dog uses the principle of inertia to shake the water from itself.

"Neat," Rebecka said. "Where'd you get that stuff, Mr. Ling?"

"I thought up the questions over time," David said. "The more I study, the more examples I find. . . . That's what we're here for. We study science so we can learn how the world around us works."

• • ● • •

Intellectual Rewards While emotional rewards almost certainly motivate them as well, many people choose to teach because they are interested in a certain subject matter and want to share their interest and excitement with others. Our survey found that "interest in a content or subject matter field" and "the opportunity for a lifetime of self-growth" were important reasons for considering teaching, ranking 3 and 4 out of 9. Acquiring knowledge and seeing students get excited about the same things we do are some of the intellectual rewards of teaching. Not surprisingly, such rewards are also important reasons veteran teachers remain in the field. One researcher studying exemplary veteran teachers concluded, "Without exception intellectual stimulation is a burning need of the teachers I interviewed" (Williams, 2003).

Extrinsic Rewards

In addition to emotional and intellectual rewards, **extrinsic rewards**—*rewards that come from outside oneself*—also attract people to teaching. The extrinsic rewards of teaching include job security (ranked 6 in our survey) and summer vacations (ranked 7).

The job security found in teaching is greater than that in most other occupations. For example, after a short probational period—usually about 3 years—teachers are typically awarded tenure. Originally designed to attract good people and protect them from political pressures, tenure provides teachers with job security and is a concrete extrinsic reward. (You will study teacher tenure in detail in Chapter 9.)

For some, working in a profession with long vacations is rewarding. According to an old joke, a student was asked to identify three reasons for going into teaching. After pondering the question and being unable to think of any better reasons, the student finally wrote, "June, July, and August." In addition to the summer, teachers have vacations throughout the year at times when vacations are most attractive—the Friday after Thanksgiving, the winter holiday season, and spring break, for example.

In addition to job security and vacations, additional extrinsic rewards include the following:

- *Convenient work schedules.* Teachers' schedules are similar to those of students, so, for example, teachers' own children don't have to go home to empty houses after school.
- *Autonomy.* **Autonomy,** *the capacity to control one's own existence*, has been identified as a basic human motivational need (R. Ryan & Deci, 1998). Teachers have a great deal of autonomy in their work. In spite of growing concerns about increased regulation and external control (van den Berg, 2002), they largely decide what and how to teach, and they make crucial decisions about students' lives. Their autonomy allows teachers to express themselves personally and creatively in the classroom and, significantly, has been linked to job satisfaction (Stamouli, 2002).
- *Occupational status.* Despite perceptions to the contrary, the teaching profession enjoys considerable occupational status; the public views teaching as not only demanding but also prestigious (National Education Association, 1993; Rowan, 1994). If you have doubts about teachers' status, think about how parents feel as they approach a parent–teacher conference. They want nothing more than to hear that everything is okay in school and that their child is growing socially and intellectually. Into no other profession's hands is so much care of young people placed.

Increasing Understanding 1.2

Consider medicine, law, and engineering, three other prominent professions. Are the extrinsic rewards in teaching likely to be higher or lower than they are in these professions? Explain.

These intrinsic and extrinsic rewards are not mutually exclusive, of course. The decision to teach or stay in teaching is influenced by a number of interacting factors, and most people choose teaching for both intrinsic and extrinsic reasons.

Case STUDY Kevin was having a difficult time in James Washington's class. He had missed several days during the grading period, was disruptive, and seldom turned in his homework.

James had tried to contact Kevin's mother, a single working parent; he left three messages on her answering machine during the last week alone. She hadn't called back.

With a large number of underachieving students in the school, principal Janet Levy was under heavy pressure from the district leadership to raise student test scores and was putting similar pressures on the teachers.

"What does Mrs. Levy expect?" James complained to Manuela Martinez, a colleague, after school one day. "Kevin, for example, is gone more than he's here; he never turns in his homework; and his mom won't call me back. And I'm supposed to get him to learn like those kids in Orange Park (an affluent suburb). I'm not making enough money to be this stressed. No wonder everyone is trying to transfer out of here."

Difficulties in Teaching

James's lament is more common than we would like it to be. In many parts of the country, and particularly in some rural areas and inner cities, teachers face daunting problems. Two of the most common issues involve working conditions and salaries. Let's look at them.

Working Conditions Working conditions are a concern for many teachers and a major reason many beginning teachers leave the profession (Ingersoll & Smith, 2003). Some school leaders, like Janet Levy, may be unsympathetic; parents or other caregivers, like Kevin's mother, may be unresponsive and may not support teachers' efforts; and

Time spent in administration or noninstructional activities can drain teachers' time and energy.

students are sometimes unmotivated or disruptive. Conditions like these lead to teacher stress.

Teacher stress has been linked to reduced job satisfaction, poorer relationships with students, decreased teacher effectiveness, and teacher burnout. It is a major reason teachers leave the profession (Abel & Sewell, 1999).

Other difficulties exist. For example, teachers complain about spending so much time on nonteaching requirements and duties—filling out student progress reports and other paperwork, monitoring hallways before and after school, checking restrooms to prevent misbehavior, and taking students to and from lunch—that they don't have the time, or energy, to teach effectively. A common lament is, "If they would only give me the time and resources I need, I could teach these students something!"

CW

Increasing Understanding 1.3

How do the salaries in your state compare with the national averages? with the salaries in neighboring states? What do the data tell you about regional trends in teachers' salaries?

Salaries Teacher salaries are another concern. Low salaries are frequently cited as a major reason people either avoid teaching as a career or leave teaching after a few years (Ingersoll & Smith, 2003; Metropolitan Life Insurance Company, 1995). Salaries are improving, however. For instance, the average teacher salary in the United States for the 2001–2002 school year was $44,367, ranging from a high of $54,348 in California to a low of just above $31,000 in South Dakota. In the same year, the average beginning salary was slightly under $31,000 (American Federation of Teachers, 2003a). Table 1.2 lists the average and beginning teacher salaries for each state in 2001–2002.

Table 1.2 Beginning and Average Teacher Salaries for U.S. States and Territories in 2001–2002

State	Average Salary	Beginning Salary
Alabama	$37,206	$29,938
Alaska	49,028	36,035
Arizona	38,510	27,648
Arkansas	36,026	27,565
California	54,348	34,180
Colorado	40,659	28,001
Connecticut	52,376	34,551
Delaware	49,011	32,868
District of Columbia	51,000	31,982
Florida	39,275	30,096
Georgia	43,933	32,283
Guam	35,038	28,054
Hawaii	44,306	31,340
Idaho	39,194	25,316
Illinois	49,679	31,761
Indiana	44,609	28,440

Table 1.2 Beginning and Average Teacher Salaries for U.S. States and Territories in 2001–2002 (*continued*)

State	Average Salary	Beginning Salary
Iowa	38,230	27,553
Kansas	37,059	26,596
Kentucky	37,951	26,813
Louisiana	36,328	28,229
Maine	37,300	24,054
Maryland	48,251	31,828
Massachusetts	48,732	32,746
Michigan	52,497	32,649
Minnesota	42,175	29,998
Mississippi	33,295	24,567
Missouri	36,053	27,554
Montana	34,379	22,344
Nebraska	36,236	26,010
Nevada	44,621	28,734
New Hampshire	39,915	25,611
New Jersey	50,115	35,311
New Mexico	36,716	27,579
New York	51,020	34,577
North Carolina	42,118	29,359
North Dakota	32,468	20,988
Ohio	44,266	29,953
Oklahoma	32,870	27,547
Oregon	46,033	31,026
Pennsylvania	50,599	31,866
Puerto Rico	22,164	18,000
Rhode Island	51,619	30,272
South Carolina	39,923	27,268
South Dakota	31,383	23,938
Tennessee	38,515	28,857
Texas	39,230	30,938
Utah	38,153	26,806
Vermont	39,771	25,229
Virgin Islands	34,784*	22,751*
Virginia	41,752	31,238
Washington	43,470	28,348
West Virginia	36,775	25,633
Wisconsin	41,056	27,397
Wyoming	37,853	26,773
U.S. AVERAGE	**$44,367**	**$30,719**

*2000–01 salaries.
Source: American Federation of Teachers (2003a).

Union officials call the salary picture a "mixed bag" (American Federation of Teachers, 2003a). Although teacher salaries have risen an average of 3 percent over the last 5 years, they still fall well below the starting salaries of other occupations like engineering and accounting, where salary increases in the last 5 years have outperformed teachers' by about 10 percent (American Federation of Teachers, 2003a).

Your salary will depend on a number of factors, such as the local cost of living and the location of the school district. As you'll see in Chapter 9, local property taxes are the major funding source for schools, so teachers' salaries depend, in large part, on property values. Also, urban districts typically have higher salaries than rural districts because of a higher cost of living.

Although low salaries are cited as a negative aspect of teaching, other economic factors add to the attractiveness of teaching. For example, annual salary increases are virtually guaranteed, and as noted earlier, vacation periods are ideal. Medical, dental, and retirement benefits are often provided, and job security is high. In addition, teachers are often paid supplements for extra duties, such as club sponsorships, coaching, chairing departments (such as chairing the English department in a middle school), and mentoring beginning teachers (Darling-Hammond, 1997). In schools with year-round schedules, teachers work 11 months of the year—versus 9 or 10—and are paid accordingly.

Merit Pay Currently most teacher salary increases are based on number of years of experience and the number of graduate and in-service credit hours. Recently, however, there has been increased interest in **merit pay,** *a supplement to a teacher's base salary to reward superior performance.* Proponents of merit pay argue that exemplary teaching performance should be rewarded and that money can provide incentives for teacher excellence (Odden, 2003).

Merit pay takes several forms. Some merit systems reward individual teachers based on their students' performance on tests. Others reward individual teachers based on principal observations or teaching artifacts such as exemplary lessons or student work. A third type of merit pay rewards entire schools for student test performance. A fourth variation provides teachers with extra pay for teaching in high-need areas such as math and science or at challenging sites such as high-poverty, low-performing urban schools (Keller, 2002; Odden, 2003).

Despite the intuitive appeal of paying better teachers more money, a number of problems exist. Critics contend that merit pay is divisive, damaging the cooperation and collegiality of teachers who work together in a school. In addition, critics point to methodological problems in identifying exemplary teachers. Research in the area of teacher evaluation supports this criticism; it is quite difficult to document minimal teacher competence, much less excellence (K. Peterson, 2000).

Teachers generally oppose merit pay plans, but they object more strongly to merit pay for teachers in high-need areas than to merit pay as a concept. In a recent national poll, 80 percent opposed paying more to science, math, and technology teachers, but only 49 percent opposed the idea of merit pay itself (Langdon, 1999).

Despite these criticisms, both large- and small-scale merit pay experiments are being attempted across the country: A statewide California system, for instance, provided schools with bonuses ranging from $10,000 to $30,000, based on improvement in student scores (Sack, 2002a). Schoolwide committees consisting of parents, teachers, and administrators could then use the bonus money to purchase anything from library books to athletic gear. In a smaller scale trial, the city of Cincinnati is experimenting with an individual teacher merit plan in which teams of teachers and administrators assess teaching excellence (Blair, 2001). Initial reports suggest the process is more difficult than designers first thought.

It is likely that the national interest in school reform will result in increased interest in the merit pay concept. If teachers are central to increased student achievement, excellent teachers need to be rewarded for their efforts, proponents contend. You may encounter some variation of this idea during your teaching career.

Private School Employment

You might also consider teaching in a private school; approximately 10 percent of all students attend private schools (National Center for Education Statistics, 2000a). Average starting salaries for private school teachers are about 30 percent lower than those in public schools, however, and the difference increases to more than 40 percent for maximum salaries (Ingersoll, 1997). In addition, private schools usually don't provide the same insurance benefits that public schools provide. One survey, for example, indicated that nearly half of all public schools provided paid medical, dental, and retirement benefits, whereas only about a fifth of private schools did (Ingersoll, 1997).

Given these disparities, you might ask, "Why would a teacher choose to teach at a private school?" Some answers include the following:

- Lack of a licensing requirement
- Commitment to an ideal
- Smaller school bureaucracy
- Smaller classes with fewer students
- Greater parental involvement

Teachers often choose to work in private schools because they aren't required to take the professional education courses needed for licensing; private schools often waive the licensing requirements that public school teachers are required by law to meet. In addition, teachers sometimes choose private school employment because the school is dedicated to religious or intellectual principles consistent with the teacher's beliefs, communication between administrators and teachers is easier, and parents whose children attend private schools tend to be more involved in school activities than those in public schools. Deciding to teach in a public or private school is ultimately an individual decision, influenced by a person's values and needs.

Putting Rewards and Difficulties into Perspective

The rewards and difficulties you face in teaching will strongly depend on the specific situation in which you work (Darling-Hammond, 2003; S. Johnson & Birkeland, 2003). For instance, some schools feel open and appealing from the moment you walk in the front door. They're well equipped, and teachers' routine needs, such as duplicating materials for students, are easily and efficiently met. Students are generally well behaved and eager to learn, and parents, colleagues, and administrators are cooperative and supportive. Other schools have problems similar to those James Washington encountered with Kevin, his mother, and the principal.

The size of your classes will also affect your work environment. A survey conducted by the National Center for Education Statistics (1998a) showed that student-teacher ratios range from 13:7 to 24:1 across the states. These figures can be misleading,

Increasing Understanding 1.4

As you anticipate a teaching career, do you believe working in the profession is more or less difficult than it was 10 years ago? Explain.

however, because school administrators, counselors, and special educators are counted as "teachers" in the statistics. The actual ratios can be considerably higher; 30 students or more in K–12 classes are common. A lower ratio will allow you to better meet the needs of individual students, and your teaching may be more rewarding. A higher ratio is associated with discipline problems, and dealing with student behavior could become one of the most prominent parts of your job. Your opportunities to get to know students as individuals could also be diminished. Each of these factors will strongly influence student learning and your satisfaction with teaching (National Education Association, 1997; Stamouli, 2002).

The Teaching Profession

What does it mean to be a professional? Are teachers professionals? Is professionalism more important now than it has been in the past? We try to answer these questions in this section.

Dimensions of Professionalism

Why are occupations such as medicine and law considered professions? Researchers examining these and other established professions have identified the following dimensions of **professionalism,** or *professional character*:

- A specialized body of knowledge
- Emphasis on decision making
- Reflection
- Autonomy
- Ethical standards for conduct (Ingersoll, 1997; Labaree, 1992)

Let's look at these dimensions and their presence in teaching.

A Specialized Body of Knowledge Professionals understand and utilize a specialized body of knowledge in serving their clients (Figure 1.1). A physician, for example, understands and can recognize symptoms of diseases and other ailments and is able to prescribe medications, surgical procedures, or other forms of therapy to eliminate both the symptoms and their causes. People seek the advice and help of physicians because of their specialized knowledge.

Figure 1.1 Professionalism Requires a Specialized Body of Knowledge

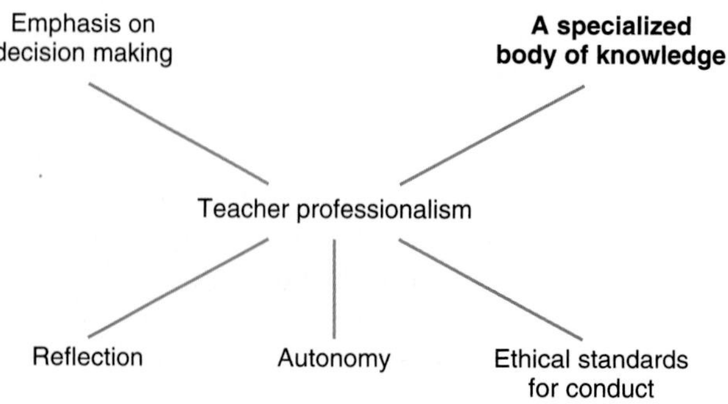

Do teachers possess specialized knowledge? Research indicates that expert teachers possess at least four kinds of knowledge (Borko & Putnam, 1996):

- *Knowledge of content:* A thorough understanding of a content area such as math, science, geography, or literature
- *Pedagogical content knowledge:* The ability to illustrate abstract concepts, such as *equivalent fractions* in math or *nationalism* in history, in ways that are understandable to students
- *General pedagogical knowledge:* Knowledge of general principles of teaching and learning, such as the ability to maintain an orderly and learning-focused classroom or guide student learning with questions
- *Knowledge of learners and learning:* Knowledge of theories of development and learning, such as understanding that learners, even in high school, tend to be egocentric, seeing the world from their own perspectives and often ignoring the views of others

To these we add *knowledge of the profession*, which includes an understanding of the social, historical, philosophical, organizational, and legal aspects of teaching, together with the ability and inclination to continue to learn. Just as physicians must continually upgrade their knowledge of therapies, medications, and surgical procedures, teachers must stay abreast of recent research in their field. For instance, it intuitively makes sense to encourage students who aren't successful to work harder, but research indicates that this suggestion can be counterproductive. Young children generally believe they are already working hard, so they're bewildered by the suggestion, and older students often believe the need to work hard is an indicator of low ability (Tollefson, 2000). Effective teachers stay abreast of research in their fields and adapt their teaching in response to their increased knowledge.

Much of this text is designed to help you develop your knowledge of the profession. We describe these different forms of knowledge in greater detail in Chapter 13 when we analyze the process of developing as a teacher.

Extended Training for Licensure. To develop the different forms of knowledge, extended training for licensure is required. As with physicians, lawyers, and engineers, teachers must earn a license that allows them to practice their profession. The license is intended to certify that the teacher is knowledgeable and competent, and as with other professions, teachers must renew their license periodically to confirm that they are staying current in their fields. Teachers need at least a bachelor's degree prior to licensure, and in many states they must complete the degree in a content area, such as math or English, before they begin teacher preparation experiences (Blair, 2000). Licensure also requires clinical experiences, such as internships, which are designed to ensure that teachers can apply the professional knowledge they have acquired in the real world of schools.

Emphasis on Decision Making To begin this section, let's return to Suzanne, our middle school science teacher introduced at the beginning of the chapter.

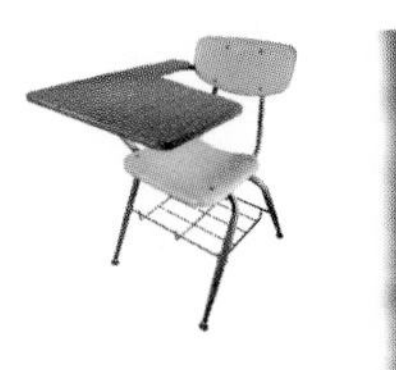

Case STUDY Suzanne came into her seventh-grade life science class on Monday morning carrying a cooler. After completing her beginning-of-class routines, she said, "Okay everyone, look up here," and reached into the cooler and pulled out a live lobster.

"Ooh," "Wow," "Yuk," "Gross," "Cool," and "What's that?" were among the many comments students made when they saw what she was holding.

Professional knowledge allows teachers to make the split-second decisions essential for effective teaching.

"Take out a piece of paper," Suzanne directed. She waited a few seconds until all the students had papers and pencils in front of them and then began walking around the room with the lobster.

"Touch it and observe it carefully," Suzanne said as she walked, "and then write at least three observations on your papers."

After the students finished writing their observations, she continued, "Okay, give us one of your observations, . . . Tiffany."

"Cold."

"Good. What else? . . . Josh?"

"It felt hard."

"Cory?"

"It looks like it has eyes."

"Yes, good," Suzanne said, pointing. "Here they are."

Suzanne asked for several more observations and then reached back into her cooler and took out several large shrimp. She told the students to work with their partners (she had partners seated near each other), gave each pair one shrimp, and instructed the students to observe the shrimp carefully and write down at least three similarities between the shrimp and the lobster.

"Give us one of your similarities, Javier," Suzanne directed after all the students had finished making their comparisons and had turned their attention back to the front of the room.

"They both are cold," Javier responded.

"What else, . . . Tamika?"

"They both have a shell on the outside."

Suzanne continued her questioning and guided the students to identify *cold-blooded, exoskeleton, three body parts,* and *jointed legs* as characteristics of arthropods, the animals they were learning about today.

She then showed the students a beetle, a spider, and a clam and asked the students if they were arthropods. After some discussion the students concluded that the beetle and spider were arthropods but the clam was not.

• • ● • •

Figure 1.2 Professionalism Requires an Emphasis on Decision Making

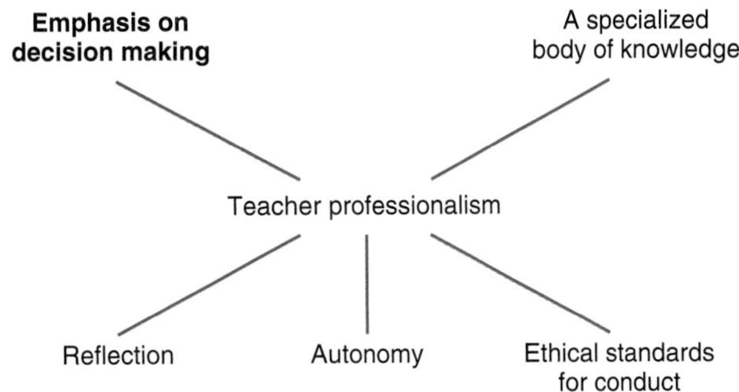

Let's look now at Suzanne's decision making, an important dimension of professionalism (Figure 1.2). Her lesson included decisions about the following:

- *Her topic and goal.* She decided to teach the topic *arthropods*, and she wanted students to understand that arthropods are cold-blooded and have three body parts, jointed legs, and an exoskeleton. She could have decided to skip the topic of arthropods completely or dealt with the topic only briefly instead.
- *The organization of her classroom.* She had partners seated near each other, for example, so that making transitions into and out of group work would be quick and smooth. She might have decided, instead, to have students work in groups of four and to have the groups move to different locations around the room.
- *The sequence of the learning activities.* Suzanne decided that she would begin the lesson by presenting examples and guiding the students to the characteristics of arthropods. She also decided to carry the lobster around the room herself. She could have decided to present the characteristics of arthropods first and then ask the students if her examples fit these characteristics and were arthropods. And she could have decided to let the students pass the lobster from one to another.
- *Her examples.* She chose real examples. She could have decided on an easier course of action, simply using pictures or verbal descriptions of the animals.
- *Learning activities.* She decided to use both small-group and whole-class work. Instead she could have conducted the entire lesson as a whole-group activity. Also, each question she asked involved a decision about the form of the question itself and who she would call on to answer it.

Now, let's look at Suzanne's reasoning as she planned and conducted her lesson. For example, she knew that the thinking of her middle school students was likely to be concrete rather than abstract, so she decided to use "real" examples rather than pictures or verbal descriptions. She knew that students learn more when they're directly involved in a learning experience, so she decided to have them conduct part of the activity in pairs. And, knowing that questioning is one of the most effective ways to actively involve students in learning (Eggen & Kauchak, 2004), she asked many questions throughout the lesson.

Suzanne based each of these decisions on her professional knowledge. Less knowledgeable teachers might have decided to simply show the students some pictures of arthropods and describe the characteristics for the students, or to simply describe arthropods without any examples. Either alternate decision would have resulted in less learning for the students.

Figure 1.3 Factors Influencing Teacher Decision Making

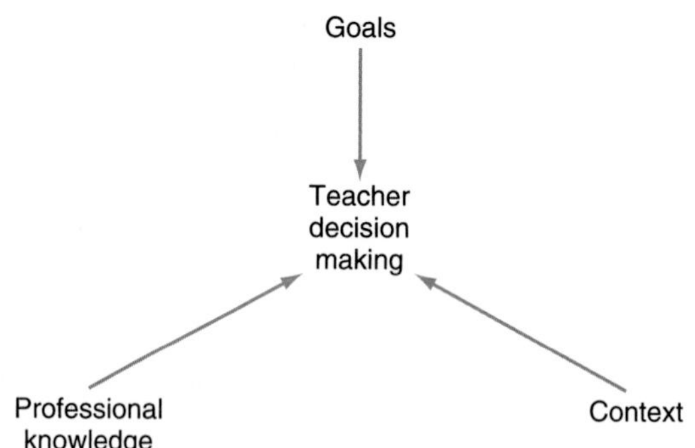

Promoting learning is a complex and ill-defined task, as we saw with Suzanne's lesson. A professional knowledge base allows expert teachers to make decisions in complex and ill-defined situations, and this decision-making process is one of the differences between a professional and a **technician,** *a person who uses specific skills to complete well-defined tasks*, such as an electrician wiring an outlet. Skills, such as questioning and the ability to organize learning activities, are important in teaching, but professionals also know when and why to implement different skills and strategies and how to adapt them when situations warrant. Thus, **decision making** involves *goal-oriented problem solving based on professional knowledge.*

Professional decision making is influenced by three factors:

- Goals
- Professional knowledge
- Context

These factors are illustrated in Figure 1.3 and discussed in the paragraphs that follow.

Increasing Understanding 1.5

What kind of teacher knowledge is primarily involved in effective questioning? How do the other forms of knowledge also influence a teacher's decision making during interactive questioning?

Suzanne's decision making was guided by her goal and professional knowledge. She wanted students to understand arthropods—her goal—and her decisions about the examples she used and the conduct of the lesson were guided by her professional knowledge about how best to reach that goal.

The context in which she planned and conducted the lesson also influenced her decisions. For instance, the ages and characteristics of students are two important contextual factors. Knowing that her students had little hands-on experience with cold-blooded animals further led to her decision to use real-world examples of arthropods. Had she been working with experienced high school biology students, she might have covered the topic more quickly and without as much emphasis. She also knew that middle school students can have limited interest in topics that have little direct impact on them, like arthropods, so she sought to increase their motivation by using a real lobster and real shrimp.

Decision making in teaching is incredibly complex. From our discussion of Suzanne's work with her students—and this was only one lesson—we begin to see how demanding teaching can be. Imagine engaging in decision making all day long, every day of the school year. In his classic study of elementary classrooms, Jackson (1968) found that teachers make more than 800 decisions a day; Murray (1986) estimated the number at 1,500. Just the conservative figure translates into more than 130 decisions per hour in a 6-hour, interactive teaching day! Being able to rely on a fund of professional knowledge is essential in helping teachers manage this complexity.

Figure 1.4 Professionalism Requires Reflection

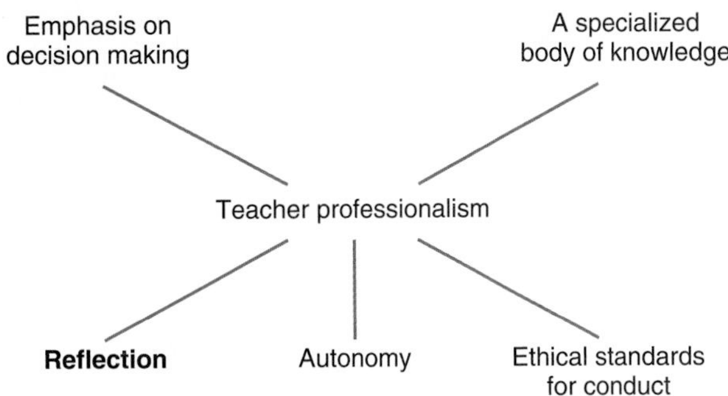

Increasing Understanding 1.6

One of your students is obviously more interested in her friends than in the topic you're teaching, and you can't seem to keep her from talking. You call on her; she doesn't hear the question. Should you reprimand her, repeat the question, or go on to another student? Explain your reasoning. (The feedback for this question will give you a research-based answer.)

We emphasize the central role of decision making in professionalism by concluding each chapter with a feature called *Decision Making: Defining Yourself as a Professional.* This feature frames chapter topics in ways that will help you decide what kind of teacher you want to become.

Reflection If teaching involves making an enormous number of decisions, most of which can't be reduced to simple rules, how do teachers know if their decisions are wise and valid? Most teachers receive little feedback about the effectiveness of their work. They are observed by administrators a few times a year at most and receive only vague, sketchy, and uncertain feedback from students and parents. In addition, they get virtually no feedback from their colleagues, unless the school has a peer coaching or mentoring program (Darling-Hammond, 1996). To develop as a professional, teachers must be able to continually assess their own classroom performance.

The ability to conduct this self-assessment requires that teachers develop a disposition for continually and critically examining what they're doing. This is the essence of a simple, yet powerful idea called **reflection** (Cruickshank, 1987; Schon, 1983), *the act of thinking about what you're doing* (Figure 1.4). Reflective teachers are thoughtful, analytical, even self-critical about their teaching. They plan lessons thoughtfully and take the time to analyze and critique them afterward.

Reflection is important in teaching not only because it improves our effectiveness as teachers but also because it helps us develop as professionals. By continually thinking about themselves and their work with students, reflective teachers develop a coherent philosophy of teaching that helps them integrate theory and practice and continually refine their practice (Rodgers, 2002).

Recall that one of our goals in writing this book is to help you decide what kind of teacher you want to become. Reflecting on the content of this book as you think about yourself and the students you'll teach will help you shape an image of yourself as a teacher.

Autonomy With knowledge also comes *autonomy.* Professionals have the authority to make decisions based on their specialized knowledge (Figure 1.5). When a person sees a physician because of stomach pains, for example, no set of standards mandates specific treatments or medications; doctors are given the authority to treat patients as they see fit. Some suggest that teaching isn't a profession because states and districts, instead of teachers, prescribe *what teachers teach* (the **curriculum**) as well as *how student understanding is measured* (**assessment**). This lack of autonomy, they assert, makes teachers technicians instead of professionals.

Reflection provides opportunities for teachers to think about and improve their practice.

Figure 1.5 Professionalisms Requires Autonomy

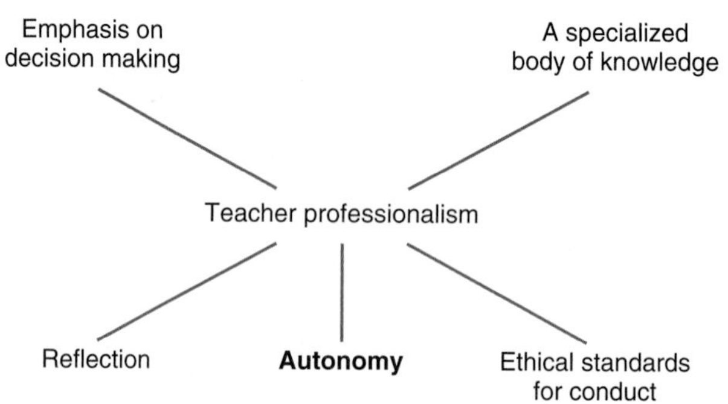

Indeed, states and districts are prescribing **standards,** *statements specifying what students should know and what skills they should have upon completing an area of study*, and students must meet these standards before being allowed to move from one grade to another or graduate from high school (Falk, 2002). However, in spite of these mandates, teachers still have a great deal of control over what is taught, how they teach it, and how students are assessed. Each day teachers make an enormous number of decisions by relying largely on their own professional judgment.

Ethical Standards for Conduct To begin this section, consider the following scenarios:

· · • · ·

An ardent advocate of gun control, you believe that access to guns should be strictly regulated, and you have said so in class. Eric, one of your students, brings a newspaper editorial to school in which a compelling argument *against* gun control is made. Because of your beliefs, you don't allow the student to share the editorial with the class.

· · • · ·

Autonomy requires that teachers use professional decision making in their interactions with students.

Greg is a very difficult student in one of your classes. He is continually disruptive and periodically shouts insults at other students and sometimes even at you. You've tried everything you know to control his behavior, but you've been unsuccessful. Finally, in exasperation one day, one of the students tells him, "Shut up! I can't think!" after one of his outbursts. Surprisingly, Greg is embarrassed and sits quietly for the remainder of the period. Now, finding that public embarrassment seems to be the only way to keep Greg from being disruptive, you use it as a technique to manage his behavior.

• • ● • •

Have you behaved "ethically" in these examples? How do you know? **Ethics** are *a set of moral standards for acceptable professional behavior*, and all professions have a code of ethics intended to guide professionals as they make decisions about how to act (Figure 1.6). In its code of ethics, the National Education Association (NEA), the

Figure 1.6 Professionalism Requires Ethical Standards for Conduct

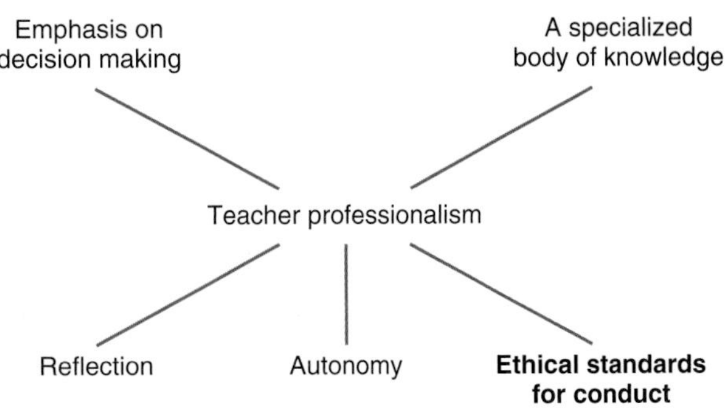

Professional ethics guide teachers in their interactions with students, parents and caregivers, and colleagues.

largest professional organization in education, addresses the behavior of teachers working with their students (Figure 1.7).

Let's evaluate your actions based on the information in the NEA Code of Ethics. Item 2 of the *Commitment to the Student* principle (Principle I) in the code states that a teacher "shall not unreasonably deny the student access to varying points of view." In our first example, you didn't let Eric share the editorial with the other students, so you have denied them access to varying points of view. Whether or not your denial was "unreasonable" is open to interpretation, as is the case with ethical standards in any profession.

In the second example, you were desperately searching for a way to manage Greg's behavior, and by chance you found that embarrassment was the only thing that seemed to work. However, Item 5 of Principle I says a teacher "shall not intentionally expose the student to embarrassment or disparagement." This case is clear; in your desperation and frustration, you intentionally used embarrassment as a strategy with Greg, so you are in violation of the ethical code.

Increasing Understanding 1.7

What is the relationship between a teacher's knowledge of the NEA code and the other components of teacher professionalism—decision making, reflection, and autonomy?

Some additional examples of ethical lapses commonly seen in the teaching profession include retaliating against students for alleged slights or offenses by grading unfairly or making unfair placement decisions, accepting fees for tutoring one's own students, and cheating on state tests by giving students more than the prescribed time or by giving them clues and/or answers (Raths & Lyman, 2003). Ethical standards are so important to professionals that they are often written into employment contracts. The standards provide an important basis for professional decision making.

Reflect on This

To analyze a case study examining issues involved in professional ethics, go to the Companion Website at **www.prenhall.com/kauchak**, then to this chapter's *Reflect on This* module.

Are Teachers Professionals?

Not everyone agrees that teaching is a profession and teachers are professionals. Their arguments include the following:

- Lack of rigorous training
- Lack of autonomy
- Lack of accountability

Figure 1.7 National Education Association Code of Ethics

Preamble

The educator, believing in the worth and dignity of each human being, recognizes the supreme importance of the pursuit of truth, devotion to excellence, and the nurture of democratic principle. Essential to these goals is the protection of freedom to learn and to teach and the guarantee of equal educational opportunity for all. The educator accepts the responsibility to adhere to the highest ethical standards.

The educator recognizes the magnitude of the responsibility inherent in the teaching process. The desire for the respect and confidence of one's colleagues, of students, of parents, and the members of the community provides the incentive to attain and maintain the highest possible degree of ethical conduct. The Code of Ethics of the Education Profession indicates the aspiration of all educators and provides standards by which to judge conduct.

The remedies specified by the NEA and/or its affiliates for the violation of any provision of this Code shall be exclusive and no such provision shall be enforceable in any form other than one specifically designated by the NEA or its affiliates.

Principle I—Commitment to the Student

The educator strives to help each student realize his or her potential as a worthy and effective member of society. The educator therefore works to stimulate the spirit of inquiry, the acquisition of knowledge and understanding, and the thoughtful formulation of worthy goals.

In fulfillment of the obligation to the student, the educator—

1. Shall not unreasonably restrain the student from independent action in the pursuit of learning.
2. Shall not unreasonably deny the student access to varying points of view.
3. Shall not deliberately suppress or distort subject matter relevant to the student's progress.
4. Shall make reasonable effort to protect the student from conditions harmful to learning or to health and safety.
5. Shall not intentionally expose the student to embarrassment or disparagement.
6. Shall not on the basis of race, color, creed, sex, national origin, marital status, political or religious beliefs, family, social or cultural background, or sexual orientation unfairly:
   a. Exclude any student from participation in any program;
   b. Deny benefits to any student;
   c. Grant any advantage to any student.
7. Shall not use professional relationships with students for private advantage.
8. Shall not disclose information about students obtained in the course of professional service, unless disclosure serves a compelling professional purpose or is required by law.

Principle II—Commitment to the Profession

The education profession is vested by the public with a trust and responsibility requiring the highest ideals of professional service.

In the belief that the quality of the services of the education profession directly influences the nation and its citizens, the educator shall exert every effort to raise professional standards, to promote a climate that encourages the exercise of professional judgment, to achieve conditions which attract persons worthy of the trust to careers in education, and to assist in preventing the practice of the profession by unqualified persons.

In fulfillment of the obligation to the profession, the educator—

1. Shall not in an application for a professional position deliberately make a false statement or fail to disclose a material fact related to competency and qualifications.
2. Shall not misrepresent his/her professional qualifications.
3. Shall not assist entry into the profession of a person known to be unqualified in respect to character, education, or other relevant attribute.
4. Shall not knowingly make a false statement concerning the qualifications of a candidate for a professional position.
5. Shall not assist a noneducator in the unauthorized practice of teaching.
6. Shall not disclose information about colleagues obtained in the course of professional service unless disclosure serves a compelling professional purpose or is required by law.
7. Shall not knowingly make a false or malicious statement about a colleague.
8. Shall not accept any gratuity, gift, or favor that might impair or appear to influence professional decisions or actions.

Source: From National Education Association. (1995). Code of Ethics of the Education Profession, NEA Representative Assembly. Reprinted by permission.

Portfolios provide opportunities for teachers to demonstrate their skills and professional knowledge.

Lack of Rigorous Training The academic rigor of teachers' professional training has historically been criticized (Gross, 1999; R. Kramer, 1991). Entrance into teaching isn't as highly competitive as entrance into professions such as medicine or law, and many proposed reforms suggest that pedagogical content knowledge, general pedagogical knowledge, and knowledge of learners and learning be de-emphasized in favor of knowledge of content (Gross, 1999). The argument is often made, though not supported by research (Berliner, 2000), that the only thing that teachers need is knowledge of the subjects they are teaching.

Lack of Autonomy In the last section we argued that teachers have a great deal of autonomy. Although we maintain this position, we also acknowledge that teachers have less autonomy than other professionals. For example, unlike physicians and lawyers, teachers are supervised and evaluated by their immediate school administrators, and a substantial portion of the curriculum is mandated by states or districts. Teachers have little to say about the standards for licensure, and many teachers even have to sign in at the beginning of the day and sign out at the end.

Lack of Accountability Critics also argue that teachers are not accountable for student learning. If a student is unable to read at the end of the third grade, for example, little consequence exists for the third-grade teacher. Further, when teachers achieve tenure, they are secure in their jobs. Barring a sexual offense or clear incompetence, removing a tenured teacher is extremely difficult.

Putting Teacher Professionalism into Perspective

The issue of whether or not teaching is a profession is controversial and won't be resolved in the near future. Without question, the training required for professions such as medicine and law is more extensive and rigorous than the training required for teaching, although rigor in teacher education is on the rise (Olson, 2000a). Prospec-

CLASSROOMS IN ACTION: THE REAL WORLD OF TEACHING

Having looked at the reasons people choose to teach, the rewards and difficulties in teaching, and teacher professionalism, you now have the opportunity to view videos of three teachers in action.

In the first episode a kindergarten teacher uses questioning to help her students think about plants and gardening. In the second episode a middle school teacher attempts to teach his students about Bernoulli's principle by actively involving them in hands-on experiments. In the third episode a high school English teacher uses role playing and discussion to teach about the characters in Nathaniel Hawthorne's *Scarlet Letter*.

To complete this activity, do the following:

- Go to the DVD, which accompanies this book, and view the video episodes titled "Classrooms in Action: The Real World of Teaching."
- Answer the questions you'll find on the DVD.

To answer the questions online and receive immediate feedback, go to the Companion Website at **www.prenhall.com/kauchak**, *then to this chapter's* Classroom Windows *module.*

tive teachers are expected to know and do more, and their understanding and skills are being increasingly assessed with tests.

With respect to autonomy, a battle is currently being fought on both sides of the issue (Meier, 2002). Some would curtail teachers' autonomy by mandating what and how to teach, as well as specifying how to assess student learning. Others argue that this technical view of teaching is unfeasible and unproductive because teaching requires too many decisions to be reduced to mandates and attempts to do so discourage creative people from considering teaching as a career (Kohn, 2000).

Also, the argument about lack of accountability doesn't apply only to education. Admittedly, teachers don't lose their jobs if their students perform poorly on standardized tests, but similar examples exist in other professions. For instance, physicians don't lose their right to practice medicine if they prescribe an antibiotic for an ear infection, but the infection doesn't go away, and attorneys don't lose their right to practice law if they lose a case. These individuals retain their professional status despite an apparent "lack of accountability" in instances such as these.

It is clear that teachers share many of the characteristics used to describe members of established professions: They possess a specialized body of knowledge, they make numerous important decisions in the course of performing their work, and they have a significant amount of autonomy. Many teachers take time to reflect on their actions and take care to follow the ethical standards set forth by educational leaders. Are teachers professionals? At this time, many educational commentators seem to be saying "not quite." To truly "professionalize" teaching, they believe a number of reforms are necessary. We discuss these reforms next.

The Modern Reform Movement

You're beginning your teacher-preparation experience in one of the most tumultuous periods in the history of American education. Critics, both inside and outside the profession, are calling for **reforms,** *suggested changes in teaching and teacher preparation* *intended to increase the amount students learn.* To implement these reforms, teachers must be well-prepared, and leaders in education are saying that we need to professionalize teaching (Blair, 2000). We examine the implications of these reform efforts in this section.

To place recent reform efforts in perspective, we should point out that the process of change and reform has been a part of education throughout its history. From colonial times to the present, schools and the teachers in them have been fair game for outside critics. The openness and accessibility of teaching make it a unique profession. Most anyone who has been in school has an opinion about how to improve education. When you study the history of education in Chapter 5, you will see how different reforms have shaped education over the years.

The modern reform movement is often traced to 1983, when the National Commission on Excellence in Education published *A Nation at Risk: The Imperative for Educational Reform.* This widely read document suggested that America was "at risk" of being unable to compete in the world economic marketplace because our system of education was inadequate. The terms "at-risk students" and more recently "students placed at-risk" were subsequently used to refer to students at risk of not acquiring the knowledge and skills needed for success in our modern, technological society. Since 1983 a great many other suggestions have been made for improving our nation's schools and the teachers who work in them.

Because discussions of reform are so important in education today, we have made *reform* a theme of this book. To help you understand the scope of reforms in education, we examine two prominent ones, which are currently occurring at both state and federal levels:

- Changes in teacher preparation
- Accountability and high-stakes testing

We close the section with a look at the results of one statewide reform effort.

Changes in Teacher Preparation

Increased emphasis on professionalism, as well as criticisms that too many unqualified teachers enter teaching (Raths & Lyman, 2003), have resulted in a number of reforms in teacher education, most of these at the state level. These reforms include the following (Blair, 2000):

- Raising standards for acceptance into teacher training programs
- Requiring teachers to take more rigorous courses than they have in the past
- Expanding teacher preparation programs from 4 years to 5
- Requiring experienced teachers to take more rigorous professional development courses
- Requiring higher standards for licensure, including teacher competency tests

The emphasis on professionalism is further reinforced through a new federal law, the *No Child Left Behind Act of 2001*, a major provision of which is a call for improved teacher quality. By 2005–2006 all teachers must be fully qualified, and paraprofessionals working in schools must have 2 years of college or demonstrate equivalent knowledge on a competency test (Hardy, 2002). This provision of the law is a direct result of research showing that teachers have a powerful effect on student achievement (Gallagher, 2002) and that many poor, minority, or inner-city children are frequently taught by underqualified teachers (J. Jennings, 2002).

Competency Testing Teacher quality will be assessed primarily through competency testing, which means it is very likely that you will be required to pass a test to be admitted to the profession. At the present time, teacher evaluation takes several forms:

- Thirty-four states require prospective teachers to pass a basic skills test.
- Thirty states require high school teachers to pass a test of subject matter knowledge they plan to teach.
- Twenty-seven states require school principals to evaluate new teachers. (Olson, 2000a; Wayne & Youngs, 2003)

Praxis: Comprehensive Teacher Testing. The most common form of teacher testing is the Praxis Series, published by the Educational Testing Service. The Praxis Series (*praxis* refers to putting theory into practice) is currently being used in 35 states and consists of three components (Educational Testing Service, 2001):

- *Praxis I: Academic Skills Assessments*—designed to measure basic or "enabling" skills in reading, writing, and math that all teachers need.
- *Praxis II: Subject Assessments*—designed to measure teachers' knowledge of the subjects they will teach. In addition to 70 content-specific tests, Praxis II also includes the Principles of Learning and Teaching (PLT) tests, which measure professional knowledge.
- *Praxis III: Classroom Performance Assessments*—use classroom observations and work samples to assess beginning teachers' ability to plan, instruct, manage, and understand professional responsibilities. In addition, Praxis III assesses the teacher's sensitivity to learners' developmental and cultural differences.

You are most likely to encounter Praxis I during your teacher preparation, Praxis II after its completion, and Praxis III during your first year of teaching.

An important part of the Praxis Series are the general Principles of Learning and Teaching (PLT) tests, specifically designed for teachers seeking licensure for different grade levels (K–6, 5–9, and 7–12). The topics these tests cover are outlined in the Praxis Correlation Matrix at the beginning of this text.

Each of the grade-level tests has two parts (Educational Testing Service, 2001). The first part consists of multiple-choice questions similar to those in the test bank that accompanies this text. The second part presents "case histories" that you will be asked to read and analyze. The PLT cases are similar to the case studies you'll find in each chapter of this text.

There are two types of items in the case-based part of each PLT exam: constructed response and document based. In the first you read a case study and are then asked to analyze it, responding to short-answer *Constructed Response Questions* (Educational Testing Service, 2001). In the *Document-Based Analysis Questions* you evaluate student- or teacher-prepared documents, such as student work, excerpts from student records, teachers' lesson plans, assignments, or assessments. We have designed this text to help you pass your Praxis PLT test by including both types of case-based formats in the Praxis Practice exercises at the end of each chapter. Suggestions on how to succeed on the Praxis can be found in Keys to Success on the Praxis at the front of this text.

Portfolios: Individual Teacher Accountability A **portfolio,** or *a collection of materials representative of one's work*, provides an alternate way to document teacher competence. Just as a portfolio of artwork is prepared by an artist to illustrate talents and accomplishments, a **professional portfolio** is *produced by a prospective teacher to document developing knowledge and skills.* (*Student portfolios* are discussed in Chapter 11 in our coverage of alternative assessment.)

As you proceed through your professional program, you will likely be required to prepare a portfolio to document your developing professional competence, and it will be a tool you can use during job interviews to describe who you are and what skills you possess. Online Portfolio Activities are found at the end of each chapter of this text, and guidelines for beginning a professional portfolio can be found in Appendix A.

Whether reforms such as teacher testing and the use of portfolios to document competency will result in the hoped-for improvements in education remains to be seen, and will continue to be debated. One thing is virtually certain, however; efforts to reform schools, teachers, and the way teachers are prepared will continue, and you will begin your career as a teacher in the midst of these changes.

INTASC: Standards in Teacher Education

In addition to increased testing and portfolios, standards are also being used to increase the rigor of teacher preparation programs. In the past, learning to teach was easier, and the demands on beginning teachers were not as great. This has changed—a rapidly expanding body of research consistently demonstrates that teaching now requires professionals who are highly knowledgeable and skilled (Berliner, 2000).

The profession is responding. Created in 1987, the *Interstate New Teacher Assessment and Support Consortium* (INTASC) was designed to help states develop better teachers through coordinated efforts of support and assessment. INTASC (1993) has raised the bar by setting rigorous standards for new teachers in important areas such as planning, instruction, and motivation. These standards describe what you should know and be able to do when you first walk into a classroom.

To date, INTASC has prepared general, or "core," standards organized around 10 principles (Table 1.3) and is preparing standards for various subject-matter areas and specific student populations. A Test for Teaching Knowledge (TTK) is also being developed. Each of the Online Portfolio Activities found at the end the chapters is linked to the INTASC core standards.

Increasing Understanding 1.8

Analyze the 10 INTASC principles in Table 1.3 in terms of the different kinds of professional knowledge described earlier. Which are emphasized the most? the least?

The principles are expanded by describing the knowledge, dispositions, and performances all teachers are expected to possess and demonstrate. For instance, with respect to the first principle, Knowledge of Subject, teachers should understand how students' misconceptions in an area—such as believing that the earth is closer to the sun in the summer (in the Northern Hemisphere)—can influence their learning (knowledge), they should be committed to continuous learning (disposition), and they should be able to employ a variety of instructional strategies to make topics understandable to students (performance), such as using demonstrations, pictures, technology, and classroom discussion to help students understand the causes of the seasons. Similar knowledge, dispositions, and performances are described for each principle.

The INTASC standards are demanding, but this is as it should be. If you expect to be treated as a professional, you should have the knowledge and skills that allow you to make the decisions expected of a professional. Being able to meet the INTASC standards is a good beginning.

To learn more about INTASC, go to the Companion Website at **www.prenhall.com/kauchak**, then link to the *INTASC* module.

Table 1.3 The INTASC Principles

Principle	Description
1. Knowledge of subject	The teacher understands the central concepts, tools of inquiry, and structures of the discipline(s) he or she teaches and can create learning experiences that make these aspects of subject matter meaningful for students.
2. Learning and human development	The teacher understands how children learn and develop and can provide learning opportunities that support their intellectual, social and personal development.
3. Adapting instruction	The teacher understands how students differ in their approaches to learning and creates instructional opportunities that are adapted to diverse learners.
4. Strategies	The teacher understands and uses a variety of instructional strategies to encourage students' development of critical thinking, problem solving, and performance skills.
5. Motivation and management	The teacher uses an understanding of individual and group motivation and behavior to create a learning environment that encourages positive social interaction, active engagement in learning, and self-motivation.
6. Communication skills	The teacher uses knowledge of effective verbal, nonverbal, and media communication techniques to foster active inquiry, collaboration, and supportive interaction in the classroom.
7. Planning	The teacher plans instruction based upon knowledge of subject matter, students, the community, and curriculum goals.
8. Assessment	The teacher understands and uses formal and informal assessment strategies to evaluate and ensure the continuous intellectual, social, and physical development of the learner.
9. Commitment	The teacher is a reflective practitioner who continually evaluates the effects of his/her choices and actions on others (students, parents, and other professionals in the learning community) and who actively seeks out opportunities to grow professionally.
10. Partnership	The teacher fosters relationships with school colleagues, parents, and agencies in the larger community to support students' learning and well-being.

Source: From Interstate New Teacher Assessment and Support Consortium. (1993). *Model standards for beginning teacher licensing and development: A resource for state dialogues.* Washington, D.C.: Council of Chief State School Officers. Reprinted by permission.

Teaching in an Era of Reform

We said earlier in this section that we have made *reform* a theme of this book. To actively involve you in examining prominent reforms throughout the text, we include a feature in each chapter called *Teaching in an Era of Reform.* We introduce the feature in this chapter and illustrate how you can use it to increase your understanding of educational reforms in the United States.

The feature includes the following elements:

- A reform issue, such as retaining students who don't pass tests in the same grade (Chapter 7) or *learner-centered* versus *teacher-centered* instruction (Chapter 11), is presented and discussed.
- The issue is "put into perspective" by presenting arguments for and against the reform.
- You are then asked to take a position by responding to the issue personally.

We illustrate this process in the accompanying feature, using "accountability and high-stakes testing" as the reform issue.

Teaching in an Era of Reform

THE ACCOUNTABILITY AND HIGH-STAKES TESTING ISSUE

In response to concerns about students graduating from high school without the skills needed to succeed either in college or the workplace, reformers have called for greater accountability for both students and teachers. **Accountability** is *the process of requiring students to demonstrate that they have met specified standards or that they demonstrate understanding of the topics they study as measured by standardized tests, as well as holding educators at all levels responsible for students' performance.* Calls for accountability were prompted by evidence indicating that students were being promoted from grade to grade without mastering essential content; some students were graduating from high school barely able to read, write, and do mathematics effectively; and even more had limited scientific literacy and a general lack of understanding of our world.

No Child Left Behind

One of the most far-reaching accountability reforms is the No Child Left Behind (NCLB) Act of 2001, which one expert called "the most significant change in federal regulation of public schools in three decades" (Hardy, 2002, p. 201).

Signed by President George W. Bush, NCLB officially reauthorized the Elementary and Secondary Education Act, which began in 1965 and resulted in billions of dollars being spent on compensatory education programs for disadvantaged students. Several key provisions of NCLB address teacher preparation, standards, accountability, and testing, and these provisions will influence teachers' professional lives in the years to come.

NCLB calls for accountability at several levels. For example, states are required to create standards for what every child should know and learn for all grades. Standards for math and reading must be developed immediately, and standards for science must be developed by the 2005–2006 school year. States must implement these standards in order to receive continued federal funding. School districts will be responsible for implementing these standards and gathering information about their attainment. Individual schools will be held accountable for ensuring that every child in that school has achieved satisfactory progress toward the standards. Schools, districts, and states must keep records of performance to document achievement of different groups of students by race, ethnicity, gender, and English proficiency.

If a school fails to make adequate yearly progress with any of these student subgroups for 2 consecutive years, students may transfer to another school. After 3 years of sub-par performance, students within underachieving schools are entitled to outside tutoring at district expense. After 4 years the school will be placed on probation and corrective measures taken. States, districts, individual schools, and teachers are already feeling the pressures of accountability (Christie, 2003).

High-stakes tests are *assessments used to determine whether or not students will be promoted from one grade to another, graduate from high school, or have access to specific fields of study.* When students aren't allowed to graduate from high school because they fail a test, for example, the "stakes" are very high, thus the term *high-stakes tests.* In a similar way, when districts and specific schools within them are singled out as failing or "leaving children behind," the stakes are also very high.

High-stakes testing was widespread before NCLB and will become even more so with its implementation, as the following facts illustrate:

- All states must create testing programs designed, in large part, to measure how well students perform on standards created to meet NCLB requirements.
- All states must issue overall ratings of their schools based on the test performance of their students.
- At least 18 states currently have the authority to close, take over, or overhaul schools that are identified as failing (Olson, 2000b). NCLB will increase this figure to all 50 states.

The key to NCLB accountability is testing. By 2005–2006 each child in grades 3 through 8 will be tested yearly in math and reading; children will be tested at least once more in grades 10–12. By 2007–2008 students will also be assessed in science at least once in their academic career. These test scores will be used to hold schools accountable for student achievement.

The Issue

As you might expect, accountability through high-stakes testing is very controversial, with critics arguing that these tests fail to accurately assess student learning and narrowly limit the curriculum (Behuniak, 2002; Meier, 2002). Critics believe that, faced with pressures to help students achieve in math, reading, and science, teachers will underemphasize other subjects like social studies, art, music, health, and physical education (Mathis, 2003). This narrowing of the curriculum deprives students of valuable learning opportunities necessary for growth and development. It also hinders teacher creativity because teachers spend too much time teaching only test content and helping students practice for the tests. Teachers also report that testing programs have forced them to teach in ways that contradict sound instructional practices. For example, despite knowing that computers can be an effective tool for teaching writing, many teachers have abandoned technology because the state writing test is handwritten (Pedulla et al., 2003).

The pressure for students to perform well on the tests also produces adverse consequences. To avoid test-related sanctions, teachers in states with high-stakes tests frequently request transfers out of grades that are tested, and experts fear that veteran teachers will transfer out of high-poverty and high-minority schools, depriving students of the experienced teachers they need (Lynn, 2003). The pressure is so great that some teachers and administrators have been driven to cheat; they help students with the tests or even give them answers (Viadero, 2000a). In Massachusetts high-stakes testing became so controversial that the state's largest teacher union, in a highly unusual move, launched a $600,000 television campaign that sharply criticized the Massachusetts Comprehensive Assessment System exam, a test students in the state must pass to graduate (Gehring, 2000a).

Critics also contend that current tests are not adequate for crucial decisions about students' lives (Neill, 2003; Popham, 2003) and that cut-off scores are often arbitrary and capricious. For example, when the state of Virginia decided to require one fewer correct answer to earn a passing score, 5,625 failing scores turned into passes (Bracey, 2003b)!

Advocates of testing, while conceding that teacher preparation, instructional resources, and the tests themselves need to be improved, argue that these tests are the fairest and most effective means of achieving the aims of democratic schooling—namely, successful learning for all. Further, they assert, evidence indicates that educational systems that require content standards and use tests that thoroughly measure the extent to which the standards are met greatly improve the achievement for all students, including those from disadvantaged backgrounds (Bishop, 1995, 1998). However, other experts disagree, asserting that high-stakes tests decrease motivation and encourage higher dropout rates (Amrein & Berliner, 2003). Hirsch (2000) summarized the testing advocates' position: "They [standards and tests that measure achievement of the standards] are the most promising educational development in half a century" (p. 64).

You Take a Position

Now it's your turn to take a position on the issue. State in writing whether you feel that accountability and high-stakes testing will improve the quality of education or harm it, and provide a two-page rationale for your position. For additional references and resources, go to the Companion Website at **www.prenhall.com/kauchak**, then to this chapter's *Teaching in an Era of Reform* module. You can respond online or submit your response to your instructor.

A major element of many current reform efforts, including No Child Left Behind, is increased emphasis on testing in the schools.

Exploring Diversity

CULTURAL MINORITIES AND HIGH-STAKES TESTS

As we have seen, high-stakes tests are highly controversial. One part of the controversy focuses on critics' claims that these tests are destructive for cultural minorities, particularly Hispanic and African American students who consistently score lower on standardized tests than do their White and Asian agemates (Bowman, 2000a; Viadero & Johnston, 2000). The controversy flaired in 1999 when the *Mexican American Legal Defense and Educational Fund* (MALDEF) filed a federal lawsuit seeking to end the practice of requiring students to pass a test to graduate from high school in Texas. MALDEF argued that the Texas Assessment of Academic Skills (TAAS) is unfair to thousands of Hispanic and Black students (Wildavsky, 1999).

The MALDEF lawsuit was just one case in a long line of controversies over race and testing. All raise the same question: As standardized tests are increasingly used to measure student performance and hold students accountable—with important consequences for not measuring up—will historically lower-scoring Black and Hispanic students be treated fairly?

MALDEF's answer to the question is, of course, no, but not all educators—including some in Texas—agree. For example, one school district in Houston made increased scores on the TAAS a high priority, which resulted in dramatic improvement in the performance of its students, of whom 86 percent were Hispanic and 88 percent were economically disadvantaged (R. Johnston, 2000a).

Other educators have suggested comprehensive strategies for decreasing the achievement gap between minority and nonminority students, and testing is an integral part of those strategies. These educators have made increasing minority achievement their goal and assert that eliminating tests will not in-

Results of One Statewide Reform: The Kentucky Education Reform Act Will reform efforts produce the hoped-for results? One of the most ambitious and well-known state reform efforts, the *Kentucky Education Reform Act* (KERA), was precipitated by a 1989 Kentucky Supreme Court ruling that declared that the state's system of funding public schools was unconstitutional. Funding disparities between rich and poor school districts had resulted in a system that was inequitable and inefficient. The state legislature responded with a comprehensive educational reform bill that attempted to address several of the issues, such as accountability and standards, discussed in this chapter. The major components of the effort, and the changes that resulted, are found in Table 1.4 on page 34.

As you can see from Table 1.4, KERA affected every student and every teacher in the state. To fund these reforms, the Kentucky legislature approved a $1.3 billion tax increase, and public school expenditures increased 50 percent over the first 5 years of implementation (Holland, 1997; "Will KERA," 2003).

How successful was this "most sweeping statewide education reform plan ever enacted" (Rothman, 1997)? Evaluations range from "success beyond all expecta-

crease achievement as test critics seem to assume (Viadero & Johnston, 2000).

Despite the negative effects of some reform efforts, teachers still have considerable autonomy in their classrooms.

Many issues related to high-stakes testing with minority students remain unanswered. One is whether the accuracy of these tests is sufficient to make important decisions about students' academic lives (Kohn, 2000). A second issue relates to eliminating test bias when testing minorities, as well as English language learners (Abedi, 1999; R. Land, 1997). High-stakes test designers need to ensure that test scores reflect differences in achievement rather than cultural or language differences. Finally, deciding student grade promotion or graduation solely on the basis of one score is being increasingly criticized by a number of prestigious professional organizations, both within and outside of education, including the American Educational Research Association and the American Psychological Association.

Unquestionably, testing is necessary to measure the learning progress of all students, both minorities and nonminorities. Whether or not progress from one grade to another or graduation from high school should be linked to performance on the tests remains an open and troubling question.

tions" to "dismal failure" (Petroska, Lindle, & Pankratz, 2000). Research suggests that this reform *did* improve student performance; between 1992 and 1996, 92 percent of Kentucky's schools showed improvements in achievement (Rothman, 1997). These increases were especially evident at the elementary level in math, reading, and social studies (Petroska et al., 2000). In addition, the preschool programs for students placed at-risk appeared to have long-lasting benefits for young students.

As with all reforms, however, the Kentucky plan was not without its critics. Conservatives argued that it cost too much, and as often happens with education reforms, funding for the program was significantly decreased (D. Hoff, 2003b). In addition, teachers now question whether the emphasis on accountability has narrowed the curriculum and forced teachers to "teach to the test," a common complaint when high-stakes testing is implemented. In many respects KERA, with its emphasis on systemic reform and accountability, was a precursor of the No Child Left Behind Act, the federal reform effort that is now changing educational systems in every state in the nation.

Table 1.4 Major Provisions of the Kentucky Education Reform Act

Reform Component	Result
Curriculum guides	Clearly defined student learning goals for key areas such as math, reading, and social studies
Assessment and accountability systems	Created a statewide testing system that held schools accountable for student learning
Ungraded primary program for K–3	Eliminated grade levels and used multiage grouping to educate primary students
Extended school services for students placed at-risk	Provided extra instruction after school and in the summer for students placed at-risk
School-based decision making	Created school-level councils consisting of parents and teachers to provide input on how schools were run
Preschool program for children placed at-risk	Created developmentally appropriate preschool programs for students eligible for free or reduced lunches or those who were developmentally delayed
Family and youth resource centers	Provided links between schools and families and offered information on other government agencies

Decision Making

Defining Yourself as a Professional

Because decision making is so important in teaching, we close each chapter by asking you one or more questions designed to help you make decisions about yourself as a developing professional. And, because we focused this chapter on the question "Do I want to be a teacher?" we address it again here.

"Do I want to be a teacher?" is the first and most basic decision you must make about teaching. This chapter described factors that will influence your decision, but ultimately you still must make it. In addition to reading this text, you can take some other steps to help you decide.

First, you can directly experience what it's like to work in schools as a teacher. Your teacher preparation program will probably have a field experience component; learn as much as possible from it. You can also volunteer to work in a classroom or tutor students outside of school. Your instructor can suggest options available in the local community. You should seek out and talk to people who are teachers and ask them about their experiences.

Second, try to learn as much as you can about where teaching is headed, as these trends will affect your satisfaction with the profession. Three of the most important trends were discussed in this chapter: changes in teacher preparation, demands for greater teacher accountability and more student testing, and a push to professionalize teaching.

Compared to teachers in the past, you will be expected to know more English, math, science, and content in other areas. The general education requirements for teachers will almost certainly increase, and your knowledge of content in a specialty area, as well as your pedagogical content knowledge, general pedagogical knowledge, and knowledge of learners and learning, will have to be deep and thorough. In 2001, 34 states required prospective teachers to pass tests of basic skills, 30 required them to pass a test of subject matter knowledge, and 25 required tests of pedagogical knowledge (Wayne & Youngs, 2003). Your performance on these tests may determine whether or not you will be allowed to teach. You must decide if you believe you have the academic capability to pass these courses and tests.

Requirements for accountability and testing will become an important part of life for all teachers in the future. The No Child Left Behind Act will fundamentally change teaching. For instance, if you become an elementary teacher, your students will be tested every year; if you become a secondary teacher, pressure to achieve and maintain high levels of student performance will also exist. Teachers at all levels are already experiencing increased performance pressures from government officials and public commentators (van den Berg, 2002), some of whom propose providing merit pay for teachers of high-performing students and sanctions for teachers of low-performing students (Bradley, 2000b; Hoff, 2000c; J. Jennings, 2002). Ask yourself whether you'll be happy living with accountability as a fact of your future professional life.

Increased emphasis will continue to be placed on making teaching a true profession. If you don't applaud this trend, you may be passed over in hiring for those who do. Although professional organizations in education have fought against high standards in the past, this is now changing (Blair, 2000). In general, people get as much professional respect as they deserve; *if you expect to be treated as a professional, then you must act like a professional.* We recommend that you voice your criticisms of courses with low standards and limited substance; they detract from teaching as a profession and don't provide you with the knowledge you need to make decisions that will help your students learn as much as possible. Commit yourself to academic excellence. Make every effort to thoroughly understand the body of knowledge in your profession. Endorse high standards for licensure. Finally, take your professional code of ethics seriously. Anything less detracts from the profession and detracts from you as a person and your status as a professional.

Deciding to become a professional educator is one of the most important decisions of your life, both for you and the teaching profession. We hope this text can assist you in this decision.

Summary

Do I Want to Be a Teacher?

Research indicates that people most commonly choose to teach because of their desire to work with young people and make contributions to society. Other reasons to enter teaching include intellectual growth and interest in a content area.

Rewards and Difficulties in Teaching

Teaching is both rewarding and difficult. Intrinsic rewards include helping young people grow emotionally, socially, and intellectually, and extrinsic rewards include desirable vacation times, autonomy, and status.

Difficulties include students who aren't motivated and are difficult to manage, as well as unresponsive parents, administrators who aren't supportive, and the great many nonteaching duties associated with the job.

The Teaching Profession

Professionals in any field understand a specialized body of knowledge, use this knowledge in decision making and reflection, have considerable autonomy in their actions, and use ethical standards to guide their professional conduct.

Some people argue that teachers are not professionals, suggesting their training isn't rigorous, they lack autonomy, and they aren't held accountable for poor performance. Others contend that teaching is a developing profession that is still evolving.

The Modern Reform Movement

The current reform movement in education emphasizes greater accountability for learners and teachers. New federal legislation in the form of the No Child Left Behind Act makes educators accountable for the children they teach. Prospective teachers will also encounter a number of reforms calling for higher standards, more rigorous training, and increased testing.

Important Concepts

accountability (p. 30)
assessment (p. 19)
autonomy (p. 9)
curriculum (p. 19)
decision making (p. 18)
ethics (p. 21)
extrinsic rewards (p. 8)
high-stakes tests (p. 30)
intrinsic rewards (p. 6)
merit pay (p. 12)
portfolio (p. 27)
professional portfolio (p. 28)
professionalism (p. 14)
reflection (p. 19)
reforms (p. 25)
standards (p. 20)
technician (p. 18)

Developing as a Professional

Praxis Practice

Read the following case study, and then answer the questions that follow.

Marissa Anderson entered the teacher's lounge and collapsed in a large over-stuffed chair.

"I'm bushed," she began, smiling at her friend, Anthony, another third-year teacher at her school.

"Late night partying?" he asked, examining a brown paper bag for the remains of his lunch.

"Don't I wish. Those evening classes are killing me, but I almost have my ELL (English language learner) endorsement. If I weren't learning so much, I'd start to wonder."

"Anything good that I can use?" Anthony asked.

"Well, we talked last night about the importance of verbal language in learning to read and how important it is to provide lots of opportunities for kids to practice their developing English skills."

"Hmm. That makes sense, but it doesn't sound much like the reading program our district wants us to use. It has a lot of individual worksheets and stresses teacher-centered instruction."

"I know. I've been thinking about that. Our reading program probably works for students who speak English, but how can my kids do worksheets when they can't even read the directions? So I've got a dilemma—do what the district says or do what I know and what research shows is best for my kids. For now I'm just going to shut my door and do the right thing. Down the line I need to talk with Jan (the school principal) and see if she can help me resolve this dilemma."

Analyze this case in terms of the following dimensions of professionalism. In your analysis, identify specific parts of the case that related to professionalism and explain the connection.

1. Specialized body of knowledge ____

   ____

2. Training for licensure ____

   ____

3. Decision making ____

   ____

4. Reflection ____

____

5. Autonomy ____

____

6. Ethical standards of conduct ______________________________

____

To receive feedback on your responses to the Praxis Practice exercises, go to the Companion Website at **www.prenhall.com/kauchak**, then to this chapter's *Praxis Practice* module.

Discussion Questions

1. Do the reasons cited in the chapter for becoming a teacher change with the grade level or content area targeted by teachers? Why?
2. Do you believe teaching is more or less rewarding than it was in the past? Is it more or less difficult? Why do you think so?
3. Which of the intrinsic and extrinsic rewards in teaching are likely to become more important in the future? Less important?
4. For which group of teachers—teachers of elementary school students (grades K–5), middle school students (grades 6–8), or secondary students (grades 9–12)—are emotional rewards likely to be the greatest? Why?
5. For which group of teachers—elementary school, middle school, or secondary school teachers—are intellectual rewards likely to be the greatest? Why?
6. Is teaching a profession? If not, what would be necessary to make it one?
7. Will the move toward teacher professionalism be beneficial for teachers? Why or why not?

Video Discussion Questions

The following discussion questions refer to video segments found on the Companion Website. To answer these questions online, view accompanying video clips, and receive immediate feedback on your answers, go to the Companion Website at **www.prenhall.com/kauchak**, then to this chapter's *Video Discussion* module.

1. Dr. Uri Treisman is a professor of mathematics at the University of Texas at Austin and director of the Charles A. Dana Center for Math and Science Education. His work focuses on school reform and ways that schools can be helped to improve. He is concerned that both individual school and teacher autonomy often conflict with centralized testing programs.
   a. What does Dr. Treisman believe is the proper balance between these two forces?
   b. Do you think centralized testing jeopardizes school and teacher autonomy? Explain.
2. Theodore Sizer is the Director of the Coalition for Effective Schools, which attempts to reform high schools. As we've seen in this chapter, testing is being pro-

posed as a major reform tool.

a. In Dr. Sizer's opinion, what questions should people ask when considering using standardized tests to assess student learning?

b. Do you think his cautions are justified? Explain.

Going into Schools

1. Interview two teachers; if possible, choose a first-year teacher and a veteran with at least 5 years' experience. Ask them the following questions:

   a. Why did you choose to teach? What are all the reasons that influenced your decision?

   b. What are some of the most rewarding aspects of teaching? Can you give me some specific examples?

   c. What are some of the most difficult parts of teaching? Can you give me some specific examples?

   d. Are you more or less confident in your ability to help kids learn than you were before you started teaching?

   e. How effective was your preservice teacher-preparation program in helping you learn to teach? What would have made it more effective?

   f. Do you plan to stay in teaching, or do you plan to move to a different job or profession? If you plan to leave teaching, what are your reasons for leaving?

   g. If you were asked to describe the process of teaching in one sentence, how would you describe it?

   h. Do you believe that teaching is a profession? Why or why not?

   i. Please use the following scale to rate the importance of each of the three types of knowledge listed.

      1 = Not at all important
      2 = Not very important
      3 = Somewhat important
      4 = Quite important
      5 = Extremely important

      1. Knowledge of content, such as math, science, or language arts
      2. Knowledge of teaching techniques, such as questioning and classroom organization.
      3. Knowledge of students, such as how they learn and what motivates them.

      Of the three types of knowledge, which is the most important? least important? Or are they all equally important?

   Compare the two teachers' responses and analyze them in terms of the content in this chapter.

2. Interview a teacher by asking him or her the following questions:

   a. To what extent do accountability and testing influence what is taught and how it is taught in your school?

   b. What are some concrete examples of how accountability is influencing your life as a teacher?

   c. Have the accountability and high-stakes testing movements been good or bad for education? Why do you feel this way?

   d. Will testing and the accountability movement increase or decrease in importance in the next 5 to 10 years? Why do you think so?

e. How have the testing and accountability movements affected your satisfaction as a teacher? How and why?

Now summarize the teacher's responses and compare with your personal views on accountability and testing.

Virtual Field Experience

If you would like to participate in a Virtual Field Experience, go to the Companion Website at **www.prenhall.com/kauchak**, then to this chapter's *Field Experience* module.

CW

Online Portfolio Activities

CW

This section, found in every chapter, is designed to begin you on the process of developing your own professional portfolio. In addition to documenting your developing competence as a teacher, portfolios can also include evidence of changes in your thinking, such as personal reflections about your reasons for becoming a teacher (which we suggest in the first activity of this chapter). You might want to include these writings in a personal journal, which you may or may not share with others and which you can return to during the course of your teacher preparation to reflect on your own growth as a teacher.

In addition to personal reflections, portfolios can include letters of commendation and recommendation, teaching units you've prepared, and videotapes of lessons you've taught. What you choose to include depends on your personal and professional judgment.

The following are suggested activities that will help you begin. Each of the activities is linked to an INTASC principle. As you continue in your program, you will add a great many items to your portfolio, and you may choose to delete some that you had initially selected.

To complete these activities online, go to the Companion Website at **www.prenhall.com/kauchak**, then to this chapter's *Portfolio Activities* module.

Portfolio Activity 1.1

Why I Want to Become a Teacher

INTASC Principle 9: Commitment

Personal Journal Reflection

Look again at your responses to the Interest in Teaching Inventory found at the beginning of this chapter. For each of the items that you marked with a 6 (Agree) or a 7 (Strongly Agree), write a brief explanation for your choice. For example, if you marked 7 for Item 2, "My family has strongly influenced my decision to become a teacher," a possible response might be the following:

> My dad is a teacher. He didn't directly encourage me to teach, but I remember how excited he would be when he came home and talked about some kid who finally "got it." Also, he was always telling some funny story about a kid he worked with. I could see how much fun he had teaching.

Now look at each of the items that you marked with a 1 (Strongly Disagree) or a 2 (Disagree). Again, write a brief explanation for your choice. What do your responses to these items tell you about your personal reasons for becoming a teacher?

Portfolio Activity 1.2

Self-Analysis and Reflection on INTASC Principles

All INTASC Principles

Review the INTASC principles in Table 1.3. For which of these principles do you already have evidence? How could you make this evidence concrete so you could include it in your portfolio? Examine descriptions of the courses in the remainder of your teacher preparation program. How will these courses help you address additional INTASC standards?

Portfolio Activity 1.3

Professional Standards and Teaching

INTASC Principle 3: Adapting Instruction

In the chapter you saw how standards are increasingly being used to guide what teachers do and what students learn. Table 13.5 contains the Web site addresses for a variety of education-related professional organizations, such as the International Reading Association and the Council for Exceptional Children. Find an organization that interests you, go to its site, and find the organization's professional standards. Summarize the standards in a paragraph, and then explain how they could guide your development as a professional. Provide specific, concrete examples to illustrate your explanations.

Chapter 2

The Teaching Profession

The lives of teachers are complex. In a typical school day teachers are asked to make a great many decisions and fulfill roles ranging from instructor to caregiver to public ambassador. These decisions and roles make teaching demanding but also very satisfying.

Compared to teachers in the past, you'll be asked to perform roles that are changing, and you'll work with people who are changing as well. Teacher retirements and demographic changes in the United States will create a different teaching force for tomorrow's schools. We examine these changes in this chapter as we try to answer the following questions:

- What is it like to be a teacher?
- What are the roles that teachers perform?
- Who will your colleagues be?
- How will increased emphasis on professionalism affect your life as a teacher?

Let's begin by looking at two teachers' experiences.

This logo appears throughout the chapter to indicate where case studies are integrated with chapter content.

Case STUDY Maria Lopez, a third-year teacher at Grover Elementary, pulled into the school parking lot at 7:30 AM. As she walked through the main office, she checked her mailbox and greeted the school secretary. "Any news on Antonio?" she asked, checking on a student she had referred for testing for special services. When the secretary replied, "Not yet," Maria nodded with a concerned look on her face and headed down the empty halls to her classroom.

Unlocking her door, she remembered that this was going to be a busy workday. It would begin with a fourth-grade team meeting and end with a district in-service workshop. She glanced at the clock and thought, "I'd better scurry. Jana (the team leader) has a fit when we're late."

At 7:46 she entered Jana Torry's classroom and smiled with relief when she noticed that she wasn't the last person there. Jana began the meeting at 7:50, and someone asked about the possibility of grouping all the fourth graders for reading. The team discussed the question at length but couldn't arrive at a decision. Next, the teachers addressed the new statewide assessment test for math. After several questions were resolved, the team members asked Maria if she would be willing to compare the test with their current math textbook to determine similarities and differences and to report on what she finds at the next meeting. As the meeting adjourned, Maria glanced at her watch and realized that she had just enough time for a quick visit to the bathroom before the kids arrived.

Back in her classroom, Maria opened her plan book.

"Hmm. A school assembly. They're going to be wired today, so I need to keep them busy," she thought.

She updated the schedule she kept permanently displayed on a board in the room:

8:30 – 10:00	Language Arts (Spelling, writing, grammar)
10:00 – 11:00	Math
11:00 – 11:15	Break (Recess)
11:15 – 11:45	Science
11:45 – 12:10	Lunch
12:10 – 1:40	Reading
1:40 – 1:50	Break (Bathroom)
1:50 – 2:15	Social Studies (Safety Assembly)
2:15 – 3:00	Art/Music/P.E. (Safety Assembly)

To be sure her students wouldn't forget to write down their homework at the end of the day, Maria added the next day's assignments to the schedule.

At 8:25 the bell rang and students streamed into her classroom.

"Good morning, Mrs. Lopez" and "Hi, Mrs. Lopez" greeted her as she hurried around the room, making last-minute preparations for her math and science lessons. From 8:30 to 10:00 she worked with small groups of students on language arts, calling five or six students at a time to one corner of the room while others worked quietly at their desks. While teaching the groups, she was sure to keep one eye on the rest of the class, and she periodically got up to answer questions or remind students to finish their work. Kevin required several reminders, and Maria remembered that she would be meeting with his mother and the special education referral team after school.

Math went smoothly. After explaining some commonly missed problems on the previous day's homework, Maria handed out kits of multicolored blocks and had groups of students use the blocks to solve and illustrate problems involving place value.

After supervising the fourth graders at recess (the teachers rotated this duty weekly), Maria began science. The class was studying ecosystems, and Maria monitored student groups as they investigated ecosystems around the world on the Internet and began preparing reports, which they would later share with the whole class.

Lunch gave Maria some time to relax for a few minutes with her colleagues. After walking her class to the cafeteria, she ducked into the teachers' room, grabbed her lunch bag, and fell into a comfortable stuffed chair. The teachers talked about a variety of topics, ranging from families and kids to the new math tests, local politics, and the possibility of getting a new principal.

When her students returned from lunch, Maria assigned a story from their literature book and asked them to answer questions written on the overhead. As the class read, Maria helped small groups of students with book reports that had been assigned earlier. A busy hum told Maria the students were working productively. Suddenly, the public address system announced that classes should get ready for the safety assembly. Maria had her class quickly put away their projects and line up.

The assembly was a zoo. The guest police officer and firefighter talked steadily, and although they were well-intentioned, much of the information they presented was over the students' heads. The students grew restless, and Maria tried to quiet them with eye contact and fingers to the lips. She wasn't upset with them, since she was also bored. Mercifully, at 2:45 the program ended, and Maria had 15 minutes to prepare her class for departure. Maria reminded students of their homework and then watched to be sure they wrote the assignments in their notebooks. Student teams cleaned up the room. When the last straggler left at 3:15, Maria sat in her chair and sighed, "Whew, what a day!"

Her relaxation was quickly interrupted by a knock at the door. It was Kevin's mother, there for the meeting to discuss testing Kevin for a learning disability. The meeting ended at 4:00, giving Maria just enough time to hop into her car and drive to her in-service class. Her day was not over yet.

· · • · ·

Dave Loft, a second-year English teacher at Hillcrest High, arrived at school at 6:45, just as the sun peaked over the horizon. A departmental meeting had been called so that he and his colleagues could analyze the new state English guidelines to see what implications they would have for their high school's curriculum.

After checking his mailbox, he unlocked his classroom door and read his e-mails. He was experimenting with a program in which parents volunteered to read assignments from his basic sophomore English courses, and he used e-mail to supplement after-school phone calls to coordinate the system. Although having parents read and make comments on papers saved Dave some time, he still read and scored each paper, and coordinating the project was time consuming.

At the departmental meeting, Dave and his colleagues discussed using a number of works of recent fiction to meet the new state standards. Dave found the discussion stimulating and thought to himself, "Ah, this is why I became a teacher." However, he kept looking at his watch, remembering everything he had to do to get ready for the day's classes.

After the meeting, Dave hurried to his classroom, just beating the bell that announced 5 minutes until Advisory Homeroom, an experiment designed to make the school more friendly and person-oriented. Every morning Dave met with his first-period English class for 15 minutes before the formal class began. During this time he took care of routine duties such as taking attendance and making announcements, and he also tried to use the time to learn more about his students. It seemed to be working—his first-period class, though not his highest achieving group, was his favorite. He had fewer management problems in the class, and because he knew his students better, class discussions were more lively and productive.

Dave worked with students from 8:00 until noon without a break, as was usual. Four of his six classes were in the morning, and he taught 55-minute periods with only 5-minute intervals in between. Even the interval times were busy, with both incoming and exiting students wanting to talk about assignments, grades, and sometimes even ideas.

Lunchtime also served as Dave's prep period, so he graded papers as he wolfed down a sandwich. He had given up his formal planning period to take an additional class for extra pay. The money helped, but the extra class also left him with many more papers to grade.

"Why did I ever go into English?" he muttered as he started on his next pile of student essays.

He recalled the exchange he had the other day with Ricardo, another second-year teacher. They were discussing the relative merits of different kinds of assessments, and Ricardo was extolling the benefits of short-answer and multiple-choice tests that could be scored quickly.

"Maybe Ricardo was right," Dave thought. "But how will students ever learn to write if they don't do a lot of writing?"

The final bell rang at 3:15, giving Dave 15 minutes to prepare materials for Debate Club, which he sponsored. He enjoyed working with the students but jokingly reported to his wife that the $800 supplement he received for the work would amount to less than minimum wage if divided by the time he spent.

"And all this time I thought you were doing it for the money," she joked in return.

· · • · ·

Teaching: A Time Perspective

Let's think about Maria and Dave. What were their days like? How did they spend their time? How do their days compare to a typical one for you?

In this section we use time as a lens through which we can view teaching. Time is a useful lens for at least three reasons. First, most people spend more of their waking hours in activities related to work than in activities related to any other part of their lives. Once you begin teaching, how you use your time will greatly influence your satisfaction with your career. Second, the way we allocate our time indicates what is important to us, and third, time is a useful way to investigate different teaching situations.

The School Year

Let's begin by looking at the school year. For students, a typical school year in the United States lasts 180 days, beginning a few days before or after Labor Day in September and ending in early June. (Some districts are now starting school in early August, so that the first semester is completed before the winter holiday.) For teachers, the school year is slightly longer, with several days at the start of the year allocated to planning, attending meetings, and getting classrooms ready (e.g., putting up bulletin boards, counting books, and requisitioning everyday supplies like paper and scissors) and several at the end of the year devoted to finalizing grades, packing up the classroom, and getting organized for next year.

Lengthening the School Year Proposals for increasing the amount of time students spend in school have been raised. It is intuitively sensible that the more time students spend in learning activities, the more they will learn, and this conclusion is confirmed by research (Karweit, 1989; Nystrand & Gamoran, 1989). One way to meet this goal is to lengthen the school year. Advocates of a longer school year point out that students in Japan, who attend school 240 days a year, and students in Germany, who at-

Time provides a useful lens through which to analyze the lives of teachers.

tend 216 days, perform better than U.S. students in international comparisons (Stigler et al., 1999). Advocates also note that the United States ranks near the bottom among industrialized nations in the number of days that children attend school (H. Cooper, Valentine, Charlton, & Melson, 2003).

A second way to meet the goal is to offer additional coursework in the summer, which, in effect, also lengthens the school year. Summer school is particularly popular as a means of remediation for low achievers: "Powerful national movements to end the automatic promotion of students who aren't ready for the next grade and to hold all students to stricter academic standards have converged to swell the ranks of summer school" (Gewertz, 2000b, p. 1). Currently 27 percent of school districts around the nation have some type of mandatory summer program for failing students, and this number is increasing as testing and accountability become more prominent (Gewertz, 2000b). In the summer of 2000, for example, 650,000 students in New York—nearly a fourth of the district's enrollment–were enrolled in summer school, a sevenfold increase over 1999. Detroit schools experienced a fourfold increase from 1999 to 2000 (Gewertz, 2000b). The impact of summer school on overall achievement remains unknown.

The lengthening school year can have implications for you as a teacher. For instance, you may have the opportunity to teach summer school or may even be pressured to do so. Teaching in the summer has the advantage of supplemental income but the possible disadvantages of burnout from teaching year-round, reduced time for vacations, and the loss of summer as a time to work on an advanced degree.

The School Week

Although a 40-hour workweek is the norm in the United States, teachers average about 46 hours per week in school-related activities (Cypher & Willower, 1984; Metropolitan Life Insurance Company, 1995; National Center for Education Statistics [NCES], 1997a). They are required to be at school about 33 hours of this time, with the remainder spent helping students before or after school, scoring papers, and planning. These are just averages. Thirty-five percent of teachers in one study reported working more than 55 hours per week (NCES, 1997a), and beginning teachers and those changing level or assignment (such as teachers moving from first to fourth grade or from math to science) spend considerably more time per week than the average in additional planning.

The average length of a teacher's workweek compares favorably with the workweeks of others who hold bachelor's degrees. People in managerial positions worked the most hours per week (46), followed by salespeople and service workers, such as social workers (44 hours), and those in administrative support positions, such as administrative assistants (42 hours) (NCES, 1997a). As we'll see shortly, working conditions and the specifics of teaching vary considerably between states, districts, and even schools within a district. These differences can affect your personal satisfaction with a teaching career, so you need to be aware of them when you seek your first position.

Teaching involves hard work and long hours. Unlike workers in some occupations, teachers don't punch a time clock and leave their jobs behind at the end of the school day. Teachers often discuss their work with spouses and friends, and many teachers even report dreaming about their classes. If you are looking for a simple 9 to 5 job with few emotional entanglements, teaching may not be for you.

A Typical Workday

What is a typical workday for teachers? How do Maria's and Dave's experiences compare with those of other teachers? Let's look at some national statistics. As we can see from Table 2.1, teachers spend the largest part of their day working with students.

Teaching in an Era of Reform

THE MODIFIED CALENDAR ISSUE

One reform suggests changing the traditional school calendar. The 9-months-on, 3-months-off calendar has its historical roots in our agrarian past, when children were needed to work on farms in the summer. Today only about 3 percent of American livelihoods are tied to agriculture, and air conditioning makes it possible to provide comfortable learning environments year-round (H. Cooper et al., 2003). As a result, there is a move toward **modified school calendars,** *calendars that eliminate long summer holidays without changing the total length of the school year.* For example, in the academic year 2000–2001 more than 2 million students in 45 states attended over 3,000 schools that operated on modified calendars (National Association for Year-Round Education, 2000). About three fourths of these students were in elementary schools, with the other quarter equally divided between middle and high schools. The most common modification in the calendars are "9 weeks on, 3 weeks off" (about 30%) and "12 weeks on, 4 weeks off" (another 30%). The remainder varies from "5 weeks on, 1 week off" to "18 weeks on, 6 weeks off." The largest numbers of students in modified calendar schools were in California, followed by Hawaii, Arizona, Nevada, and Texas, probably because these states are also experiencing rapid population increases.

The Issue

Proponents of a modified school calendar make two primary arguments: They assert that public money is used more efficiently when schools operate year-round and, perhaps most significant, that summer vacations negatively impact learning (sometimes called "summer loss") (Fairchild, 2003). The long vacation breaks up the continuity of instruction and requires teachers to spend significant time in the fall reviewing material covered the previous year. Some research indicates that summer loss equals at least one month of instruction (H. Cooper, Nye, Charlton, Lindsey, & Greathouse, 1996). This problem is particularly acute for students who are economically disadvantaged, those with special needs, and learners who are not native English speakers (Jamar, 1994).

Opponents of modified calendars make several arguments of their own. For example, they note that

Table 2.1 How Teachers Spend Their Time

Activity	Percentage of Day
Working with students	
Instruction	28.5
Testing and monitoring	10.1
Supervision	7.8
Total working with students	46.4
Peer interactions	25.2
Desk and routine work	19.8
Travel	5.3
Private time	3.5

Source: From "The Work Behavior of Secondary School Teachers" by T. Cypher and D. Willower, 1984, *Journal of Research and Development in Education, 18*, pp. 19–20. Reprinted by permission.

proponents have little evidence supporting the claim that public money is better used in year-round schools. The fact that school support staff, such as maintenance workers and office staff, must be paid 12-month rather than 9-month salaries weakens this claim, they say.

Second, opponents argue that modified calendars do not significantly enhance learning. Shorter, more frequent breaks actually give students more time to forget information and lead to more time spent in review than would occur with a traditional calendar. Opponents cite research indicating that modified calendars influence learning less than resources and the economic and ethnic backgrounds of the students, and they further argue that modifying the calendar fails to address the most important components of learning, such as effective teaching methods, parental involvement, and appropriate curricula (H. Cooper et al., 2003).

Finally, modified calendars interfere with nonacademic plans for summer. Many parents want to use the summer months for family vacations and summer camps, and they resist intrusions on this family time. Teachers often object because many use the time in the summer to supplement their salaries or work on recertification, new areas of certification, or master's degrees (Time to Learn, 1996).

Some economic interests, such as amusement parks, camping associations, and the day-care industry, have even weighed in against the modified calendars, because of concerns about lost revenues that might result from eliminating the long summer break (Worsnop, 1996).

You Take a Position

Now it's your turn to take a position on the issue. State in writing whether you favor a modified school calendar over a traditional calendar, or vice versa, and provide a two-page rationale for your position. For additional references and resources, go to the Companion Website at **www.prenhall.com/kauchak**, then to this chapter's *Teaching in an Era of Reform* module. You can respond online or submit your response to your instructor.

Increasing Understanding 2.1

In what kind of districts or schools are you most likely to encounter year-round schools? Why? How might year-round schools affect you personally?

To answer the Increasing Understanding questions online and receive immediate feedback, go to the Companion Website at **www.prenhall.com/kauchak**, *then to this chapter's* Increasing Understanding *module. Type in your response, and then study the feedback.*

Although instruction occupies most of that time (28.5%), other student-related activities, such as monitoring and supervision, also take up major chunks of teachers' time. Maria, for example, was expected to monitor students on the playground, take her class to lunch, and supervise her students during the assembly. Dave's afternoons were spent supervising students in the Debate Club.

Peer interactions occupy the next largest chunk of teacher time (25.2%). Maria and Dave both had meetings with colleagues before school, and Maria had another after school. Teachers are increasingly being asked to provide input into curricular and instructional issues, a trend connected to the move toward greater teacher professionalism (Rowan, 1994). In addition, teachers spend a large amount of their day (20%) planning, preparing for instruction, and grading student papers and work. It is likely that both Maria and Dave took batches of papers home with them when they finally left their school buildings.

Teachers report that they often get ideas for lessons while they're driving or shopping (McCutcheon, 1982). And most teachers spend time grading papers as the rest of the family goes about their regular evening activities. A teacher's job is virtually never done.

Class Scheduling Schools, particularly middle and high schools, are experimenting with different ways of scheduling classes during the day to maximize learning. A typical day in these schools consists of seven or eight periods of about 45–50 minutes each. One or two of the periods are often used for study hall and lunch activities (Gould, 2003). Many schools, however, have begun using **block scheduling,** *an alternate form of scheduling that increases the length of classes, often doubling typical periods.* Block scheduling aims to minimize disruptions caused by bells and transitions and to provide teachers with more flexibility and extended periods of time for instruction. Block schedules can work well in areas such as science, home economics, and art, where labs and projects often take longer to complete than the traditional period.

Two types of block schedules are common (Gould, 2003). In a **four-by-four block schedule,** *students take four classes a day of approximately 90–100 minutes for one semester.* Courses that take a year in the traditional system are completed in one semester in the four-by-four plan. In an **alternating-day block schedule,** *classes are approximately 90–100 minutes long, students take a traditional number (6–8) of classes a semester, and classes meet every other day.* In an alternating-day schedule, students might attend Algebra II class on Monday, Wednesday, and Friday of one week; Tuesday and Thursday of the next week; Monday, Wednesday, and Friday of the third week; and so on.

Like most proposed changes, block scheduling is controversial. Advocates argue that longer periods promote greater in-depth learning, fewer management problems, and better use of teacher time. Opponents counter that the longer periods fail to account for limitations in students' attention spans and do not provide adequate time for the assimilation of understanding (particularly in the four-by-four schedule). Further, long gaps between courses in core areas, such as math and English, make it more likely that students will forget the general knowledge needed to progress in these areas. Although the controversy is likely to continue, research indicates that few differences exist either in student learning or even in teacher preferences.

> The brouhaha over schedules does not seem nearly so important as the many other variables that contribute to sound educational practices. Based on existing research, neither block nor traditional schedules by themselves are going to perform miracles. Conversely, and in response to each side's detractors, neither choice is going to do much harm either. (Gould, 2003, p. 35)

CW

Increasing Understanding 2.2

The time percentages in Table 2.1 are averages for various types of teachers. Explain how these percentages might change for teachers working in pull-out programs. How might they change for teachers in self-contained classrooms? Describe the implications of workday structure for a person considering a teaching position.

Grade-Level Differences

The way teachers spend their day differs by grade level, and these differences have important implications for you, a prospective teacher. The majority of elementary teachers (62%) work in self-contained classrooms, whereas only 6 percent of secondary teachers do (these are usually resource or special education teachers) (NCES, 1997a). The remaining elementary teachers teach in team (9%), enrichment (11.2%), or pull-out programs (10.5%). At the secondary level, more than 84 percent of teachers work in departmentalized settings where students rotate to different classes throughout the day.

The differences in teachers' workdays can help you choose the grade level in which you'll teach. The elementary level, with its emphasis on self-contained classrooms, is a more personal environment because you work with the same group of students all or most of the time. As we saw in Chapter 1, relationships formed with students are a major source of satisfaction in teaching, so having a chance to know your students well is an advantage.

The secondary level also has advantages. Departmentalization allows you to focus on content areas of interest and share this interest with your students. Recall from Chapter 1 that interest in a content area and intellectual stimulation are prominent reasons for choosing teaching as a career. Departmentalization also places you in contact with colleagues who share your academic interests. In a secondary school, the time you spend meeting with colleagues is more likely than in an elementary school to be focused on issues related to course content. In the case at the start of this chapter, Dave found it intellectually stimulating to discuss the new English curriculum with his colleagues. Intellectual rewards are a major factor influencing teachers to remain in the profession.

Which grade level is better for you? One of the reasons you're taking this course is to help you decide.

Teaching Schedules in Other Countries

It is interesting to compare teaching schedules in the United States with those in other countries, especially Japan and China, where students outperform their U.S. counterparts in essential areas such as math and science (Calsyn, Gonzales, & Frase, 1999; Stigler, Gonzales, Kawanaka, Knoll, & Serrano, 1999). The typical teacher in Japan, for example, arrives at school around 7:30 AM, as teachers in the United States do, but stays there until 6:00 PM (Sato & McLaughlin, 1992). Most U.S. teachers are free to leave a half hour after students depart, and many teachers do so, preferring to grade papers and plan at home. (This is why you seldom see teachers leaving school empty-handed—bags, briefcases, and boxes contain the evening's work.)

Teachers in Japan work a 240-day school year, but their annual salaries are only about 95 percent of what U.S. teachers make for slightly more than 180 school days. (However, some research indicates that American primary teachers spend more hours working per year than do teachers in other countries. For example, one study indicated that primary teachers in 20 other industrialized countries worked an average of 829 hours per year, whereas primary teachers in the United States averaged 958 [NCES, 1997a].)

Teachers from other countries also spend their workdays differently than do teachers in the United States (L. Ma, 1999; Sato & McLaughlin, 1992). For example, teachers in Japan spend about half as much time as U.S. teachers in direct classroom instruction. The rest of their time is spent in professional planning, conferring with colleagues, and helping to govern their schools. Although some reformers advocate moving toward this Asian model, with its emphasis on teacher autonomy, governance, and professionalism, doing so would take teachers away from their first love—working with students (Lortie, 1975).

Deciding how teachers should best spend their time presents a dilemma, for both individual teachers and the profession. For example, do you want to spend the bulk of your time working with students or working with other teachers on curriculum projects and school governance? More teacher involvement in governance is viewed as one way to increase teacher autonomy and professionalism, but more time spent on governance and working with other teachers means less time with students (Rowan, 1994).

Without a doubt, teachers *do* want input into decisions that influence their professional lives, and they resent being told to do things without being consulted. Research indicates that teachers' satisfaction and their commitment to their school

Increased teacher input into school decisions may positively influence teacher autonomy and professionalism, but it may also pull teachers away from classrooms and students.

depend on their involvement in school decision making (Sergiovanni, Burlingame, Coombs, & Thurstone, 1999). When you interview for your first position, you may want to ask the principal how teachers in the school are involved in decision making and assess the principal's response based on your own professional goals.

Decision Making: Responding to the Complexities of Teaching

What does it feel like to actually teach? What challenges do classrooms and students present, and how do teachers deal with them? Let's begin to answer these questions by looking at the experiences of three teachers at three different grade levels.

Case STUDY Ken, an elementary teacher in a third/fourth-grade split classroom, shared the following incident in his teaching journal:

March 3: My class is sitting in a circle. I look up and notice one of the girls, Sylvia, is crying. Joey, she claims, has called her a fat jerk. The rest of the students all look at me to watch my response. I consider the alternatives: send Joey to hallway and talk to him in a few minutes; have Joey sit next to me; ask Joey to apologize; direct Sylvia to get a thick skin; ask Sylvia, "How can you solve this problem?"; send Joey to principal; have Joey write an apology letter; ask Joey, "Why did you do this?"; ignore the situation completely; keep Sylvia and Joey in for recess for dialogue; put Joey's name on board; yell at Joey; send Sylvia and Joey in hallway to work out problem; tell them to return to their seats and write in journals about problem.

It took me about 10 seconds to run through these alternatives, and after each one I thought of reasons why it wasn't a good idea. By the time I look up at Sylvia after this brief introspection, she had stopped crying and was chattering away with a friend about something else. On surface, the problem had gone away. (Winograd, 1998, p. 296)

• • • • •

Kerrie, a first-year middle school English teacher, experienced the following management struggles on the first day back after a 4-day holiday (veteran teachers will attest that students are typically wired the day before and after a long school holiday).

She was correct—the students were excited, difficult to settle down, wild. All around her, students chatted happily about their weekends and showed one another items they had brought from home, as she vainly shushed and urged them to quiet down. Some students wandered in late. It was going to be a long day. Finally, she got them settled down and began the day's lesson, but it was a struggle to keep them on-task.

Throughout the day the struggle continued. She was constantly surrounded by students who needed help or who did not listen carefully enough to her directions. As the day progressed, her frustration grew. By afternoon she was nearly frazzled; the students were winning. Seventh period finally arrived, and the end of the day was within sight: Announcements from the office were supposed to begin the period, but often they came late so the teachers never knew quite when to begin class. Kerrie waited, while the students talked noisily. Finally the announcements began. Once these were over, she gave the students a quiz on a movie they had seen. This quieted them down. However, as they finished the quiz, the noise level began to creep up. As Kerrie struggled to get them to begin an independent seat-work assignment, two students were wrestling, and most were chatting. The team leader, whose class was also noisy, walked by and commented, "It's so noisy in here, I'm going crazy!" Finally, after five minutes of near chaos, Kerrie got them settled down, continuously shushing them and commenting, "It's too noisy!" For about 10 minutes they remained settled, but then the noise level again began to rise and yet another play fight suddenly erupted, this time between two girls. When Kerrie's back was turned, some children threw things around the room, and a boy with a cast and a girl with long blonde hair began running about. When the buzzer sounded, indicating day's end, Kerrie had "had it," rather than hold them after class as she had threatened earlier, she let them go, just to get rid of them.

It was, in Kerrie's words, a day that nearly drove her "crazy." She was angry and frustrated. "Today they were just screwing off! All these little toys they have. Wanting to look at each other's stuff. Combs. Brushes. I should take them and hit them on the head with the stupid things! It drives you nuts." She sounded tired, discouraged. (Bullough, 1989, pp. 72–73)

• • • • •

Two high school student teachers discuss their frustrations in taking attendance on the day of a special school dance held during regular class hours:

Cheryl: One boy comes in, he's dressed up. He says "I have to go to the dance." Comes in early and tells me, good kid. I'm like, "OK, that's fine Aaron." Then, Kent comes in five minutes late. This is tall Kent, has his own band and never lets me mark him tardy even though he's always tardy, "I'm, going to the dance!" After I've already started class! "Ahem. Thank you, Kent. Please sit down." So he's wanting to leave but I can't let him go because he just interrupted my class and . . . I was so mad at him. So I say, "Do you have a ticket?" And he's like, "Well, yeah," and pulls out a ticket that goes to the movie he went to on Friday night and I say, "No, that's not the right ticket." He wasn't . . .

Dani: What color was it?

Cheryl: Pink.

Dani: What was the color for the . . . ?

Cheryl: The other guy who was legit had a gray one. But then, then, I don't know. And I mean WHO KNOWS! I said, "You're not on my excused list" but neither was the other guy and I'm like . . .

Dani: I didn't even get an excused list! I didn't even know this dance was — I kind of heard something over the intercom. (Dulude-Lay, 2000, p. 4)

• • ● • •

Characteristics of Classrooms

What do these vignettes have in common? Each illustrates the bewildering and sometimes frustrating world of teaching. Researchers have identified several characteristics of classroom life that make it complex and demanding (W. Doyle, 1986). They found the following:

- *Classrooms are multidimensional.* The large numbers of events and tasks make classrooms complex places.
- *Classroom events are simultaneous.* Many things happen at once.
- *Classroom events are immediate.* Things occur rapidly.
- *Classrooms are unpredictable.* Events often take unexpected turns.
- *Classrooms are public.* Teachers must do their jobs in "fishbowls."

In Chapter 1 we emphasized that the ability to make decisions in ill-defined situations is an important aspect of professionalism, and these characteristics illustrate the need for that ability. Expert teachers possess the background and experience that allow them to make necessary decisions quickly and routinely, and this is a reason we've placed so much emphasis on professionalism in this book. Let's look at these characteristics in more detail.

Classrooms Are Multidimensional Think about all the different roles you'll perform today. You're a student, but you're probably also a friend, coworker, or even a parent. Your life is multidimensional. A classroom is as well; when you teach, you will need to attend to a number of different events and perform various roles. For instance, while you're involved with a small group of students, others will be working on various assignments. Students with special needs may be pulled out of your classroom. When you conduct learning activities, some students will be attentive and involved, others will tend to drift off, and disruptions may occur. Ken found this out when he tried to begin his lesson.

External events, such as announcements, assemblies, and school functions, also add to the complexity of classroom life and take time away from instruction. For example, Kerrie, Cheryl, and Dani had to adjust their teaching plans because of announcements and a school event (the dance). Teachers often say, "If I only had time to teach." This complaint is likely to become more common as teachers are increasingly held accountable for their students' learning through standards and increased testing.

Classroom Events Are Simultaneous In addition to occurring in large numbers, many classroom events occur at the same time. While Cheryl and Dani were trying to take roll and begin class, for example, students came in needing immediate attention,

Classrooms are complex places requiring split-second decision making by teachers.

asking questions, showing hall passes, and presenting admission slips. While Kerrie and Ken were trying to teach, management problems arose. Knowing which problem to attend to first can be challenging, if not bewildering.

CW

Increasing Understanding 2.3

Reexamine Table 2.1, which describes how teachers spend their time. Which of the time categories are subject to the dimension of immediacy? Explain.

Classroom Events Are Immediate We learned in Chapter 1 that teachers make somewhere between 800 and 1,500 decisions every day. Beyond the sheer numbers, the need to make the decisions *right now* adds to the demands on the teacher. Sylvia is crying; Ken needs to immediately decide whether or not to intervene. Kent comes in with a bogus hall pass; Cheryl needs to decide immediately whether or not to honor it. Unfortunately for new teachers, the immediacy of classroom life requires split-second decision making.

Classrooms Are Unpredictable Every teacher plans for both instruction and classroom management. Experts plan extensively in an attempt to anticipate unpredictable events.

• • ● • •

One first-grade teacher, attempting to involve students in a lesson about a story they had read about shoes, brought a shoe into class. Pulling it out of a bag, she began, "What can you tell me about this shoe?"

"It's red," Mike responded.

The shoe was black—there was no sign of red on it anywhere!

• • ● • •

The teacher had planned extensively, even bringing in a concrete object to illustrate ideas and themes in a story. But she hadn't planned for this response. In a similar way, neither Ken nor Cheryl and Dani could have predicted some of the events that required split-second decision making. Often, teachers have little time for thoughtful analysis and consideration of alternatives. After the fact, it is often easy to see what we should have done differently, but in the heat of the moment we must respond immediately to unanticipated events. Classrooms are exciting, unpredictable places—a major reason people find teaching both interesting and challenging.

Classrooms Are Public That fact that we teach in front of people is obvious. In a sense, we're on stage, and our triumphs and mistakes occur in public for all to see. And mistakes are inevitable. One of your authors had this experience in his first year of teaching:

• • ● • •

I was having a rough time quieting my class as they worked on an assignment. After several futile attempts, I said loudly, "All right, this is it! I don't want to hear one more peep out of this class!" From behind the cover of a held-up textbook came a squeaky "Peep." The class watched and waited while I quickly (and publicly) sorted out my options. Finally, I smiled and said, "Very funny. Now let's get down to work." This seemed to break the ice, and the students finally settled down. I had learned an important public lesson on ultimatums.

• • ● • •

As we work with students, we are bound to make mistakes, and our actions can have unintended consequences. Ken ignored one incident of misbehavior—Joey calling Sylvia a "fat jerk." Did he unintentionally communicate that verbal abuse is acceptable? Cheryl considered allowing one student slip out of her class with a bogus pass. If she had, would other students try the same thing? A fishbowl is an apt metaphor for classroom teaching; as we swim through our day, both students and other teachers watch us and form judgments about our actions.

Will your first year of teaching necessarily consist of a series of unpredictable situations? Probably. Learning to teach is a journey filled with unanticipated events, and your first year will be exhausting and, at times, overwhelming. One book about the experiences of first-year teachers is aptly named *The Roller Coaster Year* (K. Ryan, 1992). It may help to remember, however, that thousands of other beginning teachers have not only survived but flourished.

Your teacher education program can help prepare you for the complexities of classroom decision making in two important ways. First, your coursework will teach you concepts that will help you understand how experienced teachers appear to work so effortlessly. *Withitness* and *overlapping* are two such concepts. **Withitness** is *a teacher's awareness of what is going on in all parts of the classroom at all times and the communication of this awareness to students both verbally and nonverbally.* Expert teachers describe withitness as "having eyes in the back of your head." Here are a positive and a negative example of the concept:

Case STUDY Ron Ziers was explaining the procedure for finding percentages to his seventh graders. While Ron illustrated the procedure, Kareem, in the second desk from the front of the room, was periodically poking Katilyna, who sat across from him. She retaliated by kicking him in the leg. Bill, sitting behind Katilyna, poked her in the arm with his pencil. Ron didn't respond to the students' actions. After a second poke, Katilyna swung her arm back and caught Bill on the shoulder. "Katilyna!" Ron said sternly. "We keep our hands to ourselves! . . . Now, where were we?"

• • ● • •

Karl Wickes, a seventh-grade life science teacher in the same school, had the same group of students. He put a transparency displaying a flowering plant on the overhead. As the class discussed the information, he noticed Barry whispering something to Julie, and he saw Kareem poke Katilyna, who kicked him and loudly whispered, "Stop it." As Karl asked, "What is the part of the plant that produces fruit?" he moved to Kareem's desk, leaned over, and said quietly but firmly, "We keep our hands and materials to ourselves in here." He then moved to the front of the room, watched Kareem out of the corner of his eye, and said, "Barry, what other plant part do you see in the diagram?" (Eggen & Kauchak, 2004, p. 444)

• • ● • •

Notice the ways in which Karl, but not Ron, demonstrated to his students that he had withitness:

- *Identifying the misbehavior immediately.* Karl responded quickly to Kareem. Ron did nothing until the misbehavior had spread to other students.
- *Correctly identifying the original cause of the incident.* Karl realized that Kareem was the instigator. Ron reprimanded only Katilyna, leaving the students with a sense that the teacher didn't know what was going on.
- *Responding to the most serious infraction first.* Kareem's poking was more disruptive than Barry's whispering, so Karl first responded to Kareem and then simply called on Barry, which drew him back into the activity, making further intervention unnecessary.

Withitness involves more than dealing with misbehavior after it happens. Teachers who are withit also quickly react to evidence of student inattention or confusion. They walk over to or call on inattentive students to bring them back into lessons, and they respond to quizzical looks with questions such as "I see uncertain looks on some of your faces. Do you want me to rephrase that question?" Their awareness allows them to make adjustments that ensure all students are as attentive and successful as possible.

Overlapping is *a teacher's ability to attend to more than one classroom activity at a time,* and this concept was also illustrated in Karl's work. As the class discussed the information, Karl noticed Barry whispering and saw Kareem poke Katilyna. He asked, "What is the part of the plant that produces fruit?" as he simultaneously moved to Kareem's desk and brought him back into the activity. He then watched Kareem as he moved to the front of the room and continued his questioning. The ability to perform these actions concurrently illustrates *overlapping.*

Expert teachers routinely demonstrate withitness and overlapping; as a result, they seem to manage student behavior effortlessly, and their classrooms appear to function

Structured clinical experiences during your teacher education program will provide you with opportunities to experiment with different teaching strategies and ideas.

like well-oiled machines. Acquiring withitness and overlapping skills takes time and effort (Berliner, 1994), but becoming aware of these concepts in your undergraduate preparation program will provide a foundation on which you can build when beginning your career.

The second way your teacher education program will help you develop decision-making expertise is by providing clinical experiences in schools (McIntyre, Byrd, & Foxx, 1996). You will observe teachers in action, talk with them about what they're doing and why, and watch students' reactions to their instruction. Also, you will likely have the opportunity to work with students and try ideas for yourself. Both will help you acquire the professional knowledge that will start you on the road to expertise.

The Multiple Roles of Teaching

As you saw in previous sections, teachers perform many roles. In this section we examine these multiple roles and discuss the implications they have for you as a prospective teacher. Some of the most important teacher roles are the following:

- Caring professional
- Creator of productive learning environments
- Ambassador to the public
- Collaborative colleague
- Learner and reflective practitioner

Caring Professional Teachers are people who care about their students. Researchers have documented the importance of caring for students as a central dimension of teaching (Brint, 1998; Noddings, 1992). **Caring** refers to *a teacher's ability to empathize with and invest in the protection and development of young people* (Chaskin & Rauner, 1995). Teachers who are available to students, and who like, understand, and empathize with them, have learners who behave better and are more emotionally and intellectually involved in classroom activities than those rated lower in these areas (McCombs, 1998; Skinner & Belmont, 1993). Further, students who perceive personal support from their teachers report more interest in their classwork and describe it as more important than students whose teachers are more distant (Goodenow, 1993). In addition, students who view their teachers as supportive are more likely to develop social responsibility (Wentzel, 1996). Collectively, these findings suggest that a classroom environment in which each student is valued regardless of academic ability or performance contributes to both learning and motivation (Stipek, 2002).

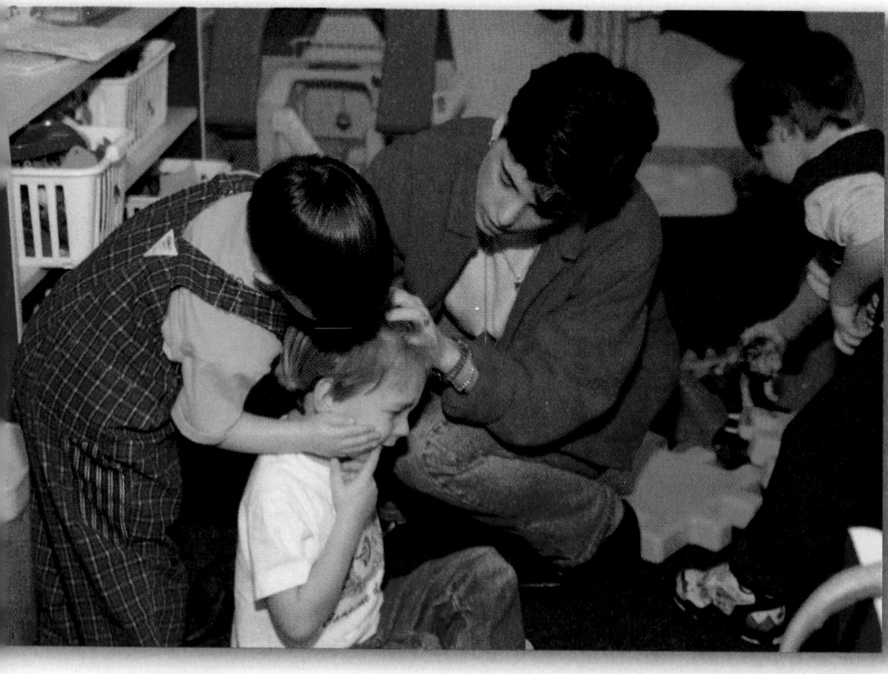

Caring teachers attend to the physical and emotional needs of their students.

How does caring reveal itself in a fourth-grade classroom? Let's listen to one teacher's perspective:

• • ● • •

I may not be on the same social studies textbook chapter as the other fourth-grade teachers, and I'll probably be late returning standardized tests to the assistant principal, but I think my kids know they're important to me. I see it in tiny, fleeting moments. I see it when a student says, "Mrs. Carkci, I wish you could come to my house for the weekend. That would be fun." I see it when a boy writes to me to ask if I will take him to the movies, or when a girl gives me a goofy smile after I've led the class down the hall taking giant, silly steps. I'm proud that a girl believes it is okay to ask "Why in America do people speak lots of languages, while in Vietnam, they only speak one language?" Or that a boy knows I will encourage him to pursue his question, "Who invented the planets?" (Carkci, 1998, p. C3)

• • ● • •

The importance of caring to students is captured in this fourth grader's comment: "If a teacher doesn't care about you, it affects your mind. You feel like you're a nobody, and it makes you want to drop out of school" (Noblit, Rogers, & McCadden, 1995, p. 683). Students can tell whether or not teachers care, as this dialogue with a high school student makes clear:

> *Nichole:* People here don't have many people to talk to. I don't. The teachers . . . some of them don't care about their students. They say, "They [administrators] want me to teach and I'm going to do it no matter what." I don't like that. I like them to say, "I'm here to teach and help you because I care." That's what I like. But a lot of them are just saying, "I'm here to teach so I'm gonna teach." I don't think that's right.
>
> *Interviewer:* Do they actually say that?
>
> *Nichole:* It's more an attitude, and they do say it. Like Ms. G. She's like . . . she never says it, but you know, she's just there and she just wants to teach, but she doesn't want to explain the whole deal.
>
> *Interviewer:* How do you know that?
>
> *Nichole:* I could feel it. The way she acts and the way she does things. She's been here seven years and all the kids I've talked to that have had her before say, "Oooh! You have Ms. G.!" Just like that.
>
> *Interviewer:* But a teacher who really cares, how do they act?
>
> *Nichole:* Like Mr. P. He really cares about his students. He's helping me a lot and he tells me, "I'm not angry with you, I just care about you." He's real caring and he does teach me when he cares. (Kramer & Colvin, 1991, p. 13)

Increasing Understanding 2.4

How does the caring dimension of teaching relate to how teachers spend their time during the day (see Table 2.1)? In terms of this table, what are some different ways that teachers show they care? Explain or defend your answer.

Caring is important for all students; for students on the margins it often makes the difference between success and failure, between staying in school or dropping out.

Communicating caring. How do teachers communicate caring to students? Although the ways are individual, research has identified two common threads: devoting time and showing respect (Freese, 1999; Noddings, 1999; Wentzel, 1997).

Everyone has 24 hours a day, and the way we allocate those hours is the most accurate indicator of our priorities. Caring teachers make time with students a priority. Spending extra time and effort to ensure that all students understand a topic, helping students who are struggling with an assignment, or calling a parent after school hours communicates that teachers care about student learning. Spending personal time to ask about a baby brother or compliment a new hairstyle communicates caring about a student as a human being. Devoting time to students communicates caring better than any other single factor.

Caring teachers respect students as individuals. They often communicate respect in subtle ways, such as the way they look at students and how long they wait for students to answer questions. One of the most important ways that teachers show they care, however, is by maintaining high standards, as one expert in the field of motivation observed:

> One of the best ways to show respect for students is to hold them to high standards—by not accepting sloppy, thoughtless, or incomplete work, by pressing them to clarify vague comments, by encouraging them not to give up, and by not praising work that does not reflect genuine effort. Ironically, reactions that are often intended to protect students' self-esteem—such as accepting low quality work—convey a lack of interest, patience, or caring. (Stipek, 2002, p. 157)

Respect is a two-way street. Teachers should model respect for students, and in turn they have the right to expect students to respect them and one another. "Treat everyone with respect" is a rule that should be enforced in every classroom. Occasional or accidental incidents of disrespect can be overlooked, but teachers should communicate that chronic disrespect will not be tolerated.

Caring sometimes extends to teachers ensuring that students' rights are upheld as well as guarding students' safety. For example, when Maria Lopez checked on the testing status of one of her students and met with the parent of another student suspected of needing special services, she was supporting the right of these students to receive an education designed to meet their individual needs. If teachers don't detect special student needs, often no one will. One way teachers can guard student safety is by learning the signs of abuse or neglect. There are clear guidelines that require teachers to report student abuse in any context, and as we'll see in Chapter 9, teachers are legally required to report suspected abuse. Teacher caring takes many forms.

Creator of Productive Learning Environments Creating productive learning environments is another essential teaching role. A **productive learning environment** is *an environment that is orderly and focuses on learning*. In schools and classrooms that are productive learning environments, students feel safe, both physically and emotionally, and the day-to-day routines—including the values, expectations, learning experiences, and both spoken and unspoken rules and conventions—are designed to help students learn as much as possible (Tishman, Perkins, & Jay, 1995).

In productive learning environments, classroom order and effective instruction are interdependent (W. Doyle, 1986). It is virtually impossible to maintain an orderly learning environment in the absence of effective instruction and vice versa. (We discuss classroom order and effective instruction in more detail in Chapter 11.)

Motivating students to learn within and outside school can be a challenging task. Let's examine the efforts of Tangia Anderson, a teacher in a large urban high school:

Case STUDY We have to dig deep down inside and reach for new strategies and teaching methods that relate to what our students have to face day to day when they are not in a school environment. We often have a student or groups of students who make teaching a challenge. The best thing to remember is to continue to provide a meaningful lesson for the entire class. The student or students who are challenging the teacher may want to use a different strategy. My immediate goal is to get the students participating without making a big issue. For example, in teaching students how to type without looking at their

Effective teachers create productive learning environments that motivate students to learn.

fingers, I always had students that were not motivated to learn the keyboard. So I made the typing assignment like a racing game and told the students to see if they could type without looking at their fingers while racing their classmates. The first three times I participated in the race and then I noticed that my previously idle students started typing to see if they could win. Before I knew it, they were racing with the class and I didn't say a word. Next time we did it, they wanted to start the next race. (T. Anderson, personal communication, 3/23/99)

Increasing Understanding 2.5

Identify at least two teacher roles that Tangia demonstrated in her work with her students.

• • ● • •

In working with students, actions often speak louder than words. Here are Tangia's comments on the importance of modeling, or "practicing what we preach":

Case STUDY Effective teachers model the expected behaviors or outcomes they want their students to know or learn. Times have long changed from "Do as I say and not as I do," because students will often do the opposite. They will do exactly what they see. When a teacher models for his or her students, students see that the teacher believes in what he or she is doing and the teacher really wants the student to understand the concept or idea. From day one in the classroom, I try to demonstrate the expected behaviors and attitudes I want my students to have. For example, respect for others is an important value I try to teach in my classes. When I teach, I use, as well as visually provide, positive words on the board for my students to use when talking with others, and I consciously avoid negative words. Respect for other people's feelings is important, and I want my students to know that we can communicate in a positive way to get what we need accomplished without being negative. (T. Anderson, personal communication, 5/28/99)

• • ● • •

Handling students' many different needs in a class can be complex and challenging. To maintain lesson momentum and make the constant transitions required both within and between lessons, teachers need both withitness and overlapping skills

(Kounin, 1970). Tangia demonstrated her ability in these areas when she was observed in her classroom:

Case STUDY Tangia stood outside her classroom door, observing students as they moved to their next class. She warmly greeted each student who entered her class while also monitoring the activities of students already in her room. Her students settled into their seats before the next bell rang. Several students asked her questions while entering the classroom. As Tangia monitored both the hallway and classroom and listened to her students, she noticed one student approach her own desk, which was at the back of the classroom, away from the lesson area. The student eyed a candy jar on Tangia's desk, along with other personal items, including a gift that had been placed there the previous period. When the student turned to see if Tangia was watching, he found her looking right at him as she answered questions in the doorway. The student waited a few seconds until Tangia was done speaking and then pointed at her candy jar.

"Mrs. Anderson, can I have one of these?" the student asked.

Tangia saw the opportunity to address the student's sloppy attire, which was evident in his slouching pants and untucked shirt.

"Yes, if you tuck in your shirt," Tangia replied.

The student complied, smiling, took a piece of candy, and went to his seat. When the passing-period bell rang, Tangia proceeded to the front of her class and began her lesson.

To begin, Tangia pointed to a chart of "Acceptable Business Phrases" at the front of her class and discussed different contexts in which the different expressions should be used. Students had to identify those different contexts on the phone, using voice tone and vocabulary to judge the state of mind and response of the persons they called. Tangia asked students to identify words and tones that indicated receptivity by the call receiver, versus those which might be indicators of nonreceptivity.

"How could you tell my receptivity when you entered class?" she asked to illustrate the difference.

"You greeted us when we came in and said 'Good morning' in a friendly voice," a student responded.

When asked how an unwelcome call receiver might sound, several students raised their hands. Tangia called on one student and patiently waited while he slowly collected his thoughts and explained them. Two males and one female started talking over the selected student, interfering with his response. Tangia silently pointed at each of the interrupters to indicate the need for their silence and patience. When the first student had finished his response, Tangia then called on another student, who had been waiting silently with a raised hand. The lesson continued with students calling each other—on actual business phones that had been donated to their classroom—and reading from scripts to simulate problems that might occur in the work world.

CW

Increasing Understanding 2.6

How did Tangia demonstrate caring in this teaching episode?

• • ● • •

By actively involving students in realistic problem solving, Tangia was making sure that students' school world was preparing them for the real world.

Teachers often have to struggle with overcrowded classrooms and inadequate resources. Resourceful teachers find ways to accomplish challenging teaching tasks, such as finding materials for concrete demonstrations of a concept or volunteers to assist with classroom activities. Tangia drew on her resourcefulness by creating business education lessons that used real office equipment donated by a local business. Tangia needed to place several calls and make visits to corporate offices in her city, but her efforts paid off in increased learning and motivation.

As we better understand learning and how important concrete examples and student involvement are in maximizing it, resourcefulness becomes ever more important. After one of your authors was hired for a public school job, the principal told him that he had been chosen largely because of his resourcefulness. The principal was impressed when he described in the interview how he used the leftovers from a lobster dinner as the focal point of a language arts lesson during his internship.

Ambassador to the Public Another important role that teachers perform is "ambassador to the public"; they are the most visible representatives of the schools in which they teach. To parents and the public at large, teachers *are* the school; they represent the primary link to their children's education. When parents assess their children's schools, only safety is rated as more important than the ability of teachers (Olson, 1999a). Teachers are under constant public scrutiny, and their perceived competence is continually discussed. Sometimes this public scrutiny is both critical and negative (Allison, 1995; Bullough & Baughman, 1997). Knowing this, teachers can take steps to publicly demonstrate their students' and their own accomplishments. In doing so, they communicate that students' academic and emotional growth are their primary concerns and that they and parents are on the same team.

Learning is a cooperative venture, and teachers, students, and parents are in it together. In a comprehensive review of factors affecting student learning, researchers concluded the following:

> Because of the importance of the home environment to school learning, teachers must also develop strategies to increase parent involvement in their children's academic life. This means teachers should go beyond traditional once-a-year parent/teacher conferences and work with parents to see that learning is valued in the home. Teachers should encourage parents to be involved with their children's academic pursuits on a day-to-day basis, helping them with homework, monitoring television viewing, reading to their young children, and simply expressing the expectation that their children will achieve academic success. (M. Wang, Haertel, & Walberg, 1993, pp. 278–279)

Communication with parents or other primary caregivers is not an appendage to the teaching process; it is an integral part of the teacher's job.

Home–school cooperation results in at least four benefits for students:

- Higher academic achievement
- More positive attitudes and behaviors
- Better attendance rates
- Greater willingness to do homework (Cameron & Lee, 1997; Marzano, 2003)

These outcomes likely result from parents' increased participation in school activities, their more positive attitudes about schooling, and teachers' increased understanding of learners' home environments. Responding to a student's unresponsive behavior is easier, for example, when his teacher knows that his mother or father has just lost a job, his parents are going through a divorce, or there's a serious illness in the family.

Barriers to parental involvement. Involving parents in the education of their children is a desired goal, but it doesn't happen automatically. Economic, cultural, and

Teachers serve as ambassadors to parents, helping them understand how schools can help their children learn.

language barriers are often difficult to overcome. Teacher understanding is a first step in resolving these difficulties.

Communication and involvement take time, and economic commitments often come first out of necessity. First among these is employment; holding two and even three jobs often prevents parents from helping their youngsters with homework (Ellis, Dowdy, Graham, & Jones, 1992). Parents may be unable to pay for child care, transportation, telephone service, or other things that would allow them to participate in school activities. Parents want to be involved in their children's schooling, but schools need to be flexible and provide help and encouragement.

Discontinuities between students' home cultures and the culture of the school can also be barriers to home–school cooperation (Delgado-Gaitan, 1992; Harry, 1992). Students' parents may have experienced schools that were very different from the ones their children attend. Also, some parents may have gone through only the elementary grades or may have had negative school experiences. One researcher described the problem this way:

> Underneath most parents is a student—someone who went to school, sometimes happily, sometimes unhappily. What often happens when the parent-as-adult returns to school, or has dealings with teachers, is that the parent as child/student returns. Many parents still enter school buildings flooded with old memories, angers, and disappointments. Their stomachs churn and flutter with butterflies, not because of what is happening today with their own children, but because of outdated memories and past behaviors. (Rich, 1987, p. 24)

Parents like these will require encouragement and support to become involved.

Language can be another potential barrier to effective home–school cooperation. Parents of bilingual students may not speak English, making home–school communication difficult. In these situations, children often have the responsibility of interpreting messages. Homework poses special problems because parents are unable to interpret assignments or provide help (Delgado-Gaitan, 1992).

Schools often compound the problem by using educational jargon when they send letters home. The problem is especially acute in special education, where the language of legal and procedural safeguards can be bewildering. For example, parents often don't understand individualized education programs or even remember that they've signed one (Harry, 1992).

Reflect on This

To analyze a case study examining questions about involving parents in their children's education, go to the Companion Website at **www.prenhall.com/kauchak**, then to this chapter's *Reflect on This* module.

Strategies for involving parents. Parents often feel ill-prepared to assist their children with school-related tasks, but suggestions from school describing specific strategies in the home can be effective in bridging the home–school gap (Gorman & Balter, 1997; Hoover-Dempsey, Bassler, & Burow, 1995). The National Parent Teacher Association (PTA) has issued standards for parent/family involvement programs that emphasize the central role that parents and caregivers play in their children's education (the PTA's standards are presented in Chapter 7). Researchers in this area suggest five important ways schools can involve parents:

- Help parents create better learning environments in the home.
- Create effective home–school and school–home communciation lines.
- Recruit and organize parent volunteers.
- Involve parents in school decision making.
- Identify and integrate community resources to complement and supplement school goals. (Epstein, Sanders, Simon, Salinas, Jansorn, & Van Voorhis, 2002)

Although many of these efforts occur at the school level, individual teachers are often asked to provide leadership in these areas and are the human link to students' homes (Feuerstein, 2000).

Virtually all schools have formal communication channels; these include interim progress reports, which tell parents about their youngster's achievement at the midpoint of each grading period; open houses, during which teachers introduce themselves and describe school procedures; parent–teacher conferences; and, of course, report cards. Although these processes are schoolwide and valuable, as an individual teacher you can do more to enhance the communication process:

- Send a letter home at the beginning of the school year describing your expectations and how parents can assist in their children's learning. You can enlist the aid of students, other teachers, or parents to translate the letter into students' home languages if necessary.
- Maintain communication by sending student work home regularly. Short notes describing upcoming topics and projects as well as ways that parents can assist their children communicate caring and also create a learning partnership with parents and caregivers.
- Invite parents and caregivers to visit your classroom and contact you if they have questions or concerns.
- Involve parents in school activities, such as by inviting them to talk to classes about their occupations and by asking them to participate in music and sports booster clubs.

One first-year teacher had this experience in calling parents:

I started [calling] because I had some kids right off who really had trouble. So, I felt like I needed to call just so they wouldn't get totally lost so soon. I had to deal with them, somehow. I really like parent/teacher conferences a lot. I've discovered that a phone call is just as good. I've been getting [very] positive feedback from . . . parents. Like, "Oh, I'm so glad you called. Not one teacher called me ever last year. He had so much trouble." I just . . . decided I'm going to call a couple of parents every night. It's really [having a] positive [effect on] what's happening in the classroom. I'm also going to call some parents for positive reasons. There are some kids who really deserve to have a teacher call and say [something good]. (Bullough, 1989, p. 112)

CW

Increasing Understanding 2.7

Refer again to Table 2.1. Identify an additional barrier to increased home–school cooperation. What are some things teachers can do to overcome this barrier?

Research indicates that parents want to be involved in their children's education (Elam & Rose, 1995). Teachers can capitalize on this desire by providing opportunities for parents to learn about and participate in their children's education.

Technology provides another channel for improving communication. A voice-mail system, for example, allows teachers and parents to communicate despite their busy schedules (Cameron & Lee, 1997). One voice-mail system, called the Bridge Project, enables teachers to post daily assignments and event reminders on a bulletin board that parents can access 24 hours a day, seven days a week. E-mail is also an excellent tool for maintaining communication, especially in school communities in which most families make use of this technology.

Collaborative Colleague As we saw earlier, a significant portion of a teacher's time (almost 26%) is spent working with peers. Effective teachers are parts of teams that work for the benefit of school districts, individual schools, and students. They work cooperatively on the many tasks that make their classrooms and schools productive

WORKING WITH PARENTS: A PARENT–TEACHER CONFERENCE

Having examined barriers to parental involvement as well as strategies for involving parents, you now have the opportunity to view a video of a teacher conducting a parent–teacher conference.

In this episode fifth-grade teacher DeVonne Lampkin conducts a conference with a parent of a student who is struggling in her class. The parent is somewhat defensive at different points in the conference, and DeVonne attempts to simultaneously support and disarm the parent by grounding her discussion with specific facts about the student's performance.

To complete this activity, do the following:

- Go to the DVD, and view the video episode titled "Working with Parents: A Parent–Teacher Conference."
- Answer the questions you'll find on the DVD.

CW *To answer the questions online and receive immediate feedback, go to the Companion Website at* **www.prenhall.com/kauchak**, *then to this chapter's* Classroom Windows *module.*

places to learn. Collaboration is important for educators in all levels of education. Administrators begin to assess teachers' ability and inclination to collaborate in the initial job interview, and many principals view collaboration as essential to the effectiveness of a teacher and the well-being of a school. Students considering teaching as a career might want to ask themselves the following question:

Am I the kind of person willing and able to enter a profession subject to all kinds of pressures, criticisms, and calls for change, secure as I can be at my stage of the game that besides being responsible for the education of students in my classroom, I have a responsibility to gain a voice in whatever decisions are made that affect the school as a social-education organization? (Sarason, 1993, p. 6)

To be productive in today's schools, as in many other workplaces, teachers need collaboration and negotiation skills and the ability to communicate dissenting views in inoffensive ways. Being knowledgeable and well informed also assists teachers in their professional negotiations.

Learner and Reflective Practitioner Teachers are also learners. Expert teachers continually update their "knowledge of students, conceptions of learning, pedagogical content knowledge, and knowledge of goals and curriculum" (Hillocks, 1999, p. 109). In other words, they refine and expand the specialized body of knowledge needed for professional status: "A professional is someone who has something to profess. Your obligation to yourself and your profession is to know what is going on, that is, what others are experiencing, studying and writing" (Sarason, 1993, p. 138). Tangia Anderson comments on this essential teacher role:

As a teacher, I continually look for new ways of reaching and teaching my students. Learning how to become a more effective teacher is a good feeling. To be a teacher, you want to continue learning new ways to keep lessons interesting, manage your classroom, assist other teachers, and communicate effectively with parents. When teachers learn new ways to make their lessons more meaningful, they enjoy teaching. (T. Anderson, personal communication, 5/27/99)

In looking for new ways of reaching her students, Tangia must make many decisions, most of which can't be reduced to simple rules. How does she know if her decisions are wise? As mentioned in Chapter 1, teachers receive little feedback about the effectiveness of their work. They are observed infrequently by administrators, receive only uncertain feedback from students and parents, and get virtually no feedback from their colleagues (Darling-Hammond, 1996, 1997). To improve, teachers must be able to think about and assess their own classroom performance. They must be *reflective practitioners.*

A **reflective practitioner** is *a professional continually involved in the process of examining and evaluating his or her own practice* (Cruickshank, 1987; Schon, 1983). Reflective teachers are thoughtful, analytical, even self-critical about their work (Palmer, 1998). They plan lessons carefully and take the time to analyze and critique them afterward. Very simply, they constantly think about what they're doing and ask themselves how they might improve. Questions for reflective teachers might include the following:

- Did I have a clear goal for the lesson? What was the goal?
- Was the goal important? How do I know?

- Was my learning activity consistent with my goal?
- What examples could I have used to make the lesson clearer for the students?
- What could I have done to make the lesson more interesting?
- How do I know if the students understand what I taught? What would be a better way of finding out?

More important than the specific questions themselves is the inclination to ask them. If teachers keep questions such as these in mind, they can avoid the trap of teaching in a certain way because they've always taught that way. Openness to change and the desire for improvement are two of the most important characteristics for a professional. Reflection may be the most significant thing you can do to grow professionally.

Increasing Understanding 2.8

How does reflection relate to the other dimensions of professionalism—a specialized body of knowledge, emphasis on decision making, autonomy, and ethical standards—presented in Chapter 1?

A journal is a useful tool for reflection, which is why we've encouraged you to keep one as you move through this course. You may recall that Ken's reflection about his responses to the "fat jerk" incident was an excerpt from his teaching journal.

Developing the ability and inclination to be reflective is difficult and demanding: "The pressures on teachers, together with a school culture that generally values action above reflection, make it difficult for teachers to find the time and opportunities for reflection" (Calderhead, 1996, p. 715). With commitment and effort, however, you can become a skilled reflective practitioner, and observing your own professional growth can be one of the most rewarding aspects of your teaching experience.

Who Will Your Colleagues Be?

In this section we examine the teaching workforce. Knowledge of teacher demographics can be helpful to you in at least two ways. First, it gives you a snapshot of your future colleagues—the people you'll work with. Second, it can provide you with information about possible job opportunities. For example, minority teachers, in general, and male teachers at the elementary and preschool levels are in short supply. These teachers will be actively recruited when they graduate from college.

In 2000 there were 3.5 million teachers in the United States, with slightly less than 90 percent of these teaching in public schools (Hussar & Gerald, 2001). To put this figure into perspective, the number of K–12 teachers represents about 2.1 percent of the total U.S. workforce, slightly lower than in other industrialized countries (NCES, 1997a). Surprisingly, teachers make up only 52.1 percent of the total school staff, with the remainder consisting of administrators and support staff (e.g., secretaries, custodians, and other instructional staff such as counselors and school psychologists).

In contrast, teachers comprise more than three fourths of all public education employees in Japan, Belgium, and Italy and more than 60 percent in most other industrialized countries (Darling-Hammond, 1997). One comparison between Riverside, California, and Zurich, Switzerland, two districts with approximately the same number of students, revealed that Zurich had almost twice as many teachers (2,330 versus 1,223). Critics contend that U.S. schools are top heavy, with too many resources going to bloated bureaucracies.

The number of new teachers required to meet workforce demands is projected to increase by 4 percent each year until the year 2009, resulting in 2.2 million new teachers (Hussar & Gerald, 2001). This increase will result from factors such as increases in the K–12 student population, increased expenditures for education, attempts to decrease class sizes, and the reform movements you read about in Chapter 1.

You've all experienced the teaching profession from the other side of the teacher's desk. To see how accurate your perceptions are of the "average" teacher, answer the questions that follow:

A Demographic Profile of the Teaching Force

1. Approximately what percentage of the teaching force is male?
   a. 10%
   b. 25%
   c. 35%
   d. 50%
2. How old is the average teacher?
   a. 25
   b. 35
   c. 45
   d. 55
3. Approximately what percentage of the teaching force is minority?
   a. 5%
   b. 10%
   c. 15%
   d. 20%
4. New teachers, directly out of college, differ from the rest of the teaching force. They are
   a. Younger, more likely to be female, less likely to be minority, and less likely to be married
   b. Younger, less likely to be female, less likely to be minority, and less likely to be married
   c. Younger, more likely to be female, more likely to be minority, and less likely to be married
   d. Younger, more likely to be female, less likely to be minority, and more likely to be married

Read the following sections to see how accurate your perceptions are.

Gender

Most teachers are female, a historical trend that has continued since the 1800s. At one time the percentage of female teachers reached 85 percent, but today the figure is closer to 75 percent. This figure is higher than in most industrialized countries, where the average is about 65 percent (NCES, 1997a). As you can see from Table 2.2, this percentage varies by grade level and content area. The highest percentage of women are found at the elementary level, in English/language arts, and in special education. The highest percentages of male teachers are found in social studies, math, and science. Despite attempts to attract male teachers to elementary schools, the percentage of men at this level hasn't changed significantly in the last 10 years (Deneen, 2002). In preschools the percentage is even lower—less than 5 percent of early childhood teachers are men (Galley, 2000a).

CW

Increasing Understanding 2.9

How could a beginning teacher use the information in Table 2.2 to maximize the possibility of obtaining a teaching position? What are the advantages and disadvantages of this strategy?

Table 2.2 Public School Teachers' Gender by Assignment

Area	Percentage of Females	Percentage of Males
Elementary	91	9
Math/Science	52	48
Social Studies	38	62
English/Language Arts	80	20
Special Education	84	16

Source: National Center for Education Statistics (1997a).

Age

The teaching population is aging, and this has implications for prospective teachers. In 1993 the average age of schoolteachers was 43, with proportionally more older teachers in high-demand areas such as math and science (Darling-Hammond & Sclan, 1996). The average teacher had more than 15 years of teaching experience, and greater than 47 percent of teachers held master's degrees or higher (NCES, 1997a). Only 13 percent of the teaching force had less than 3 years' experience; 65 percent had 10 years or more, and 34 percent had 20 or more years. Because of the aging teaching population and projected increases in the K–12 student population, forecasters have predicted that more than 200,000 new teachers will need to be hired annually for the next decade (A. Bradley, 2000a).

Race and Ethnicity

The majority (87%) of U.S. teachers are White, with the largest numbers of minority teachers being either African American (8%) or Hispanic (4%). Recently, the per-

The ability to communicate ideas and the ability to work collaboratively with colleagues are essential teacher skills.

CW

Increasing Understanding 2.10

What are some possible reasons for the decline in the percentage of minority teachers? Is the percentage of minority teachers likely to increase or decrease in the future? Why?

centage of minority teachers has declined slightly, a trend that has many educators concerned, because the percentage of minority youth in our schools is steadily increasing. A third of all public school students in the United Students are of African American, Asian, or Hispanic descent. The proportion of students from non-European backgrounds approaches 90 percent in many large urban areas (Darling-Hammond, 1996).

New Teachers

In 1998, 200,545 new teachers graduated from college, a whopping 49 percent increase from 1983. How do new teachers hired differ from the existing teacher pool? The answer to this question is more complex than it appears at first because the pool of "new" teachers actually includes newly graduated teachers (approximately 34% of the total), recently graduated candidates who delayed entry into teaching (19%), persons reentering the teaching force (30%), and transfers from other teaching positions (17%) (Darling-Hammond & Sclan, 1996). So, at the "new teacher" orientation meeting on your first job, you are likely to find that only some of your new colleagues have not taught before; a good number of others will be transfers and reentries into the profession.

Market forces both within and outside education influence the mix of people entering the teaching profession. For example, during the 1980s teaching positions were hard to find, leading many new teachers to accept positions in business and other fields. In the 1990s, as the demand for teachers increased, the profession saw more delayed entrants and reentrant teachers.

Newly graduated teachers differ from the existing teaching force in several ways. They are more likely to be female (79% versus 74% for the total teaching force), White (91% versus 87%), and younger (28 years old versus 43 years old) (Darling-Hammond & Sclan, 1996). A small but increasing number of "newly minted" teachers do not fit this profile, however. These teachers entered teacher education programs immediately after graduating from college in other areas. (Today, 65 percent of teacher education programs have special programs for post-baccalaureate students, and about 9 percent admit these students only.) Individuals in this subgroup of new teachers tend to be older—about 30—and are more likely to be male than teachers who studied education as undergraduates.

What Happens to New Teachers? Many new teachers end up leaving the profession. About 15 percent leave teaching after their first year, another 15 percent after their second year, and still another 10 percent leave after their third year (Croasmun, Hampton, & Herrmann, 1999). They leave for a variety of reasons, including the following:

- Better jobs or other careers (39%)
- Dissatisfaction with teaching as a career or with their specific jobs (29%)
- School staffing actions, such as cutbacks in staff, layoffs, terminations, school reorganizations, or school closings (19%)

Of the people who listed dissatisfaction with teaching as a career, 75 percent listed low salaries as a major factor. An even higher percentage who said they were dissatisfied cited working conditions, such as student discipline problems, lack of support from the school administration, low student motivation, and lack of teacher influence over schoolwide and classroom decision making as sources of their dissatisfaction (Ingersoll & Smith, 2003).

Exploring Diversity

MINORITY TEACHERS AND WHAT THEY BRING TO THE PROFESSION

As the number of minority students in U.S. schools continues to grow, attempts to recruit minority teachers have also increased. Nearly a third of school-age children in the United States are members of cultural minority groups, compared to only 12 percent of the teaching force (Archer, 2000a). Efforts to recruit more minority teachers include early recruitment programs aimed at high schoolers, specially targeted scholarship programs, and programs designed to attract older workers interested in a career change.

Why all this interest and effort? What do minority teachers bring to classrooms that is so important? Researchers attempting to answer this question have focused on three areas:

- The need for minority role models
- The need for effective instructors
- The need for alternative perspectives

Let's look at them.

Minorities as Role Models

Research clearly indicates that effective role models increase motivation and learning for all children (Bruning, Schraw, Norby, & Ronning, 2004; Schunk, 2000). This is particularly important for members of cultural minority groups. Minority teachers demonstrate to minority students that success and professional status are attainable for all people—including cultural minorities. Equally important, they can demonstrate that success doesn't detract from cultural identity—a concern of many youngsters.

In one study, the presence of a minority teacher helped *students* regain their cultural identities. Yup'ik Eskimos in rural Alaska were losing their native language because young children were either not interested in or ashamed of speaking it (Lipka, 1998). When a native Yup'ik teacher was hired at the local school, the pattern was reversed:

> We lived right next to the school, and my sister lived with us for the year. We spoke only Yup'ik all of the time, so by the end of the year many of the students were no longer ashamed either to speak, or learn to speak, Yup'ik. My husband and I felt we had really done something good for those students because they began to identify themselves as Yup'ik and acquired their own language. (Lipka, 1998, p. 50)

Minority teachers themselves will attest to the importance of modeling. Many say that, as students, their own experience with minority teachers was a powerful influence on their decision to choose teaching as a career (Gordon, 1993; Toppin & Levine, 1992). When students see adults from their own cultural backgrounds performing effectively in the classroom, they begin believing that they too can succeed academically and can become teachers.

Minorities as Effective Instructors

Researchers also suggest that minority teachers may bring increased understanding of minority students' backgrounds and needs to learning activities (Villegas, 1991). For example, in one study of instructional styles, effective African American teachers used standard English to give directions and regulate behavior but used "performances," stylized ways of speaking that resembled African American

Despite these obstacles, a recent Public Agenda survey found that more than two thirds of new teachers "get a lot of satisfaction from teaching," and three fourths "view teaching as a lifelong choice" (Public Agenda, 2000b). Interestingly, although three fourths of new teachers considered themselves "seriously underpaid," when given a choice between schools with better pay or better working conditions, they chose better working conditions.

In spite of the problems facing beginning teachers, more than half of them stay in the profession, and you may very well be in that half. We have presented the problems

preaching styles, to motivate students during lessons (Foster, 1992). In the study of Yup'ik instruction mentioned earlier, a Yup'ik teacher used an interdisciplinary unit on smelting (drying fish for the winter) as a means to teach geography, science, mathematics, sanitation, family traditions, and cultural values (Lipka, 1998). Students took part in smelting in the classroom through observation, practice, and teaching other students. Students responded with a high degree of interest and participation, presumedly because the unit was relevant to their lives and culture.

Minority Teachers Bring Unique Perspectives to the Profession

Teachers from cultural minority groups also bring valuable alternative perspectives to teaching. Many minority teachers view teaching as a "calling" in which they have opportunities to work with and help minority students (Gordon, 1993). For example, one Chicana student teacher reported the following:

> I began my student teaching experience thinking that minority students had to be saved from a harsh and cruel world which was existent in the schools. Consequently, when I saw the faces of many minority students, I set out to make a difference in their lives. (Kauchak & Burbank, 2000, p. 6)

This commitment permeated the teacher's work with students, making her an important advocate for them.

Minority teachers can also help nonminority teachers understand students who look at the world from perspectives different than their own. Because teachers from diverse backgrounds have had firsthand experience in minority communities, they can become effective spokespersons for students from those communities (Gordon, 1993; Kauchak & Burbank, 2000; Toppin & Levine, 1992).

Unquestionably, like all students, minority students need role models with whom they can identify. Further, diversity and the perspectives of people from different backgrounds have always been strengths in American culture. However, none of this suggests that White teachers cannot be effective role models or instructors for Black, Hispanic, Native American, Asian, or other minority students. Any knowledgeable and sensitive teacher can design lessons that are meaningful and motivating to specific groups of minority students.

Minority teachers serve as effective role models for minority youth and bring unique and valuable perspectives to teaching.

Just as student diversity can enrich learning for every student, diversity among teachers can add perspectives that make every teacher more effective. The key, which is one of the themes of this book, is professionalism. Professionals—minority and nonminority—have a shared vision; they communicate with and learn from each other, and they're committed to providing the best for all students, not just those whose ethnic and cultural backgrounds are similar to their own.

because they give you a realistic look at the world of teaching and can help you make decisions about whether you want to be a teacher and, if you do, where you might want to work.

You now know some of the characteristics of new and existing teachers—the people who will be your colleagues. When you interview for a teaching position, you might want to make a special effort to meet the people you'd work with at the school. They can provide valuable insights into the school environment, and your discussions can help you decide whether your work with them will be productive and enjoyable.

Decision Making

Defining Yourself as a Professional

Defining yourself as a professional requires that you take a hard look at the devastating attrition rates facing new teachers. Research shows that only 60 percent to 70 percent of newly prepared teachers enter teaching jobs after they graduate, and large numbers (experts estimate almost 50%) leave within 5 years of entering the profession (Croasmun et al., 1999; Darling-Hammond, 2001). Attrition rates for new teachers are often 5 times those of experienced teachers (Archer, 2003). These figures reflect a significant loss both nationally and personally. At the individual level these figures often represent personal frustration and failure.

What can you, a prospective teacher, do to address these problems and increase the odds that your entry into the profession will be a successful one? The first and most obvious strategy is to take full advantage of the learning opportunities that present themselves during your teacher training program. Beginning teachers who are well prepared, who understand the professional literature, and who have extensive clinical experiences in a number of school settings perform better in the classroom and are more likely to survive the rigors of the first years of teaching (Darling-Hammond, 2001, 2003). In essence, work hard, study hard, and learn as much as you can.

A second survival strategy is to choose the right school for your first teaching job. Schools vary considerably in their treatment of beginning teachers (S. Johnson & Birkeland, 2002; Stevens & Parkes, 2001). Some throw beginning teachers into the most difficult teaching positions, giving them an unreasonable number of classes to prepare for. Others nurture their teachers by providing induction programs and collegial support. Successful induction programs can smooth the transition into the first year of teaching by providing special help and assistance to beginning teachers. When you interview for your first teaching position, ask about the existence of induction programs. If possible, talk with other new teachers in the school about the kinds of support they received.

In addition to selecting the right school, finding a mentor, an experienced teacher who can guide you during your first year, is also important. Many districts now have formal mentoring programs in which beginning teachers are assigned to an experienced colleague who provides both technical and psychological support (J. Wang & Odell, 2002). First-year teachers in schools where these programs don't exist often succeed by finding a "pro" down the hall who is willing to share his or her knowledge and experience. The human dimension of this assistance often makes the difference between giving up in frustration and growing through the challenge.

The first year of teaching is demanding, but your teacher education program can do much to prepare you for the uncertainties of that year. In addition to studying hard, you should actively seek out experienced teachers in your clinical experiences who can help you not only connect theory and practice but also make the giant step from novice to expert.

Summary

Teaching: A Time Perspective

Teachers work within specified frameworks of time. The school year typically consists of 180 days, although this is changing in many areas with year-round schooling and summer school. The average teacher's workweek is slightly longer than the national 40-hour norm, and much of this time is spent outside the classroom and school building. During the school day teachers spend most of their time working with students, but peer interactions and desk work eat up significant chunks of teachers' days.

Decision Making: Responding to the Complexities of Teaching

Classrooms are multidimensional, with many events occurring immediately and simultaneously. These events occur in the public eye, and they're often unpredictable. These classroom characteristics make teaching both challenging and rewarding.

Teachers assume a number of roles. Foremost, they must be caring professionals. They can best communicate this caring by devoting time to their students and by demonstrating respect and expecting it in return. Teachers are also responsible for creating orderly classrooms that focus on learning.

Three teacher roles occur outside the immediate classroom. As ambassadors to the public, teachers communicate classroom accomplishments and help create effective home–school linkages. As collaborative colleagues, they work with other teachers to make their schools more effective. As learners and reflective practitioners, they continue their professional growth throughout their careers.

Who Will Your Colleagues Be?

The currently aging teaching force has implications for beginning teachers. As more teachers retire, a number of teaching position openings will occur. The typical U.S. teacher is White, female, and 43. These demographics change with teaching level and location and also are expected to change over time.

New teachers differ from the existing teaching force in several ways. They are more likely to be White, female, and younger. A surprisingly low number of teachers (61%) enter teaching immediately after graduation, and almost one half leave the profession within 5 years. Understanding who your colleagues will be can make your first teaching position more enjoyable and rewarding.

Important Concepts

alternating-day block schedule (p. 50)
block scheduling (p. 50)
caring (p. 58)
four-by-four block schedule (p. 50)
modified school calendar (p. 48)
overlapping (p. 57)
productive learning environment (p. 60)
reflective practitioner (p. 67)
withitness (p. 56)

Developing as a Professional

Praxis Practice

Read the case study, and then answer the questions that follow.

"Why are you leaving so early?" Jim Davis asked his wife, Judy, a fourth-grade teacher, on Wednesday morning. "It's quarter to seven."

"We have a grade-level meeting this morning," she returned. "We start at seven fifteen, and we go exactly 45 minutes. Jan, Kim, and Helen have been really sweet about getting to school early for the meetings, because I told them that I needed to work with Cassie and Manuel before school each morning. Neither one of them spoke a word of English when school started, but they're really coming along.

"By the way, how does this look?" Judy asked, showing Jim a letter.

"I can't read it."

"Of course not," she said, smiling. "It's in Spanish, and your Spanish stinks. . . . It's a letter to the parents telling them what we're going to be doing next semester and inviting them to come in any time. The kids helped me put it together, since my Spanish isn't so hot either."

"Looks great," Jim smiled.

Judy gathered her papers and headed off for school.

"I don't think this math curriculum they want us to consider puts enough emphasis on basic skills," Kim asserted during the grade-level meeting. "A bunch of our kids still don't know their times tables."

"I think you're right, Kim," Judy said, nodding. "It really does a good job with word problems, though. I actually found myself interested in some of the problems. Maybe we should all commit ourselves to some drill and practice on the times tables each day, so we could sort of have the best of both worlds."

"Good idea, Judy. I agree that the curriculum does a good job with real-world problems, and that's what we constantly struggle with every year," Helen added.

Later that day, Judy prepared her class for their science lesson.

"Put your writing papers away for now," Judy directed just before 11:00. "It's time for your bathroom break, and then we have science."

"Excellent job," Judy smiled at 11:05. "Each one of you is seated and ready to learn. That's doing a very good job of being responsible. . . . Now, what have we been talking about . . . Sonja?"

"Physical changes," Sonja answered.

"Give us an example, Darren."

"Tearing paper."

"Another one . . . Cassie?"

"Melting ice," Cassie responded hesitantly.

"Good, Cassie," Judy said, smiling.

"And what is a physical change? Raulo?"

"A change in the size . . . or shape . . . or the state of something," Raulo responded, the wheels seemingly turning in his head.

"Now look," Judy directed as she brought out a soft drink bottle about a third full of clear liquid (vinegar). "I'm going to put this powder into a balloon and then place the balloon over the top. Let's see what happens."

She covered the mouth of the soft drink bottle with the balloon, held the balloon up, and let a white power (baking soda) drop into the liquid.

Amidst cries of "Ooh," "Ahh," "Cool," and "What's happening?" the powder began to fizz and the balloon to expand.

Suddenly, the balloon blew off the top of the bottle, and a combination of fizz, vinegar, and baking soda sprayed all over Judy's desk. The students howled with laughter.

Judy stepped back, paused briefly, and then smiled.

"How many of you think I did that on purpose?"

"Yeh," "No way," "Sure," "Unh uh," followed her question.

"No, I didn't," Judy confessed as she used some paper towels to wipe off the table. "But let's think about this. . . . Was this an example of a physical change? . . . Think about it everyone, and also decide *why* you think it was or wasn't. Remember, knowing why is every bit as important as the answer itself."

1. Identify at least three characteristics of classrooms that were illustrated in the case study. Which of the characteristics was most prominently illustrated?
2. Describe one way that Judy demonstrated the teaching role of caring professional.
3. Identify two examples from the case study that illustrated Judy in the role of creator of productive learning environments.
4. Describe how Judy demonstrated the role of ambassador to the public.
5. Describe how Judy demonstrated the teaching role of collaborative colleague.

To receive feedback on your responses to the Praxis Practice exercises, go to the Companion Website at **www.prenhall.com/kauchak**, then to this chapter's *Praxis Practice* module.

Discussion Questions

1. If you could change any dimension of the way teachers spend their time (see Table 2.1), what would you change? Why?
2. Which of the school calendar and scheduling alternatives—year-round schools, longer school year, block scheduling—have the most potential for increasing student learning? Which are most attractive to you personally as a prospective teacher? The least attractive?
3. Are the complexities of teaching likely to become greater or less in the future? Why?
4. Is caring more important at some levels (e.g., elementary versus secondary) than others? Why or why not?
5. Is the importance of teachers working with parents likely to increase or decrease in the near future? Why?
6. What are the pros and cons of making hiring decisions based on demographic information about the teaching force (e.g., the shortage of males in elementary school, females in social studies)?

Video Discussion Questions

The following discussion questions refer to video segments found on the Companion Website. To view the accompanying video, answer the questions online, and receive immediate feedback, go to the Companion Website at **www.prenhall.com/kauchak**, then to this chapter's *Video Discussion* module.

1. Dr. Uri Treisman is a professor of mathematics at the University of Texas at Austin and Director of the Charles A. Dana Center for Math and Science Education. He believes teachers and their professional development are central to school reform. What does Dr. Treisman believe are some concrete things teachers can do within their own schools to further their professional development? Which do you think have the most potential for furthering teachers' professional development?
2. As we saw in this chapter, involving parents is important for school success. How does Dr. Treisman believe that parents can be enlisted as political allies in school reform efforts? Which of these strategies would be most useful to you as a teacher?
3. Dr. John Goodlad is a professor emeritus and co-director of the Center for Renewal at the University of Washington and president of the Independent Institute for Educational Inquiry. He believes that caring is essential to effective teaching. What does Dr. Goodlad feel are some concrete ways in which teachers can structure their classrooms to facilitate the development of caring relationships? Which of these strategies will be most useful to you as a teacher?

Going into Schools

1. Interview a teacher concerning local experiments with time and scheduling. Ask about the existence of the following in the teacher's district:
   a. Year-round schooling
   b. Extended school year
   c. Summer school
   d. Alternate (e.g., block) schedules

   How prevalent are these? How effective are they? How popular are these? Analyze the teacher's response, and decide whether these experiments with time are beneficial for education.
2. Interview a teacher to find out if his or her day differs from the one depicted in Table 2.1.
   a. Are these percentages typical? If not, where are they different and why?
   b. To what extent does the teacher's time allocation fluctuate from these averages from day to day? What causes these fluctuations?
   c. If the teacher could change the allocation of his or her time in one way, what would it be?

   Analyze the teacher's responses using information from this chapter.
3. Observe a teacher interacting with students, and identify instances in which the following characteristics of classrooms are evident:
   a. Classrooms are multidimensional.
   b. Events are simultaneous.
   c. Events are immediate.
   d. Classrooms are unpredictable.
   e. Classrooms are public.

Which characteristic appears to present the greatest challenge to teachers? The least challenge? In a paper describe how these different classroom characteristics affect the professional lives of teachers.

4. Interview two teachers about the teacher roles named in this chapter (i.e., caring professional, creator of productive learning environments, etc.). Ask them to list the roles in order of importance and to explain why they ranked them the way they did. Compare the two teachers' responses in a paper, and describe how their rankings differ from yours.
5. Visit a school district office or a state office of education, and ask to see the statistics on the current teaching force in your area. How does it differ from national averages? Why? Describe these differences, and explain how they might affect your employment opportunities in this area.

Virtual Field Experience

If you would like to participate in a Virtual Field Experience, go to the Companion Website at **www.prenhall.com/kauchak**, then to this chapter's *Field Experience* module.

Online Portfolio Activities

To complete these activities online, go to the Companion Website at **www.prenhall.com/kauchak**, then to this chapter's *Portfolio Activities* module.

Portfolio Activity 2.1

Parental Involvement

INTASC Principle 10: Partnership

Personal Journal Reflection
Write a one-page paper that explains your philosophy on involving parents and caregivers in their children's education. Include the following in your paper:

- Why you believe parental involvement is important
- Specific ways in which you will communicate your students' learning progress with parents or other caregivers
- Specific ways in which you will involve parents or other caregivers

Portfolio Activity 2.2

Caring

INTASC Principle 2: Learning and Human Development
INTASC Principle 5: Motivation and Management

Explain why the students of a caring teacher will learn more than those taught by a teacher who isn't caring. List at least four specific, concrete things teachers can do to demonstrate that they care about their students.

Portfolio Activity 2.3

Time and Learning

INTASC Principle 7: Planning

On the Companion Website, go to Chapter 2's *Portfolio Activities* module and click on "Time and Organization." Read the information, and then write a one- or two-paragraph summary of the section. Then offer at least two specific, concrete ways in which teachers can maximize their *instructional time* and at least two specific, concrete ways in which teachers can maximize *engaged time.*

Part 2

Students

Chapter 3

Learner Diversity

Differences in Today's Students

Teachers begin their careers expecting to find classrooms like the ones they experienced when they were students. In some ways classrooms are the same. Students go to school to learn, but they also want to have fun and be with their friends. They expect to work but often need encouragement from their teachers. They're typical kids.

Classrooms are changing, however; the population of our schools is becoming increasingly diverse. Students come from different cultures and speak many different languages at home; they possess a range of abilities and talents; and issues involving differences between boys and girls are receiving increased attention. In this chapter we examine this diversity as we try to answer the following questions:

- What is cultural diversity, and how does it influence student learning?
- How are the educational experiences of boys and girls different?
- How do schools accommodate ability differences in learners?
- What are learning styles, and how should teachers respond to them?
- Who are learners with exceptionalities, and how can schools best meet their needs?

Let's see how learner diversity influences the lives of teachers.

This logo appears throughout the chapter to indicate where case studies are integrated with chapter content.

Case STUDY

Shannon Wilson, a fifth-grade teacher in a large urban elementary school, walked around her classroom, helping student groups as they worked on their social studies projects. A number of hands were raised, and she felt relieved that she had Maria Arguelas, her special education resource teacher, to help her. Shannon had 27 students in her class, seven of whom did not speak English as their first language. Five of the seven were Hispanic, and fortunately Maria was able to assist them in their native language. Shannon often spent extra time with Kwan and Abdul, the other two non-English speakers. Maria also assisted Shannon by working with four of her students who had learning disabilities.

Shannon's class was preparing for Parents' Day, an afternoon in which parents and other caregivers would join the class in celebrating the students' ancestral countries. The students would present information about the countries' history, geography, and cultures in their projects. The class had already prepared a large world map with pins marking the students' countries of origin. While several of the pins were clustered in Mexico and Central and South America, the map showed that students also came from many other parts of the world. Each student was encouraged to invite a family member to come and share a part of the family's native culture. The parents could bring food, music, and native dress from their different homelands.

Figure 3.1 Dimensions of Diversity

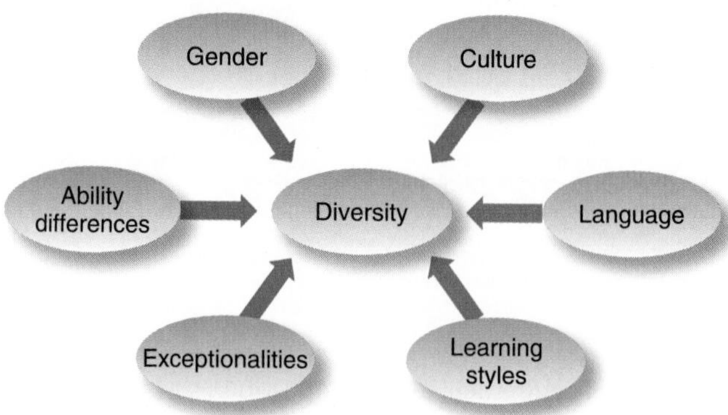

Your first classroom is likely to be comprised of students from a variety of backgrounds, primarily because student diversity in today's schools is rapidly increasing (Hodgkinson, 2001) but also because new teachers are more likely to find jobs in schools that serve diverse populations (Olson, 2003a). This diversity has several sources (Figure 3.1), and it presents both challenges and opportunities.

To meet these challenges, teachers need to develop a deep understanding of diversity and adopt teaching strategies that address the learning needs of students from varying backgrounds. In some instances they will require professional knowledge in specialized areas such as English language learning or special education. Acquiring such professional knowledge, however, gives teachers additional tools for increasing learning for all students, and it presents enormous opportunities for professional growth. This chapter is designed to help you start the journey toward meeting the challenges and capitalizing on the opportunities of the diverse classroom.

Cultural Diversity

What kinds of clothes do you wear? What types of music do you like? What foods do you eat? Your clothing, music, and foods, along with other factors such as religion, family structure, and values, are all part of your culture. **Culture** refers to *the attitudes, values, customs, and behavior patterns that characterize a social group* (Banks, 2001).

The enormous impact of culture is illustrated by its influence on all aspects of our lives (Gollnick & Chinn, 2002). An activity as basic as eating is one example:

• • ● • •

Culture not only helps to determine what foods we eat, but it also influences when we eat (for example, one, three, or five meals and at what time of the day); with whom we eat (that is, only with the same sex, with children or with the extended family); how we eat (for example, at a table or on the floor; with chopsticks, silverware, or the fingers); and the ritual of eating (for example, in which hand the fork is held, asking for or being offered seconds, and belching to show appreciation of a good meal). These eating patterns are habits of the culture. (Gollnick & Chinn, 1986, pp. 6–7)

• • ● • •

Culture influences people's responses to other basic needs, such as the need for shelter and clothing, and it influences school success through the attitudes, values, and ways of viewing the world embedded in it.

Figure 3.2 Changes in School-Age Population, 2000–2020

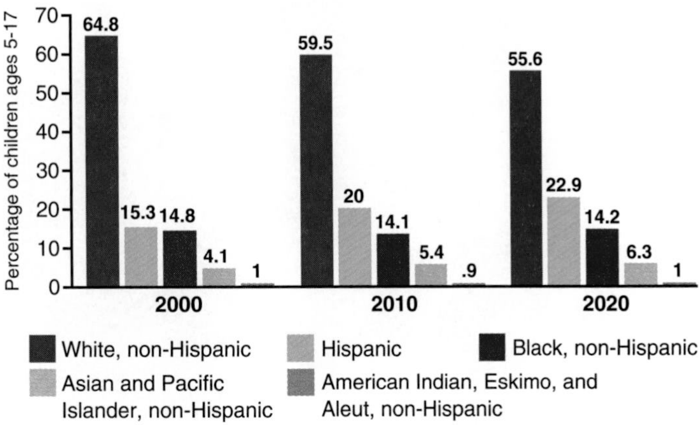

Source: U.S. Bureau of Census (1998b).

An important part of culture is a person's ethnic background. **Ethnicity** refers to *a person's ancestry; the way individuals identify themselves with the nation from which they or their ancestors came* (deMarrais & LeCompte, 1999; Gollnick & Chinn, 2002). Members of an ethnic group have a common identity defined by their history, language (although sometimes not spoken), customs, and traditions.

Increasing Understanding 3.1

What ethnic group or groups do you belong to? How is your heritage evidenced in the foods you eat, the holidays you celebrate, and the language spoken in your community?

To answer the Increasing Understanding questions online and receive immediate feedback, go to the Companion Website at **www.prenhall.com/kauchak**, then to this chapter's *Increasing Understanding* module. Type in your response, and then study the feedback.

More than 14 million people immigrated to the United States during the 1970s and 1980s. Between 1980 and 1994, America's classrooms underwent the following changes:

- An increase in Asian American students of almost 100 percent
- An increase in Hispanic students of 46 percent
- An increase in African American students of 25 percent
- An increase in Caucasian students of 10 percent (Kent, Pollard, Haaga, & Mather, 2001; U.S. Bureau of Census, 1996)

By the year 2020, the U.S. school-age population will see many more changes (Figure 3.2). Experts predict considerable increases in the percentages of Hispanic students and Asian/Pacific Island students, while the percentage of African American students will remain essentially the same. During this time the proportion of White students will decrease from 64.8 percent to 55.6 percent of the total population (U.S. Bureau of Census, 1998b; U.S. Department of Education, 2000c). By 2020, almost half of the U.S. school population will consist of members of non-Caucasian cultural groups. Each of these groups brings a distinct set of values and traditions that influences student learning.

Cultural Attitudes and Values

Increasing Understanding 3.2

How do the foods Americans eat reflect this growing cultural diversity?

Students come to school with a long learning history. Cultural patterns exist in their dress, family roles, interactions with parents and peers, and attitudes and values. When they enter our classrooms, they bring these attitudes and values with them. Some complement learning; others conflict with it.

Language is an example. Students are sometimes hesitant to drop the use of nonstandard English dialects in favor of "school English" because doing so might

The increasing cultural diversity of our students provides teachers with both opportunities and challenges.

alienate their peers (Ogbu, 1999). The same problem occurs in second-language learning. Research indicates that programs encouraging students to drop their native language in favor of English can cause students to distance themselves from their parents, many of whom cannot speak English (Wong-Fillmore, 1992).

Even school success can be an issue. To succeed in school is interpreted by some as rejecting a native culture; to become a good student is to become "White"—to uphold only White cultural values. Students who study and become actively involved in school risk losing the friendship and respect of their peers. John Ogbu, an anthropologist who studies the achievement of minority students, believes that in many schools peer values either don't support school learning or actually oppose it; students form what he calls "resistance cultures" (Ogbu & Simons, 1998). Low grades, management and motivation problems, truancy, and high dropout rates are symptoms of this conflict.

Cultural attitudes and values can also complement school learning. In a cross-cultural study comparing Chinese, Japanese, and American child-rearing practices, researchers found significant differences in parental support for schooling (Stevenson, Lee, & Stigler, 1986). More than 95 percent of native Chinese and Japanese fifth graders had desks at home on which to do their homework; only 63 percent of the American sample did. Also, 57 percent of the Chinese and Japanese parents supplemented their fifth graders' schoolwork with additional math workbooks, as compared with only 28 percent of the U.S. parents. Finally, 51 percent of the Chinese parents and 29 percent of the Japanese parents supplemented their children's science curriculum with additional work, compared with only 1 percent of American parents.

A study attempting to understand the phenomenal successes of Indo-Chinese children in U.S. classrooms further documents the effects of home values on learning (Caplan, Choy, & Whitmore, 1992). In examining the school experiences of Vietnamese and Laotian refugees who had been in the United States for a relatively short time (an average of 3½ years), the researchers found amazing progress. The Indo-Chinese children received better than a B average in school, and their scores on standardized achievement tests corroborated the grades as reflecting true achievement, not grade inflation.

In attempting to explain this encouraging pattern, the researchers (Caplan et al., 1992) looked to the attitudes and values in the families. They found heavy emphasis on the importance of education, hard work, autonomy, perseverance, and pride. These values were reinforced with a nightly ritual of family homework in which both parents and older siblings helped younger members of the family. Indo-Chinese high schoolers spent an average of 3 hours a day on homework, and junior high and elementary students spent an average of 2½ hours and 2 hours, respectively. In comparison, non-Indo-Chinese junior and senior high students spent 1½ hours a day on homework.

Cultural Interaction Patterns

Cultural conflict can occur in the interaction patterns typically found in most classrooms. Let's look at an example:

Case STUDY A second-grade class in Albuquerque, New Mexico, was reading *The Boxcar Children* and was about to start a new chapter. The teacher said, "Look at the illustration at the beginning of the chapter and tell me what you think is going to happen." A few students raised their hands. The teacher called on a boy in the back row.

He said, "I think the boy is going to meet his grandfather."

The teacher asked, "Based on what you know, how does the boy feel about meeting his grandfather?"

Trying to involve the whole class, the teacher called on another student—one of four Native Americans in the group—even though she had not raised her hand. When she didn't answer, the teacher tried rephrasing the question, but again the student sat in silence.

Feeling exasperated, the teacher wondered if there was something in the way the lesson was being conducted that made it difficult for the student to respond. She sensed that the student she had called on understood the story and was enjoying it. Why, then, wouldn't she answer what appeared to be a simple question?

The teacher recalled that this was not the first time this had happened, and that, in fact, the other Native American students in the class rarely answered questions in class discussions. She wanted to involve them, wanted them to participate in class, but could not think of ways to get them to talk. (Villegas, 1991, p. 3)

• • ● • •

Why did this happen? One explanation suggests that Native American children are not used to the fast-paced, give-and-take patterns that characterize many American classrooms. When involved in a discussion like the one just described, they are uncomfortable and, as a result, reluctant to participate.

Studies have found interaction differences between White and African American students as well (Heath, 1989, 1982). For instance, Heath (1982) looked at students' responses to teacher directives such as "Let's put the scissors away now." Accustomed to this indirect way of speaking, White students interpreted the directive as a command; African Americans, used to more direct commands like "Put your scissors away, now," did not. Teachers viewed a student's failure to comply as either a management or a motivation problem, when instead the problem arose from the mismatch between home and school cultures.

Heath (1982) found other cultural differences that also caused problems during instruction. White children, accustomed to being asked direct questions in the home, knew how to answer questions requiring specific answers, such as "Where did the puppy go?" and "What's this story about?" African American children, by contrast, were accustomed to questions that were more "open-ended, story-starter" types that didn't have single answers. In addition, in their homes, African American children "were not viewed as information-givers in their interactions with adults, nor were they considered appropriate conversation partners and thus they did not learn to act as such" (Heath, 1982, p. 119). When teachers learned to use more open-ended questions in their instruction, participation of African American students increased. In addition, over time African American students began to understand that answering teacher questions was part of the educational game, designed to increase their involvement and learning.

Educational Responses to Cultural Diversity

Historically, social commentators have used different metaphors to describe the relationship between diverse cultures in the United States. The "melting pot" was one of the first. Those who saw the United States as a melting pot emphasized **assimilation,** *a process of socializing people so that they adopt dominant social norms and patterns of behavior.* Assimilation attempted to make members of minority cultural groups "similar" to those belonging to the dominant cultural group—typically Whites of European descent.

The melting pot metaphor was especially popular in the early 1900s, when large numbers of immigrants from southern and eastern Europe entered the United States. Society assigned schools the task of teaching these immigrants how "Americans" were supposed to think, talk, and behave. Immigrants, eager to become "American" and share in this country's economic wealth, generally accepted efforts to assimilate them.

About the middle of the twentieth century, a shift in thinking occurred. People realized that assimilation had never totally worked and that there was no "melting pot," as indicated by neighborhoods and groups that continued to speak their home languages, celebrate their unique cultural festivals, and maintain their cultural habits (such as eating certain foods). The contributions of different cultural and ethnic groups were increasingly recognized, and leaders began to realize that some educational practices aimed at assimilation were actually counterproductive. For example, in an effort to encourage English acquisition, schools in the Southwest frequently didn't allow students to speak Spanish, even on playgrounds. Schools became hostile places where students had to choose between family and friends, and school. The policy probably did as much to alienate Hispanic youth as it did to encourage English language development.

To remedy these problems, educators began developing new approaches to addressing cultural diversity. **Multicultural education** is *a catch-all term for a variety of strategies schools use to accommodate cultural differences and provide educational opportunities for all students.* Instead of trying to create a melting pot, these approaches align with new metaphors that describe America as a "mosaic" or "tossed salad" in which each culture's unique contributions are recognized and valued. Multicultural education seeks to recognize and celebrate cultural differences and contributions to our American way of life.

Controversies over Multiculturalism Multicultural education has become highly controversial. Critics contend that it is divisive because it places too much emphasis on differences between cultural groups and not enough on our common characteristics (Schlesinger, 1992). Textbooks have been scrutinized; in 2000, a spokesperson for

Culturally responsive teaching builds on students' cultural backgrounds, accepting and valuing differences and accommodating different cultural learning styles.

the American Textbook Council criticized modern history textbooks as emphasizing multicultural themes at the expense of basic information about history (Sewall, 2000). Conservative columnists in the popular press, such as *U.S. News and World Report,* consistently criticize multiculturalism and concepts associated with it, such as identity politics and political correctness.

Proponents of multicultural education assert that building upon students' cultures is nothing more than sound teaching; by recognizing, valuing, and utilizing students' cultures and languages in their instruction, teachers help students link the topics they're studying to what they already know, a process consistent with effective teaching and learning (Eggen & Kauchak, 2004; Ormrod, 2003). In addition, proponents of multicultural education point out that the United States has always been a nation of immigrants and that this diversity has long been recognized in a number of ways. For example, American society embraces the music, holidays (St. Patrick's Day, Mardi Gras, Chinese New Year), and foods of many cultures. Good multicultural education continues this tradition by recognizing and building on students' diverse cultural heritages.

Increasing Understanding 3.3

Use American's eating habits to explain why the "mosaic" and "tossed salad" metaphors are more accurate than the "melting pot" metaphor.

Like all educational approaches, multiculturalism will undoubtedly evolve as educators decide what works and what doesn't in the classroom. One promising approach to working with diverse student populations is called *culturally responsive teaching*.

Culturally Responsive Teaching **Culturally responsive teaching** is *instruction that acknowledges and accommodates cultural diversity in classrooms* (Gay, 1997). It attempts to accomplish this goal in at least three ways:

- Accepting and valuing differences
- Accommodating different cultural interaction patterns
- Building on students' cultural backgrounds

Accepting and valuing differences. By recognizing and accepting student diversity, teachers communicate that all students are welcome and valued. This is particularly important for cultural minorities, who sometimes feel alienated from school. As a simple example, Shannon, in our opening case study, attempted to meet this goal by having her students identify their ethnic homelands on the map. This showed an interest in each student as an individual and helped students see similarities and differences in other students' backgrounds.

Genuine caring is an essential element in this process. Teachers can communicate caring in several ways, including the following:

- By devoting time to students—for example, being available before and after school to help with schoolwork and discuss students' personal concerns
- By demonstrating interest in students' lives—for example, asking about Jewish holidays, Muslim holy days, and festivals like Kwanzaa
- By involving all students in learning activities—for example, calling on all students as equally as possible

Each of these suggestions communicates that all students are welcome and valued.

Accommodating cultural interaction patterns. Teachers who are sensitive to possible differences between home and school interaction patterns can adapt their instruction to best meet their students' needs. For example, we saw earlier that the communication patterns of Native Americans may clash with typical classroom practices. Recognizing that these students may not be comfortable in teacher-centered question-and-answer activities, teachers can use additional strategies, such as cooperative learning, to complement teacher-centered approaches.

Similarly, knowing that White and African American students sometimes have different communication patterns, teachers can incorporate more open-ended questions in their lessons and can word instructions more directly ("Put your scissors away, now").

As another example, when a teacher learned that her Asian American students were overwhelmed by the bustle of American schools, she tried to keep her classroom quiet and orderly and encouraged shy and reluctant students to participate with open-ended questioning, extra time to respond, and gentle reminders to speak a bit louder (C. Park, 1997). Another teacher reported the following:

• • ● • •

I traditionally end every day with the students lining up and receiving a hug before they leave. My Vietnamese kids were always the stiff huggers until October. Through my understanding of their cultures, I now give all students the choice of a hug, handshake, or high five. This simple act may make children feel more comfortable interacting with me. (McAllister & Irvine, 2002, p. 440)

• • ● • •

Through increased sensitivity to each cultural group's learning needs, teachers can make their classrooms safe and inviting learning environments for all students.

Accommodating different cultural interaction patterns can result in "accommodation without assimilation," the process through which minority students adapt to the dominant culture (including that of schools) without losing their cultural identities (Ogbu, 1987). Other terms for this process include "alternation"—the ability to comfortably function in both cultures (Hamm & Coleman, 1997) and "code switching"—talking differently in different contexts (DeMeulenaere, 2001). The challenge for teachers is to help students learn about the "culture of schooling"—the norms, procedures, and expectations necessary for success in school—while honoring the value and integrity of students' home cultures.

CW

Increasing Understanding 3.4

To which metaphor—"melting pot" or "tossed salad"—does the concept of accommodation without assimilation most closely relate? Explain.

Building on students' backgrounds. Effective teachers also learn about their students' cultures and use this information to promote personal pride and motivation in their students, as the teacher in the following example did:

• • • • •

In one third-grade classroom with a predominately Central American student population, youngsters are greeted most mornings with the sound of salsa music in the background, instruction takes place in both English and Spanish, magazines and games in both languages are available throughout the classroom, maps of both the United States and Latin America line one wall, with pins noting each student's origin, and every afternoon there is a Spanish reading lesson to ensure that students learn to read and write in Spanish as well as English. (Shields & Shaver, 1990, p. 9)

• • • • •

CW

Increasing Understanding 3.5

In this chapter's opening case study, what does Shannon do to build upon her students' cultural backgrounds? Provide at least two specific examples.

The benefits of building on students' cultural backgrounds are felt in both the classroom and the home. Students achieve more in the classroom, and parents become more positive about school, which in turn enhances student motivation (Shumow & Harris, 1998). Shannon recognized this when she invited parents and other caregivers to share their cultural heritages with her class. Students bring to school a wealth of experiences embedded in their home cultures. Sensitive teachers build on these experiences, and all students benefit.

Reflect on This

To analyze a case study examining issues involved in attempting to adapt instruction to cultural differences, go to the Companion Website at **www.prenhall.com/kauchak**, then to this chapter's *Reflect on This* module.

Language Diversity

One of the most prominent parts of any culture is its language, and because language diversity is so important to learning, and the responses to it are so controversial, we devote a major section to it.

Immigration has brought increasing numbers of students with limited backgrounds in English to U.S. classrooms. The number of English language learners (ELLs) in the United States increased by more than 50 percent between 1985 and 1991. Between 1991 and 1993, the language minority population increased 12.6 percent, compared to an increase of only 1.02 percent in the general population (Weaver & Padron, 1997).

There are more than 3.2 million students in U.S. schools whose first language is not English, and in many states, these students now make up a significant proportion of the student body. For example, California's 1.4 million ELL students comprise 35 percent of the state's school-age population; ELL students comprise 30 percent of the population in New Mexico, 28 percent in Texas, and 23 percent in New York (U.S. Bureau of Census, 1998b). Nationwide, the number of ELL students is expected to triple during the next 30 years. The most common language groups for these students are Spanish (73%), Vietnamese (4%), Hmong (1.8%), Cantonese (1.7%), and Cambodian (1.6%).

Language Diversity: The Government's Response The federal government, through legislation and court rulings, has attempted to address the needs of English language learners. For example, in 1968 Congress passed the Bilingual Education Act, which provided federal funds for educating non-native English speakers. In 1974 the U.S. Supreme Court ruled unanimously, in the controversial San Francisco case *Lau v. Nichols*, that the San Francisco School District unlawfully discriminated on the basis of students' national origin by failing to address children's language problems. More recently the English Acquisition part of the No Child Left Behind Act of 2001 mandated that the primary objective of U.S. schools should be the teaching of English without any attempt to preserve minority languages (No Child Left Behind Act of 2001). Accordingly, the previous Office of Bilingual Education became the Office of English Acquisition.

Language Diversity: Schools' Responses Schools across the country have responded to the challenge of language diversity in several ways, outlined in Table 3.1. All of the programs are designed to ultimately teach English, but they differ in how fast English is introduced and to what extent the first language is used and maintained. *Maintenance language programs* placed the greatest emphasis on using and sustaining the first language. For example, in one bilingual program in Houston, students ini-

Table 3.1 Different Programs for ELL Students

Type of Program	Description	Advantages	Disadvantages
Maintenance	First language maintained through reading and writing activities in first language while English introduced.	Students become literate in two languages.	Requires teachers trained in first language. Acquisition of English may not be as fast.
Transition	Students learn to read in first language and are given supplementary instruction in English as a second language. Once English is mastered, students are placed in regular classrooms and first language discontinued.	Maintains first language. Transition to English eased by gradual approach.	Requires teachers trained in first language. Acquisition of English may not be as fast.
Immersion	Students learn English by being "immersed" in classrooms where English is the only language spoken.	When effective, quick transition to English. Does not require teachers trained in second language.	Loss of native language. "Sink or swim" approach hard on students.
English as a Second Language (ESL) Programs	Pull-out programs in which students are provided with supplementary English instruction or modified instruction in content areas (also called *sheltered English programs*).	Easier to administer when dealing with diverse language backgrounds.	Students may not be ready to benefit from content instruction in English. Pull-out programs segregate students.

Bilingual education maintains students' first language, using it as the foundation for learning English.

tially received 90 percent of instruction in Spanish and 10 percent in English (Zehr, 2002a). The amount of English then increased in each grade. In contrast with maintenance programs, ***immersion*** and ***English as a second language (ESL) programs*** emphasize rapid transition to English. *Transition programs* maintain the first language until students acquire sufficient English. The current viability of maintenance programs is questionable, given the English Acquisition Act, which discourages such programs.

CW

Increasing Understanding 3.6

Which approach to helping English language learners is most culturally responsive? Least? Explain why in each case.

Logistics are often a factor when schools consider which type of program to use. When there are large numbers of ELL students who speak the same language (such as Spanish-speaking students in Los Angeles), transition programs are feasible because one teacher who speaks the students' native language can be hired. When several different first languages exist in the classroom, however, it isn't feasible to find teachers who speak all of the languages. High schools, with students going from one content classroom to the next, also present logistical challenges, and ESL programs are more likely to exist at this level.

Language Diversity: Implications for Teachers How will language diversity affect you as a teacher? First, bilingual education is likely to be a subject of hot debate for years. Second, although bilingual programs have been reduced, the need for teachers with ELL expertise will only increase. Experts estimate that an additional 290,000 teachers with ELL certification will be needed to meet the demands of these students (Zhao, 2002). Teaching candidates who speak two languages, especially Spanish, are in high demand across the country.

Third, you will almost certainly have non-native English speakers in your classroom, and your ability to make informed professional decisions will be essential for their learning success. In working with students from diverse backgrounds, your professionalism will be tested perhaps more than in any other area of your work.

Research offers the following suggestions:

- Attempt to create a warm and inviting classroom environment by taking a personal interest in all students and involving everyone in learning activities.

Teaching in an Era of Reform

THE BILINGUAL EDUCATION ISSUE

Bilingual education has been the focus of several reform efforts. Through the Bilingual Education Act in 1968 and guidelines drafted as a result of *Lau v. Nichols* in 1974, the federal government has demonstrated its commitment to providing services for nonnative English speakers.

A counterreform occurred in California in 1998 when voters passed Proposition 227, a ballot initiative that sharply reduced bilingual education programs, replacing them with English-only immersion programs for ELL students. Similar measures passed in Arizona in 2000 and Massachusetts and Colorado in 2002, and other states, such as Utah, are considering similar initiatives (K. Gutiérrez et al., 2002; Schnaiberg, 1999a; Zehr, 2000a, 2000b). These initiatives have sharply curtailed the use of bilingual education in these states. For example, before the initiatives occurred in Arizona and California, about one third of ELL students were taking bilingual education classes; after, the numbers plummeted to 11 percent in both states (Zehr, 2002b). In addition, 26 states have passed laws making English the official language (U.S. English, Inc., 2000). Although these laws are mostly symbolic because they have few concrete implications, they do illustrate public sentiment in favor of English and highlight fears about losing English as a common cultural bond.

In addition, in 2002 the U.S. Congress failed to renew the Bilingual Education Act, instead packaging funds for English language learners into the No Child Left Behind Act, which requires students to attain "English fluency" in 3 years and requires schools to teach students in English after that time period.

The Issue

The essence of bilingual programs is an attempt to maintain students' native languages while they learn English. Proponents make several arguments in support of bilingual education. First, they contend that the programs make sense because they provide a smooth and humane transition to English by building on students' first languages. They also argue that being able to speak two languages has practical benefits; a bilingual person is able to live and communicate in two worlds, which can increase economic and career opportunities. They also cite research. A study conducted in the early 1990s indicated that students in bilingual programs scored higher in math and reading and had more positive attitudes toward school and themselves (Arias & Casanova, 1993). In a more comprehensive study, researchers found significant benefits for bilingual programs on standardized tests in reading (Zehr, 2002b). Contrary to arguments that newcomers to the United States are learning English more slowly than in previous generations, the opposite appears to be true (Waggoner, 1995). Fur-

- Avoid situations that draw attention to students' lack of English skills and cause embarrassment. One student commented:

> I think it is a bad strategy to make [ELLs] read aloud in front of other kids when they really can't. Teachers should give them time and make them more welcome by talking to them in Spanish first and later in English. They shouldn't expect them right away to do everything in English. (Thompson, 2000, p. 85)

- Mix teacher-centered instruction with learner-centered approaches, such as cooperative learning, where students can interact informally and practice their language skills at the same time as they study content.

ther research indicates that knowledge and skills acquired in a native language—literacy in particular—are "transferable" to the second language, providing students with a better understanding of the role of language in communication and how language works (K. Gutiérrez et al. 2002; Krashen, 1996).

Proponents of bilingual education also contend that immersion programs are ineffective because they place unrealistic language demands on learners. They note that conversational English, such as that spoken on the playground, is learned quite quickly, but the cognitively demanding language needed for academic success is learned much less rapidly (Peregoy & Boyle, 2001).

Finally, the magnitude of the challenges involved in requiring students to attain "English fluency" in 3 years, as mandated by No Child Left Behind, is enormous. For example, in Arizona an estimated 37 percent of the state's ELL students were enrolled in bilingual programs in 1999, and in California roughly one third of the state's 1.4 million ELL students were enrolled in such programs (Schnaiberg, 1999a, 1999b). The Los Angeles Unified School District alone had more than 100,000 of its 310,000 ELL students enrolled in bilingual education programs.

Critics of bilingual education have attacked it on several grounds. They contend that it is

- Divisive, encouraging groups of non-native English speakers to remain separate from mainstream American culture
- Ineffective, slowing the process of acquiring English for English language learners
- Inefficient, requiring expenditures for the training of bilingual teachers and materials that could better be spent on quality monolingual programs

Critics also cite their own research. For instance, one California school district reported that standardized test scores for students in the early grades—those most affected by the move from bilingual to immersion programs—improved from the 35th to the 45th percentile after students spent just one year in an immersion program, and additional research found similar positive results across California (Barone, 2000).

For a report on "The Initial Impact of Proposition 227 on the Instruction of English Learners," go to the Companion Website at **www.prenhall.com/kauchak**, *then to this chapter's* Web Links *module.*

CW

You Take a Position

Now it's your turn to take a position on the issue. State in writing whether you feel that schools should make efforts to retain students' native languages or whether it makes more sense to move students into English as quickly as possible, and provide a two-page rationale for your position.

For additional references and resources, go to the Companion Website at **www.prenhall.com/kauchak**, *then to this chapter's* Teaching in an Era of Reform *module. You can respond online or submit your response to your instructor.*

CW

- Provide peer tutoring and "buddy" programs where students more proficient in English can help classmates who are less proficient. Peer tutoring not only increases learning but also helps ELL students feel at home in the classroom. One student recalled:

One day, while everyone else was working, my teacher called a young boy and me up to her desk. She told him something and then he glanced at me. All of a sudden, he asked me my name in Cambodian. I was so happy to know that there was someone else that spoke my language. So, I answered him back in Cambodian. Then, he told me that he was my partner in the class. In only a week, I memorized the alphabet. (Thompson, 2000, p. 84)

Schools can be frightening places for ELLs; having a learning partner can help in the transition to English.

- Use many examples and illustrations to provide concrete referents for new ideas and vocabulary. (Echevarria & Graves, 2002; Peregoy & Boyle, 2001)

These strategies represent good instructional practice for all students; for English language learners, they are essential.

Gender

Case STUDY What Geri Peterson saw on her first day of teaching advanced-placement calculus was both surprising and disturbing. Of the 26 students watching her, only four were girls, and they sat quietly in class, responding only when she asked them direct questions. One reason that Geri had gone into teaching was to share her interest in math with other females, but this situation gave her little chance to do so.

. . ● . .

Lori Anderson, the school counselor at an urban middle school, looked up from the desk where she was working on her annual report to the faculty. From her coursework at the university and her internship, she knew that boys traditionally outnumber girls with respect to behavioral problems, but the numbers she was looking at were disturbing. In every category—referrals by teachers, absenteeism, tardies, and fights—boys outnumbered girls by a more than 2 to 1 margin. In addition, the number of boys referred to her for special education testing far exceeded referrals for girls. This was a problem that her faculty needed to think about.

. . ● . .

Gender and Society

The fact that males and females are different is so obvious that we usually don't think about it. Some important differences between the sexes may not be readily apparent, however. Researchers (Feingold, 1995; Halpern & LaMay, 2000) have found, for example, that women generally are more extroverted, anxious, and trusting; they're less assertive and have slightly lower self-esteem than males of the same age and background; and their verbal and motor skills tend to develop faster than boys' skills do. In addition, the play habits of boys and girls are different; boys typically prefer more "rough and tumble" play.

Why do these gender differences exist? Research suggests the causes are a combination of genetics and environment (Berk, 2003). Genetics result in physical differences such as size and growth rate and may also influence other differences such as temperament, aggressiveness, and early verbal and exploratory behaviors.

Environment plays a part as well. From the day they are born, boys and girls are treated differently (Berk, 2003, 2004; McDevitt & Ormrod, 2002). Often, girls are given pink blankets, are called cute and pretty, and are handled delicately. Boys are dressed in blue, are regarded as handsome, and are seen as tougher, better coordinated, and hardier. Fathers are rougher with their sons and involve them in more physical stimulation and play; they tend to be gentler with their daughters and offer more sex-stereotyped toys, such as dolls and stuffed animals. Not surprisingly, boys and girls grow up looking and acting differently.

Gender and Schooling

The differences between boys and girls should generally be celebrated. They're problems only when societal or school forces limit the growth and academic potential of students—either male or female.

Consider these findings which suggest that schools are failing to meet the educational needs of girls:

- In the early grades, girls are ahead of or equal to boys on almost every standardized measure of achievement and psychological well-being. By the time they graduate from high school or college, they have fallen behind on these standardized measures.
- In high school, girls score lower than boys on the SAT and ACT, two tests that are critical for college admission. The greatest gender gaps occur in science and math, and the gaps are more pronounced at the upper end of scores.
- Women score lower on all sections of the Graduate Record Exam, required to get into most graduate programs; the Medical College Admissions Test; and admission tests for law, dental, and optometry schools (P. Campbell & Clewell, 1999; Sadker, Sadker, & Long, 1997).

Other research suggests that schools also fail to meet the learning needs of boys:

- Boys outnumber girls in remedial English and math classes, are held back in grade more often, are 3 to 5 times more likely to be labeled learning disabled, and are 2 to 3 times more likely to be placed in special education classes.
- Boys consistently receive lower grades than girls, receiving 70 percent of the Ds and Fs on report cards, and they score lower than girls on both direct and indirect measures of writing skills.
- Boys are more likely to be involved in serious school misbehavior. They account for 71 percent of all school suspensions.
- The proportion of both bachelor's and master's degrees earned favors women by a ratio of 54 to 46. (Hunsader, 2002; Riordan, 1999)

Let's examine some possible explanations for these findings. Again, a combination of genetics and environment is likely at work. Because little can be done about genetics, more attention has been given to environment, particularly **gender-role identity differences,** *expectations and beliefs about appropriate roles and behaviors of the two sexes.*

Gender issues are controversial. For instance, in 1992's *How Schools Shortchange Girls,* the American Association of University Women (AAUW) argued that different treatment of boys and girls by both teachers and society was seriously hampering the educational progress, self-esteem, and career choices of girls and women. In 1998's *Gender Gaps: Where Schools Still Fail Our Children,* the AAUW reiterated many of its earlier claims.

Counterclaims have also been made. For example, Christina Sommers, author of *The War Against Boys: How Misguided Feminism Is Harming Our Young Men* (Sommers, 2000), has pointed out that—in addition to having lower achievement, more frequent misbehavior, and more frequent placement in special education classes—boys are less likely to do their homework and are more likely to cheat on tests, wind up in detention, and drop out of school. Yet it's the myth of the fragile girl that continues to receive the lion's share of attention, she has argued.

Is differential treatment of girls and boys really to blame for these problems? The controversies are likely to continue. It's important to point out that gender-role identity differences aren't a problem unless they perpetuate stereotypes or negatively influence behavior, learning, or expectations for school success. Research indicates that this may be happening, particularly in math, computer science, and engineering (J. Campbell & Beaudry, 1998; O'Brien, Kopola, & Martinez-Pons, 1999).

Gender and Career Choices Look around the classroom you're in for this course. If it's a typical education course, probably three fourths of the students in it are women. The same would be true in nursing classes, but you would find the opposite in math, science, and computer-related fields.

Differences in students' views of gender-appropriate careers appear as early as kindergarten (Kochenberger-Stroeher, 1994). In spite of strong and systematic efforts to address the needs of both boys and girls in today's schools, when asked about future potential career options, boys continue to be more likely to choose doctor and engineer and girls are more likely to mention nurse or secretary (Riordan, 1999). Significantly, when kindergarten children chose nontraditional roles for males or females, their choice was based on personal experience (e.g., "My friend's dad is a nurse").

Where do the stereotypes of "appropriate" careers for boys and girls originate? Society and the media perpetuate stereotypes, but ironically, the most powerful source is parents, particularly mothers. For instance, one study found that mothers who held negative gender-stereotyped attitudes about girls' ability in math adversely influenced their daughters' achievement in, and their attitudes toward, math (J. Campbell & Beaudry, 1998).

Parents can also have powerful positive influences on their children. One female chemistry software developer reported:

> My mother always engendered in me the attitude that I could do absolutely anything I ever want to do. So she really gave me the confidence that is a big part of success in academics and maybe in other things—sometimes you get to a point where you don't have that much either skill or knowledge, and you have to just go on your guts or your confidence. You have to just kind of push your way through something until you have the time to accumulate the knowledge. And I think that that's something she engendered in me just by always being herself so confident of my abilities, rightly or wrongly. And my father certainly never detracted from that. He always portrayed her as being the smarter of the two. So I was raised in an environment where women were not only capable but were even potentially very well and highly regarded. (Zeldin & Pajares, 2000, p. 229)

Gender-stereotypic views can also negatively influence career decisions. Girls are less than half as likely as boys to pursue careers in engineering and physical and computer sciences (AAUW, 1998). At the high school level only 11 percent of students taking the College Board advanced placement test in computer science in 2001 were women (Stabiner, 2003). The percentages of female physicians (26%), lawyers (27%), and engineers (8%), as well as professors in science-related fields (36%), remain low as well (U.S. Bureau of Census, 1998b; U.S. Department of Education, 1998b). The problem of gender-stereotypic views of math, science, and computer science careers is especially acute for minority females (O'Brien et al., 1999).

Role models are effective in preventing students from forming gender-stereotypic views about appropriate careers.

Single-Gender Classrooms and Schools One response to gender-related problems has been the creation of **single-gender classes and schools,** *where boys and girls are segregated for part or all of the day* (Mael, 1998; Vail, 2002). One researcher found that middle school girls were more likely to ask and answer questions in girls-only math classes than in other coeducational classes (Streitmatter, 1997). The girls also preferred this type of learning environment, saying that it enhanced their ability to learn math and their view of themselves as mathematicians.

Research on single-gender schools has revealed other positive effects—for both girls and boys. Girls who attend single-gender schools are more apt to assume leadership roles, take more math and science courses, have higher self-esteem, and have firmer beliefs that they are in control of their destinies (Datnow, Hubbard, & Conchas, 2001). Advocates of all-male schools claim that they promote male character development and are especially effective with males from low-income and minority families.

CW

Increasing Understanding 3.7

In single-gender classrooms and schools, should the teachers be the same gender as the students? Explain alternate positions, using the information in this section.

Although research shows that single-sex schooling has positive effects on both general achievement and achievement in gender-stereotyped fields such as math and science, this research also raises other issues (Datnow et al., 2001; Vail, 2002). For example, because boys and girls are isolated from one another, single-gender schools and classes can exacerbate stereotypic views of the opposite sex (Datnow et al., 2001) and fail to prepare students for the "real world" in which males and females must work together. In addition, some critics question the legality of single-sex classrooms and schools based on Title IX, a federal law that prohibits discrimination on the basis of gender (Zehr, 2000c). More research is needed about the long-term effects of these experiments and the ways in which they may (or may not) help students learn and develop.

Gender and Schooling: Implications for Teachers What can you do to prevent gender inequities in the classroom? To begin, you should be aware that you may have stereotypical attitudes of your own. Attitudes influence behavior, and you will need to monitor how you interact with the boys and girls in your classroom. Research indicates that teachers typically call on boys more often than girls, probably because boys are more verbally assertive or aggressive, and boys are more likely to ask questions and make comments about ideas being discussed in class (Altermatt, Jovanovic, & Perry, 1998; Sadker, Sadker, & Klein, 1991). These differences increase as students move through school. In the extreme, these patterns can result in girls becoming less involved in learning activities.

As a teacher, what can you do? Several possibilities exist:

- Communicate openly with students about gender issues and concerns. Simply telling your students that teachers often treat boys and girls differently and that you're going to try to treat them equally is a positive first step. Continue to explain why and how you are attempting to make your classroom gender-fair.
- Encourage equal participation in all classes, particularly in math and science classes. One demanding but extremely effective technique is to call on everyone in your classes individually and by name, regardless of whether or not their hands are raised.
- Arrange to have science and computer experiments and demonstrations, which tend to be dominated by boys, prepared and conducted by both boys and girls equally.
- Make an effort to present cases of men and women in nonstereotypical roles, such as women who are engineers and men who are first-grade teachers.
- Encourage girls to pursue science-related careers. Significantly, girls who did so reported that the encouragement received from teachers was an important factor in their career decisions (AAUW, 1992).

The powerful influence that teachers can have on students is captured in the following remembrance from a 42-year-old female mathematics professor:

• • ● • •

It was the first time I had algebra, and I loved it. And then, all of a sudden, I excelled in it. And the teacher said, "Oh no, you should be in the honors course," or something like that. So, there's somebody who definitely influenced me because I don't think I ever even noticed. I mean, I didn't care one way or the other about mathematics. It was just something you had to do. I remember she used to run up and down the aisle. She was real excited. . . . She said,"Oh, you gotta go in this other class. You gotta." And she kind of pushed a little bit, and I was willing to be pushed. (Zeldin & Pajares, 2000, p. 232)

• • ● • •

When teachers believe in their students, students start believing in themselves.

No one is suggesting that boys and girls are, or should be, the same. Teachers should, however, attempt to provide the same academic opportunities and encouragement for all.

Sexual Harassment

Hey, babe. Lookin' good in that sweater!
Hey, sugar. Want to make me happy tonight?

Comments like these, heard in many classrooms and hallways in our nation's schools, may constitute sexual harassment. A problem that affects both males and females, **sexual harassment** is "*unwanted and unwelcome sexual behavior that interferes*

Sexual harassment often occurs in school hallways, and teachers can play a powerful role in preventing it there and in the classroom.

with your life" (AAUW, 1993, p. 6). It can also interfere with a student's learning and development. In one survey, 4 out of 5 teenagers (grades 8–11) reported some type of sexual harassment in schools (AAUW, 1993). Sexual comments, gestures, and looks, as well as touching and grabbing, were most commonly cited (Figure 3.3).

Several aspects of the AAUW survey are disturbing. One is the high incidence of sexual harassment that occurs in the schools; schools and classrooms should be safe places for learning. Another is a finding that only 7 percent of the harassment cases were reported. In addition, only 26 percent of students were aware of school policies regarding sexual harassment.

A more recent survey (AAUW, 2001) found that sexual harassment continues to be a problem in schools. Both boys (79%) and girls (83%) continue to report problems with sexual harassment, and the figures don't differ for urban, suburban, or rural schools. However, there has been a sea change in awareness of school policies toward sexual harassment. The 2001 study found that 69 percent of students were aware that school policies on sexual harassment existed. This is an encouraging first step, but more needs to be done to make schools safe for all students.

Harassment is a particularly acute problem for homosexual students (Meyer & Stein, 2002). One national survey found that 91 percent of homosexual students had encountered anti-gay comments, 69 percent had been verbally abused, and 34 percent were verbally abused on a daily basis (Galley, 1999). Sometimes the abuse isn't only verbal:

• • ● • •

When I was changing classes, I had all the books in my hands. . . . I'd hear someone mutter "faggot" and have my books knocked down. People are walking over me as I'm trying to gather my books. I don't have time to turn around to see who said it. (Sears, 1993, p. 129)

• • ● • •

Students report that treatment such as this makes them feel "sad and worthless" and "powerless" (Shakeshaft et al., 1997). This harassment contributes to higher rates of depression, substance abuse, and suicide for gay students (Berk, 2003).

Figure 3.3 Sexual Harassment in U.S. Schools

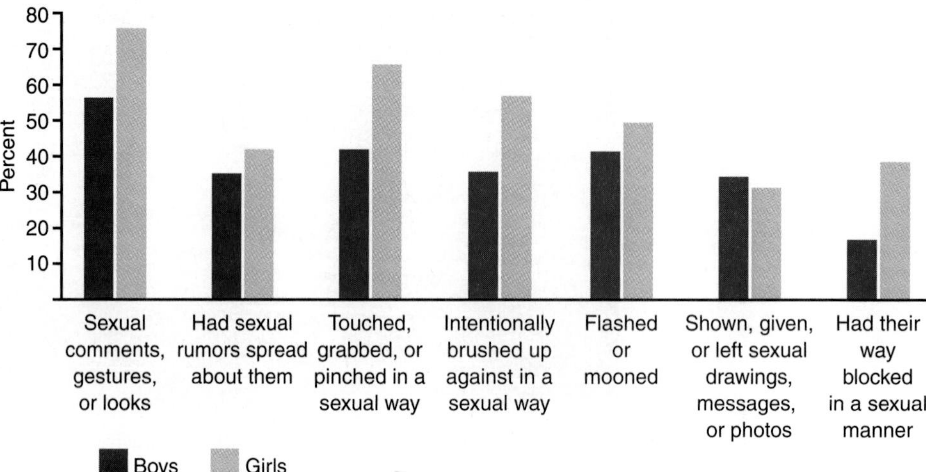

Source: From American Association of University Women (1993). *Hostile hallways: The AAUW survey on sexual harassment in America's schools.* New York: Louis Harris and Associates. Reprinted by permission.

Schools and teachers need to do a better job of making classrooms and hallways safe. Teachers are likely to encounter increased attention to the problem in light of a U.S. Supreme Court ruling that found school districts legally responsible in cases where sexual harassment is reported but not corrected (N. Stein, 2000). Research also suggests that teachers may require additional help understanding the problem and what their professional and legal obligations are (Meyer & Stein, 2002).

All students—boys and girls, heterosexual and homosexual—have a right to harassment-free schools. Teachers have an important role in ensuring that this happens. Talk with your students about the problem, and emphasize that no form of sexual harassment will be tolerated.

Ability Differences

When you look out over your first class, you'll see obvious similarities and differences. Your students will be about the same age, and their dress and hairstyles will probably be similar. They'll come from different cultural backgrounds, and you'll have both boys and girls. Less obvious, however, will be differences in their ability to learn. In virtually any class, you'll work with students who master the content effortlessly as well as other students who struggle just to keep up. In this section we examine ability differences and how schools accommodate them.

What Is Intelligence?

To begin this section, try to answer the following questions, and then decide what they have in common.

1. On what continent is Brazil?
2. A coat priced $45 is marked 1/3 off. When it still doesn't sell, the sale price is reduced by half. What is the price after the second discount?

3. Who was Albert Einstein?
4. How far is it from Seattle to Atlanta?
5. How are a *river* and a *plateau* alike?

The common feature of these questions may surprise you. Each resembles an item found on the Wechsler Intelligence Scale for Children–Third Edition (Wechsler, 1991), one of the most widely used intelligence tests in the United States. In other words, experts believe that the ability to answer questions such as these is an indicator of a person's *intelligence.*

We all have intuitive notions of intelligence; it's how "sharp" people are, how much they know, how quickly and easily they learn, and how perceptive and sensitive they are. These casual definitions would not satisfy the experts, however. They more precisely define **intelligence** as *the capacity to acquire knowledge, the ability to think and reason in the abstract, and the ability to solve problems* (Snyderman & Rothman, 1987; Sternberg, 1986). It is these three dimensions that intelligence tests seek to measure. The test questions at the start of this section are interesting, however, because they tell us about something *else* that is needed to perform well on most intelligence tests: experience and background knowledge (Halpern & LaMay, 2000; Perkins, 1995). Indeed, research has consistently indicated that experience and background knowledge are essential to the development of problem-solving ability in general as well as the ability to think in the abstract (Bruning et al., 2004).

Increasing Understanding 3.8

If experience is crucial to performance on tests of learning ability, how might performance be affected by growing up in a minority culture?

Changes in Views of Intelligence

Historically, researchers believed that intelligence was a unitary trait and that all people could be classified along a single continuum of general intelligence. Thinking has changed, however, and some researchers now believe that intelligence is composed of several distinct dimensions that, unlike the unified dimensions in our traditional definition of intellience, may occur alone or in various combinations in different individuals.

One of the most well-known proponents of the idea that intelligence is composed of more than one factor is Howard Gardner (1983, 1999), a Harvard psychologist who did groundbreaking work in this area. He proposed a theory of **multiple intelligences,** which *suggests that overall intelligence is composed of eight relatively independent dimensions* (Table 3.2).

Gardner's theory makes intuitive sense. For example, we all know people who don't seem particularly "sharp" analytically but who excel in getting along with others. This ability serves them well, and in some instances they're more successful than their "brighter" peers. Other people seem very self-aware and can capitalize on their personal strengths and minimize their weaknesses. Gardner would describe these people as high in interpersonal and intrapersonal intelligence, respectively.

Despite the theory's popularity with teachers (Viadero, 2003c), most classrooms focus heavily on the linguistic and logical-mathematical dimensions and virtually ignore the others. If the other dimensions are to develop, however, students need experiences with them. For example, cooperative learning activities can help students develop interpersonal intelligence, participation in sports or dance can improve bodily-kinesthetic abilities, and playing in a band or singing in choral groups can improve musical intelligence.

Increasing Understanding 3.9

If educators were to apply Gardner's theory, what would an elementary-level report card look like? A high school report card?

Ability: Nature Versus Nurture

No aspect of intelligence has been more hotly debated than the relative contributions of heredity versus environment. The extreme **nature view of intelligence** *asserts that*

Table 3.2 Gardner's Eight Intelligences

Dimension	Description	Individuals Who Might Be High in This Dimension
Linguistic intelligence	Sensitivity to the meaning and order of words and the varied uses of language	Poet, journalist
Logical-mathematical intelligence	The ability to handle long chains of reasoning and to recognize patterns and order in the world	Scientist, mathematician
Musical intelligence	Sensitivity to pitch, melody, and tone	Composer, violinist
Spatial intelligence	The ability to perceive the visual world accurately, and to re-create, transform, or modify aspects of the world on the basis of one's perceptions	Sculptor, navigator
Bodily-kinesthetic intelligence	A fine-tuned ability to use the body and to handle objects	Dancer, athlete
Interpersonal intelligence	An understanding of interpersonal relations and the ability to make distinctions among others	Therapist, salesperson
Intrapersonal intelligence	Access to one's own "feeling life"	Self-aware individual
Naturalist intelligence	The ability to recognize similarities and differences in the physical world	Biologist, anthropologist

Source: Checkley (1997).

intelligence is primarily determined by genetics. The **nurture view of intelligence** *emphasizes the influence of the environment.*

Differences between the nature and nurture views are controversial when race or ethnicity is considered. For example, research indicates that in the United States, children from some cultural minority groups collectively score lower on intelligence tests than White children (Brody, 1992; McLoyd, 1998). People who emphasize the nurture view explain this finding by arguing that minority children have fewer stimulating experiences while they are developing. People adhering to the nature view argue that heredity is the more important factor. In their highly controversial book, *The Bell Curve,* Herrnstein and Murray (1994) concluded that the contribution of heredity outweighed environmental factors in influencing the intelligence test scores of minority populations, especially African Americans. Methodological problems, such as inferring causation from correlational data, caused other experts to reject this position (Jacoby & Glauberman, 1995; Marks, 1995).

In considering the nature–nurture debate, most experts take a position somewhere in the middle, believing that ability is influenced by both heredity and the environment (Petrill & Wilkerson, 2000; Shepard, 2001). In this view, a person's genes provide the potential for intelligence, and stimulating environments make the most of the raw material.

If learning environments don't provide enough stimulation, however, children may not reach their full potential (Berk, 2003; McDevitt & Ormrod, 2002). For example, researchers tracked children born of low-income parents but adopted as infants into high-income families. Children in the high-income homes received more adult attention, went on more outings, and were exposed to a greater variety of playthings and reading materials. The children in these enriched environments scored an average of 14 points higher on intelligence tests than their siblings in the low-income environments (Schiff, Duyme, Dumaret, & Tomkiewicz, 1982).

School experiences can also lead to increases in intelligence test scores (Ceci & Williams, 1997). A longitudinal study of disadvantaged, inner-city children indicated that early stimulation provided in school settings can have lasting effects on IQ (F. Campbell & Raney, 1995). In addition, attempts to directly teach the skills measured by intelligence tests have been successful with preschool and elementary students (Bronfenbrenner, 1999), adults (Whimbey, 1980), and students with learning disabilities (A. Brown & Campione, 1986).

Ability Grouping and Tracking

The most common way schools respond to differences in learner ability is by **ability grouping,** *the practice of placing students of similar aptitude and achievement histories together in an attempt to match instruction to the needs of different groups* (Holloway, 2001; Lou, Abrami, & Spence, 2000).

Ability grouping is popular in elementary schools and typically exists in two major forms. **Between-class ability grouping** *divides all students in a given grade into high, medium, and low groups.* **Within-class grouping** *divides students within one classroom into ability groups.* Most elementary teachers endorse ability grouping, particularly in reading and math.

In middle, junior high, and high schools, ability grouping goes further, with high-ability students studying advanced and college preparatory courses and lower ability classmates receiving vocational or work-related instruction. In some schools students are grouped only in certain areas, such as English or math. In other schools the grouping exists across all content areas; this practice, called **tracking,** *places students in a series of different classes or curricula on the basis of ability and career goals.* Some form of tracking exists in most middle, junior high, and high schools (Braddock, 1990), and tracking has its most negative effects on minorities in the lower tracks (Davenport et al., 1998; Mickelson & Heath, 1999).

Increasing Understanding 3.10

Considering his theory of multiple intelligences, do you think Howard Gardner would favor ability grouping? Explain. How might he modify ability grouping?

Why is ability grouping so common? Advocates claim that it increases learning because it allows teachers to adjust methods, materials, and instructional pace to better meet students' needs (Gladden, 2003). Because lesson components, as well as assessments, are the same (or similar) for students in a particular group, instruction is also easier for the teacher.

Research has uncovered the following problems, however:

- Homogeneously grouped low-ability students achieve less than heterogeneously grouped students of similar ability (Good & Brophy, 2003).
- Within-class grouping creates logistical problems for teachers, because different lessons and assignments are required, and monitoring students in different tasks is difficult (Good & Brophy, 2003).
- Improper placements occur, and placement tends to become permanent. Cultural minorities are underrepresented in high-ability classes and overrepresented in lower classes and tracks (Davenport et al., 1998; Mickelson & Heath, 1999; Oakes, 1992).
- Low groups are stigmatized, and the self-esteem and motivation of students in these groups suffer (Good & Marshall, 1984; Hallinan, 1984).

In addition to decreasing students' self-esteem and motivation to learn, placement in low groups increases absentee rates. One study found that absenteeism increased from

Teachers minimize the negative effects of ability grouping by using it only when absolutely necessary, such as in reading or math, and by adapting instruction to meet the needs of all students.

8 percent to 26 percent after students' transition to a tracked junior high (Slavin & Karweit, 1982), with most of the truants being students in the low-level classes. Tracking can also result in racial or cultural segregation of students, impeding social development and the ability to form friendships across cultural groups (Oakes, 1992).

The negative effects of grouping are related, in part, to the quality of instruction. Presentations to low groups are more fragmented and vague than those to high groups; they focus more on memorizing than understanding, problem solving, and "active learning." Students in low-ability classes are often taught by teachers who lack enthusiasm and stress conformity versus autonomy and the development of self-regulation (Good & Brophy, 2003; Ross, Smith, Loks, & McNelie, 1994).

Teachers can avoid the problems associated with ability grouping and tracking by working with students in heterogeneous groups whenever possible. Instructional adaptations will be needed, however, to ensure the success of students of varying abilities. Some effective strategies include the following:

- Breaking large assignments into smaller ones and providing additional scaffolding and support for those who need it
- Giving students who need it more time to complete assignments
- Providing peer tutors for students requiring extra help
- Using small-group work in which students help each other learn
- Providing options on some assignments, such as giving students the choice of presenting a report orally or in writing (Nyberg, McMillin, O'Neill-Rood, & Florence, 1997; Tomlinson & Callahan, 2001)

Effective teachers adapt instruction to meet the needs of all students; the need for these adaptations is especially acute for low-ability students (Tomlinson & Callahan, 2001).

Learning Styles

Case STUDY One thing Chris Burnette remembered from his methods classes was the need for variety. He had been primarily using large-group discussions in his junior high social studies class, and most of the students seemed to respond okay. But others seemed disinterested, and their attention often drifted.

Today, Chris decided to try a small-group activity involving problem solving. The class had been studying the growth of American cities, and he wanted the class to think about solutions to some of the problems of big cities. As he watched the small groups interact, he was amazed at what he saw. Some of the quietest, most withdrawn students were leaders in the groups.

"Great!" he thought. But at the same time, he noted that some of his more active students were sitting back and not getting involved.

• • ● • •

How do you like to study? Do you learn most effectively in groups or alone? Do you prefer teacher presentations or reading a textbook? Your answers to these questions reflect your unique **learning style,** or your *preferred way of learning or processing information.*

Teachers often see differences in cognitive learning styles when they present problems to students. For example, some students jump in and try to solve a problem through trial and error, whereas others sit back and carefully analyze the problem. In learning style theory, **impulsive students** are *students who work quickly but often make errors* and **reflective students** are *students who analyze and deliberate before answering.* Impulsive students emphasize speed and take chances; reflective students think more carefully and consider alternatives before they answer. Impulsive students perform better on activities requiring factual information; reflective students have an advantage in problem solving.

Another difference in learning style involves **field dependence/independence,** *an individual's ability to identify relevant information in a complex and potentially confusing background* (Kogan, 1994). *Field-dependent* people see patterns as wholes; *field-independent* people are able to analyze complex patterns into their constituent parts. In mathematics, for example, a field-independent student would be better at breaking a complex word problem into subcomponents and using relevant information to solve the problem.

Research has also revealed learning style differences between introverts and extroverts (Nussbaum, 2002). During small-group discussions, extroverts were more likely to challenge others' ideas, whereas introverts were more likely to work cooperatively with others to develop solutions to problems. Teachers using these research findings might strategically group these different types of students together so that they could learn from and complement each other.

One of the oldest and most popular approaches to learning styles is that proposed by Rita and Kenneth Dunn (1992a, 1992b). Through their work in schools, they observed differences in the ways students responded to instructional environments. Some liked to learn alone, whereas others preferred learning in groups or from a teacher. Dunn and Dunn identified a number of key dimensions on which they suggested student learning styles differed. In an attempt to systematically measure these dimensions, the researchers constructed a learning styles inventory that asked students to respond to statements such as the following (Dunn & Dunn, 1992a, 1992b):

- I study best when it is quiet.
- I like to study by myself.
- I do my best work early in the morning.
- The things I remember best are things I hear.

CW

Increasing Understanding 3.11

Would a field-independent person more likely be impulsive or reflective? Why?

According to Dunn and Dunn, teachers should try to provide optimal learning environments for each student based on responses to the inventory.

Despite the popularity of learning styles theory, there is little research evidence linking learning style accommodations to increases in student achievement. In practice, making accommodatations for individual styles in a class of 25 or 30 students

Teachers can meet students' different learning styles by offering a variety of learning options.

can be quite difficult. A more practical idea may be to teach students to adapt their learning strategies to different tasks and environments. High achievers demonstrate this adaptive flexibility to a greater extent than do lower achievers (Eggen & Kauchak, 2004).

Cultural Learning Styles

Learning styles are also influenced by culture and gender. In typical U.S. classrooms, individual initiative and responsibility are emphasized and reinforced by grades and competition. Competition demands successes and failures, and the success of one student is often linked to the failure of another (D. Campbell, 2000).

Contrast this orientation with the learning styles of the Hmong, a mountain tribe from Laos that immigrated to the United States after the Vietnam War. The Hmong culture emphasizes cooperation, and Hmong students constantly monitor the learning progress of their peers, offering help and assistance. Individual achievement is deemphasized in favor of group success.

• • • • •

When Mee Hang has difficulty with an alphabetization lesson, Pang Lor explains, in Hmong, how to proceed. Chia Ying listens in to Pang's explanation and nods her head. Pang goes back to work on her own paper, keeping an eye on Mee Hang. When she sees Mee looking confused, Pang leaves her seat and leans over Mee's shoulder. She writes the first letter of each word on the line, indicating to Mee that these letters are in alphabetical order and that Mee should fill in the rest of each word. This gives Mee the help she needs and she is able to finish on her own. Mee, in turn, writes the first letter of each word on the line for Chia Ying, passing on Pang Lor's explanation.

Classroom achievement is never personal but always considered to be the result of cooperative effort. Not only is there no competition in the classroom, there is constant denial of individual ability. When individuals are praised by the teacher, they generally shake their heads and appear hesitant to be singled out as being more able than their peers. (Hvitfeldt, 1986, p. 70)

• • • • •

Think about how well Hmong students would learn if instruction were competitive and teacher centered, with few opportunities for student help and collaboration.

Some research suggests that Native American, Mexican American, Southeast Asian, and Pacific Island students experience similar difficulties in competitive classrooms (Greenfield, 1994; Triandis, 1995). Cooperation is more important to these groups than competition, which they view as silly, if not distasteful. When students come to school and are asked to compete, they may experience cultural conflict. Getting good grades at the expense of fellow students seems both strange and offensive. Raising hands and jousting for the right to give the correct answer isn't congruent with the ways in which students interact at home. If forced to choose between two cultures, some young people may conclude that schools are not for them.

Although cultural learning styles can provide insights into why some students think and act the way they do, multicultural experts caution against cultural stereotyping:

Increasing Understanding 3.12

From a nature–nurture perspective, how might cognitive and cultural learning styles differ?

> The notion that certain learning styles are associated with different ethnic groups is both promising and dangerous. Promise lies in the realization that low academic achievement among some ethnic minorities may sometimes be attributed to conflicts between styles of teaching and learning, not low intelligence. This leads to the possibility that teachers will alter their own instructional styles to be more responsive to the learning needs of students. Danger lies in the possibility that new ethnic stereotypes will develop while old ones are reinforced, as in "Blacks learn aurally," "Asians excel in math," "Mexican American males can't learn from female peer tutors," and "Navajos won't ask a question or participate in a discussion." (Bennett, 1999, p. 63)

Keeping these cautions in mind, new teachers can use information about different minority groups as springboards to think about the individuals in their classrooms.

Instructional Responses to Learning Styles

Unquestionably, individual students come to school with different ways of learning and solving problems. The key question is "What should teachers do in response to these differences?" or perhaps, more realistically, "What *can* teachers do about these differences?"

One position would take all instruction and tailor it to the distinctive needs and predispositions of individual students. Field-independent students, for example, would be allowed to work on independent projects, whereas field-dependent students would be allowed to work in small groups. The opposite position strives for balance—for example, by attempting to make impulsive students more reflective ("Now think a minute. Don't just blurt out the answer!") and vice versa.

Neither of these positions is realistic; in a class of 25 to 30 students, it is virtually impossible to individualize your teaching to meet the distinct learning style preferences of all students. Further, research evidence doesn't support the practice of tailoring teaching to students' individual learning styles (Curry, 1990).

So why do we study the concept of learning styles? We believe it has three implications for teachers. First, and most important, the existence of learning styles suggests the need to vary our instruction. Evidence supports the notion that teachers who vary the way they teach are more effective than those who repeatedly use the same strategies (Shuell, 1996). Individual projects, student presentations, small-group discussion, and cooperative learning all provide alternatives to teacher-led activities and provide flexibility in accommodating individual learning styles. Second, considering learning styles reminds us that our students are, indeed, individuals and helps us become more sensitive to differences in the way they act and learn. In turn, we are less apt to interpret these differences as unimportant or inappropriate, and our classrooms become models of tolerance that provide positive learning environments for all students.

Finally, discussing learning styles gives teachers the opportunity to encourage students to think about their own learning and, as a result, to develop metacognition. **Metacognition** refers to *students' awareness of the ways they learn most effectively and their ability to control these factors.* For example, a student who realizes that studying with a stereo on reduces her ability to concentrate, and then turns the stereo off, is demonstrating metacognition. Students who are metacognitive are better able to adjust strategies to match learning tasks than are their less metacognitive peers, and consequentially are more successful students (Eggen & Kauchak, 2004). By encouraging students to think about how they learn best, teachers provide students with a powerful learning tool that they can use throughout their lives.

Students with Exceptionalities

As we've seen in this chapter, students differ in several important ways, and effective teachers consider these differences when they plan and teach. In some cases, additional support is required. **Students with exceptionalities** are *learners who need special help and resources to reach their full potential.* Exceptionalities include disabilities as well as giftedness. Help and resources can include special schools, self-contained classrooms designed especially for these students, resource rooms where students can go to receive supplemental instruction, and inclusion in regular classrooms with the support of specially trained professionals.

Special education refers to *instruction designed to meet the unique needs of students with exceptionalities.* The terms *children with exceptionalities, special education students, children with handicaps, students with special needs,* and *individuals with disabilities* have all been used to describe students needing additional help to reach their full potential.

About 6.5 million students in the United States are enrolled in special education programs, two thirds of them for relatively minor problems (Galley, 2000b; Heward, 2003). Approximately 12 percent of students in a typical school receive special education services (U.S. Department of Education, 2002b).

Federal legislation has created categories to identify students eligible for special education services, and educators use these categories in developing programs to meet students' needs. The use of categories and the labeling that results is controversial, however (King-Sears, 1997). Advocates argue that categories provide a common language for professionals and encourage specialized instruction that meets the specific needs of students (Heward, 2003). Opponents claim that categories are arbitrary, many differences exist within them, and categorizing encourages educators to treat students as labels rather than as people. Despite the controversy, these categories are widely used, so you should be familiar with the terms. The federal law that describes the educational rights of students with disabilities, the *Individuals with Disabilities Education Act* (discussed later in this chapter), lists 13 disability categories:

- Autism
- Deaf-blindness

- Developmental delay
- Emotional disturbance
- Hearing impairments including deafness
- Mental retardation
- Multiple disabilities
- Orthopedic impairments
- Other health impairments
- Specific learning disabilities
- Speech or language impairments
- Traumatic brain injury
- Visual impairments including blindness

Three categories make up more than 70 percent of the population of students with exceptionalities who have disabilities (U.S. Department of Education, 2002b):

- Students with mental retardation
- Students who have specific learning disabilities
- Students with behavior disorders

In addition, a large number of students are gifted and talented. Accurate figures on the number of students in this category are difficult to come by, and state averages range from less than 2 percent of the total student population in Washington to 15 percent in Wisconsin (National Center for Education Statistics, 2001). Figures are not always comparable because of state-by-state differences in the definition of "gifted and talented." Despite these differences, it is safe to assume that there are a substantial number of students who are gifted and talented in most classrooms.

Gifted and Talented

Although we don't typically think of gifted and talented students as having exceptionalities, they often have learning needs not met by the regular education curriculum. **Gifted and talented** is *a designation given to students at the upper end of the ability continuum who need special services to reach their full potential.* At one time the term *gifted* was used to identify these students, but the category has been enlarged to include both students who do well on intelligence tests and those who demonstrate above-average talents in a variety of areas such as math, creative writing, and music (Callahan, 2001; G. Davis & Rimm, 1998).

The first step in meeting the needs of gifted and talented students is early identification. Experts recommend using a variety of methods for identification, including standardized test scores, teacher nominations, creativity measures, and peer and parent nominations (G. Davis & Rimm, 1998; Shea, Lubinsky, & Benbaw, 2001). As a teacher, you will have an important role in this process. Although the majority of states require that schools identify students who are gifted and talented, in 2003 only 27 had laws requiring that schools provide services to them (Shaunessy, 2003). Nine states, however, required that schools prepare an individualized education program, like those used for students in special education, detailing specific goals for meeting a gifted student's educational needs.

The regular education teacher may be responsible for adapting instruction for students who are gifted and talented, or students may attend special programs.

Table 3.3 Acceleration and Enrichment Options for Students Who Are Gifted and Talented

Enrichment Options	Acceleration Options
1. Independent study and independent projects	1. Early admission to kindergarten and first grade
2. Learning centers	2. Grade skipping
3. Field trips	3. Subject skipping
4. Saturday and summer programs	4. Credit by exam
5. Simulations and games	5. College courses in high school
6. Small-group inquiry and investigations	6. Correspondence courses
7. Academic competitions	7. Early admission to college

Increasing Understanding 3.13

Using information from this chapter, explain why standardized testing might fail to identify many minority students who are gifted and talented.

Programs are typically based on either **acceleration,** which *keeps the curriculum the same but allows students to move through it more quickly,* or **enrichment,** which *provides richer and varied content through strategies that supplement usual grade-level work* (Callahan, 2001; Feldhusen, 1998). Table 3.3 lists some acceleration and enrichment options. Failure to address the needs of these students can result in gifted underachievers, with social and emotional problems linked to boredom and lack of motivation (Dai, Moon, & Feldhusen, 1998; Louis, Subotnick, Breland, & Lewis, 2000).

Mental Retardation

Students with **mental retardation** have *an exceptionality that includes limitations in intellectual functioning, as indicated by difficulties in learning, and problems with adaptive skills, such as communication, self-care, and social ability* (Turnbull et al., 2002). Prior to the 1960s, definitions of mental retardation were based primarily on below-average scores on intelligence tests, but this approach had at least three problems. First, errors in testing sometimes resulted in misdiagnoses, and second, disproportionate numbers of minorities and non-English-speaking students were identified as mentally retarded (Hallahan & Kauffman, 2003; Hardman, Drew, & Egan, 2002). Third, individuals with the same intelligence test scores varied widely in their ability to cope with the real world, and these differences couldn't be explained based on the tests alone (Heward, 2003). Because of these limitations, adaptive functioning was added to the definition.

Learning Disabilities

Students with **learning disabilities** have *exceptionalities that involve difficulties in acquiring and using listening, speaking, reading, writing, reasoning, or mathematical abilities* (National Joint Committee on Learning Disabilities, 1994). Problems with reading, writing, and listening are most common, and disparities between scores on standardized IQ tests and scores on achievement tests (representing classroom performance) are often used for identification. However, experts caution that language-intensive IQ tests may not adequately identify learning disabilities in students who are English language learners (Gunderson & Siegel, 2001). Learning disabilities are assumed to be due to central nervous system dysfunction.

Students with learning disabilities make up the largest group of students with exceptionalities—approximately half of the special education population (U.S. Department of Education, 2002b). The category first became widely used in the early 1960s, and the number of school-age children diagnosed as learning disabled has continually increased since then.

Students with learning disabilities have the following problems:

- Uneven performance (e.g., capabilities in one area, extreme weaknesses in others)
- Hyperactivity and difficulty in concentrating
- Lack of follow-through in completion of assignments
- Disorganization and tendency toward distraction

CW

Increasing Understanding 3.14

Identify at least one similarity and one difference between learning disabilities and mental retardation.

Many of these characteristics are typical of general learning problems or immaturity. Unlike developmental lags, however, problems associated with learning disabilities tend to increase over time instead of disappearing. Students fall further behind in achievement, behavior problems increase, and self-esteem decreases (Hardman et al., 2002; Heward, 2003). Lowered achievement and reduced self-esteem intensify each other, resulting in significant learning problems.

Behavior Disorders

Students with **behavior disorders** have *exceptionalities involving the display of serious and persistent age-inappropriate behaviors that result in social conflict, personal unhappiness, and school failure.* The term *behavior disorders* is often used interchangeably with *emotional disturbance, emotional disability,* or *emotional handicap,* and you may encounter these terms in your work. In the definition, the words *serious* and *persistent* are important. Many children occasionally fight with their peers, and all children go

SAFE HAVEN: HELPING EMOTIONALLY TROUBLED KIDS GET BACK ON TRACK

The trend in special education is to include students with exceptionalities in the regular education classroom, but some students require extra structure and support to cope with the demands of schooling. This ABC News video examines a day school that assists teens with serious emotional problems.

Think About This

1. How well would these students function in regular schools and classrooms?
2. How does this approach to helping students with special needs compare with inclusion? What are the advantages and disadvantages?
3. How could schools and classrooms be adapted to help these students make a successful transition back into a regular classroom?

CW *To answer these questions online and receive immediate feedback, go to the Companion Website at* **www.prenhall.com/kauchak**, *then to this chapter's* Video Perspectives *module.*

through periods when they want to be alone. When these patterns are chronic and interfere with normal development and school performance, however, a behavior disorder may exist.

CW

Increasing Understanding 3.15

Identify at least one similarity and one difference between learning disabilities and behavior disorders.

Estimates of the frequency of behavior disorders vary (Hardman et al., 2002). Some suggest that about 1 percent of the total school population and about 9 percent of the special education population have these disorders (U.S. Department of Education, 2002b), whereas others suggest that it's closer to 6 percent to 10 percent of the total population (Hallahan & Kauffman, 2003). Identification is a problem because the characteristics are elusive, making diagnosis difficult (Turnbull et al., 2002).

Changes in the Way Schools and Teachers Help Students with Exceptionalities

In the past, students with exceptionalities were separated from their peers and placed in segregated classrooms or schools. However, instruction in these settings was often inferior, achievement was no better than in regular education classrooms, and students didn't learn the social and life skills they needed to function well in the real world (D. Bradley & Switlick, 1997). Educators and lawmakers looked for other ways to help these students.

In 1975 the U.S. Congress passed Public Law 94-142, the *Individuals with Disabilities Education Act (IDEA)*, which mandates a free and public education for all students with exceptionalities. This law helped ensure consistency in how different states addressed the needs of students with exceptionalities. IDEA, combined with recent amendments, provides the following guidelines for working with students having exceptionalities:

- Identify the needs of students with exceptionalities through nondiscriminatory assessment.
- Involve parents in developing each child's educational program.
- Create an environment that is the least restrictive possible for promoting learning.
- Develop an individualized education program (IEP) of study for each student.

The impact of IDEA can be seen in the large numbers of students with exceptionalities now being served. For example, in 1976–1977, just after the law's passage, the nation educated about 3.3 million children with exceptionalities; presently the schools serve more than 6 million, an increase of nearly 82 percent (Sack, 2000). IDEA has affected every school in the United States and has changed the roles of general and special educators.

The Evolution Toward Inclusion As educators realized that segregated classes and services were not meeting the needs of students with exceptionalities, they searched for alternatives. The first was **mainstreaming,** *the practice of moving students with exceptionalities from segregated settings into regular education classrooms, often for selected activities only.* Popular in the 1970s, mainstreaming began the move away from segregated services; however, because students with exceptionalities were often placed in regular classrooms without adequate support and services, results were unsatisfactory (Hardman et al., 2002).

Inclusion attempts to integrate students with special needs into the regular classroom through instructional adaptations that meet their special needs.

In attempting to solve these problems, educators developed the concept of the **least restrictive environment (LRE),** *one that places students in as normal an educational setting as possible while still meeting their special academic, social, and physical needs.* Broader than the concept of mainstreaming, the LRE allows a greater range of placement options, from full-time placement in the regular classroom to placement in a separate facility, if parents and educators decide that this environment best meets the child's needs.

As educators considered mainstreaming and the LRE, they gradually developed the concept of **inclusion,** *a comprehensive approach to educating students with exceptionalities that advocates a total, systematic, and coordinated web of services.* Inclusion has three components:

- Including students with special needs in a regular school campus
- Placing students with special needs in age- and grade-appropriate classrooms
- Providing special education support within the regular classroom

Initially, students with exceptionalities received additional services to help them function in regular school settings (Turnbull et al., 2002). Gradually the concept of coordination replaced this additive approach. Special and regular education teachers collaborate closely to ensure that learning experiences are integrated into the regular classroom curriculum. For example, rather than pulling a student with special needs out of the classroom for supplementary instruction in math, a special education teacher would coordinate instruction with the general education teacher and then work with the student in the regular classroom on tasks linked to the standard math curriculum.

Inclusion seeks to make all educators responsible for creating supportive learning environments for students with exceptionalities. When inclusion is properly implemented, general education teachers receive help from trained specialists when they have students with special needs in their classrooms.

Inclusion is controversial. The specialized help teachers are supposed to receive often isn't provided, so teachers are left to cope with students' special needs on their own. Some parents criticize the practice, because they worry that their children will get lost in regular classrooms. Even special educators don't agree on inclusion (Turnbull et al., 2002). Advocates contend that placement in a regular classroom is the only way to eliminate the negative effects of segregation, whereas opponents argue that inclusion is not for everyone and that some students are better served in separate special classes for parts of the day (Hardman et al., 2002; Holloway, 2001).

What does all this mean for you as a teacher? You are virtually certain to have students with exceptionalities in your classroom, and you will be expected to do the following:

- Aid in the process of identifying students with exceptionalities.
- Adapt your instruction to meet the needs of students with exceptionalities, actively seeking out the help of special educators in the process.
- Maintain communication with parents, school administrators, and special educators about the progress of students in your classroom who have special needs.

For up-to-date national information and statistics on the implementation of IDEA, go to the Companion Website at www.prenhall.com/kauchak, then to this chapter's *Web Links* module.

Decision Making

Defining Yourself as a Professional

As you think about the kind of professional you want to become, you will need to make a number of decisions related to the diversity of today's students. One of the most important is deciding how you will personally approach issues involving culture, gender, ability, and exceptionalities. For example, one of the paradoxes of culture is that people tacitly believe their cultural views are the "normal" or right ways to look at the world, and as a consequence, they tend to see others in narrow, stereotypical ways. But if you are to help all students grow as much as possible, you will need to avoid stereotypes and think of each student as an individual.

How can you grow in these areas? A number of possibilities exist. For instance, travel can expose you to different cultures, in both the United States and other countries. Gathering experiences in working with cultural minorities, either through volunteer or part-time work, provides another opportunity for growth. Schools that serve high numbers of students who are members of cultural minority groups are constantly seeking adults to work with students both during and after school. Learning another language can lead to personal and professional growth. Teachers who can speak foreign languages, especially Spanish, not only learn about other cultures but also make themselves more marketable.

Similar learning experiences can help teachers deepen their understanding of gender issues. Coaching girls' athletic teams, for example, can provide you with valuable insights into how girls think and interact. Talking with other skilled teachers can give you ideas about how to encourage students to consider nontraditional occupations and how to maintain gender equity in the classroom.

You will need to make many decisions about how diversity will affect your instruction. Many people view instruction as a simple dissemination of information and learning as a process of absorbing that information. In other words, teachers simply explain topics to their students, and students remember the explanations. Research indicates that learning is more complex than this simplistic view, however, and learners are much more than empty vessels to be filled with knowledge; they bring with them a wealth of background experiences, beliefs, and language capabilities that all influence learning. When you enter your first classroom, you will need to build upon your students' cultural and linguistic backgrounds, forging bridges between their communities and the school community.

To build on students' strengths, you must discover what these are. Effective teachers do this in a number of ways, including talking with students' previous teachers, examining students' cumulative folders, and giving comprehensive pre-assessments at the beginning of the school year. The most successful teachers go beyond these traditional strategies and establish communication links by reaching out to their students as human beings (Obidah & Teel, 2001). Suggestions for creating these links include the following:

- Have students write about themselves and their families at the beginning of the school year. Ask them to share their hopes and uncertainties about the new year and some personal information about themselves and their families, such as their favorite foods and leisure activities, the number of brothers and sisters they have, and how long they've lived in the area.
- Spend time with students at lunch and on the playground. This provides you with opportunities to learn about how they act and feel outside the classroom.
- Make yourself available before and after school for academic help. Teachers who do this often find that students want to talk about much more than homework problems.

The most important component of a student's education is you, the teacher: "The beliefs, intentions, and personalities of all teachers play a more significant role in the success of individual students than the curriculum, materials, class size, and [other factors]" (Obidah & Teel, 2001, p. 107). Becoming the kind of teacher that can promote the most possible growth for all students will require a great deal of effort, but it can also provide you with some of the most satisfying experiences that you will ever have.

Summary

Cultural Diversity

Due to demographic trends, our schools are becoming increasingly diverse. In the past, schools responded to diversity with the goal of assimilation, hoping to "Americanize" students as quickly as possible. Multicultural education, by contrast, attempts to recognize the contributions of different cultures and build on students' cultural strengths in the classroom.

This increase in diversity is also seen in the languages students bring to our classrooms. Different approaches to dealing with this language diversity place different amounts of emphasis on maintaining the first language versus learning English as quickly as possible.

Gender

Evidence suggests that both boys and girls encounter problems in today's schools. For girls these problems focus more on achievement, especially in math, science, and computer science, whereas for boys the problems are more behavioral and connected to learning problems. Suspected causes of these problems range from societal and parental expectations to differential treatment in classrooms. Teachers play a major role in ensuring that gender differences don't become gender inequalities. Sexual harassment is a problem for both males and females and occurs most often in environments where teachers and administrators allow it to occur.

Ability Differences

A third dimension of diversity found in today's classrooms focuses on students' different abilities to learn. Earlier perspectives viewed ability as unidimensional and unchanging; current perspectives view ability as multifaceted, malleable, and adaptable.

Ability grouping is one of the most common responses to this dimension of diversity. Despite its popularity, ability grouping is associated with a number of problems, ranging from inappropriate and rigid placements to substandard instruction in some low-ability classrooms.

Learning Styles

Cognitive learning styles emphasize differences in the ways students process information and prefer to learn in the classroom. Cultural learning styles reflect the variety of ways that different groups learn and interact. The concept of learning styles reminds us that all students learn differently; effective teachers are sensitive to these differences and adapt their teaching accordingly.

Students with Exceptionalities

Students with exceptionalities require extra help to reach their full potential. The majority of students with exceptionalities who have disabilities fall into three major categories—students with mental retardation, learning disabilities, and behavior disorders—and a substantial number of students are gifted and talented. Inclusion is changing the way schools assist students with exceptionalities, providing them with a supporting network of services.

Important Concepts

ability grouping (p. 105)
acceleration (p. 112)
assimilation (p. 88)
behavior disorders (p. 113)
between-class ability grouping (p. 105)
culturally responsive teaching (p. 89)
culture (p. 84)
English as a second language (ESL) programs (p. 92)
enrichment (p. 112)
ethnicity (p. 85)
field dependence/independence (p. 107)
gender-role identity differences (p. 97)
gifted and talented (p. 111)
immersion programs (p. 92)
impulsive students (p. 107)
inclusion (p. 115)
intelligence (p. 103)
learning disabilities (p. 112)
learning style (p. 107)
least restrictive environment (LRE) (p. 115)
mainstreaming (p. 114)
maintenance language programs (p. 92)
mental retardation (p. 112)
metacognition (p. 110)
multicultural education (p. 88)
multiple intelligences (p. 103)
nature view of intelligence (p. 103)
nurture view of intelligence (p. 104)
reflective students (p. 107)
sexual harassment (p. 100)
single-gender classes and schools (p. 99)
special education (p. 110)
students with exceptionalities (p. 110)
tracking (p. 105)
transition programs (p. 92)
within-class ability grouping (p. 105)

Developing as a Professional

Praxis Practice

Read the case study, and answer the questions that follow.

Diane Henderson, a fifth-grade teacher at Martin Luther King Elementary school, began her language arts class by saying, "Class, look up at the overhead. What do you notice about the two sentences?"

He gave the gift to her.

John sent him the letter.

She called on Naitia.

"The second one has a proper noun."

"Okay. What else?" Diane said, smiling. . . . "Sheila?"

"Both verbs are past tense."

"Indeed they are!" Diane nodded and smiled again. "What else, Kelvin?" she asked quickly.

"The first has a pronoun for the subject."

"That's true," Diane confirmed. "Does everyone see that?" she asked energetically.

"Now, let's look more closely at the first sentence. What is the direct object in that sentence? . . . Randy?" Diane asks as she walks down the aisle.

"*Her*?" Randy responded.

"Hmm. What do you think, Luciano?"

"*Gift*?" answered Luciano, hesitating.

"Class, what do you think? Is the direct object in sentence one *her* or *gift*? Think about that one for a moment.

"Okay, Todd, do you want to try?"

"Uh, I think it's *gift*."

"That's correct. But why is *gift* the direct object, Theresa?"

"Because that's what he gave," Theresa replied.

"Good answer, Theresa. The direct object takes the action from the verb. But now, what about *her*? What is *her*?" Diane asked, looking around the room. "Well, that's what we are going to learn about today. *Her* is an indirect object. An indirect object receives the action. So, in the first sentence, *gift* is the direct object and *her* is the indirect object. Now let's look at the second sentence. It has both a direct object and an indirect object. Who can tell us which is which? Heather?"

"The direct object in the second sentence is *letter*," Heather responded hesitantly.

"Yes, good," Diane said and smiled reassuringly.

"So what is the indirect object? Jason?" Diane continued.

"It must be *him*."

"Very good, Jason! And why is *letter* the direct object? . . . Laura?"

"Because that's what John sent."

"And how about *him*? Why is it the indirect object. . . . Jana?"

"'Cause that's who received the letter."

"Good! Now look at this sentence and tell me which is the direct and indirect object."

The batter hit the shortstop a line drive.

"Katya?"

"Umm . . . "

"Oh, I know," Tom blurted out.

"That's great, Tom, but remember what we said about giving everyone in the class a chance to answer? Go ahead, Katya."

"I think *line drive* is the direct object."

"Good, Katya. That's right. Now who can tell us why it's the direct object? . . . Angie?"

"Because that's what the batter hit."

"And what's the indirect object, Kareem, and why?"

"I think it's *shortstop* because that's who the batter hit the line drive to."

"Yes, good answer." Diane nodded and then wrote an additional sentence on the overhead:

Jim passed the papers back to Mary.

"What is the indirect object in this sentence? . . . Sean?"

Sean looked up suddenly at the sound of his name. "Could you repeat the question?"

"Sure, Sean. What is the indirect object in this sentence?" Diane repeated, pointing to the overhead.

"Is it *Mary*?" Sean asked tentatively.

"Okay. Good, Sean. And why is it the indirect object? . . . Spence?"

"Because that's who Jim passed the papers to."

"And so, what is the direct object in this sentence? . . . Debbie?"

"*Papers.*"

"And just for review, what is the subject? . . . Maria?"

"*Jim.*"

"And what about the tense? What tense do we have here? . . . Sara?"

"Past."

"Very good, everyone."

"Now, look," Diane continued.

She reached back and took a tennis ball from her desk.

"I want you to pair up with your partner and write a sentence about this tennis ball that contains a direct and indirect object. When you're done, decide which of you will present your sentence."

As the students began writing their sentences, Diane walked up and down the rows, looking at each student's work.

"Now let's look at some sentences," Diane announced after a few minutes. "Someone volunteer a sentence, and I'll write it on the chalkboard. . . . Okay, Rashad?"

"She threw him the tennis ball," Rashad volunteered.

"Very good, Rashad. And which is the direct object in your sentence?"

"*Tennis ball*?"

"Good, Rashad. And so, what is *him*? Jacinto?"

"It's the indirect object."

After discussing several more student examples, Diane continued, "That's excellent. Now I want each of you to write a paragraph that has in it at least two examples of indirect objects and at least two other examples that are direct objects. Underline them in each case and label them. If you are having problems getting started, raise your hand and I'll be by in a minute."

While the students wrote their paragraphs, Diane circulated among them, periodically stopping to comment on students' work and to offer suggestions. Todd, a student who had been receiving extra help from a resource teacher, sat with his head on his desk.

"What's the problem, Todd?"

"I can't do this," Todd replied with a shrug.

"Well, getting started is often the hardest part. Why don't you write down one sentence and then raise your hand, and I'll help you with the next step."

At 1:40, Diane announced, "All right, everyone. Please turn in your paragraphs; we're going to get ready for social studies."

The students passed their papers forward. By 1:45, the students had turned in their papers and had their social studies books out and waiting.

1. To what extent did Diane display culturally responsive teaching in her lesson?
2. To what extent did Diane's teaching reflect sensitivity to gender issues?
3. What did Diane do to accommodate differences in learning ability and learning styles?

To receive feedback on your responses to the Praxis Practice exercises, go to the Companion Website at **www.prenhall.com/kauchak**, then to this chapter's *Praxis Practice* module.

Discussion Questions

1. Is multicultural education more important at some grade levels than in others? Why? Is multicultural education more important in some content areas than in others? Why?
2. Experts debate whether teachers should adjust instruction to match student learning styles or teach students to broaden their learning repertoires. Which approach is more desirable? Why?
3. Which approach to teaching English to ELL students makes the most sense in the teaching setting in which you hope to find yourself in your first job? Why?
4. Are single-gender classrooms a good idea? Why or why not?
5. What are the advantages and disadvantages of full-time inclusion in the regular education classroom? Should it be used with all students with exceptionalities?
6. What implications does Gardner's theory of multiple intelligences have for you as a teacher? In answering this question, be sure to relate your answer to the grade level and content area(s) in which you plan to teach.

Classroom Observation Guide

Before You Begin: The purpose of these observation activities is to help you understand how classroom teachers adapt their instruction to meet the needs of diverse learners. Several of the items ask you to combine your observations with teacher interviews, which will allow you access to teachers' professional thinking.

1. Observe a classroom, and focus on several students from cultural minority groups.
   a. Where do they sit?
   b. Who do they talk to and make friends with?

c. Do they attend to the class, and are they involved?

d. Do they participate in classroom discussions?

Ask the teacher how these students perform in class and what he or she does to build upon the differences in these students. Analyze the teacher's response on the basis of the information in this chapter.

2. Observe a class during an interactive questioning session.

a. Note the number of boys and girls in the class.

b. Where were the boys and girls seated?

c. Did boys and girls raise their hands to respond equally?

d. Record the number of times boys and girls were called on. Were they equal?

e. Did the number of management interventions vary by gender?

How gender-neutral was the class? What can teachers do to make their classes more gender-neutral and a better place for both boys and girls to learn?

3. Observe a class working on an in-class assignment. As you do this, circulate around the room so you can observe the work progress of different students. Note the following:

a. Beginning times—Do all students get immediately to work, or do some take their time starting?

b. On-task behaviors—What percentage of the class stays on task throughout the assignment?

c. Completions—Do all students complete the assignment? What do they do if they don't?

d. What forms of help or assistance are there for students who need it?

e. Options—What options are there for students who complete their assignments early?

On the basis of your observations, how diverse is this class in terms of learning ability? What concrete steps could a teacher take to address this diversity?

Going into Schools

1. Interview a teacher about the diversity in his or her classroom. How do students differ in terms of the following:

a. Culture

b. Home language

c. Learning styles

d. Multiple intelligences

e. Learning ability

What does the teacher do to accommodate these differences? Summarize these responses, and analyze them using information from this chapter.

2. Ask the teacher to identify several cultural minority students. Interview these students, and ask the following:

a. How long have you been at this school?

b. What do you like most about school?

c. What do you like least about school?

d. What can teachers do to help you learn better?

On the basis of students' responses, suggest several things a teacher could do to make the classroom a better learning environment for these cultural minority students.

3. Interview a teacher to investigate his or her use of the following strategies to address differences in learning ability: flexible time requirements, grouping, strategy instruction, and peer tutoring and cooperative learning. Answer these questions:
   a. Are differences in learning ability a problem for the teacher? Explain.
   b. Does the teacher use any of the strategies mentioned in the book? Which ones work and why? Have any been tried that didn't work?
   c. Does the teacher employ any other strategy for dealing with differences in learning ability?

   What implications do the teacher's responses suggest for you, and how you would teach in your future classroom?
4. Interview a teacher about working with students with exceptionalities in the classroom. Answer the following questions:
   a. Which students are classified as exceptional? What behaviors led to this classification? What role did the teacher play in identification?
   b. In working with students with exceptionalities, what assistance does the classroom teacher receive from the following people?
      - Special education teacher
      - School psychologist or school counselor
      - Principal
   c. Ask the teacher to share an individualized education program. What are its major components? How helpful is an IEP to the teacher when working with exceptional students in the classroom?
   d. What is the biggest challenge the teacher faces in working with students with exceptionalities?

   In a paragraph or two, describe what your approach will be in working with students who have exceptionalities.

Virtual Field Experience

If you would like to participate in a Virtual Field Experience, go to the Companion Website at **www.prenhall.com/kauchak**, then to this chapter's *Field Experience* module.

Online Portfolio Activities

To complete these activities online, go to the Companion Website at **www.prenhall.com/kauchak**, then to this chapter's *Portfolio Activities* module.

Portfolio Activity 3.1

Exploring Diversity

INTASC Principle 9: Commitment

Personal Journal Reflection

The purpose of this activity is to encourage you to think about your own personal experiences with the different dimensions of diversity you have encountered during your educational experiences. First, analyze yourself in terms of the different dimensions of diversity identified in Figure 3.1, "Dimensions of Diversity." How have these different dimensions of diversity influenced your development as a person? Next, think about your personal experiences with these different dimensions of diversity during your education. Finally, reflect on how these different personal experiences with diversity will influence your effectiveness as a teacher of diverse students, and think about things you can do to fill in any learning gaps.

Portfolio Activity 3.2

Exploring Cultural Diversity

INTASC Principle 3: Adapting Instruction

The purpose of this activity is to introduce you to the cultural diversity in an area where you might teach. Contact the State Office of Education in a state where you're thinking of teaching (addresses and Web sites can be found in Appendix B). Or contact a district in which you might teach (school district telephone numbers can be found in the White Pages of the telephone directory, in the Business Section under "Schools"). Ask for demographic information on cultural minorities and ELL students. Summarize the information briefly, identifying major cultural groups and possible implications for your teaching.

Portfolio Activity 3.3

Exploring Careers in Special Education

INTASC Principle 9: Commitment

This activity is designed to acquaint you with teaching career options in special education. Visit the Web site for the Council for Exceptional Children, the national professional organization for special educators (the address can be found in Chapter 3's *Web Links* module on the Companion Website at **www.prenhall.com/kauchak**). Click on "Student CEC" for information on Tools You Need, Career Info, Goals, Chapter Directory, and Regional Contacts. The *Career Info* module contains additional information on résumé writing, interviewing, and building a professional portfolio. Write a brief description of career opportunities in special education and how your talents and personality might match these.

Chapter 4

Changes in American Society

Their Influences on Today's Schools

Teaching today is more challenging than at any point in our history. In addition to the increasing diversity we discussed in Chapter 3, challenges also come from changes in our society and our students, who have different characteristics than in the past. Consider these statistics from a survey of high school students (Grunbaum et al., 2002):

- Forty-seven percent consumed alcohol within 30 days prior to the survey; 13 percent drove after drinking, and 31 percent rode in a car when a driver had been drinking.
- Twenty-four percent used marijuana during the previous month; 10 percent had tried marijuana before age 13.
- Nine percent attempted suicide within the last 12 months; 19 percent had seriously contemplated it.
- Twenty-nine percent of males and 6 percent of females reported carrying a weapon to school on one or more days during the preceding month; 33 percent were in physical fights on school property during the same time period.

Fewer of today's students come from "traditional" homes, where the father is the breadwinner and the mother works in the home as the primary caregiver. More come to school hungry, tired, or emotionally drained because of conditions in their homes and communities. They are more sexually active, and they use alcohol and other drugs more often than students did in the past. The magnitude of the problems facing teachers is reflected in the following lament from an elementary teacher in Atlanta, Georgia:

• • ● • •

I just don't know what I'm going to do. Every year, my first grade class has more and more of these kids. They don't seem to care about right or wrong, they don't care about adult approval, they are disruptive, they can't read and they arrive at school absolutely unprepared to learn. Who are these kids? Where do they come from? Why are there more and more of them? I used to think that I was a good teacher. I really prided myself on doing an outstanding job. But I find I'm working harder and harder, and being less and less effective. A good teacher? Today I really don't know. I do know that my classroom is being overwhelmed by society's problems and I don't understand it. What's happening to our schools? What's happening to society? I don't understand all of this and I sure don't know what we're going to do about it. (Barr & Parrett, 2001, p. 1)

• • ● • •

This chapter attempts to answer the following questions:

- How have societal changes affected the students you'll work with?
- Who are students placed at-risk, and what can teachers and schools do to help them learn?
- What implications do changes in our students have for prospective teachers?

Let's begin by examining how the answers to these questions influence the lives of real teachers.

This logo appears throughout the chapter to indicate where case studies are integrated with chapter content.

Case STUDY It was the end of August. Carla Ramirez, a second-year teacher, was excited about the new school year. Relocating to the Midwest because of her husband's job, she had been assigned a first-grade classroom in a large city. She spent the summer constructing units in the different content areas and was eager to get started.

Two weeks later Carla shuffled into the faculty lounge on her lunch break.

"You look tired. Been getting enough sleep?" her hallmate, 20-year veteran Rae Anne Johnson, asked.

"No, I'm not tired," Carla responded, collapsing in a chair. "Just a little discouraged."

"Anything you want to talk about?" Rae Anne asked after a moment.

Carla hesitated and then replied, "It's my class. I had such high hopes. I had my room all set up with learning centers and neat stuff. I knew what I was going to teach, and I was really looking forward to it. But these kids . . . I don't know. I'm really struggling, and now I'm beginning to wonder if it's me."

Rae Anne shrugged. "Maybe, but you're so conscientious. . . . I doubt it. What's got you so down?"

"I can't quite figure it out. Some of the kids are really squirrelly. It's hard to get them to sit down at all. Others literally fall asleep in the middle of lessons. I've got four thumb-suckers, and frankly, some of them just don't seem ready for first-grade work. I hand out a worksheet, and they look at it like I wrote it in Greek or something."

"You might be right. . . . I know it's tough. I have some of the same problems. One of my kids was all upset yesterday, so I sat her down at recess, and she told me that her parents had had a big fight the night before. And then there's Johnny . . . he's always so droopy, so I asked him if he'd had breakfast this morning. He said he never eats it, so I called his home and told his mother about the school's free breakfast program. I had to call three times to get her—I didn't want to just leave a message on the machine. She was all apologetic about sending him to school without it, but she works weird hours, and she's a single mom, so I know it's tough for her too. It's hard for a lot of kids."

"I guess you're right, but they didn't prepare me for this. I was so eager, and, I guess, idealistic about making a difference. Now, I'm not so sure."

• • ● • •

A Changing Society

Our goal as teachers is to provide the best education possible for all students. We want them to enjoy school and learn as much as they can. This happens for some students. They come from stable, supportive families, and they have experiences that prepare them to achieve.

Unfortunately, for other students this isn't the case. Problems in their families, neighborhoods, and even communities limit their chances for success. Additional in-

Figure 4.1 A Changing Society

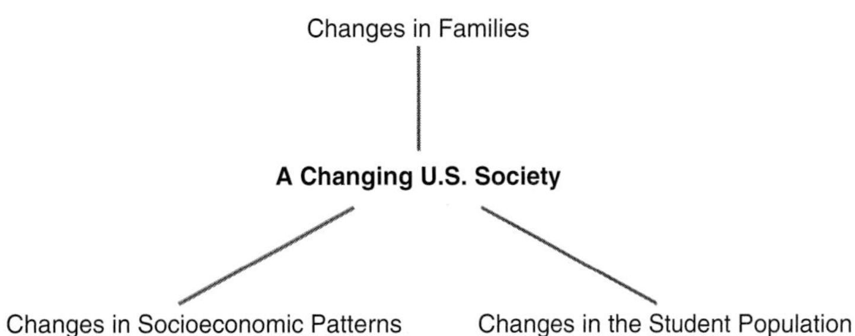

fluences, such as changes in the economy, the workplace, and society's attitudes toward schools and schooling, all impact our students' ability to benefit from schooling.

Being a professional requires that teachers understand these changes so they're equipped to accommodate them in their decision making. For example, if you are an elementary teacher and you understand how poverty and homelessness affect learning, you are better able to serve as a student advocate and perhaps even influence important policy decisions such as making free breakfast and lunch programs available to disadvantaged students. If you're a middle or high school teacher and you understand how alcohol and other drugs affect both learning and healthy development, you are better able to help your students avoid these pitfalls. To help students learn as much as possible and grow up as healthy adults, teachers need to understand the homes and neighborhoods in which their students live.

In this chapter we examine our changing society and the implications these changes have for teachers and schools. They're illustrated in Figure 4.1 and discussed in the sections that follow.

Changes in Families

With head resting on his hands, Brad looked puzzled when he was asked how many brothers and sisters he had—a seemingly simple question, but not so easy for Brad to answer. He scrunched his face, paused, pushed back in his chair, pursed his lips, rolled his dark eyes, and began counting on his fingers slowly, deliberately, then said, "Let's see, hmmm, six." "Six?" "Wait, seven." "Seven?" "Wait, eight." "That's a hard question." It wasn't meant to be. Brad explained: "I didn't count my sister Mary or my sister Kerrie." "Oh?" "My dad was married to four different ladies and has had quite a few kids." Brad had a hard time remembering when he last saw two of his siblings, who are older and live in other states. Even with his best effort, he was off one child. (Bullough, 1999, p. 10)

Brad's story, while extreme, illustrates some of the ways in which American family structure has changed. In spite of these changes, the family is still the institution primarily responsible for meeting the needs of young people and helping them adapt to the world. This was true in colonial times and remains true today. But the ways that families care for and educate their children are shifting.

The "traditional" American family—a husband who is the primary breadwinner, a mother who doesn't work outside the home, and two school-age children—made up only 6 percent of the total households in the United States in 1998. Census data from 1998 reveal some additional facts about families and households with children:

- Families headed by married couples made up 55 percent of all households, compared to 71 percent in 1970.
- Seven out of 10 women with children were in the workforce.
- The divorce rate quadrupled from 1978 to 1998.
- Sixty-eight percent of all births to teenagers occurred out of wedlock.
- The incidence of poverty among single-parent families was between 7 and 8 times higher than in families headed by married couples.
- Sixty percent of teenage families lived in poverty, but only 14 percent of the total population did. (U.S. Bureau of Census, 1998a).

CW

Increasing Understanding 4.1

Identify at least two things teachers could do to help parents work with their children more effectively on homework and other academic activities.

To answer the Increasing Understanding questions online and receive immediate feedback, go to the Companion Website at **www.prenhall.com/kauchak**, then to this chapter's *Increasing Understanding* module. Type in your response, and then study the feedback.

In addition, in 2000, 22 percent of children lived with only their mothers, 4 percent lived with only their fathers, and 4 percent lived with neither (Federal Interagency Forum on Child and Family Statistics, 2001).

Poverty, divorce, single parents, families where both parents work, and teenage pregnancies pose challenges to parents, their children, and teachers. Because of work demands, single parents and couples who work outside the home spend less time with their children in general, as well as less time helping and supervising homework. Many parents in today's fast-paced world are spending up to 40 percent less time with their children than parents did a generation ago (Kamerman & Kahn, 1995). Even when they have time, many parents are uncertain about how to help their children with schoolwork (Gorman & Balter, 1997).

What does this information imply for teachers? Let's look at an example. One of your authors went to a first volleyball team meeting with his daughter. The team was lined up on the floor, and members were asked to introduce themselves and their parents. The first girl introduced both parents; the second, whose father wasn't there, felt obligated to explain. From that point every girl followed precedent by "explaining" the absence of a parent, and some were embarrassed because their parents were divorced. Teachers can make situations like these easier for students by using words such as "Would you please introduce your parent, or parents, or caregivers?" or "Please introduce the people you brought with you today." On the surface it may seem like a minor issue, but it is important to students.

Being flexible with meeting times for parent–teacher conferences is another way teachers can accommodate working or single parents. It communicates that you care about your students, you're committed to their education, and you're aware of the pressures of work schedules. As teachers, we should be sensitive to changes in family structures and communicate to our students that we accept and support all types of family patterns.

Child Care When a single parent or both parents work outside the home, students often spend time in child care. The trend is away from in-home care; in the mid-1990s only 25 percent of the children of working parents were cared for in the home compared to 57 percent in 1958 (Leach, 1995).

People have long raised questions about the effects of child care on the emotional and intellectual development of children. Critics contend that young children need the presence of a mother in the home, and child care is not an adequate substitute. Supporters of child care counter that children can adapt to different care patterns and are not jeopardized by varying child care arrangements.

Researchers examining this issue have focused on the quality of the child care instead of the larger issue of parents working. When children are placed in well-run and supervised child-care facilities, few adverse effects seem to exist (Berk, 2003, 2004).

Latchkey children often face long hours of unsupervised care.

Unfortunately, many child-care facilities are not well run and well supervised.

Latchkey Children **Latchkey children,** *children who go home to empty houses after school and who are left alone until parents arrive home from work*, are another work-related problem. Almost three quarters of today's children live in households where both parents work or the primary caregiver works full-time (Federal Interagency Forum on Child and Family Statistics, 2001). Experts estimate that close to 4 million children return home to an empty house or apartment after school. The problem is complex, ranging from concerns about children's safety to questions of supervision, excessive time spent watching television, and lack of help with homework.

Some schools respond with after-hours programs, but a more common solution is for schools to cooperate with community agencies, such as YMCAs or youth clubs, to offer after-school programs. In addition to providing safe, supervised environments, these programs teach children how to respond to home emergencies, use the phone to seek help, make healthful snacks, and spend time wisely.

Changes in Socioeconomic Patterns

Researchers have found that parents and caregivers from different backgrounds think about and prepare their children for school in different ways. One of the strongest indicators of these differences is **socioeconomic status (SES),** *the combination of income, occupation, and level of education that describes a family or individual.* Teachers, for example (in spite of what we sometimes hear), have relatively high socioeconomic status; they make middle-class incomes, work in professional occupations, and hold bachelor's or higher degrees. Plumbers, in comparison, tend to have lower socioeconomic status because they don't work in professional occupations and usually don't have college degrees (even though they often make more money than teachers).

Socioeconomic status is commonly described using three levels—upper, middle, and lower class—with finer distinctions within each. The **upper class** *is composed of highly educated (usually a college degree), highly paid (usually above $100,000) professionals who make up about 15 percent or less of the population.* Though only a small part of the total population, the upper class controls a disproportionate amount of the wealth, and the gap between the upper and other classes is growing. For example, in 1979 corporate chief executives earned 29 times as much as their employees; by 1988 the figure had grown to 93 times (Phillips, 1990).

The **middle class** *is composed of managers, administrators, and white-collar workers who perform nonmanual work.* Teachers are in this category. Middle-class incomes typically range between approximately $30,000 and $70,000, and about 40 percent of the population falls into this category. (Upper-middle-class groups are in the $70,000 and $100,000 range.)

Families in the lower class typically make less than $20,000 per year, have a high school education or less, and work in blue-collar jobs. About 45 percent of the U.S. population is in this category, and the percentage is increasing. People in the lowest-earning segment of this category often depend on public assistance to supplement their incomes and are often the third or fourth generation to live in poverty. The term "**underclass**" describes *people with low incomes who continually struggle with economic* *problems.* Research indicates escaping this situation is very difficult (Lind, 1995; Reich, 1995).

CW

Increasing Understanding 4.2

Do you think most new teaching positions will occur in schools populated by students from upper-, middle-, or lower-SES backgrounds? Why do you think so?

Socioeconomic status can have powerful effects both on K–12 learning and success in college. For example, 13-year-old students whose parents had not graduated from high school scored 9 percent lower on math achievement tests and 12 percent lower on reading achievement tests than students whose parents had at least some college (U.S. Department of Education, 2000a). Average scores for 9-year-olds whose parents had some college were roughly comparable to those of the 13-year-olds. About 25 percent of high school graduates from the lower SES levels go to college and earn a degree, whereas nearly 80 percent of the graduates from the highest SES levels do (Mortenson, 2001).

Poverty

When Sally gets a spare moment (and there are precious few of them), she loves to draw, mostly fantasy creatures. "What is your favorite thing to draw?" "A mermaid thing, cuz it's not real—there's no such thing as a mermaid—but I like to draw things that aren't real. Fairy tales. Fairies, monsters." She lights up talking about her creations. But Sally's life is not a fairy tale. With her brother she hurries home from school, immediately does her homework, and "I mean *right* after my homework I have to clean up my room and do the dishes for dinner and cook dinner." "You cook dinner? Every day?" Staring straight across the table separating us, and without blinking her blue eyes, Sally responded slightly defensively, "I'm a good cook." For all the talk about food, Sally's greatest fear, she said, was that she will not get enough to eat and will get sick. Who would take care of the family, then? "I worry. . . I [will] end up getting too skinny and die cuz I'm really skinny." (Bullough, 1999, p. 13)

Sally has to do all this work because her mother, who has severe diabetes, works 10 hours a day as a waitress. When her mother returns home from work, she collapses on the sofa exhausted. When Sally gets home from school, this is how she usually finds her. Life is not easy for Sally.

Poverty can exert a powerful negative influence on school success.

The lowest end of the SES continuum is characterized by pervasive poverty. The federal government determines who is poor by establishing **poverty thresholds,** *household income levels that are meant to represent the lowest earnings needed to meet basic living needs.* In 2001 the poverty level for a family of four was $18,267 (U.S. Bureau of Census, 2002).

Research on poverty revealed the following patterns at the end of the twentieth century:

- The United States had the highest rate of child poverty (estimates ranged from 17% to 22%) of developed countries.
- Almost 19 million children, or 26 percent, were growing up in households where neither parent had a full-time job.
- Poverty was most common in small towns and suburban areas (46% of all impoverished families lived in small towns; 28 percent lived in suburban areas; and less than 9 percent lived in inner cities).
- Children, while only 27 percent of the total population, constituted 40 percent of the poor.

Figure 4.2 Poverty Levels by Ethnicity

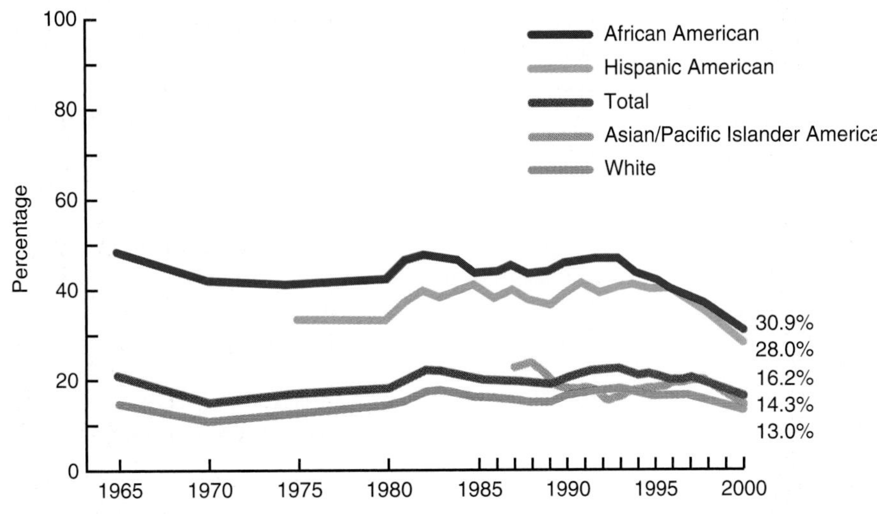

Source: U.S. Bureau of Census (2002).

- Poverty was most common in families headed by single mothers.
- Poverty was more prevalent among minorities than nonminorities (Figure 4.2). (Annie E. Casey Foundation, 2001; Hodgkinson, 2002; U.S. Bureau of Census, 2002)

Some of these findings are surprising. For example, many people think that poverty is most prevalent in cities, and most don't realize that 40 percent of children—our potential future leaders—are living in poverty.

The powerful effect that poverty can have on learning is reflected in a program implemented by Wake County District in North Carolina. The district developed a busing program to ensure that no more than 40 percent of a school's enrollment would be students eligible for the federal free or reduced-price lunch program (Johnston, 2000e). San Francisco proposed a similar strategy to battle both economic and racial segregation (Kahlenberg, 1999). These programs are based on the belief that high concentrations of students from impoverished backgrounds detract from a school's ability to successfully meet students' learning needs.

Homelessness One direct result of poverty is the increase in homelessness. Experts estimate that between one half to one million children are homeless; accurate figures are hard to obtain because of the transient nature of the population (Rafferty, 1995). Homeless children often come from unstable families, suffer from inadequate diets, and lack medical care (Gracenin, 1993). The majority of homeless children (estimates run as high as 63%) fail to regularly attend school (Sandham, 2000).

Effective schools attempt to respond to the problem in several ways. Recognizing that students' home situations are difficult, they remove barriers by making school admission, attendance, and course requirements flexible (Vissing, Schroepfer, & Bloise, 1994). They also provide outreach services such as counselors, after-school programs, and financial aid for transportation. School officials coordinate their efforts with other community agencies to ensure that basic needs, such as food and shelter, are met.

One elementary school in Phoenix, Arizona, targets homeless children as its primary clients (Sandham, 2000). It sends school buses around the city to pick up these children and maintains a clothing room that students can visit to get clean underwear and changes of clothes. Volunteer pediatricians staff an on-site clinic that provides free medical care and immunizations. The school even hands out alarm clocks (old-fashioned windups because many of the children don't have access to electricity) to help the children get to school on time in the morning. Teacher dedication and effort make the school work. One teacher commented, "There's something about watching the buses roll out of here, with all the kids' faces pressed against the windows. I get this feeling it's what I should be doing" (Sandham, 2000, p. 29).

CW

Increasing Understanding 4.3

What is the most effective thing teachers can do to demonstrate that they care about a student?

As a teacher, what can you do about homeless children? While seemingly simple and insignificant, the most important responses are to be caring and flexible. Demonstrating that you genuinely care about students and their learning is important for all children. For those that are homeless, it's essential.

Socioeconomic Status and School Success Socorro is a fifth grader who is struggling in school. When a researcher went to her house to find out why, here is what he found:

• • • • •

When interviewing Socorro's mother, Nick passed through the apartment apparently returning to work after taking a brief break. The phone rang. Socorro's 5-year-old stepbrother curled up in his mother's lap and began talking into her ear. The television was on. There is a television in every room; one is Socorro's. Cable. The apartment is spotlessly clean. Life is busy, very busy. Once off the phone, the mother exclaims, proudly, "I let her do whatever she wants . . . she does whatever she wants." Working two jobs, one in housekeeping at a nearby hospital and another, an evening job as a parking lot attendant to obtain money for a promised trip to Disneyland, leaves her no option: She is not home often. Socorro's father pays regular child support. While not at work, her mother's brother, who lives with the family and spends much of his day watching television, tends the children when they are home. Irritated, Socorro said that her uncle expects to be waited on, and she doesn't like it. "I want to support my kids," the mother says, and this requires that she is "never home for them." She works very hard.

Socorro's problem in school, her mother asserts, is that "her mind wanders." Her teachers tell another tale: Socorro cannot read and is struggling. Her mother seems unconcerned that Socorro frequently misses school. As her teacher said: "She is out of school more than she is in it." Attending school irregularly, Socorro is slipping further and further behind her classmates. Concerned, teachers made arrangements to place Socorro for part of the day with the special education teacher. They didn't know what else to do, having failed to gain the mother's help in getting Socorro to school regularly. (Bullough, 2001, p. 33)

• • • • •

Socioeconomic status is related to school success in several ways. For example, compared to students from low-SES backgrounds, high-SES students score higher on intelligence and achievement tests, get better grades, miss less school, and have fewer suspensions (Macionis, 2003). School dropout rates for students from poor families are twice those of the general population; for students from the poorest families, they exceed 50 percent. In summarizing the powerful influence of SES on learning, one researcher noted that "the relationship between test scores and SES is one of the most widely replicated findings in the social sciences" (Konstantopoulos, 1997, p. 5).

What might cause these differences? At least five factors related to socioeconomic status influence student performance:

- Fulfillment of basic needs
- Family stability

- School-related experiences
- Interaction patterns in the home
- Parental attitudes and values

Fulfillment of basic needs is something that many families in the United States take for granted. Many low-SES families, however, lack adequate medical care, and an increasing number of children are coming to school without proper nourishment and adequate rest.

The quality of home life influences student learning and performance. In some low-SES families daily struggles and economic problems lead to parental frustration, anger, and depression. These pressures can also lead to marital conflicts that result in unstable home environments (Conger et al., 1992). Children then come to school without a sense of safety and security, and they are less equipped to tackle school-related challenges.

Children's exposure to school-related experiences influences their learning as well. For example, high-SES parents are more likely than low-SES parents to provide their children with educational activities outside of school (such as visits to museums, concerts, bookstores, and libraries), to have materials at home that support learning (such as computers, calculators, newspapers, encyclopedias, and dictionaries), and to arrange for formal educational experiences outside of school (such as music or dance lessons, religious instruction, or computer classes) (Economic Policy Institute, 2002). These experiences provide a learning base that helps students succeed in school activities. Minority and low-SES students, however, are less likely to participate in enriching activities in the community as well as in extracurricular activities provided by schools (McNeal, 1997), often because of work demands, transportation problems, or a simple lack of awareness that the opportunities exist.

The ways in which parents interact with their children can help or hinder learning (Chance, 1997). Experts estimate that by the age of 3, children with professional parents have heard 30 million words, children with working-class parents have heard 20 million, and children with parents on welfare have heard 10 million. Low-SES parents are more likely to "tell" rather than explain and are more likely to emphasize conformity and obedience instead of individual responsibility or initiative. Their language is less elaborate, their directions are less clear, and they are less likely to encourage problem solving. High-SES parents talk more with their children, explain ideas and the causes of events, encourage independent thinking, and emphasize individual responsibility (Berk, 2003, 2004; Macionis, 2003). These discussions promote language development and prepare children for the kind of verbal interaction found in the schools (Heath, 1989). Sometimes called "the curriculum of the home," these rich interaction patterns, together with the enrichment experiences described in the previous paragraph, provide a foundation for reading and vocabulary development.

Finally, parental attitudes and values about schooling and learning shape students' attitudes and values. As mentioned earlier, reading materials are more likely to be found in high-SES homes. Parents who enjoy books, newspapers, and magazines communicate that the information they contain is valuable and that reading itself is a useful activity. When children see their parents read, they imitate the behavior, which influences learning. Students who read at home show larger gains in reading achievement than those who do not (E. Hiebert & Raphael, 1996).

Parents also communicate their attitudes through the expectations they hold for their children and through their involvement in children's activities. High-SES parents and caregivers are more likely to expect their children to graduate from high school and attend college, and they communicate these expectations in conversations.

CW

Increasing Understanding 4.4

What do "instructional structure" and "motivational support" mean? Give an example of each to illustrate your explanation.

They also send the message that they believe in a well-rounded education by attending curricular and extracurricular activities. One mother commented, "When she sees me at her games, when she sees me going to open house, when I attend her Interscholastic League contests, she knows I am interested in her activities. Plus, we have more to talk about" (Young & Scribner, 1997, p. 12).

To succeed in schools, low-SES students often need more instructional structure and motivational support than their high-SES peers (Eggen & Kauchak, 2004). In addition, they may need help in seeing connections between learning tasks and the outside world, as well as understanding that effort leads to accomplishment.

Changes in the Student Population

In previous sections we saw how the American family and socioeconomic patterns have changed and how these changes impact students' chances for success. We now turn to changes in the students themselves, as we examine sexuality, use of alcohol and other drugs, violence, suicide, and child abuse. These factors are outlined in Figure 4.3 and discussed in the sections that follow.

Sexuality In the past, we tacitly thought of our teenagers as either asexual or restrained. We knew they were going through puberty but assumed that they weren't sexually active (or chose not to think about it).

The facts suggest otherwise. In 2001 nearly one half of teens reported being sexually active by the end of high school, and nearly 1 in 10 said they had sex before age 13. Almost 13 percent of tenth graders said they had four or more sex partners (Grunbaum et al., 2002). Sexual activity such as this poses a number of risks, including teenage pregnancy and sexually transmitted diseases.

Teenage pregnancy. Although the teenage birthrate has been declining steadily (almost 30 percent from 1991 to 2002), the United States still has the highest rate of teenage pregnancy and births in the Western industrialized world (National Campaign to Prevent Teen Pregnancy, 2003). Thirty-five percent of young women become pregnant at least once before the age of 20—about 850,000 a year. Eight in 10 of these pregnancies are unintended, and 79 percent are to unmarried teens. These pregnancies take a terrible toll on both the mother and the child.

Figure 4.3 Changes in the Student Population

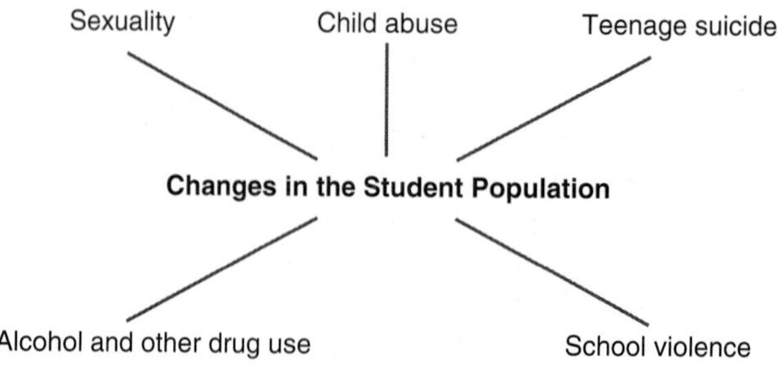

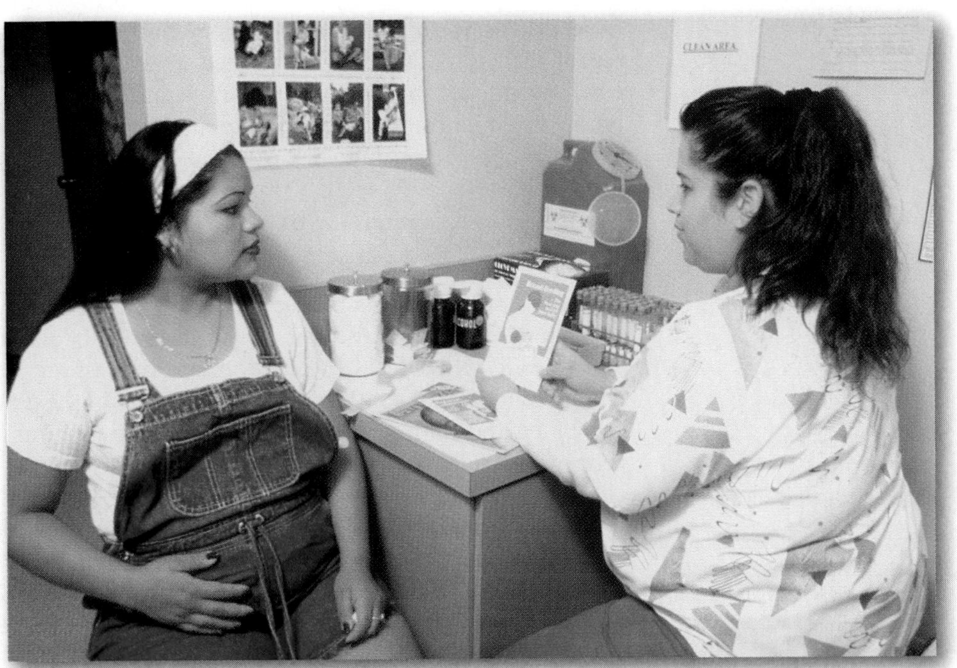

Teen pregnancies force students to mature too rapidly, diverting attention from their own personal development.

Becoming a teenage parent forces students to mature too quickly, diverting energy from their own development to the care of a baby. Economics is also a problem; more than half of the households headed by teen mothers live in poverty. Many mothers drop out of school, develop poor work skills, and have limited employment opportunities. They are forced to juggle children with work. The babies also fare poorly. Because of inadequate prenatal care, they are often born prematurely or with health problems.

For a full report on the latest statistics on teenage sexual behavior, go to the Companion Website at **www.prenhall.com/kauchak**, then to this chapter's *Web Links* module.

Efforts to deal with the problem of teenage pregnancy focus on programs that encourage mothers to complete their educations through home instruction or programs in which mothers bring their babies to school and attend child-care as well as regular classes. Despite these efforts, the majority of teen mothers drop out of school.

CW

Increasing Understanding 4.5

Identify one advantage and one disadvantage of home instruction for teenage mothers. Do the same for in-school programs.

Sexually transmitted diseases. One in 4 sexually active teens will contract a sexually transmitted disease. Unfortunately, many have sex without protecting themselves from sexually transmitted diseases, such as herpes, genital warts, syphilis, and gonorrhea. AIDS (acquired immune deficiency syndrome), which can be transmitted through sexual activity, has made the problem more urgent and deadly. In 1999 AIDS-related illnesses were the sixth leading cause of death among 15- to 24-year-olds in the United States (U.S. Department of Health and Human Services, 1999).

Although almost half of teenagers report being sexually active and 1 in 7 have had four or more sex partners, only 51 percent of sexually active females and 65 percent of sexually active males reported using condoms (Grunbaum et al., 2002), the only reliable defense, other than abstinence, against sexually transmitted diseases. While it was first believed that the virus was transmitted primarily through sexual contact between male homosexuals and through intravenous drug use, it is now well known that HIV is also spread through heterosexual sex. Nine percent of the HIV/AIDS cases reported in 1995–1996 were attributed to heterosexual contact (Centers for Disease Control and Prevention, 1996).

Homosexuality. Experts have estimated that between 5 percent and 10 percent of U.S. students are homosexual. Gay and lesbian students commonly face rejection, which leads to feelings of alienation and depression. Perhaps as a result, drug use among homosexual youth is much higher than in the heterosexual population (Sears, 1991). Further, although homosexual students account for only 5 percent to 10 percent of the student population, they commit 30 percent of the youth suicides annually (Gibson, 1989).

Increasing Understanding 4.6

What could teachers do on the first day of class to minimize peer sexual harassment? Throughout the school year?

Although these problems have no easy solutions, teachers can do much to shape attitudes toward homosexual students (Shakeshaft et al., 1997). For example, they can define appropriate behaviors and maintain "zero tolerance" for harassment. Schools and classrooms must be emotionally safe places for *all* students.

Increasing Understanding 4.7

Identify at least two different kinds of background knowledge teachers must have to effectively teach about sexuality. (Hint: Recall the different kinds of professional knowledge discussed in Chapter 1.)

Sex education. In response to teenagers' increasing sexual activity, many school districts have implemented some form of sex education. The form and content of instruction varies from state to state and community to community. Controversy over sex education usually centers on two important questions: (1) What is the proper role of the family versus the schools in sex education? and (2) what content should go into these programs?

Polls have indicated that the majority of parents favor some type of sex education (Mulrine, 2002), and courts have upheld school districts' rights to offer sex education courses (Fischer, Schimmel, & Kelly, 2003). Parents who object are free to take their children out of the programs. You'll read more about different curricular approaches to sex education in Chapter 10.

Use of Alcohol and Other Drugs After a 20-year period of decline, use of alcohol and other drugs by teenagers has either leveled off or been on the rise in recent years (Figure 4.4). In a study of high school seniors conducted in 1997, 84 percent reported using alcohol, 26 percent said they had tried marijuana, and 16 percent said they had sniffed or inhaled intoxicating substances such as glue or paint spray. This pattern of drug use starts early—21 percent of eighth graders, 33 percent of tenth graders, and 39 percent of twelfth graders reported drug or alcohol use in the past year (L. Johnson, Bachman, & O'Malley, 2001). In another study 60 percent of high school students and 30 percent of middle schoolers said that drugs are kept, used, and sold in their schools (National Center on Addiction and Substance Abuse, 2001). Research indicates that, in 1998, 10.5 million U.S. youth, age 12–20, used alcohol and 4.1 million 12- to 17-year-olds smoked (Coles, 1999b). Alcohol and drug use are often associated with other risk factors such as poverty, low SES, family instability, and academic problems at school, such as low achievement and truancy (Bryant & Zimmerman, 2002).

For information from the Substance Abuse and Mental Health Services Administration, a federal agency, go to the Companion Website at **www.prenhall.com/kauchak**, then to this chapter's *Web Links* module.

Figure 4.4 Student Drug and Alcohol Use

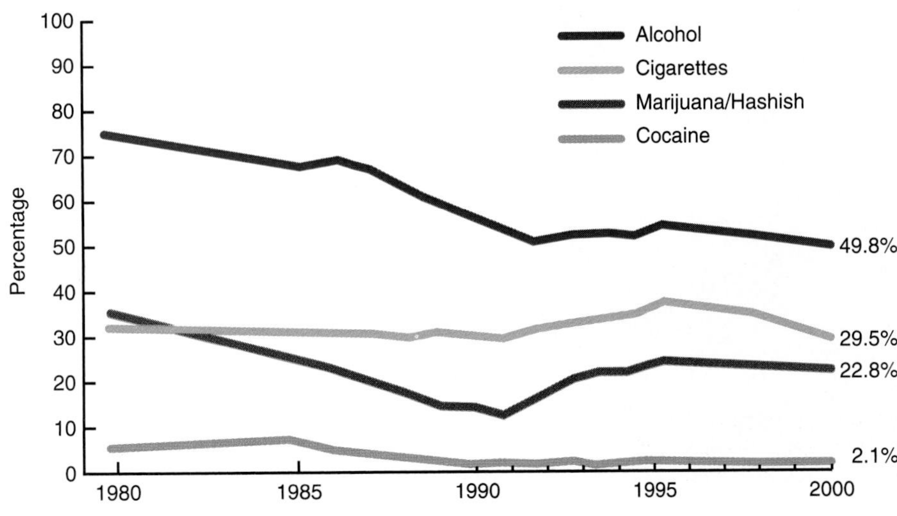

Percentage of High School Seniors Reporting Use in the Previous 30 Days

Source: L. Johnson et al. (2001).

Despite the stereotyped belief that drug use is primarily an inner-city problem, drug-use problems are actually most acute in rural areas (Coles, 2000). Rural teens are more likely to use a variety of drugs, ranging from cocaine to amphetamines to alcohol.

What leads teenagers to alcohol and drug use? Some people blame the mixed messages teens receive. Although educators and parents talk about the dangers of these substances, the media, and particularly teenage pop culture, often glorify alcohol and other drugs, implying that they are not just acceptable but are the preferred ways of dealing with problems such as stress, loneliness, or depression. Unfortunately, as teenagers become drug dependent, they place themselves at risk for problems such as suicide, poor health, and automobile accidents, and they also fail to develop healthy mechanisms for coping with life's problems (Berk, 2003, 2004). Dependence on drugs can also reinforce feelings of alienation and encourage students to drop out of school. As is intuitively sensible, students who have little attachment to school and devalue its importance are those most likely to use drugs during school hours (K. Finn, Willert, & Marable, 2003).

Increasing Understanding 4.8

Identify two specific ways in which alcohol or other drug use interferes with learning.

Efforts to curtail drug use include programs that teach students facts about drugs while helping them learn to make their own decisions and understand and avoid peer pressure. They also work to develop students' self-esteem. Probably best known is the Drug Abuse Resistance Education (DARE) program, which started in California and spread across the country. Research on these programs is mixed, however, and experts agree that delivering the "Just Say No" message without further intervention efforts is almost always ineffective (Portner, 1993; Schlozman, 2002b). More recent efforts to revise DARE and focus on middle schoolers' ability to understand and refuse drugs appear promising (Bowman, 2002).

Similar criticisms have been directed at the U.S. Department of Education's Safe and Drug-Free Schools program, which provides more than $500 million annually to local school districts with virtually no strings attached. A review of the program found that taxpayer dollars paid for a variety of questionable practices, such as providing

Drug and alcohol education programs attempt to help students avoid harmful and addictive substances.

motivational speakers, puppet shows, dunking booths, magicians, clowns, and tickets to Disneyland. Even though two federal reports were highly critical of the program and the Congressional Budget Office recommended eliminating it, Congress continues to fund it. This is one example of the problems involved in "throwing" money at educational problems. The need is there, the intent is good, but the implementation is lacking.

Other research suggests that intense coordinated efforts can curtail teenage smoking (Portner, 1999a). The state of Florida combined an aggressive anti-smoking advertising campaign, increased law enforcement efforts aimed at minors, and a 50-cents-per package increase in the price of cigarettes. Cigarette use among middle schoolers dropped 19 percent, and smoking declined 8 percent among high schoolers. Despite these results, the Florida legislature, under pressure from tobacco lobbies, cut funding for this program from $70 million to $45 million.

Crime and Violence

· · ● · ·

For the past few months, Juan and his mother have been in hiding, the entire time he has attended Lafayette Elementary. His 29-year-old mother has been in gangs since she was twelve, and her sons, including Juan, grew up believing that at some point they would gain membership for themselves, and in gaining membership would enjoy status and achieve a measure of safety for themselves and their families. One bloody evening, however, crushed her and Juan's worldview, leaving behind a fearful, small boy and a mother overwhelmed with regret. (Bullough, 1999, p. 22)

Juan's uncle was shot and killed in a drive-by shooting; his uncle's girlfriend still wears a metal brace on her leg from the incident. Juan not only witnessed the shooting but had the presence of mind to pull the uncle's two children to the ground to protect them from danger. Juan's school principal, unaware of this and similar incidents, wonders why Juan is so angry in school.

· · ● · ·

Safety is a basic need for all individuals. Unfortunately, in recent polls 1 in 4 students reported some kind of violence-related problem in their schools (Louis Harris & Associates, 1999, 1996), and 40 violent school-related deaths occurred during the 1997–1998 school year (Portner, 1999b). An average of 14 children die each day from gunfire in the United States—approximately one every 100 minutes (Children's Defense Fund, 1999). The problem of school violence came to national attention in 1999 with the Columbine, Colorado, tragedy in which two students went on a rampage, gunning down 13 students before killing themselves.

On a list of concerns about school quality, parents, taxpayers, and educators rated school safety highest (Olson, 1999b). The costs of school crime and vandalism are staggering, more than $200 million a year, according to some estimates (Geiger, 1993). Theft is most common; in 1997 it constituted 62 percent of all crimes against students, and nearly 5 percent of teachers reported theft crimes (U.S. Department of Education, 1998c). In addition, about 4 out of every 1,000 teachers were victims of violent crime at school. During the 1996–1997 school year, 6,093 students were expelled for possession or use of a firearm (U.S. Department of Education, 1998c).

For up-to-date information on national efforts to curb violence in schools, go to the Companion Website at **www.prenhall.com/kauchak**, then to this chapter's *Web Links* module.

CW

Increasing Understanding 4.9

Why might student concerns about safety and violence peak at the eighth-grade level? What implications does this have for middle schools? For middle school teachers?

Student concerns about safety and violence are highest at the eighth-grade level and decline as students get older. Urban students are more likely (33%) to report serious problems with violence than suburban (22%) or rural (18%) students, and concerns about violence are greatest in high-poverty areas (Louis Harris & Associates, 1996).

School violence is often associated with gangs, but the proportion of young people that actually join gangs is small. The Justice Department estimated that in 1995 the number of youth gang members numbered only 250,000 out of 47 million American youths aged 12 to 25 (Stepp, 1996).

School uniforms. Largely in response to students wearing gang colors, a growing number of public schools are requiring students to wear uniforms. Proponents claim that gang clothing and designer sports clothes contribute to violence, fights, and overall delinquency. In addition, clothes serve as a visual reminder of the economic disparities between students. Long Beach School District in California started the school uniform trend, and about 20 percent of the nation's school districts—including Chicago, Miami, and Phoenix—allow individual schools to require uniforms (Portner, 1999b).

The results of the Long Beach experiment with school uniforms are impressive. After the uniform policy was implemented, school crime dropped by 76 percent, assaults by 85 percent, and weapons offenses by 83 percent. Attendance figures rose. Proponents argued that these results were due to students being required to wear uniforms.

However, critics of school uniforms point to research indicating school uniforms have no direct result on behavioral problems or attendance (Brunsma & Rockquemoro, 1999). Instead, they argue, the positive effects are due to greater parental involvement in the school and a visible and public symbol of commitment to school improvement and reform.

Bullying A more subtle form of school violence, bullying, is receiving increased attention, as educators are realizing its damaging effects on students, as well as possible links to suicide and school shootings. One U.S. Secret Service study found bullying to be a factor in two thirds of school shooting incidents (Viadero, 2003d). Another study found that both bullies and victims were more likely to carry a weapon, bring it to school, and become involved in serious fights (Viadero, 2003e). In response to school shootings and lawsuits brought against schools by victims of bullying, 11 states—California, Colorado, Georgia, Louisiana, Minnesota, Nevada, New Hampshire, Oklahoma, Oregon, Vermont, and Washington—have mandated that schools take steps to reduce bullying (D. Cooper & Snell, 2003).

All of us remember teasing and taunting in the halls and school playgrounds, and many parents and educators considered this to be a normal rite of passage. Recent research, however, links bullying to a number of antisocial and aggressive behaviors that can have negative consequences for both bullies and victims. People who bully take advantage of imbalances in power, such as greater size or physical strength, higher status, or the support of a peer group. The bullying itself can be a face-to-face attack, threats, teasing about perceived sexual orientation, or telling someone in a mean way that he or she can't participate or play. It can also include behind-the-back behaviors, such as starting or spreading malicious rumors, writing harmful graffiti, or encouraging others to exclude a particular child (D. Cooper & Snell, 2003; Kerr, 2000).

Bullying is more common than many adults realize. In a survey of middle school students, 1 in 4 reported being bullied several times in a 30-month period, and 1 in 10 said the bullying occurred once a week or more (Institute for Families in Society, 1997). In other studies, nearly one third of students reported that they had been bullies, victims, or both in the last month (Viadero, 2003e), and 9 percent of teenagers reported avoiding at least one place in school because of concerns for their personal safety (Kaufman et al., 1999). Experts say that the actual incidence of bullying may be higher than reported. Bullying most commonly occurs in areas where students interact informally with little adult supervision, such as playgrounds, hallways, cafeterias, and school buses (Astor, Meyer, & Pitner, 2001).

Adults often fail to take steps to address the problem because of a series of misconceptions, which include the following:

- *Everyone knows what bullying is.* In fact, adults often mistake aggression for rough-and-tumble play and misperceive bullying incidents in as many as 1 in 5 episodes (Boulton, 1996).
- *Boys will be boys.* Although people often perceive bullying as physical aggression committed by boys, girls bully as often as boys (Craig, Pepler, & Atlas, 2000). Girls tend to use more subtle forms of bullying, however, such as malicious gossip and social exclusion (Crick & Grotpeter, 1995).
- *Only a small number of students are bullied.* Nearly every student in a school can be affected by bullying, and estimates indicate that 10 percent are victims of chronic bullying (D. Cooper & Snell, 2003).
- *Adults are already doing all they need to do.* This is one of the most serious misconceptions. Students often don't tell adults when they've been bullied, because they believe that adults won't intervene. Research supports these students' beliefs: Adults rarely intervene in bullying incidents (Craig et al., 2000).
- *Students are just tattling.* Adults often dismiss students' reports of bullying as simply tattling, which perpetuates students' beliefs that adults don't take incidents of bullying seriously. Adults need to learn to recognize the difference between tattling—an attempt to get someone into trouble—and reporting—an attempt to keep someone safe (D. Cooper & Snell, 2003).

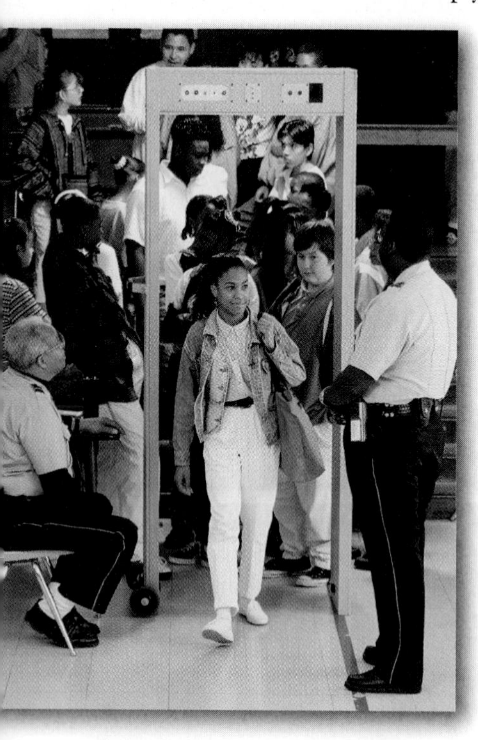

Schoolwide security programs attempt to make schools safe places to learn.

Attempts to prevent bullying focus on changing both individuals and the school climate. Bullying behaviors are often learned, with modeling and reinforcement by parents and peers playing major roles (McDevitt & Ormrod, 2002). For example, bullies often come from homes where parents are authoritarian, hostile, and rejecting. The parents often have poor problem-solving skills and advocate fighting as a solution to conflicts (X. Ma, 2001). In addition, some children who bully may have deficits in the ability to understand others' perspectives, empathy, moral development, and emotional self-regulation (Eisenberg & Fabes, 1998). Efforts to eliminate bullying at the individual level attempt to help students understand the consequences of their negative behaviors and also attempt to teach alternative prosocial behaviors (McDevitt & Ormrod, 2002). Schoolwide efforts are described in the next section.

Schoolwide Safety Programs Schoolwide safety programs are designed to make schools safe havens for teaching and learning. One way to do this is through comprehensive anti-bullying programs (Galley, 2002). Successful programs require commitment from parents, administrators, and teachers to take a proactive stance against bullying and monitor areas where bullying is most common—playgrounds, lunchrooms, and hallways.

In other attempts to increase school safety, many schools are adopting comprehensive security measures, such as having visitors sign in, closing campuses during lunch, and controlling access to school buildings. Many schools are adding prevention policies that include use of hallway police, student photo ID badges, transparent book bags, hand-held metal detectors, and breathalyzers to check for alcohol consumption. Students are being warned to avoid jokes about violence and given hotline numbers to anonymously report any indications that a classmate could turn violent. Schools are also making discipline more strict, creating peer buddy systems and adult mentorship programs, and teaching conflict resolution skills (Bender & McLaughlin, 1997; Sauter, 1995).

School Violence and Teachers As a teacher, you will be asked to deal with the problems of aggressive students and the possibilities of violence. Involving parents is an important first step (Powell, McLaughlin, Savage, & Zehm, 2001; Vergon, 2001). The vast majority of parents (88%) want to be notified immediately if school problems occur (L. Harris, Kagay, & Ross, 1987). You will need to consult with school counselors and psychologists, social workers, and principals, all of whom are trained to deal with these problems and can provide advice and assistance. Experienced teachers can provide you with information about how they've handled similar problems. You won't have to face persistent or serious problems of violence or aggression alone, and as you continue with your teacher preparation program, you'll be taught specific skills you can use in a variety of classroom discipline situations.

Although violence and aggression may seem frightening, they should be put into perspective. The incidence of school violence has actually decreased since 1993, and students are at much greater risk of suffering from violence outside rather than inside schools (Schlozman, 2002a). Violence remains a possibility, but the majority of your day-to-day teaching problems will be issues of student cooperation and motivation. Most problems can be prevented, others can be dealt with quickly, and some will require individual attention. We all hear about students carrying guns to school and

ACTION, REACTION, AND ZERO TOLERANCE

This ABC News video examines the effects of zero tolerance policies on schools and students. The news crew first visits an elementary school in Irvington, New Jersey, where an 8-year-old boy was expelled for playing cowboys and Indians with a paper gun. Next the program focuses on a high school in Virginia where the school mascot, a Spartan, is not allowed to wear a cardboard sword.

Think About This

1. What are the major goals of zero tolerance policies?
2. What are the advantages and disadvantages of zero tolerance policies?
3. What could schools do to minimize the negative effects of zero tolerance policies?

CW *To answer these questions online and receive immediate feedback, go to the Companion Website at* www.prenhall.com/kauchak, *then to this chapter's* Video Perspectives *module.*

Teaching in an Era of Reform

THE ZERO TOLERANCE ISSUE

The enormous publicity generated by school shooting incidents has led many schools around the country to experiment with new approaches to making our schools safer places to learn and work. One of the most controversial approaches involves the issue of zero tolerance.

Zero tolerance policies *call for students to receive automatic suspensions or expulsions as punishment for certain offenses, primarily those involving weapons, threats, or drugs.* Such policies have become increasingly popular across the nation (Skiba & Peterson, 1999). The era of zero tolerance began in 1994 when Congress passed the Gun-Free Schools Act, which required states receiving federal funds to expel for one year any student who brought a weapon to school (N. Stein, 2000). Recently, more than three quarters of all schools reported having zero tolerance policies; these policies were more common in school districts with large minority populations (Holloway, 2001/2002).

The need for safe schools is obvious, and the premise behind zero tolerance policies—that students who seriously endanger or disrupt the learning environment for the majority of the school population should be removed—also is intuitively sensible. Students can't learn when they're worried about either their physical or emotional well-being. Not surprisingly, both parents and other taxpayers have ranked school safety as the most important characteristic of an effective school (Olson, 1999b).

However, despite their popularity, zero tolerance policies also have problems (Ayers, Dohrn, & Ayers, 2001). One negative consequence is that the annual U.S. suspension rate went from 3.7 percent to 6.9 percent between 1974 and 1998, an 86 percent increase (Johnston, 2000d). During the 1996–1997 school year, the most common reasons students were expelled were bringing firearms or other weapons to school (94% and 91% of expelled students, respectively); possessing drugs (88%), alcohol (87%), or tobacco (79%); and committing acts of violence (79%). During that same period, 6,093 students were expelled for bringing weapons to school. The majority of the expulsions occurred in high schools (56%), although middle schools/junior highs and elementary schools also expelled students (34% and 9%, respectively) (Bushweller, 1998).

In addition, because these policies don't discriminate between major and minor disruptions, schools sometimes punish students for trivial and innocent transgressions. For example, one fifth grader was suspended for bringing a miniature plastic gun to school with his G.I. Joe action figure, and in another case a 6-year-old was suspended for kissing one of his classmates (Cornelius, 2002; Skiba & Peterson, 1999).

When expulsions occur, only 56 percent of students are sent to an alternative placement; the remainder are sent home to fend for themselves, making the likelihood of truancy and crime even greater

CW

Increasing Understanding 4.10

Parents consistently rate discipline and safety among their top concerns about schools (Rose & Gallup, 2002). Are these concerns justified? Defend your position with information from this section.

incidents of assault on teachers in the news. Statistically, however, considering the huge numbers of students that pass through schools each day, these incidents remain very infrequent.

Suicide The suicide rate among adolescents has quadrupled in the last 50 years; after accidents and homicide, suicide is now the third leading cause of teen death (Bostic, Rustuccia, & Schlozman, 2001). Each year about 5,000 youths take their own lives, and 2 percent of girls and 1 percent of boys make suicide attempts

(Skiba & Peterson, 1999). One student described the problem in this way:

> When they suspend you, you get in more trouble, 'cause you're out in the street. . . . And that's what happened to me once. I got into trouble one day 'cause there was a party, and they arrested everybody in that party. . . . I got in trouble more than I get in trouble at school, because I got arrested and everything. (Skiba & Peterson, 1999, p. 376)

Expelled students typically fall further behind, experience increased social difficulties, and sometimes never return to complete school (Barr & Parrett, 2001).

Critics of zero tolerance also point to the disproportionate number of minorities affected by the policies. African American students made up 17 percent of all students in the 1998–1999 school year but accounted for 33 percent of students suspended, whereas White students made up 63 percent of enrollments and 50 percent of suspensions. Also, Native American and Hispanic males were 1.2 times more likely to be suspended than White males (Vergon, 2001), and students with disabilities were suspended at twice the rate of those without disabilities (Holloway, 2001/2002). Explanations for these uneven rates range from higher rates of poverty and misbehavior, to inexperienced teachers, crowded classrooms, and academically sterile learning environments.

School leaders can significantly influence the implementation of zero tolerance policies (Johnston, 2000d; Vergon, 2001). For instance, one middle school in Dade County, Florida, had an expulsion rate of 34 percent, whereas another—serving basically the same student population—had a rate of only 2.8 percent. Students at the second school who were involved in a fight, for example, were given alternative punishments (such as in-school suspensions) or work assignments (such as cleaning the cafeteria), instead of suspensions. School leaders increase the effectiveness of discipline programs by clearly communicating policies to both students and parents (Vergon, 2001).

As with all reforms, efforts to increase school safety are neither totally positive or negative. Unquestionably, schools must be safe. How this should be accomplished remains controversial. Despite problems, zero tolerance programs are, in all likelihood, here to stay. As experts in this area concluded, "eliminating zero tolerance policies is a hard sell because the concept is *simple* to understand, sounds *tough*, and gives the impression of *high standards* for behavior" (Curwin & Mendler, 1999, p. 120). As a professional, you need to be as knowledgeable as possible about these issues so that you can implement policies in ways that benefit students and can make informed contributions to the decision-making process.

You Take a Position

Now it's your turn to take a position on the issue. State in writing whether you feel that zero tolerance programs make schools safer and better places to learn, and provide a two-page rationale for your position.

CW

For additional references and resources, go to the Companion Website at **www.prenhall.com/kauchak**, *then to this chapter's* Teaching in an Era of Reform *module. You can respond online or submit your response to your instructor.*

(Bostic et al., 2001). For every teenager who commits suicide, 100 more will try (Portner, 2000a). Although girls are more likely than boys to attempt suicide, boys are 4 times more likely to succeed. Boys tend to employ more lethal means, such as shooting themselves, whereas girls choose more survivable methods, such as overdosing on drugs.

Causes of teen suicide vary, but most are related to the stresses of adolescence. They include family conflicts, parental unemployment and divorce, drug use, failed peer relationships, and peer harassment (especially for homosexual youngsters).

Increasing Understanding 4.11

Why are teachers so important in identifying potential suicide victims?

Potential suicide indicators include the following:

- An abrupt change in the quality of schoolwork
- Withdrawal from friends or classroom and school activities
- Neglect of personal appearance or radical changes in personality
- Changes in eating or sleeping habits
- Depression, as evidenced by persistent boredom or lack of interest in school activities
- Student comments about suicide as a solution to problems

Teachers play a critical role in identifying child abuse.

Teachers observing these signs should contact a school counselor or psychologist immediately; early intervention is essential.

Child Abuse Child abuse is another serious problem in today's society. In 2001 child protective services agencies received 2.7 million reports of child abuse; investigation of these cases confirmed that more than 900,000 children had been victims of abuse or maltreatment (U.S. Department of Health and Human Services, 2003). Because abuse and neglect are often hidden or not reported, reliable figures are difficult to obtain. Almost three fifths of abuse victims suffer from neglect, about one fifth experience physical abuse, and about one tenth are sexually abused. When sexual abuse occurs, it most commonly involves a family member or friend. Although child abuse can occur at any level of society, it tends to be associated with poverty and is often linked to parental substance abuse.

Teachers are in a unique position to identify child abuse because they work with children every day. Symptoms of abuse include the following:

Increasing Understanding 4.12

Is child abuse easier to detect at the elementary or secondary level? Why?

- Neglected appearance
- Sudden changes in either academic or social behavior
- Disruptive or overly compliant behavior
- Repeated injuries such as bruises, welts, or burns

Teachers in all 50 states are legally bound to report suspicions of child abuse. Teachers and schools are protected from civil and criminal liability if the report is made honestly, and includes behavioral data, such as observations of the symptoms just listed.

Reflect on This

To analyze a case study examining issues involved in reporting child abuse, go to the Companion Website at **www.prenhall.com/kauchak**, then to this chapter's *Reflect on This* module.

Students Placed At-Risk

The conditions we've been describing in this chapter—changing families, poverty, violence, abuse of alcohol and other drugs, suicide, and child abuse—are serious problems. In many instances, two or more problems occur together, placing students at-risk for academic failure. **Students placed at-risk** are *those in danger of failing to complete their education with the skills necessary to survive in modern society* (Slavin, Karweit, & Madden, 1989). The term *at-risk* is borrowed from medicine, where it is used in describing individuals who have conditions or habits that make them likely to develop a specific disease; for example, an overweight person with high blood pressure is described as being at-risk for a heart attack. The term became widely used after 1983, when the National Commission on Excellence in Education proclaimed the United States a "nation at risk" (National Commission on Excellence in Education, 1983), emphasizing the growing link between education and economic well-being in today's technological society.

The problem of students dropping out or leaving school has significant economic implications. For example, between 1979 and 1996 the real earnings of 25- to 34-year-old male dropouts fell by 28 percent (Murnane & Tyler, 2000). In 2000, 11 percent of U.S. youth 16 to 24 years old either were not enrolled in a high school program or had not completed high school (Kaufman, Alt, & Chapman, 2001). Hispanic youths are the most likely to become dropouts. It has been estimated that, of the youth that will drop out of school, 28 percent will be Hispanic, 13 percent will be African American, 7 percent will be White, and 4 percent will be Asian American. Dropout rates are also strongly affected by poverty; students from low-income families are 6 times more likely to drop out than those from high-income families (Kaufman et al., 2001).

In recent years much attention has been focused on problems and issues involving students placed at-risk (Barr & Parrett, 2001). Table 4.1 outlines some of the academic, social, and emotional problems students placed at-risk experience. Almost certainly, you will have some of these students in your classes.

The presence of "male" as a background factor should be clarified. Although males are more likely to experience difficulties in school and to drop out, girls who do drop out are more likely to end up in poverty than male dropouts (American Association of University Women, 1992). In addition, many girls who drop out are pregnant and are left with the burden of single parenting on a below-the-poverty-level income. Being placed at-risk is a problem facing both male and female students.

Before continuing, we want to offer an additional note of caution. Some critics contend that using the term *at-risk* is ill-advised (Benard, 1994; Franklin, 1997), arguing

Table 4.1 Characteristics of Students Placed At-Risk

Background Factors	Educational Problems
Low SES	High dropout rates
Inner city	Low grades
Male	Retention in grade
Transient	Low achievement
Minority	Low participation in extracurricular activities
Non-native English speaker	Low motivation
Divorced families	Poor attendance
	High rate of drug use
	Misbehavior in classes
	Low self-esteem
	High criminal activity rates
	Low standardized test scores
	Lack of interest in school
	High suspension rates

that teachers form low expectations of labeled students, which contributes to underachievement. As teachers, we need to be sensitive to the possibility of negative stereotyping and continually ask ourselves, "Am I demanding as much as possible from these students, and am I providing every opportunity for their success?" The following sections describe different ways to increase the likelihood of this happening.

It Takes a Village: The Community-Based Approach to Working with Children Placed At-Risk

This chapter has focused on changes in society that can influence student learning and success, such as poverty, violence, and drug use. Responses to these negative influences have varied from denial to making our schools "fortresses"—safe havens in troubled communities. More recent approaches have focused on actively involving parents and other adult members of the community in redesigning schools to better meet the needs of children placed at-risk (Comer, Haynes, Joyner, & Ben-Avie, 1996; Frank & Walker-Moffat, 2001).

One example is the School Development Program, created by Yale psychiatrist James Comer (Comer, 1994). It integrates schools and the community by bringing principals, teachers, and parents together in school planning and management teams. School services, such as counseling and support for students with learning problems, are coordinated through teams of psychologists, counselors, and special educators. This coordination is important because services for students are often fragmented. For example, one depressed, pregnant, drug-using teenager saw three different counselors each week: a suicide prevention counselor, a parenting counselor, and a drug abuse counselor. None of them talked to each other (Tyson, 1999). Educational programs need to focus on educating the whole child by attending to children's physical, social, emotional, and academic growth through coordinated efforts.

From its start in New Haven, Connecticut, the School Development Program has spread to more than 500 schools across the country. Evaluations indicate that the program is effective. Achievement has increased significantly, student self-concepts have improved, and absences, suspensions, and management problems have declined in the schools where the program is fully implemented (Comer, 1994).

Promoting Student Resilience

In this chapter we've presented research examining societal factors that place students at-risk for school failure. More recent studies, however, have focused on **resilient students,** *students placed at-risk who have been able to rise above adverse conditions to succeed in school and in other aspects of life* (M. Wang, Haertel, & Walberg, 1995). Researchers became interested in resilience for both theoretical and practical reasons. From a theoretical perspective, studying resilience helps us understand the process of development, especially in youth placed at-risk, and practically, it identifies practices that foster healthy, academically successful learners.

Resilient children have well-developed "self systems," including high self-esteem and feelings that they are in control of their destinies. They set personal goals, possess good interpersonal skills, and have positive expectations for success (Benard, 1993; Wang et al., 1995). These strengths result in higher academic achievement, motivation, and satisfaction with school (Waxman & Huang, 1996).

How do students' adaptive skills develop? First, resilient children have relationships with caring adults who hold high moral and academic expectations for them (Frank & Walker-Moffat, 2001). (Think about the impact you might have on a student; you could be that caring adult.) Second, they come from schools that are both demanding and supportive; in many instances, schools serve as homes away from home. Let's look more closely at how schools and teachers help develop resilience in students.

Effective Schools for Students Placed At-Risk Effective schools for students placed at-risk focus on mutual respect between teachers and students, personal responsibility, and cooperation (Barr & Parrett, 2001; Griffith, 2002). They emphasize the following:

- A safe, orderly school climate in which students understand the meaning behind and the purpose of school and classroom rules
- Academic objectives focusing on mastery of content
- Caring and demanding teachers and high expectations for all students
- Cooperation, a sense of community, and prosocial values
- Student responsibility and self-regulation; decreased emphasis on external controls
- Strong parental involvement

Increasing Understanding 4.13

Explain how these characteristics of effective schools could contribute to resiliency in students placed at-risk.

These same strategies seem to work in other countries and cultures; a study of students placed at-risk in Israel arrived at essentially the same conclusions about which schools were effective (Gaziel, 1997).

Effective Teachers for Students Placed At-Risk Well-run and academically focused schools are important, but they aren't sufficient. Professional teachers who are highly skilled and sensitive are critical (Haberman, 1995, Jordan, 2001). In Chapter 1 we said that professionals are skilled in making decisions in ill-defined situations. This ability is essential in working with students placed at-risk because their needs and personal sensitivities make them particularly vulnerable to failure, personal slights, hints of favoritism, and questions about the relevance of school.

What makes a teacher effective with students placed at-risk? How can teachers help students develop resilience and make connections between their lives and the classroom? Let's have students tell us. A ninth grader gave this view:

• • ● • •

Well it's like you're family, you know. Like regular days like at home, we argue sometimes, and then it's like we're all brothers and sisters and the teachers are like our guardians or something.

And the teachers really get on you until they try to make you think of what's in the future and all that. It's good. I mean it makes you think, you know, if every school was like that I don't think there would be a lot of people that would drop out. (Greenleaf, 1995, p. 2)

• • ● • •

Interviews with other high school students offer additional perspectives about effective teachers:

Melinda: I act differently in his [Appleby's] class—I guess because of the type of teacher he is. He cuts up and stuff. . . . He is hisself—he acts natural—not tryin' to be what somebody wants him to be . . . he makes sure that nobody makes fun of anybody if they mess up when they read out loud.

Bernard: [I like him] just by the way he talk, he were good to you . . . he don't be afraid to tell you how he feels—he don't talk mean to you, he just speak right to you . . . some teachers only likes the smart people—and Coach Appleby don't do that. (Dillon, 1989, pp. 241–242)

Schools and teachers exert a powerful influence on the development of resilience in their students.

Another student noted:

. . ● . .

She listens to us! She respects us! She lets us express our opinions! She looks us in the eye when she talks to us! She smiles at us! She speaks to us when she sees us in the hall or in the cafeteria! (Ladson-Billings, 1994, p. 68)

. . ● . .

Alienation from school is a problem for students placed at-risk (Barr & Parrett, 2001). Boredom, lack of involvement, and feelings that they are unwelcome keep them on the fringe, prevent them from participating in school experiences, and lower motivation. When bright spots appear, they are usually the result of teachers who care about these students as people and learners (Drajem, 2002; Jordan, 2001).

How do effective teachers communicate this caring? First, they make a special effort to know all of their students.

. . ● . .

I think with children one of the things you have to do first is to get to know them. Even with those you find a little bit hard to like at first, you have to find something that you really appreciate about that child so that you can really teach them, because if you don't you're not going to get any place. (Darling-Hammond, 1997, p. 81)

. . ● . .

Individual kids' needs, awarenesses, and differences are part of understanding the whole teaching process. Whether you have a kid sitting in the front row because he has a visual problem and you have to have an auditory contact, a kid back there who doesn't speak English, a kid who has parents who are breaking up, a kid over here who has just been in a fight with somebody outside the classroom, or a kid who has physical handicaps, it all depends on the situation. . . . There are all types of problems and, of course, the more you know, it puts you in a better situation. (Darling-Hammond, 1997, p. 81)

. . ● . .

Knowing our students both helps us relate to them as people and helps us adapt instruction to their special needs.

A study examining the practices of teachers working with urban junior high students placed at-risk can help us understand differences between teachers who are more and less effective in working with youth placed at-risk. The study by Kramer-Schlosser (1992) used the terms *high-impact* and *low-impact* to describe the teachers. **High-impact teachers** *create caring, personal learning environments and assume responsibility for their students' progress.* They talk with students, find out about their families, and share their own lives. They maintain high expectations, use questioning to involve students in lessons, and emphasize success and mastery of content. They motivate students through personal contacts, and attempt to link school to students' lives. They create vibrant, interesting, and supportive learning environments where teachers grant students no excuses for not succeeding (Weiner, 2002).

Low-impact teachers, in contrast, *are authoritarian, distancing themselves from students and placing primary responsibility for learning on them.* They view instructional help as "babying the student" or "holding the student's hand." Instruction is teacher-directed and lecture-oriented, and students hold the primary responsibility for their own motivation.

Students think of low-impact teachers as adversaries, to be avoided if possible, tolerated if not. In contrast, they seek out high-impact teachers, both in class and out. In the Kramer-Schlosser study, teacher caring, communication, and investment in relationships affected the behaviors and attitudes of marginal students; the students reported losing interest in learning when teachers distanced themselves (Kramer-Schlosser, 1992; Weiner, 2002). Other studies have found effective teachers for students placed at-risk to be ap-

Caring teachers with high expectations for success help students placed at-risk achieve in school.

proachable, pleasant, easy to relate to, accepting, concerned, caring, and sensitive to students' needs (D. Brown, 2002; Sanders & Jordan, 1997). Personalized, caring learning environments are important for all students; for students placed at risk, they are essential. But beyond the human element, what else can teachers do?

Effective Instructional Structure and Support

Case STUDY When students entered Dena Hine's classroom after recess, they saw a review assignment on the chalkboard. As Dena took roll, students got out their books and started on the assignment.

Five minutes later, Dena began with a brief review of the previous day's lesson. Because the students were able to answer her questions quickly and correctly, she felt that the class knew the content and was ready to move on.

As she introduced two-column subtraction, she explained the new idea and gave each student bundles of 10 Popsicle sticks bound together with rubber bands. She guided students through the steps by having them take apart the bundles to illustrate the process, asking many questions as she went along. She also used questioning to help them link the manipulatives—the Popsicle sticks—to the numerals she wrote on the board. Then she had students solve problems on their own mini-chalkboards and hold them up to allow her to check their solutions. Whenever mistakes occurred, she stopped, explained the errors, and helped students correct them.

When 90 percent of the class was correctly solving the problems, Dena started the students on additional practice problems, which they checked in pairs when they were done. As they worked, she helped those still having difficulty, moving around the room to respond to pairs who disagreed with each other or had questions.

• • ● • •

How should teachers adapt their instruction to meet the needs of students placed at-risk? The overall suggestion is to offer more structure and support, as Dena did, while still challenging students and emphasizing concrete and real-world applications. Research consistently supports the need for instruction that is challenging, motivating, and connected to students' lives (Corbett & Wilson, 2002; Easton, 2002; Thompson, 2002).

Teachers of students placed at-risk don't need to teach in fundamentally different ways; instead, they need to apply effective strategies more systematically (Eggen &

Kauchak, 2004). They need to provide enough instructional support to ensure success while at the same time teaching students active learning strategies that allow them to take control of their own learning. Effective practices for teaching students placed at-risk include the following:

CW

Increasing Understanding 4.14

Which of these instructional practices would be most effective in promoting student resilience? Why?

- Communicating high expectations for student success
- Emphasizing student responsibility
- Giving frequent feedback and ensuring high success rates
- Using interactive teaching with frequent questions
- Increasing structure and support through use of clear teacher explanations and modeling (Gladney & Greene, 1997; M. Wang et al., 1995)

Communicating high expectations for student success is a key practice that influences the effectiveness of all the others. But how is this accomplished? One student recalls a former teacher:

• • • • •

My sixth-grade teacher was a coach. She could yell, scream, cajole, and nag with the best of them. But we knew that the constant pushing was for our benefit. "You know you can do better," was her favorite phrase. We laughed about her repeating it so often. On the playground and in our neighborhoods we would tease each other when we were not successful at stickball or double Dutch. "You know you can do better," we would sing and quickly dissolve into laughter. Funny, the sound of her voice repeating that phrase haunted me as a college student, as a graduate student, and as a university professional: "You know you can do better!" (Ladson-Billings, 1994, p. 25)

• • • • •

Through her daily interactions with students, this teacher was able to instill in them the feeling that they truly could do better.

Reflect on This

To analyze a case study examining instructional issues relating to teaching students placed at-risk, go to the Companion Website at **www.prenhall.com/kauchak**, then to this chapter's *Reflect on This* module.

Decision Making

Defining Yourself as a Professional

Working with today's students requires redefined roles for teachers. This redefined role will require teachers to refocus their efforts and perhaps seek additional training to address new challenges. Traditionally, teachers' efforts were limited to their work in classrooms, and their focus was on academics. Today's student population requires teachers to think more broadly and to consider students' overall emotional and physical development in addition to their academic growth.

Protecting and Nurturing Students

Schools are being increasingly asked to safeguard children's well-being. They're required to report suspected cases of child abuse and neglect. Many provide free breakfasts and lunches for the children of poverty. Effective schools are islands of safety and security in an often chaotic and sometimes dangerous world. Teachers often play a crucial role in ensuring that all of children's needs—physical, social, emotional, and intellectual—are being addressed.

Expanded Instructional Roles

Teachers' instructional roles are also changing. In an ideal world, students come to school motivated and prepared to learn. Many students do. For those who do not, however, teachers must consciously plan to motivate and involve them—in addition to helping them understand school topics. Stagnant teaching strategies, such as lecturing, that place students in passive listening roles won't work. Many students simply stop listening, and some put their heads down on their desks, making no pretense of paying attention.

Teachers are also being asked to make personal contact with students—not as "buddies," but rather as concerned caregivers committed to the total well-being of students. Effective professionals have always taken a personal interest in their students, but this dimension of teaching has become more important as more students come to our schools feeling unwelcome. Teachers play an essential role in creating schools that are student-friendly and classrooms that are warm and caring.

Involving Parents and Connecting with Homes

Today's teachers are also being asked to move outside the classroom. Learning is a cooperative venture, and teachers, students, and parents are in it together. In a comprehensive review of factors affecting student learning, researchers concluded the following:

> Because of the importance of the home environment to school learning, teachers must also develop strategies to increase parent involvement in their children's academic life. This means teachers should go beyond traditional once-a-year parent/teacher conferences and work with parents to see that learning is valued in the home. Teachers should encourage parents to be involved with their children's academic pursuits on a day-to-day basis, helping them with homework, monitoring television viewing, reading to their young children, and simply expressing the expectation that their children will achieve academic success. (M. Wang et al., 1993, pp. 278–279)

Communication with parents or other primary caregivers is not an appendage to the teaching process; it is an integral part of a teacher's job. Through their involvement in outreach programs, teachers can encourage parents to become actively involved in their child's education (Hoover-Dempsey & Sandler, 1997; Shumow & Harris, 1998). Teachers may be asked to work with other people in the community as well. Working with tomorrow's students will be more difficult and more challenging. It can also be more rewarding.

Summary

A Changing Society

Society is changing in a number of ways, and these changes have important implications for schools. Traditional family configurations have evolved into alternative patterns that include single-parent and extended families. The majority of mothers now work, raising concerns about child care and latchkey children. Poverty presents a number of challenges, ranging from hunger to homelessness.

Teenagers themselves are also changing. They are becoming sexually active at an earlier age, placing themselves at-risk for pregnancy and sexually transmitted disease. The use of alcohol and other drugs, violence, suicide, and child abuse all present challenges to youth as well as the teachers who work with them.

Students Placed At-Risk

Students placed at-risk face a number of challenges to school success. Community-based approaches to working with students placed at-risk actively involve parents in the community in designing and implementing educational programs. Effective schools for students placed at-risk create a safe, orderly learning environment in which academic goals are foremost. Studies of successful or resilient children suggest that caring home and school environments with supportive, understanding adults can help these students withstand societal challenges. Effective teachers for students placed at-risk combine interpersonal contacts with instructional structure and support. In working with at-risk students, teachers are advised to combine challenge with this support.

Important Concepts

Developing as a Professional

Praxis Practice

Read the case study, and answer the questions that follow.

Kari Statler sat, taking notes, alongside the seven other new teachers hired at John F. Kennedy Middle School, a large urban school serving a diverse and often at-risk student population. The assistant principal was going over schoolwide procedures to follow as students entered the school after the morning bell and transitioned from class. She explained that the school's tradition of having teachers at the door to greet students not only made the hallways safer and more orderly but also helped to make students feel more welcome. Next, she transitioned into the student advisor program. The program was designed to provide middle schoolers with a place where they felt connected—both to their homeroom teacher and to their classmates. The homeroom met for 20 minutes every day and provided teachers with an opportunity to get to know their students better. The meeting concluded with a discussion of the new parental involvement program, which asked students to accompany their parents to parent-teacher conferences in order to explain their portfolios and sometimes translate for their parents.

Back in her room, Kari looked at the stack of books on her desk. "Whew, this is going to be a busy year," she thought to herself. "All I keep hearing is *tests, tests, tests.* First the district, then the state, and maybe even a new one by the English department. Hmm, I had all these great ideas about teaching creative writing to students, but now it looks like all they want me to teach is grammar and punctuation. I can't just do that. My kids deserve more than that. They'll learn punctuation and grammar, but they'll also learn to write—and maybe even to enjoy it. I know they can do both, and that's my goal for the year—everyone writing clearly, with correct punctuation and grammar—and liking it besides!" A smile crossed her face.

The first week was a whirlwind of students, bells, and forms to fill out. By the second week, Kari had settled into an instructional routine. Every day began with a short assignment to assess the content discussed the day before. Students graded their own papers, and Kari stressed the need for student honesty and responsibility. When the grading was complete, Kari asked for a show of hands to see how well everyone had done. She also collected the papers so she could analyze them for any individual or group patterns or trends and so that she could adjust her instruction if need be.

To begin her unit on writing, she passed out two paragraphs, one clearly written and the other not. She asked students to pair up and analyze the two, looking for similarities and differences. In the whole-class discussion that followed, Kari used interactive questioning to establish the need for a topic sentence, supporting sentences that related to the topic, and a summarizing sentence that pulled together all the related ideas in the paragraph.

Next, Kari had each student write a paragraph on their favorite subject in school. Students wrote these on clear transparencies, which Kari would collect and display anonymously for the class to evaluate. "So far, so good," Kari thought as she circulated among her working students.

1. What characteristics of an effective school for students placed at-risk did Kari encounter?
2. What characteristics of an effective teacher for students placed at-risk did Kari display?
3. What aspects of Kari's instruction were effective for students placed at-risk?

To receive feedback on your responses to the Praxis Practice exercises, go to the Companion Website at **www.prenhall.com/kauchak**, then to this chapter's *Praxis Practice* module.

Discussion Questions

1. How would your role as a teacher change if you worked in an upper-SES suburb? in a lower-SES part of a city?
2. How would your actual instruction change if you worked in an upper-SES suburb? in a lower-SES part of a city?
3. What role should schools play in dealing with teenage sexuality?
4. What role should schools play in dealing with drug and alcohol abuse?
5. What strengths do students placed at-risk bring to the classroom? How can teachers take advantage of these strengths?
6. What will be your biggest challenges in working with the parents of students placed at-risk?

Video Discussion Questions

The following discussion question refers to video segments found on the Companion Website. To view the accompanying video, answer the question online, and receive immediate feedback, go to the Companion Website at **www.prenhall.com/kauchak**, then to this chapter's *Video Discussion* module.

1. Theodore Sizer is the director of the Coalition for Effective Schools, which attempts to reform high schools. A major challenge of high school reform efforts is helping students placed at-risk develop resiliency. From Mr. Sizer's perspective, what is the most important thing schools can do to foster resiliency in students? How do these suggestions compare to information in this chapter?

Going into Schools

1. Ask a teacher to identify a student who is at-risk for school failure. Arrange to interview the student, and ask questions like those that follow:
   a. Personal characteristics: What do you like to do when not in school (hobbies, music, sports, friends, activities, favorite foods, etc.)? Do you work? Do you like what you're doing? What do you want to do when you graduate? Do you intend to graduate? If not, why not?
   b. School: What about school do you like? dislike? How could schools be changed to make them better?

c. Class: What do you like about this class? What do you dislike? How could the class be changed to make it more pleasant? to make it a better learning environment?
d. School subjects: Which is your favorite? least favorite? Why?
e. Teachers: Which kinds of teachers do you like? dislike? What advice do you have for me as a new teacher?
f. Learning: How do you learn best? What do teachers do that helps students learn? What do they do that interferes with learning?
g. Motivation: What motivates you in school? out of school? How important are grades? In which classes do you work the hardest? Why?

What do the student's responses suggest about teaching students placed at-risk?

2. Interview a teacher who works with students who are at-risk. Ask the following questions:
   a. How are at-risk students similar to and different from other students?
   b. What strengths do at-risk students bring to the classroom?
   c. How do you adapt your teaching to meet the needs of at-risk students?
   d. What successful strategies do you use in working with the parents of at-risk students?
   e. What are the rewards and challenges of working with at-risk students?

   How do the teacher's responses compare with research in this chapter? What do these responses suggest about teaching students placed at-risk?
3. Interview a counselor at a school that enrolls a significant number of students placed at-risk. Ask the following questions:
   a. What proportion of the students in the school are considered at-risk? How does the school identify them?
   b. What special programs within the school are designed for these students?
   c. What kinds of outreach activities does the school have for connecting with the community?
   d. What kinds of different roles do teachers play in this school?

   How effective is this school in addressing the needs of students placed at-risk? On the basis of the information in this chapter, how might this school be changed to better address students' needs?
4. Identify a classroom with a high number of at-risk students. Observe a lesson in that class, and analyze it in terms of the following:
   a. Emotional tone of the classroom (e.g., supportive, warm, etc.)
   b. Student–teacher interactions
   c. Teacher expectations
   d. Interactive teaching (e.g., questioning, groupwork)
   e. Frequency of feedback

   Analyze the interaction on the basis of the recommendations in this chapter. Make suggestions for changes.

Virtual Field Experience

If you would like to participate in a Virtual Field Experience, go to the Companion Website at **www.prenhall.com/kauchak**, then to this chapter's *Field Experience* module.

Online Portfolio Activities

To complete these activities online, go to the Companion Website at **www.prenhall.com/kauchak**, then to this chapter's *Portfolio Activities* module.

Portfolio Activity 4.1

Personal Experiences with Societal Changes

INTASC Principle 9: Commitment

Personal Journal Reflection

The purpose of this activity is to encourage you to think about your own personal experiences with the societal changes described in this chapter. First, analyze your own personal development in terms of the following societal elements: family structure, child care, socioeconomic status, alcohol and drugs, and crime and violence. How have experiences with these various elements influenced your development? Next, think about how your experiences influenced the kind of education you received. Finally, reflect on how your personal experiences with societal changes will influence your effectiveness as a teacher, and think about things you can do to prepare yourself to work with students placed at-risk.

Portfolio Activity 4.2

Investigating Title I Programs and Students

INTASC Principle 3: Adapting Instruction

Locate the Web sites for your state's office of education or for several local school districts. (Phone numbers for local school districts can be found under "Schools" in the commercial White Pages at the back of a phone book. The offices you call will provide Web site addresses.). Browse the sites for information on Title I programs, and answer the following questions:

a. Which districts or schools offer the largest number of these programs?
b. What kinds of students (i.e., students from which cultural minority groups) are found in these programs?
c. What is the curriculum in these programs?
d. What is instruction like in these programs?

Based on this information, what are some ways that you can prepare yourself to teach in schools that have high percentages of Title I students?

Portfolio Activity 4.3

School Safety and Security

INTASC Principle 5: Motivation and Management

This activity is designed to familiarize you with school safety and security procedures in your area. Locate the Web sites of several local school districts. Browse the sites for information on student conduct policies and procedures, and read how each district handles discipline and safety issues. How are the procedures similar and different? How would they affect your life as a teacher?

Part 3

Foundations

Chapter 5

Education in the United States

Its Historical Roots

Education in the United States is unique. The organization of the schools, the content we teach, and our teaching methods all differentiate us from other countries around the world. History has been a major factor in shaping these differences. Our purpose in writing this chapter is to help you understand how our schools have evolved to their present state by examining the history of education in the United States. This knowledge will not only help you understand the schools you'll be working in but can also help you decide on the kind of teacher you want to become.

In this chapter we try to answer the following questions:

- How have European roots influenced American education?
- Why is religion a controversial issue in American education?
- What are the historical roots of a free, public education for all students?
- How have schools historically responded to different minority groups?
- What role should the federal government play in education?

Let's see how answers to these questions influence the lives of real teachers in our schools today.

This logo appears throughout the chapter to indicate where case studies are integrated with chapter content.

Case STUDY

"Phew, I think I've had it," Dave Carlisle, a first-year teacher, said as he plopped into an overstuffed chair in the teachers' lounge.

"Having a bad day?" Monica Henderson, one of Dave's colleagues at Westmont Middle School, asked.

"Bad day. You could say that," Dave replied. "We had lunch money missing again today. And I'm pretty sure there was cheating on the test I gave last week. It's like these kids have no moral compass. I think they could use a healthy dose of religion."

"We already tried that," Monica replied, looking up from the papers she was grading.

"When? Before I got here?" Dave asked.

"No," Monica replied. "Back in our country's history, and often since then."

"Oh, no. Not more of that history of ed stuff you're learning in that class you're taking."

"Hey, can I help it if I'm learning some interesting stuff that makes me think about what we're trying to do?" Monica replied with a smile.

"Yeah, I know, 'Those that don't know history are destined to repeat it,'" Dave said, rolling his eyes, "but how can history help me with my cheating and stealing problems?"

• • • • •

Studying the history of our country's educational system may not give teachers answers to their daily classroom problems, but it can provide them with a broader perspective on what they're doing and help them become more effective in their decision making. Understanding the role of religion in teaching, for example, can help teachers make professional decisions about the extent to which they can or should share deeply held religious beliefs with their students. In this chapter we examine the history of education in the United States and how that history can shed light on some of our most perplexing educational dilemmas.

The Colonial Period (1607–1775)

Character education, seen as a way to provide moral guidance in a confusing world filled with drugs, sex, and violence, is receiving increased attention in schools today (D. Doyle, 1997; Kohn, 1997). Educators generally agree that some form of moral education is needed in schools, but they disagree about the form and shape it should take. Some advocate linking character education closely to religious values that are normally taught in homes and churches. Others argue that this religious foundation is neither desirable nor possible given the religious diversity in the United States (Wynne, 1997). The roots of character education, as well as controversies about the shape it should take, can be found in the colonial period of education in America.

Parents who believe schools should teach values and emphasize student discipline often send their children to private, parochial (church-supported) schools. Should these schools receive federal assistance—money supported by general tax revenue? Proponents claim that parochial schools have as much right to federal education monies as any other schools. Opponents claim that federal support of parochial schools violates the principle of separation of church and state set forth in the First Amendment to the Constitution. The controversy about the proper place of religious schools in the United States is also rooted in the colonial period.

Religion and schools are closely linked in many states. Some Alabama public schools, for example, allow prayers in classrooms, hold religious assemblies, and distribute Bibles to students (Walsh, 1998a). Critics claim these practices also violate the principle of separation of church and state. Proponents counter that schools should teach family, spiritual, and moral values and that religion promotes these values. The issue, debated in court numerous times, reflects a continual tension in U.S. schools over the proper role that religion should play in public education. This tension has its beginnings in the colonial period.

These controversies illustrate the powerful role that religion plays in American education. Why is its role so powerful? The answers go back to the dawn of our country.

The beginnings of the relationship between religion and education in America can be traced to the founding of Jamestown in 1607. Before that time, New World explorers were primarily interested in "gold and glory"—conquering the New World for riches and adventure. The Jamestown settlers, in contrast, brought families and wanted to start new lives. Like parents today, they believed that the family was central to helping children grow up straight and strong, but they saw that they also needed help from schools. Colonial schools were formed in response to this need, and they laid the foundation for many of the controversies and structures in place today.

Although settlers came to the colonies for different reasons—in search of political independence, religious freedom, or simply a better life—they all brought with them values and beliefs derived from their European roots. As a result, schooling in colonial America had the same class and gender distinctions common in Europe at the time. Formal education was usually reserved for wealthy White males and ignored for females and those less wealthy. As in Europe, religion was an integral part of education, but the way this played out differed by region.

Differences in Colonies

Education in America has always been a process of people adapting and creating schools to meet their unique needs. Although the original 13 colonies shared some similarities, such as their cultural links with Europe and people's desire for better lives, there were regional differences, influenced by geography, economics, and the reasons the colonists came to America. Let's look at them.

The Southern Colonies Life in the Southern colonies—Maryland, Virginia, the Carolinas, and Georgia—centered around agriculture, much of which existed on large plantations where African slaves and indentured servants worked land owned by wealthy landlords. Poor White settlers worked small farms on the margins, barely scratching out an existence.

Life for most people in the colonial South was hard, and formal education was a luxury reserved for the wealthy (Cremin, 1970). Private tutors often lived on plantations, or parents would pool their resources to hire a tutor to teach the children of several families. Private schools sponsored by the Church of England and boarding schools for the wealthy were often found in the larger Southern cities, such as Charleston and Williamsburg. The English tradition of education for the wealthy few made an easy leap over the Atlantic to the Southern colonies.

CW

Increasing Understanding 5.1

From a student's perspective what were the advantages and disadvantages of receiving instruction in one's native language? From a national perspective, what were the advantages and disadvantages?

To answer the Increasing Understanding questions online and receive immediate feedback, go to the Companion Website at www.prenhall.com/kauchak, then to this chapter's *Increasing Understanding* module. Type in your response, and then study the feedback.

The Middle Colonies The middle colonies—New York, New Jersey, Delaware, and Pennsylvania—were more diverse than the colonies in the South. Although English-speaking people were the majority, substantial pockets of Dutch in New York, Swedes in Delaware, and Germans in Pennsylvania also existed. Also, whereas most of the Southern colonists were members of the Church of England, middle colonists belonged to a number of different religious groups. They were Dutch Reformists, Quakers, Lutherans, Baptists, Roman Catholics, and Jews (Cremin, 1970; Pulliam & Van Patten, 1999). Because religious freedom was a major reason for coming to America, and religion played such a central role in people's daily lives, it was difficult to create public schools that satisfied everyone.

In response to this diversity, families in the middle colonies created parochial schools. Students learned in their native languages, and local religious beliefs were an integral part of the curriculum.

The New England Colonies The New England colonies—Massachusetts, Connecticut, and New Hampshire—differed from the other colonies in two important ways. First, they were culturally and religiously homogeneous, which made consensus about school goals easier to achieve. Second, industry and commerce encouraged the clustering of people into towns, which allowed the formation of common schools.

As an example, let's look at Massachusetts. Puritans, the followers of John Calvin, settled in Massachusetts. As with colonists in the other regions, religion played a major role in the Puritans' lives. They came to America because of conflicts resulting from their attempts to reform the Church of England. Puritans believed that humans are inherently evil, having fallen when Adam and Eve committed original sin. Education helped people follow God's commandments and resist the devil's temptations. By

Religion was a major reason the Pilgrims came to America and a major force in shaping early schools.

learning to read and write, people gained access to God's word through the Bible. In addition, religious education contributed to a person's general character by promoting industry, resourcefulness, punctuality, and thrift. According to the Puritans, education was important because it made people more righteous.

The Puritans' views shaped the schools they created. Children were seen as savage and primitive, requiring education (religion) to become civilized and God-fearing. Play was viewed as idleness, children's talk was seen as prattle, and corporal punishment was commonly used to ensure conformity. Students were beaten with switches, forced to kneel on hard pebbles, and made to wear heavy wooden yolks as punishments for unacceptable behavior. It's easy to see why "Idle minds are the Devil's workshop" and "Spare the rod and spoil the child" were principles of Puritan education.

Religion also influenced curriculum and instruction. Reading, writing, arithmetic, and religion ("the four Rs") made up the curriculum. The *New England Primer* taught children the alphabet through rhymes such as the following:

> A—In *Adam's* Fall
> We Sinned all.
> B—Thy Life to Mend
> This *Book* Attend.

Instruction focused on memorization and recitation; children were expected to sit quietly for long periods of time, and they were discouraged from expressing opinions and asking questions. Teachers had no formal preparation about how or what to teach, and curriculum materials were scarce, if not nonexistent.

Paradoxically, a landmark piece of legislation, the *Massachusetts Act of 1647*, arose from this grim educational landscape. Also known as the **Old Deluder Satan Act,** it was *a law designed to create scripture-literate citizens who would thwart Satan's trickery.* It required every town of 50 or more households to hire a teacher of reading and

Table 5.1 Changes in Educational Thought in Europe

Thinker	Educational Views
John Amos Comenius (1592–1670) Czech philosopher	Questioned the effectiveness of memorization and recitation, emphasizing instead the need to base teaching on children's interests and needs
John Locke (1632–1704) English philosopher	Emphasized the importance of firsthand experiences in helping children learn about the world
Jean Jacques Rousseau (1712–1778) French philosopher	Viewed children as innately good and argued that teachers should provide children with opportunities for exploration and experimentation
Johann Pestalozzi (1746–1827) Swiss philosopher	Criticized authoritarian educational practices that stifled students' playfulness and natural curiosity and recommended that teachers use concrete experiences to help students learn

writing. The historical significance of this act is enormous, because it provided the legal foundation for public support of education. It gave birth to the idea that the public good was enhanced by government-sponsored efforts at public education, and it became a cornerstone of American education.

European Crosscurrents

As we've seen, American colonists brought many ideas from Europe, such as the view that education should be reserved for wealthy White males. Also, because schooling existed for religious purposes or for preparing the wealthy to be leaders, few attempts were made to relate the curriculum to the average person's practical needs or the long-term needs of a growing nation. As we also saw, teaching methods emphasized passive learning in the form of memorization and recitation.

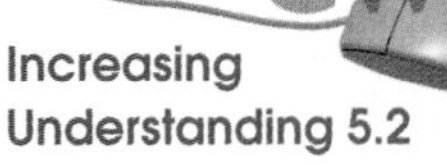

Increasing Understanding 5.2

How would these philosophers have reacted to the New England schools? What changes would they have recommended?

Forces of change were altering education in Europe, however, and these ideas slowly made their way across the Atlantic. Some of the prominent philosophers and their thinking are outlined in Table 5.1.

As we see in Table 5.1, the ideas came from different places, but all involved a more practical, humane, and child-centered view of education. These philosophers are important because they planted the seeds of educational change that would fundamentally alter the way students were taught in the United States.

The Legacy of the Colonial Period

The colonial period shaped American education in at least three ways. First, with few exceptions, poor Whites, females, and minorities such as Native Americans and African Americans were excluded from schools (Spring, 2001). William Berkeley, the aristocratic governor of Virginia, supported this exclusion and in 1671 railed against both free public education and access to books: "I thank God, *there are no free schools nor printing*, and I hope we shall not have them these hundred years, for *learning* has brought disobedience, and heresy, and sects into the world, and *printing* has divulged them, and libels against the best government" (Pulliam & Van Patten, 1999, p. 56). European ideas of class structures and privilege did not die easily in the New World. Given attitudes such as Berkeley expressed, it's easy to see why equality of educational opportunity wasn't realized until the mid-twentieth century. Some present-day critics argue that today's schools are still racist and sexist (Spring, 2001).

Second, the colonial period shaped our current system of education through actions that planted the seeds for public support of education (the Old Deluder Satan Act) and local control of schools. These two ideas have become important foundations of our present educational system.

Third, and perhaps most significantly, the relationship between religion and schooling prevalent in the colonial period influenced attitudes about education for many years. Examining that history helps us understand why religion continues to be an important issue in education. Let's take a closer look at religion in schools.

Religion in Schools Considering the colonial legacy and the courts' evolving interpretation of the First Amendment principle mandating separation of church and state (written just after the colonial period), it is easy to see why controversies about religion in schools exist. Three questions are commonly raised today:

- Should prayer be allowed in schools?
- Should federal dollars be used to provide instruction in religious schools?
- What role should religion play in character education?

Let's look at them.

Should prayer be allowed in schools? In colonial times prayer was an integral part of the curriculum. Today this question has become so controversial that the issue has been thrown to the courts, and their answer has generally been no. A federal court in Alabama, for example, ruled that praying in schools, holding religious assemblies, and giving students Bibles all violate separation of church and state (Walsh, 1998c). However, in a case involving graduation speeches, prayers were ruled legal, because they were voluntary and given by students (Walsh, 1998a). Further, some members of the House of Representatives sponsored a bill in 1998 that would have allowed organized voluntary prayers in the schools, but it fell 61 votes short of the 224 necessary for a two thirds majority (Walsh, 1998d). This legislative action revealed that prayer in U.S. schools was not a dead issue. More recently the U.S. Supreme Court ruled 6–3 that student-led prayers at Texas football games were unconstitutional, this time concluding that the prayers did violate separation of church and state (Walsh, 2000a).

Should federal dollars be used to provide instruction in religious schools? This wasn't an issue in the colonial period, because most schools were private and religion was an integral part of the curriculum. Today, however, the role of government funding for religious instruction is less clear and more controversial. For example, courts have generally ruled in favor of using federal monies to provide supplementary instruction for poor students or students with special needs who attend parochial schools (Walsh, 1998c). The Supreme Court also ruled that religious schools could receive government aid in the form of computers and library books (Walsh, 2000a).

Funding vouchers for parochial schools is another legally contentious matter, however. **Vouchers,** *checks or written documents that parents can use to purchase educational services,* have been promoted as one way to increase parental choice and involvement (Reinhard, 1997, 1998). Parents in Cleveland and Milwaukee, sites of two well-known voucher experiments, want to use vouchers (public monies) to send their children to parochial schools. Opponents contend this violates separation of church and state. Recently the U.S. Supreme Court, in a divided 5–4 vote, approved the use of public school funds for vouchers to religious and private schools (Walsh, 2002b). The next battlefield for the issue of public funds for religious schools will be the states, where 37 state constitutions currently forbid state aid to religious schools (Gehring, 2002b).

GOD AND EVOLUTION IN KANSAS CLASSROOMS

This ABC News video examines a recent controversy in which the Kansas Board of Education decided to drop the teaching of evolution from the required coursework in the state's public schools. It features interviews with Sue Gamble, a candidate for the school board, who questions this decision, as well as two experts on the topic.

Think About This

1. What are some reasons that religion is such a hotly debated topic in American education?
2. In what areas of the curriculum are teachers most likely to encounter debate over religious issues?
3. What are the advantages and disadvantages of including religion in our schools?

To answer these questions online and receive immediate feedback, go to the Companion Website at **www.prenhall.com/kauchak**, *then to this chapter's* Video Perspectives *module.*

What role should religion play in character education? **Character education** is *an approach to developing morality that suggests moral values and positive character traits, such as honesty and citizenship, should be emphasized, taught, and rewarded.* In colonial times, religion and character education were synonymous, and in some cases the primary purpose of education was religious training. The link between the two is controversial today, however, and religious diversity is one reason why. Although in a recent survey 87 percent of Americans said they considered themselves Christian, 5 million Muslims, 1 million Hindus, and almost a million Buddhists live in the United States, in addition to many people of Jewish faith and other smaller religious groups (Gibsen, 1998). Further, considerable religious diversity, ranging from liberal to ultraconservative denominations, exists within the Christian ranks. Given these differences, consensus about the role of religion in the development of students' character is extremely difficult.

The Early National Period (1775–1820)

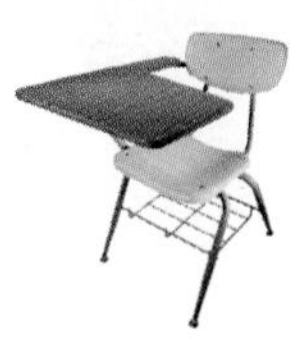

Case STUDY

Teresa Sanchez moved with her family from a large urban center in the Northeast to a large, sprawling city in the South. Although the teenager encountered changes in climate and lifestyle, she found her new high school surprisingly similar to the one she had previously attended. The two buildings and their physical layout were similar, with long hallways lined with lockers and interspersed with classrooms. Even the central office seemed the same, and the guidance counselor who worked with her assured her that she wouldn't lose any credits from the move.

But there were differences. Teresa rode a district school bus instead of using public transportation. The students, while friendly, talked differently and were interested in different things than her friends back home. And the textbooks she received, while covering the same basic material, did so in different ways.

Her mother, an elementary teacher, also noticed similarities and differences in the educational systems. She landed a new teaching position almost immediately but was told that her teaching certificate was only temporary and that she would have to take additional coursework for it to become permanent. The textbooks she was given were different, but the principal's emphasis on testing at the end of the year wasn't. Some things never change.

• • ● • •

The United States, at first glance, appears homogeneous. A McDonald's restaurant in California appears much like one in Ohio, for example, and television programs across the country are very similar. However, a closer look reveals both regional and state differences in the ways people look, act, and talk.

The same paradox occurs in education. Although schools across the country appear similar, a closer look reveals important regional and state differences. For example, students in Texas study Texas state history and take specially constructed tests to determine grade advancement. Bilingual education exists in many states with large numbers of English language learners, but its use in California has been severely limited by a statewide initiative. Why do these state-to-state differences occur? Some answers can be found by studying the early national period of our country.

Before about 1775 the United States was a loose collection of separate colonies that looked mostly to Europe for trade and ideas. During the 45 years of the early national period (1775–1820), however, the colonies became the United States of America, and this country shaped its future through the Constitution and the Bill of Rights. These laws shaped the future of American education as well.

Redefining American Education: Religion and the Schools

Religion, so important during the colonial period, posed a problem for our new nation. Many of the original colonists came here seeking religious freedom—freedom from state-sponsored or imposed religion. Because of the religious diversity that existed in the colonies, the framers of the Constitution refused to create a national reli-

The proper role of religion in schools continues to be a controversial issue.

gion, such as existed in England, the country colonists had just defeated in the Revolutionary War.

Our country's leaders dodged this thorny problem with the First Amendment to the Constitution, which prohibits Congress from making any law respecting the establishment of religion or any law prohibiting religious practice. As we saw earlier in the chapter, this amendment established the principle of *separation of church and state.* While religious freedom was ensured, religious ties with government were severed. Originally a driving force behind education, religion could no longer be government approved and sanctioned.

Educational Governance: Whose Responsibility?

The severing of governmental ties between religion and education raised an important question: Who would be responsible for organizing and running education in our new country? A national system of education was one option (Pulliam & Van Patten, 1999). Proponents argued that, in addition to developing an enlightened citizenry, a national system would best meet the country's agricultural, industrial, and commercial needs. Opponents cited the monolithic and unresponsive systems in Europe in their arguments against a national system. They also argued that the beginnings of viable local and state systems, such as those in Massachusetts, already existed. Why create another level of bureaucracy and control when it wasn't needed? The Constitution's framers sidestepped the issue with the Tenth Amendment, which said that areas not explicitly assigned to the federal government would be the responsibility of each state.

The Tenth Amendment was important for two reasons. First, it implicitly removed the federal government from a central role in running and operating schools, and second, it passed this responsibility on to the individual states. To support the educational efforts of the states, Congress passed the *Land Ordinance of 1785* and the *Northwest Ordinance of 1787.* The goal of these acts was to promote settlement of the present-day Midwest, which was then an undeveloped area of the country (K. Alexander & Alexander, 2001). These ordinances divided the land into townships, each 6 miles square and consisting of 36 sections; in each township, the income from one section was reserved for support of public education. The rationale for this financial support was contained in the text of the Northwest Ordinance: "Religion, morality, and knowledge being necessary to good government and the happiness of mankind, schools and the means of education shall forever be encouraged." This encouragement came in the form of federal land that states could use to support education. Although not directly involved in governing or operating schools, the federal government provided material support for schools and education, a tradition that persists to this day. With respect to education, the lines of responsibility between state and federal governments were already being blurred.

The Legacy of the Early National Period

The early national period shaped the schools of the future and planted the seeds of controversies to come. Three important actions that occurred during the period have had far-reaching effects on our educational system:

- The link between religion and schools was severed by the First Amendment to the Constitution, which established the principle of separation of church and state.
- Control of education was given to the states, rather than the federal government.
- The federal government expressed the view that education was essential for improving the quality of people's lives and helping the nation grow.

The influence of these three actions is still readily apparent in the policies and views of education in effect today. In education cases the U.S. courts have repeatedly upheld the principle of separation of church and state, and decisions about what occurs in the classroom are primarily made by individual states and local school districts (although public schools must adhere to federal laws and do receive some federal funding).

Although education remains in the hands of the states, it is increasingly viewed as an instrument of national goals and purposes, just as it was in the early national period (Tyack & Cuban, 1995). When the economy sputters and trade deficits mount, a national commission is often formed, and education is examined. The publication of *A Nation at Risk: An Imperative for Reform* (National Commission on Excellence in Education, 1983) is an example. The report suggested that American education was so poor that the nation was "at risk" of not being able to compete in the world marketplace. Some leaders argue that we need a national test to accurately assess the true state of the nation's schools. Both measures—national commissions and national tests—argue for a greater federal role in education, a highly controversial issue.

Reflect on This

To analyze a case study examining issues related to standardized testing and control of the curriculum, go to the Companion Website at **www.prenhall.com/kauchak**, then to this chapter's *Reflect on This* module.

The Common School Movement (1820–1865)

Case STUDY

Many of you reading this text will become teachers of elementary students and will work in public schools. Let's think for a moment about these schools. First, the children you'll teach will be required by law to be there; virtually all states require students to attend school until they are 16. Second, your salary and the salaries of other teachers and administrators, the building itself, your materials and supplies, the buses that will take kids to and from school, and even some of your students' lunches will be publicly supported, meaning a portion of local taxes will pay for these items. (Parents who choose to send their children to a private school pay tuition to defray these costs.)

Typically, your school will be organized into grade levels. Five-year-olds will be in kindergarten, 6-year-olds will be in the first grade, and so on. Some of the schools will include sixth graders; others will go only through grade 5. You will have a designated grade to teach; you'll be a first-grade teacher, or you'll teach fourth grade, for example.

To get a teaching job, you'll be required to be licensed. You'll have to complete a specified set of university courses (which is one reason you're in this class) and complete some clinical experiences in schools, including an internship. You'll probably also have to take a standardized test (the content of which will vary from state to state) to assess your competency as a teacher.

What are the origins of these practices and policies, and what are the historical roots that shaped a free public education for all students in the United States?

• • ● • •

Although developing a literate citizenry was a goal during the early national period, American education in the early 1800s remained a patchwork of schools designed primarily for the wealthy; the vast majority of children received little or no formal education. The common school movement changed that.

Historians commonly describe the period from 1820 to 1865 as the "Age of the Common Man." Andrew Jackson, a popular and down-to-earth person who gained fame as a general in the War of 1812, was elected president in 1828. Westward expansion provided opportunities for people and changed the social landscape; the poor and landless could start over by pulling up stakes and heading west. The land area of the United States nearly doubled between 1830 and 1865, and the population increased from 13 to 32 million, 4 million of whom were new immigrants (U.S. Government Printing Office, 1975).

CW

Increasing Understanding 5.3

Where do recent immigrants to the United States come from? Where do most immigrants in your specific region come from? How will immigrants' countries of origin affect schools and the teachers in them?

This expansion presented both opportunities and challenges. Industrialization created jobs and contributed to the growth of cities such as New York and Boston, but it also resulted in pollution, crime, and the development of urban slums. Many new immigrants didn't speak English and were unaccustomed to American ways of living. The country needed a citizenry that could participate in decisions and contribute to the nation's economy, but most people were functionally illiterate. America turned to its schools for help.

The Common School Movement: Making Education Available to All

As we saw in the last section, the American educational system at the beginning of the nineteenth century was a patchwork of private and quasi-public schools. Those defined as "public" often charged partial tuition, discouraging all but the wealthiest from attending. States didn't coordinate their efforts, and the quality of education was uneven at best (Butts & Cremin, 1953; Pulliam & Van Patten, 1999).

About 1830, educational changes began to occur (Kaestle, 1983). These changes marked the beginning of the **common school movement,** *a historical attempt to make education available to all children in the United States.* The following are some of the events that occurred during this period:

- Citizens were directly taxed to support public schools. Attempts were made to increase the attendance of underrepresented groups such as the urban poor and freed slaves.
- State education departments were created, and state superintendents of instruction were appointed.
- Schools were organized by grade level, and the curriculum was standardized.
- Teacher preparation was improved.

The Contributions of Horace Mann Horace Mann, a lawyer turned educator, was a key figure in the common school movement. Secretary of the Massachusetts State Board of Education from 1837 to 1848, he was an outspoken advocate for public education, believing that it was the key to developing the country and improving the quality of life for all people.

Under Mann's influence, Massachusetts moved to the cutting edge of education in America. During the common school period, Massachusetts doubled state appropriations for education, built 50 new secondary schools, increased teacher salaries by 50 percent, and passed the nation's first compulsory school attendance law in 1852. (By 1900, 32 other states had passed similar laws.) Perhaps Mann's biggest legacy,

The common school movement made education accessible to the common person.

however, was the idea that public education, in the form of tax-supported elementary schools (common schools), should be a right of all citizens.

Expansion of the Common School Movement Despite some obstacles—such as business interests that feared a loss of cheap child labor, citizens who objected to increased taxes and having to pay to educate other people's children, and competition from private and parochial schools—the common school movement prospered. The following are some of the reasons for its success:

- Parents began envisioning better lives for their children through education.
- National and local leaders saw education as the vehicle for assimilation of immigrants and improvement of national productivity.
- The growth of industry and commerce required an increasingly educated populace.

Fifty percent of children were enrolled in public schools by the beginning of the Civil War, and by 1865, 28 of 35 states had established state boards of education. During the common school movement, tax-supported public elementary schools were firmly established as a cornerstone of the U.S. educational system. (New Jersey eliminated the need for parents to pay for an elementary education in 1871; it was the last state to do so.)

CW

Increasing Understanding 5.4

How would you justify the need or legality of school taxes to citizens without children? How is paying school taxes similar to or different from paying taxes to support a police or fire department or a mail system?

Issues of Quality and Quantity in Teacher Education Although the common school movement dramatically increased access to education, quality was a problem. During the early to mid–1800s,

> teachers' workloads were heavy, and only the fundamentals were taught. For the most part, school buildings and equipment were very poor, even in the private schools and academies. Textbooks, blackboards, and all working materials were in extremely short supply. Buildings were not kept up, lighting was not adequate, and quite often one poorly trained teacher was in charge not only of one school but also of an entire district.
>
> Teachers who possessed only an elementary school education were frequently hired. (Pulliam & Van Patten, 1999, p. 98)

Then, as now, teachers were seen as keys to improving our schools. The creation of **normal schools,** *2-year institutions developed in the early 1800s to prepare prospective elementary teachers,* was perhaps the most significant attempt to solve this problem. Before normal schools existed, the typical teacher was a man, either preparing for or waiting for a position in the ministry. Because these teachers had no training in education, they used primitive methods, such as memorization and recitation, and they maintained order with stern disciplinary measures, including corporal punishment. Normal schools, in contrast, targeted women as potential teachers, and they attempted to provide both content background and pedagogical training beyond the high school level.

School quality also increased when larger elementary schools began dividing up students into grade levels, which eliminated congested conditions and the overlapping curricula often found in one-room schools. Grade differentiation also resulted in more age-appropriate instruction and allowed content to be taught in greater depth for older students. Finally, as paper and printing presses became more common, more textbooks were available and educational materials improved.

The Legacy of the Common School Movement

The common school movement was a turning point in American education. The idea of universal access to a tax-supported education was planted and took root. Although not all children attended elementary schools, the number who did increased steadily during this period, and public support for the idea grew. State governance and control of education was institutionalized with the creation of state departments of education, and teacher training and quality improved with the development of normal schools.

Despite these advances, the common school movement left at least two controversial issues that remain today. One issue involves the inequitable funding of education from state to state and from district to district, both of which indirectly affect quality. In *Savage Inequalities* (1991), Jonathon Kozol addresses this issue:

. . . Americans abhor the notion of a social order in which economic privilege and political power are determined by hereditary class. Officially, we have a more enlightened goal in sight: namely, a society in which a family's wealth has no relation to the probability of future educational attainment and the wealth and station it affords. By this standard, education offered to poor children should be at least as good as that which is provided to the children of the upper-middle class. (p. 207)

The education offered to poor children often isn't on par with that offered to upper-middle-class children, however. Wide differences in funding exist between states and among districts within states. For example, during the 2001–2002 school year, average per-pupil expenditures ranged from under \$4,769 in Utah to \$10,725 in New York ("State of the States," 2003). In that same approximate time period, the poorest districts in Illinois spent an average of \$4,330 per pupil, whereas the wealthiest spent \$7,249 (Johnston, 1998). (You will study more about issues related to school funding in Chapter 8.)

Teacher quality is the second contentious issue from the common school era, and the question of what constitutes a well-educated and qualified teacher remains controversial. Efforts to increase teacher professionalism, a theme of this text, and alternative routes to licensure are recent responses to this historical issue of teacher quality. Alternative routes to certification have become popular, especially in high-demand areas such as math, science, and special education, and in rural areas and inner cities, where it is difficult to recruit teachers. Proponents of alternative certification contend that it helps districts address critical needs while attracting talented people, such as retired military personnel, scientists, and engineers seeking a second career.

Critics of alternative certification programs contend that the programs don't provide adequate preparation (Darling-Hammond, Berry, & Thoreson, 2001; Laczko-Kerr & Berliner, 2003). All too often the programs involve inadequate coursework, abbreviated clinical experiences, and inadequate supervision, support, and mentoring. Alternate certification teachers have higher dropout rates, both during their program

Table 5.2 A Summary of Historical Periods in American Education

Period	Significant Features	Issues That Remain Today
The Colonial Period, 1607–1775	• Education reserved for wealthy White males • Seeds planted for public support of education • Religion at the core of education	• Whether or not prayer should be allowed in schools • Tax support for religious schools • The relationship between religion and character education
The Early National Period, 1775–1820	• The principle of separation of church and state established • Control of education given to the states, rather than the federal government • Education viewed as crucial for furthering the national interest	• The role of the federal government in education • National testing of students • A national curriculum
The Common School Movement, 1820–1865	• Access to tax-supported education for all established • Grade levels introduced in elementary schools • Normal schools created for the preparation of teachers	• Inequities in funding among states and school districts • Teacher quality and alternative routes to teacher certification

and in their first year of teaching, are less satisfied with their training, and are less confident in their ability to teach (Laczko-Kerr & Berliner, 2003).

The question of what constitutes a well-educated and qualified teacher remains under debate, as evidenced in two contradictory movements in education today. One is the effort to open up entrance to the teaching profession through alternative routes; the other is to make entry into teaching more rigorous and difficult through increased coursework and testing (Darling-Hammond, 2000). How the issue will be resolved in the future is unclear. (You will examine the alternative licensure issue in greater depth in Chapter 13.)

We've now taken a look at important events in our country's early history that have shaped education. Table 5.2 provides a summary of these events, the periods during which they occurred, and the issues they have left with us.

The Evolution of the American High School

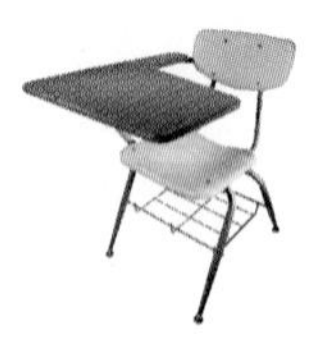

Case STUDY Kareem and Antonio walked to high school together, had lockers that were side by side, and even had the same homeroom period. But that is where their contact ended. Kareem was in a college-preparation track, along with about a third of the other students in his school. As he went from class to class, he would see many of the same students. Antonio was in a vocational track, and many of his classes were designed to introduce him to specific career options. A technology class focused on business applications of computers and introduced him to jobs in the computer field. A metalworking class included welding and even allowed him to work on his family's car as a class project. Once Kareem and Antonio left homeroom, they often didn't see each other until the very end of the day, at football practice.

• • ● • •

Some of you studying this text graduated from high school only a year or two ago, whereas others finished several years back. Either way, think about your experience. The majority of you probably attended a unique American invention, the **comprehensive high school,** *a secondary school that attempts to meet the needs of all students by housing them together and providing curricular options (such as vocational or college-preparatory programs) geared toward a variety of student ability levels and interests.* For example, some of you took honors classes in English, history, chemistry, or biology. Others were in "standard" classes, designed for students of average ability. Perhaps you enrolled in some vocational courses, such as word processing or woodworking, designed to provide you with immediately marketable skills. You may have even taken driver's training or other "life management" courses. All of these are part of a comprehensive American high school. How did the modern, comprehensive high school evolve?

Because a high school education prepares students for a job or entrance to college, today it is seen as essential to success in life. This wasn't always the case. Before the turn of the twentieth century, less than 10 percent of the population went beyond elementary school (U.S. Department of Education, 1995). By contrast, in the year 2000, 96 percent of all teenagers attended high school. A high school education has evolved from a luxury to a right to a necessity.

Historical Roots of the Comprehensive High School

The American high school as it exists today is the result of a long evolutionary history. A timeline illustrating this development appears in Figure 5.1 and is discussed in this section.

The first American "high school" was a decidedly European institution aimed at the colonial elite. The *Boston Latin School,* established in Boston in 1635, was a **Latin grammar school,** *a type of college-preparatory school originally designed to help boys prepare for the ministry or, later, for a career in law.* Women didn't attend, since they could be neither ministers nor lawyers. The narrow curriculum and high cost made Latin grammar schools largely unattainable and irrelevant for the vast majority of Americans.

In reaction to this narrow, academic orientation, Benjamin Franklin opened the first academy, the Academy of Philadelphia, in 1751. Free of religious orientation and

Figure 5.1 The Evolution of the American High School

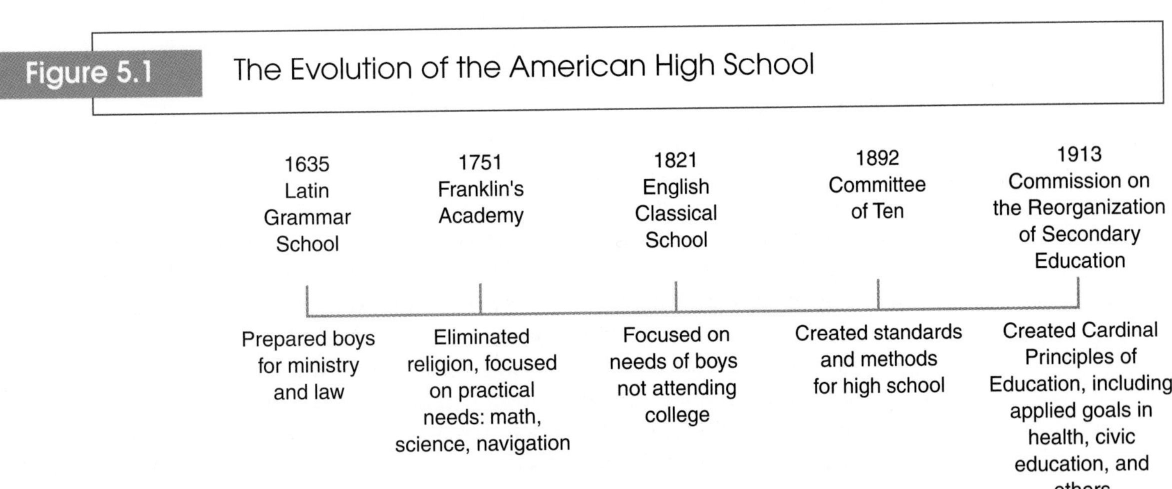

Today's modern comprehensive high school can be traced back to academies, such as Franklin's Academy of Philadelphia, and English classical schools, such as the English High School in Boston.

uniquely American, an **academy** was *a type of secondary school that focused on the practical needs of colonial America as a growing nation.* Math, navigation, astronomy, bookkeeping, logic, and rhetoric were all taught, and both boys and girls attended. The students selected courses from this menu, which set the precedent for electives and alternative programs at the secondary level.

Merchants and craftsmen, who had questioned the emphasis on Latin and Greek in the Latin grammar schools, enthusiastically supported this broader, more applied curriculum. By 1860 a quarter of a million students were enrolled in 6,000 tuition-charging academies, and they were more numerous than high schools until about 1890 (Butts & Cremin, 1953).

The academies were a significant addition to American education for at least three reasons. First, they emphasized a practical curriculum, suggesting that schools should continuously adapt to changes in society. Second, they eliminated religion from the curriculum, further widening the division between church and state, and third, they were partially supported by public funds, which established a trend that flourished in the common school movement. These characteristics—practical, secular, and public—were themes that would be revisited again and again in American education.

In addition to the academies, another uniquely American educational institution appeared. In 1821 Boston established the first **English classical school,** *a free secondary school designed to meet the needs of boys not planning to attend college.* The *English Classical School of Boston* offered studies in English, math, history, science, geography, bookkeeping, and surveying and, to reflect this practical emphasis, changed its name to the *English High School* in 1824.

Schools modeled after the English High School spread slowly, partly because of competition from the academies and public opposition to taxes needed to support the schools. Taxpayers did not view secondary schools as free and natural extensions of elementary education. In addition, the schools were uncertain about their role. Unable to decide whether their mission was practical or college preparatory, the schools responded by offering both types of classes. This uncertainty also affected students; in 1900 only one tenth of the students said they expected to attend college, but the majority took a college-preparatory curriculum. As we'll see in the next section, this confusion about the American high school's role and mission continued into the twentieth century and persists even today.

Redefining the High School

The American high school at the end of the nineteenth century was an institution in search of an identity. Begun as an elitist, college-preparatory institution, its curriculum evolved into a disorganized mix of college-preparatory, terminal, and vocational courses. Educational leaders recognized that something needed to be done.

In 1892, in response to this need, the National Education Association (NEA) appointed a group called *The Committee of Ten* to examine the high school curriculum and make recommendations about standards, programs, and methods. The committee concluded that students who planned to go no further than high school needed content and teaching methods that were the same as those who were college bound—an idea that is generally viewed as erroneous.

CW

Increasing Understanding 5.5

Explain how the Committee of Ten membership and faculty psychology influenced decisions about the curriculum for non-college-bound students. How might the inclusion of parents on the committee, especially immigrant parents, have changed the nature of the recommendations?

There were probably three reasons the committee reached its conclusion (Spring, 2001). First, no high school teachers or parents were included on the committee. It was composed of college professors and administrators only, so the bias toward a college-preparatory curriculum wasn't surprising. Second, the committee members believed in *faculty psychology*, the view that exercising powers of the mind promoted learning. Everyone, regardless of where they were heading in life, could practice mental discipline to achieve a "stronger" mind.

A third factor influencing the committee was the large numbers of non-English-speaking immigrants and growing lower class that threatened to create divisions in American society. The committee felt that a different curriculum for college and non-college-bound students might create a class-based system of education and damage national unity (Spring, 2001).

The committee recognized, however, that the college-preparatory curriculum wasn't providing prospective workers with the occupational skills needed for increasingly complex jobs. In an attempt to resolve this dilemma, in 1913 the NEA appointed a second committee, called *The Commission on the Reorganization of Secondary Education*. In 1918 this commission issued a report, the *Cardinal Principles of Secondary Education*, that included goals in basic skills such as reading and math, vocational education, personal health, worthy home membership, civic education, effective use of leisure time, and ethical character. To accommodate these more applied goals, the commission proposed the idea of comprehensive high schools, with different tracks for different students. The hope was that the diverse student body separated into different tracks would be integrated by sports and other extracurricular activities (Spring, 2001).

Efforts to solve the problems of intellectual and other forms of diversity persist today. Although the practice of tracking was designed to provide a customized education for all students, it has resulted in unanticipated negative consequences. As you learned in Chapter 3, the curriculum in the non-college-bound tracks often offers little intellectual challenge, and teachers tend to have low expectations for students and use primitive and ineffective teaching methods, such as lecture and seatwork (Oakes, 1985; Tucker & Codding, 1998).

Junior High and Middle Schools

While groups such as the Committee of Ten and The Commission on the Reorganization of Secondary Education wrestled with curricular issues, other educators questioned the effectiveness of the 8–4 organizational pattern (8 years of elementary, 4 of high school). Critics of the pattern argued that too much emphasis was being placed on basic skills in the upper elementary grades, a time that could be better spent learning content in depth. Developmental psychologists pointed out that early adolescence is a time of intellectual, emotional, and physical transition, and students undergoing these transitions require a different kind of school. In response to these arguments, **junior high schools,** *schools that provide a unique academic curriculum for early adolescent youth*, were created. The first junior high, which encompassed grades 7, 8, and 9, opened in Columbus, Ohio, in 1909. The concept spread quickly, and by 1926 junior highs had been set up in 800 school systems (Gruhn & Douglass, 1971).

The 6–3–3 organizational pattern (6 years of elementary school, 3 of junior high, and 3 of high school) was more a change in form than substance, however. Most "junior" highs were exactly that—imitations of high schools with a fragmented curriculum, emphasis on academic disciplines, and little attention to the developing needs of adolescents.

In spite of these weaknesses, junior highs remained popular until the 1970s, when continued criticisms caused fundamental change. The response to these criticisms was middle schools. **Middle schools** are *schools, typically for grades 6–8, specifically designed to help students through the rapid social, emotional, and intellectual changes characteristic of early adolescence.* Specifically, middle schools provided opportunities for teachers to get to know students by creating student and teacher teams. Working together on teams, teachers could share information about learner progress and problems as well as design interdisciplinary units that explored connections between different content areas. The curriculum became more applied and more focused on adolescents' emotional development. In addition, teachers were encouraged to move away from the lecture-dominated instruction so common in high schools and toward more student-centered instruction, such as cooperative learning and problem-based learning.

The middle school philosophy has grown in popularity. The number of junior highs decreased from 7,200 in 1968 to 1,000 in 1996 (Viadero, 1996), with an accompanying increase in middle schools. (You will study junior highs and middle schools in more detail in Chapter 7.)

American Secondary Schools: Future Directions

The history of American secondary schools helps us understand some of the questions facing educators today. Begun as college-preparatory institutions, high schools became comprehensive in an effort to meet the needs of all students. To help adolescents make the transition from elementary to high school, junior highs were created; when they failed to fulfill that mission, middle schools were created. The academic pendulum has now swung back, however, and some leaders are calling for a redesign of middle schools to make them more academic and rigorous (A. Bradley, 1998).

Have American secondary schools been too trendy and overly responsive to changing conditions in society, first zigging one way and then zagging another? Or have they been too traditional and conservative, hanging on to outmoded academics in the face of dramatic changes in society? These questions are reexamined in the next section when we discuss the progressive era in American education.

The Progressive Era

Case STUDY Cassie Jones walked through the halls of the inner-city middle school where she is the principal and listened to the sounds coming from the different classrooms. As she walked by Ben Carlson's social studies class, she heard him say, "Yesterday we talked about the strengths and weaknesses of the North and South at the outbreak of the Civil War. Who remembers one of these?"

As Cassie moved down the hall, she stopped in front of Sarah McCarthy's science class. Sarah was at the front of the room swinging a set of keys from a piece of string. "Hmm," Cassie thought, "no wonder her class is so quiet—she's got them hypnotized." As she listened further she heard Sarah ask, "Class, this is a simple pendulum, just like the one we find in grandfather clocks. Who can tell me what factors influence the rate at which a pendulum swings?"

"Good question," Cassie thought. "Maybe that's why her kids are so quiet."

When Cassie turned the corner, she was greeted by a steady stream of student voices arguing about something.

"I don't care what you say, stealing is wrong."

"But his family didn't have enough to eat. They were hungry—he couldn't let them starve!"

"What's Hector up to today?" Cassie thought as she listened more closely to Hector Sanchez's English class.

"Class," Hector broke in, "it's not enough just to disagree with your partners. You have to explain why. Remember, one of the reasons we read books like *Sounder* is to help us understand our own lives. So, you have three more minutes in your discussion groups to explain why the father was right or wrong to steal food for his family."

Cassie chuckled as she heard Hector's class rejoin the battle. "He's sure got them stirred up today. I guess I'm lucky to have such a talented teaching staff that has so many different strengths." (Jacobsen, Eggen, & Kauchak, 2002, p. 171)

• • ● • •

Observe a typical classroom, and at some point you're likely to see students involved in a variety of learning activities. Some are busy in small-group work; the teacher moves among the groups, talking briefly and then rotating to another group. Toward the end of the period, the class reconvenes and the teacher leads a discussion that summarizes the day. The teacher doesn't seem to be "teaching" in the traditional sense of the term. No lectures are given, and students do more talking than the teacher. What are the historical roots of these practices?

From 1890 to 1920, the American educational system experienced dramatic growth (U.S. Department of Education, 1982). The school-age population increased 49 percent, and school enrollments, fueled by accessibility and compulsory attendance laws, increased 70 percent. The number of teachers grew by 80 percent. The basic structure of the American education system was in place. The combination of structure and growth provided an opportunity for educators to reexamine their goals.

The country was also in a state of transition. Excesses in industry and business had led to unsafe working conditions and poverty-blighted city slums. Reform-minded journalists exposed these problems and asked government to intervene. The Progressive Era began.

Within this broader political backdrop, educators began to reexamine schooling practices. They questioned the value of teacher-centered instruction that asked students to passively absorb information. Ideas from early reformers such as Locke, Rousseau, and Pestalozzi received increased attention. At the center of this reform movement was the philosopher John Dewey.

Dewey first encountered progressive teaching practices through his children, who attended an experimental lab school in Chicago. He became so fascinated with student-centered teaching that in 1896 he established his own lab school connected to the University of Chicago, where he worked. The lab school became the birthplace of **progressive education**, *an educational movement, which gained prominence during the early to mid-twentieth centuries, that advocates a child-centered curriculum that encourages individual problem solving.* For Dewey, classrooms became microcosms of a democratic society. Goals like personal growth and preparation for participation in a democratic society were met through an activity-oriented curriculum that emphasized realistic problems. For example, student concerns about a stray dog might lead to a group investigation of pets in general as well as an investigation of strays in an urban environment. Content, which historically was an end in itself, now became a tool for solving problems.

Dewey's ideas created both excitement and criticism. To some, seeing learners actively involved in solving real-world problems was exciting. To others, progressive

CW

Increasing Understanding 5.6

Would progressive ideas be more compatible with a junior high or a middle school? Why?

education seemed to inappropriately de-emphasize content and cater to student whims. For instance, critics would assert that a social studies class should be learning important historical names and dates, not studying the problems of pets in an urban setting. Further, successfully integrating problem-based learning and essential content required teachers who were knowledgeable in content and skilled in connecting the content to students' interests—abilities many teachers lacked (Ravitch, 1983).

Although aspects of progressive education remain today, interest in it as a general movement waned after the mid-twentieth century. The movement became divided by factions and a well-intentioned but misguided attempt at fostering "life adjustment." The life adjustment movement, which flourished in the 1950s, sought to meet the needs of high school students who weren't in either college-preparatory or vocational tracks—a majority of students. Courses like "Developing an Effective Personality" and "Marriage and Living" were designed to provide students with life skills. Critics howled, denouncing the life adjustment curriculum as watered down and devoid of content and intellectual rigor. Their cries were amplified by the Russian launching of *Sputnik* in 1957. Russia had beaten America to outer space! Critics concluded that there must be something wrong with our educational system, and that something was progressive education in the form of life adjustment.

Although the progressive education movement declined, it rekindled interest in two important questions: What content is most valuable, and how should that content be taught? These questions have been debated in our country for more than 300 years, and the debate continues. Conservative educators argue that a body of essential knowledge exists and all students must master that knowledge in order to function effectively in society (Adler, 1982; Hirsch, 1987). Social studies, for example, should emphasize history and particularly western civilization. Language arts should focus on grammar and writing and time-tested works of literature, such as those by Shakespeare. Students should be asked to master math and science concepts before worrying about their applicability.

Reformers counter that times have changed and schools should change accordingly. The revolution in technology, which has given most people access to personal computers and information networks, requires a different curriculum and different teaching methods. Students should be taught about this technology and how to use it in their daily lives. In addition, schools should help students understand and deal with problems such as crime, violence, drugs, and sexually transmitted diseases. To do otherwise ignores reality and places our students at risk.

Positions about what and what not to teach are grounded in philosophy, and when you study Chapter 6, you'll examine them again in that context.

Searching for Equality: The Education of Cultural Minorities

> The first thing to do was to clean them [Native Americans] thoroughly and to dress them in their new [military] attire. . . . [then] everything except swallowing, walking, and sleeping had to be taught; the care of person, clothing, furniture, the usages of the table, the carriage of the body, civility, all those things which white children usually learn from their childhood by mere imitation, had to be painfully inculcated and strenuously insisted on. In addition to this, they were to be taught the rudiments of an English school course and the practical use of tools. (U.S. Bureau of Indian Affairs, 1974, p. 1749)

The story of American education we've presented so far has been generally positive. Despite lurches and false starts, education has improved in quality and has become more accessible to American young people. The story isn't so positive for cultural minorities, however. In this section we outline the evolution of education for cultural minorities as we consider the education of Native Americans, African Americans, Hispanic Americans, and Asian Americans.

Two themes have been pervasive in the education of cultural minorities: assimilation and "separate but equal." In our discussion of multicultural education in Chapter 3, we defined **assimilation** as *a process of socializing people so that they adopt dominant social norms and patterns of behavior.* For much of history, educators sought to bring minorities into the mainstream of American life—to assimilate them—by teaching basic skills and instilling White middle-class values. In the process of asking for assimilation, educators also asked minorities to reject important aspects of their own histories and cultures; this rejection is apparent in the quote about Native Americans that introduces this section.

The second theme, **separate but equal,** was *a policy of segregating minorities in education, transportation, housing, and other areas of public life if opportunities and facilities were considered equal to those of nonminorities. In education, the policy was evidenced by separate schools with different curricula, teaching methods, teachers, and resources.* The policy was particularly applied to the education of African American students. Some historians believe that these efforts were well intentioned but misguided, whereas others argue that they were inherently racist (Spring, 2001).

Let's turn now to a look at the education of specific minority groups.

Education of Native Americans

The history of Native American education is a story of generally unsuccessful attempts to assimilate different tribes into the American mainstream. To achieve assimilation Native Americans were expected to exchange their tribal customs and values for mainstream American values. The process left Native American students asking the question "Who am I?" It was a difficult question to answer.

Like American education in general, the education of Native Americans began with a religious orientation. During the 1700s and 1800s, mission schools run by various protestant denominations provided a common school curriculum that focused on basic skills, agriculture, vocational education, and religion. Although instruction was given in the native language, mission schools attempted to help Native Americans bridge the gap between tribal, communal life and one in which individuals owned land, had jobs, and followed the dominant culture's way of life (Butts, 1978; Spring, 2001).

From 1890 to 1930, the federal government became involved in Native American education through boarding schools run by the Bureau of Indian Affairs. Children were forced to live at the schools, English was spoken and taught, and native languages and customs were forbidden. The best way to "Americanize" the children, leaders thought, was to remove them from tribal settings and provide them with a strict program of cultural transformation (Adams, 1995).

CW

Increasing Understanding 5.7

How would progressive educators react to the Native American boarding schools? What adaptations might they suggest?

The failure of the boarding schools was evidenced by low participation rates (only 300 of a possible 4,000 to 5,000 eligible Navajo children attended these schools in 1901), high dropout rates (many children ran away), and a tendency for students to return to the reservation after graduation because the curriculum wasn't applicable to Native American culture or interests (Button & Provenzo, 1989).

Despite the failure of boarding schools, federal control of Native American education continued through the 1960s. Tribal schools, which included Native American culture in the curriculum, opened in 1965, but financial dependence on the federal government, limited instructional materials, and poorly paid teachers were difficult problems to overcome.

More recently, the federal government shifted responsibility for Native American education from the Bureau of Indian Affairs and tribal schools to public schools. In the 1990s, 91 percent of Native Americans attended public schools (National Center for Education Statistics, 1997b). Despite this shift, and increased involvement by tribal governments, the problems in Native American education persist. Underachievement, absenteeism, and dropout rates of almost 50 percent in grades 8–12 indicate that current educational practices remain unsuccessful (U.S. Department of Education, 1996b).

Education of African Americans: Up from Slavery to . . .

The first African Americans arrived in the United States in the early 1600s, shortly after the founding of Jamestown. Brought as slaves, they had few educational opportunities prior to the Civil War. In 1850 fewer than 2 percent of African Americans attended schools (about 4,000 in slave states and 23,000 in free states), and the literacy rate was low, ranging between 5 percent and 10 percent (U.S. Government Printing Office, 1975; West, 1972).

Educational accessibility improved after the Civil War. As a result of religious, philanthropic, and governmental efforts, school participation rates increased from 2 percent of the African American population in 1850 to 10 percent in 1870 and 35 percent in 1890 (U.S. Government Printing Office, 1975). Literacy rates increased from the 5–10 percent at the time of the Civil War to 40 percent by 1890 and 70 percent by 1910 (U.S. Bureau of the Census, 1990).

Near the end of the 1870s, events took a negative turn, however. The federal government shifted the responsibility for educating African Americans back to state and local governments, particularly in the South, where the vast majority still lived. Segregated and substandard schools were predominant, and funding for African American schools was consistently lower than for White schools. In 1877, for example, expenditures for African American students in the South were less than half those for Whites; by the 1940s they had dropped to a fifth (J. Anderson, 1988). In 1907 White teachers in Alabama were paid five times more than African American ones. In Georgia in the late 1920s, 99 percent of the money budgeted for teaching equipment went to White schools, even though African Americans made up 34 percent of the state's student population (Bond, 1934). In 1952 Arkansas spent $102 to educate each White child but only $67 for each African American child (Pulliam & Van Patten, 1999). Schools for African Americans were clearly not separate but equal; they would more accurately be called ***separate and unequal.***

Proposed Solutions to the Problem The education of African Americans was clearly inferior to that of Whites, but a solution to the problem remained elusive. Finally, two leaders, with sharply different perspectives, emerged.

Booker T. Washington (1856–1915) was born a slave and taught himself to read. Educated at Hampton Institute, an industrial school for African Americans, he gained prominence for successfully establishing the Tuskegee Institute in 1881. Short of supplies and resources, he had his students build the school themselves. This hands-on approach to learning exemplified his strategy for bettering the education and lives of African Americans in the South. He believed that hard work, practical training, and economic cooperation with Whites were the keys to success. His philosophy became popular, and he was often invited to address White audiences on the topic of African

American education. At one of these appearances he summarized his philosophy in this way: "In all things that are purely social we can be as separate as the finger, yet one as the hand in all things essential to mutual progress" (Washington, 1932). Washington encouraged his students to become teachers; he felt that attempting to enter other professions or politics was premature and would lead to conflict with the White power structure in the South.

Although Washington was accepted by many African Americans and popular with Whites, his policy of accommodating segregation angered other African American leaders. W.E.B. Dubois (1868–1963) was an important opponent whose resistance to Washington's stance was predictable, given the differences in their backgrounds. Dubois was born in Massachusetts and educated in integrated schools. He attended colleges and universities in the United States and Europe and was the first African American to receive a Ph.D. in the United States (Spring, 2001; Watkins, 2001).

Dubois was committed to changing the status of African Americans and advocated a determined stand against segregation and racism. He wanted to focus educational energies on students achieving in the top 10 percent, believing that these students would provide leadership and create opportunities for the rest of the African American population. He also felt that this group could take their place among the business, professional, and intellectual leaders of the White population. Dubois believed that Washington's separatist approach implied inferiority and, while expedient in the short term, would retard the educational progress of African Americans in the long run. He advocated social activism and was a leader in helping establish the National Association for the Advancement of Colored People (NAACP). This organization has played a major role in the advancement of African Americans in the twentieth century.

The Courts Examine "Separate But Equal" Prior to the Civil War, African Americans lived apart from the White majority because of slavery, legal restrictions, or

Early efforts at educating African Americans were often substandard due to inadequate funding and resources.

de facto (not stipulated by law) segregation. Segregation continued after the Civil War because of the policy of "separate but equal." The policy justified segregation by claiming that African Americans were receiving different but equal treatment under the law. The principle was first legally challenged in Massachusetts in 1850 when an African American student wasn't allowed to attend a White school. At that time, the state court ruled that having separate but equal facilities was legal (Spring, 2001).

A federal challenge to the policy of "separate but equal" came in Louisiana in 1896 in a court case involving segregated railroads. In *Plessy v. Ferguson*, the U.S. Supreme Court ruled that separate but equal railroad facilities did not violate the Constitution (Spring, 2001). This decision was also applied to education, and "separate but equal" stood for almost 50 years. (We examine the federal government's response to the "separate but equal" policy in education in our section on exploring diversity later in the chapter.)

Education of Hispanic Americans

Hispanic is a label that refers to a diverse group of people who are of Latin American or Caribbean heritage or who speak Spanish (Banks, 2003; Nieto, 1996). Mexican Americans in the Southwest, Puerto Rican Americans in the Northeast, and Cuban Americans in Florida are all included in this group. The term *Hispanic* is more popular in the Northeast, with groups in the Southwest preferring *Latino* (*Latina*, female). The term *Chicano* (*Chicana,* female) refers to Hispanics of Mexican American heritage.

Hispanics are the fastest growing minority group in the United States. At the turn of the twenty-first century they made up more than 13 percent of the nation's school-age children and were the largest minority group in California, Texas, and Florida (Zehr, 2000b). By the year 2025, 1 in 4 children in U.S. elementary schools is predicted to be of Hispanic origin.

Hispanic education in America began with Catholic mission schools in the Southwest, but it shifted to public schools after the Mexican-American War in 1848. Unlike African American segregation, segregation of Hispanics was not mandated by law, but it occurred nevertheless. Hispanic students were often taught in separate schools or classes, with poorer facilities, fewer well-trained teachers, and smaller budgets. Migrancy also contributed to educational problems. In the late 1900s, Hispanics constituted 17 percent of the migrant workforce (C. Bennett, 1999), and attendance at school often suffered because of family work demands that led to transiency.

Initially, assimilation was the educational focus. Classes were taught in English, Spanish was forbidden, and students' own Hispanic heritage was ignored (Banks, 2003; Spring, 2001). Apathy and resistance to school, as occurred with Native Americans, were pervasive, and dropping out was common. In 1999, 30 percent of the Hispanic school-age population left school before graduation, compared to 12 percent for African Americans and 11 percent for Whites. The dropout rate for 16- to 24-year-old Hispanics born outside the United States was even higher—44 percent, compared to 7.2 percent for non-Hispanics (Johnston, 2000a). Also, only 12 percent of 22-year-old Hispanics have a bachelor's degree, compared to 30 percent for Whites and 15 percent for African Americans (Bowman, 2000c). When Hispanics go to college, they are much more likely to attend a 2-year institution than other groups (Pew Hispanic Foundation, 2003).

Language differences have been the source of many problems in the education of Hispanics. Language symbolizes differences between Hispanics and the dominant cul-

CW

Increasing Understanding 5.8

Why wasn't bilingual education a major issue with Native American education? with African American education?

ture, and instruction in English interferes with students' learning. Some experts have argued that Hispanic students have historically scored lower on intelligence tests, which are commonly language based, because of language barriers (Bowman, 2000c; Viadero & Johnston, 2000).

The federal government addressed the problem of language differences in the *Bilingual Education Act* in 1968, which provided money for bilingual programs ($160 million by 1979). However, voters in California and Arizona have recently voted to restrict the use of bilingual programs, so the future of the programs is uncertain. (Bilingual education was discussed in detail in Chapter 3.)

Education of Asian Americans

Like Hispanics, Asian Americans are a diverse group of people with varied histories (Banks, 2003). The first Asian Americans were Chinese who came to the United States to work in the California gold mines and on the first transcontinental railroad. Japanese immigrants came to California and Hawaii in the late 1800s as agricultural workers. More recently, Korean and Southeast Asian immigrants have come to the United States seeking a better life and an escape from the Korean and Vietnam Wars.

Asian immigrants were initially welcomed because they relieved an acute labor shortage in the West. However, competition for jobs, together with racism, resulted in a series of changes in immigration laws that prevented further Chinese immigration in 1882 and then Japanese immigration in 1924 (Spring, 2001). Perhaps the darkest page in Asian American history came during World War II when more than 100,000 Japanese Americans were forced out of their homes near the Pacific coast and into internment camps in barren areas of the West.

Like other minority groups, Asian Americans experienced discrimination. For example, in 1906 San Francisco established segregated schools for Asian Americans. Instruction was in English, which resulted in problems similar to those Native Americans and Hispanics encountered. A federal court ruled in 1974 (in *Lau v. Nichols*) that the San Francisco school system had violated the rights of Chinese American students and that students who find their educational experience "wholly incomprehensible" must be taught in the first language if that language is not English.

As a group, Asian Americans have fared better than other cultural minority groups in the American educational system. In 1994 Asian American students had the highest average SAT scores of any group in the country (U.S. Department of Education, 1996a), and the proportion of Asian Americans in colleges and universities is higher than the proportion in the general population. This success has led some educators to label this group "the model minority," but more recent immigrants from Southeast Asian countries such as Cambodia, Laos, and Vietnam have experienced greater challenges in the U.S. educational system.

The Search for Equality: Where Are We Now?

As we said at the beginning of this section, two themes—assimilation and "separate but equal"—have been central to the education of minorities in the United States. The policy of "separate but equal" has been banned by the courts, but where does assimilation now stand?

Assimilation has always required that ethnic groups sacrifice a portion of their cultural identity to become "American." At the extreme, success meant creating a "melting pot" in which the diverse cultures of America had blended into a uniform and homogeneous society. This uniform society has never been achieved, as evidenced,

Increasing Understanding 5.9

Describe a "melting pot" approach to teaching American history. Describe a "tossed salad" approach.

for example, in the present-day diversity of religions in America and holidays such as Kwanzaa, St. Patrick's Day, and the Jewish and Muslim religious holidays.

In educational circles a "tossed salad" metaphor has replaced the metaphor of the melting pot; in this salad, different ethnic and cultural groups contribute unique tastes and perspectives. The extent to which Americans should share common values and beliefs is still controversial, with some arguing for greater uniformity (Schlesinger, 1992) and others advocating an America built around diversity and shared values (Takaki, 1993).

The federal government's role in the education of cultural minorities remains poorly defined. In the past, federal courts have played a major role in desegregation, but in recent times they have been increasingly reluctant to impose busing and other legal mechanisms to achieve integration (Kahlenberg, 2002; Orfield, Frankenberg, & Lee, 2002/2003). The same is true in the legislative branch; senators and members of the House of Representatives can't decide what role the federal government should play in the quest for equity and equality (D. Hoff, 1998). We examine this changing federal role in education in the next section.

To analyze a case study examining issues involved in motivating cultural minority students, go to the Companion Website at **www.prenhall.com/kauchak**, then to this chapter's *Reflect on This* module.

The Modern Era: Schools as Instruments for National Purpose and Social Change

The modern era in education began at about the end of World War II and continues to the present. It is characterized by an increased emphasis on education, which is now viewed as the key to both individual success and the progress of the nation. Given this perspective, it isn't surprising to see the federal government more actively involved in education than it was in the past. This increased involvement occurred in at least three areas:

- The government's response to the cold war
- The government's War on Poverty and search for the "great society"
- The government's role in equity issues

Let's look at these areas.

The Cold War: Enlisting America's Schools

Increasing Understanding 5.10

Why were educational efforts during the cold war focused on science, math, and foreign languages?

We commonly think of the cold war as a stalemate with the Soviet Union, with ever more powerful weapons being stockpiled on both sides. It was also significant in education's history.

The Russian launching of the satellite *Sputnik* in 1957 was the key event of the period. Believing the United States was losing the technology war, our government responded by authorizing a fivefold increase in the funding of the National Science Foundation, which had been created in 1950 to support research and improve science education. Congress also passed the National Defense Education Act (NDEA) in

1958, which was designed to enhance "the security of the nation" by improving instruction in math, science, and foreign languages. The NDEA provided funds for teacher training, new equipment, and the establishment of centers for research and dissemination of new teaching methods. During this period, Admiral Rickover, the father of the American nuclear navy, called education "our first line of defense."

The War on Poverty and the Great Society

During the 1960s, leaders began to realize that despite the economic boom following World War II, many Americans were living in poverty. America was becoming a nation of "haves" and "have nots," and the problem was exacerbated by an economy that required ever-increasing skills in its workers.

For the unfortunate, a cycle of poverty began with inadequate education, which decreased employment opportunities, leading to a poorer quality of life that resulted in lowered achievement in the next generation. To break this cycle and create a "great society" in which all could participate and benefit, President Lyndon Johnson, in his 1964 State of the Union address, stated that "this administration today, here and now, declares unconditional war on poverty in America."

Emphasis on education was a major thrust in the **War on Poverty,** *a general term for federal programs designed to eradicate poverty during the 1960s.* During this period the central government's involvement increased significantly. Initiatives included the following:

- *Increased federal funding.* Federal funds for K–12 education went from $900 million and about 4.4 percent of the total spent on education in 1964 (prior to LBJ's initiatives) to $3 billion and 8.8 percent of the total educational budget by 1968.
- *The development of the Job Corps.* Modeled after the Civilian Conservation Corps of the 1930s, the Job Corps created rural and urban vocational training centers, which helped young people learn marketable skills while working in government projects.
- *The creation of the Department of Education in 1979.* Originally part of the Department of Health, Education and Welfare, education was considered so important that it was elevated to its own cabinet-level position during President Carter's administration.
- *Support for learners with exceptionalities.* In Chapter 3 you learned that the federal government passed Public Law 94–142, the Individuals with Disabilities Education Act (IDEA), in 1975. In 1976–1977, just after the law's passage, the nation educated about 3.3 million children with exceptionalities; presently the schools serve more than 6 million, an increase of nearly 82 percent (Sack, 2000).
- *The creation of national compensatory education programs.* Let's look at these programs in more detail.

Increasing Understanding 5.11

How was the War on Poverty similar to other educational efforts aimed at minorities? How was it different?

Compensatory Education Programs **Compensatory education programs** are *government attempts to create more equal educational opportunities for disadvantaged youth.* These programs provide supplementary instruction and attempt to prevent learning problems before they occur. The two best known are Head Start and Title I.

Head Start. Part of the Economic Opportunity Act of 1964, **Head Start** is *a federal compensatory education program designed to help 3- to 5-year-old disadvantaged children enter school ready to learn.* It has two goals: (1) to stimulate the development and academic achievement of low-income preschoolers and (2) to educate and involve parents in the education of their children. In 1997, for example, more than 94,000 children were involved in the program, which had a budget of nearly $5 billion (U.S. Department of Education, 1999b). Head Start has served almost 17 million children since its inception.

The Head Start curriculum focuses on basic skills such as counting, naming colors, and pre-reading skills, as well as social skills such as turn-taking and following directions. Parenting goals include helping parents develop their children's literacy skills by encouraging parents to read and talk to their children and provide experiences (like trips to zoos, libraries, and museums) that increase their readiness for school.

In general, Head Start 4-year-olds perform better than comparable 4-year-olds who haven't participated in the program, and almost 90 percent of parents surveyed said they are very satisfied with their children's experiences (U.S. Department of Health and Human Services, 1997). In the more effective Head Start programs, such as the Perry Preschool Program in Ypsilanti, Michigan, researchers have found long-term positive effects ranging from fewer special education placements to higher numbers of high school graduates and lower crime and teen pregnancy rates (D. Cohen, 1993).

The success of Head Start has been mixed, however, and some programs have had little impact on children's readiness to learn. Poor program quality and inadequate budgets are the most commonly cited reasons (Merrow, 2002).

Title I. **Title I** is *a federal compensatory education program that funds supplemental education services for low-income students in elementary and secondary schools.* Between 1965 and 2000, more than $120 billion was spent on Title I, and these monies reached almost all of our nation's schools. Presently funded at $10 billion per year, Title I serves 11 million low-income children in 45,000 schools (Borman, 2002/2003). This figure represents only 3 percent of total expenditures for elementary and secondary education, however, and only about 50 percent of eligible students receive

Compensatory education programs such as Title I and Head Start created improved educational opportunities for disadvantaged children.

Title I help ("Educational Excellence for All Children Act," 1999; J. Jennings, 2000). Two-thirds of the money goes to elementary schools, and 15 percent of the highest poverty schools receive 46 percent of Title I funds. Title I currently serves 300,000 migrant children, 200,000 homeless, and 2 million English language learners. Approximately 35 percent of the recipients are White, 30 percent are Hispanic American, and 28 percent African American ("Educational Excellence for All Children Act," 1999).

As with Head Start, the outcomes of Title I programs have been uneven. Part of Title I's ineffectiveness resulted from initial design problems (Borman, 2002/2003). Because the funds initially targeted only low-income students, "pull-out" programs—where students were taken out of their regular classrooms for supplementary instruction—prevailed. During the late 1990s, 60 percent of the instruction in these pull-out programs was conducted by unlicensed aides, or paraprofessionals, and more than 40 percent of these Title I aides spent half or more of their time without the supervision of a licensed teacher (U.S. Department of Education, 1999a). The recent No Child Left Behind Act attempts to address this problem by specifying qualifications for Title I paraprofessionals. By 2005–2006 current paraprofessionals are to have finished 2 years of college or demonstrated competence through passing a rigorous test; newly hired paraprofessionals must meet this standard at the time of hire (J. Jennings, 2002).

Pull-out Title I programs have had other problems as well. Removing students from their classrooms causes logistical problems; the students who are pulled out miss regular instruction, and teachers have trouble helping them catch up. Also, pull-out instruction often focuses on low-level skills with few links to the regular curriculum.

In response to these criticisms, Title I programs have been redesigned to focus on total school improvement, rather than instruction in pull-out programs (Borman, 2002/2003). Newer programs attempt to achieve schoolwide improvement in a variety of ways. For example, James Comer's *School Development Program* (see Chapter 4) focuses on involving parents and providing improved family services such as counseling and social services (Comer, 1994). Another example, *Success for All*, attempts to prevent school failure by emphasizing family involvement and by laying a strong foundation in reading, writing, and math during the early grades (Slavin et al., 1996).

Putting compensatory education programs into perspective. Critics wanting to do away with compensatory education programs first point to their uneven quality. This criticism underscores the general dilemma of federal aid to education. This aid is usually given with only broad guidelines that allow schools and districts to spend the money essentially as they see fit. This necessary flexibility also results in uneven quality.

Critics also argue that the programs have failed to eliminate achievement differences between participants and other students. This criticism is more debatable. Expecting schools, alone, to solve the social problems associated with poverty, such as drug use, violence, unstable families, and unhealthy neighborhoods, is unrealistic. And a long history of research consistently demonstrates that these factors adversely affect learning (Macionis, 2003).

Putting Federal Efforts into Perspective So, how has federal intervention affected the struggle for equality in education? With respect to integration, progress is uncertain. For example, in the South in 1988, nearly 44 percent of African American students attended integrated schools, up from virtually none in 1954. However, by 1996 the figure had shrunk back to about 35 percent (Hendrie, 1999). In the North, segregated housing patterns led to segregated schools. This problem has been exacerbated in urban areas by "White flight" to the suburbs. For example, the African

Exploring Diversity

THE FEDERAL GOVERNMENT'S ROLE IN PURSUING EQUALITY

Consider the following statistics. The average twelfth-grade low-income student of color reads at the same level as the average eighth-grade middle-class White student (Kahlenberg, 2000). The high school graduation rate for White students is 88 percent, but for Hispanics it is 56 percent (U.S. Bureau of Census, 2000a). As a group, African Americans have the lowest achievement test scores of any minority, are over-represented in special education classes, and have a high school completion rate of 86 percent (National Center for Education Statistics, 1996). Close to 30 percent of Hispanics live at or below the poverty line, nearly 30 percent drop out of high school, and college attendance rates are substantially below the general population (National Education Association, 1995; U.S. Bureau of Census, 1997).

In terms of gender equality, while more women attend college and receive bachelor's degrees than do men, their participation in high-status fields remains low. In 1995 women earned only 28 percent of the bachelor's degrees in computer or information sciences, and only 9 percent of the bachelor's degrees in engineering-related technologies (AAUW Education Foundation Commission on Technology, Gender, and Teacher Education, 2000). The percentages of women who are doctors (27%), lawyers (28%), and engineers (11%) continue to remain low, and women earn only 70 percent of what men do (U.S. Bureau of Census, 2000b).

The struggle for equality in education is an important area in which the federal government's role has increased. Civil rights and equity for women are two important areas.

The Civil Rights Movement

Linda Brown was an 8-year-old African American student in Topeka, Kansas, in 1951. Instead of walking 5 blocks to an all-White elementary school, she was forced to cross unguarded and potentially dangerous railroad tracks to catch a bus to a school for African Americans 21 blocks away. In addition to objecting to the distance, her father believed that the African American school had substandard resources and programs. With the help of the National Association for the Advancement of Colored People (NAACP), he went to court to change this.

We saw earlier in the chapter that the policy "separate but equal" was put into place after the Civil War. It remained a guiding principle in education until 1954, when Thurgood Marshall, who later became the first African American on the U.S. Supreme Court, represented the NAACP in arguing against the doctrine that forced Linda Brown to attend a segregated school. In a unanimous decision, the Supreme Court ruled in the famous watershed case, *Brown v. Board of Education of Topeka* (1954), that separate educational facilities are inherently unequal and that racially segregated schools generated "a feeling of inferiority." The days of segregated education for African American students were supposed to be over.

However, in some areas, Whites so strongly resisted integration that it had to be forced. For example, in 1957 President Eisenhower sent federal troops to an all-white high school in Little Rock, Arkansas, to enforce the Supreme Court's antisegregation decision and allow nine African American students to attend the school in safety. In spite of these efforts, discrimination remained widespread because the responsibility for desegregation was left to individual school districts, many of which resisted change.

Congress responded with the Civil Rights Act of 1964, which prohibited discrimination against students on the basis of race, color, or national origin in all institutions receiving federal funds. The federal government now had a mechanism to both encourage and enforce integration efforts.

Federal efforts through legislation such as Title IX have increased funding and participation in girls' athletics.

Equity for Women

As we saw at the beginning of the chapter, in the early periods of U.S. history women were generally excluded from education, and historically, they have been underserved by our nation's schools. The federal government became involved in gender equity issues by enacting Title IX of the Education Amendments of 1972. The purpose of this legislation was to eliminate gender bias in the schools and states:

> No person in the United States shall, on the basis of sex, be excluded from participation in, be denied benefits of, or be subjected to discrimination under any education program or activity receiving federal financial assistance.

The law has had its largest impact on physical education and sports: The number of girls participating in high school athletics increased from 295,000 in 1970 to more than 2.7 million in 1998–1999 (White, 1999a). However, participation is still well below that of boys (3.8 million in 1998–1999), and in most schools women's teams still do not receive comparable funding, facilities, equipment, publicity, travel budgets, or practice opportunities.

Title IX has become very controversial at the college and university level. Critics of Title IX argue that in order to achieve an equal number of male and female athletes, schools have had to eliminate many of the "minor" men's sports, such as wrestling, swimming, gymnastics, and tennis (M. Davis, 2003). Supporters of Title IX argue that the extraordinary cost of college football skews the issue, and a modest cut in football expenditures would allow for a greater investment in women's sports with no cuts to other men's sports.

Increasing Understanding 5.12 CW

How does the concept of "separate but equal" relate to education for women and students with exceptionalities?

Teaching in an Era of Reform

THE FEDERAL GOVERNMENT ISSUE

Reforms result from various sources, such as professional organizations, states, and local districts. One of the most powerful sources of reform is the federal government. As we've seen, during the twentieth century the federal government expanded its role in influencing education. The government initiates or encourages national reforms in three primary ways:

- Setting standards
- Creating testing programs
- Offering financial incentives

Standards

A logical way for the federal government to start influencing education is by setting standards, which provide common goals for educational efforts. One prominent example occurred in 1989, when President Bush and the nation's governors collaborated in an Education Summit and created eight National Education Goals. The goals became the centerpiece of the *Goals 2000: Educate America Act*, which was later funded by Congress. Major provisions of the act are found in Table 5.3.

Goals 2000 guided federal reform efforts until the No Child Left Behind Act was signed into law. One key element of this act is that each state must guarantee that 100 percent of its students be proficient in reading and math by the year 2014. This federal legislation also requires each state to establish its own standards and create tests to assess the extent to which its students meet those standards.

Testing Programs

Begun in 1969, the National Assessment of Educational Progress (NAEP) testing program, also known as "the Nation's Report Card," was designed to provide an objective, external measure of how students in the United States are performing (D. Hoff, 2000b). The program recommends periodic assessments of students in fourth, eighth, and twelfth grades in the areas of math, science, reading, writing, the arts, and the social studies areas of civics, geography, and U.S. history. Because of concerns about undue federal influence and the confidentiality of scores, testing is voluntary and only group scores are reported. In 2003 all 50 states participated in some aspect of the program. In addition to providing a nationwide snapshot of the competence of U.S. students, NAEP also provides state profiles and comparisons of test scores.

Financial Incentives

If national goals are worth pursuing, and tests can measure progress towards these goals, rewarding districts that make significant progress is a logical next step. This is exactly what President George W. Bush recommended during his presidential campaign and what Congress enacted in the 2001 No Child Left Behind Act (Hardy, 2002; J. Jennings, 2002). Low-performing schools that receive federal funds can be put into a 5-year schedule of remediation, and if scores don't improve, the schools could be taken over by the state or reconstituted.

The Issue

No Child Left Behind provides worthy ideals to which the country can aspire. Who would oppose, for example, the idea of every student in the nation reaching proficiency in reading and math by 2014? However, goals such as this—or more accurately, ideas about setting national goals—have been controversial with both political conservatives and liberals, although for different reasons. As Chester Finn, former Assistant Secretary of Education under President Reagan, observed, "Republicans oppose any proposal with the word 'national' in it; Democrats oppose anything with the word 'standards' in it" (quoted in D. Doyle, 1999, p. 56). No Child Left Behind partially dodges this issue by making states responsible for setting proficiency levels in math and reading.

National testing is also controversial. On one hand, knowing how our students are doing and how states compare to one another seems sensible. How can we improve our education systems if we don't know how much our students are learning? On the other hand, those who oppose testing say it leads teachers to "teach to the test," which narrows the curriculum and detracts from an overall education. One critic of the NAEP testing program commented, "What gets tested must be taught. [With national testing] We're one step shy of a national curriculum and we're moving fast in that direction" (D. Hoff, 2000a, p. 29).

Financial incentives also make sense intuitively. Why shouldn't teachers and schools be rewarded for increasing the amount their students learn (and punished when learning doesn't occur)? Nevertheless, critics charge that such incentives will further encourage teachers to teach to the tests, and states and districts will align their curricula with the content being tested—in essence, creating a de facto national curriculum.

You Take a Position

Now it's your turn to take a position on the issue. State in writing whether you favor an increased federal role in school reform that includes setting standards, creating testing programs, and offering financial incentives, and provide a two-page rationale for your position.

For additional references and resources, go to the Companion Website at **www.prenhall. com/kauchak**, *then to this chapter's* Teaching in an Era of Reform *module. You can respond online or submit your response to your instructor.*

CW

Table 5.3 Major Provisions of the Goals 2000 Act

By the year 2000:

- All children in America will start school ready to learn.
- The high school graduation rate will increase to 90 percent.
- Students will master challenging subject matter in all the disciplines.
- The nation's teaching force will have access to high-quality professional development.
- American students will be first in the world in math and science.
- All adult Americans will be literate and possess the skills to compete in a global economy.
- Schools will be safe places to learn.
- Parental involvement and participation in schools will increase.

American student population in inner-city Detroit schools increased from 71 percent in 1975 to 94 percent in 1996 (Kunen, 1996). At the end of the twentieth century, a third of African American students attended schools where minorities made up more than 90 percent of the enrollment. It was recently reported that more than three fourths of Hispanic students attend schools populated predominantly by members of cultural minorities and nearly 4 in 10 attend schools that are 90 percent to 100 percent minority (Borman, 2002/2003).

Various strategies have been proposed to achieve greater racial diversity in schools. Compensatory education, school boundary realignments, and mandatory busing are some. In the 1970s **magnet schools**, *public schools that provide innovative or specialized programs and accept enrollment from students in all parts of a district*, were developed to aid in the integration of White and minority students. Magnet schools have been used in a number of large cities, including Boston, Dallas, Houston, Minneapolis, and San Diego (Black, 1996; Viadero, 1999b).

In spite of strong governmental support ($739 million for experimentation with magnet programs), magnet schools are not always meeting their original intent. For instance, they tend to attract the highest-achieving minority students, which robs other students of role models. When they are successful in attracting bright students from different cultural groups, they are sometimes unable to attract high-performing White students into the same schools. Social class differences between wealthier and poorer students and cultural differences within magnet schools also work to minimize true integration and the development of cohesive learning communities (Dickinson, Holifield, Holifield, & Creer, 2000).

Civil rights and women's equity efforts continue to be highly controversial. Some minority leaders and women's groups assert that progress for cultural minorities and women has been too slow, and the government should do more. On the other hand, conservative leaders—including both African Americans and Whites—contend that civil rights efforts have gone too far. They charge that women and minorities are receiving inappropriately preferential treatment (reverse discrimination). These debates are likely to continue in the future as critics on various sides become increasingly vocal and polar in their positions.

Decision Making

Defining Yourself as a Professional

You've now completed your study of important historical trends that have shaped our country's educational system. These trends have important implications for you as a developing professional.

First, educational goals are becoming more complex and controversial. Early in American history, schools were satisfied with teachers who could teach "the three Rs" and instill religious beliefs in their students. Today's teachers are faced with more complex goals and more demands on the curriculum they are expected to teach. Teachers are expected to use more sophisticated teaching methods, utilize technology, teach higher order and critical thinking, help students become effective problem solvers, effectively manage group work, make learning relevant, and motivate reluctant learners. These increased demands will require teachers to continually improve their teaching skills through ongoing professional development.

Second, education will become more important as technology advances and international economic competition increase. Advances in technology have changed both our personal lives and the U.S. economy. At one time, a strong back and willingness to work were the major prerequisites for employment in America. Today, however, less than 3 percent of the population makes its living on farms, and industries like auto and steel manufacturing employ a declining percentage of the workforce. People who are well educated, understand technology, and can adapt to change are needed in the future. The growing importance of education is clear. Schools and teachers will face increasing pressures to ensure that all students possess an adequate education. These pressures will come in the form of increased emphasis on testing and accountability. As a teacher, you will need to become skilled at translating standards into instruction that will help your students meet those standards.

Third, teachers of the future will be working with student populations that are becoming ever more challenging. Teachers and schools are being increasingly asked to respond to societal problems influencing diverse student populations. Societal problems can be seen in areas such as working with the children of poverty, identifying incidents of child abuse, helping learners cope with violence and anger, and a host of other problems. Teachers no longer simply teach; they counsel, diagnose, keep records, and confer with parents, helping them participate in their children's learning. Teachers will also be expected to respond to the needs, motivations, and sensitivities of students with different cultural and experiential backgrounds. You will need to make continual efforts to learn about the strengths and weaknesses of the different groups of students you'll be working with.

Finally, this chapter reminds us that all teachers contribute to the moral and character development of their students. Sometimes this occurs implicitly through our interactions with students and the rules we establish and the ways we enforce them. Other times teachers explicitly focus on moral issues, whether they involve an altercation on the playground or the interpretation of a historical event such as the Vietnam War or the civil rights movement. As you prepare to become a teacher, you need to think about your own views of morality and how those views will influence your teaching and ultimately your students.

Summary

The Colonial Period (1607–1775)

Religion played a central role in colonial education. The first place public funds were used to support education was in colonial New England. Despite humanistic influences from Europe, colonial education was influenced by negative views of children and learning.

The Early National Period (1775–1820)

During the early national period, the framers of the Constitution made two important decisions. One was to separate religion from government. The other was to place the primary responsibility for funding and governing education in the hands of state and local governments.

The Common School Movement (1820–1865)

During the years leading up to the Civil War, the foundations of universal access to tax-supported schools were set. State departments of education were established to govern schools, and normal schools were built to advance the idea of professional training for teachers.

The Evolution of the American High School

The history of the comprehensive American high school began with the Boston Latin School, the first Latin grammar school in the colonies. The college-preparatory institution focused on the classics. Benjamin Franklin's Academy of Philadelphia introduced the idea of a practical curriculum. The English High School targeted non-college students and was supported by public funds. The comprehensive American high school evolved as a compromise out of a tug-of-war between committee reports that advocated either academic or applied orientations. Current middle schools started as more traditional junior highs created in the early 1900s.

The Progressive Era

During the Progressive Era, educators reexamined goals and methods. Emphasis on teacher-centered academics was replaced by a more student-centered approach to democratic problem solving. A conservative reaction to life adjustment courses signaled the end of this movement.

Searching for Equality: The Education of Cultural Minorities

The education of minorities in the United States, aimed at assimilation, attempted to be separate but equal but generally failed. Native American education efforts attempted to assimilate students through boarding schools. African American education had a long history of separate but unequal treatment that was finally challenged in the Supreme Court in 1954. Bilingual education has been a central controversy in the education of Hispanics and Asian Americans.

The Modern Era: Schools as Instruments for National Purpose and Social Change

During the modern era, the federal government took a more active role in education. During the cold war with Russia, the federal government spent large amounts of money improving math, science, and foreign language education. The federal government also used courts and federal spending to battle poverty and inequalities in the schools.

Important Concepts

academy (p. 176)
assimilation (p. 181)
character education (p. 167)
common school movement (p. 171)
compensatory education programs (p. 187)
comprehensive high school (p. 175)
English classical school (p. 176)
Head Start (p. 187)
junior high schools (p. 177)
Latin grammar school (p. 175)
magnet schools (p. 194)
middle schools (p. 178)
normal schools (p. 172)
Old Deluder Satan Act (p. 164)
progressive education (p. 179)
separate but equal (p. 181)
Title I (p. 188)
vouchers (p. 166)
War on Poverty (p. 187)

Developing as a Professional

Praxis Practice

Read the case study, and answer the questions that follow.

"Oh, my aching feet!" Dave Carlisle (the first-year middle school teacher from the opening case for this chapter) moaned as he sank onto the sofa.

"Out late dancing again?" Monica asked, looking up from the lesson plans she was working on.

"Yeah, right. Don't I wish. I've been on my feet all morning lecturing on Newton's laws of motion."

"Newton's laws of motion? Isn't that stuff they'll get in high school physics?" Monica asked.

"Yeah, but I just want to be sure that they'll be ready for it when they get there. About half of the kids in my morning class are really sharp and should go on to college. They'll need this stuff," Dave replied.

"How come you're lecturing so much? I thought we agreed we'd try more problem-based learning to get the kids involved. Lecturing is not only hard on you, it's difficult for them—especially the ones struggling in science."

"Yeah, I know that, but I'm torn. Science is really important. Especially for those going on to college. Do I aim for the average student and punish my high achievers, or teach to the college bound and hope the others come along for the ride? Any ideas?"

"Sounds like we better talk about this in our next team meeting," Monica replied with a frown.

1. Analyze Dave's comments in terms of the history of the middle school and junior high school. Where would Dave's teaching more clearly fit?
2. In which type of earlier school—Latin grammar school, academy, or English classical school—would Dave's teaching fit the best? least?
3. Which report, the report from the Committee of Ten or the *Cardinal Principles of Secondary Education*, would Dave agree with more? Why?
4. What evidence of progressive education is there at Dave Carlisle's middle school?

To receive feedback on your responses to the Praxis Practice exercises, go to the Companion Website at **www.prenhall.com/kauchak**, then to this chapter's *Praxis Practice* module.

Discussion Questions

1. What is the proper relationship between education and religion? Is the connection between religion and education likely to get closer or farther apart over the next 10 years? Why do you think so?
2. Will trends that emphasize *choice*, such as the use of school vouchers and enrollment in magnet schools, likely increase or decrease in the future? Why do you think so? Will choice positively or negatively influence education?
3. What is your position on bilingual education? Should it be generally banned as it has been in California, or did California make a mistake? Explain your position.
4. How would you attempt to solve the problems of Native American education?
5. Do you believe that racial discrimination remains a major problem for society? What could or should schools do to alleviate this problem?
6. Would our educational system be better if control were at the national level instead of the local and state levels? Why or why not?

Going into Schools

1. Interview a teacher who has been teaching for more than 20 years, and ask him or her to describe educational changes in the following areas.
   a. Emphasis on character or moral education and religion in the schools
   b. Diversity of students and implications for teaching
   c. Gender equity efforts
   d. Federal programs and their effects on the schools

   Analyze responses in terms of the content in this chapter. Specifically, have the experiences of this teacher been similar to or different from national trends?
2. Interview a Title I teacher about the program in which he or she teaches, and explore the following areas.
   a. What student populations are served?
   b. What is the curriculum, and who determines it?
   c. How does the Title I curriculum connect with the regular curriculum?
   d. What instructional strategies are used and why?
   e. What suggestions does the teacher have for improving the program?

   Analyze these responses, decide how effective Title I has been in the War on Poverty, and make suggestions for making it more effective.
3. Examine two textbooks for the same class (e.g., social studies or literature). One should be a recent one, and the other should be at least 20 years old. (Textbooks can be obtained from the curriculum library at your college, local school district, or state.)
   a. How does the content differ?
   b. What changes can you find in the books' coverage of women?
   c. What changes can you find in the books' treatment or coverage of minorities?
   d. What do these changes suggest about changing priorities in education?
4. Interview a junior high or middle school teacher about ways that the school attempts to meet the needs of developing adolescents. Ask about the following:
   a. Teaming by teachers
   b. Modifications in the curriculum

c. Interactive teaching strategies such as cooperative learning or problem-based learning

d. Extracurricular activities

Analyze the teacher's responses in terms of the reasons for which middle schools were created.

5. Interview a high school teacher about the success of the school in creating a comprehensive high school. The following questions might guide your interview:

a. Are there different tracks or programs in the school?

b. What percentage of students are in each track, and what are these students like?

c. How is the curriculum different for each track?

d. How is instruction different for each track?

e. How much do students from different tracks interact? What does the school do to encourage this?

Analyze the teacher's responses in terms of the successes and challenges facing comprehensive high schools.

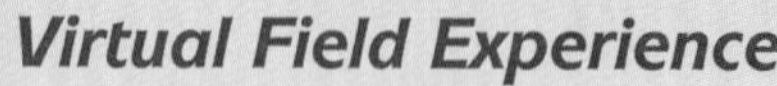

Virtual Field Experience

If you would like to participate in a Virtual Field Experience, go to the Companion Website at **www.prenhall.com/kauchak**, then to this chapter's *Field Experience* module.

Online Portfolio Activities

To complete these activities online, go to the Companion Website at **www.prenhall.com/kauchak**, then to this chapter's *Portfolio Activities* module.

Portfolio Activity 5.1

Character Education

INTASC Principle 2: Learning and Human Development

Personal Journal Reflection
The purpose of this activity is to help you to begin thinking about the role of moral or character education in your own teaching. Research different views on character education, and take a personal position on the issue. (You'll find additional information on the topic in Chapter 10.) In this position statement, make sure you include:

a. Your definition of character education

b. The proper role that religion, parents, and other nonschool institutions should play in it

c. What teachers can or should do in this regard

Portfolio Activity 5.2

Progressive Education

INTASC Principle 4: Strategies

The purpose of this activity is to help you understand the important role that the progressive movement played in American education. Research the text section "The Progressive Era," and write a personal evaluation of the movement. (You'll find additional information and resources on the topic in Chapter 6.) In your evaluation, address the following issues or questions:

a. What was progressive education?
b. What were its strengths and weaknesses?
c. What positive aspects of it would you include in your teaching?
d. How is it related to the present movement in instruction of constructivism (see Chapter 11)?

Portfolio Activity 5.3

Ability Grouping and Tracking

INTASC Principle 3: Adapting Instruction
INTASC Principle 7: Planning

The purpose of this activity is to help you form an opinion about the proper role of grouping and tracking in education. Ability grouping and tracking are found in many schools. Investigate the research on ability grouping, and answer the following questions.

a. What are the advantages and disadvantages of these practices in general and at the specific level at which you'll teach?
b. What can teachers do to minimize the potential negative effects of these practices? (You'll find additional information on the topic in Chapters 3 and 7.)

Chapter 6

Educational Philosophy

The Intellectual Foundations of American Education

Philosophy often seems rather remote and disconnected from everyday life, but this isn't at all the case. We each have a "philosophy of life." For many people it is tacit and unclearly defined, but for others it is well articulated. Our philosophy is the set of principles we have chosen to live by; it's what guides us in our daily actions.

As with individuals, professions and professionals have philosophies that guide their practice. This is the topic for this chapter, as we try to answer the following questions:

- What is philosophy?
- How does philosophy influence teacher professionalism?
- How do traditional philosophies influence the process of learning to teach?
- What are the most prominent philosophies of education, and how do they affect teaching and learning?
- How can you, a prospective teacher, begin to form a philosophy of education?

Let's begin by looking in on a conversation between two teachers.

This logo appears throughout the chapter to indicate where case studies are integrated with chapter content.

Case STUDY

"What's happening?" Brad Norman asked Allie Skinner as he walked into the teachers' lounge during the lunch period.

"Working on this quiz," Allie mumbled, glancing up at him.

"You sure do test the heck out of your kids, don't you? Every time I come in here you're either writing a quiz or scoring one, or recording grades, or something."

"Well, it isn't that I love tests so much, but . . . well, you know what I think."

"Yeah, yeah, I know," Brad replied, waving his hand. "If you don't challenge them, they don't learn. . . . I guess I'm just more interested in trying to motivate them."

"Wait a minute," Allie interrupted. "I'm as interested in motivation as you are; it's just that I have some different views about how you get there."

"I know you think that *pushing* the kids . . . " Brad began again.

"High expectations," Allie interrupted with a wry smile.

"Whatever," Brad shrugged. "I know you think that having *high expectations,*" he continued, rolling his eyes at the words, "is important, but I don't see how testing and all that stuff relates to motivation."

"Do you want to hear about it?" Allie asked. "Might be boring."

"Sure, but keep it brief," Brad smiled.

"Well, this is what I believe, . . . and you've got to be true to what you believe, I think, or you just blow back and forth like a leaf in the wind. I've given all this a lot of thought, and this is the best I've been able to come up with so far. I mean, I'll change my mind when I get some evidence that I'm wrong."

"You were going to keep it brief."

"Yeah, yeah, . . . well . . . anyway, I know kids have changed over the last however many years. They don't come to school with the same sort of desire to learn as they once did. Now, I do still believe that kids want to learn, or maybe more specifically, they want to believe they did learn something when they're finished with a topic, or class, or year of school, or whatever. On the other hand, they're not intrinsically motivated, and by that I mean, I don't think they're motivated to study stuff for it's own sake. I think they're often extrinsically motivated, motivated to study as a means to some end, like a good grade, or recognition from their classmates, or compliments from the teacher or something like that.

"Now, I was reading in one of my journals a while back, and the authors were talking about the link between achievement and self-esteem, and it really made sense. I thought about what they said, and I do believe that kids feel good when they learn something, particularly if it's challenging. I also think that the more they know about a topic, the better they like it. For example, wouldn't you agree that an expert in some area, like a person who really understands literature, or poetry, or physics, is more motivated in that area than a novice, a person who doesn't know much about literature?

"Look at yourself; you're really into surfing the Internet; you talk about it all the time. . . . The better you've gotten at it, the more you like it, and the more you want to do it."

"Yeah, probably, . . . I guess so," Brad shrugged.

"So, my goal is to get students to learn as much as possible about everything, like I mean the topics I'm teaching. The more they learn, the more intrinsically motivated they're going to be, and they're going to be motivated because they're getting good at the topic, and they're acquiring expertise about it.

"Now, there's real, practical stuff out there that they need to know, and there's only one way they're gonna learn it. . . . That's practice and experience. So, I've got to get them to study and practice. One way of doing that is to give them a lot of quizzes. They study for the quizzes, they get lots of feedback, and they tell me they learn a lot. Ultimately they like it, and further, their self-esteem improves, and it improves because they've learned a lot. That's the way it works. It's a win–win all the way around. . . . That's how I think the world works. I'm getting paid to help kids learn. If I don't do my very best to make that happen, I'm not earning my salary."

"Some of what you're saying makes sense," Brad acknowledged. "However, your view is a bit narrow for me. First, much of what I read suggests that kids would be intrinsically motivated if school wasn't so boring. How motivated would you be if you had to sit and listen to dry teachers drone on all day, every day?

"I like the idea of kids knowing stuff too, but school involves more than that. Where in your scheme do kids learn to solve problems and make choices and wise decisions? A head full of facts may be great if your goal in life is to be good at quiz shows, but the person who really succeeds is the one who continues to learn and is able to adapt to changes in the world by solving the large and small problems they encounter. So, . . . the only way they're going to get good at making decisions is to be put in situations where they're forced to make decisions. They need lots of experience in making decisions and solving problems. That's what life's all about.

"Plus, thinking about doing my job, it would be a heck of a lot easier to just make the kids cram some stuff in their heads, but I would be doing them, their parents, and ultimately our whole society a disservice if I didn't bite the bullet and prepare them for life outside of school.

"And, as long as I'm at it," Brad continued, holding up a hand to prevent Allie from interrupting, "exactly what is *real?* You said ' there's real, practical stuff out there that they need to know.' For instance, let's say that, based on this conversation, you conclude that I'm naive and idealistic. On the other hand, I conclude that I'm actually more practical than you are, because I think schooling should help kids learn to make wise decisions and be adaptable, which requires learning activities where they're forced to make decisions. What is the reality? Am I naive, or am I practical? Who's to say? Reality is in fact this: To you, I'm naive, and you will operate based on that belief. To me, I'm not. So, reality is what we perceive it to be, and there's no objective source *out there* to decide which view is the 'right one.'"

"Aw, c'mon," Allie countered. "Sure I acknowledge your point, but look at that oak tree outside the window. You can perceive it to be anything you want, but it's still an oak. And it doesn't matter what anybody thinks, two plus two is four—not three, not five, not anything in between.

"Plus, I'm not talking about a 'head full of facts.' Knowing stuff means that they understand it well enough so they can apply it to whatever situation comes up. For instance, you want them to make wise decisions. They can't make a *wise* decision if they don't know anything."

Just then the bell rang, announcing the end of the teachers' planning period and signaling the transition to the next class. Allie and Brad left, agreeing to disagree and promising (or threatening) to continue the discussion later.

• • ● • •

Let's consider Brad's and Allie's conversation. They were discussing ideas at the heart of learning and teaching, and they obviously disagreed on several of them. However, both had given a good deal of thought to what is important in teaching and why it's important. The result was a philosophy of education that guided their work. This is what our chapter is about.

Philosophy and Philosophy of Education

What is philosophy, and what does "philosophy of education" mean? At its most basic level, philosophy is described as a search for wisdom (Ozmon & Craver, 2003), but in a more formal sense, **philosophy** is *a study of theories of knowledge, truth, existence, and good* (Jacobsen, 2003).

We see evidence of this study in Allie's and Brad's reflections. Allie, for example, said, "I've given all this a lot of thought, and this is the best I've been able to come up with so far. I mean, I'll change my mind when I get some evidence that I'm wrong." She was describing knowledge, truth, and what she believed was good in her statements. Although his beliefs and conclusions were different, Brad was pursuing the same goal. This is why philosophy is important for teachers. A **philosophy of education** *provides a framework for thinking about educational issues, and it guides professional practice.* How is this framework acquired?

Philosophy and Teacher Professionalism

All professions have "philosophies" that help guide practitioners in their thinking and actions. For example, the famous architect Frank Lloyd Wright came from the "organic" school of architecture. According to this school, homes and other structures should be a part of the environment; they shouldn't exist apart from their surroundings. In the photo on the left on page 206 we see that the house blends into its background so well that it almost appears to be a natural part of the setting. A contrasting architectural philosophy holds that "form follows function." This view suggests that structures must first be functional, and the way they're built then depends on that function. The photo on the right on page 206 reflects this belief.

Philosophy exerts a powerful influence on other professions, such as architecture.

Other professions have their own philosophies—their systems of beliefs that guide their decisions about professional practice. For example, the shift in emphasis from treating illness after it's occured to preventing illness through lifestyle changes reflects a philosophical change in medicine. Holistic medicine, where patients' beliefs and emotions, in addition to their physical symptoms, are taken into account in diagnosis and treatment, represents another philosophical shift. Similar competing philosophical systems could be described for all professions.

In their conversation Allie and Brad expressed different views, but their contrasting positions share common features, and they closely relate to teacher professionalism (see Figure 6.1). For example, both Allie and Brad reflected on their practice, and they made decisions about what topics were most important to study and how to best help students understand those topics. Allie, for example, stated her belief that "there's real, practical stuff out there that they need to know, and there's only one way they're gonna learn it." She decided to emphasize what she believed was essential knowledge, and she further decided to frequently assess her students to help them acquire this knowledge. Brad's reflection led him to decide that involving students in learning activities was the best way for students to gain essential knowledge.

Both Allie and Brad based their decisions on specialized knowledge—another aspect of professionalism. For example, Allie said, "Now, I was reading in one of my journals a while back, . . . and it really made sense." She didn't base her decisions on intuition or whim; she based them on professional knowledge. The same was true for Brad, as indicated by his comment, "First, much of what I read suggests that. . . ." He disagreed with Allie, but his decisions were also based on knowledge.

Figure 6.1 Elements of Professionalism in Allie's and Brad's Philosophies

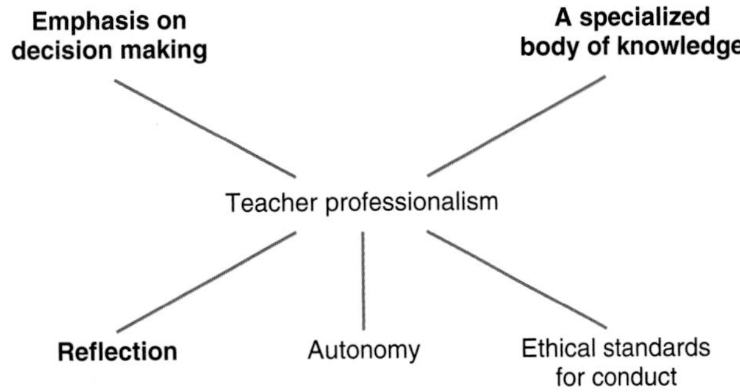

Increasing Understanding 6.1

Figure 6.1 emphasizes knowledge, decision making, and reflection. Explain how autonomy is also illustrated in Allie's and Brad's conversation.

To answer the Increasing Understanding questions online and receive immediate feedback, go to the Companion Website at www.prenhall.com/kauchak, then to this chapter's *Increasing Understanding* module. Type in your response, and then study the feedback.

We posed the question, "How is this framework acquired?" at the close of the last section. Teachers acquire a philosophical framework to guide their practice by becoming knowledgeable and reflective, which allows them to make professional decisions that promote as much growth in their students as possible. Philosophy is an essential part of this professional knowledge.

The Relationship Between Philosophy and Theory

Philosophy and theory overlap in many ways, and the distinction between the two is often blurred. In fact, our definition describes philosophy as the study of *theories*, specifically theories of knowledge, truth, existence, and good (Jacobsen, 2003). A philosophy and a theory are not the same, however.

A **theory** is *a set of related principles that are based on observation and are used to explain additional observations.* Let's say we see a boy wearing a prominent sports figure's football jersey. Psychology's *social cognitive theory* tells us that "people tend to imitate behavior they observe in others" and also that "individuals are more likely to imitate someone with high status than someone with low status." These principles, which are based on psychologists' observations, help us explain what we observe in the boy, and we conclude that he is imitating a high-status model.

CW

Increasing Understanding 6.2

We said that philosophy guides practice. Does theory also guide practice? Explain.

Philosophies are based in part on theories. For example, Allie's emphasis on high expectations is based in part on theories of motivation. Philosophy goes beyond theory, however, to not only explain the way things are, such as why the boy wears the jersey and why students are motivated, but to also suggest the way things *ought to be,* and to analyze theories, ideas, and beliefs. Allie, for example, suggested that schools ought to emphasize knowledge and understanding, whereas Brad thought they ought to focus on decision making and problem solving. Further, Allie expressed the *belief* that kids basically want to learn but that they're not intrinsically motivated. Brad expressed the opposite belief. In this regard, both Allie and Brad stepped beyond theory into the realm of philosophy.

Philosophies in other professions also suggest what ought to be. Using the examples cited earlier, one school of architecture suggests that structures ought to be a part of the environment, whereas another believes that being functional is the highest priority. In medicine one school of thinking emphasizes prevention through healthy lifestyles, while another focuses on healing through medication and other treatments. *A description of the way something ought to be*—such as the way educators, architects, physicians, or other professionals ought to practice—is called a **normative philosophy.**

Branches of Philosophy

Just as other areas of inquiry, such as biology, geography, or literature, have different areas and topics of study, so does philosophy. In philosophy these include the following:

- Epistemology
- Metaphysics (ontology)
- Axiology
- Logic

Let's examine them.

Epistemology

Let's look again at Allie's and Brad's discussion. Allie stated, "Now, there's real, practical stuff out there that they need to know, and there's only one way they're gonna learn it. . . . That's practice and experience. So, I've got to get them to study and practice." She argued that *the way learners come to know* the ideas they learn is through practice and experience.

Allie was making an epistemological argument. **Epistemology** is *a branch of philosophy that examines questions of how we come to know what we know.* A variety of ways of knowing exist. The scientific method, in which a problem is tested by collecting facts through observation and experiment, is one. Intuition, authority, and even divine revelation are others.

CW

Increasing Understanding 6.3

A woman shopping for a new car makes her choice by reviewing the cars' mileage ratings, their repair records, and evaluations from organizations such as the American Automobile Association. Is her "way of knowing" primarily the scientific method, intuition, or authority? Explain.

Constructivism, a prominent learning theory, raises interesting epistemological questions. Constructivism argues that, instead of behaving like tape recorders, which reproduce words and music in their original form, people "construct" understanding that makes sense to them, For example, many people have "constructed" the idea that places in the northern hemisphere are warmer in summer than winter because they are closer to the sun then. (In reality, the northern hemisphere is farther away from the sun in summer, but the sun's rays are more direct.) In thinking this way, people draw analogies between proximity to a candle or a bonfire and the sun's distance to the earth (Mayer, 1998). The way we come to understand why summer is warmer than winter is to construct ideas—sometimes faulty ideas—that make sense to us.

Increasing Understanding 6.4

With respect to epistemology, are Allie's and Brad's views quite similar or quite different? Explain, citing evidence from the case study to support your position.

Epistemology is important for teachers because our beliefs about how students gain knowledge affect our choice of teaching methods. Teachers who believe in constructivism, for example, provide a variety of experiences for learners and lead discussions that will help them construct valid understandings of the way the world works. In contrast, teachers who believe that listening to an expert is the most important way of knowing are likely to lecture students and expect them to reproduce what they've heard on tests.

Metaphysics

Whereas epistemology examines *how* we know, **metaphysics**—or **ontology**—is *a branch of philosophy that considers what we know* (Osborne, 1996). Metaphysics considers questions of reality and, ultimately, what is real (Jacobsen, 2003). With respect to metaphysics, Allie and Brad are far apart. Allie argued that "there's real, practical stuff out there that [students] need to know," but Brad countered that "reality is what we perceive it to be, and there's no objective source *out there* to decide which view is the 'right one.'" Allie believes in a reality independent of our perception, but Brad believes that perception and reality are inextricably intertwined.

Our metaphysical beliefs influence both the way we teach and the goals we establish. For instance, because Allie believes in a reality independent of people's perceptions, her goal is for students to understand that reality. In contrast, because Brad believes less strongly in an objective reality, his goals more strongly emphasize students learning to critically examine their own thinking. The teaching methods both Allie and Brad use will be those that best help students reach these goals.

Axiology

CW

Increasing Understanding 6.5

Character educators see learners as unsocialized and in need of moral discipline. In contrast, moral educators see learners as undeveloped, needing stimulation to construct more mature moral views. Are these contrasting positions more closely related to metaphysics or to epistemology? Explain.

Axiology is *a branch of philosophy that considers values and ethics,* and axiological issues are now prominent in American education. Because of problems such as drug abuse, teen pregnancy, and juvenile violence and crime, educators generally agree that some form of moral education is needed in schools (Bebeau, Rest, & Narvaez, 1999; Wynne, 1997). They disagree, however, on the form it should take. Some favor **character education** (introduced in Chapter 5), *an approach to developing morality that suggests moral values and positive character traits, such as honesty and citizenship, should be emphasized, taught, and rewarded* (Benninga & Wynne, 1998; D. Doyle, 1997). Other educators prefer **moral education,** *an approach to developing morality that emphasizes the development of students' moral reasoning but doesn't establish a preset list of values that learners should acquire* (Kohn, 1997). Almost all educators, however, believe that the development of moral thinking and moral behavior are important goals for schools.

How does axiology influence teachers? Let's look again at Allie's and Brad's conversation. Allie argued, "I'm getting paid to help kids learn. If I don't do my very best to make that happen, I'm not earning my salary." Brad retorted that "it would be a heck of a lot easier to just make the kids cram some stuff in their heads, but I would be doing them, their parents, and ultimately our whole society a disservice if I didn't bite the bullet and prepare them for life outside of school." Both teachers argued that they wouldn't be behaving ethically if they weren't true to their beliefs about what is important. Although they were probably unaware of it, this part of their conversation was concerned with axiology.

Logic

Some of Allie's comments to Brad demonstrate a particular thinking process. Although these are not Allie's exact words, the following statements represent Allie's sequence of thoughts:

> "The more people learn, the more intrinsically motivated they become."
>
> "You [Brad] have learned a lot about the Internet."
>
> "You want to surf the Internet more now than ever before because you're more intrinsically motivated."

Logic is *a branch of philosophy that examines the processes of deriving valid conclusions from basic principles,* and Allie was illustrating a form of logic called *deductive reasoning.* Deductive reasoning begins with a proposition, called a major premise, which could be a principle or generalization such as "The more people learn, the more intrinsically motivated they are." The major premise is followed by a fact, called a minor premise, such as "You have learned a lot about the Internet." A deductive reasoning sequence ends with a conclusion that follows from the two premises. In Allie's case the conclusion was an explanation for why Brad spent time surfing the Internet.

Inductive reasoning is the counterpart to deductive reasoning. For instance, when students see that a rock and paper clip and a baseball and golf ball hit the floor at the same time if they're dropped simultaneously from the same height, they conclude that objects fall at the same rate regardless of weight (if air resistance is negligible). On the basis of the specific instances (such as the fall of the rock and the clip), the students make a general conclusion about falling objects.

CW

Increasing Understanding 6.6

You're being asked to respond to margin questions, such as this one. We have concluded that questions such as these will increase your understanding of this book. Identify a major premise and a minor premise on which this conclusion could be based.

Logic helps both teachers and learners examine the validity of their thinking. For instance, in social studies we try to help students see that if we stereotype a specific cultural group based on the behavior or appearance of a few members of the group, we're using faulty inductive reasoning. Similarly, many controversies in education and other aspects of life exist because proponents and critics disagree on the validity of conclusions, which are the products of deductive reasoning. For example, critics of character education conclude that it emphasizes indoctrination (Kohn, 1997). They base this conclusion on the premise that a system that relies on rewards indoctrinates rather than teaches (a major premise) and character education utilizes rewards (a minor premise). Proponents of character education disagree with both the major premise and the conclusion.

Traditional Schools of Philosophy

Throughout history philosophers have struggled to systematically describe how the world works; that is, they've tried to answer questions about reality and what is real (metaphysics), how we know (epistemology), what is good and valuable (axiology), and whether or not our thinking is clear and accurate (logic). These efforts have resulted in four cohesive philosophies, considered by many to be the traditional philosophies that undergird most educational decisions (Jacobsen, 2003):

- Idealism
- Realism
- Pragmatism
- Existentialism

We turn to them now.

Idealism

Consider one of Brad's arguments in his conversation with Allie:

[L]et's say that, based on this conversation, you conclude that I'm naive and idealistic. On the other hand, I conclude that I'm actually more practical than you are, . . . What is the reality? Am I naive, or am I practical? . . . To you, I'm naive, and you will operate based on that belief. To me I'm not. So, reality is what we perceive it to be, and there's no objective source *out there* to decide which view is the "right one."

CW

Increasing Understanding 6.7

Would idealists support the scientific method, or would they be critical of it? Explain. To which of the four branches of philosophy is this question most closely related? Explain.

Brad was making an argument consistent with **idealism,** *a traditional philosophy asserting that, because the physical world is constantly changing, ideas are the only reliable form of reality.* Idealism is the oldest of the Western philosophies, having originated with Plato, the great Greek philosopher.

Plato was born at the height of Greek civilization into an aristocratic family in Athens (his birth date is estimated to be 428 BC). Along with Socrates (Plato's teacher and mentor) and Aristotle, Plato was one of the three philosophers of ancient Greece that laid the philosophical foundations of Western culture.

Idealism emphasizes great works of literature, music, and art, which contain powerful ideas from important contributors to our culture.

> *Plato wrote imaginary dialogues between Socrates and his students in order to faithfully represent Socrates' thinking. In the dialogues Socrates questions students' beliefs and assumptions about truth, beauty, and other philosophical topics. Plato's portrayal of the questioning led to the modern concept of the* Socratic method, *or* Socratic questioning.

To idealists, ultimate reality exists in the world of ideas, so they believe that teaching and learning should focus on ideas. A curriculum based on idealism emphasizes mathematics, because of its logic, precision, and abstraction. It also emphasizes great works of literature, art, and music, because of their enduring contributions. Great men and women in history are studied in order to examine their thinking and the ideas they offered.

Teachers fill a critical role for idealists. Learners are unlikely to understand many important ideas without support and guidance. Teachers provide this guidance by helping students become more precise and logical thinkers and by helping them understand the important ideas that have endured throughout history.

Idealism has been criticized for being elitist and overemphasizing cold, rational ideas at the expense of human emotions and intuition. It is elitist because the ideas chosen for analysis often come from a small, wealthy, and privileged part of the population. It is considered coldly cognitive because it emphasizes the rational and logical over other dimensions of human experience.

Realism

In contrast with idealism, which argues that ideas are the ultimate reality, **realism** *holds that the features of the universe exist whether or not a human being is there to perceive them.* Realism is also an ancient philosophy, originating from the work of Aristotle and others. In the following statements, Allie's thinking is consistent with realism: "[L]ook at

that oak tree outside the window. You can perceive it to be anything you want, but it's still an oak. And it doesn't matter what anybody thinks, two plus two is four—not three, not five, not anything in between." Realists argue that there are important ideas and facts that must be understood and they can only be understood by studying the material world. Realists emphasize science and technology and strongly endorse the scientific method. They argue that ignorance of information about diet, disease, and natural disasters, for example, has caused much of the suffering in human history and that accumulation of knowledge in areas such as science and medicine has improved the quality of life for many people.

Born in Greece in 384 BC, Aristotle studied at Plato's Academy. The great thinker and teacher is believed to have participated in the education of Alexander the Great, one of the greatest military leaders in history.

Aristotle studied and wrote about an amazing array of topics ranging from logic, philosophy, and ethics to physics, biology, psychology, and politics. Deductive reasoning and the scientific method were both influenced by his thinking.

Critics who claim that American education is in decline because the curriculum has been "dumbed down" with too many superfluous courses and too much emphasis on self-esteem are expressing views consistent with realism. A curriculum consistent with realism emphasizes essentials, such as math, science, reading, and writing, because they are tools to help us understand our world. The periodic national focus and refocus on basic skills is also consistent with this view.

Teachers working within the philosophy of realism emphasize observation, experimentation, and critical reasoning. Their goals are for learners to think clearly and understand the material world. They tend to de-emphasize formal emphasis on feelings and other personal factors, arguing that positive feelings and the improvement of self-esteem are an outgrowth of knowledge and understanding.

Critics of realism, like critics of idealism, argue that the philosophy is inappropriately narrow. It fails to take the whole person—physical, emotional, and social sides, in addition to the intellectual domain—into account in the learning process.

Pragmatism

Although it has ancient roots, pragmatism is considered a modern—even American—philosophy, with John Dewey being one of its primary proponents. Dewey (1902, 1906, 1923, 1938) wrote extensively on education, and his work has arguably had more impact on American education than that of any other philosopher. His ideas continue to be actively debated by educators today (e.g., see Prawat, 1998; Proefriedt, 1999). (See Chapter 5 for a discussion of Dewey's role in the progressive movement in education.)

John Dewey (1859–1952) may be the most important American philosopher in history. Educated in his native Vermont and at Johns Hopkins University, Dewey enjoyed a long career as an educator, psychologist, and philosopher. He initiated the progressive laboratory school at the University of Chicago, where his reforms in methods of education were put into practice. As a result, progressivism, *a prominent educational philosophy, is associated with his work.*

Pragmatism is *a traditional philosophy that rejects the idea of absolute, unchanging truth, instead asserting that truth is what works.* The term *pragmatism* shares a root with *pragmatic*, which means "practical" in common usage. Pragmatism shares some views with realism but is less rigid. For example, our primitive ancestors needed and

Pragmatists attempt to connect subject matter to children's interests.

CW
Increasing Understanding 6.8

Are Allie's views or Brad's views, as expressed in our opening case study, more closely related to pragmatism? Cite evidence from the case to support your contention.

ate a diet high in fat, because it might be a long time between meals, and they were very active as hunter–gatherers. Now, we have a problem. Our evolved selves still enjoy—even crave—fat, but we no longer need as much because we've become sedentary. Long ago, truth was that fat was important and healthy; today, truth is fat is less important and too much is unhealthy. A high-fat diet no longer "works."

For pragmatists, *experience* is a key idea. As we've gathered experiences with respect to diet, for example, we've observed the consequences of those experiences and have adapted (or are trying to adapt) accordingly. Pragmatists contend that truth isn't an abstract idea, nor is it simply a material aspect of the world. Rather, it represents the interaction between the individual and the environment. Further, truth is personal and relative. Some people, for example, need more fat in their diet than do others.

Because truth changes, individuals need methods for dealing with these changes. As a result, teachers adhering to pragmatism place the processes involved in learning on an equal plane with content. Direct experiences and problem solving are emphasized. Information needed to solve problems comes from many sources, so studying content areas in isolation isn't effective or practical; interdisciplinary education that focuses on using various academic disciplines to analyze and solve problems is more "pragmatic." In addition, lectures focusing on abstract ideas are rejected in favor of hands-on, concrete experiences.

Critics contend that pragmatism too strongly emphasizes student interests at the expense of essential knowledge (Ravitch, 2000). A conservative faction blames pragmatism, with its educational counterpart, progressivism (discussed later in the chapter and introduced in Chapter 5), for the decline in performance by American students as compared to students in other industrialized countries.

Defenders of pragmatism, and particularly of Dewey's work, argue that the critics either misrepresent Dewey or don't understand him.

• • ● • •

He saw clearly that to ask, "Which is more important: the interests of the child or the knowledge of subject-matter?" was to ask a very dumb question indeed. The teacher's task, for Dewey, was to create an interaction between the child's interest and the funded knowledge of the adult world (Proefriedt, 1999, p. 28).

• • ● • •

Pragmatism doesn't de-emphasize the importance of knowledge but instead attempts to connect it to children's interests.

Existentialism

Compared to idealism, realism, and pragmatism, existentialism is quite radical. **Existentialism** is *a traditional philosophy suggesting that humanity isn't part of an orderly universe; rather, individuals create their own realities in their own unique ways.* Influenced by the horrors of World War II, existentialist writers, such as Jean-Paul Sartre, have a pessimistic view of humanity, seeing it as essentially meaningless on a small, isolated planet in an uncertain universe where nothing is determined. If nothing is determined, people have total freedom—freedom to take advantage of others, promote racial strife, or cause conflicts, for example. Conversely, we're also free to conduct ourselves morally, promote peace and harmony, and so on. With total freedom comes total responsibility. Unwise choices can't be blamed on God's will, other people, or prior experiences.

> *Jean-Paul Sartre (1905–1980) was educated at Paris and Göttingen, Germany. He participated actively in the French resistance to German occupation in World War II, and the experience of the war, combined with his study of earlier existentialist writers, strongly influenced his thinking. He wrote philosophy, fiction, and political treatises, becoming one of the most respected leaders in post-war French culture.*

Existentialism makes a contribution to education because it places primary emphasis on the individual, and in doing so, it reminds us that we don't teach math, science, reading, and writing; rather, we teach people, and the people we teach are at the core of learning.

Existentialists would have us change our attitudes about education. Education isn't something a student is filled with and then tested for; education is an individual's search for personal understanding. Existentialist educators decry tracking, testing, and standardization, arguing that these practices detract from individuals' opportunities for growth. Schools, they suggest, should be places where students are free to engage in activities because these activities are interesting to them and help students define who they are.

Whereas science and technology are important for realists and pragmatists, existentialists place more emphasis on the humanities, because these studies examine the human struggle for meaning, relationships between people, and tragedy as well as triumph.

Existentialism has influenced the thinking of humanistic educators, such as Carl Rogers (1967) and Abraham Maslow (1968, 1970), who advocate a learner-centered and nondirective approach to education. Empathy is an important teacher characteristic, and teachers, they argue, should care for their students unconditionally, helping students feel like worthy individuals. In their quest for meaning, teachers should be students, and students should be teachers. Current emphases on communities of learners, in which teachers and students work together to accomplish learning goals, are consistent with this view.

Critics of existentialism remind us that we all live in a social world, which, whether we like it or not, has rules; total freedom is impossible. However, even critics acknowledge the existentialist position that personal freedom carries with it personal responsibility.

Teacher Decision Making: Applying the Traditional Philosophies in Classrooms

How do the traditional philosophies influence teaching? To answer this question, let's listen in on a conversation among a group of teachers relaxing in the workroom after school one day.

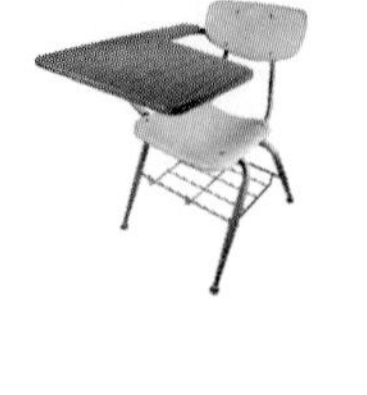

Case STUDY

"I love this time of the year," Greg Chiesa, an English teacher, commented. "I'm going to have my kids read *Moby Dick*, and then we're going to read *Les Miserables*. You wouldn't think the kids would be that crazy about them, but they really get into the discussions of good and evil that Melville examines with Captain Ahab and the white whale, and they also like the whole morality issue in *Les Miserables*. I think they're attracted to dealing with these time-honored issues. From now to the end of time, issues of good and evil will be with us, so they're forever new."

"My history classes also wrestle with issues of good and evil," Jaclyn Holt, a colleague, responded. "So, were we good or were we evil when we dropped the atomic bomb on Hiroshima and Nagasaki in World War II? Many people argue that we saved a lot of lives by dropping the bombs, but others describe it as a quantum leap forward in man's inhumanity to man. I have my kids spend a couple periods discussing that issue and the related issue of war, but I don't try to impose my view on them. I want them to understand that we, as people, are ultimately responsible for what we make of life, and the same thing applies to nations. It may seem like pie in the sky but I want the kids to grapple with the ideas and make their own decisions about whether or not wars are justified and whether we were right to drop the bombs."

"That sounds nice, but I want kids to examine those kinds of issues in depth, doing their own research and coming up with their own answers. That's why I put my students in teams and let them use the Internet to research important questions," Justin Bruinsma, another history teacher, added.

"You people are too far out for me," Edna Chatman, a math and physics teacher, said, laughing. "I admit that I'm biased because I'm a math and science teacher, but I spend most of my time trying to help the kids learn important math skills and develop their critical thinking so they won't be duped by propaganda and promotions when they're out in the real world. Making conclusions based on evidence is what I spend most of my time on."

• • ● • •

Decision making is an essential part of a professional teacher's role. Let's look at the decisions that each of the teachers made to see how those decisions were influenced by philosophy. Greg decided to have his students read classic literature, because it dealt with timeless issues, such as good and evil. He made this decision based on a personal philosophy grounded in idealism. Jaclyn's thinking was a bit different. She too was interested in a moral issue—whether or not the United States government was morally justified in dropping the atomic bombs in World War II—but her goal was for students to make decisions about the issues on their own. Her decision about the most appropriate way to deal with the topic was more nearly grounded in existentialism.

Justin held another view, and it had an important influence on his decisions concerning instruction. Because he took a pragmatic view of knowledge, he had his students actively engaged in problem solving on the Internet. Finally, Edna's focus on essential knowledge and critical thinking was grounded in realism.

As we said earlier, philosophy may seem distant and remote from where you are, particularly at this point in your teacher preparation program, but it is an essential part

Table 6.1 The Traditional Schools of Philosophy

	Idealism	Realism	Pragmatism	Existentialism
Metaphysics	Reality is the world of unchanging ideas.	Reality is the physical world.	Reality is the interaction of the individual and the environment.	Reality is the subjective interpretation of the physical world.
Epistemology	Knowing is the personal rethinking of universal ideas.	Knowing is observing and understanding natural laws.	Knowing is the result of experience based on the scientific method.	Knowing is making personal choice.
Axiology	Values are absolute based on enduring ideas.	Values are absolute based on natural law.	Values are relative.	Values are chosen by the individual.
Educational Implications	Curricula focus on content that emphasizes time-honored ideas.	Curricula focus on content that emphasizes natural laws.	Curricula and instruction focus on problem solving and the scientific method.	Instruction emphasizes discussion designed to increase individual self-awareness.

of teacher professionalism. As we saw in the case, teachers' philosophical views guide their decisions about how classroom time is spent, which strongly influences what and how much students learn. Differences among the traditional philosophies are summarized in Table 6.1.

Philosophies of Education

The traditional philosophies presented thus far are comprehensive views of life and thought; they weren't developed as philosophies of education, even though each has implications for teaching and learning. We now examine philosophies that focus specifically on education. As you analyze these philosophies, look for relationships between them and the traditional philosophies you've studied.

In this section we examine four philosophies of education:

- Perennialism
- Essentialism
- Progressivism
- Postmodernism

Perennialism

Let's think about the term *perennial* for a moment. It is an adjective meaning "perpetual" or "long-lasting." **Perennialism** is *an educational philosophy suggesting that nature—including human nature—is constant.* In this regard, perennialism has roots in both idealism and realism (Jacobsen, 2003). Both idealists and realists believe in the enduring and constant nature of reality; idealists believe in enduring ideas, and realists recognize the constancy of the physical universe.

Consistent with the beliefs of idealism and realism, perennialists believe in a rigorous intellectual curriculum for all students. For perennialists, education is preparation for future life, and the extent to which students find their studies relevant isn't crucial. Math, science, and particularly literature are important in a perennialist curriculum because they expose learners to both the rigors of logical thought as well as the great ideas that have endured throughout history. The ideal perennialist curriculum would have students study classic works ranging from Homer's *Iliad* to Darwin's *The Origin of Species* (which introduced the theory of evolution), together with a host of works in between. After reading these works, students would be engaged in discussions that encouraged them to analyze and evaluate the ideas expressed (Billings & Fitzgerald, 2002).

CW

Increasing Understanding 6.9

Think about Allie's philosophical position in the opening case study. In what way or ways are her views consistent with perennialism? In what way or ways are they inconsistent? Explain.

Perennialism experienced a mild and brief renaissance in the early 1980s with the publication of Mortimer Adler's (1982) *The Paideia Proposal: An Educational Manifesto*. Adler advocated a general curriculum, for all students, that included math, science, history, geography, literature, and fine arts. Understanding the content of these subject areas was a means to an end, however, and not an end in itself. The goal in studying them was to develop intellectual skills, such as writing, speaking, computing, and problem solving. The content, together with these intellectual skills, would lead to higher-level thinking, reflection, and awareness.

Increasing Understanding 6.10

Would perennialists favor or oppose vocational education? Explain.

Adler's ideas received considerable attention from the popular press, but their application in schools was limited. Critics argued that Adler's proposals were elitist, aimed primarily at students with the highest ability (Ozmon & Craver, 2003). They also questioned the value of distant and abstract ideas for poorly motivated and intellectually unprepared students. Adler's efforts remain alive, however, with the reissue of his book (Adler, 1998) and renewed interest in student discussion and dialogue as a vehicle for learning (Billings & Fitzgerald, 2002).

Essentialism

We've all heard of "back to the basics" movements, which occur in education on a somewhat cyclical basis. "Back to the basics" means that learning should focus on essential basic skills, such as reading, writing, mathematics and, to a certain extent, science and geography. (Many educational leaders now include technology use and technological literacy as a basic skill.) People who support "back to the basics" movements periodically write newspaper editorials sounding the alarm about American students' ignorance of the world around them, their inability to communicate either orally or in writing, and their lack of ability to do rudimentary math (American Council of Trustees and Alumni, 2000; Ravitch, 2000). These views are consistent with essentialism.

Essentialism is *an educational philosophy suggesting that there is a critical core of information that all people should possess.* Schools should emphasize basic skills and academic subjects, and students should be expected to master these subjects. Essentialists want to ensure that the educational system produces a literate and skilled workforce able to compete in a technological society. Therefore, they are concerned about a general "dumbing down" of the curriculum, they decry social promotion of students, and they are wary of student-centered curriculum and instruction.

Many of the reform efforts over the last 20 or more years have arisen from essentialist views. In the 1980s reform was spurred by *A Nation at Risk* (National Commission on Excellence in Education, 1983), the widely publicized report that recommended that all high school students master core requirements in five "basics"—English, math, science, social studies, and computer science. The federal No Child Left Behind Act (Hardy, 2002; J. Jennings, 2002), passed in 2002, drives many of the changes occurring in schools today; it emphasizes the basic skills of reading and math and uses extensive testing as an accountability tool.

Essentialist philosophy is also found in teacher education programs. As a prospective teacher, you may read books such as *Knowledge Base for the Beginning Teacher*

Exploring Diversity

PHILOSOPHY AND CULTURAL MINORITIES

To this point in the chapter, the philosophies we've examined have been "Western," meaning their origins are European or American. Two principles undergird this Western orientation. The first is the preeminence of the individual, as seen in the individual's search for truth in both idealism and realism, the interaction of the individual with the environment in pragmatism, and the individual's search for a meaningful life in existentialism. The second is rational thought and respect for objectivity, science, and the scientific method. Realism and pragmatism, in particular, emphasize science as a way of knowing.

Some philosophers criticize the Western emphasis on individuality and rationality and point to its undesirable consequences in American life. Americans are working more hours per week than they ever have in the past, technology dominates their lives, and they're chronically sleep deprived, for example. Critics of this Western orientation assert that valuable alternatives can be found in the philosophies of other cultures.

Some philosophies, such as those embedded in certain Native American cultures, use the shared folklore of elders and knowledge that comes from the heart as their sources of wisdom (Morton, 1988). Because people in these cultures have a long history of living in harmony with the land, their philosophies place emphasis on ecological as well as interpersonal harmony. The emphasis on harmony and cooperation results in valuing individual achievement primarily as it contributes to a group's overall well-being. Competition and individual displays of achievement are frowned upon. Understanding these differences can help explain why Navajo students, for example, are sometimes reluctant to participate in the competitive verbal give-and-take of fast-paced questioning sessions that require individuals to demonstrate how much they know (Tharp, 1989; Villegas, 1991).

Similarly, for some African cultures, feelings and personal relationships are equally or more important ways of knowing than science and rational thought (Nieto, 1996). Art and music are important means of expression and seeking knowledge. This philosophical view helps explain why music was such a prominent part of slaves' lives in America, why African Americans have made such a strong contribution to modern and impressionistic art, and why African influences can be seen in much of the contemporary music in Europe and the Americas.

Many Asians also value harmony. A desire to achieve harmony with nature, life, family, and society leads to reverence for elders, respect for authority, and adherence to traditions. Because harmony is so important, being polite is highly valued, and feelings and emotions tend to be controlled in order to maintain order and proper social relationships (McDermott, 1994). Understanding these perspectives helps teachers understand characteristics commonly attributed to Asian American students. For instance, they are often described as being shy, reluctant to speak out in class, and restrained in their nonverbal behavior, which

(Reynolds, 1989), you'll be required to take a specified sequence of courses, and you'll be expected to demonstrate mastery of essential teaching skills. These requirements reflect the belief that a core of knowledge exists that all preservice teachers should master.

Essentialism and perennialism share the view that knowledge and understanding are preeminent, and both are wary of the emphasis on learner-centered education and the focus on learner self-esteem. Essentialists don't share perennialists' emphasis on universal truths through the study of classical literature, however. Instead, they emphasize knowledge and skills that are useful in today's world. From an essentialist per-

sometimes makes reading students' nonverbal cues difficult (C. Park, 1997).

Alternate philosophies remind teachers of the need to view each child as an individual with unique needs and interests.

Although teachers can gain valuable insights from the cultural perspectives just described, they should never be used as the sole bases for making conclusions about minority students. Critics argue that the descriptions are little more than stereotypes that grossly oversimplify the complexities of alternative philosophies. For example, some Americans simplistically think of Africa as a country, not realizing that it is a vast continent, more culturally and linguistically diverse than North or South America. To speak of a singular "African philosophy"—or Native American or Asian philosophy, for that matter—does an injustice to diverse groups of people and their philosophies. Further, people are people, and categorizing them on the basis of sweeping and uncertain philosophical generalizations is questionable at best and perhaps even potentially damaging (Diamond, 1999).

Rather than viewing students as Hispanic, Native American, African American, or as representative of any other cultural or ethnic group, we should see students as individuals. Concluding that Ted Chang, for example, doesn't speak out in class because of the influence of his Chinese culture—and leaving it at that—might be educationally dangerous. What if you are wrong? If you get to know Ted as a person, you'll not only learn why he is quiet, you'll also gain knowledge you can use to involve him in learning activities, just as you would try to involve any student in your classes (Banks, 2002).

Respecting and valuing cultural differences is important. Making decisions that may detract from learning, based on overgeneralizations about these differences, is not. If you realize that not all people share the same philosophical orientations, as a teacher you'll be more sensitive to the important individual differences in your students.

spective, taking the required sequence of courses and mastering certain competencies or skills in your teacher preparation program will help you become a better teacher in today's world.

In addition to learner-centered instruction, essentialists essentialists also criticize interdisciplinary approaches to teaching. In the social studies area, for example, they decry the use of an integrative approach that uses history, geography, economics, sociology, psychology, and anthropology to understand human events (Manzo, 2003a). Politics has entered the battle, with conservatives in Congress targeting $100 million in 2001 for a history-only curriculum emphasizing positive aspects of U.S. history.

Increasing Understanding 6.11

A recent trend is to require students to pass standardized tests before they're allowed to advance in grade or graduate from high school. Would essentialists react negatively or positively to such "high-stakes" testing? Explain.

Because of its emphasis on practical, usable knowledge, the essentialist curriculum is more likely to change than is the perennialist curriculum. For instance, as our society becomes increasingly diverse and researchers better understand how diversity affects learning, teacher preparation programs place greater and greater emphasis on working effectively with learners from diverse backgrounds. This means you will likely take a course in multicultural education or that topics in multicultural education will be included in several of your courses. This emphasis wouldn't have existed 20 years ago. The same is true for technology; most teacher education programs now have some type of technology component. Whether arrived at implicitly or consciously, these shifts in emphasis reflect essentialist thinking.

To analyze a case study examining philosophical issues involved in working with cultural minorities in the classroom, go to the Companion Website at **www.prenhall.com/kauchak**, then to this chapter's *Reflect on This* module.

Progressivism

Think for a moment about some of the practices emphasized in education today. For instance, we encounter "learner-centered curricula," which emphasize learners' interests and needs (Lambert & McCombs, 1998). We also see hands-on learning activities, particularly in science, where children work with batteries, bulbs, magnets, plants, soil, and a variety of other materials. Learners are given blocks and other manipulatives to help them solve problems and learn concepts in math, and they are asked to write about their own experiences in language arts. Learners are then encouraged to collaborate with one another. Teachers don't simply deliver information; they guide learners and facilitate the learning process (Eggen & Kauchak, 2004).

These practices are philosophically rooted in progressivism, an educational philosophy grounded in pragmatism. **Progressivism** is *an educational philosophy emphasizing curricula that focus on real-world problem solving and individual development.* (See Chapter 5 for a discussion of the history of the progressive movement in education.)

In the opening case study, Brad expressed views consistent with progressivism:

[T]he person who really succeeds is the one who continues to learn and is able to adapt to changes in the world by solving the large and small problems they encounter. . . . They need lots of experience in making decisions and solving problems. That's what life's all about.

In our discussion of epistemology, we briefly examined the constructivists' view that, rather than record understanding, students construct it based on their experiences and background knowledge. Constructivism is consistent with progressivism and its precursor, pragmatism. All three emphasize concrete experiences, real-world tasks, and the central role of the individual in determining reality and promoting learning. As you analyze learning in educational psychology, you will undoubtedly study constructivism in detail. As you do, remember that it's rooted in pragmatism and progressivism.

Progressivism is controversial. As with pragmatism, critics contend that the pendulum has swung too far in the direction of children's interests and self-esteem and that knowledge and understanding have been sacrificed (Ravitch, 2000). Some of these criticisms are justified and in fact draw attention to misapplications of Dewey's ideas. For

Postmodern philosophy raises questions about culture and gender bias in our schools.

example, progressives complained that schools organized subject matter in a detached manner, alien to the interests and abilities of young children:

> But these same progressives made no sustained effort to develop or understand alternate ways of organizing knowledge so that it would be more accessible or useable to the learner. They recognized the shortcomings of assigning the learner to a passive, receptive role, but too often substituted for it a set of educationally purposeless activities. (Proefriedt, 1999, p. 28)

Both progressivism and pragmatism—when properly interpreted—suggest that effective education isn't a matter of process *or* content; it is a matter of process *and* content.

Postmodernism

During the 1960s the United States went through major cultural upheavals. The Vietnam War was unpopular, and many Americans, even those outside of the anti-war movement, grew skeptical of authority and leadership. Other movements—such as the civil rights movement, the feminist movement, and gay and lesbian crusades—encouraged critiques of American culture, society, and education. Postmodern philosophy emerged among these critiques.

Postmodernism is *an educational philosophy that contends that many of the institutions in our society, including schools, are used by those in power to control and marginalize those who lack power.* The powerful are typically White males, and those marginalized (lacking power) are unskilled workers, women, and cultural minorities. The curricula in elementary, secondary, and postsecondary schools, postmodernists argue, are racist, sexist, and imperialist.

Postmodernists target the continued curricular emphasis on the study of Shakespeare as an example. Shakespeare, a White European male, figures prominently in most high school literature programs. Emphasis on Shakespeare and other White male authors has resulted in little room left for literature written by women, minorities, or people from other cultures. Because White males make curricular decisions, marginalizing those without power continues unabated.

Increasing Understanding 6.12

Of the traditional philosophies—idealism, realism, pragmatism, and existentialism—which would be most acceptable to postmodernists? Explain.

A postmodern curriculum would reverse these trends. Literature written by women and cultural minorities, such as African Americans, would be elevated to a position as prominent or more prominent than traditional literature. Further, traditional literature would be critically examined to see how it has historically shaped our notions of race, gender, and other differences among people. Issues such as the use of power, personal and group identities, cultural politics, and social criticism would enjoy prominent positions. Historical events would be examined from the perspective of power, status, and the struggles of marginalized groups in those contexts (Abowitz, 2000). For instance, Columbus's arrival in the New World has historically been presented as a critical point in European expansion and colonization and the beginning of modern history in North and South America. Postmodernism would recognize that fact but would emphasize the brutalization of Native Americans by the Spaniards, the ravaging of the indigenous people by European diseases such as smallpox (for which Native Americans had no natural immunities), their enslavement, and the fact that conquering and colonization were two major goals for explorers.

Teaching in an Era of Reform

THE ESSENTIAL KNOWLEDGE ISSUE

American students are being increasingly criticized for their lack of knowledge about the United States and the world. Editorial headlines, such as "Historical illiteracy plaguing many in high schools and colleges," are appearing with greater frequency. The facts cited are disheartening at best. For example, only 1 in 3 college seniors randomly chosen from 55 top-rated colleges and universities could identify George Washington as the American general at Yorktown, and only 22 percent could identify the Gettysburg address as the source of the words "Government of the people, by the people, for the people" (American Council of Trustees and Alumni, 2000). These facts were so alarming that the U.S. Congress introduced a resolution warning that lack of historical knowledge is dangerous for our country's future. In other surveys only 42 percent of college seniors could place the Civil War in the correct half century, and most adult Americans couldn't find the Persian Gulf on a map (Bertman, 2000). The situation is no better in math. For example, one study asked American fifth graders to solve the problem 45 × 26 = ?, but only 54 percent were successful (Stigler et al., 1999).

In response to these problems, standards have been written in virtually every content area. **Standards** are *statements specifying what students should know and what skills they should have upon completing an area of study.* Nearly every state has specified standards, and to hold students and schools accountable, they have created tests to measure the extent to which the standards are being met. At the federal level the No Child Left Behind legislation requires all states to create standards for what every child should understand about different subjects (Hardy, 2002; J. Jennings, 2002). Standards for math and reading must be developed immediately, and standards for science must be developed by the 2005–2006 school year. Standards apply to teachers as well: 39 states now require teachers to pass exams in order to be licensed.

The Issue

Those who support standards believe that there are well-defined skills and bodies of knowledge that all people should master, a view grounded in essentialist educational philosophy. E. D. Hirsch (1987), author of the controversial but widely read book *Cultural Literacy: What Every American Needs to Know,* illustrates this position. Hirsch identified a vast list of facts, concepts, and people that he believed all citizens should know in order to function effectively in American society. Since then, he has produced a series of edited paperbacks that contain what he calls "The Core Knowledge" curriculum. Books such as *What Your Third Grader Needs to Know: Fundamentals of a Good Third-Grade Education* (Hirsch, 1994) and similar titles for each of the grade levels K–6 are meant to be used by both teachers and parents.

Research on learning indicates that background knowledge is crucial for developing understanding of new content (Bruning et al., 2004; Eggen & Kauchak, 2004). All new learning builds on what learners already know. For instance, to understand the relationships among people's growing distrust of government and authority, the civil rights movement, and the Vietnam War, learners must know facts about each situation, such as when events happened, who was involved, what views were prominent, and so on. Similarly, to understand the problems of sub-Saharan Africa, learners must also understand European colonialism, as well as the geography and climate of this vast area. Knowledge builds on knowledge, and when knowledge is lacking, learning suffers.

Citizens agree that knowledge is important and that our young people lack it. Hirsch's Core Knowledge series is popular with both parents and teachers, and many reviewers have responded positively to it. Criticisms that the series focuses on rote memory rather than understanding have gone largely unnoticed or have been refuted.

On the other hand, if increased knowledge means that learners should memorize more facts, this has already been proven unsuccessful, critics counter. For example, K–12 students already are exposed to a considerable amount of American history (they take at least one American history course during middle school and another in high school, plus smatterings during their elementary years). But, critics note, they apparently retain little of the content, as indicated by the survey results cited earlier. So the issue is more complex than simply requiring more content and courses. Students apparently aren't learning from the courses they do take.

The essential knowledge debate raises important questions about curriculum—what is taught in schools—as well as instruction.

Critics of the essential knowledge position also cite research indicating that personal motivation and the ability to use strategies to acquire knowledge are better predictors of later success than is the accumulation of facts (McCaslin & Good, 1996).

> It is the affective and motivational characteristics of workers that our employers worry most about. They depend on employees to show up on time, to get along with others, to care about doing well on the job. . . . They do not find the technical ability of the workforce to be a problem for them. (Berliner, 1992; pp. 33–34)

Critics also question whether increased knowledge makes people happier and more productive workers, and they cite motivational research suggesting that increasing learner readiness and eagerness to learn should be the primary goals of schools (Pintrich & Schunk, 2002). This position is more consistent with pragmatism and progressivism than with essentialism.

Finally, the question of what knowledge is "essential" is hard to determine (R. Gutiérrez, 2002). For example, Hirsch (1987) identifies such information as "Who was Spiro Agnew?" and "What is a carnivore?" as essential. Why is this information more important than knowing, for instance, who Cesar Chavez was or what macrobiotic means (Marzano, Kendall, & Gaddy, 1999)? Further, the sheer amount of knowledge called for by standards is overwhelming. Nearly 14,000 benchmarks in 14 subject areas have been written, resulting in "far too many standards and not enough time in the day or year to teach them all" (Marzano et al., 1999, p. 68).

You Take a Position

Now it's your turn to take a position on the issue. State in writing whether you favor or oppose the emphasis on essential knowledge, and provide a two-page rationale for your position.

For additional references and resources, go to the Companion Website at **www.prenhall.com/kauchak**, *then to this chapter's* Teaching in an Era of Reform *module. You can respond online or submit your response to your instructor.*

Table 6.2 Classroom Applications of the Educational Philosophies

	Perennialism	Essentialism	Progressivism	Postmodernism
Traditional Philosophy Most Closely Related	Idealism, realism	Idealism, realism	Pragmatism	Existentialism
Educational Goals	Train the intellect; moral development	Acquire basic skills; acquire knowledge needed to function in today's world	Acquire ability to function in the real world; develop problem-solving skills	Critically examine today's institutions; elevate the status of marginalized people (women and cultural minorities)
Curriculum	Emphasis on enduring ideas	Emphasis on basic skills	Emphasis on problem solving and skills needed in today's world	Emphasis on the works of marginalized people
Role of the Teacher	Deliver clear lectures; increase student understanding with critical questions	Deliver clear lectures; increase student understanding with critical questions	Guide learning with questioning; develop and guide practical problem-solving activities	Facilitate discussions that involve clarifying issues
Teaching Methods	Lecture; questioning; coaching in intellectual thinking	Lecture; practice and feedback; questioning	Problem-based learning; cooperative learning; guided discovery	Discussion; role play; simulation; personal research
Learning Environment	High structure; high levels of time on task	High structure; high levels of time on task	Collaborative; self-regulated; democratic	Community-oriented; self-regulated
Assessment	Frequent objective and essay tests	Frequent objective, essay, and performance tests	Continuous feedback; informal monitoring of student progress	Collaborative between teacher and student; emphasis on the exposure of hidden assumptions

CW

Increasing Understanding 6.13

Throughout this text you've been asked to respond to margin questions, such as this one. The fact that these questions exist and the types of questions best reflect which of the educational philosophies? Explain.

Postmodernism has sparked hot debate. As postmodernists have risen to positions of power in some universities, for example, the study of Shakespeare and other time-honored American and British authors has decreased or been eliminated from the curriculum, whereas the study of female authors, minority authors, and cultural issues has proliferated. This has caused outrage among perennialist and essentialist thinkers. They argue that postmodernism has resulted in the abandonment of schools as places for intellectual pursuits, instead using them for political purposes. They contend further that postmodernism is as control-oriented as traditional philosophies and institutions; it merely wants to establish controls more to their liking (Ozmon & Craver, 2003). Classroom applications of the educational philosophies are summarized in Table 6.2.

To analyze a case study examining issues involved in classroom applications of educational philosophies, go to the Companion Website at **www.prenhall.com/kauchak**, then to this chapter's *Reflect on This* module.

EXAMINING PHILOSOPHIES OF TEACHING

Having examined both traditional and educational philosophies, and considering your own philosphy of education as developed in the Decision Making feature below, you now have the opportunity to view a video of two lessons that reflect two different educational philosophies.

In the first lesson, a junior high geography teacher uses interactive questioning to guide her students' analysis of a matrix containing information about different regions in the United States. In the second lesson, a high school history teacher explores the events that led up to the Vietnam War.

To complete this activity, do the following:

- Go to the DVD, and view the video episode titled "Examining Philosophies of Teaching."
- Answer the questions you'll find on the DVD.

To answer the questions online and receive immediate feedback, go to the Companion Website at **www.prenhall.com/kauchak**, *then to this chapter's* Classroom Windows *module.*

Decision Making

Defining Yourself as a Professional

You've now studied the traditional philosophies idealism, realism, pragmatism, and existentialism, along with the educational philosophies perennialism, essentialism, progressivism, and postmodernism. This study is intended to help you make one of the most important decisions of your professional life: deciding what kind of teacher you want to be by forming your own philosophy of education. This decision will influence the kinds of knowledge you emphasize in your classes, the instructional decisions you make as a teacher, and the criteria you use to reflect on and analyze your teaching (see Figure 6.1 on p. 207).

Philosophy is also important because it will help you explain and defend your educational goals—what you will try to accomplish in your classroom. Your goals reflect the kind of teacher you want to be, and being able to explain and defend them means that you're knowledgeable and reflective. Professionals are able to articulate what they're doing and why. For instance, if you walked into a classroom, saw students working on basic skills, and asked the teacher why she was involving her students in this activity, she should be able to give you a clear and specific answer. If she were an essentialist, the answer might be that basic skills are part of a core of knowledge that learners need to function effectively in the world. However, some teachers do an activity simply because it is next in the text or curriculum guide sequence or because they did it last year. These are clearly inadequate and unprofessional reasons.

When teachers are clear about their philosophies, they can make systematic changes when they conclude that their teaching practices need improvement. If their philosophies aren't clear, they are less likely to make needed changes, or they make changes at random. In either case, professional growth doesn't occur. This is one reason professionals make decisions grounded in philosophy.

As you begin to form your own personal philosophy of education, keep at least three ideas in mind. First, any philosophy is evolving and dynamic. This means that it will change as you learn and gather experience. So don't be concerned if your philosophy is initially uncertain and loosely formed; it will crystalize and become clearer as you think about and use it over time. Second, your personal philosophy is likely to include elements of more than one traditional or educational philosophy. Third, be willing to change your views. People have a tendency to cling to the first ideas they form; they then feel that changing their minds is a sign of weakness or fuzzy thinking. Nothing could be further from the truth. In fact, changing your views is an indicator of the open-mindedness necessary for personal and professional growth.

The Role of Beliefs in a Philosophy of Education

Early in the chapter we said that philosophy *provides a framework for thinking, and it guides professional practice.* To begin establishing this framework for thinking, first try to identify and examine your beliefs. Allie and Brad both did a good job of describing their beliefs about teaching and learning. Allie's comments, in particular, show that her beliefs were well thought out:

> "They [kids] don't come to school with the same . . . desire to learn as they once did."
>
> "[T]hey want to believe they did learn something when they're finished with a topic, or class."
>
> "[T]hey're not intrinsically motivated."
>
> "I do believe that kids feel good when they learn something, particularly if it's challenging."
>
> "[T]he more they know about a topic, the better they like it."
>
> "[T]here's real, practical stuff out there that they need to know, and there's only one way they're gonna learn it. . . . That's practice and experience."

The following questions might help you get started in the process of identifying your own beliefs.

- What is the purpose of schooling? Should students focus on content, or is the development of self-concept, interpersonal skills, and other personal qualities more important?
- Are students basically good and trustworthy, or do they need constant monitoring?
- Is motivating students part of my job, or should motivation come from within the students?
- Is my role as a teacher to pass knowledge on to students, or should I be guiding students as they learn on their own?
- How do people know things? Is intuition important and valuable? How important are feelings? Is evidence always, or often, necessary?
- How do students best learn? Should I push them, or should they be left largely on their own?

Examining Your Beliefs

Once identified, beliefs should be examined and analyzed. This is where philosophy and knowledge become important. How does Allie know that her beliefs are valid? Do they "feel" right? Do they make sense intuitively? Is feeling or intuition adequate to justify the belief, or must she have research evidence to indicate that they're valid?

CW

Increasing Understanding 6.14

Throughout this book we've cited reference sources for the information we've presented. What does this imply about our epistemological beliefs? What does this imply about our axiological beliefs? Explain in each case.

If Allie is an existentialist, intuition and feelings are perfectly acceptable in validating her beliefs. However, if Allie is a realist or a pragmatist, feelings and intuition are not adequate or trustworthy; she must have evidence.

From this discussion we can see why understanding philosophy is important. For instance, if Allie describes herself as an essentialist but then accepts feelings and intuition as validation for her beliefs, her thinking is inconsistent, and she should reconsider what she really believes about knowing, learning, and teaching.

Forming a Philosophy

My job is to help these kids learn as much as they can about the topics I teach, so that's what I try to do every day. Kids basically want to learn. They may not be too crazy about it initially, and some of them might be in it mostly for grades to start with, but the more they learn about the topics, the better they like what they study. Relevance isn't as critical to the kids' motivation as understanding and success are. If the kids understand the stuff, they'll like it, and they'll feel better about themselves.

So, my goal is to get them to learn, really learn, not just memorize information. I want them to know why, how they know, and what might happen if conditions changed. If I get them to learn, really learn, motivation and self-esteem take care of themselves.

I know that I can get them to learn. We're going to have class discussions, do homework, go over it, have quizzes, and go over them. If I do my job, they'll learn.

What you've just read is a succinct description of Allie's philosophy of education. It is clear, well articulated, and consistent with her beliefs. The relationships between her beliefs and components of her philosophy are outlined in Table 6.3.

Because Allie's philosophy is clear and well articulated, it can effectively guide her thinking as she defines her goals and designs learning activities and assessments.

Table 6.3 An Analysis of Allie's Philosophy of Education

Belief Statement	Component of Her Philosophy
"They [kids] don't come to school with the same . . . desire to learn as they once did."	"They may not be too crazy about it initially."
"[T]hey want to believe they did learn something when they're finished with a topic, or class."	"Kids basically want to learn."
"[T]hey're not intrinsically motivated."	[S]ome of them might be in it mostly for grades to start with."
"[K]ids feel good when they learn something, particularly if it's challenging."	"If the kids understand the stuff, they'll like it, and they'll feel better about themselves." "I want them to know why, how they know, and what might happen if conditions changed."
"[T]he more they know about a topic, the better they like it."	"The more they learn about the topics, the better they like what they study. Relevance isn't as critical to the kids' motivation as understanding and success are."
"[T]here's real, practical stuff out there that they need to know, and there's only one way they're gonna learn it. . . . That's practice and experience."	"We're going to have class discussions, do homework, go over it, have quizzes, and go over them."

Dialoguing with other professionals can help beginning teachers shape their own personal philosophy of education.

CW

Increasing Understanding 6.15

Look again at Brad's thinking, as expressed in his conversation with Allie. On the basis of this information, summarize Brad's philosophy of education. Explain how the philosophy is based on his beliefs.

Her philosophy helps ensure that all three—goals, learning activities, and assessments—are consistent with one another. Although you may or may not agree with Allie's goals or the rationale for them, the fact that she's clear in her thinking increases the likelihood that her students will reach the goals, and she will be more likely to make conscious choices to change and improve her teaching when she sees evidence that change is needed.

You now have the following information:

- The description of Allie's philosophy
- Your own description of Brad's philosophy from your response to Increasing Understanding 6.15
- Your analysis of your own beliefs

Using this information, you're now ready to compile them into a personal philosophy that will guide your thinking and actions.

We said earlier that your philosophy will likely incorporate elements from more than one traditional and educational philosophy. We see this in Allie's thinking. Her view that an objective reality exists, independent of the world of ideas, is consistent with realism; from essentialism she drew the belief that a body of important information exists that all students need to know in order to function effectively in today's world; and her concerns for her students' personal needs, emotions, and self-esteem most closely relate to existentialism. In constructing your personal philosophy, you will combine traditional and educational philosophies in the same way.

We hope that this chapter has provided you with the background needed to begin your journey toward developing a personal philosophy and that it has encouraged you to think about teaching in a different way. At this point you won't have all the answers you need to decide what education should be and how you can help make it that way. But if you are now able to begin asking some important questions, then our goal for the chapter has been fulfilled. Good luck.

Summary

Philosophy and Philosophy of Education

Philosophy is a search for wisdom. In forming a philosophy, a professional teacher searches for the wisdom to maximize learning for all students.

Philosophy provides a framework for thinking, and it guides professional practice. Philosophy and theory overlap but are not the same. Theories are used to explain events and behavior, as they are, whereas philosophies go further to suggest the way events and behaviors ought to be.

Branches of Philosophy

Epistemology is the branch of philosophy that describes how we know what we know. Metaphysics, or ontology, considers what we know and addresses questions of reality and, ultimately, what is real. Axiology considers values and ethics, and logic is the process of deriving valid conclusions from basic principles.

Traditional Schools of Philosophy

Idealism, realism, pragmatism, and existentialism are often called the traditional philosophies. Their views of reality, ways of knowing, and what is valuable and good often differ considerably.

Each philosophy has implications for teaching and learning. Idealists would create a curriculum focusing on absolute and time-honored ideas. Realists would also emphasize absolutes, but in contrast with idealists, their absolutes would focus on natural laws. Pragmatists see the world in relative terms and would emphasize experience and practical understanding, validated by the scientific method. Existentialists would take a more extreme position and support a curriculum emphasizing personal awareness, freedom, and responsibility.

Philosophies of Education

The educational philosophies perennialism, essentialism, progressivism, and postmodernism are rooted in the traditional philosophies. Perennialism, as with idealism and realism, focuses on time-honored absolutes. Progressivism, rooted in pragmatism, views goals as dynamic and emphasizes that learning should be experience-based and relevant to students' lives. Postmodernism sees schools and other institutions in need of restructuring, with marginalized people and their works elevated to more prominent positions in the content of schooling.

Important Concepts

axiology (p. 209)
character education (p. 209)
epistemology (p. 208)
essentialism (p. 217)
existentialism (p. 214)
idealism (p. 210)
logic (p. 209)
metaphysics (ontology) (p. 208)
moral education (p. 209)
normative philosophy (p. 207)
perennialism (p. 216)
philosophy (p. 205)
philosophy of education (p. 205)
postmodernism (p. 221)
pragmatism (p. 212)
progressivism (p. 220)
realism (p. 211)
standards (p. 222)
theory (p. 207)

Developing as a Professional

Praxis Practice

Look again at the discussion between the teachers Greg, Jaclyn, Justin, and Edna, presented on p. 215. We have already examined the teachers' thinking in the context of the traditional philosophies. Now, read this discussion again and decide which *educational philosophy* is best illustrated in each of the teacher's comments.

1. Which educational philosophy is best reflected in Greg's comments? Explain.
2. Which educational philosophy is best reflected in Jaclyn's comments? Explain.
3. Which educational philosophy is best reflected in Justin's comments? Explain.
4. Which educational philosophy is best reflected in Edna's comments? Explain.

To receive feedback on your responses to the Praxis Practice exercises, go to the Companion Website at **www.prenhall.com/kauchak**, then to this chapter's *Praxis Practice* module.

Discussion Questions

1. Four basic areas of philosophy are epistemology, metaphysics, axiology, and logic. Which of these is most useful for teachers? Least useful?
2. Technology is becoming increasingly important in society as well as education. Which of the four philosophies of education—perennialism, essentialism, progressivism, or postmodernism—is most compatible with applications of technology in education? Least compatible?
3. Students are becoming increasingly diverse. How well do the different philosophies of education address issues of student diversity?
4. Which philosophy of education has the most current support in the geographic area in which you plan to teach? What evidence do you have for your conclusion?
5. Of the different educational philosophies discussed in this chapter, which is most valuable in framing issues for preschool children? middle school students? high school students? Does one particular philosophy fit with a content area that you will be teaching?

6. Public school teachers rated educational goals as follows (U.S. Department of Education, 1993):

Goal	*Rank*
Building literacy skills	1
Promoting personal growth	2
Promoting good work habits and self-discipline	3
Encouraging academic excellence	4
Promoting occupational or vocational skills	5

What do these rankings tell us about teachers' philosophical positions?

Classroom Observation Guide

Before You Begin: The purpose of these observation activities is to provide you with some classroom examples of how philosophy affects teachers' work with their students. Observe a lesson at a grade level or in a content area you are interested in. Describe the teacher's classroom and lesson with respect to the following:

1. The arrangement of desks: For example, are the desks arranged in rows, at tables, in a semicircle, or in some other arrangement?
2. Teaching method: Does the teacher primarily lecture and explain, or does the teacher ask a large number of questions?
3. Student motivation: Does the teacher provide a rationale at the beginning of the lesson that explains why it's important, or does he or she simply begin the lesson?
4. Use of examples: Does the teacher use examples or other ways of representing the topic he or she is teaching, or is the information presented primarily in verbal form?
5. Classroom order: Are the students orderly and attentive during the lesson? How does the teacher attempt to accomplish this?
6. Assessment: How does the teacher measure student understanding?

Describe what you believe these indicators suggest about the teacher's educational philosophy. If possible, share your analysis with the teacher and discuss your conclusions.

Going into Schools

1. Interview an elementary teacher about his or her learning goals and instruction. As a guide, you might want to ask the following questions:
   a. What are your most important learning goals for your students? Why do you believe these goals are most important?
   b. What do you emphasize the most in your curriculum? For example, do you believe that having the students develop basic skills is most important, or do you emphasize other aspects of the curriculum?
   c. What is the primary teaching method that you use? Why do you use it?
   d. How do you assess student learning?
   e. What do you see as your major role as a teacher?
   f. What are your major classroom management goals? How do you implement them?

   Based on the teacher's responses, which of the educational philosophies is most nearly reflected in his or her teaching? If possible, share your analysis with the teacher and discuss your conclusions.

2. Interview a middle school or secondary teacher about his or her learning goals and instruction. As a guide, you might want to ask the questions listed in item 1. Based on the teacher's responses, which of the educational philosophies is most nearly reflected in his or her teaching? How do the responses of the elementary teacher compare to the responses of the middle or secondary teacher? If possible, share your analysis with the teacher and discuss your conclusions.
3. Locate a social studies or literature text for a level at which you'll be teaching (e.g., elementary versus high school). Examine the relative contributions of males versus females, minorities versus nonminorities. Does the inclusion of topics or literary selections suggest a perennialist or postmodern philosophy? Defend your answer with specific examples from the text.
4. Locate a teacher's edition of a textbook for a subject or grade level you'll teach. Every book series comes with a teacher's edition that contains suggestions on how to teach the subject; these can be obtained from a teacher, in a school district curriculum library, or at the curriculum library at your college or university. Read the introduction to the text, and identify elements of the following educational philosophies: perennialism, essentialism, progressivism, and postmodernism. How well does the text match your own developing educational philosophy?

Virtual Field Experience

If you would like to participate in a Virtual Field Experience, go to the Companion Website at **www.prenhall.com/kauchak**, then to this chapter's *Field Experience* module.

Online Portfolio Activities

To complete these activities online, go to the Companion Website at **www.prenhall.com/kauchak**, then to this chapter's *Portfolio Activities* module.

Portfolio Activity 6.1

Describing Your Philosophy of Education

INTASC Principle 9: Commitment

Personal Journal Reflection
The purpose of this activity is to assist you in developing your own philosophy of education. List your beliefs about learning, learners, and teaching. Then, based on the list, write a two-page description of your philosophy of education as it presently exists.

Portfolio Activity 6.2

Assessing Your Philosophy of Education

INTASC Principle 9: Commitment

The purpose of this activity is to help you begin to develop a philosophy of education. Complete the survey, and then answer the questions.

Philosophy of Education Survey

For each statement, circle the number that best represents your beliefs at this time. Use the following scale in responding:

4 = Strongly agree
3 = Agree
2 = Disagree
1 = Strongly disagree

1. The primary focus in the school curriculum should be basic skills, such as reading, writing, and math. 1 2 3 4
2. The school curriculum should be the same for all students and should emphasize math, science, and good literature. 1 2 3 4
3. The personal growth of students—such as the development of their values and beliefs, understanding who they are as people, and their place in the world—should be the primary goal of schooling. 1 2 3 4
4. The essential aim of education should be the development of students' critical thinking abilities. 1 2 3 4
5. Teachers should emphasize that correctness of answers is more often a matter of personal opinion than a function of general standards of accuracy. 1 2 3 4
6. Teachers should guide students' developing understanding with questioning instead of relying on teacher explanations to promote learning. 1 2 3 4
7. Classic content, such as the works of Shakespeare, Hawthorne, Mark Twain, and Steinbeck, should be a primary emphasis in the school curriculum. 1 2 3 4
8. Schools should emphasize practical knowledge and understanding, such as the ability to write clearly and persuasively or do basic math operations, that can be immediately applied to the world of work outside of schools. 1 2 3 4
9. Teachers should take students' needs and interests into account when making decisions about what to teach. 1 2 3 4
10. The examination of social injustices, such as racism, sexism, and economic inequality, should be an essential goal for education. 1 2 3 4
11. The development of students' problem-solving skills should be one of teachers' most important goals. 1 2 3 4
12. The primary emphasis in the school curriculum should be on core knowledge, such as the way our government works, the geography of our country and the rest of the world, and science concepts and skills. 1 2 3 4

Now add up the numbers indicating your responses to the following items:

Group A: Items 2 + 4 + 7
Group B: Items 1 + 8 + 12
Group C: Items 6 + 9 + 11
Group D: Items 3 + 5 + 10

If your score was highest for Group A, the survey indicates that your philosophical orientation tends toward perrenialism. If it was highest for Group B, your orientation is essentialism; for Group C, progressivism; and for Group D, postmodernism.

1. Do you think the survey results accurately reflect your philosophy of education? Why or why not?
2. How are the results from this survey similar to and different from your philosophy of education as you described it in Portfolio Activity 6.1?
3. Why do you think the differences exist?
4. Now, using your scores as the basis, summarize what this survey suggests about your developing philosophy of education.

Portfolio Activity 6.3

Assessing an Instructor's Philosophy of Education

INTASC Principle 9: Commitment

The purpose of this activity is to help you to see how educational philosophies influence teaching practices. Think about an instructor in one of your classes. Based on your observations of the instructor and the way he or she teaches, describe in one page what you believe to be the instructor's philosophy of education.

After you've completed the description, share it with the instructor. Ask if he or she considers the description accurate and, if not accurate, to explain why.

Chapter

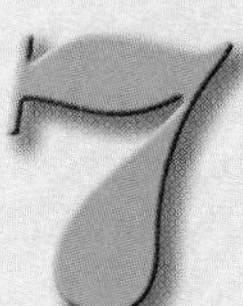

The Organization of American Schools

We've all attended schools and experienced them as students, so we're familiar with the basic ways in which they're organized. Elementary schools lead to middle or junior high schools followed by high schools. But what do schools look like from a teacher's perspective?

In this chapter we examine the organization of schools in the United States from a teacher's perspective and in the process try to answer the following questions:

- What is a school?
- Why are schools divided into elementary, middle or junior high, and high schools?
- Why is the organization of elementary schools different than the organization of middle, junior high, and high schools?
- How will the organization of schools influence your life as a teacher?
- What is an effective school?

To begin answering these questions, let's look at one teacher in a junior high school.

This logo appears throughout the chapter to indicate where case studies are integrated with chapter content.

Case STUDY

"Wow, noon. I need to get going," Chris Lucio said to his colleague April Jackson as he jumped up from the couch in the teacher's lounge, finishing the last bite of his lunch. "My kids will be chomping at the bit trying to get into the room."

Chris hurriedly left the lounge, stopped by the main office to quickly check his box for notes, phone messages, and mail, and then walked across the courtyard to his building.

The courtyard sits at the center of the somewhat atypical campus of Lakeside Junior High. Created 30 years earlier as a middle school for grades 6–9, Lakeside is now one of three junior high schools housing seventh through ninth graders in Orange Park, a suburb of a large eastern city. Four main buildings surround the courtyard: an administrative building and three classroom buildings. The administrative building contains the principal's and administrators' offices, a cafeteria—with a stage at one end—that doubles as an auditorium, and a media center and computer lab holding 30 computers. A gymnasium and fine arts building, built 10 years ago when Lakeside became a junior high, and athletic facilities (tennis courts and baseball, softball, and soccer fields) are positioned outside the main buildings.

Chris walked briskly to the room where he teaches seventh-grade geography.

"Okay everyone, the bell is going to ring in a couple minutes. . . . Find your seats quickly," Chris called out, unlocking the door to his room.

"Mr. Lucio, can I go to the bathroom?" Armondo asked as he stood by the open door.

"Hurry—you don't want to be tardy," Chris answered and smiled at him.

"Are you going to come to our track meet this afternoon?" Devon, another of Chris's students asked as he entered the room. "We're going to kick butt on Ridgeview."

"Wouldn't miss it," Chris returned and thought to himself, "Yikes, I almost forgot. . . . I promised Joe and Karen (the boys' and girls' track coaches) that I'd be a timer for the 100- and 200-meter races."

"What time does it start?" Chris asked Devon.

"Right after school—4 o'clock, I think."

As the bell signaled the start of the period, Chris moved to the front of the room and started taking roll.

• • ● • •

What Is a School?

CW

Increasing Understanding 7.1

Would a *family* be considered a social institution? Why or why not?

To answer the Increasing Understanding questions online and receive immediate feedback, go to the Companion Website at www.prenhall.com/kauchak, then to this chapter's *Increasing Understanding* module. Type in your response, and then study the feedback.

We've all gone to school; in fact, if you're in your mid-twenties or younger, you've spent more than half of your life in school. But exactly what is a school, and what does it mean to teach and learn in one? We consider these questions in this section.

As a concept, *school* has several meanings. At a simple level, a school is a physical place—a building or set of buildings. At another level, school is a place where students go to learn. For example, churches have vacation Bible *school*, and we've all heard of students being home*schooled*.

At a third level, school is a **social institution,** *an organization with established structures and rules designed to promote certain goals.* Schools are social institutions whose goals are to promote both students' growth and development and the well-being of a country and its citizens. Other social institutions include churches, religions, and governments. They are all organizations intended to make society a better place in which to live.

Using social institutions as a framework, we examine the ways in which schools are organized and how their organization is designed to help meet their goals. Some ways of organizing schools are better than others, and these differences influence how much students learn and how they develop. These differences will also influence your life as a teacher.

Every school operates as a relatively independent unit within a **school district,** *an administrative unit within a state that is defined by geographical boundaries and is legally responsible for the public education of children within those boundaries.* A school district may encompass an entire county, or large counties may be divided into more than one district.

Districts are important because schools are embedded within them, and their rules and policies affect teachers' lives. Some districts are quite bureaucratic and hierarchical, controlling major elements of curriculum and instruction. Other districts attempt to give more of the decisions about what and how to teach to individual schools and teachers. When you interview for a job, you will want to talk to teachers about their perceptions of the district and how its administrators treat teachers.

To learn more about school districts where you might want to teach, go to the Companion Website at **www.prenhall.com/kauchak**, then to this chapter's *Web Links* module.

Let's turn now to the organization of individual schools.

The Organization of Schools

Think about the schools you attended as a student or schools you've visited as part of your teacher preparation program. If the organization was typical of schools in the United States, you first went to an elementary school, which began with kindergarten, or even pre-kindergarten, followed by first grade, second grade, and so on. You then went to a middle school or junior high, and finally to a high school. As we look at how these schools are organized and why, we'll examine the following:

- Personnel
- The physical plant
- Curriculum organization

Personnel

No school is better than the people who work there. School personnel includes all the people—the administrators, the support staff, and the teachers—who help make a school an effective social institution.

Administrators and Support Staff Elementary, middle, junior high, and high schools all have **administrators,** *individuals responsible for the day-to-day operation of a school.* The administrators include a **principal,** *the individual given the ultimate administrative responsibility for the school's operation*, and, if the school is large, an assistant principal, vice principal, or both, who support the principal in his or her work. Lakeside Junior High, the school in the case study at the beginning of the chapter, has a principal, vice principal, and two assistant principals. The vice principal's responsibilities include scheduling, collecting student records (such as grade reports) from teachers, keeping master records for the school, and maintaining communication with district-level administrators and parents. One of the assistant principals manages the physical plant, arranging the distribution of lockers to students, coordinating the duties of the custodial staff, and overseeing all maintenance and construction. The other assistant principal is in charge of discipline—including referrals made by teachers and both in-school and out-of-school suspension of students—ordering and distributing textbooks to department heads, and maintaining in-service records for teachers.

Depending on the size of the school and the financial status and organization of the school district, schools may also have guidance counselors, school psychologists, and health care providers, such as school nurses. Lakeside Junior High, for example, has two full-time guidance counselors and a school psychologist it shares with other schools. The guidance counselors schedule and coordinate the statewide assessment tests and provide information to students about course offerings and career options. The school psychologist administers individualized intelligence tests and other tests used in making decisions about whether students qualify for special education or programs for the gifted and talented. The school psychologist also provides individual counseling for students having emotional problems and makes recommendations for further mental health assistance.

CW

Increasing Understanding 7.2

What is the most likely reason that school policies on administering medication are so rigid?

Lakeside also has a full-time licensed practical nurse. She maintains all student health records, is trained in administering CPR, supervises medical evacuations, and dispenses all medications to students. Students at Lakeside are forbidden from taking even an over-the-counter painkiller, such as aspirin, on their own, and teachers may not give students any form of medication.

The central office is the school's nerve center; the office staff plays an important role in greeting guests and assisting both teachers and students.

In addition, all schools have support staff, such as the following:

- Secretaries and receptionists, who greet visitors to the school
- Administrative and instructional support staff, who complete paperwork for the principal and other administrators, duplicate tests and handouts for teachers, maintain payroll records, and perform other functions
- Media center specialists, who handle books and different forms of technology
- Physical plant staff, such as custodians who clean the rooms and buildings and cafeteria workers who prepare school lunches

Curriculum Specialists Many elementary schools have teachers who specialize in a particular area, such as technology, art, or music, and who coordinate their efforts with classroom teachers. For example, a class of students may visit a computer center to work with the technology specialist for a certain amount of time each day or week.

Why have we presented this information? In other words, why do teachers need to know about other school personnel and their roles? A school is a complex social institution, and all the people working in a school contribute to making it run smoothly. As a professional, your ability to work with the other personnel will influence how effective you and the school can be. For example, if you have a student who is so unruly that you can't work with him or her in your classroom, you will need the support of the assistant principal and perhaps the advice of the school psychologist to help you address the problem. Although you may teach without another adult in your classroom, your effectiveness will depend on your ability to coordinate your efforts with many different people in your school.

A common adage suggests that you can tell a great deal about the social and emotional climate in a school by observing the way a school receptionist greets students and

Teachers' responsibilities extend beyond their classrooms and include ensuring that the total school facility is a safe and productive place to learn.

visitors when they enter the main office. Likewise, the way you treat support staff will also help set the tone for a positive and supportive school climate. For example, requesting—instead of demanding—services, such as having a test duplicated, communicates to support staff that you value their contributions to the overall functioning of the school. The most effective schools are those in which all personnel work together for the benefit of students.

The Physical Plant

Schools have classrooms, hallways that allow students to move from one room to another, a central administrative office, and one or more large rooms, such as auditoriums, gymnasiums, music rooms, and cafeterias. Many schools have a simple boxlike structure, with hall upon hall of separate cells, that has been criticized as promoting isolation between teachers and fragmentation in the curriculum. When teachers retreat into their classrooms and close their doors, no one else knows what goes on in there. Open school designs, with movable walls and large communal spaces, have gone in and out of popularity and are usually resisted by teachers because of noise and lack of privacy.

CW

Increasing Understanding 7.3

Strong efforts are being made in many areas to eliminate the use of temporaries. Identify at least two reasons these buildings might be considered undesirable.

An elementary school property usually includes a staff parking area, playground, and driveway used for dropping off and picking up students. Middle, junior high, and high schools have athletic facilities, such as playing fields, stadiums, and sometimes swimming pools, although some middle schools were intentionally designed to leave out gymnasiums or other facilities that support competitive activities. High schools also have parking spaces available for students who drive their own cars to school.

School enrollments often increase so rapidly that physical plants can't keep up. As a result, many schools have "temporaries" or "modulars," individual buildings on the perimeter of school campuses that provide additional classroom space.

What will the physical arrangement of schools mean for you as a teacher? First, it will separate you from your colleagues. When you're in your classroom and you shut the door (as many teachers do), you'll essentially be on your own. You'll be responsible for 20–30 second graders, for example, all day, every day. If you teach in middle or high school, you'll spend most of your workday in the confines of your classroom, where you'll be responsible for the education and safety of five or six different classes of students. Second, although your primary responsibility will be to teach students in your classroom, you'll also be expected to carry out nonteaching activities in other areas of the school. If you teach in an elementary school, you may need to escort your students to and from the cafeteria or the media center, for example. If you're a middle or secondary teacher, you'll be expected to monitor students as they move through the corridors and attend auditorium assemblies. You may also be asked to sell tickets at football games, attend track meets, and go to band concerts. A teacher's responsibilities result, in part, from the way schools are physically organized.

Curriculum Organization

Schools are social institutions designed to help young people grow and develop and to prepare them to function effectively in today's (and tomorrow's) world. To function effectively in today's technologically oriented and fast-changing world, students need to acquire essential knowledge and skills. The task for educators is to organize the curriculum in a way that maximizes students' opportunities for learning and development. Theorists offer a variety of definitions of *curriculum*, and no single one is generally accepted (Armstrong, 2003; Parkay & Hass, 2000). For our purposes in this chapter, however, we define **curriculum** as *what teachers teach and what students learn*. (We examine school curriculum in detail in Chapter 10.)

A curriculum is organized around learning goals, such as the following:

- Students will recognize the letters of the alphabet.
- Students will read and understand sentences with compound subjects, such as "Antonio and Carol worked together on their art project."
- Students will use the correct order of operations to simplify expressions such as $9 + 4(7 - 3)/2$.
- Students will understand the concepts of mass and inertia.

Historically, educators have decided that the most efficient way of helping students reach goals such as these is to classify what teachers teach according to different grade levels, ages of students, and subject areas. For instance, children in kindergarten are expected to reach the first goal, third graders the second, seventh-grade pre-algebra students the third, and eleventh-grade physics students the fourth. Learning goals for grade levels and subject areas are part of a school's general curriculum, and they provide teachers with direction as they make decisions about what to teach.

School Organization and the Curriculum How should teachers and students be grouped to help students most effectively learn the content of the curriculum? For example, does it make sense to have 6-year-olds in the same building and walking the same halls as 17- or 18-year-olds? Safety, as well as seemingly mundane concerns like the height of drinking fountains and toilets, suggests no.

Most school systems are organized into three levels: elementary schools for younger children, middle or junior high schools for young adolescents, and high schools for later adolescents. The grades included at each level vary from place to place, however, and as a teacher you may encounter various organizational patterns. Table 7.1 outlines some of the most common patterns.

Table 7.1 Common Ways to Organize Schools

School Level	Grade Ranges
Elementary school	K–2 K–3 K–5 K–6
Middle school	5–8 6–8 7–8
Junior high school	7–8 7–9 8–9
High school	9–12 10–12

What factors do educators consider when making decisions about organizing schools? For example, why do middle schools typically include grades 6–8 or grades 7 and 8? Two factors are most common: (1) the developmental characteristics of students and (2) economics and politics.

Developmental Characteristics of Students **Development** refers to *the physical changes in children as well as changes in the way they think and relate to their peers that result from maturation and experience.* For example, fifth graders are bigger, stronger, and more coordinated than first graders; that is, they are physically more *developed*. Similarly, fifth graders think differently than do first graders. When shown the following drawing, typical first graders conclude that Block A is heavier than Block B, because their thinking tends to focus on size—the most obvious aspect of the balance and blocks. Fifth graders, on the other hand, are more likely to realize that the blocks have the same weight, because they recognize that the balance is balanced (level). Their thinking is more *developed* (Eggen & Kauchak, 2004).

Increasing Understanding 7.4

Elementary schools were first organized into grade levels during the common school movement, which began about 1830 (see Chapter 5). What was the rationale, at that time, for organizing elementary schools this way?

Differences in social development also exist. For example, when faced with a disagreement about who in a group gets to report on which topic, a fifth grader is more likely to step back, recognize the others' perspectives, and compromise. Socially, fifth graders are more capable of considering where a classmate is "coming from," whereas first graders tend to be more self-centered in their thinking (Berk, 2003, 2004; McDevitt & Ormrod, 2002). Advances in social development allow teachers to use instructional strategies, such as cooperative learning, that are more effective with older children than with those who are younger or less developed socially.

Similar differences can be found between fifth graders and tenth or eleventh graders. Many older students are physically young men and women, some think quite abstractly, and they can be socially skilled. These developmental differences influence the ways in which schools are organized. For example, students in elementary schools are typically assigned to one teacher who looks after the cognitive, social, and emotional growth of the students. In some schools **looping,** *the practice of keeping a teacher with one group of students for more than a year,* is used to help individual teachers further nurture the children. Older students are more capable of learning on their own and fending for themselves, so they are assigned to a number of teachers who also serve as subject-matter specialists.

Economics and Politics Economics and politics are also factors that influence decisions about school organization. For example, both influenced the development of Lakeside, Chris Lucio's school, first in its creation as a middle school and later in its conversion to a junior high. At the time Lakeside was developed, the elementary schools in Orange Park had become overcrowded because of rapid population increases in the city, and the process of building additional elementary schools didn't keep up with demand. Creating middle schools temporarily solved the problem, because sixth graders could be moved into the middle schools. This was a decision based on economics.

Also, the middle school movement was gathering momentum at this same time, and Mary Zellner, who was to be Lakeside's first principal, was an outspoken proponent of middle schools. She was a respected leader in district politics, and because of her influence, Lakeside was built according to middle school philosophy. This philosophy de-emphasized competition among students, and as a result, the school didn't have competitive athletics, which was the reason the school didn't originally have a gymnasium. Although Mary Zellner's advocacy of middle schools was grounded in research, the district-level decision to avoid competitive activities at Lakeside was a result of her political influence.

The issues then became further complicated. Coaches at Orange Park High complained that potential athletes came to them from the middle schools without the athletic experiences students attending competing schools enjoyed. (These pressures occur nationwide; about 80 percent of middle-level schools in the United States offer organized competitive sports [Swain, McEwin & Irvin, 1998].) A bigger problem was that Orange Park High, the only high school in the district, had become overcrowded. District officials solved both problems by converting the middle schools into junior highs, moving ninth graders from the high school to the junior highs, and sending sixth graders back to elementary schools. By this time, the elementary schools were able to accept the additional students because a number of new elementary schools had recently been built in the city. The decision to convert middle schools to junior highs was based on both economics and politics; it had little to do with the developmental needs of students. This is not uncommon in education.

It will be helpful to keep these factors in mind as we look at schools at different levels in more depth. We begin by looking at early childhood programs and elementary schools and then turn to schools for older students—high schools, junior highs, and middle schools.

Early Childhood Programs

Most of you reading this book probably attended kindergarten, and some of you may have even gone to a pre-kindergarten program. However, one of your authors, educated in a small town in a predominantly rural area, attended neither, because they weren't offered there at the time.

Early childhood education is *a catch-all term encompassing a range of educational programs for young children, including infant intervention and enrichment programs, nursery schools, public and private pre-kindergartens and kindergartens, and federally funded Head Start programs.* Early childhood education is a mid-twentieth century development in the United States, although its philosophical roots go back 250 years. The French philosopher Rousseau, for example, gave this advice about educating young children:

• • ● • •

Do not treat the child to discourses which he cannot understand. No descriptions, no eloquence, no figures of speech. . . . In general, let us never substitute the sign for the thing, except when it is impossible for us to show the thing. . . . Things! Things! I shall never tire of saying that we ascribe too much importance to words. (Compayre, 1888)

• • ● • •

Rousseau was arguing that young children need to play and work with concrete objects ("Things! Things!") rather than being taught with abstract words. This idea is consistent with the need for concrete experiences that the famous developmental psychologist Jean Piaget (1952, 1970) emphasized, and it is at the core of developmentally appropriate kindergarten and early childhood programs.

Developmental programs *accommodate children's developmental differences by allowing children to acquire skills and abilities at their own pace through direct experi-*

ences. Visitors in a developmental classroom are likely to see learning centers around the room with activities for the children. For instance, one center might have a tub of water and items that the children test to see if they sink or float. Another might have a series of big books with pictures and large-print words. A third might have a series of blocks that children use to construct towers and other structures. Instead of traditional teacher-centered instruction, the teacher's role is to provide experiences for children and encourage exploration.

For more information about early childhood education programs, visit the Web site of the National Association for the Education of Young Children (NAEYC), the largest professional association for early children education. A link to the site can be found in this chapter's *Web Links* module of the Companion Website at www.prenhall.com/kauchak.

The need for learning-related experiences early in life is well recognized (Berk, 2003; Hartnett & Gelman, 1998), and the benefits of early intervention programs are long-lasting. The Perry Preschool study tracked 123 poor African American children who either attended 3 years of preschool or did not (the program did not have room for all applicants) (Bracey, 2003a). Dramatic differences were found between the preschool students and students in the control group. By the time these students turned 27, 71 percent of the preschool group had attained a high school diploma or GED, but only 54 percent of the control group had. Forty-two percent of the males in the preschool group reported making more than $24,000 a year, compared to only 6 percent of the males in the control group. Thirty-six percent of the preschool group, but only 13 percent of the control group, owned their own homes. Control group members had twice as many arrests as those who attended the preschool, and five times as many of the control group had been arrested five or more times. Clearly, the Perry Preschool program had long-lasting beneficial effects on the children it served.

A more ambitious program in North Carolina provided nutritional help and social services from birth, as well as parenting lessons and a language-oriented preschool program (Bracey, 2003a; Jacobsen, 2003). Follow-up studies revealed that participants scored higher on intelligence and achievement tests, were twice as likely to attend postsecondary education, and delayed having children by 2 years versus nonparticipants. Early childhood education programs pay off, not only in terms of immediate school success but also later in life. David Broder, a prominent *Washington Post* columnist, observed: "The evidence that high-quality education beginning at age 3 or 4 will pay lifetime dividends is overwhelming. The only question is whether we will make the needed investment" (quoted in Bracey, 2003a, p. 32).

By the mid-1990s, less than half of all 5-year-olds were attending full-time preschool, day-care, or other programs (U.S. Department of Education, 1996a), but this is rapidly changing. Much greater emphasis is now being placed on high-quality early intervention programs in all settings. As full-time pre-K programs become increasingly common, job opportunities in these areas will grow.

For more information about early intervention programs, go to the Companion Website at www.prenhall.com/kauchak, then to this chapter's *Web Links* module.

Elementary Schools

To begin our examination of the organization of elementary schools, let's look at the schedules of two elementary teachers. Read the schedules in Table 7.2, and see what you notice.

Self-contained elementary classrooms attempt to meet young students' developmental needs.

Some observations might include the following:

- Both teachers are responsible for all the content areas, such as reading, language arts, math, science, and social studies.
- The schedules are quite different. Although both teachers teach young children, Sharon begins with language arts, for example, while Susie begins by having the children practice their previous day's math and language arts.
- The amount of time the teachers allocate to each of the content areas is a personal decision. Sharon, for example, devotes 50 minutes to math, whereas Susie teaches math for 75 minutes a day.

Table 7.2 Schedules for Two Elementary School Teachers

Sharon's First-Grade Schedule

8:30 AM	School begins
8:30–8:45	Morning announcements
8:45–10:30	Language arts (including reading and writing)
10:30–11:20	Math
11:20–11:50	Lunch
11:50–12:20	Read story
12:20–1:15	Center time (practice on language arts and math)
1:15–1:45	Physical education
1:45–2:30	Social studies/science
2:30–2:45	Class meeting
2:45–3:00	Call buses/dismissal

Susie's Third-Grade Schedule

8:30 AM	School begins
8:30–9:15	Independent work (practice previous day's language arts and math)
9:15–10:20	Language arts (including reading and writing)
10:20–10:45	Snack/independent reading
10:45–11:15	Physical education
11:15–12:15	Language arts/social studies/science
12:15–12:45	Lunch
12:45–2:00	Math
2:00–2:30	Spelling/catch up on material not covered earlier
2:30–2:45	Read story
2:45–3:00	Clean up/prepare for dismissal

In conversation both teachers noted that the schedules in Table 7.2 were approximate and often changed depending on their perception of students' needs and the day of the week. For example, if students were having trouble with a math topic, they might devote more time to math on a given day (S. Mittelstadt, personal communication, July 26, 2003; S. Van Horn, personal communication, July 28, 2003).

If you observe in elementary classrooms, you're likely to see a schedule that varies from the ones in Table 7.2. This individual teacher freedom and autonomy is characteristic of elementary school organization.

Why are elementary schools organized this way? In the very first elementary-level schools in early America (see Chapter 5), a single teacher was typically responsible for all of the content areas. Until about the mid-1800s, elementary schools weren't even organized into grade levels. In many rural, one-room schools, a single teacher was responsible for all the grade levels and content areas. So, history has influenced the way elementary schools are organized.

The developmental characteristics of students have also influenced the organization of elementary schools. We saw earlier that young children look, think, and interact with their peers in ways that are different from older students. Educators have historically believed that young children need the stability of one teacher and a single classroom to function most effectively in school. Schools can be frightening places for little children, and self-contained classrooms provide emotional security. Further, simply moving from room to room, as middle and secondary students do, can be difficult for young children. Imagine, for example, a first grader going to Room 101 for math, 108 for language arts, and so on. Rotating schedules, which are becoming increasingly popular under block scheduling, would be even more confusing.

CW

Increasing Understanding 7.5

In both Sharon's and Susie's schedules, reading, language arts, and math are strongly emphasized. On which of the educational philosophies that you studied in Chapter 6 is this emphasis most likely based?

The idea of a single classroom and teacher is being questioned by some educators. Expecting one teacher to be sufficiently knowledgeable to effectively teach reading, language arts, math, science, and social studies is asking almost the impossible, they say. A common situation is that some content areas—typically science, social studies, art, and music—are de-emphasized by teachers who feel uncomfortable teaching in these areas. So educators, teachers, and parents face a dilemma: Is social and emotional well-being more important than content for elementary students? Historically, the answer has been yes.

WITHIN-SCHOOL COORDINATION: A GRADE-LEVEL MEETING

Having examined the ways in which elementary schools are organized, you now have the opportunity to view a video showing how teachers deal with this organization.

In this episode DeVonne Lampkin, a fifth-grade teacher, leads a grade-level meeting with her colleagues as they discuss various issues related to their duties as teachers in an elementary school.

To complete this activity, do the following:

- Go to the DVD and view the video episode titled "Within-School Coordination: A Grade-Level Meeting."
- Answer the questions you'll find on the DVD.

CW *To answer the questions online and receive immediate feedback, go the Companion Website at* **www.prenhall.com/kauchak,** *then to this chapter's* Classroom Windows *module.*

High Schools, Junior Highs, and Middle Schools

To see differences between elementary schools and middle, junior high, and high schools, we need only compare Chris's experiences (in the chapter opening case) to Susie's and Sharon's. We saw that elementary teachers typically teach all the content areas and set their own schedules. Also, they are responsible for monitoring their students outside the classroom, such as by walking with them to the cafeteria.

In contrast, as a middle school teacher, Chris teaches only one subject (geography), and he (along with all the other teachers in his school) follows a specific, predetermined schedule. The lengths of class periods are uniform for all the content areas, and the beginnings and endings are signaled by a bell. Also, Chris is not responsible for monitoring his students as they move from place to place on the Lakeside campus, but he is involved in extracurricular activities (such as the track meet), which are part of middle schools, junior highs, and high schools.

CW

Increasing Understanding 7.6

Think again about your study of Chapter 5. Identify three reasons educational leaders decided that all students—college-bound and non-college-bound—should take the same curriculum.

Why are upper-level schools organized in this way? To answer this question, think back to our description of school as a social institution designed to promote the development of children and the welfare of society. Also recall from Chapter 5 that views about educational goals have changed over time. For instance, in colonial times, people felt that society would benefit most from having students learn to read and understand the Bible. Much later (near the end of the nineteenth century), educators felt that having both college-bound and non-college-bound students take the same curriculum would serve society. This view was based on the belief that mental discipline was the most important function of education. Also, schools were organized to accommodate the large influx of immigrants and help them assimilate into American society.

As educational thinking evolved, leaders felt that society needed citizens well schooled in a variety of academic subjects. This emphasis on the mastery of subject matter resulted in the departmentalization found in the middle or junior highs and high schools that you most likely attended. Let's look at the organization of these schools, beginning with high schools.

Extracurricular activities provide valuable learning opportunities not typically tapped by traditional classrooms.

The Comprehensive High School

Most of you probably attended a **comprehensive high school,** *a secondary school that attempts to meet the needs of all students* (see Chapter 5 for a discussion of the history of high schools). In *The American High School* James Conant (1959) argues persuasively that the most effective high schools are ones large enough to offer diverse academic courses and diverse facilities. In attempting to do this, most high schools are organized into tracks (Oakes, 1992, 1995). For example, students in a college-preparatory track take courses designed to get them ready for college-level work. A college-prep track might include honors or advanced placement classes in core subject areas. **Advanced placement classes** are *courses taken in high school that allow students to earn college credit,* making college less time-consuming and expensive. A general track composed of "standard" classes is designed for students of average ability who may or may not go on to college. Students in this track may take some vocational courses, such as word processing or woodworking, designed to provide them with practical skills they can use immediately after graduating. A vocational track specifically targets students not going to college, preparing them for careers in such areas as automobile repair or technology.

A comprehensive high school also offers extracurricular activities (such as band, chorus, and theater) and athletics (such as football, swimming, soccer, and tennis). These options are intended to help all students develop personally, socially, and intellectually. Educational leaders believe that the more fully developed students are when they leave high school, the better equipped they will be to succeed in college or immediately contribute to society.

Criticisms of the Comprehensive High School Can a comprehensive high school be all things to all students? Critics say no and focus on three factors: tracking, size, and departmentalization.

A paradox of the comprehensive high school is that different tracks, designed to present quality alternatives, often produce exactly the opposite. Instead of providing freedom and choice, tracking limits choices and segregates students, often leaving many with substandard educational experiences (Oakes, 1995). Lower-ability, minority, and low-SES students are often steered into vocational or lower-level tracks, where the curriculum is less challenging and instruction is often poor. Instead of effectively preparing students for the world of work, lower tracks often segregate students from their college-bound peers and communicate that challenge and deep understanding are not for them. Some critics charge that tracking should be eliminated completely and that all students should be prepared as much as possible for college work (Vander Ark, 2003).

A second criticism of high schools relates to size of enrollment, which exceeds 1,000 students in many U.S. high schools. As schools become larger, they tend to also become more impersonal and bureaucratic. They virtually become shopping malls in which students mill around looking for entertainment and educational bargains. Like smart shoppers, the brighter students (or their parents) know what they want and quickly find the more challenging, college-preparatory courses. Lower achievers get lost in the shuffle, spending time but not receiving a quality education. One critic remarked that because of their unwieldy size, "our high schools are the least effective part of the American education system" (Vander Ark, 2003, p. 52).

According to critics, departmentalization, or the organization of teachers and classes into separate academic areas, is another problem of the comprehensive high school. Departmentalization fragments the curriculum and interferes with learning:

> While the adults organize as separate departmental entities isolated from one another, however, their teenage students seek interconnectedness and relevancy in their school experience. What they get instead is math with no relationship to social studies, science without any connection to literature, and so forth. This relevancy-starved approach continues year in, year out with no alternatives, and any "reforms" seen in public education are invariably found at the elementary or middle school level. (Cooperman, 2003, p. 30)

To prevent such fragmentation, some educators suggest that schools cluster teachers and classes into interdisciplinary teams where connections between disciplines are emphasized. Other concrete solutions to the problems of large high schools include creating "smaller learning communities" within large schools, allowing students to keep the same guidance counselor throughout high school, and offering specific opportunities for students and teachers to get to know one another (Sack, 1999). These ideas are discussed further in the section on school size later in the chapter. Interestingly, they are similar to the suggestions offered to make junior highs and middle schools more user-friendly. Let's examine them.

Junior High and Middle Schools

As described in Chapter 5, schools in the early twentieth century were organized into eight elementary and four high school grades. This 8–4 organization changed when emphasis shifted away from basic skills, such as reading and math, and toward the more intensive study of specific content areas, such as history, literature, and science. This intensive study required teachers who were subject-matter experts. In addition, a growing recognition of the unique needs of early adolescents was being realized. The result was the development of the "junior" high school.

Most junior high schools today have a variety of offerings, although not as comprehensive as those in high schools, and they include competitive athletics and other extracurricular activities. Although initially designed to help students make the transition between elementary and high schools, they are in every sense of the word "junior" high schools.

Think back to the friends you knew when you were in the sixth, seventh, or eighth grades. Some of the girls were young women, fully developed physically and emotionally, whereas others were still little girls. Some boys needed to shave, whereas others looked like fifth graders. Many of the boys and girls were becoming more and more attracted to each other, and others were attracted to the other sex but didn't know why. This was the transitional period of early adolescence.

Because of rapid physical, emotional, and intellectual changes, early adolescence is a unique period in a child's development. At no other time in a person's life, except infancy, is change so rapid or profound. As a result, many educators believe that schools for young adolescents should be organized to meet the unique needs of these students (Clark & Clark, 1993; National Middle School Association, 1995). This thinking, and the fact that junior highs weren't meeting early adolescents' needs, led to the formation of **middle schools,** *schools, typically for grades 6–8, specifically designed to help students through the rapid social, emotional, and intellectual changes characteristic of early adolescence.*

What is teaching in a middle school like? Let's look at an example.

Case STUDY Robin West is an eighth-grade teacher in an inner-city middle school. She teaches physical science, and she and her team members have a common planning period. They teach the same group of students and often spend their planning period discussing the students and the topics they are teaching. A number of their students are not native English speakers, and their discussions often center on what can be done to help students with language problems. In addition, Robin has four students with learning disabilities in her classroom. The teachers try to integrate topics across as many of the four areas as often as possible.

"Can you help me out with anything on graphing?" Mary, the math teacher, asked the others one Monday. "The kids just see graphs as some meaningless lines. I explain the heck out of them, but it doesn't seem to help all that much."

"I know what I can do," Robin offered, after thinking for a few seconds. "I'll do some simple demonstrations and then have them link the demonstration to a graph. . . . Here, look."

She held out her pen and dropped it. She then drew a graph on a piece of paper:

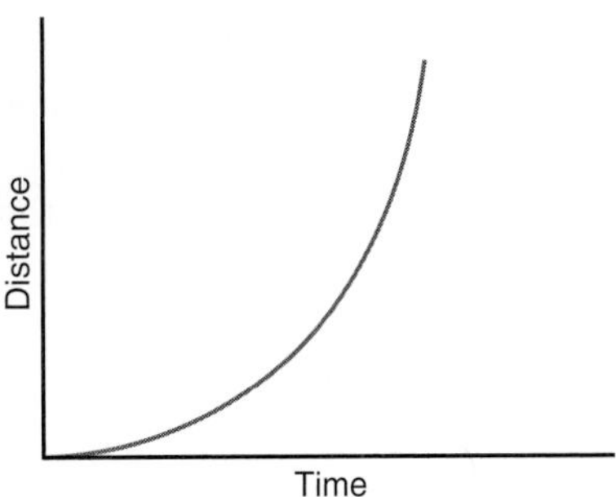

"The graph represents the relationship between the distance the pen falls and the time it takes to fall," she explained. "Time is on the horizontal axis, and distance is on the vertical axis. . . . I'll do this with the kids, and you can refer to what I did when you do your work on graphs," she added, nodding to Mary.

"Great. Thanks. . . . When will you do it?"

"We're between units now, so I can do it tomorrow. . . . Then you and I can talk about it after school for a few minutes, and I'll let you know how it went. . . . By the way, how is Lorraine Williams doing in math?"

"Not good," Mary responded. "In fact, I was going to ask you all about her. She hasn't been turning in her homework, and she seems only 'half there' in class."

"Same thing in history," Keith, the history teacher, added. "We'd better see what's going on. . . . I'll call her parents tonight."

• • ● • •

As this short scenario suggests, middle schools do things differently than junior high and high schools. Effective middle schools make the following adaptations. (National Middle School Association, 1995):

- *They organize teachers and students into interdisciplinary teams.* For example, a team composed of a math, science, English, and social studies teacher instructs the same group of students and works together to coordinate topics.
- *They attempt to create and maintain long-term teacher–student relationships with attention to emotional development.* Many middle schools implement an "advisor–advisee" period, in which the homeroom teacher meets with students each day to discuss a variety of nonacademic topics. Through these advisory periods teachers get to know students on an individual basis and can more carefully track their academic progress.
- *They use interactive teaching strategies.* Teachers are encouraged to move away from the lecture-dominated instruction so common in high schools and toward instruction based on interactive questioning and student involvement. In addition, greater emphasis is placed on study strategies, such as note taking and time management.
- *They eliminate activities that emphasize developmental differences, such as competitive sports.* In middle schools everyone is invited to participate in intramural sports and clubs.

When done well, these adaptations have a positive influence on students (MacIver & Epstein, 1993). For instance, interdisciplinary teams allow teachers to efficiently plan for the integration of topics across different content areas, as Robin and Mary did with math and science. Also, when teachers have the same students, they can more carefully monitor students' progress, as the team did with Lorraine. Forming relationships with students helps them adjust to an atmosphere less personal than that in

Teaching in an Era of Reform

THE GRADE RETENTION ISSUE

U.S. schools are organized so that children progress from grade to grade as they grow older. It makes sense to expose students to increasingly complex ideas as they develop. But what should happen when a student isn't able to master course content?

Educators have shown an increased interest in **grade retention,** *the practice of having students repeat a grade if they don't meet certain criteria.* An important plank in current reform efforts is the elimination of "social promotion"—that is, promoting low-achieving students to the next grade so they can be with their social peers. When then-president Clinton called for an end to social promotion in the late 1990s (Clinton, 1998, 1999), many education professionals interpreted his remarks as a mandate to retain students who fail to achieve at prescribed levels (Jimerson, 2001).

Grade retention is not new, but its popularity as a reform tool is growing (Jimerson, Ferguson, Whipple, Anderson, & Dalton, 2002). In the past, 5 to 7 percent of public school children (about 2 children in every classroom) were retained each year (Shepard & Smith, 1990). However, research published in the last decade of the twentieth century indicates that by ninth grade some 30 percent to 50 percent of students will have been retained at least once in their academic careers (K. Alexander, Entwisle, & Kabbani, 1999; McCoy & Reynolds, 1999). Overall, it has been estimated that about 2.5 million students are retained each year at a cost to U.S. taxpayers of more than $14 billion annually (Dawson, 1999). The number of retentions is likely to grow even further. A number of states and several large school districts (including New York City, Los Angeles, and Chicago) are either considering or have implemented systems in which students must pass a test to progress to the next grade (Robelen, 2000; White, 1999b).

The Issue

Proponents of grade retention point to the inherent sensibility of retaining students in a grade until they've acquired the knowledge and skills for that level. For example, allowing students to move from the fourth to the fifth grade when they haven't mastered the content and abilities expected of typical fourth graders is counterproductive because students are less likely to succeed in the fifth grade. Spending a second year in a grade gives learners another chance to acquire the necessary understanding and skills and sends the message that schoolwork is important.

CW

Increasing Understanding 7.7

Are middle schools more like elementary or high schools? Why?

their elementary schools. And eliminating competitive sports encourages greater participation in athletic activities and minimizes the advantages early-maturing students have over their later-developing classmates.

Interactive teaching strategies can be particularly important in middle school. These strategies actively involve students in learning activities that can also develop their thinking and social interaction skills. Research indicates that motivation often drops during the early adolescent years, and some researchers believe that this drop is due to increased use of teaching strategies, such as lecturing, that place students in passive roles (Pintrich & Schunk, 2002; Stipek, 2002). Interactive teaching strategies are discussed in more depth in Chapter 11.

The number of middle schools continues to increase. By the start of the twenty-first century, middle schools outnumbered junior highs by a ratio of 4 to 1 (National Center for Education Statistics, 2002). However, critics suggest that many middle schools, rather than implementing the intended adaptations just listed, still largely resemble the junior high schools they were intended to replace (Bailey, 1997).

The impact of this position is illustrated in Louisiana, where all fourth and eighth graders must pass a test to progress to the next grade level. In 1999 about 38,000 students—about one third of the students taking the test—failed. Those students were offered summer school and a second chance to pass. Those not passing were required to repeat fourth or eighth grade (Robelen, 2000).

Opponents of grade retention argue that holding students back does not improve their academic performance. They point to studies indicating that students retained in grade tend to perform lower on subsequent achievement tests than their nonretained classmates (Jimerson, 2001) and are also more likely to later drop out of school (Hauser, 1999; Jimerson, Anderson, & Whipple, 2002). They note that school dropouts are five times more likely to have repeated a grade than students who complete high school and that the probability of dropping out for students who repeat two grades is nearly 100 percent. They further note that minorities and low-SES children are much more likely to be retained than their White, wealthier counterparts. In Texas this fact sparked a lawsuit challenging the state's pass-or-don't-graduate policy (Zehr, 1999b).

Opponents further argue that grade retention causes emotional problems. In one study children rated the prospect of repeating a grade as more stressful than "wetting in class" or being caught stealing. Going blind or losing a parent were the only two life events that children said would be more stressful than being retained (Shepard & Smith, 1990). Opponents note that the psychological effects of grade retention are especially acute in adolescence, where physical size differences and peer awareness exacerbate the problem (G. Anderson, Jimerson, & Whipple, 2002).

Finally, opponents suggest, there are better alternatives to social promotion. Before- and after-school programs, summer school programs with reduced class sizes, instructional aides who work with low-achieving children, and peer tutoring are all possibilities. Each is less expensive than the thousands of dollars spent on having children repeat what they have already experienced, and students in alternative programs are more likely to meet standards than those who have repeated grades (Hauser, 1999).

You Take a Position

Now it's your turn to take a position on the issue. State in writing whether you do or do not believe that grade retention is needed and is likely to increase student learning, and provide a two-page rationale for your position.

CW

For additional references and resources, go to the Companion Website at **www.prenhall.com/kauchak**, *then to this chapter's* Teaching in an Era of Reform *module. You can respond online or submit your response to your instructor.*

What Is an Effective School?

You're either planning to teach or are thinking about teaching; this is the reason you're taking this course. As you consider job offers from different schools, some important questions to ask are "How good is this school?" and "What would it be like to work in this school?" How can you determine whether or not a school is good? What does "good" mean? We try to answer these questions in this section.

Although people commonly refer to schools as good or not so good, as in "Lakeside is a very *good* junior high school," researchers use the term *effective* instead. An **effective school** is *a school in which learning for all students is maximized.* In simple terms, an effective school is one that promotes learning. But what makes a school effective for promoting student learning? Researchers attempting to answer this question identified schools that, despite challenging circumstances, produced more learning in their students than comparable schools (Marzano, 2003). They also looked at poor-performing schools as negative examples. Let's see what these researchers found.

Research on Effective Schools

Research has identified several characteristics of schools that maximize learning for all students (Bransford, Brown, & Cocking, 2000; Herman, 1999; Taylor, Pressley, & Pearson, 2002). They are outlined in Figure 7.1 and discussed in the sections that follow.

Optimal School and Class Size This chapter focuses on school organization, and the way schools are organized has a significant effect on learning. An important dimension of this organization is size—the size of the school and the size of classes.

School size. Are small schools better than big ones, or is the reverse true? As it turns out, the relationship between size and quality isn't simple or direct. Schools must be large enough to provide the varied curricular offerings needed to help students learn in different content areas, but not so large that students get lost.

How big is too big? The largest high school on record, DeWitt Clinton High School in the Bronx, boasted 12,000 students in 1934 (Allen, 2002). (Can you imagine what it must have been like to be a freshman walking into that school on the first day of the school year?) At the other end of the spectrum are one-room elementary schools; for example, one K–4 elementary school in Grantville, Vermont, had 18 students in 2002 (Shelley, 2003). School size relates to level, with elementary schools being the smallest and high schools the largest. In the 2000–2001 school year, the average elementary school in the United States had 482 students; the average secondary school had 795 students (National Center for Education Statistics, 2002). More than 70 percent of U.S. high school students, however, attend schools of 1,000 students or more, and a number of urban districts have high schools of over 5,000 students (Allen, 2002). Research suggests the ideal size for a high school is between 600 and 900 students (Lee, 2000).

School size affects low- and high-SES students differently. For example, the decrease in learning in very large or very small high schools is greater for low-SES than it is for high-SES students. The only schools not fitting this pattern are elite private schools that enroll students with similar backgrounds and provide extensive resources, such as well-equipped science and computer labs. Unfortunately, a disproportionate

Figure 7.1 Characteristics of Effective Schools

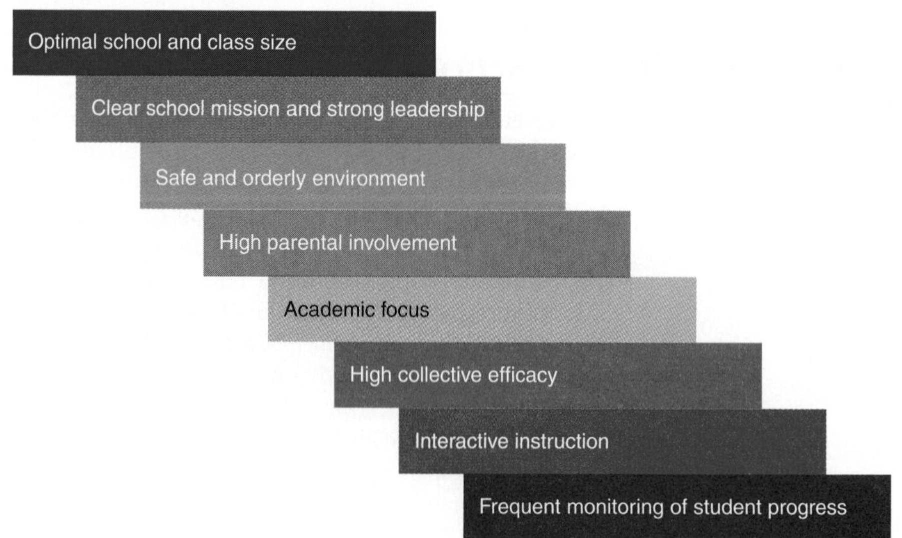

CW

Increasing Understanding 7.8

Explain why school size more strongly influences low-SES students than high-SES students. Think about the characteristics of students placed at-risk presented in Chapter 4.

number of low-SES students attend either very small or very large high schools. Examples include small rural schools in sparsely populated states, such as Wyoming or Montana, and large, urban schools in major cities such as New York or Los Angeles.

How does school size influence student learning? Researchers suggest that school size, in itself, doesn't cause students to learn less than they would in an ideally sized school. Rather, size influences other factors (Lee, 2000). As schools becomes larger, for example, it becomes more difficult to create learning communities that promote a sense of physical and emotional safety in students. In large schools education is less personal, and it is harder for teachers and students to get to know one another and to work together.

Both parents and teachers want smaller schools, but the cost of building them is a major deterrent to taxpayers. In a national survey, parents said they felt their children received a more rigorous and personalized education in smaller schools, and teachers said that, all too often, students fell through the cracks in larger schools (Public Agenda, 2002). Research also supports smaller schools, showing that they have significantly higher graduation and college attendance rates, as well as fewer discipline and safety issues, than large schools (Vander Ark, 2002).

One solution to the problem of large schools is to create schools within schools, smaller learning communities where both teachers and students feel more comfortable. For example, Creekland Middle School in Georgia has more than 3,100 students, many more than experts recommend for any school, much less a middle school (Jacobson, 2000). To address this issue, Creekland is divided into five learning communities, each with its own assistant principal, school counselor, and faculty. Students are assigned to one of these communities for the 3 years they attend the middle school, and faculty make a special effort to integrate students into their community.

Class size. Class size also influences a school's effectiveness. Classes of 20 or fewer students are considered optimal, but many classes are much larger, especially in middle school and high school. Although critics argue either that class size doesn't matter or that reducing class size isn't worth the cost, research consistently indicates that reducing class size does indeed increase learning for all students, and the effects are particularly pronounced in the lower grades and for students placed at-risk (J. Finn, 2002; Gilman & Kiger, 2003).

Class-size reduction can be an effective tool to increase achievement.

Reductions in class size can have both short- and long-term positive effects (Nye, Hedges, & Konstantopoulos, 2001; Viadero, 1999c). In Tennessee, where class sizes were reduced from 25 to 15 students, researchers found immediate gains in reading and math scores. Follow-up studies revealed that the positive effects lasted through twelfth grade. Students in the smaller class dropped out of school less frequently, took more challenging courses, and were more likely to attend college than their counterparts in larger classes. These positive effects were especially strong for African American students.

Smaller class sizes also positively affect teachers' lives (Muñoz & Portes, 2002). When class sizes are reduced, teachers' morale and job satisfaction increase. In smaller classes teachers spend less time on discipline and more time on small-group work and diagnostic assessment. Researchers caution, however, that these positive changes don't occur automatically; teachers need to be trained to adjust their instruction to take advantage of the smaller number of students in their classrooms.

The politics of reducing class size were recently seen in the state of Florida (Richard, 2002a). Voters in that state approved a constitutional amendment in 2002 to reduce class size by two students per class. Conservatives, including the governor, Jeb Bush, claimed the amendment would be too costly to implement. Under pressure from parents and educational groups, the legislature appropriated $468 million to fund class-size-reduction programs in districts. In addition, the Florida legislature added $600 million in construction bonds to help districts increase or renovate classroom space for the smaller classes. Reducing class sizes requires money, and both taxpayers and politicians must be willing to pay the price.

Clear School Mission and Strong Leadership In effective schools, a clearly stated mission exists. This mission is clearly communicated, and it remains at the forefront of the thinking of the entire school staff. For example, if developing literacy is emphasized in the mission of an elementary school, evidence of this theme appears in teachers' instruction. Reading comprehension is emphasized in all classes, not simply when the explicit focus is on reading, and children are given extensive practice in putting their understanding of math, science, and other content into words. The same is true for other aspects of the school mission. In effective schools, teachers share an understanding of and commitment to instructional goals, priorities, and assessment procedures, and they accept responsibility for students meeting the school's curricular goals.

Strong leadership is essential to the success of a school. In effective schools, the principal understands learning and teaching and acts as an instructional leader who can advise staff and serve as a resource to parents and students. Faculty meetings focus on instructional issues, and learning and effective teaching are continually discussed topics.

Safe and Orderly Environment In a national survey asking students to identify serious problems in their school, 45 percent identified fighting, 54 percent targeted bullying, and 38 percent pointed to stealing. When asked whether noisy students disrupting class, cheating, and stealing were problems at their school, the majority of fourth, fifth, and sixth graders (88%, 66%, and 51%, respectively) said yes (Boyer, 1995). Schools, which should be sheltered communities for learning, often mirror the problems of society. Marzano (2003) noted, "If teachers and students do not feel safe, they will not have the necessary psychological energy for teaching and learning" (p. 53).

The need for safe and orderly schools is supported by both research and theory. Researchers describe effective schools as places of trust, order, cooperation, and high morale (Marzano, 2003; Rutter, Maughan, Mortimore, Ouston, & Smith, 1979). Students need to feel emotionally safe in schools for learning to occur (P. Alexander & Murphy, 1998).

Theories of learner development, which we briefly discussed earlier in the chapter, suggest that the need for order is innate (Piaget 1952, 1970). In other words, people are born with a desire to live in an orderly rather than chaotic world. In addition, the psychologist Abraham Maslow (1968), who described a hierarchy of human needs, argued that only the need for survival is more basic than the need for safety. Studies of classroom management also confirm the need for order; orderly classrooms

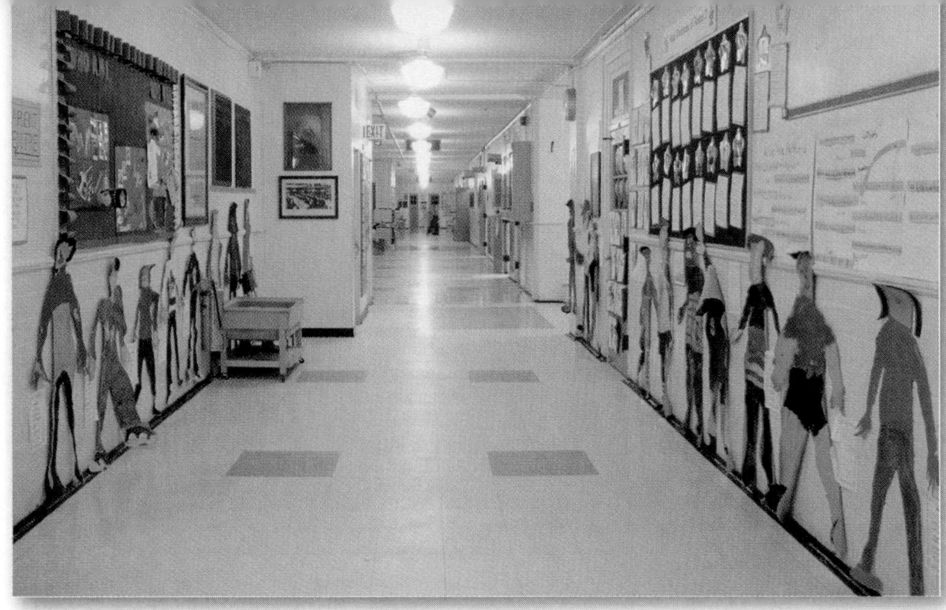

One essential characteristic of an effective school is hallways that are safe and orderly.

promote both learning and student motivation (Emmer, Evertson, & Worsham, 2003; Evertson, Emmer, & Worsham, 2003).

High Parental Involvement Schools, no matter how well they're organized, won't be effective if parents aren't involved in their children's education (Marzano, 2003). Learning is a cooperative venture, and teachers, students, and parents are in it together.

Research indicates that students benefit from home–school cooperation in a number of ways, including the following:

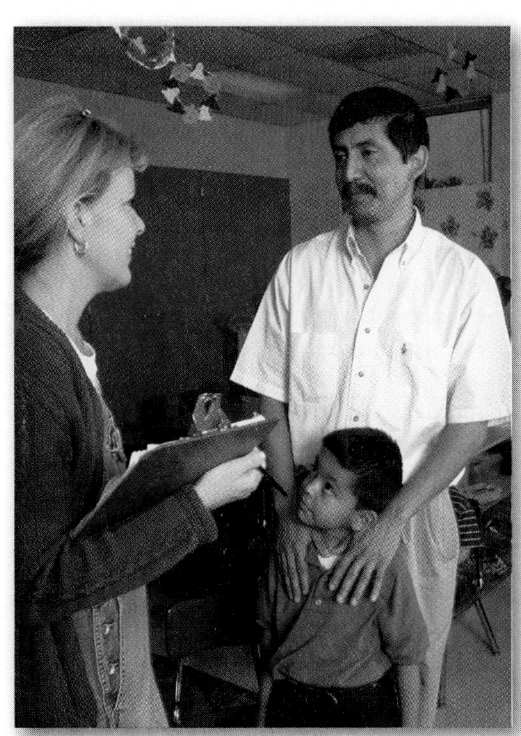
Effective schools develop mechanisms to allow parents and teachers to work together.

- When parents are involved, students achieve more, regardless of socioeconomic status, ethnic/racial background, or the parents' levels of education. The more extensive the parental involvement, the higher the student achievement.
- When parents are involved in their children's education, students earn higher grades and test scores, attend school more regularly, and complete homework more consistently.
- When parents are involved, students exhibit more positive attitudes and behavior.
- Educators hold higher expectations for students whose parents collaborate with teachers. They also hold higher opinions of those parents.
- Student alcohol use, violence, and antisocial behaviors decrease as parental involvement increases. (López & Scribner, 1999; U.S. Department of Education, 2001b)

These outcomes likely result from parents' increased participation in school activities, their more positive attitudes about schooling, and teachers' increased understanding of students' home environments.

Parental involvement is so important that the National PTA established the National Standards for Parent/Family Involvement Programs (National Parent Teacher Association, 1998) presented in Table 7.3.

Table 7.3 National Standards for Parent/Family Involvement Programs

Standard	Description
I. Communicating	Communication between home and school is regular, two-way and meaningful.
II. Parenting	Parenting skills are promoted and supported.
III. Student Learning	Parents play an integral role in assisting student learning.
IV. Volunteering	Parents are welcome in the school, and their support and assistance are sought.
V. School Decision Making and Advocacy	Parents are full partners in the decisions that affect children and families.
VI. Collaborating with Community	Community resources are used to strengthen schools, families, and student learning.

Source: Reprinted/excerpted with permission from National PTA's *National Standards for Parent/Family Involvement Programs*, © 1998.

Increasing Understanding 7.9

Earlier we stated that a disproportionate number of low-SES students are enrolled in large schools. Are low-SES parents likely to be more or less involved in their children's schools than high-SES parents? Explain. (Hint: Think about the influence of SES on learning that was discussed in Chapter 4.)

To learn more about the National Standards for Parent/Family Involvement Programs and read suggestions for involving parents in their children's education, go to the Companion Website at **www.prenhall.com/kauchak**, then to this chapter's *Web Links* module.

Academic Focus The essence of academic focus is promoting learning for all students. Promoting learning is the central mission of effective schools, and as we saw earlier, this mission is clear to the teachers in the school, and the tone is set by the school principal and other administrators. In academically focused schools, teachers have high expectations, and they maximize the time available for instruction. Students are directly involved in learning activities for as much of the day as possible, and instruction remains focused on essential content and skills. An array of clubs, sports, and other extracurricular offerings exist and are important, but they don't take precedence over learning. In effective schools, for example, classes are not canceled so students can attend sporting events, and class time isn't used for club meetings.

One study investigating the effects of academic focus on learning concluded, "Students learn more in schools that set high standards for academic performance, that use their instructional time wisely, and that use student learning as a criterion for making decisions" (Lee & Smith, 1999). Schools with an academic focus are also more positive places in which to work because both students and teachers feel that learning is occurring. You will want to look for signs that academic focus is present in the schools in which you're considering working.

High Collective Efficacy In the last sections we saw how school size, safety and order, parental involvement, and school focus all influence a school's effectiveness and the amount students learn. Teachers are central to a school's effectiveness, and their attitudes and beliefs strongly influence the way they teach and the amount students learn.

One of the most important ways a teacher can contribute to an effective school is through **personal teaching efficacy,** *a teacher's belief that he or she can promote learning in all students regardless of their backgrounds.* Teachers who are uncertain of their teaching abilities have low personal teaching efficacy. Teachers with high efficacy are influential forces in the schools in which they teach. Bruning, Schraw, and Ronning (2004) described the characteristics of these teachers:

High-efficacy teachers possess a greater sense of personal accomplishment, convey more positive expectations to their students, and are more likely to take personal responsibility for the choices and decisions. . . . There is higher student accountability and more time focused on academic learning. High-efficacy teachers also show more confidence in working with parents. (p. 115)

Of these characteristics, the most significant is the tendency of high-efficacy teachers to take responsibility for the success or failure of their own instruction (Lee, 2000). In other words, if students aren't learning as much as they should be, rather than blaming students' lack of intelligence, poor home environments, uncooperative administrators, or some other cause, high-efficacy teachers conclude that they could be doing a better job and look for ways to increase student learning.

Let's look at an example.

Case STUDY "What are you doing with those cake pans?" Jim Barton asked his wife, Shirley, a fifth-grade teacher, as he saw her hard at work constructing some cardboard (cakes).

"What do you think?" she grinned at him. "Do they look like cake?" she asked, holding up rectangular cardboard pieces drawn to resemble two cakes cut into pieces, with the pieces intended to be used to illustrate fractions.

"Actually, they almost do," he responded.

"My students didn't score as well as I would have liked on the fractions part of the Stanford Achievement Test last year, and I promised myself that they were going to do better this year."

"But you said the students aren't as sharp this year."

"That doesn't matter. I'm pushing them harder. I think I could have done a better job last year, so I swore I was really going to be ready for them this time."

Jim walked back into the living room shaking his head and mumbling something about thinking that teachers who have taught for 11 years were supposed to burn out. (Eggen & Kauchak, 2001, p. 463)

Shirley is a high-efficacy teacher; she accepts responsibility for the amount her students learn, and she is increasing her efforts to be sure that learning occurs.

High-efficacy teachers help create high-efficacy schools. **High-collective-efficacy schools,** are *schools in which most of the teachers are high in personal teaching efficacy.* As a result, as shown in Figure 7.2, all learners have higher achievement (Goddard, Hoy, & Hoy, 2000; Lee, 2000).

Three findings illustrated in Figure 7.2 are important. First, students from all socioeconomic levels—high, middle, and low—learn more in high-collective-efficacy schools than they do in schools where collective efficacy is lower. This, in itself, isn't surprising; it make sense that the more teachers strive for student learning, the more students will learn. Second, and more important, low-SES students in high-collective-efficacy schools have achievement levels nearly as high as high-SES students in low-collective-efficacy schools. Third, differences in achievement levels among low, middle, and high-SES students in high-collective-efficacy schools are smaller than they are in low-collective-efficacy schools (Lee, 2000). In other words, high-collective-efficacy schools help reduce achievement differences between groups of students who typically benefit quite differently from schooling.

Figure 7.2 Achievement Gains in High-Collective-Efficacy Schools Versus Low-Collective-Efficacy Schools

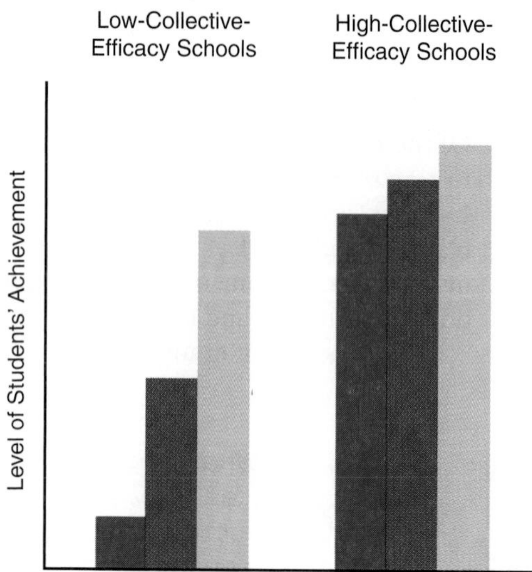

Source: From Lee, V. (2000). Using hierarchical linear modeling to study social contexts: The case of school effects. *Educational Psychologist, 35,* 125–141. Adapted by permission.

How do high-efficacy teachers and high-collective-efficacy schools accomplish these results? A number of factors contribute, but two are essential: (1) interactive instruction and (2) frequent monitoring of student progress.

Interactive Instruction Imagine that you're walking through the hallways of a school and the doors of classrooms are open. You glance inside as you walk by each classroom. Can you determine anything about the effectiveness of the school with a simple glance? The answer is yes. If the prevailing pattern is one in which teachers are asking large numbers of questions and students are involved in discussions, the likelihood that the school is effective increases. In contrast, if you see teachers primarily lecturing or students spending most of their time working alone and doing seatwork, the school is less likely to be effective. Evaluating schools in this way is admittedly simplistic, and many additional factors influence how much students learn. Nevertheless, interaction between teacher and students and students with one another is an essential ingredient for learning (Eggen & Kauchak, 2004).

Not only is interactive teaching essential for learning, it is also important for motivation (Pintrich & Schunk, 2002). In a study where students were asked to rate different methods of promoting learning, teacher lectures and memorization were rated lowest (Boyer, 1995). In another study, middle schoolers rated hands-on science and independent research projects as their most memorable schoolwork (Wasserstein, 1995). Effective schools provide opportunities for students to become actively involved in their learning.

CW

Increasing Understanding 7.10

Do high-SES or low-SES students need interactive instruction more? Explain, using the information from Figure 7.2 as the basis for your answer.

Teachers high in personal teaching efficacy—who believe that they can make a difference in student learning—are more likely to promote high levels of teacher–student interaction than low-efficacy teachers: "Such teachers view teaching and learning as an interactive process with students cast as active participants, rather than as a one-way flow of information" (Lee, 2000, p. 135).

Frequent Monitoring of Student Progress Another essential factor differentiating more from less effective schools is the extent to which teachers frequently assess learning and provide students with feedback. Experts suggest that effective learning environments are assessment-centered (Bransford, Brown, & Cocking, 2000). In other words, assessment isn't tacked on at the end of an instructional period, as when teachers give a test every other week; rather, it is an integral part of the entire teaching–learning process. Teachers in effective schools collect a great deal of information about students' learning progress. They regularly collect work samples and give frequent quizzes and tests, and the assessments measure more than recall of facts. Teachers return the assessments shortly after they're given, and test items are thoroughly discussed to provide students with feedback about their responses (Brookhart, 1997; Dochy & McDowell, 1997; Tuckman, 1998). The need for assessment-centered classrooms also helps us understand why interactive instruction is so essential. Teachers can gather a great deal of information about students' understanding by listening to their attempts to describe their thinking.

CW

Increasing Understanding 7.11

Look again at the characteristics of effective schools and effective teachers for students placed at-risk (Chapter 4, pp. 146–152). The characteristics are very similar to the characteristics of effective schools discussed here. Explain why this is the case.

Parents' and Other Taxpayers' Perceptions of Effective Schools

How do parents and taxpayers view effective schools? On what do they base their perceptions? What do they most commonly look for in judging a school? Let's take a look.

The results of research examining parents' and other taxpayers' perceptions of effective schools are not surprising. As would be expected, people react most strongly to factors that are concrete and observable. For example, as a result of highly publicized incidents of school violence, school safety is a primary concern, and both parents and other taxpayers have ranked it as the most essential characteristic of an effective school (Olson, 1999a).

Parents and other taxpayers also look for qualified teachers and indicators of student and school performance (Olson, 1999a). The desire for qualified teachers isn't surprising, since teachers represent schools and are the people who work most directly with parents' sons and daughters. To determine how children and schools are doing, parents and others turn to standardized test scores and school report cards. Currently, under the federal No Child Left Behind Act, all states are required to test students annually and publish report cards on their schools (Hardy, 2002); in 1998, 48 of the 50 states were already regularly testing students, and 36 states were publishing annual report cards on individual schools (Olson, 1999c). Olson (1999b) summarized parents' views of effective schools: "In short, parents and taxpayers view school safety and the presence of qualified teachers as two essential ingredients of education. Once those basic conditions are met, they want results" (p. 34).

These results are consistent with the characteristics of effective schools discussed earlier. For instance, we saw school safety on both lists. Other factors, such as teaching efficacy, interactive instruction, and monitoring of student progress, are more complex and harder to understand for people outside the profession.

Reflect on This

To analyze a case study examining questions about school organization and school effectiveness, go to the Companion Website at **www.prenhall.com/kauchak**, then to this chapter's *Reflect on This* module.

Exploring Diversity

SCHOOL ORGANIZATION AND THE ACHIEVEMENT OF CULTURAL MINORITIES

Emphasis on higher standards and increased accountability is perhaps the most prominent reform in education today. Change, however, can have unintended outcomes, and one outcome of this reform has been a widening gap between the achievement of cultural minorities—particularly African American and Hispanic students—and the achievement of their White and Asian counterparts (Hoff, 2000b). Between 1970, when the National Assessment of Educational Progress first began systematically measuring students' achievement, and 1980, African American and Hispanic students made great progress in narrowing the achievement gap that had separated them from their White peers. This progress stopped abruptly in the late 1980s, however, and since then the gap has either remained constant or widened (Jencks & Phillips, 1998).

A number of factors have been cited to explain these differences in achievement, including poverty, peer pressure, and parental values (Viadero, 2000b). These are all likely candidates, but research has also identified two aspects of school organization that are believed to influence the achievement of minority students: tracking and class size.

Cultural Minorities and Tracking

We saw earlier in the chapter that comprehensive high schools have been criticized for the practice of tracking, because evidence indicates that educational experiences on lower-level tracks are often substandard (Oakes, 1992, 1995). This evidence is particularly relevant for cultural minorities, because they tend to be underrepresented in higher-level tracks and overrepresented in lower-level tracks. The problem is exacerbated by the fact that minority students tend not to enroll in more demanding classes (Jencks & Phillips, 1998). As shown in Table 7.4, the students least likely to enroll in such classes are also least likely to graduate from college (Viadero, 2000b).

Tracking can result in the segregation of cultural minorities into low-level classes where instruction tends to be less challenging.

Table 7.4 Percentages of Students Taking Advanced Math Courses and Graduating from Four-Year Colleges

Race/Ethnicity	1992 High School Graduates Who Completed Algebra 2 and Geometry (%)	Freshmen at Four-Year Colleges Who Graduate Within Six Years (%)
Asian American	55.5	65
White	53.1	59
Hispanic American	41.9	46
Native American	35.7	37
African American	35	40

Source: Data from Johnston & Viadero (2000).

Tracking and minority achievement have a form of negative synergy; that is, student achievement in low-level classes is reduced compared to the achievement of students of comparable ability in high-level classes. Because decisions about tracking are based on students' records of past achievement, minority students continue to be placed in lower-level tracks, and the negative relationship between achievement and tracking is magnified. Unfortunately, school leaders haven't been able to identify a satisfactory solution to this problem.

Cultural Minorities and Class Size

The relationship between class size and minority achievement is more encouraging. Earlier we said that research supports the contention that student achievement is higher in smaller classes. This research is important, because the beneficial effects of reducing class size are greater for cultural minorities than for nonminorities (Gewertz, 2000c; Robinson, 1990).

Two studies are particularly significant. First, an assessment of a major class-size-reduction project in Tennessee found the following (Illig, 1996):

- Children in small classes (about 15 students per class) consistently outperformed children in larger classes.
- Inner-city children (about 97% of whom were minorities) in small classes closed some of the achievement gap between themselves and nonminority children in large classes.
- Children in small classes outperformed children in larger classes, even when teachers in the large classes had support from aides.

In the second study, a 4-year experiment with class-size reduction in Wisconsin, researchers found that the achievement gap between minorities and nonminorities shrank by 19 percent in smaller classes, whereas in regular classrooms it grew by 58 percent (Molnar, Percy, Smith, & Zahorik, 1998). The results of the class-size-reduction experiment were so compelling that the Wisconsin legislature appropriated $59 million beginning in 2000 to expand the program to 400 schools (Gewertz, 2000c).

If the other characteristics of an effective school don't exist, however, reducing the number of students in classes, by itself, won't increase achievement. Narrowing the achievement gap requires the systematic implementation of all the effective school characteristics.

Decision Making

Defining Yourself as a Professional

Decision making as an essential element of professionalism is a theme for this text, and this chapter leaves you with a number of decisions that you'll need to make as you begin to define yourself as a professional. Perhaps the most basic is the decision about the level at which you want to teach. In this chapter you read important information about teaching at different levels. For example, elementary teachers enjoy considerable autonomy in scheduling their day but are also faced with the challenges of teaching all subjects. Secondary specialists, by contrast, can focus on one or two content areas, but their lives are more controlled by bells, and because of the greater number of students, they have fewer opportunities to get to know them well.

Your decision to teach in a particular school will strongly affect your satisfaction as a developing professional. When a school interviews you for a job, you will also be interviewing the school. (We discuss this process in detail in Chapter 13.) You must carefully assess the effectiveness of the school principal and the rest of the administrative staff, as well as the overall effectiveness of the school.

A positive school climate is an essential ingredient of an effective school (J. Johnson, Livingston, Schwartz, & Slate, 2000; Wolf, Borko, Elliott, & McIver, 2000). It not only influences how much students learn but also how much teachers enjoy working in that school. School climate will be important to you, as a new teacher, because it may mean the difference between growing and developing or hiding in your room to escape the other teachers (Marx, 2001).

How can beginning teachers assess school climate? Earlier in the chapter we suggested observing how staff in the central office treat students and visitors. Are visitors to the office made to feel welcome? Other indications of school climate include the following:

- *Teacher involvement in decisions about the school's instructional agenda.* Are teachers consulted about decisions that affect what and how they teach?
- *Openness, informality, and dialogue among teachers.* Do teachers talk about their work and share their problems and concerns?
- *The physical appearance of the school.* For example, are hallways clean and bright and decorated with student work?
- *Teacher attrition rates.* Is this a school that teachers want to work and stay in?

When you are looking for a job, you should take the time to visit in a prospective school. Ask to visit with the teachers you'll be working with to find out their impression of the school.

The leadership of the school principal shapes the school culture, which in turn influences school climate (Colley, 2002). His or her leadership style—whether democratic and involved or autocratic and distant—can have a powerful effect on the school (Wolf et al., 2000). A basic question to ask principals is how they view themselves as instructional leaders. A basic question to ask teachers is whether they trust the principal and like working for him or her.

The school you choose may also influence your salary and vacation plans. For example, you may be expected to spend more time teaching than teachers have in the past. The school year may start earlier, end later, and you may be asked to teach summer school. You may choose to teach in a year-round school. As far back as the early 1990s, more than a million and a half students in over 2,000 schools attended year-round programs (Harp, 1993). In 1999 about half of the nation's big-city districts offered remedial summer programs (White & Johnston, 1999). The New York City School District had more than 300,000 students attending summer school in 2000, two thirds for remedial work and one third for enrichment programs (R. Johnston, 2000b). If you're looking for ways to augment your academic year salary, this is good news (the New York City program alone required 16,000 teachers). However, if you want the freedom of a summer vacation, you may feel pressured to work during these summer months.

Schools as social institutions influence the lives of the people who learn and work in them. The better you understand how they operate, the better you will be able to grow within them and facilitate the growth of your students.

Summary

What Is a School?

A school is a social institution, organized to promote student growth and development, as well as the welfare of society. All societies have a number of social institutions in addition to schools, such as churches and governments. Schools are organized within districts, administrative units with the responsibility of educating children within geographic areas.

The Organization of Schools

Personnel in the total school organization include the school principal and other administrators, support staff (such as administrative assistants, custodians, and cafeteria workers), and teachers (including curriculum specialists).

The physical plant includes the buildings that house classrooms, the library, computer labs, the cafeteria, and the administration. In addition, junior highs and high schools usually have gymnasiums, playing fields, sometimes swimming pools, and may even have buildings devoted to fine arts.

What is taught—the curriculum—is typically organized into grade levels, and content is intended to be taught to students of different ages.

Early Childhood Programs

Educators have come to realize the importance of early learning experiences—at home and in programs such as preschools and kindergartens—for long-term school success. Developmentally appropriate programs attempt to match classroom instruction to the learning needs of young children.

Elementary Schools

Elementary schools are organized so that a single teacher is responsible for all, or most, of the instruction in the different content areas. Elementary teachers arrange their own schedules, and the amount of time they allocate to different content areas can vary widely. Typically, elementary teachers emphasize reading, language arts, and math in their instruction, and they de-emphasize content areas such as science, social studies, and the arts.

High Schools, Junior Highs, and Middle Schools

High schools, junior highs, and middle schools are organized very differently than elementary schools. Teachers in these schools have content specialties, and they teach only in these specialty areas.

The comprehensive high school attempts to meet the needs of all students through different tracks. Unfortunately, some research suggests that tracking doesn't work and that large comprehensive high schools may be too impersonal to provide a positive learning environment.

Junior highs are aptly named; they are "junior" high schools, with similar curricular offerings and similar extracurricular activities.

Middle schools are intended to meet the developmental needs of early adolescents, who are going through major physical, emotional, and intellectual changes. Middle schools are organized so that teachers can help students more readily make the transition from the cloistered environments of elementary schools to the less personal settings common in high schools.

What Is an Effective School?

Effective schools promote learning for all students. Size is important. Effective elementary schools keep class sizes below 20 students per class, and effective high schools have enrollments in the 600–900 range.

In addition, effective schools are safe and orderly, academically focused, and involve parents. Teachers in effective schools take responsibility for student learning, maintain high levels of interaction with students, and continually monitor student progress.

Polls indicate that parents and other taxpayers emphasize school safety and order, highly qualified teachers, and student scores on standardized tests as indicators of an effective school.

Important Concepts

administrators (p. 239)
advanced placement classes (p. 248)
comprehensive high school (p. 248)
curriculum (p. 242)
development (p. 243)
developmental programs (p. 244)
early childhood education (p. 244)
effective school (p. 253)
grade retention (p. 252)
high-collective-efficacy schools (p. 259)
looping (p. 243)
middle schools (p. 250)
personal teaching efficacy (p. 258)
principal (p. 239)
school district (p. 238)
social institution (p. 238)

Developing as a Professional

Praxis Practice

Read the case study, and answer the questions that follow.

Donna Barber, an eighth-grade teacher at Lincoln Middle School, a school of about 1,200 students, teaches three sections of standard physical science and two sections of advanced. Donna's schedule is as follows:

Period 1 (Advanced)	7:45–8:40
Period 2 (Standard)	8:45–9:40
Period 3 (Advanced)	9:45–10:40
Period 4 (Standard)	10:45–11:40
Lunch	11:45–12:40
Period 5 (Standard)	12:45–1:40
Period 6 (Planning)	1:45–2:40

Her fifth-period class has been studying the make-up of the atom and now is moving to a discussion of static electricity.

"C'mon," Susan says to a group of students at 12:43 as they're standing outside the classroom. "The bell is going to ring, and we'll be late."

"Did you finish your homework?" Jay asks Patricia as they walk in.

"Are you kidding? You miss a homework assignment in this class, and you're a dead duck," Amy interjects.

"Yeah," Chris nods. "You don't dare come without it. You know how Mrs. Barber is constantly saying that she wants to find out how well we understand this stuff."

At 12:44 Ken comments, "Boy, Mrs. Barber, you had my whole family on the ropes last night. I had both my Mom and Dad helping me find examples of the elements you assigned us."

"That's great," Donna smiles back. "I know it was a tough assignment, but it makes you think. And besides, it was designed to be practical. It will get easier the more you work at it."

Danielle, who had been standing in front of the room taking roll, hands the roll slip to Donna as the bell rings.

"Thanks, Danielle," Donna smiles, taking the slip and moving to the front of the room. "Class, just a reminder," she continues, "we're having a notebook check tomorrow, and your last test with your parents' signature on it must be in the notebook. I want to be sure your parents know what we've been studying. . . . Also, tell them to e-mail or call me if they have any questions about your score. . . . What are we in school for?"

"Learning!" the students nearly shout in unison, repeating a theme they hear from Donna on a regular basis.

"Yes," Donna smiles at their response. "And Mrs. Garnett (the principal) commented on that again in our last assembly when she emphasized that all of you can understand what you're studying and you can all be successful if you're willing to work. All the teachers in our school feel the same way."

At 12:47 Donna begins, "We've been talking about elements. Let's see what we remember. Look at the model. What element does this represent? . . . Allen?"

". . . Lithium," Allen responds.

"Good, and how do we know, . . . Kathleen?"

"There are three protons in there."

"All right! Very good.

"Now let's switch gears. We've been dealing with the nucleus of the atom, but now we're going to focus on the electrons. . . . What do we know about them? . . . Armondo?"

"They're out around the nucleus."

"Yes, good. We've said that the numbers of electrons and protons are equal, and the electrons are in orbit around the nucleus. Are they tightly or loosely attracted to the nucleus? Janice?"

"Sort of loosely, I think."

"Yes, good. We can 'scrape' electrons off," Donna continues, "so we think of them as being loosely attached. Now keep that in mind, because it's important. We can get electrons off the atoms fairly easily with heat or even by simply rubbing them, but the nucleus is very hard to break up.

"Now let's take a look," Donna says as she steps quickly over to her file cabinet and takes out an inflated balloon and a wool sweater. "Watch." She rubs the balloon vigorously with the sweater, steps over to Michelle, and holds the balloon over her hair. "What do you notice here? . . . Vicki?"

"The balloon is making Michelle's hair stick up," Vicki responds to the giggles of the class.

Donna explains that their goal for the day is to understand why the balloon makes Michelle's hair stick up. She then takes another inflated balloon, holds it against the chalkboard, and lets it go. "What happened here? Joe?"

"It just fell down," Joe shrugs.

"Let's try it again," Donna continues and rubs the balloon on the sweater and again holds it against the board.

"Now what? . . . Melody?"

"It's stuck up there now."

Donna uses a series of questions to guide the students into concluding that some of the electrons were rubbed off the sweater and collected on the balloon, so the balloon had more electrons than protons and the extra electrons attracted the protons in Michelle's hair and the board.

Donna reminds the students that this is called static electricity, and she continues, "Two everyday examples of static electricity are clothes sticking together in the dryer and getting a shock after you walk across a carpet and touch a doorknob.

"For tomorrow," she says in conclusion, "I want you to write a one-paragraph explanation for each of these using the ideas we've discussed here today."

At 1:38 she says, "OK, everyone. It's time to head for your next class. Collect any paper or other scraps around your desk and get ready to go. We'll start right where we left off tomorrow."

1. Identify at least five characteristics of Lincoln Middle School that are also characteristics of an effective school. Take evidence directly from the case study when describing each characteristic.

2. Identify one characteristic of Lincoln Middle School that is not consistent with an effective school.
3. Identify one characteristic of an effective school for which direct evidence doesn't exist in the case study.

To receive feedback on your responses to the Praxis Practice exercises, go to the Companion Website at **www.prenhall.com/kauchak**, then to this chapter's *Praxis Practice* module.

Discussion Questions

1. Based on the organization of typical elementary schools, what are the primary advantages and disadvantages of teaching in an elementary school? How could elementary schools be organized differently to improve the education of all students?
2. Based on the organization of typical middle schools, what are the primary advantages and disadvantages of teaching in a middle school? How could middle schools be organized differently to improve the education of all students?
3. Based on the organization of typical high schools, what are the primary advantages and disadvantages of teaching in a high school? How could high schools be organized differently to improve the education of all students?
4. In which kind of school—elementary, middle, junior high, or high school—do teachers have the most autonomy? the least autonomy? What implications does this have for you as a prospective teacher?
5. Consider what you know about the organization of elementary, middle, junior high, and high schools. Which type of school is best suited to your academic and personal characteristics? Why do you think so?

Video Discussion Questions

The following discussion questions refer to video segments found on the Companion Website. To view the accompanying video, answer the questions online, and receive immediate feedback, go to the Companion Website at **www.prenhall.com/kauchak**, then to this chapter's *Video Discussion* module.

1. Dr. Uri Treisman is a professor of mathematics at the University of Texas at Austin and director of the Charles A. Dana Center for Math and Science Education. His work focuses on school reform and ways that schools can be helped to improve. He believes principals are essential to effective schools. What does Dr. Treisman believe is the single most important thing that principals can do within a school to promote learning? Do you agree with him?
2. Theodore Sizer is the director of the Coalition for Effective Schools, an organization that attempts to reform high schools. From his perspective, what are some arguments against grouping students together by age? How practical do you think the alternatives are?
3. Dr. John Goodlad is professor emeritus and co-director of the Center for Renewal at the University of Washington and president of the Independent Institute for Educational Inquiry. How does Dr. Goodlad believe that students suffer psychologically from grade retention? What alternatives are there to grade retention? Which of these do you think are most effective?

Going into Schools

1. Go to an elementary and either a middle, junior high, or high school. Interview a teacher in each school. Ask the teacher to describe the school administration and support staff and to explain the duties of each person. This might include some or all of the following (as well as others):
   - Principal
   - Vice principal
   - Assistant principal
   - Dean
   - School psychologist
   - Guidance counselor
   - School nurse
   - Media center director
   - Curriculum specialists (such as a technology specialist)

   In addition, ask each teacher how the school is organized and how the organization of the school could be improved so that all students could learn more. Report your results in a paper comparing the two types of schools.
2. Visit a school in which you plan to teach. How does the receptionist greet you? Is she pleasant and cordial, or cool and businesslike? As you're standing in the school reception area, watch the receptionist. How does she treat students when they come into the area? Again, is she pleasant and cordial, or cool and businesslike? What does this tell you about the school from a student's perspective? From a teacher's perspective?
3. Visit a school and stand in a hallway as students are moving to or from lunch, or from one class to another. Describe the behavior of the students and the teachers as students are making these transitions. In particular, look for the following:
   a. How orderly is the movement? Do students move quickly and with a minimum of confusion?
   b. Are teachers monitoring the students' movement? What are the teachers saying? Is the general tone of the teachers comments and directives pleasant and cordial, or harsh and critical?
   c. Do students move into classrooms in an orderly way? Are they in their seats and waiting when instruction is scheduled to begin?

   What does this information tell you about this school as a learning environment?
4. Interview a teacher; place special emphasis on questions about the teacher's students. You might include some or all of the following questions:
   a. How capable of learning are the students?
   b. What are their lives like at home?
   c. Can you overcome home problems if they exist? Please explain.
   d. What could be done to organize the school so that learning could be increased for all students?
   e. What is the toughest part of your job?
   f. What is the easiest part of your job?
   g. What is the most distasteful part of your job?
   h. What is the most pleasant or rewarding part of your job?

   What do the teacher's responses tell you about teaching in a school like this?
5. Observe the class of the teacher you interviewed to learn the answers to the following questions:
   a. Does the teacher ask a large number of questions, or is most of the instructional time spent lecturing?
   b. How much of the teacher's time is spent in instruction (explaining and lecturing or question and answer)?

c. How much time do the students spend doing seatwork?
d. How much time do students spend in nonlearning activities, such as visiting with each other or moving around the room?

On the basis of your observations, decide how well the organization of this classroom promotes learning.

Virtual Field Experience

If you would like to participate in a Virtual Field Experience, go to the Companion Website at **www.prenhall.com/kauchak**, then to this chapter's *Field Experience* module.

Online Portfolio Activities

To complete these activities online, go to the Companion Website at **www.prenhall.com/kauchak**, then to this chapter's *Portfolio Activities* module.

Portfolio Activity 7.1

Involving Students with Diverse Backgrounds

INTASC Principle 9: Commitment

Personal Journal Reflection
The purpose of this activity is to help you begin thinking about the grade level you will be most effective and happy working at. On a sheet of paper or online, create four columns with the headings "Elementary Teachers," "Middle School/Junior High Teachers," "High School Teachers," and "Me." Think about effective teachers you've known, and list their characteristics in the appropriate columns. In the last column, list the personal strengths you think you'll bring to the teaching profession. Compare this personal list with the school-level ones, and decide which educational level best fits your personal strengths.

Portfolio Activity 7.2

Effective Schools

INTASC Principle 5: Motivation and Management

The purpose of this activity is to encourage you to think about your own vision of an effective school. Use information in this chapter to write a two-page description of an effective school at the level in which you plan to teach. Explain how this organization would influence your life as a teacher.

Portfolio Activity 7.3

Involving Parents

INTASC Principle 10: Partnership

Write a two-page description of your philosophy regarding parents' involvement in their children's education. Include in the description a minimum of four suggestions for involving parents.

Chapter 8

Governance and Finance

Regulating and Funding Schools

School governance and the way schools are funded may seem irrelevant to beginning teachers, but veterans know otherwise. The way schools are run and school districts' use of money make big differences in the quality of teachers' professional lives. In addition, reform efforts aimed at addressing funding inequalities, increasing decision making at the school level, and providing more choice to parents are changing teaching today. To help you understand these changes, we try to answer the following questions in this chapter:

- How are schools regulated and run?
- How does the governance of schools affect teachers?
- How are schools funded?
- How can different ways of funding schools result in inequalities in education?
- How will school-choice reforms such as vouchers and charters change education as well as teachers' lives?

Let's see how the answers to these questions can influence your life as a teacher.

This logo appears throughout the chapter to indicate where case studies are integrated with chapter content.

Case STUDY

Carla Buendia sat at her desk, looking at the pile of books and papers covering it. "I better get this one right as it'll be our only chance," she thought to herself.

Carla was a member of Unified Metropolitan School District's Elementary Math Steering Committee. Unified Metropolitan is a large district in the Midwest. The Steering Committee had been meeting regularly over the last 2 years to study the elementary math curriculum in the district. Test scores had been declining, especially in the areas of applications and problem solving, and the committee was asked to make a recommendation to the district's school board. Tonight was the night.

"Just don't be nervous," Carla kept telling herself, but her advice wasn't working. She had been to school board meetings as a spectator, when teacher salaries and contracts were being discussed, and she was clearly nervous about getting up in front of the hundred or more people who would be in attendance. "Why did I ever say I'd do this?" she thought. "Too late for that. I just better have my act together when it's my turn to speak."

• • ● • •

It can be startling to go into two schools within a few miles of each other and experience striking differences in how they look and feel. One is bright, cheerful, and clean, with student projects and works of art prominently displayed. The other is dark, depressing, and dirty, and the hallways are cluttered with candy wrappers and other trash. These differences are testimony to the influence that governance and finance can have on teachers' working conditions and students' educational experiences.

Governance and finance also influence the resources available to teachers. To experience a major difference in resources, simply drive across the state line from New Mexico, where the average spending per pupil in 2001 was $7,093, to Utah, where per pupil spending was $4,769 (U.S. Department of Education, 2002a). Politicians argue that money doesn't influence the quality of education, but evidence suggests otherwise (Biddle & Berliner, 2002; Flanagan & Grissmer, 2002). Money buys paper, supplies, and equipment, for example, and allows students to *do* science experiments rather than simply read about them. Perhaps most importantly, money helps reduce class size, which can make the difference between teaching as crowd control and personalized teaching that maximizes student learning (Krueger & Whitmore, 2002; Molnar, Zahorik, Smith, Halback, & Ehrle, 2002).

Let's see how school governance affects the lives of teachers and students.

Governance: How Are Schools Regulated and Run?

In a few short years, you will walk into your own classroom, look around, and think, "At last, my own classroom; it's all mine." That's a good feeling, and it *will* be all yours—sort of. Although teachers have considerable professional autonomy in creating and implementing their own vision of good teaching, they also operate within a specified governance framework.

Governance: A Legal Overview

Unlike in many other countries, where the federal government is responsible for schools, in the United States the Tenth Amendment to the Constitution clearly assigns legal responsibility for the education of its citizens to the 50 states.

Because the 50 states differ significantly in geography, history, economics, and politics, you might think that they would also differ in their approaches to governing education, but they don't. Each of the states has a surprisingly similar organizational structure. These structures are outlined in Figure 8.1 and described in the section that follows.

State Governance Structures

In every state a constitution outlines the roles and responsibilities of state officers with respect to education. Governors focus public attention on educational issues and attempt to solicit public support for educational funding. State legislatures meet annually to debate school finance and other issues. These legislative sessions are important to teachers because states supply about 45 percent of a district's education budget, and legislative actions (or inactions) influence teacher salaries, class sizes, supplies, and equipment (Brimley & Garfield, 2002).

State Board of Education Because a governor and legislators have an entire state to run, they turn most of the responsibility for steering their state's schools to the **state board of education,** *the legal governing body that exercises general control and supervision of the schools in a state.* The state boards are similar in purpose to district school

Figure 8.1 State Administrative Organizational Structure

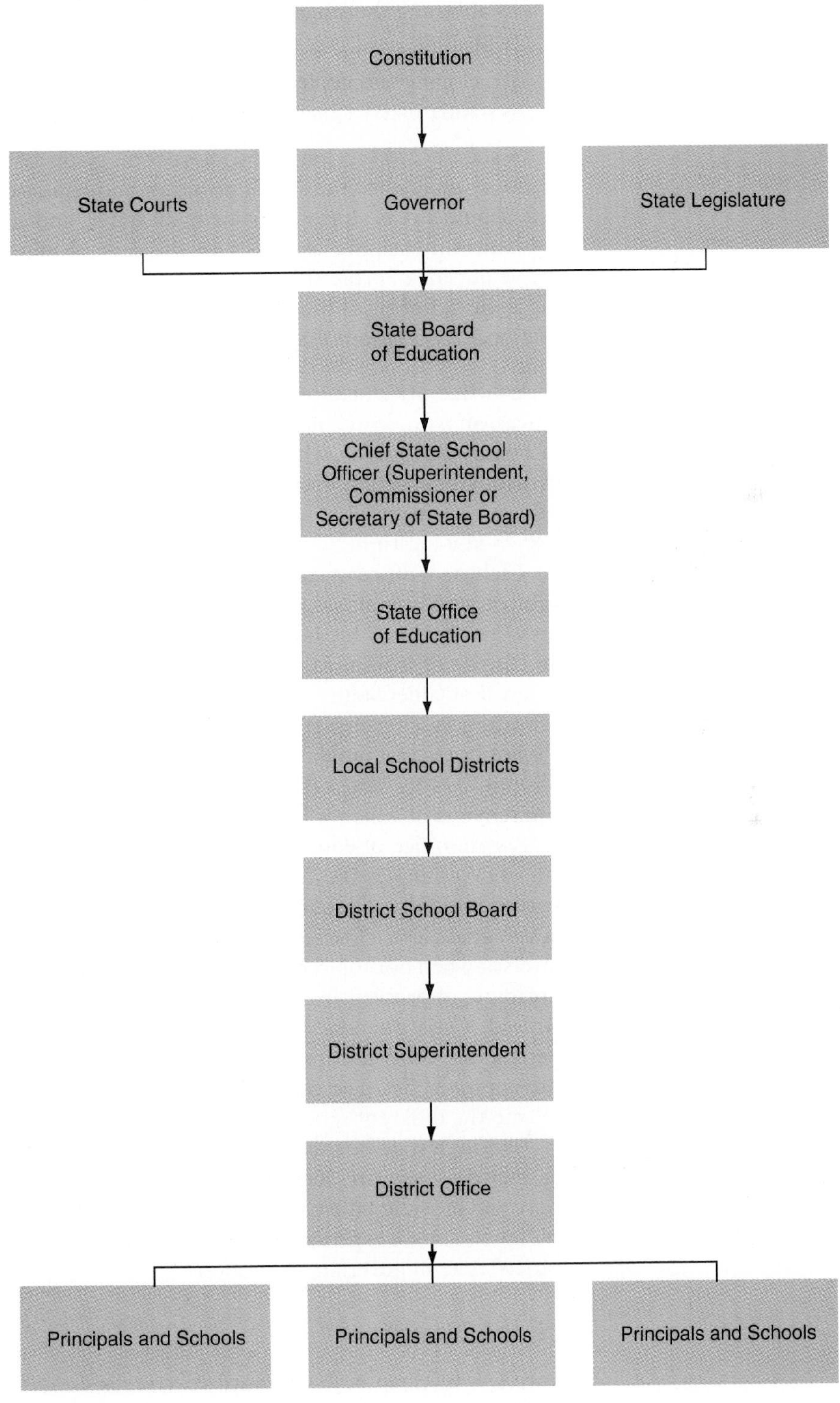

boards and perform both regulatory and advisory functions. State boards regulate education by

- Issuing and revoking teaching licenses
- Establishing the length of the school year
- Publishing standards for approving and accrediting schools
- Developing and implementing uniform systems for gathering education data, such as standardized achievement test scores, enrollment trends, and demographics

A state board sets long- and short-term goals for its state and helps create an educational agenda for the state's governor and legislature. For example, the No Child Left Behind Act is a pressing issue in all states, and state boards assist governors and legislatures in shaping responses to this federal initiative. State board members are people outside of professional education. They are usually appointed by the governor, but about a fourth of the states elect these officials, who typically serve without pay (National Association of State Boards of Education, 2004).

Increasing Understanding 8.1

What do the arrows pointing downward in Figure 8.1 suggest about the line of authority in school governance? Who do teachers most directly answer to?

To answer the Increasing Understanding questions online and receive immediate feedback, go to the Companion Website at **www.prenhall.com/kauchak**, then to this chapter's *Increasing Understanding* module. Type in your response, and then study the feedback.

State Office of Education A state board of education makes policy; a **state office of education** *is responsible for implementing education policy on a day-to-day basis.* In contrast with state boards, which are composed of lay members who meet periodically to discharge their duties, state offices of education are staffed by full-time education professionals, virtually all of whom have been teachers and most of whom have advanced degrees in education.

Each state office of education is headed by a chief state officer with the title of superintendent, commissioner, or secretary of the state board. In 2003 chief state officers were appointed by the state board of education or another board in 24 states and the District of Columbia, elected in 15 states, and appointed by the governor in 11 (Council of Chief State School Officers, 2003). The state office is responsible for implementation of teacher and administrator licensing, curriculum supervision, approval of school sites and buildings, and collection of statistical data. As a new teacher, you will apply to your state office of education for an initial teaching license, the form and requirements of which will have been determined by the state board.

A state office of education also plays a major role in determining curricula in its state. For example, the textbooks used by individual schools must be on a state-approved list. Usually states offer districts a choice of several acceptable text series for a given grade level. The textbook selection process can be highly politicized and controversial when hot topics such as evolution in science, phonics versus whole language in reading, or problem-based versus computationally oriented approaches to math are involved. Carla Buendia's Elementary Math Steering Committee, mentioned in the opening case study for this chapter, began its search for a math series by looking at the state-approved list. The committee then conferred with the state's math specialist to evaluate the different series.

Although state boards and state offices of education influence teaching and learning, they do so at arm's length; the day-to-day responsibility for getting kids into classrooms and providing them with materials and qualified teachers is a district responsibility. This is why Carla's experience at a district school board meeting is relevant. Let's look at districts' roles in governing education.

School Districts

As we saw in Chapter 7, a **school district** *is an administrative unit within a state that is defined by geographical boundaries and is legally responsible for the public education of children within those boundaries*; with respect to educational governance,

it's where the action is. School districts hire and fire teachers, and they determine the nature of the content (the curriculum) and the kinds of learning experiences (instruction) students will have as they attend school. That's why Carla was making her presentation to the district school board. She was involved in the process of making decisions about the district's elementary math curriculum. Decisions like these are usually made at the district level, and school districts also determine what books will be used and ensure that they will be available to students at the beginning of the school year.

School districts differ dramatically in size. For example, there are approximately 15,000 school districts in the United States, and if they were divided equally among states, there would be about 300 per state. But states have differing views about the ideal number and size of districts. For example, the whole state of Hawaii constitutes one school district, whereas Texas has more than 1,000 districts. In 2000–2001 the New York City School District had more than 1 million students, but more than a third of U.S. school districts (3,265) had 300 or fewer students. Almost half of the districts (48%) in 2000–2001 enrolled fewer than 1,000 students per year. The largest 4 percent—districts enrolling 10,000 to 1 million students each—were educating more than half the students in this country (National Center for Education Statistics, 2002).

The historical trend has been consolidation into fewer and larger districts. For instance, in 1930 the United States had more than 130,000 school districts; 70 years later, it had only 14,859 (U.S. Department of Education, 2000b). The primary reason for consolidation is efficiency; larger districts can offer broader services and minimize duplication of administrative staff. For example, one medium-sized district with a superintendent and district staff of 10 people is more efficient than two small districts that require a superintendent and a staff of six to eight people each.

Which are better, bigger or smaller districts? From a teacher's perspective, both types offer advantages and disadvantages. Small districts are less bureaucratic and easier to influence, but they typically lack resources and instructional support staff. For example, Carla's committee functioned in a large district. As committee members did their work, they were assisted by a district math coordinator, a testing specialist, and technology experts who helped them evaluate the claims of different commercial math programs. This type of assistance doesn't exist in very small districts.

Large districts also have problems. They tend to be hierarchical and bureaucratic, and getting things done takes time. Teachers sometimes feel like nameless and faceless cogs in large, impersonal organizations. Teachers can often rely on face-to-face contacts to make things happen quickly in smaller districts; in larger districts, however, decision making is placed in the hands of large and sometimes contentious committees. From a teacher perspective, the ideal district is an administrative structure that is supportive and responsive but also leaves teachers alone to do what they love most—work with students.

CW

Increasing Understanding 8.2

From a beginning teacher's perspective, what might be some advantages and disadvantages of starting in a large district? a small district?

Every school district has a local school board, a superintendent, and central staff. These are the people who make the district-level decisions about teaching and learning in their district's schools. Let's see how they will influence your life as a teacher.

The Local School Board A **local school board** is *a group of elected lay citizens responsible for setting policies that determine how a school district operates.* With respect to governance, what kinds of rules and regulations do school boards pass? Who are the members of these boards? How are school board members selected? Since they will influence your life as a teacher, you should know the answers to these questions.

School boards, consisting of lay people, are legally responsible for school governance in states and districts.

Functions of school boards. The major functions of school boards occur in five areas, outlined in Figure 8.2 and discussed in the paragraphs that follow.

Perhaps the most important (and contentious) school board function involves the district budget. School boards are responsible for raising money through taxes and disbursing funds to the schools within the district. They also make decisions about various district services, such as providing buses and maintaining lunch programs. School boards directly influence teachers by making decisions about salary increases and the benefits teachers receive. They also affect teachers indirectly by making budget decisions that impact class size and the amount of instructional materials available. Wrestling with each year's budget occupies more than a quarter of a school board's time and energy; it's a continual process that begins in the fall and ends in the spring (Odden, Monk, Nakib, & Picus, 1995).

Personnel responsibilities are closely aligned with financial decisions. School boards are legally responsible for hiring and firing all school personnel, including teachers, principals, custodians, and school bus drivers. Your teaching contract will be offered by a school board that has the legal authority to hire and fire teachers.

The curriculum—what teachers teach—is a third area of school board jurisdiction. School boards, assisted by district administrators, are responsible for specifically defining the curriculum and implementing the general guidelines developed by states. In virtually all districts, teachers are consulted about the curriculum; in the better ones, teachers are directly involved in curriculum decisions. For example, Carla's committee helped make the decision about what math curriculum the district would adopt.

Figure 8.2 Functions of Local School Boards

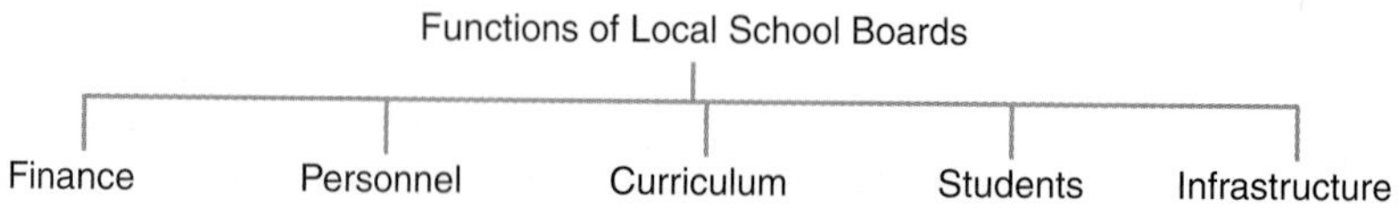

Decisions that impact students are also made by school boards. They set attendance, dress, grooming, conduct, and discipline standards for their districts. For example, the issue of school uniforms has been debated at district, state, and national levels, but the decision is ultimately made (sometimes after contentious debate) by local school boards.

School boards also determine extracurricular policies—from the mundane to the controversial. For example, some districts require students to maintain minimal grade levels to participate in sports, a policy critics contend doubly punishes struggling student athletes by failing them in the classroom and not allowing them to participate in extracurricular activities. Supporters of no-pass/no-play policies argue that they improve motivation to learn by providing incentives for academic success (Camerino, 2003). Another topic that has generated controversy at school board meetings is the question of whether or not to grant gay and lesbian clubs equal status with other school-sponsored organizations. When controversial issues are on school board meeting agendas, attendance rises as various citizens' groups attempt to influence board decisions.

CW

Increasing Understanding 8.3

Which of the school board functions is likely to be most important to a teacher? Least important? Explain.

Finally, school boards make decisions about district infrastructure. For example, they ensure that school buildings and school buses are well maintained and safe, and they approve plans and hire contractors when new schools are built.

Not surprisingly, student achievement has been school board members' primary concern in recent years—fueled by the reporting demands of the No Child Left Behind Act—followed by budget issues, and increasing enrollment pressures ("School Leaders," 1998). Interestingly, student achievement wasn't even listed in school board members' top 10 concerns as recently as the late 1980s. Reform efforts and the national trend toward greater school accountability have strongly impacted the ways that school boards operate.

Members of school boards and their selection. Who serves on school boards, and how do they get there? Nearly all (about 96%) school boards consist of members elected for 3- or 4-year terms; the remainder have members appointed by large city mayors or city councils (D. Land, 2002). School board elections can be controversial for at least two reasons. First, the voter turnout for most school board elections is embarrassingly low; as few as 5 to 10 percent of eligible voters often decide school board membership. This results in boards that don't represent the citizens in the district, critics contend. The second controversy involves the question of whether school board elections should be at-large or limited to specific areas within a city. In a limited-area election, only citizens who live in a specific part of the city are allowed to vote for candidates representing that area. At-large elections tend to favor wealthy, White majority candidates who have either more money to run an election campaign or benefit from White majority voting pools (D. Land, 2002). Area-specific elections provide greater opportunities for minority candidates to represent local, ethnic minority neighborhoods.

Who serves on school boards? The typical school board member is male, White, older, and wealthy, although membership is slowly growing more diverse in some areas. For example, in 1987, 61 percent of board members were male and 94 percent were White, whereas in 1998 the percentage of board members who were male remained the same, but the number who were White had dropped by more than 10 percent (down to 81%)(National School Boards Association, 2000). However, 86 percent are 40 or older, and 85 percent make more than $40,000 per year. Thirty-eight percent have graduate degrees, and another 29 percent have 4-year degrees; only 7 percent have a high school degree or less (Carr, 2003).

Disparities exist between the characteristics of school board members and those of the people they're elected to serve. For example, only 19 percent of board members are cultural minorities, but 33 percent of the nation's students are minorities, and that figure is projected to rise to 42 percent by the year 2010 (U.S. Department of

Education, 2003). Also, 45 percent of school board members are business people or professionals, and 85 percent make more money than the average teacher (Carr, 2003; National School Boards Association, 2000). Critics contend that wealthy school board members are unable to empathize with the financial hardships that teachers and community members often experience. Critics also question the ability of male-dominated school boards to effectively represent the teaching force, which is almost three-fourths female.

The Superintendent The school board makes policy, and the **superintendent,** ***the district's head administrative officer,*** along with his or her staff, is responsible for implementing that policy in the district's schools. The division of labor between the board and the superintendent isn't simple and well defined, however. Because most board members have little or no background in professional education, the superintendent often plays a central role in leading the board and helping set the agenda.

Superintendents are hired by school boards. Most hold an advanced degree in education (National School Boards Association, 2000), but some districts are now going outside of education to find superintendents. For example, in the summer of 2000, Roy Romer, a former governor of Colorado with no experience in educational administration, was picked to lead the Los Angeles schools, the nation's second largest system with an enrollment of more than 710,000 students (Richard, 2000a). The superintendents of the three largest districts in the country—New York City, Chicago, and Los Angeles—all came from outside the field of education, as school boards tend to increasingly value management experience over knowledge of education. Whether this trend will continue is uncertain.

As they are on school boards, females and minorities are underrepresented as superintendents (Carr, 2003; Richard, 2000b). Thirteen percent are women, compared to 75 percent of the teaching force and 51 percent of the general population. Of the 15 largest districts, only one, Palm Beach County in Florida, is headed by a woman. Persons of color make up only 5 percent of superintendents, in contrast to the number of minority students (33 percent) and teachers (13 percent).

When power and authority are shared, as is the case with school boards and superintendents, conflicts are inevitable, and when they occur, the superintendent usually loses. Nationally, the average tenure for superintendents is just under 6 years; in urban districts it is slightly less than 5 years (Borja, 2002). Recently a superintendent in Denver, Colorado, resigned after serving a mere 9 months; apparently, "board members had lost confidence in him . . . because they believed his day-to-day skills in running the 70,000-student district were not up to par" (Gewertz, 2000a, p. 3).

Disputes with school boards, politics, and bureaucracy are major obstacles that superintendents face. When controversy flares over issues such as student drug use, school violence, desegregation, and lagging student achievement, a community looks to the superintendent for answers. Superintendents get caught in the crossfire of politics and public opinion and, unable to quickly solve these problems, are either terminated or feel obliged to resign, as happened in Denver.

What are superintendents paid for this frustrating and insecure job? Pay varies considerably with both location and district size; the average 2001–2002 salary was $121,794, but competition for superintendents in larger districts has resulted in salaries that are considerably higher (A. Williams, 2002). For example, in 2000, Dallas, Texas, paid its new superintendent $260,000 plus benefits (Johnston, 2000c).

The District Office The district office assists the superintendent in translating school board policies into action (see Figure 8.1). It is also responsible for coordinating the myriad of curricular and instructional efforts within the district (Grove, 2002). It is responsible for the following:

- Ordering textbooks and supplies
- Developing programs of study
- Ordering, distributing, and analyzing standardized tests
- Evaluating teachers and assisting those with difficulties

The district office is instrumental in translating abstract state and school board mandates into reality. The manner in which it does this can give teachers a sense of empowerment or can make them feel like hired hands.

The district office also plays an important role for new teachers (Grove, 2002). It typically provides new-teacher orientations, which may include an overview of the district's curriculum, any districtwide instructional initiatives, and district assessment programs. These policies and procedures are important because they frame the district's work expectations for new teachers. In addition, the central office coordinates mentoring and assessment programs for new teachers, which helps them make the transition from university students to working professionals.

The School Principal As you saw in Chapter 7, the school **principal,** *the individual given the ultimate administrative responsibility for a school's operation,* is the district administrator who has the greatest impact on teachers' lives. Many larger schools have a vice principal and two or more assistant principals as part of the administrative staff. The makeup of this staff will depend on the size and organization of the school. Middle schools and high schools almost always have assistant principals; elementary schools, if they are large, may.

A demographic profile of principals (see Table 8.1) mirrors that of school board members. Most are White at all levels, and males are still in the majority at

Table 8.1 Profile of School Principals

	High School Principals	Junior High and Middle School Principals	Elementary School Principals
Sex			
Male	78.8%	66.8%	44.8%
Female	21.2	33.2	55.2
Ethnic Background			
White	85.9	83.0	80.8
African American	8.4	10.5	12.0
Hispanic American	3.8	5.1	5.8
Asian American	0.9	0.7	0.7
Native American	1.1	0.8	0.7
Other	0.7	–	0.6
Highest Degree Earned			
Bachelor's	1.4	1.8	1.8
Master's	54.8	55.5	53.9
Professional diploma	31.6	33.6	34.6
Doctorate	12.1	9.1	9.7
Salary (12-month)			
	$83,944	$78,176	$73,114

Sources: Data from U.S. Department of Education (2001c); Williams (2002).

Principals are crucial in creating well-run, learning-oriented schools.

the secondary levels. Principals almost always have classroom experience, and most have at least a master's degree.

As the person who oversees the everyday operation of the school, the principal has wide-ranging duties (Sebring & Bryk, 2000; Ubben, Hughes, & Norris, 2001). The principal has the primary responsibility for teacher selection and evaluation, and his or her interview with you will be a crucial factor in whether or not you get the job. The principal is also responsible for school-level curricular and instructional leadership, community relations, and the coordination of pupil services provided by school counselors, psychologists, nurses, and others. Principals also implement and monitor the school budget and ensure that the school's physical facilities are maintained. Principals are busy, and their schedules often leave too little time for their most important function—helping teachers effectively teach.

CW

Increasing Understanding 8.4

Offer at least one reason that the percentage of male administrators is higher in high schools than in middle or elementary schools. (Hint: Think back to your study of the teaching force in Chapter 2.) Offer at least one reason that the percentage of female administrators is not higher than 55 percent at the elementary level.

Research indicates that principals are crucial in creating well-run, learning-oriented schools. Effective principals demonstrate leadership in the following ways:

- Creating a positive emotional and social climate for teaching and learning
- Helping to establish a clear school mission and maintaining focus on that mission
- Establishing high expectations for teachers and students
- Working with teachers on the curriculum and instructional improvement
- Being visible in school classrooms and hallways (Sergiovanni et al., 1999; Ubben et al., 2001)

Principals are the most important people in the district's administrative structure because they work directly with teachers and students. Effective principals can transform a mediocre school into a positive and productive learning environment, whereas ineffective principals can make a school an unpleasant place to work and learn.

Interviewing with the principal will be very important when you apply for a teaching position. It will give you an opportunity to learn about the person you'll be working for and the kind of school you'll be working in. During an interview, you should try to determine the principal's perception of his or her role (Cunningham & Cordeiro, 2000; Ubben et al., 2001). Experienced teachers want principals who see themselves as *instructional leaders* and who take a hands-on approach to the teaching–learning process (Harris & Lowery, 2002). Instructional leadership is especially important for beginning teachers, who need support, mentoring, and feedback. As we saw earlier, because of their schedules many principals become *managers* who focus primarily on the day-to-day operation of the school and forget that their most important role is to support teaching and learning (Ginsberg & Murphy, 2002).

School Finance: How Are Schools Funded?

To begin our discussion of school finance, let's revisit Carla Buendia, the teacher serving on her school's Elementary Math Steering Committee.

Case STUDY "And based on our analysis of math programs around the country, we believe this one is best for our children. Any questions?" Carla asked as she concluded her presentation to the school board.

"Let me make sure that I'm clear about this," one board member responded. "In addition to the texts themselves, students will need manipulatives. . . . I'm sorry, but I'm not sure exactly what 'manipulatives' are."

"Manipulatives are concrete objects, like uniform cubes that could be put in a box to help kids understand the concept of volume, and plastic squares that could be used to illustrate area. The success of this program depends on students seeing math ideas in action."

"Thank you. . . . And teachers will need additional in-service training to bring them up to speed on how to use these new materials. Is that right?"

"Yes. What we've read and heard is that teacher in-service is essential to the success of this program," Carla replied, as her fellow committee members nodded in agreement.

"What seems clear to me," the president of the school board added, "is that this program, along with our technology initiative and the changes in our language arts program, is going to need additional funding. We need to make sure that the public understands how and why taxes are going to go up next fall. We've all got a big job ahead of us—selling, no, explaining, why our schools need additional monies."

CW

Increasing Understanding 8.5

What is the most likely reason the board member did not know what manipulatives are? Think about the makeup of school boards in answering this question.

• • ● • •

Money is important in education. It determines teachers' salaries, professional development opportunities, and access to resources, such as computers, lab supplies, maps, and a host of other supplies. It also influences the quality of schools by allowing districts to do such things as reducing class sizes and recruiting and retaining qualified teachers (Biddle & Berliner, 2002). For 3 consecutive years, national polls have indicated that members of the public view lack of financial support and funding for education as the biggest problem facing their local schools (Rose & Gallup, 2002). In this section we look at where this money comes from, how it is spent, and what can be done to make school funding more equitable.

Increasing Understanding 8.6

Explain why the federal government's share of education funding is much less than the local and state shares.

School Funding Sources

Local, state, and federal sources all provide money for education (Brimley & Garfield, 2002). As you can see in Figure 8.3, the state and local shares are about equal and are considerably greater than the federal share, which is about 7 percent.

The proportions of education funding coming from local, state, and federal sources have changed over time (Arnold, 1998; Odden et al., 1995). For example, from 1920 to 1980 the federal share increased from virtually nothing to a peak of nearly 10 percent, and from 1980 to 1993 it declined again to less than 7 percent. The local share steadily decreased from 1920 to 1980 and then increased again in the 1990s, and the state share did just the opposite. These figures are national averages, and the federal, state, and local proportions can vary significantly from state to state. For example, only about 2 percent of Hawaii's 1994–1995 school budget came from local sources, whereas in New Hampshire local funds accounted for almost 90 percent of school funding (Arnold, 1998).

Figure 8.3 Education Revenues from Local, State, and Federal Sources

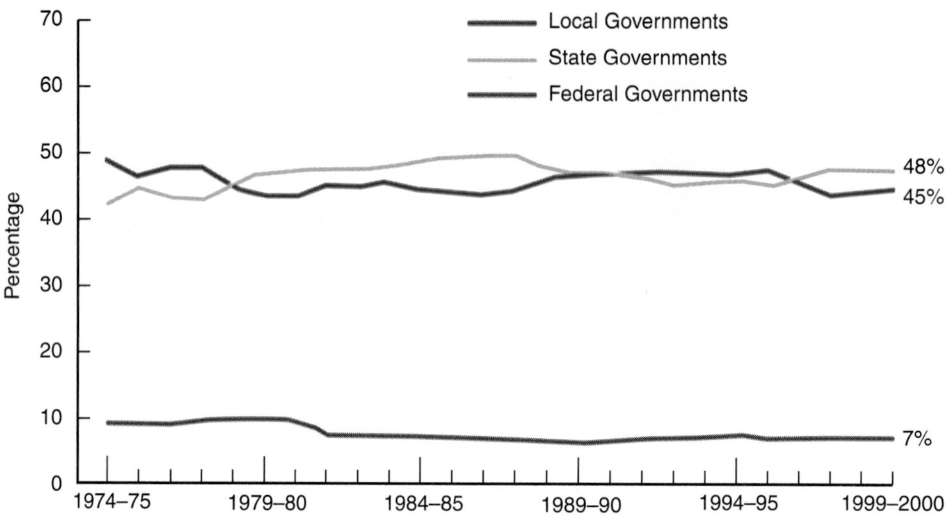

Source: Data from National Center for Education Statistics (2002).

Shifts in education funding reflect the changing views of education throughout U.S. history. In early America education was seen as a local responsibility with virtually no involvement by the federal government. In sharp contrast, twentieth-century leaders saw a direct connection between education and the country's political and economic well-being. Quality schools and a well-educated workforce became national concerns, and the federal government's role in education increased. Similarly, states began to recognize the importance of education in attracting high-tech industries and high-paying jobs. This insight, plus efforts to equalize funding within states, has led to an increasing state role in educational funding (Biddle & Berliner, 2002).

The public is undecided about the relative amounts local, state, and federal governments should contribute to educational funding. In a 1998 Gallup poll, 21 percent favored local funding through property taxes, 33 percent favored state sources, and 37 percent favored federal taxes (Rose & Gallup, 1998). In a more recent poll, 49 percent said that the federal government had too much say in decisions affecting local public schools, and 43 percent said state governments also had too much control over these decisions (Rose & Gallup, 2000). The debate over the role governments should play is likely to continue.

Let's look now at how funds are raised at each level of government and how they make their way to classrooms.

Local Funding As we saw in our discussion of school governance, financing education at the local level is the responsibility of local school boards, which is why Carla made her presentation to her local board. One of the implications of her presentation was the need for increased funding. At the local level most funding for schools comes from property taxes, which are determined by the value of property in the school district (Brimley & Garfield, 2002). Other local revenue sources include income taxes, fees for building permits, traffic fines, and user fees charged to groups that hold meetings on school facilities. In collecting property taxes, local authorities first assess the value of a property and then tax the owners a small percentage of the property's value (usually less than 1%).

The value of property in a school district directly affects how much money schools in the district will receive from local sources.

Funding education primarily through local property taxes has disadvantages, the most glaring of which is inequities between property resources in different districts (Brimley & Garfield, 2002; Rothstein, 1998). Wealthier cities or districts have a higher tax base, so they're able to collect (and spend) more money for their schools. Poorer rural and inner-city school districts find themselves on the opposite end of this continuum, with a lower tax base, resulting in lower revenues. Property taxes also place an unfair burden on older taxpayers, whose homes may have increased in value while their ability to pay taxes has remained constant or decreased. In addition, many older taxpayers resist these charges because they no longer have children in school and don't see the immediate benefit of increased spending for schools.

The property-tax method of financing schools also has a political disadvantage (Brimley & Garfield, 2002). Unlike sales taxes, which taxpayers pay in small, continual, and essentially unnoticed increments, property taxes are more visible targets for taxpayer dissatisfaction. Statements arrive once a year with a comparison to the previous year, and property-tax increases are discussed in public forums whenever school boards, like Carla's, ask their taxpayers for increased funding. Dissatisfaction with this method of funding reached a head in California in 1978 when voters passed an initiative, called Proposition 13, that limited property taxes in the state. By the 1990s, 45 other states had passed similar measures (McAdams, 1994). The effect on educational funding has been chilling. Schools and school districts have had less to spend and have had to fight harder when requesting new funds from taxpayers.

State Revenue Sources States are the second largest source of educational funding. In 2002, state income taxes and sales taxes were the two largest sources of state income, each contributing about one third of all state revenues (Federation of Tax Administrators, n.d.). Sales taxes are regressive, however, meaning they take proportionally more from lower-income families who spend a larger portion of their income on necessities, such as food, clothing, and housing. Progressive states provide some relief by excluding food from items that are taxed. Personal income tax accounts for another third of state revenues. The remaining third comes from other sources such as taxes on liquor and tobacco, oil and mining revenues, and corporate income taxes.

Recently, state lotteries and gambling have also become sources of revenue, but education is often the victim of a zero-sum shell game in which increased funding from

CW

Increasing Understanding 8.7

Liquor and tobacco taxes are often called "sin taxes" because they target commodities that either pose health risks or are viewed as socially unacceptable by a portion of the population. What are the advantages and disadvantages of "sin taxes"?

lottery monies, for example, are balanced by decreasing monies from other sources, such as sales taxes. Currently, 38 states have lotteries, but the percentage of income going to education in these states varies considerably (Sack, 2002b). States spend 33 cents of every lottery income dollar on expenses, and research indicates that these gambling ventures attract participants who are poor and have had little schooling (Brimley & Garfield, 2002). The long-term viability of gambling revenues for education is uncertain and highly controversial.

Federal Funding for Education The federal government is the third, smallest, and most controversial source of educational funding. As we saw earlier, federal funding for education was virtually nonexistent before 1920 but has increased over time to its present level of about 7 percent. The amount spent on education increased by nearly a fifth in fiscal years 2001 and 2002 and about 6 percent in 2003 (Robelen, 2003), but the total still accounts for only about 2 percent of total federal expenditures (U.S. Department of Education, 2001a).

Proponents of a greater federal role in education believe that education is essential for the country's continued progress in the twenty-first century and that the federal government should continue to exert leadership (and funds) in this area. Critics warn of increased federal control over what they believe should be a local responsibility. In addition, conservatives argue against the expansion of what they consider to be an already bloated federal bureaucracy. For these critics, less is better when it comes to federal funding. Local funding, in contrast, makes schools more efficient and responsive to local needs and wishes, they say.

Although the percentage of education funds contributed by the federal government has been small, the impact has been considerable, largely because of the use of **categorical grants,** *monies targeted for specific groups and designated purposes.* Head Start, aimed at preschoolers, and Title I, which benefits economically disadvantaged youth, are examples of categorical aid programs targeting specific needs or populations (these programs are discussed in detail in Chapter 5). Because the funds must be used for specific purposes, categorical grants have strongly influenced local education practices.

CW

Increasing Understanding 8.8

Would state offices of education and local school boards prefer categorical or block grants? Why?

During the 1980s, categorical funds were replaced by **block grants,** *federal monies provided to states and school districts with few restrictions for use.* Begun during the conservative Reagan administration, block grants purposely reduce the federal role in policy making, in essence giving states and districts control over how monies are spent. Proponents contend this makes sense—who knows local needs better than local educators? Critics contend that funds are often misspent or spent in areas where they aren't needed (Kirst, 1995).

Educational Revenues: Where Do They Go?

In 2001–2002 the states and the District of Columbia spent an average of $7,545 per pupil, but as you can see in Table 8.2, spending varied considerably from state to state (U.S. Department of Education, 2002a). The District of Columbia and New York spent the highest amounts ($11,009 and $10,725, respectively), while Utah spent the lowest ($4,769). In examining the data in Table 8.2, some regional trends are apparent. Most of the higher per-pupil expenditures are found in Northeastern and upper Midwest states, and lower expenditures are found in the South and West.

It is tempting to conclude that a state's commitment to education can be judged by its per-pupil spending, but, in fact, some states are wealthier than others, so they have a greater capacity to fund education. For example, in 1996 Utah had one of the lowest per-pupil expenditures but spent 4.2 percent of its gross state product (an indicator of a state's economic productivity) on education; in contrast, New York had

Table 8.2 State-by-State Spending per Student

State	1997–1998	2001–2002
Alabama	$4,849	$5,937
Alaska	8,271	9,430
Arizona	4,595	5,445
Arkansas	4,708	5,764
California	5,644	6,878
Colorado	5,656	6,244
Connecticut	8,904	10,517
Delaware	7,420	9,612
District of Columbia	8,393	11,009
Florida	5,552	6,232
Georgia	5,647	7,633
Hawaii	5,858	6,775
Idaho	4,721	5,789
Illinois	6,242	7,598
Indiana	6,318	8,034
Iowa	5,998	7,126
Kansas	5,727	6,906
Kentucky	5,213	6,449
Louisiana	5,188	6,270
Maine	6,742	8,160
Maryland	7,034	7,847
Massachusetts	7,778	9,883
Michigan	7,050	8,611
Minnesota	6,388	7,832
Mississippi	4,288	5,235
Missouri	5,565	6,574
Montana	5,724	7,080
Nebraska	5,958	7,547
Nevada	5,295	6,134
New Hampshire	6,156	7,926
New Jersey	9,643	9,296
New Mexico	5,005	7,093
New York	8,852	10,725
North Carolina	5,257	6,578
North Dakota	5,056	6,173
Ohio	6,198	8,308
Oklahoma	5,033	6,184
Oregon	6,419	8,280
Pennsylvania	7,209	8,673
Rhode Island	7,928	10,216
South Carolina	5,320	7,179
South Dakota	4,669	6,442
Tennessee	4,937	5,470

(continued)

Table 8.2 State-by-State Spending per Student *(continued)*

State	1997–1998	2001–2002
Texas	5,444	6,833
Utah	3,969	4,769
Vermont	7,075	9,798
Virginia	6,067	7,452
Washington	6,040	7,236
West Virginia	6,323	8,742
Wisconsin	7,123	8,654
Wyoming	6,218	8,203
AVERAGE	6,131	7,545

Source: Data from "State of the States" (2003).

one of the highest per-pupil expenditures but spent a smaller percentage (4.1 %) on education (National Center for Education Statistics, 1998a). Funding differences between states are also influenced by differences in the cost of living and the number of children that need to be educated. Utah, for example, has the highest birth rate in the nation, approximately one and a half times the national average, so whatever funds are available must be divided among more children.

The effects of funding on excellence in education is a controversial topic, with early research concluding that the amount spent has little or no influence on achievement (Hanushek, 1996). However, more recent research in this area found that higher per-pupil expenditures resulted in higher achievement, possibly because of better qualified teachers and smaller class sizes (Flanagan & Grissmer, 2002; Krueger & Whitmore, 2002). Increased expenditures seem to have their greatest effect on low-income and minority students.

The relationship between funding and learning isn't simple or precise, however. Achievement tests—the most commonly used measure of student learning—focus on core academic areas, such as math, science, and reading, and not every dollar spent on education goes to teaching these basic subjects. Some monies go to art and music, for example, which are valuable areas of the curriculum, but increased expenditures in these areas won't be directly reflected in higher test scores. Furthermore, as you see in Figure 8.4, only about 60 percent of the money allocated to education is spent on instruction, most of which goes to teacher salaries (Odden et al., 1995). The rest is spent on areas that affect achievement only indirectly.

In addition to the 60 percent that directly supports instruction, 10 percent of school district funds goes to instructional assistance needs, such as student services, curriculum development, and teacher professional advancement (Odden et al., 1995). Another 10 percent goes to administration. Of this figure, approximately one third is spent in district offices and two thirds goes to schools. Maintenance of school buildings and grounds takes up another 10 percent of the budget. Transportation (school buses) and food services (cafeteria lunches) each account for another 5 percent.

To understand the magnitude of transportation expenditures, consider these national figures. In an average school year, 450,000 yellow school buses travel 4 billion (billion, not million) miles, providing 10 billion separate rides to nearly 24 million K–12 students (Brimley & Garfield, 2002). Student activities add 5 million trips. In

A significant portion of a district's budget goes to transportation, building maintenance, and food services.

Increasing Understanding 8.9

Explain how the percentages in Figure 8.4 would be different for a new and growing school district compared to a stable rural school district.

1998 schools provided transportation to 54 percent of the nation's student population at a cost of $493 per student.

Critics often decry the large amount of monies (40%) spent on areas other than academics, but school finance experts point out that expenditures for school buses and school lunches, for example, are all part of the total education process. In addition, they note that the amounts schools spend on administration and maintenance of the physical plant compare favorably with those spent in industry (Bracey, 1999b; Odden et al., 1995).

Figure 8.4 Educational Expenditures on Different District Programs

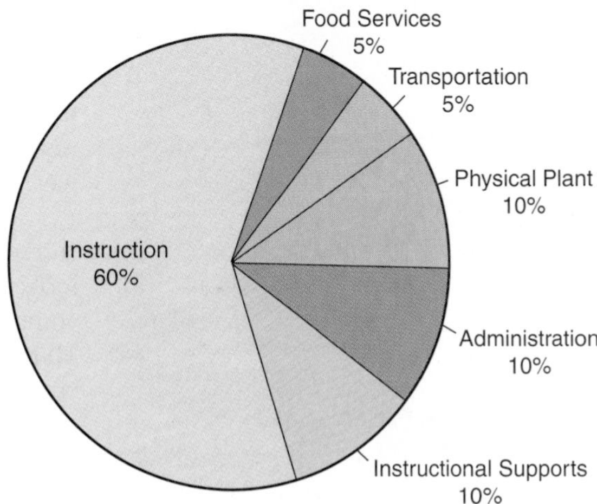

Source: Data from Odden. A., Monk, D., Nakib, Y., & Picus, L. (1995).

Reflect on This

To analyze a case study examining issues related to financial considerations and the choice of a first teaching position, go to the Companion Website at **www.prenhall.com/kauchak**, then to this chapter's *Reflect on This* module.

Emerging Issues in School Governance and Finance

As schools confront the challenges of the twenty-first century, they face a number of issues in the areas of governance and finance. Some of the most important include the following:

- Equity in funding, one of the most fundamental issues facing education
- Site-based decision making, which attempts to involve teachers and parents in the running of schools
- School choice in the form of charter schools and vouchers

Let's look at them.

Savage Inequalities: The Struggle for Funding Equity

As you saw earlier, research reveals significant differences in per-pupil expenditures both between and within states (Biddle & Berliner, 2002; Rothstein, 1998). Jonathan Kozol outlines this issue in his influential book *Savage Inequalities* (1991):

> Americans abhor the notion of a social order in which economic privilege and political power are determined by hereditary class. Officially, we have a more enlightened goal in sight: namely, a society in which a family's wealth has no relation to the probability of future educational attainment and the wealth and station it affords. By this standard, education offered to poor children should be at least as good as that which is provided to the children of the upper-middle class. (p. 207)

This standard of equality is not what Kozol found in his research on school funding. Instead, he found that many urban schools around the country were dirty and run down with peeling paint, broken toilets, lights that did not work, boarded-up windows, and antiquated or missing textbooks. Only miles away, suburban schools featured new, well-maintained buildings that were attractive and inviting learning environments. These stark contrasts gave Kozol's book its title.

Disparities in property tax revenues can result in dramatic differences in funding for schools that are quite close geographically.

In 1968 Demetrio Rodriguez, a sheet-metal worker in a poor suburb of San Antonio, Texas, looked at the schools his children were attending and compared them with those in wealthier districts only 10 miles away. He was disturbed by what he saw. His children's schools lacked textbooks and air conditioning, the top two floors were condemned, and almost half of the teachers weren't certified. The major problem was the fact that property taxes for his district produced only \$37 per student compared to \$412 per student for the wealthier suburb. These differences are not unusual. For example, in Texas during the 1980s, the 100 most affluent districts in the state spent an average of $7,233 per student, whereas the poorest 100 averaged $2,978. Faced with these inequalities, Mr. Rodriguez sued, contending that his children were being unfairly penalized by where they lived (Verstegen, 1994).

Similar patterns exist in other states. Nationally, wealthy districts spend an average of 23 percent more on their students than do poorer districts. In Alaska wealthier districts spend more than double the amount per pupil ($16,546 versus $7,379) than other districts in the state (Biddle & Berliner, 2002).

Legal challenges over funding equity have increased. The battle lines for these cases were drawn in California in 1971 when the California Supreme Court ruled in a 6–1 vote that the use of property taxes to fund education resulted in unconstitutional funding inequities in the state (*Serrano v. Priest*, 1971). In an attempt to reduce funding inequities, the state's share of education funding rose from 40 percent to 70 percent.

Serrano v. Priest set the stage for the Rodriguez suit in Texas, which went all the way to the U.S. Supreme Court. Many believed, based on the California decision, that the Supreme Court would find the spending patterns in Texas unconstitutional. However, in a 5–4 vote it did just the opposite, ruling in 1973 that the Constitution does not guarantee citizens a right to an education. The Court did point out that funding inequities may violate state constitutions, many of which *do* guarantee citizens a right to an education.

CW

Increasing Understanding 8.10

Explain why the California and Texas funding-equity cases ended up in different court systems.

The Supreme Court ruling on the Rodriguez case sent the issue back to state courts, and many other state suits followed. By mid-2002 courts had overturned existing systems in 19 states and upheld others in 20 states, with four cases still pending (Flanagan & Grissmer, 2002). Differences in state rulings are primarily the result of differences in the wording of state constitutions. Some consitutions are quite specific in guaranteeing "equal education for all," whereas others are vague in specifying that educational opportunity should be "ample" or "efficient." When rulings favored the plaintiffs, researchers found that inequities were reduced by almost 14 percent (Nelson, 1999). Decreasing or eliminating reliance on the property tax was the primary cause (Flanagan & Grissmer, 2002).

The problem of funding inequalities is complicated by the fact that not all districts in a state have the same needs (Odden & Clune, 1998; Wenglinsky, 1998). Some have a higher proportion of low-income children, non-native English speakers, or children who need special education services. These populations require extra resources. Reformers are calling for funding formulas that go beyond simply equalizing dollars; they want plans that meet the needs of all students. These proposed reforms will be expensive and controversial, as many parents from wealthier districts object to having their local taxes used to fund distant schools across the state. In addition, the problems involved in attempting to quantify educational needs in terms of dollars and cents is complex.

The role the federal government should play in reducing or eliminating funding inequities is another issue facing funding reformers. Critics of the current system point out that two thirds of funding differences occur between states rather than within states, and states receiving low levels of educational funding are clustered in the South and Southeast, areas that also have large proportions of poor and minority students. Experts estimate that it would take a minimum of $25 billion to equalize states' expenditures, a daunting figure considering current state and federal budget shortfalls (Flanagan & Grissmer, 2002).

Site-Based Decision Making

Carla made her proposal to her school board, which would ultimately decide which math series to use. Her recommendation came from a committee composed of other

Site-based decision making actively involves parents and teachers in the running of their schools.

teachers in the district whose ideas and opinions were solicited and considered. Concerned parents, whose children would use the new series, were also at the meeting and had the opportunity to ask questions and influence the decision. This appears to be democracy in action, but is it? The decision would still be made at the district level, far removed from local schools.

Critics of this "top-down," district-level form of school governance contend that too many important educational decisions are made by people far removed from schools. They argue that school board members from across town may not know what is best for a particular school, for example. **Site-based decision making** is *a school management reform movement that attempts to place increased responsibility for governance at the individual school level.* Proponents of site-based decision making believe that the people most affected by educational decisions—teachers, parents, and even students—ought to be more directly involved in those decisions (Cunningham & Cordeiro, 2000; Sarason, 1997). In addition to being more democratic, site-based decision making ought to result in better-run schools. People who help make decisions about schools are more likely to support them and help them succeed.

CW

Increasing Understanding 8.11

Explain why teachers in large urban districts might feel more strongly than those in suburban districts about teacher input into educational decisions.

Both parents and teachers desire a greater say in educational issues. National polls show that people in general, and parents in particular, overwhelmingly support the idea that parents should be involved in schools and should play a major role in shaping their children's education (V. Johnson, 1994). In one national poll, a majority of respondents said that parents, teachers, and students had too little input in decisions affecting the local public schools (Rose & Gallup, 2000). Teachers also want more say in how their schools are run. In another poll, 70 percent of teachers felt they were out of the loop in their district's decision-making process (Public Agenda, 2000a). In an earlier survey, more than half of all teachers surveyed nationally, and two thirds of teachers in large urban districts, expressed a desire for greater input into school governance (Louis Harris & Associates, 1993).

Site-based decision making is appealing from a professional perspective. It seems sensible that professional educators should have a substantial say in how learning and teaching occur in their schools. Involvement in decision making creates dilemmas for teachers, however. Teachers join the profession to work with students, and the de-

mands of extended committee work can siphon energies away from teaching (van den Berg, 2002). For example, was the effort Carla spent on the textbook selection process worth it, or would students be better served if she had been able to devote more of her time to teaching? If decisions such as these are made at the school level, will this increase duplication of effort in the district? These questions don't have easy answers.

Power relationships change too. Traditionally, principals have run schools like captains on a ship, and teachers have been expected to follow orders. Site-based decision making requires principals to share their power and teachers to exercise initiative and leadership (in addition to fulfilling their regular teacher responsibilities). It also requires teachers to redefine their relationships with parents. Authoritarian ways of communicating must be replaced with cooperative ventures requiring both patience and tact.

Site-based decision making usually exists in one of two forms. Increased community participation in advisory committees, composed of parents, teachers, community members (and sometimes students) is the most common. School boards and building administrators maintain legal control over schools, and the advisory committees provide input in areas such as setting school goals and priorities, making curricular and extracurricular decisions, and selecting and evaluating teachers and administrators.

A more radical form of site-based decision making involves actual community control of educational decisions through an elected council. When this occurs, the district school board shares decision-making power with the council in areas such as recruitment and retention of principals and teachers, the curriculum, and budgets. Experiments in several large cities have raised thorny questions about who should serve on these community councils and whether or not decentralized decision making results in better schools for children (D. Land, 2002; Walberg & Niemiec, 1994).

School Choice

The freedom to choose is a central American value. Americans can choose where and how they live and what occupation they work in, for example. Shouldn't they also have a choice in the kind of schools their children attend? As presently organized, public school systems are centralized and bureaucratic, and where students go to school is determined by the neighborhoods in which they live. In the name of efficiency, we've created a governance and finance system that begins in state capitals, runs through local district offices, and culminates in schools that are similar in form and function. Walk into most public schools across the country and you'll see teachers teaching the same content in basically the same way (Cuban, 1984; Goodlad, 1984). Even the box-like architecture of school buildings is the same.

Critics decry this uniformity, and they make several arguments in support of their position. For example, we are a nation of 50 states with unique individuals and distinctive subcultures, and our schools ought to reflect this diversity. In addition, experimentation and innovation have been central to our nation's progress, and conformity discourages innovation. From an economic perspective, the present system represents a monopoly that forces parents to send their children to neighborhood public schools (Goldhaber, 1999). Critics believe that alternatives would result in healthy competition, which would ultimately result in better schools. They also argue that the public school system has become bloated, bureaucratic, and unresponsive to individual citizens' needs. In response to these criticisms, reformers call for school choice.

What does *choice* mean? At one level, parents already have choices, because they move to neighborhoods served by particular schools. The quality of the schools is one of the major features parents consider when choosing a neighborhood. If parents don't like the schools in their neighborhood, they can send their children to private schools, something that 10 percent of parents currently do (U.S. Department of Education, 2000b). In addition, through open enrollment programs districts typically allow parents who believe their local schools are sub-par to send their children across town to better schools. Doing so requires greater time and expense, but parents still have choices.

But choice advocates point out that many poor, minority, and inner-city parents don't have the resources to vote with their wallets or their cars. They cannot afford to move to better neighborhoods with better schools, to send their children to private schools, or even to drive across town each day to transport their children to a non-neighborhood public school. In addition, some school districts are so bad, critics contend, that other schools in the district don't really provide viable alternatives. These parents deserve the right to choose just as much as more wealthy parents do.

But how can parents be provided with options? The concept of school choice has resulted in two educational innovations: charter schools and vouchers.

Charter Schools **Charter schools** are *alternative schools that are independently operated but publicly funded.* In many states, parents or others unsatisfied with the local school choices have the right to create their own alternative or specialty schools. Charter schools typically begin when a group—teachers, community members, or a private corporation—develops a plan for a school, including its curriculum, staffing, and budget. This plan or "charter" must then be accepted by the local school board or state office of education and serves as a contract with the state.

Many school districts already have alternative schools, such as magnet schools with specialized programs as well as schools designed to meet the needs of students who can't successfully function in regular schools and classrooms (for example, young, unwed mothers or children with serious behavior or emotional problems). Charter schools are similar to other alternative schools in that they offer a different curriculum or target special populations; they differ in that they are independently administered public schools and subject to less regulatory control from a district's central administration (Goldhaber, 1999).

The charter school movement began in Minnesota in 1991 when the legislature approved the creation of eight teacher-created and operated outcome-based schools. (An outcome-based school makes curricular and instructional decisions based on student performance on specified assessments.) Since that time, 35 additional states and the District of Columbia have passed charter school legislation resulting in the creation of more than 2,700 schools with more than 575,000 students (Flanigan, 2003). Nationally, the number of charter schools increased by 14 percent in 2002 (Hendrie, 2002b). Arizona is a leader in this area, having appropriated $600 million to fund more than 468 charter schools. California added 89 new charter schools in 2002, bringing its total to 452.

The focus of different charter schools varies dramatically, although most attract parents seeking smaller schools and class sizes, better quality instruction, and alternatives to public school curricula and environments (Casey, Andreson, Yelverton, & Wedeen, 2002). Some are designed by inner-city community leaders to meet the needs of urban youth. One school in Michigan, for example, focuses on developing students' African heritage through language instruction, literature, and the arts. Others attract parents who want a return to the basics, while still others focus on technology and the arts (Toch, 1998).

Teacher involvement in charter schools. Initial research on charter school teachers has revealed greater teacher involvement in school governance issues (Gresham, Hess, Maranto, & Milliman, 2000). As we can see in Figure 8.5, 62 percent of teachers in charter elementary schools reported having high levels of influence over curriculum

Figure 8.5 Perceptions of Governance Issues by Charter and Non-Charter Arizona Teachers

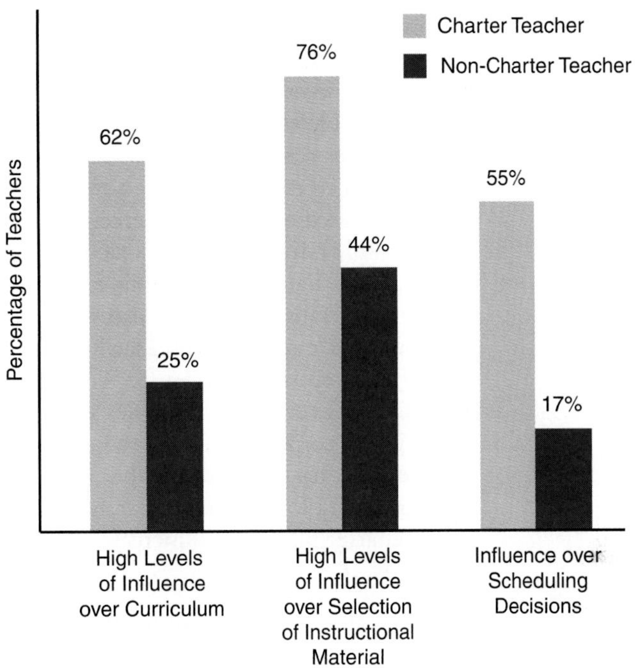

Source: Data from Gresham, A., Hess, F., Maranto. R., & Milliman, S. (2000).

decisions at their schools, whereas only 25 percent of teachers at regular schools reported such influence. Similar differences occurred in teachers' beliefs about their influence over selection of instructional materials and scheduling.

School philosophy, smaller size, and characteristics of the teachers themselves are all possible reasons for teachers' greater role in decision making. Most charter schools begin with the view that teachers are central to a quality education and actively attempt to involve teachers in school planning. Charter schools also tend to be smaller, which allows change to occur more rapidly. Finally, teachers who choose to work in charter schools are likely to be more adventurous and willing to experiment with their teaching. One charter school teacher commented, "Everyone who came was one of the best in the program from wherever they came from. There were no slackers in the group" (Brouillette, 2000, p. 31).

Issues of quality in charter schools. Considerable variation exists in the quality of charter schools, and this uneven quality is having a negative effect on the charter school movement. For example, in Texas—a leader in establishing charter schools—a panel of state lawmakers recommended a moratorium on new charter schools, citing poor student performance, financial troubles, and unexpected closures (Associated Press, 2000). In 1999 there were 193 charter schools in Texas, and the state spent \$218 million on them. However, only 59 percent of charter school students passed a state skills exam in the 1998–1999 school year, compared with the state average of 78.4 percent. In reviewing existing charter schools, the state education agency gave an "unacceptable" rating to nearly one fourth of the 103 schools it evaluated. In 2002 Texas revoked the charters of five schools for chronically poor performance on state tests; two charter schools serving 2,000 students were at the bottom of the state's accountability rankings for 3 years in a row (Hendrie, 2002a).

California, another leader in the charter school movement, has encountered similar problems (Hendrie, 2002a). A state audit revealed inadequate monitoring of charter schools and uncovered problems that included inadequately prepared teachers, poor quality instruction, and failure to administer state accountability tests.

The problem of quality is partially linked to the large numbers of unlicensed teachers in charter schools. One national study found that 43 percent of charter school teachers lacked credentials, compared to 9 percent in regular public schools, and this figure increased to nearly 60 percent in predominantly African American charters (H. Brown, 2003). In a time when teacher quality is seen as central to school improvement efforts, these figures are troubling. A major advantage of charter schools—freedom from bureaucratic oversight—also seems to be a major weakness of this reform.

Inadequate resources and facilities are also persistent problems in charter schools (Casey, Andreson, Yelverton, & Wedeen, 2002). Many lack libraries and laboratories and sometimes even basic supplies such as paper and pencils (Toch, 1998). The arrival of for-profit corporations into the charter school arena, which you'll read about in a later section, has exacerbated the problem (Hendrie, 2003a). Given these factors, it isn't surprising to find that research has been unable to demonstrate a relationship between charter schools and increased student achievement (D. Land, 2002).

CW For more information about charter schools, go to the Companion Website at **www.prenhall.com/kauchak**, then to this chapter's *Web Links* module.

Vouchers Vouchers are another approach to school choice. A **voucher** is *a check or written document that parents can use to purchase educational services.* The voucher approach is grounded in the belief that parents know what their children need and should be free to purchase the best education wherever they can find it. Some voucher plans give parents the choice of either a public or private school, whereas others limit the choice to public schools.

Vouchers are often defended by political conservatives who argue that public schools are a monopoly and that opening up schools to parental choice would allow market forces to improve education. All schools (not just those in immediate neigh-

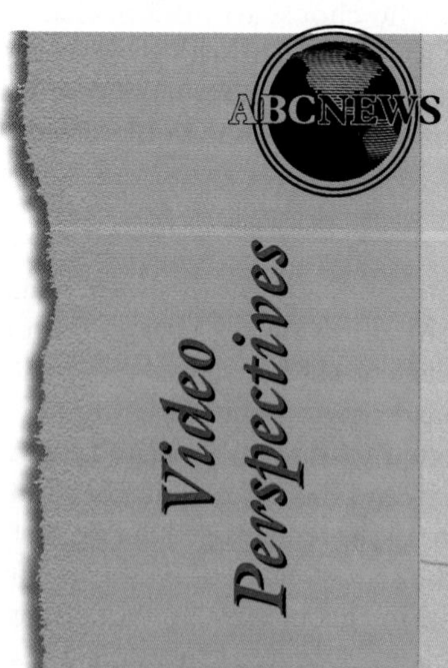

HOME ROOM: ONE LAST CHANCE

This ABC News video describes a unique kind of school, SEED Public Charter School, a public boarding school in Washington, DC. The news crew interviews the founders of the charter school, as well as teachers and students. These interviews provide insights into the promises and challenges of this innovation.

Think About This

1. How is this charter school different from ones that you've read about?
2. Why aren't there more charter schools like this across the country?
3. What positive features of this school could be transferred to other schools?

CW *To answer these questions online and receive immediate feedback, go to the Companion Website at* **www.prenhall.com/kauchak**, *then to this chapter's* Video Perspectives *module.*

borhoods) become viable alternatives. Over time, the best schools would attract more students and flourish, whereas poorer schools would be shut down by informed consumers and market forces.

Because of possible disruptive influences on public schools and issues with religious instruction, the voucher movement is highly controversial. Critics, including the National Education Association and the American Federation of Teachers, the two largest professional organizations in education, argue that vouchers increase segregation, split the public along socioeconomic lines, and drain students and resources from already struggling inner-city schools (American Federation of Teachers, 2003b; National Education Association, 2002).

Some voucher advocates would also like to use them for religious schools; critics contend that this violates the principle of separation of church and state. In Cleveland and Milwaukee, two cities that have led the country in the voucher movement, religious schools have been the major beneficiaries. For example, 82 percent of Cleveland schools participating in a voucher program were religiously affiliated, and 96 percent of participating students attended religious schools (National Association of Elementary School Principals, 2002). Nationally, almost 80 percent of private schools have a religious affiliation (Brimley & Garfield, 2002). Supporters of voucher programs ask why parents should have to pay for a quality education twice—once when they pay public school taxes and again when they pay tuition at private schools.

In 2002 the U.S. Supreme Court, in a narrow 5–4 decision, ruled that the voucher program in Cleveland did not violate separation of church and state (Flanigan, 2003; Walsh, 2002b). The idea that voucher funds went to parents rather than directly to religious schools was central to the decision. Since the Supreme Court made its decision, the number of applicants for the Cleveland voucher program has risen 29 percent, suggesting more parents are taking advantage of this educational option (Hendrie, 2002a). However, a research study conducted by a Cleveland-based nonprofit organization, Policy Matters Ohio, concluded that Cleveland vouchers served more as a subsidy for students already attending private schools than as an "escape hatch" for students eager to leave the public schools.

Three state legislatures have enacted voucher systems since 1990: Wisconsin, Ohio, and Florida. The Wisconsin and Ohio plans apply only to Milwaukee and Cleveland, respectively; Florida's is statewide. Now that the Supreme Court has approved vouchers for religious schools, the next legal battles will occur in state capitols. These battles may be difficult for voucher advocates because 37 state constitutions currently have language that prohibits state aid to religious schools (Gehring, 2002b).

The academic benefits of vouchers are unclear. Some research suggests that providing students school choice through voucher programs can lead to small achievement gains (Bowman, 2000a, 2000b; Goldhaber, 1999), but other research indicates no achievement gains or gains in some populations (e.g., African American) but not others (Gewertz, 2003a; National Education Association, 2002). A curriculum emphasizing academics, more effective instruction, and greater parental involvement are explanations offered for any gains that exist. In addition, parents provided with choice are more satisfied with the schools their children attend (Goldhaber, 1999). However, questions about the effects of choice on school diversity are continually raised, as we'll see later in the chapter.

Florida's school-choice program is interesting because of the number of options it provides (Richard, 2002b). If the state gives a school a failing grade (based on achievement test scores) twice within a 4-year period, students in that school qualify to receive vouchers. Eighty schools received failing grades in 2002, and students in ten schools became eligible for vouchers, which at the time were worth $3,891 each. Of the 9,000 students eligible in these schools, 571 switched to private schools and

Teaching in an Era of Reform

THE PRIVATIZATION ISSUE

The move towards school choice has taken an interesting turn recently, with one option being privately run, for-profit schools. Modeled after HMOs (health maintenance organizations), EMOs (education maintenance organizations) propose to run and manage either whole districts or specific schools within a district.

Aspects of school privatization are not new. Schools have been outsourcing contracts for support services, such as school lunches and transportation, for years, and more recently, districts have hired companies such as IBM and Hewlett-Packard to provide technology support (Trotter, 2002a). What *is* new is the idea of handing over control of a whole school or district to a private corporation.

Estimates indicate that 70 percent of school districts currently engage in some type of business partnership (L. Alexander & Riley, 2002). At one time, school–business partnerships often consisted of corporations buying a football scoreboard or placing an ad in the school newspaper. More recently, Channel One, a privately run school news/advertising company, offered 10 minutes of news to schools in return for 2 minutes of advertising. Incentives include free satellite disks, a schoolwide cable system, and free televisions in all classrooms. In 2001 Channel One reached 12,000 schools and 8 million students, 40 percent of the nation's 12- to 18-year-olds (Molnar & Reeves, 2001; Trotter, 2001b). This is a huge advertising market.

Corporations such as Edison Schools, Inc., and Sylvan Learning Incorporated are leaders in the school privatization movement. Edison began about 10 years ago and made its stock public in 1998 with an initial Wall Street offering of $18 per share; optimism soon propelled share prices to $38 (Woodward, 2002). Chris Whittle, its founder, predicted that by 2020 Edison would run one in every 10 schools in America, but so far the company has grown slowly. In 2002 Edison ran 150 schools across the country, serving 82,000 students (Walsh, 2003c). Edison's most visible challenge came when the school district of Philadelphia, a floundering system suffering from perennial low student achievement, offered Edison a 5-year, $60 million contract to manage 20 of its schools.

Nationwide, the privatization movement has received a big boost from the trend toward school choice. The number of privately run schools grew from 285 in 2001 to 417 in 2003 (Walsh, 2003b); of these, 74 percent were charter schools. The number of for-profit companies in the educational arena also grew from 21 in 2001 to 47 in 2003.

The Issue

As would be expected, private, for-profit schools are very controversial. Should corporations, whose primary objective is making a profit, be entrusted with the education of children?

Critics make a number of arguments against privatization. They question the ability of a corporate efficiency model to work in education and assert that corporate strategies will adversely affect both teachers and students. Further, they contend, privatized schools have a dual mission—improving test scores and making a profit—and corporate profits and education don't mix. Attention to the bottom line means that student welfare may be sacrificed in an effort to make money. Critics also claim that a narrow focus on the basics as well as neglect of non-native English speakers and students with special needs are additional problems. Teachers are treated as workers, not professionals, and are expected to implement a regimented, top-down curriculum.

Support for the critics' position can be found in Edison's efforts in Philadelphia, where controversy has existed from the beginning. Apparently, the district's call for outside help was based on an evaluation conducted by Edison itself and not sent out for competitive bids (Gewertz, 2002). In essence, the state of Pennsylvania hired Edison to conduct a study, completed in 2 months, for $2.7 million (Bracey, 2002). Not surprisingly, the Edison report concluded that external help should be sought, and the district authorized the creation of 20 Edison charter schools. After less than one year of operation, the Philadelphia School District, citing budget considerations, decided to shift $10 million of the next year's $20 million contract from Edison and other private companies to other reform projects (Gewertz, 2003b).

Teacher morale and lagging student performance in Edison schools are persistent problems. For example, in an Edison-contracted San Francisco elementary school, approximately half of the teachers left in each of Edison's 2 years of operation, citing problems with long work hours, a regimented curriculum, and overemphasis on test preparation. There were also claims that students with academic or behavioral difficulties were "counseled out" of the school in hopes of raising test scores (Woodward, 2002). San Francisco cancelled its contract with Edison; under a renewed charter contract with the state of California, the elementary school's test scores remained low, ranking last among scores from San Francisco's 75 elementary schools.

Privatization advocates argue that these problems are exceptions, that Edison works in some of the most challenging schools in the country, and that the public shouldn't expect miracles overnight. They also assert that competition from the corporate sector is good because it encourages public schools to reexamine unproductive practices. In addition, advocates claim, the same business efficiencies that have made America a world leader can also work in schools, and a focus on performance (as measured by standardized tests) can provide schools with a clear mission to increase student achievement. They also claim that privatization can inject a breath of fresh air into the educational bureaucracy.

Research has found some benefits of privatized schools. They are cleaner and more efficiently run than public schools (Hoffman, 1998). Technology is typically emphasized, and more attention is given to individualized instruction. However, companies have not been able to provide clear evidence that students learn more in privately run schools, a core assertion of privatization advocates. Some research shows improved achievement, but other research shows either no gain or declines (Shay & Gomez, 2002; Walsh, 2003c). Unfortunately, the research sponsors—either privatization backers or critics—seem to be as important as the data itself.

You Take a Position

Now it's your turn to take a position on the issue. State in writing whether you do or do not favor the operation of schools by for-profit corporations, and provide a two-page rationale for your position.

CW

For additional references and resources, go to the Companion Website at **www.prenhall.com/kauchak**, *then to this chapter's* Teaching in an Era of Reform *module. You can respond online or submit your response to your instructor.*

Exploring Diversity

SCHOOL CHOICE AND CULTURAL MINORITIES

School choice is often framed in terms of parental empowerment, or providing parents with educational alternatives. But can the process of school choice result in such unintended negative consequences as increased social and racial segregation, as some critics claim?

Research from New Zealand, which began experimenting with school choice via a quasi voucher system in 1989, raises some cautionary flags (Fiske & Ladd, 2000). Under new choice rules, schools with more student applicants than openings could essentially choose whom they admitted and served. The better schools chose academically motivated students from affluent families, leaving less popular schools with poorer achieving students. Researchers concluded that in New Zealand schools, "Choice and competition are likely to polarize enrollment patterns by race, ethnicity, socioeconomic status, and students' performance" (Fiske & Ladd, 2000, p. 38). These same researchers cautioned against unregulated choice systems that could result in "polarization of enrollment patterns and exacerbation of the problems of noncompetitive schools" (Fiske & Ladd, 2000, p. 38). In other words, choice systems have the potential of encouraging social segregation and further damaging already weak inner-city schools. The same concerns have been raised in the United States; critics contend that voucher programs and charter schools entice the best students away from poor-performing schools, leaving urban schools in particular in even worse shape than they are now (Ferguson, 2002). Furthur, offering school choice leads to segregation of students, either by income or race. One recent study supports critics' claims. Researchers found that 70 percent of African American charter school students attend intensely segregated schools, compared with 34 percent of African American students in regular public schools (Frankenberg & Lee, 2003). In almost every state studied, the average African American charter school student attended a school with a higher percentage of African American students and a lower percentage of White students.

Problems of social and cultural polarization were also found in Arizona, a leader in the charter school movement (Schnaiberg, 2000). In 1996 two charter schools opened in the small rural school district of Safford, which had approximately 60 percent Anglo and 40 percent Hispanic students. In its first year of

another 900 went to other public schools. In a second variation on vouchers, an estimated 9,000 special education students used state monies to attend private schools. A third school-choice program allows corporations to use their state income taxes to fund private schools (Goldstein, 2002). The legal status of all three programs is currently being challenged in courts.

The Florida voucher program has come under close scrutiny lately with critics charging that it fails to hold private schools receiving vouchers accountable. One case involved the Islamic Academy of Florida, which received $300,000 in state vouchers in 2002 (Zehr, 2003). Two men affiliated with the school have been indicted on charges that they had links to terrorism. Critics protested that state tax dollars were used to support terrorism. Although an extreme example, the situation does reveal the potential for problems when deregulation in education isn't accompanied by some form of oversight.

enrollment, the Triumphant Learning Center, a back-to-basics school with Christian overtones, enrolled 95 percent Anglo students. Los Milagros, a charter school with Catholic ties, enrolled 75 percent Hispanic students. Although neither school consciously chose to exclude certain types of students, "subtle signals" sent messages to parents. For example, the Triumphant Learning Center emphasized increased parental involvement by encouraging parents to volunteer in the school and by closing their doors every Friday to allow more family time. Poor Hispanic families, in which both parents worked—some holding more than one job—were not able to participate. As recently as 2000, 53 percent of Los Milagros' students were Hispanic and 90 percent of the students in the Triumphant Learning Center were Anglo, but both schools are making efforts to balance their enrollments.

Another area of concern connected with school choice has to do with equal opportunities for students with special needs and how those needs should be funded. In most voucher plans, the voucher amount is equal to the average per-pupil expenditure in the district or state, but the cost for educating children with special needs can be more than twice that amount (Odden et al., 1995). Consequently, students with exceptionalities could find themselves underfunded or even refused admittance by certain schools. This very problem occurred in Massachusetts when for-profit charter schools openly discouraged students with exceptionalities from attending (Zollars, 2000). Only 17 percent of private schools provide special education services (Ferguson, 2002), so the problem of access to choice schools may be particularly acute for students with special needs.

Supporters of school-choice programs counter that public schools are already segregated, especially in inner cities, and that choice can actually promote integration. For example, in 1999, 55 percent of all public-school twelfth graders attended classes that had either more than 90 percent or fewer than 10 percent minorities (Greene, 2000). In contrast, only 41 percent of students in choice-driven private schools were in similarly segregated classrooms. As we saw with magnet schools in Chapter 5, school choice, when designed strategically, can actually be an integration tool.

The effects of school choice on students from minority groups will remain controversial and is likely to significantly affect education in the future. Whether these effects will be positive or negative is unclear at this time (Goldhaber & Hyde, 2002). Ideally, school choice should encourage experimentation and innovation. As with all experiments, mistakes will occur. Whether these mistakes will adversely affect students and the teachers who work with them are important questions.

Public Reactions to School Choice The American public seems to be confused and uncertain about school choice, both in terms of charter schools and vouchers. In one poll, for example, only 56 percent acknowledged either reading or hearing about charter schools (Rose & Gallup, 2002). When asked to choose between improving existing public schools or providing vouchers for public or private schools, 69 percent voted for strengthening existing schools and only 29 percent favored vouchers. However, another poll found a disparity in the attitudes of African Americans and White Americans (Coles, 1997). The 1997 poll, the Public's Attitude Toward Public Schools, found that 62 percent of African Americans favored the use of vouchers. Fifty six percent of African Americans also preferred a greater role for the federal government in funding education, compared to 26 percent of Whites. These findings suggest that funding inequalities are a major concern of African Americans, many of whom live in locations where educational funding is below national averages.

Vouchers and state tax credit for private-school tuition can provide economically disadvantaged families with opportunities to choose the schools they want for their children.

In general, support for vouchers comes from dissatisfaction with existing public schools, and if public schools improve, public interest in vouchers is likely to wane. In the 2000 election, voters in California and Michigan overwhelmingly (70% in California and 69% in Michigan) voted against voucher initiatives, which opponents contend sounds a death knell for the movement (Walsh, 2000b). However, Republican legislatures in Texas, Colorado, and Louisiana are considering statewide voucher plans, primarily aimed at low-income students in poor-performing schools (Richard, 2003).

State tuition tax-credit plans are *a variation on school voucher programs in which parents are given tax credits for money they spend on private-school tuition.* Tuition tax credits have emerged in some states as a more politically viable alternative to publicly financed school vouchers. Unfortunately, research suggests that tuition tax credits primarily benefit wealthy families who are already sending their children to private schools. In Illinois, for example, tax credits cost the state more than $61 million in lost revenues in 2000 (Gehring, 2002a). Taxpayers earning more than $80,000 claimed 46 percent of that amount, whereas less than 3 percent went to households making less than $20,000. A similar problem occurred in Arizona (Bracey, 2002). Households earning more than $50,000 received 81 percent of the tax credits as well as 84 percent of the $109 million state revenues spent on tuition tax credits. More equitable ways of distributing the benefits of this form of school choice need to be designed if this reform effort is to grow.

Homeschooling **Homeschooling,** *an educational option in which parents educate their children at home*, may be the ultimate form of school choice. Homeschooling has become increasingly popular in recent years, with estimates of the number of children participating ranging from 850,000 to 2.1 million (Ray, 2003; Walsh, 2002c). Homeschoolers account for between 2 and 4 percent of the school-age population. More children are homeschooled than attend charter schools (Reich, 2002).

Parents choose to homeschool their children for a wide variety of reasons. Many do so because of concerns about the moral climate of existing schools or because of religious objections to the curriculum. Others are concerned about the lack of challenge in public schools or the absence of a particular course of study. All are seeking an alternative to existing public schools.

State laws regulating homeschooling vary greatly (Fischer et al., 2003). In most states, parents must demonstrate that their instruction is equivalent to that offered in public schools. In some states, parents must submit an educational plan documenting the equivalence. Approximately half the states require homeschooled students to participate in regular standardized testing. Homeschooled students who take these tests typically do well, scoring, on average, between the 65th and 90th percentiles on various tests (Mathews, 1999).

Despite its growing popularity, homeschooling has its critics. Some wonder whether children schooled at home will learn important social interaction skills (Galley, 2003). Other critics question whether narrow courses of study will expose children to alternative views and perspectives that are not widely accepted (Reich, 2002). One troubling trend is the tendency of some homeschool learning materials to criticize specific religious beliefs or entire religions. One study found that some of the more popular religiously oriented homeschool texts describe Islam as "a false religion," blame Hinduism for India's problems, and attribute Africa's problems to the absence of non-Christian religions (Patterson, 2001/2002). These types of messages are troubling in a pluralistic society such as ours.

Decision Making

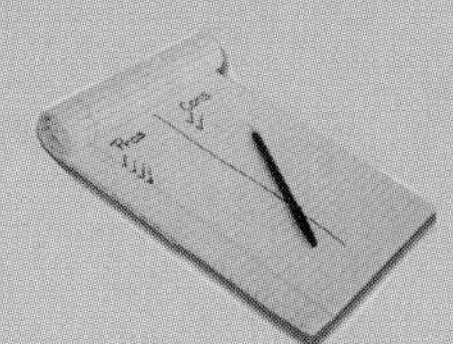

Defining Yourself as a Professional

Changes in educational governance and funding will present both opportunities and challenges to you as a new teacher. School choice, discussed from the perspective of parents and students, is also an issue for new teachers as they consider where to start their teaching careers.

School finances don't only influence student achievement. They also influence the quality of teachers' work lives in several important ways. Class size is one. The size of a class can alter the ways teachers teach, the relationships they can form with students and, ultimately, student achievement. It is obviously much more difficult to do small-group work or individual projects with classes of more than 30 students than with classes of around 20 students.

Instructional resources such as computers, as well as more basic material resources such as paper and up-to-date textbooks, also influence student achievement and teachers' work lives. It is difficult to involve students in an Internet inquiry when a teacher has only one or two computers in the classroom.

Opportunities for professional development also relate to finances. This is understandable, as 80 percent of a district's expenses are related to personnel (Brimley & Garfield, 2002). Wealthier districts can offer better mentor and induction programs for new teachers as well as sponsor more professional development opportunities for veterans.

New teachers, when considering choices between two districts, should investigate the financial investments different districts make toward their students and teachers. State offices of education collect data each year on these district-level expenditures, and this information is typically available to the public on Web sites or through print publications. A smaller financial investment in education doesn't necessarily make a district or state a poor place to teach, of course. Typically, the poorest districts and states are also the most needy. Teachers wanting to make a difference in the world might consciously choose to work in areas with fewer resources, specifically because they feel they can make a difference. This decision is laudable.

Charter schools and vouchers, too, pose both opportunities and challenges for teachers. Advocates claim that a true free market educational scene will reward quality and initiative and punish mediocrity and complacency. As this concept moves toward actual implementation, however, a number of thorny issues need to be worked out, many of which have to do with teacher job security. If voucher programs are fully implemented, there may be major shifts in individual school populations, resulting in teacher transfers to other schools or even firing through reduction in force. Likewise, teachers lose job security when charter schools fail or even close mid-year (Bowman, 2000b). Advocates say that changes in the market, although temporarily painful, will ultimately result in improvements in education. In pursuing excellence, however, teachers want the guarantee of a job next year. In experimenting with innovations, teachers need the assurance that failures, as well as successes, will be tolerated.

These are exciting and challenging times to be a teacher. Changes in governance and finance structures will require teachers to redefine both themselves and the profession. These are not easy tasks, but we believe they have enormous potential to influence teaching. They also will offer new, adventurous teachers a number of career options they never had before.

Summary

Governance: How Are Schools Regulated and Run?

The responsibility for governing schools in the United States is given to the states by the U.S. Constitution. Within each state, the governor and state legislature are aided by the state office of education in regulating school functions.

Local control of education, a uniquely American idea, occurs through individual school districts. Each district is governed by a local school board, containing lay people from the community, and administered by a district superintendent. The superintendent is responsible for running the district office as well as overseeing the operations of the individual schools within the district. Principals play a major role in shaping the instructional agendas at the individual school level.

Districts are part of a larger state governance structure determined by the state's constitution. Within this structure the state governor and legislature provide leadership through bills and initiatives. The overall responsibility for education in the state goes to the state board of education. Assisting this board is the state superintendent (or commissioner or secretary), who is assisted by and responsible for the state office of education.

School Finance: How Are Schools Funded?

Schools are funded from three different sources. Almost one half of school funds come from local sources, which typically use property taxes to collect revenues. States provide another major source of funding and typically do this through state income taxes and special taxes. The third and smallest source of school funding is the federal government.

Most education monies (60%) go to instructional services, primarily to pay for teacher salaries. The large differences in how much various states invest in education can be attributed to differing capacities to pay, as well as differences in cost of living.

Emerging Issues in School Governance and Finance

Controversies over inequities in school finance have focused on differences within, rather than between, states. The large number of court cases involving funding inequities has caused states to reexamine funding formulas and has resulted in increased state and decreased local funding. Current approaches to funding equity go beyond absolute dollar amounts to include student and district needs.

Site-based decision making has emerged as a major trend in governance reform. In site-based decision making, both parents and teachers have greater input into curricular and instructional decisions.

School choice in the form of charter schools and vouchers provides parents with greater control over their children's education. Charter schools, created by interested teachers and parents, target their efforts on specific educational goals or patrons. Vouchers, essentially tickets for educational services, allow parents to shop around for schools that fit their needs. Privatization, in which corporations contract for specific services within districts, is a growing but controversial practice. The impact of school-choice programs on cultural minorities and integration efforts is still unclear.

Important Concepts

block grants (p. 286)
categorical grants (p. 286)
charter schools (p. 294)
homeschooling (p. 302)
local school board (p. 277)
principal (p. 281)
school district (p. 276)
site-based decision making (p. 292)
state board of education (p. 274)
state office of education (p. 276)
state tuition tax-credit plans (p. 302)
superintendent (p. 280)
voucher (p. 296)

Developing as a Professional

Praxis Practice

Read the case study, and answer the questions that follow.

"Hi, Tom. How's the world treating you?" Andrea Martinez asked, as she dropped a load of books on the desk in the teachers' lounge.

"I think I'm in the wrong job," Tom replied, looking down at the newspaper he was reading. "We got a lousy 2 percent pay increase this year. That, combined with the $1^1/_2$ percent last year, puts us behind even inflation. Maybe I'll need to get a third job to make ends meet."

"I know what you mean. We're struggling, too, but the economy is tight—a lot of people are unemployed. I don't know what to do myself."

"Maybe I should run for the state legislature," Tom said. "I could tell those people what it's really like to live on a teacher's salary."

"Why the legislature? Why not our school board? They're the ones who actually decide our pay raises."

"Aw, I'm probably not cut out to be a politician anyways. I'm too honest," Tom replied with a cynical grin. "I *have* actually thought about going back to school and becoming a principal. Their salaries beat ours."

"But so do their headaches," Andrea replied. "If big bucks are what you're after, why stop there? Why not become a superintendent? Ours makes over $150,000."

"Yeah, I heard that. But I also heard he's looking for a new job. They can't seem to keep people in that job. This one's been with us 2 years. The other one lasted 3. Maybe my job isn't so bad after all. At least I know there'll be a job waiting for me next year."

1. How would you respond to Tom and Andrea's comments about who actually determines teachers' salaries?
2. How accurate was Tom's comment that principals' salaries "beat" teachers' salaries? (You may wish to refer to Table 1.2 in Chapter 1, which lists teachers' salaries across the nation.)
3. Is the experience of Tom and Andrea's superintendent unusual? What factors lead to superintendents' short tenures?

To receive feedback on your responses to the Praxis Practice exercises, go to the Companion Website at **www.prenhall.com/kauchak**, then to this chapter's *Praxis Practice* module.

Discussion Questions

1. Should legislation be passed to make local school boards mirror the populations they serve? For example, if 25 percent of the population is Hispanic, should one fourth of the school board be Hispanic? What advantages and disadvantages are there to this approach to equitable representation? What other alternatives might be better?
2. Ordinarily, teachers cannot be school board members in their own districts because of potential conflicts of interest. Would teachers make good school board members in districts in which they live but don't teach? Should a certain number or percentage of school board positions be reserved for teachers? Why or why not?
3. Should the percentages of male and female principals reflect the gender composition of the teachers at the school level in which the principals work? Why or why not?
4. Should school districts in a state be funded equally? What are the advantages and disadvantages to this approach? Should every school district in the nation receive equal funds? What are the advantages and disadvantages to this approach?
5. Will school choice be a positive or negative development in education? Why?
6. Should vouchers be made available to private religious schools? Why or why not?

Video Discussion Questions

The following discussion question refers to a video segment found on the Companion Website. To answer this question online, view the accompanying video clip, and receive immediate feedback on your answer, go to the Companion Website at **www.prenhall.com/kauchak**, then to this chapter's *Video Discussion* module.

1. Theodore Sizer is the Director of the Coalition for Effective Schools, which attempts to reform high schools. Dr. Sizer believes that parental choice and involvement are central to school reform effects. In Dr. Sizer's opinion, what are some arguments in favor of school choice? Which of these arguments are most persuasive? Do you believe school choice will improve education?

Going into Schools

1. *School board governance:* Attend a local school board meeting.
   a. What is the demographic composition (males, females, minorities, etc.) of the board? How does this compare with national figures? How does this compare with local demographics?
   b. Of the five school board functions (see Figure 8.2), which took the most time during the meeting? Least?
   c. What role did teachers play in the meeting?
   d. Were any controversial issues discussed? How did the board resolve these issues?

   Summarize your findings, and make recommendations about how school boards can be made more responsive to constituents' needs.
2. *Administrative leadership:* Interview a teacher about the principal in his or her school.
   a. Is the principal primarily a manager or instructional leader? Can the teacher give you concrete examples of either role?

b. What role does the principal play in establishing the academic climate for the school? How does the principal do this?
c. What kinds of mentoring or professional development activities does the principal promote?
d. Pose the following: "My school would be a better place to work if my principal would . . . "

What do the teacher's responses tell you about the importance of a principal for a school? What kind of principal would you like to work for?

3. *District organization:* Visit a local school district office, and ask for information about the following:
   a. Size: How large is the district in terms of schools, teachers, and number of students?
   b. School board: How big is it, and how are the members selected?
   c. District organization: What kinds of instructional support services (e.g., math specialist) are available for teachers?
   d. District budget: Where do funds come from, and how are they spent?

   How is the organization of this district similar to or different from other districts that you read about in this chapter?
4. *School choice:* Contact your state's office of education, either in person or through its Web site, and investigate the availability of choice in your state.
   a. Vouchers: Are vouchers currently in use? What restrictions are there on the use of these? What schools are being targeted?
   b. Charter schools: Does the state have charter schools? How many? Where are they located? How long have they existed? Do they have specific goals or missions? How are they monitored or governed by the state?

   Summarize your findings in a report. In this report, speculate on how school choice might influence your future life as a teacher.
5. *Site-based decision making:* Contact a teacher, and ask about the decision-making processes at his or her school.
   a. To what extent are parents involved in curricular and instructional issues?
   b. To what extent are teachers involved in curricular and instructional issues?
   c. What permanent and temporary ad hoc committees exist in the school? What are their missions? Who serves on them?
   d. Would the teacher want to be more involved in site-based decision making? Why or why not?

   In your report, indicate whether this school would be a productive place to work. Make recommendations about how it could be made a better place to work.

Virtual Field Experience

If you would like to participate in a Virtual Field Experience, go to the Companion Website at **www.prenhall.com/kauchak**, then to this chapter's *Field Experience* module.

Online Portfolio Activities

To complete these activities online, go to the Companion Website at **www.prenhall.com/kauchak**, then to this chapter's *Portfolio Activities* module.

Portfolio Activity 8.1

School Governance

INTASC Principle 9: Commitment

Personal Journal Reflection

The purpose of this activity is to help you prepare for your first interview with a principal. Review the material in this chapter on the role of the principal and site-based decision making. Construct several questions to ask during the interview that would allow you to gauge the principal's views on his or her leadership role in the school and the role that teachers play in the governance process.

Portfolio Activity 8.2

School Finance

INTASC Principle 9: Commitment

The purpose of this activity is to help you begin thinking about how school finance will influence your life as a teacher. Locate the Web site of a local school district or one you may want to teach in. Browse the site's budget section, and try to determine how much of the district's budget is allocated to teacher salaries and professional development. Also, check out the teacher salary schedule. How do these figures compare to ones mentioned in this text? Write down several questions you might want to ask about finance issues when you interview with a district (e.g., "How much of your district's budget goes to teacher professional development?").

Portfolio Activity 8.3

State Governance Structures and Licensure

INTASC Principle 9: Commitment

The purpose of this activity is to acquaint you with your state's office of education and the teacher licensure procedures in the state. Locate the Web site for your state office of education (most of these can be found in Appendix B of this text). How does the administrative structure of your state compare to the structure discussed in the chapter? What procedures do you need to follow to be licensed as a teacher?

Chapter 9

IN A YEAR ROUND CLASSROOM WITHOUT AIR CONDITI
THIS IS YOUR
CHILD'S BRAIN
We Need Local Options Now!
IT'S TIME FOR THE EDUCATION REVOLUTION
TOO MANY KIDS $ $ NOT Enough Teachers

School Law

Ethical and Legal Influences on Teaching

At this point in your preparation to become a teacher, legal issues may seem distant, unrelated to your work, and perhaps not very interesting. Imagine, however, that you're an elementary teacher and are called to the main office to talk with a parent. Can you leave your class unsupervised? Suppose now that you're a high school teacher and you find a poem that strikes you as a powerful and moving commentary on love. Do you dare share it with your students without the approval of their parents? Perhaps you're a science teacher, and you've discovered a program on the Internet that you would like to use in your classes. Can you legally download and duplicate the information? The answers to these questions can be found in the school law literature.

Decision making is a central theme of this text, and professional knowledge helps teachers make wise and efficient decisions. Our goal in writing this chapter is to help you understand how legal issues can influence your life as a teacher. In it we try to answer the following questions:

- How do the law and ethics influence teacher professionalism?
- How is the U.S. legal system organized?
- What are teachers' legal rights and responsibilities?
- What are the legal issues involving religion in the schools?
- What are students' rights and responsibilities?

Let's begin by looking at two teachers struggling with legal and ethical issues.

This logo appears throughout the chapter to indicate where case studies are integrated with chapter content.

Case STUDY

Jason Taylor is a science teacher in a suburban school in the Pacific Northwest. The town in which he teaches is considering an open-space initiative that will limit urban growth. Environmentalists support the law because they believe it will help to preserve local farms and wildlife habitat in the area; business concerns in the town oppose it because of its potential to curtail economic growth. Jason talks about the initiative in class, explaining how it will help the environment. At the end of his presentation, he mentions that he is head of a local action committee and that interested students can receive extra credit for passing out fliers after school.

Some parents complain to the principal, claiming that school time shouldn't be devoted to political activity. When the principal calls in Jason to talk about the problem, Jason is adamant about his right to involve students in local politics, claiming that a part of every course ought to be devoted to civic awareness and action. The principal, unconvinced, points out that Jason was hired to teach science, not social studies, and warns that persisting on this path could cause Jason to lose his job. What should Jason do?

• • • • •

Sasha Brown looks at the two folders in front of her and frowns. Her job is to recommend one of two students from her school for a prestigious science and math scholarship to the state university. Although the decision will ultimately be made by a committee she'll be on, she knows that her recommendation will carry a lot of weight because she is chair of the math department.

One of the candidates, Brandon, is a bright, conscientious student who always scores at the top of his class. The son of a local engineer, he has a good grasp of mathematical concepts. The other candidate, Sonia, is probably not as strong conceptually but often solves problems in creative and innovative ways. She's also a female—and a female hasn't won this award in its 6-year history. In addition, Sasha knows that Sonia comes from a single-parent family and really needs the scholarship. Knowing this does not make the selection process any easer.

• • • • •

What would you do in these situations? What personal values would you use to resolve these dilemmas? What external guidelines exist to guide you? How does all this relate to teacher professionalism?

Laws, Ethics, and Teacher Professionalism

As you've learned from other chapters, professionals are responsible for making decisions in ill-defined situations, they have the autonomy to do so, and they base their decisions on a thorough understanding of their professional literature. Most teachers devote considerable time and study to their profession. They know they must understand the content they're expected to teach, for example. They look to the literature to learn how to represent content in ways that make sense to learners, and they seek insights into the intellectual, emotional, and social needs of students.

Teachers must also be familiar with the legal and ethical aspects of their profession and have a good understanding of their professional rights and responsibilities. Unfortunately, research indicates that many teachers do not understand their rights and responsibilities and are ill-equipped to deal with the legal issues involving their roles in schools (Mayes & Ferrin, 2001; Stefkovich & O'Brien, 2001). This chapter examines the law and how it influences professional decision making. We begin by putting the legal aspects of teaching in a larger perspective.

The Law and Its Limitations

You're working in a middle school, and you see a fight between two students on the playground. Does the law address a teacher's responsibilities in a situation such as this? The answer is yes. You can't ignore the fight, because you're responsible for the safety of the children; in fact, parents have the right to sue a teacher if they can demonstrate that the teacher failed to protect students from injury, a problem labeled *negligence.* Should you physically break up the fight, or can you simply report it to the administration? As with many other situations, the law is vague and does not specify a particular correct response.

Laws regulate the rights and responsibilities of teachers, but they only partially guide our professional decision making. This is true for two reasons. First, laws are purposely general, so they can apply to a variety of specific situations. A teacher may need to protect students from injury by supervising a chemistry experiment, maintaining order at a school assembly, stopping horseplay in the locker room—not just by breaking up fights on the playground. Jason's dilemma at the beginning of the chapter is another case. The law *generally* protects a teacher's right to freedom of speech, but does it allow a teacher to campaign politically in the classroom and present issues that may not be part of the assigned curriculum? Unfortunately, the answers to these questions are not explicitly described in laws, so professional decision making is required.

A second limitation of laws is that they were created in response to problems that existed in the past, so they don't provide specific guidelines for future decisions. New situations often raise new legal questions. For example, what are the rights of students and teachers who have AIDS? (We examine this issue later in the chapter.) The use of technology (the subject of Chapter 12) provides additional examples: What kinds of materials can we legally borrow from the Internet? What are the legal limitations to software use in schools? What can be legally copied? Experts are wrestling with these issues, and preliminary guidelines have appeared, but educators must often make decisions based on their knowledge of the law and their own professional judgment. We see again why professional knowledge is so important.

CW

Increasing Understanding 9.1

Think back to your study of philosophical issues and education in Chapter 6. How does the section of text you're reading now relate to your study of that chapter? Explain specifically.

To answer the Increasing Understanding questions online and receive immediate feedback, go to the Companion Website at www.prenhall.com/kauchak, then to this chapter's *Increasing Understanding* module. Type in your response, and then study the feedback.

Ethical Dimensions of Teaching

The law tells teachers what they can do (their rights) and what they must do (their responsibilities). However, laws don't tell teachers what they *should* do. For information on appropriate conduct, they must turn to ethics. Ethics is the discipline that examines values and offers principles that can be used to decide whether or not acts are right or wrong.

Professional ethics are *a set of moral standards for acceptable professional behavior* (Corey, Corey, & Callahan, 1993). For example, the Hippocratic Oath is a code of ethics that guides the medical profession. In taking the oath, physicians pledge to do their best to benefit their patients (with both curative methods and kindness), to tell the truth, and to maintain patients' confidences. Other professions have similar ethical codes, which are designed to both guide practitioners and protect clients.

You were first introduced to the National Education Association's (NEA) code of ethics in Chapter 1 when you studied teacher professionalism (see Figure 1.7). The NEA code provides guidance to teachers in ambiguous professional situations such as the one described at the beginning of the chapter.

As with the law, codes of ethics are limited; they provide only general guidelines for professional behavior. Let's look again at Jason's dilemma to see why this is so. Under Principle I of the NEA Code of Ethics, Item 2 states that "the educator shall not unreasonably deny the student access to varying points of view." Has Jason been balanced and fair in presenting both sides of the environmental and political issue? A code of ethics isn't, and never can be, specific enough to provide a definitive answer. Jason must answer the question for himself based on his personal philosophy of education and, within it, his personal code of ethics.

The limitations of the NEA code are also apparent in the case of Sasha, the teacher who was deciding which student to recommend for a science and math scholarship. Item 6 of Principle I cautions teachers not to discriminate on the basis of race, color, creed, or sex, but it doesn't tell Sasha which student to choose. Judged strictly on academics, Brandon appears to be the better candidate. If Sasha believes that Sonia is less talented than Brandon, choosing her because she is female would be granting her an unfair advantage. On the other hand, Sasha may believe that Sonia's math talents are equal to (even if different than) Brandon's and that it is ethically valid to consider her financial need and the good that might result from giving recognition to a girl in a male-dominated area of the curriculum.

Professional ethics provide broad guidelines for teachers as they make decisions in complex situations.

CW

Increasing Understanding 9.2

Earlier we said that laws are limited because they're *general* and *reactive*—that is, written in reaction to problems in the past. Which of these two limitations also applies to professional codes of ethics?

In response to these complexities, teachers are often encouraged to "treat all students equally." However, even this edict isn't as simple as it appears on the surface. Sensitive teachers purposefully call on shy students to involve them in lessons, sometimes avoid calling on assertive students who tend to dominate discussions, and give students who have difficulty with English more time to answer questions and finish tests. Teachers treat students differently depending on their individual needs; professional ethics help teachers treat all students equitably, but not always equally.

These examples illustrate why developing your personal philosophy of education is so important. We saw in Chapter 6 that a philosophy of education provides a framework for thinking about educational issues and guides professional practice. Your personal philosophy will guide you as you make decisions about what is important and what is fair. Because the law and professional codes of ethics can provide only general guidelines, a personal philosophy will be essential in helping you make specific decisions each day in the classroom.

Having briefly examined the law, ethics, and their limitations, let's look more closely at the legal system in the United States.

The U.S. Legal System

Laws regulating schools and teachers are part of a larger, complex legal system, which exists at three interconnected levels: federal, state, and local. This legal system attempts to use peoples' rights and responsibilities to each other as the basis for defining fairness.

Federal Influences

Through amendments to the Constitution and specific laws enacted by Congress, the federal government plays a central role in defining the rights and responsibilities of teachers and students.

Constitutional Amendments Think about the following questions:

- As a teacher, how much freedom do you have in selecting topics to teach? Are you limited in what books and articles you can ask your students to read?
- Can you publicly criticize the administrators and school boards for whom you work?
- How much freedom do students have in running their school newspapers and yearbooks?

The First Amendment to the Constitution guarantees all citizens the right of freedom of speech (and as you saw in Chapter 5, it also established the principle of separation of church and state), but where do we draw the line with respect to the questions above? You certainly can't have your students read *Playboy* magazine, but how about *Catcher in the Rye,* a classic coming-of-age novel with explicit sexual references? Consideration of the second and third questions yields similar uncertainties.

The Fourth Amendment protects citizens from unreasonable searches and seizures. To what extent does this amendment protect teachers and students? For instance:

- Can school officials search students' backpacks and purses when they're on school property?
- Are students' lockers considered to be personal property, or can they be searched if school officials suspect drugs or weapons?

The Fourth Amendment provides general guidelines about search and seizure but doesn't specifically answer these two questions.

The Fourteenth Amendment states that " . . . nor shall any State deprive any person of life, liberty, or property without due process of law." What does "due process" mean in the context of schools? For example:

- Can teachers be fired without a formal hearing?
- Can students be expelled from class without formal proceedings?
- How long can a student be suspended from school, and what kinds of deliberations need to precede such a suspension?

Increasing Understanding 9.3

Which amendment is relevant to Jason's situation at the beginning of this chapter? Why?

Again, the Constitution provides general guidelines about due process, but specific decisions are left to teachers and other educators. These examples further illustrate why an understanding of legal issues is so important for beginning teachers.

Federal Laws The federal laws passed in Congress also may influence education. For example, the Civil Rights Act of 1964 states, "No person in the United States shall on the ground of race, color, or national origin, be excluded from participation in or be denied the benefits of, or be subjected to discrimination under any program or activity receiving federal financial assistance." This law was influential in ending segregation in schools around the country. Similarly, Title IX, passed in 1972, prohibits discrimination on the basis of gender and has been instrumental in helping equalize the amount of money spent on boys' and girls' sports.

State and Local Influences

States influence education by passing laws regulating teachers' qualifications, working conditions, and legal rights. For example, most states require a bachelor's degree to teach, and many are now requiring a major in an academic area.

States also create departments of education with a variety of responsibilities, such as determining the length of the school year and approving textbooks. They also pass laws creating local school districts, which are then legally responsible for the day-to-day functioning of schools.

The Overlapping Legal System

Overlapping levels of the legal system have been created to correspond to different levels of responsibility, but conflicts sometimes occur, and when they do, attempts are made to solve problems and disputes at a lower level before sending them to a higher one. Let's look at two examples.

***Case* STUDY** Brenda Taylor has been hired to teach American history at a rural high school. Three days before the school year begins, her principal informs her that she will be the debate team sponsor. She objects, saying she knows nothing about debate. When the principal insists, she looks into her contract and finds that a description of her duties includes the phrase "and related extracurricular activities." It doesn't mention the debate team. She complains again to the principal, but he is adamant. She writes a letter to the school board, which appoints a grievance committee. The committee rules in the district's favor. Brenda, not willing to back down, hires a lawyer, and her case goes to a state court.

• • ● • •

Henry Ipsinger likes his job in a suburban middle school but disagrees with the school's priorities. In college he had learned that middle schools are supposed to be for all kids, not just the academically and athletically talented. He especially objects to his school's participation in Academic Olympics, an interschool academic competition, and the school's emphasis on competitive football and basketball.

Henry isn't afraid to express his opinions, and he does so frequently at faculty meetings, to the consternation of his principal. When his concerns aren't addressed he takes his complaints to school board meetings. His complaints fall on deaf ears, though they do raise a number of eyebrows. He then tries politics, openly backing opposition candidates to the school board. Finally he goes too far; at the end of the school year, he is cited for insubordination and his contract isn't renewed.

Henry is livid. He hires a lawyer, claiming his First Amendment right to freedom of speech has been violated. The case works its way through the court system all the way to the U.S. Supreme Court.

• • ● • •

Can teachers be asked to perform duties in addition to their teaching responsibilities? Can their professional opinions cause them to be fired from their jobs? Both of these questions fall into a gray area called *school law* and are addressed by different court systems.

Because Brenda's and Henry's issues were different, their cases were dealt with in different ways and at different levels. Both cases started at the local level. Brenda's complaint involved conditions of employment, so her case moved to state courts because employment issues are state responsibilities. Henry's case went to federal courts because freedom of speech is a right guaranteed by the U.S. Constitution. In a similar court case, *Pickering v. Board of Education* (1968), the U.S. Supreme Court upheld a teacher's right to publicly criticize school district policies.

In the next section we examine teachers' rights and responsibilities, probably the most important dimensions of school law for teachers.

Teachers' Rights and Responsibilities

As citizens, teachers enjoy the same legal safeguards as all Americans, including freedom of speech and the right to due process. But because they are professionals entrusted with the care of children, they have responsibilities beyond those of other

Figure 9.1 Teachers' Rights and Responsibilities

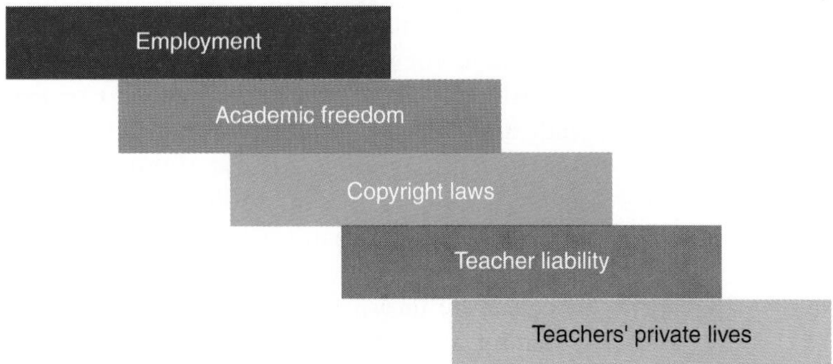

citizens, such as protecting their students from physical and emotional harm. In this section we examine five areas in which the law influences teachers' rights and responsibilities. They're outlined in Figure 9.1. Let's look at them.

Teacher Employment and the Law

One of the first things you will think about as you join the teaching profession is how to get and keep a job. Legal guidelines influence the process.

Licensure **Licensure** is *the process by which a state evaluates the credentials of prospective teachers to ensure that they have achieved satisfactory levels of teaching competence and are morally fit to work with youth.* Every state has licensure requirements, which typically include a bachelor's degree from an accredited college or university with a minimum number of credit hours in specified areas (such as those required for a teaching major or minor). In addition, prospective teachers are screened for felony arrests or a history of abusing or molesting children. Applicants who fail usually have the right to petition before a state professional practices board that considers each case individually.

Increasingly, teachers are being asked to pass competency tests that measure their ability to perform basic skills (reading, writing, and mathematics), their background in an academic area (e.g., biology, history, or English), and their understanding of learning and teaching (A. Bradley, 2000c). These tests are controversial because a disproportionate number of minorities fail them. However, when properly developed and validated, the tests have been upheld in courts (Fischer et al., 2003). Individuals who meet these requirements receive a teaching license that makes them *eligible* to teach but doesn't ensure employment.

Competency testing has become an increasingly controversial issue. For example, in 1996 lawmakers from North Carolina passed the ABCs of Public Education Law, which mandated that teachers in the state's lowest performing schools be required to take a test of general knowledge (A. Bradley, 1999a). Those who failed the test three times would be dismissed, even if they were licensed and tenured (we discuss tenure in a later section). The North Carolina Association of Educators threatened to sue, other critics argued that the tests would make it difficult to recruit teachers for low-income schools, and the state backed off.

A similar reform strategy was proposed in Massachusetts. Paul Cellucci, the governor at the time, proposed that teachers of low-performing math students be required to take a test measuring their understanding of math content (A. Bradley,

2000c). He further proposed that the results be made public but that no disciplinary actions for teachers be taken. The implementation of this proposed policy is still to be determined by the state's board of education.

Reformers' attempts to improve the performance of students by upgrading the quality of their teachers make intuitive sense. Without question, teachers must understand the content they're teaching. Further, teachers, perhaps more than any other professionals, need a broad background of general knowledge that will help them guide and inspire the students they teach.

However, although the use of tests to ensure teacher quality has been upheld in courts (Melnick & Pullin, 2000), critics argue that student performance depends on many factors other than teachers' knowledge, the most powerful being the students' own background knowledge and motivation (Kohn, 2000). Further, teacher competence can be measured in more effective ways, such as through direct observation. Watching a teacher actually work with students in teaching–learning activities—although admittedly more time-consuming and labor intensive—provides a better indication of teacher competence than a paper-and-pencil test. Politicians who pass teacher testing laws often don't understand this, however.

Contracts A **teaching contract** is *a legal employment agreement between a teacher and a local school board.* In issuing contracts, school boards must comply with laws that prohibit discrimination on the basis of sex, race, religion, or age. Contracts are legally binding for both parties. School boards can be sued for breaking one without due cause, and teachers must honor contracts they have signed (Kelly, 1998). Many states permit a teacher's certificate to be revoked for breach of contract, a practice growing more common as the competition for teachers increases (Archer, 2000b).

Teachers should carefully read their contracts and any district policies and procedures manuals covered by the contract. Extracurricular assignments, such as sponsoring school clubs or monitoring sports events, may not be specified in detail in an initial contract but can be required later. This is what happened to Brenda Taylor when her contract mentioned "and related extracurricular activities." Courts have generally upheld districts' rights to require these additional responsibilities but have also said that a reasonable connection must exist between additional assignments and a teacher's regular classroom duties. So, for example, a speech or English teacher may be obligated to sponsor a debate club but might not be legally bound to coach an athletic team if the teacher has no corresponding background experience.

Tenure **Tenure** is *a legal safeguard that provides job security by preventing teacher dismissal without cause.* Tenure is designed to protect teachers from political or personal abuses and to ensure the stability of the teaching force. It is grounded in the principle that teachers should be hired and fired on their professional merits and not because of who they know or don't support politically. Tenured teachers can be dismissed only for causes such as incompetence, immoral behavior, insubordination, or unprofessional conduct.

When any of these charges are filed, due process must be observed. The teacher must be provided with the following:

- Notification of the list of charges
- Adequate time to prepare a rebuttal to the charges
- Access to evidence and the names of witnesses
- A hearing, which must be conducted before an impartial decision maker
- The right to representation by legal counsel

- Opportunities to introduce evidence and cross-examine witnesses
- A school board decision based on evidence and findings of the hearing
- A transcript or record of the hearing
- The right to appeal an adverse decision

These safeguards, guaranteed by the Fourteenth Amendment, provide teachers with the same Constitutional protections enjoyed by the population at large.

Dismissal You'll work hard to become licensed and perhaps even harder to get a teaching position. Obviously, you won't want to lose your job; therefore, it's important to understand your rights so you'll be prepared should this possibility occur.

Most districts require a probationary period before tenure is granted (commonly 3 years). During this time teachers have a yearly contract and can be dismissed for a variety of reasons, such as believed incompetence, overstaffing, or reduced school enrollments. Although some states require districts to provide a formal hearing upon demand when a nontenured teacher is dismissed, this isn't common. Teachers uncertain about their rights during this period should check with their district, state office of education, or professional organization.

Dishonesty on the initial job application can also cause a new teacher to be dismissed. Students close to obtaining their degrees are sometimes offered positions during their internships. They agree but, due to unforeseen circumstances, are then unable to graduate or obtain a license. When districts discover the problem, they can either dismiss the teacher or lower his or her status to substitute teacher, resulting in lower pay and loss of benefits.

Reduction in force. Because of declining student numbers, budget cuts, or course or program cancellations, districts are sometimes forced to dismiss teachers. **Reduction in force** (or "riffing" as it's called in industry) is *the elimination of teaching positions because of declining student enrollment or school funds.* Typically, the district dismisses teachers with the least seniority—in other words, the last in are first out. Fortunately, "riffing" occurs infrequently and, as increasing numbers of students enter the educational system, should be even less common in the future.

Reduction in force can involve both tenured and nontenured teachers and is regulated either by state law or by collective bargaining agreements between districts and professional organizations (Fischer et al., 2003). Teachers faced with this possibility should consult representatives from their local professional organization.

Academic Freedom

Academic freedom refers to *the right of teachers to choose both content and teaching methods based on their professional judgment.* Although freedom of speech is protected by the First Amendment, professional academic freedom has limits. What are they? Consider these actual cases:

In an attempt to motivate his students, a teacher organized his classroom around a sports-competition theme called "Learnball." Dividing his students into teams, the teacher instituted a system of rewards that included playing the radio and shooting foam basketballs. His principal objected, and when the teacher refused to change his methods, he was fired. He sued to get his job back, claiming his freedom of speech had been violated. (*Bradley v. Pittsburgh Board of Education,* 1990)

An eleventh-grade English teacher was leading a discussion on taboo words. To illustrate his point, he wrote the four-letter slang word for sexual intercourse on the board. Parents complained and the teacher was dismissed. He sued to get his job back, claiming his freedom of speech had been curtailed. (*Mailloux v. Kiley,* 1971)

• • ● • •

Teachers are hired to teach a specific curriculum, whether that be first-grade math or high school English. State and district curriculum frameworks exist to guide teachers, and required textbooks are often identified. Within this general framework, teachers are free to teach topics as they see fit. Sometimes these topics and methods are controversial and may result in a teacher being disciplined or dismissed, as in the cases just mentioned.

In resolving disputes about academic freedom, the courts consider the following:

- The teacher's goal in discussing a topic or using a method
- The age of the students involved
- The relevance of the materials to the course
- The quality or general acceptance of the questioned material or methods
- The existence of policies related to the issue

Increasing Understanding 9.4

A factor considered by the courts in academic freedom cases is the age of the students involved. How do you think this factor influenced the decision in the case involving the taboo word? Would the verdict have been different if the class was in middle or elementary school? Why?

In the case of the teacher using the Learnball format, the courts upheld the district's dismissal. The court based its decision on the fact that this teaching strategy was not widely accepted and the teacher had been warned repeatedly by the administration to stop using it.

The case of the high school English teacher resulted in the opposite outcome. The teacher's job was reinstated because the court upheld the importance of two kinds of academic freedom: (1) the "substantive" right to use a teaching method that serves a "demonstrated" purpose and (2) the procedural right not to be discharged for the use of a teaching method not prohibited by clear regulations. The teacher's goal was for his students to understand taboo words and how they influenced literature, a topic that fell under the broad umbrella of the English curriculum. Had this not been the case, or if the teacher had been clearly warned against using this strategy, the outcome probably would have been different.

When considering the discussion of controversial topics or the use of controversial methods, teachers should try to decide if they fall within the scope of the assigned curriculum. If teachers choose to move forward, they should have clear educational goals in mind and be able to defend them if objections arise. Academic freedom protects knowledgeable, well-intentioned teachers working within their assigned responsibilities. If, as a beginning teacher, you're uncertain about an issue that could involve academic freedom, you should check with your principal or other school administrator.

Copyright Laws

As teachers, we want to share the most up-to-date information with our students. This can involve copying information from newspapers, magazines, books, and even television programs. Unfortunately, our desire to bring this information into the classroom can violate copyright laws (K. Murray, 1994).

Copyright laws are *federal laws designed to protect the intellectual property of authors, which includes printed matter, videos, computer software, and various other types of original work.* Just as patents protect the intellectual work of inventors, copyright laws protect the work of print writers, filmmakers, software creators, songwriters, graphic artists, and many others. To balance the rights of authors with the legitimate needs of teachers and learners, federal guidelines have been developed.

Copyright laws provide guidelines for teachers when they use technology in their teaching.

Fair use guidelines are *policies that specify limitations in the use of copyrighted materials for educational purposes.* Teachers may make a single copy of a book chapter, newspaper or magazine article, short story, essay, or poem for planning purposes, and they may copy short works (poems that are less than 250 words or prose that is less than 2,500 words) for one-time use in the classroom. However, they may not create class anthologies by copying material from several sources or charge students more than it cost them to copy the materials. In addition, pages from workbooks or other consumable materials may not be copied.

Videotapes and computer software pose unique challenges. They too were created by and belong to someone, and fair use guidelines also apply to them. For example, teachers may tape a television program, but they must use it within 10 days of taping. They may show it again for reinforcement but must erase the tape after 45 days. One copy, and no more, of software may be made as a "backup." Materials on the Internet may not be copied unless specific permission is given or unless the document is published by the federal government.

Increasing Understanding 9.5

If a copyright violation were to occur and the problem went to the courts, would these be state or federal courts? Why

These guidelines restrict teachers, but the restrictions are not usually a major handicap. Teachers may want to share the principle of fair use with students to help them understand its purpose and the ways that copyright laws help protect people.

Teacher Liability

An elementary teacher on playground duty was mingling with students, watching them as they ran around. After the teacher passed one group of students, a boy picked up and threw a rock that hit another boy in the eye, causing serious injury. The injured boy's parents sued the teacher for negligence. (*Fagen v. Summers,* 1972)

Field trips and labs pose special liability challenges to teachers as they work with their students.

A teacher was taking a group of first graders on a school-sponsored field trip to the Oregon coast. While some of the students were wading in the water, a big wave rolled in, bringing a big log with it, and one of the children was seriously injured. The parents sued the teacher for negligence. (*Morris v. Douglas County School District,* 1965)

• • ● • •

We don't often think of schools as dangerous places, but the combination of large numbers of children, small places, and youthful exuberance and energy can result in falls, scrapes, and accidents. In addition, field trips, science laboratories, woodworking shops, and physical education classes pose special risks.

Teachers are legally responsible for the children under their supervision. The courts employ the idea of *in loco parentis,* which means "in place of the parents," in gauging the limits of teacher responsibility. **In loco parentis** is *a principle that requires teachers to use the same judgment and care as parents in protecting the children under their supervision.* **Negligence** is *a teacher's or other school employee's failure to exercise sufficient care in protecting students from injury.* If negligence occurs, parents may bring a liability suit against a teacher or school district.

In attempting to define the limits of teachers' responsibilities in liability cases, the courts consider whether teachers

- Made a reasonable attempt to anticipate dangerous conditions
- Took proper precautions and established rules and procedures to prevent injuries
- Warned students of possible dangerous situations
- Provided proper supervision

In applying these principles to the rock-throwing incident, the courts found no direct connection between the teacher's actions and the child's injury. The teacher was properly supervising the children, and events happened so quickly that she was unable to prevent the accident. Had she witnessed, and failed to stop, a similar incident, or had she left the playground for personal reasons, the court's decision would probably have been different.

Field trips pose special safety and legal challenges because of the dangers of transportation and the increased possibility of injury in unfamiliar surroundings. Many school districts ask parents to sign a consent form to inform them of the trip and release school personnel from liability in case of injury. These forms don't do the latter, however; even with signed forms, teachers are still responsible for the safety of the children in their care. The courts ruled in favor of the parents in the Oregon case, because this type of accident is fairly common on beaches along the Oregon coast. The teacher, they ruled, should have anticipated the accident and acted accordingly.

CW

Increasing Understanding 9.6

How might these two factors—student age and special situations—have influenced the court's decision in the Oregon beach case?

As they supervise, teachers need to consider the ages and developmental levels of students, as well as the type of classroom activity. Young children need more direction and supervision, for example, as do some students with special needs. Science labs, cooking classes, use of certain equipment, and physical education classes pose special safety hazards. Professional organizations, such as the National Science Teachers Association, provide guidelines to help teachers avoid liability-causing situations in their classroom (D. Hoff, 2003c), and beginning teachers should be familiar with their guidelines. In addition, teachers should carefully plan ahead, anticipate potential dangers, and teach safety rules and procedures to all students.

In spite of conscientious planning, accidents can and do happen. Beginning teachers should consider the liability insurance offered by teacher organizations. These organizations also often provide legal assistance to members who are sued. In addition, for a small amount per year teachers can purchase a personal liability policy good for $1 million in damages (Portner, 2000b).

Reflect on This

To analyze a case study examining issues involved in teacher liability, go to the Companion Website at **www.prenhall.com/kauchak**, then to this chapter's *Reflect on This* module.

Child Abuse

Case STUDY Anita is a pleasant and attentive middle school student who seems socially well-adjusted. Recently, however, she has been unresponsive in class, and she comes to class somewhat disheveled. You watch her, but she will only glance back at you, refusing to maintain eye contact. You ask her to come in after school to talk, and she agrees, although reluctantly.

She nervously comes in, fidgets, and won't look at you. She replies, "Fine," when you ask her how she feels. You continue to pleasantly chat with her, but she is unresponsive, and not wanting to press her, you end the conversation by saying, "Please feel free to come in and talk any time if something is bothering you, . . . even if it's just a little thing." As she gets up to leave, you see that she moves rather stiffly.

"Anita, are you sure you're okay?"

"I fell the other day."

"But how did you hurt your back?"

Anita's expression suggests that a fall wasn't the cause.

"Did someone hurt you, Anita?" you ask firmly.

"Please, please, . . . you can't tell anyone," she blurts out.

• • ● • •

What are your responsibilities in this situation? The student begged you to say nothing. Do you honor her request? The answer is no. All 50 states and the District of Columbia have laws requiring educators to report suspected child abuse (Fischer et al., 2003). In addition, teachers are protected from legal action if they act in "good faith" and "without malice." Teachers suspecting child abuse should immediately report the matter to school counselors or administrators.

Teachers' Private Lives

Case STUDY Gary Hansen had lived with the same male roommate for several years. They were often seen shopping together in the local community, and they even went to social events together. Students and other faculty "talked," but Gary ignored the hints that he was homosexual until the principal called him into his office, confronted him with the charge, and threatened dismissal.

• • ● • •

Mary Evans had taught in Chicago for more than 8 years and didn't mind the long commute from the suburbs because it gave her an opportunity to "clear her head." She had been living with her boyfriend for several years, and everything seemed fine until one day she found she was pregnant. After lengthy discussions with her partner, she decided to keep the baby but not get married. When her pregnancy became noticeable, her principal called her in. She affirmed that she wasn't married and didn't intend to be. He asked for her resignation, suggesting she was a poor role model for her students.

• • ● • •

An individual's right to "life, liberty, and the pursuit of happiness" is one of our country's founding principles. What happens, however, when teachers' lifestyles conflict with those of the community in which they work? Are teachers' private lives really "private," or can teachers be dismissed for what they do in their free time?

In answering these questions, the courts have relied on a definition of teaching that is broader than classroom instruction. Teachers do more than help students understand English and history, for example; they also serve as role models for students. This results in greater scrutiny than most citizens receive. Other professionals, such as attorneys or physicians, might be able to lead lifestyles at odds with community values, but teachers might not. What *are* teachers' rights with respect to their private lives?

Unfortunately, clear answers in this area don't exist. Morality and what constitutes a good role model are contextual. For example, in the 1800s women's teaching contracts required them to do the following:

- Abstain from marriage
- Be home between the hours of 8:00 PM and 6:00 AM unless attending school functions
- Wear dresses no more than 2 inches above the ankle

More recently, pregnant teachers were required (even if married) to take a leave of absence once their condition became noticeable. Obviously, views of morality change. As the California Supreme Court noted, "Today's morals may be tomorrow's ancient and absurd customs" (Fischer et al., 1999, p. 296).

Moral standards also vary among communities. What is acceptable in large cities may not be in the suburbs or rural areas. Cities also provide a measure of anonymity, and notoriety is one of the criteria courts use to decide if a teacher's private activities damage their credibility as role models. **Notoriety** is *the extent to which a teacher's be-*

havior becomes known and controversial. For example, many young people are choosing to live together as an alternative to marriage. This lifestyle is less noticeable in a large city than in smaller communities.

Where does this leave teachers? Generalizations such as "Consider the community in which you live and teach" provide some guidance, as do representative court cases. Unfortunately, the law isn't clear with respect to the specifics of teachers' private behavior.

The issue of homosexuality illustrates how schools can become legal battlegrounds for people's differing beliefs. Some people believe that homosexuality is morally wrong, whereas others believe that it is either an inherited condition or a personal choice and has no relevance to schools. When the issue has gone to courts, they have generally ruled in favor of homosexual teachers.

In a landmark California case, a teacher named Marc Morrison engaged in a brief homosexual relationship with another teacher. About a year later, the other teacher reported the relationship to Morrison's superintendent, who reported it to the state board of education. The state board revoked his teaching credentials, arguing that state law required teachers to be models of good conduct, and that homosexual behavior is inconsistent with the moral standards of the people of California (*Morrison v. State Board of Education*, 1969). The California Supreme Court disagreed. The court concluded that "immoral" was so broad it could be interpreted in a number of ways and no evidence existed indicating that Morrison's behavior adversely affected his teaching effectiveness.

CW

Increasing Understanding 9.7

A teacher became involved in her city's gay rights movement, passing out leaflets at demonstrations and making speeches. Her school district warned her and then fired her for her activity. What legal issues would be involved here?

In other cases involving criminal or public sexual behavior (e.g., soliciting sex in a park), courts have ruled against teachers (Fischer et al., 2003). Notoriety was a key element in these cases. In addition, courts ask whether the conduct or behavior will directly affect the future performance of the teacher (Kelly, 1998).

The case involving the unwed mother further illustrates the murkiness of school law. A case in Nebraska in 1976 resulted in an unwed mother being fired because the

Teachers have a right to their own private lives but must meet community standards of acceptable conduct.

Teaching in an Era of Reform

THE TEACHER TENURE ISSUE

As you saw earlier in the chapter, tenure is designed to protect teachers from political or personal abuses and to ensure the stability of the teaching force. Recently, however, tenure has been under fire by some educational reformers, who believe it's holding back progress in the teaching profession. In 1997 lawmakers in Oregon eliminated tenure for teachers, replacing it with 2-year contracts (A. Bradley, 1999a). Georgia followed suit in 2000 by eliminating tenure for new teachers, and at the start of 2004 the governor of Alabama was working to pass legislation that would shorten the amount of time it takes to fire incompetent teachers (Reeves, 2004). Talk of similar measures has been heard in other states and districts across the country.

The Issue

Critics of tenure contend that it is outdated and unfair, providing teachers with protections that other professionals don't have. Further, they argue, it is unnecessary, because the present legal system provides recourse to teachers who feel they have been wrongly dismissed. Most importantly, critics assert, it is virtually impossible to remove a tenured teacher, regardless of ability. Therefore, tenure protects incompetent teachers.

One study of 30 school districts found that only slightly more than one tenth of 1 percent of teachers believed to be incompetent were either dismissed or

school board claimed there was "a rational connection between the plaintiff's pregnancy out of wedlock and the school board's interest in conserving marital values" (*Brown v. Bathhe,* 1976). In other cases, however, courts have ruled in favor of pregnant unwed teachers, including one in Ohio who became pregnant through artificial insemination (Fischer et al., 2003).

Although the law is ambiguous with respect to teachers' private sexual lives, it is clear regarding sexual relations with students (Hendrie, 2003b). Teachers are in a position of authority and trust, and any breach of this trust will result in dismissal. When teachers take sexual advantage of their students, they violate both legal and ethical standards.

Other teacher behaviors can also jeopardize teacher's jobs. Drug offenses, excessive drinking, driving under the influence of alcohol, felony arrests, and even a misdemeanor, such as shoplifting, can result in dismissal (Fischer et al., 2003). The message is clear: Teachers are legally and ethically responsible for being good role models for their students.

Teachers with AIDS In determining the rights of teachers with AIDS or HIV infection, the courts have generally used nondiscrimination as the legal principle guiding their decisions. The legal foundation for this principle was established in 1987 in a case involving an Arkansas teacher with tuberculosis (*School Board of Nassau County, Florida v. Arline,* 1987). The courts' dilemma involved weighing the rights of the individual against the public's concern about the possible spread of disease. The court ruled in favor of the teacher, considering the disease a handicap and protecting the teacher from discrimination because of it.

The Arkansas decision set a precedent for a California case involving a teacher with AIDS who had been removed from the classroom and reassigned to adminis-

persuaded to resign (A. Bradley, 1999a), and superintendents in these districts estimated that the percentage of tenured teachers who should be dismissed for poor performance is significantly higher. As another example, it took one California district 8 years and more than $300,000 in legal fees to dismiss one tenured teacher (J. Richardson, 1995). Because of difficulties such as this, districts typically respond to the issue by moving incompetent teachers from school to school instead of taking them out of classrooms.

Supporters of tenure argue that it was created to protect teachers from political or personal pressure and that it continues to serve that function. Teachers who have tenure are more likely to address controversial issues in class without fear of retribution. In addition, tenured teachers are more likely to become politically active, especially in school-related issues such as school board elections and bond issues.

Supporters also contend that teachers need protection from the potential abuse of power that can exist if a principal or other district leader, for unprofessional reasons, conducts a personal vendetta against a teacher. In addition, during times of teacher shortages, the job security that tenure provides is an incentive for teachers to go into or remain in teaching.

You Take a Position

Now it's your turn to take a position on the issue. State in writing whether or not you feel that teacher tenure should be abolished, and provide a two-page rationale for your position.

For additional references and resources, go to the Companion Website at **www.prenhall.com/kauchak**, *then to this chapter's* Teaching in an Era of Reform *module. You can respond online or submit your response to your instructor.*

CW

trative duties (*Chalk v. U.S. District Court Cent. Dist. of California*, 1988). The court ruled in favor of the teacher, using medical opinion to argue that the teacher's right to employment outweighed the minor risk of communicating the AIDS virus to children.

Religion and the Law

Religion provides fertile ground for helping us understand how conflicting views of education can result in legal challenges. The role of religion in U.S. schools is and always has been controversial, and teachers are often caught in the crossfire.

You know from your study of Chapter 5 that the First Amendment to the Constitution provides for the principle of separation of church and state. The amendment reads:

> Congress shall make no law respecting an establishment of religion, or prohibiting the free exercise thereof; or abridging the freedom of speech, or of the press; or the right of the people peaceably to assemble, and to petition the Government for a redress of grievances.

Each of the six clauses, or sections, of the amendment presents an important legal principle. The amendment begins with the **establishment clause,** *the clause that prohibits the establishment of a national religion.* The words "or prohibiting the free exercise thereof" is the **free exercise clause,** *the clause that prohibits the government from interfering with individuals' rights to hold religious beliefs and freely practice religion.*

Because religion plays an important role in many people's lives, the issue of religion in schools has become legally contentious, and teachers and administrators are often caught in the crossfire. Some of the questions that have arisen include the following:

- Can students and teachers pray in schools?
- Can religion be included in the school curriculum?
- Can religious clubs have access to public school facilities?

We answer these questions in the sections that follow.

Prayer in Schools

In the past, prayer and scripture reading were common in many, if not most, schools. In fact, they were required by law in some states. For example, Pennsylvania passed legislation in 1959 that required daily Bible reading in the schools (but exempted children whose parents did not want them to participate). The law was challenged, and the U.S. Supreme Court ruled that it violated the First Amendment's establishment clause (*Abington School District v. Schempp,* 1963). Nondenominational or generic prayers designed to skirt the issue of promoting a specific religion have also been outlawed. In a New York case, the Supreme Court held that generic prayers violated the establishment clause as well (*Engle v. Vitale,* 1962). Neither schools nor teachers can officially encourage student prayer; however, prayer is permissible when student initiated and when it doesn't interfere with other students or the functioning of the school (Walsh, 1999).

The law also forbids the official use of religious symbols in schools. For example, the courts ruled that a 2-by-3-foot portrait of Jesus Christ displayed in the hallway next to the principal's office was unconstitutional (Fischer et al., 2003). Also, the U.S. Supreme Court struck down a Kentucky law requiring that the Ten Commandments be posted in school classrooms (*Stone v. Graham,* 1981). To circumvent the law, some Kentucky educators and legislators advocated posting the Ten Commandments next to the Bill of Rights and the Magna Carta to present the commandments as an important cultural or historical document (Gehring, 1999a). The constitutionality of this strategy has yet to be determined.

Increasing Understanding 9.8

Which aspect of the First Amendment—establishment or free exercise of religion—would relate to the case involving the portrait of Jesus Christ? Explain.

These cases illustrate a legal trend: Officially sanctioned prayer and religious symbols—whether they come from school boards, principals, or teachers—are not allowed in public schools. They violate the principle of separation of church and state, which acknowledges religious diversity. Students may be Christians, Jews, Muslims, Buddhists, Hindus, or members of other religions. Imposing a particular form of prayer or religion on children in a school can be both illegal and unethical, because it can exclude children on the basis of religion.

Although the courts have been clear about denying prayer as a regular part of schools' opening ceremonies, the issue of prayer at graduation and other school activities is less clear. In a landmark case, a high school principal asked a clergyman to provide the graduation invocation and also suggested the content of the prayer. This was ruled a violation of separation of church and state by the U.S. Supreme Court (*Lee v. Weismann,* 1992). The school's involvement in the prayer was the key point; whether or not the Court would have banned the prayer if it had been initiated by students or parents is uncertain. In a more recent decision, the Supreme Court voted 6–3 against student-led prayers at football games in Texas (Walsh, 2000a). The Court concluded that students would perceive the pre-game prayer as "stamped with the school's seal of approval," thus violating separation of church and state.

Although the Constitution forbids the establishment of any particular religion in schools, a number of complex issues make this a controversial topic.

Religious Clubs and Organizations

Organized prayer in schools is illegal, but it may be legal for extracurricular religious clubs to meet on school grounds. In one instance, a student in Omaha, Nebraska, requested permission to meet with her Bible study group before school. Officials refused, concerned about the possibility of undesirable groups, such as the Ku Klux Klan, using the case as precedent. The U.S. Supreme Court ruled in the student's favor, stating that schools must allow religious, philosophical, and political groups to use school facilities in the same ways as other extracurricular organizations (*Board of Education of the Westside Community School v. Mergens,* 1990). The fact that the club was not school sponsored or initiated was central to the Court's argument.

A link between church and state may also be permissable in some situations involving religious organization: For instance, the Supreme Court recently approved the use of federally funded computers and library books for Catholic schools in Louisiana (Walsh, 2000a). The principle of separation of church and state will likely be revisited in future educational court cases.

Religion in the Curriculum

Case STUDY A high school biology teacher prefaces his presentation on evolution with a warning, stating that it is only a "theory" and that many theories have been proven wrong in the past. He encourages students to keep an open mind and offers creationism, or the Biblical version of the origin of the world, as an alternate theory. As part of his presentation, he holds up a pamphlet, published by a religious organization, that refutes evolution and argues that creationism provides a more valid explanation. He offers the pamphlets to interested students.

Where does religion fit in the school curriculum? Can a well-intentioned teacher use the classroom to promote his or her religious views? Given court decisions on school prayer, simplistic answers might be "no" or "never." But considering the enormous influence that religion has had on human history—as evidenced in art and literature—the issue becomes more complex.

Evolution is one point of tension. Concern over this issue dates back to the famous 1925 "Scopes Monkey Trial," in which a high school teacher (John Scopes) was prosecuted for violating a Tennessee state law that made it illegal to teach "any theory which denies the story of the Divine Creation of man as taught in the Bible and to teach instead that man is descended from a lower order of animals." Scopes argued that the law violated his academic freedom, contending that the theory of evolution had scientific merit and should be shared with his high school biology students. Scopes was found guilty of violating the state law and fined $100, but the decision was later reversed on a technicality.

Several states have since attempted to use legislation to resolve the evolution issue. In the 1960s the Arkansas legislature passed a law banning the teaching of evolution in that state. The U.S. Supreme Court declared the law unconstitutional, because it violated the establishment clause of the First Amendment. In 1982 the Louisiana legislature, trying to create a middle ground, passed a "Balanced Treatment Act," requiring that evolution and creationism be given equal treatment in the curriculum. The U.S. Supreme Court threw this law out, arguing that, instead of being balanced, it was designed to promote a particular religious viewpoint.

In a more recent case, the Kansas State Board of Education voted 6–4 to remove most references to evolution from state standards (Keller & Coles, 1999). State standards determine the content of state tests, so the decision gave local school boards leeway to exclude or downplay the topic. The decision, while not violating any legal statutes, was highly criticized, not only in the state, but across the country. Bill Nye, public television's "Science Guy," even joined in the criticism.

The broader issue of religion in the curriculum has also surfaced in several court cases. In one, fundamentalist parents objected to including literature such as *The Wizard of Oz, Rumpelstiltskin,* and *Macbeth* in the curriculum, arguing that these works exposed children to feminism, witchcraft, pacifism, and vegetarianism. A lower court supported the parents, but a higher federal court reversed the decision, asserting that accommodating every parent's religious claims would "leave public education goals in shreds." It supported the right of districts to use religiously controversial materials if they were useful in achieving important educational goals (*Mozert v. Hawkins County Public Schools,* 1987, 1988). Comparable cases in Alabama (*Smith v. Board of School Commissioners of Mobile County,* 1987) and Illinois (*Fleischfresser v. Directors of School District No. 200,* 1994) resulted in similar outcomes. When schools can show that learning materials have a clear purpose, such as exposing students to time-honored literature, parental objections are usually overridden.

Teaching About Religion in the Schools

Unfortunately, legal controversies have had a dampening effect on teaching about religion in the schools. Here we emphasize the difference between teaching *about* different religions and *advocating* a particular one. Religion has had an enormous impact on history (e.g., the Crusades, New World exploration) as well as art and literature. Avoiding the study of religion leaves students in a cultural vacuum that is both inaccurate and potentially dangerous (Nord & Haynes, 1998).

But how can schools teach about religion without provoking religious controversies? The U.S. Department of Education wrestled with this problem and developed the following guidelines (U.S. Department of Education, 1999c):

- Advocacy of religion by teachers and administrators has no place in public schools.
- Public schools should not interfere with or intrude upon a student's religious beliefs.
- Students may pray in private but cannot do so to a captive audience or compel other students to pray.
- Public schools may teach about the history of religion, comparative religions, the Bible as literature, and the role of religion in the history of the United States and other countries.

In addition, the directive reaffirmed students' rights to distribute religious literature and display religious messages on items of clothing, as protected by the free speech clause of the First Amendment. More recently, a provision of the No Child Left Behind Act requires states to certify that school districts don't prohibit students from praying privately during noninstructional time such as lunch and recess (Walsh, 2003d).

Increasing Understanding 9.9

A biology teacher wants his students to know how the Bible is the basis of the theory of creationism. Would this be legally permitted? Why? Under what circumstances wouldn't it?

Critics caution that the Bible should not be used as a history textbook, should not be framed and taught strictly from a Christian perspective, and should not be used to promote the Christian faith or religious values (Gehring, 2000b). The First Amendment Center (1999), a national organization promoting free speech, published the guidelines *The Bible and Public Schools: A First Amendment Guide* to address this issue. The guidelines, endorsed by the National Education Association, the American Federation of Teachers, and the National School Boards Association, recommend using secondary sources to provide additional scholarly perspectives with respect to the Bible as a historical document (Gehring, 1999b). These guidelines seem straightforward, but future legal battles over this emotion-laden issue are likely.

To view *The Bible and Public Schools: A First Amendment Guide* online, go to the Companion Website at **www.prenhall.com/kauchak**, then to this chapter's *Web Links* module.

Students' Rights and Responsibilities

As it does for teachers, the law also helps define students' rights and responsibilities. Understanding these rights and responsibilities can guide teachers and others in their treatment of students. Sharing this understanding with students allows teachers to teach them about the legal system and their rights and responsibilities as future adult citizens. Students' rights and responsibilities fall into several general areas, which are outlined in Figure 9.2 and discussed in the sections that follow.

Students' Freedom of Speech

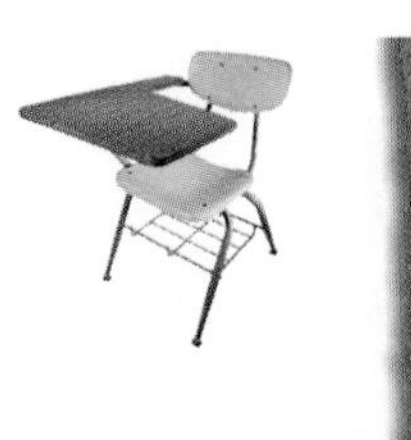

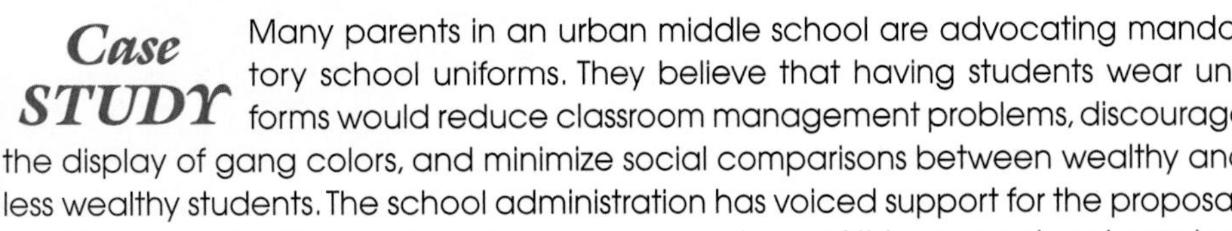

Case STUDY Many parents in an urban middle school are advocating mandatory school uniforms. They believe that having students wear uniforms would reduce classroom management problems, discourage the display of gang colors, and minimize social comparisons between wealthy and less wealthy students. The school administration has voiced support for the proposal.

The student editors of the school newspaper hear of this proposal and conduct an informal poll of students, which indicates that a majority of students are opposed to uniforms. The editors want to publish these results along with an editorial arguing for student choice in what to wear. The principal refuses to let them print the article. What are students' rights in this matter?

• • ● • •

As we've repeatedly seen, the First Amendment guarantees U.S. citizens freedom of speech, and we want our students to understand and appreciate this right as they prepare to be responsible citizens. Do they lose the right when they enter our schools? Yes and no. Yes, they have the right to express themselves in schools, provided doing so doesn't interfere with learning.

The landmark case in this area occurred in the late 1960s during the peak of the Vietnam War. As a protest against the war, three high school students wore black arm bands to school, despite the school's ban on such protests (*Tinker v. Des Moines Community School District*, 1969). When the students were suspended, they sued the school district, arguing that the suspensions violated their freedom of speech. The case went all the way to the U.S. Supreme Court, which ruled in favor of the students. The Court ruled that freedom of speech is an essential right for all citizens and that students' freedom of expression should not be curtailed if it isn't disruptive and doesn't interfere with the educational mission of the schools (Zirkel, 2001/2002).

Students' freedom of speech was tested again in 1986. During a high school assembly to nominate student government leaders, a student made a speech that contained a graphic and explicit metaphor comparing a candidate to a male sex organ. Not surprisingly, students in the audience hooted, made sexual gestures, and became disruptive. The student was reprimanded, and he sued, claiming his freedom of speech had been curtailed. This case also went to the U.S. Supreme Court, which ruled that "schools . . . may determine that the essential lessons of civil, mature conduct cannot be conveyed in a school that tolerates lewd, indecent or offensive speech" (*Bethel School District No. 403 v. Fraser*, 1986). In this instance freedom of speech did interfere with learning or the effective running of a school and could therefore be limited.

CW

Increasing Understanding 9.10

How are the two cases involving students' freedom of speech similar? How are they different?

With respect to freedom of speech, school newspapers pose a special problem. Court rulings have reflected the idea that a school newspaper is an integral part of a school's extracurricular activities and should reflect a school's goals (Zirkel, 2001/2002). In a pivotal case, students working on a newspaper wanted to print two articles, one detailing the personal stories of three anonymous, pregnant teenage stu-

Figure 9.2 Students' Rights and Responsibilities

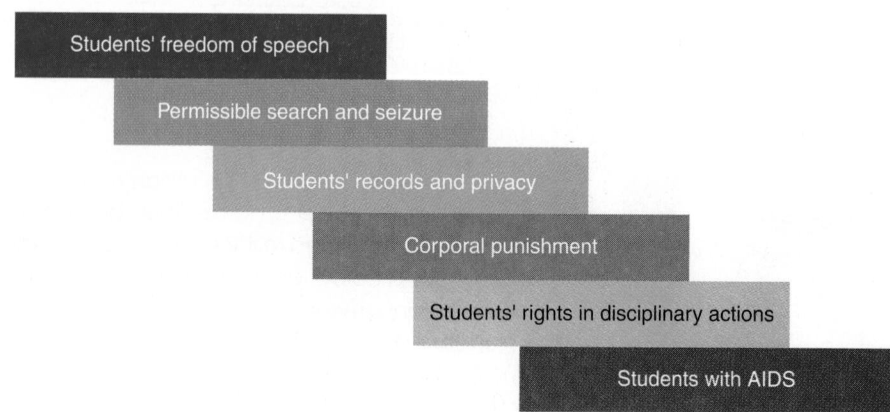

The law guarantees students' rights to freedom of speech, but students may not disrupt a school's main mission—learning.

dents, and the other dealing with the effects of divorce on children. The principal objected, arguing that the students in the first story might be identified because of the details in the articles. The newspaper authors sued, but the U.S. Supreme Court decided that school newspapers could be regulated in cases of "legitimate pedagogical concerns" (*Hazelwood School District v. Kuhlmeier*, 1988).

What should teachers communicate to students about freedom of speech? Whether publishing a newspaper, writing an essay, or giving a speech, students should be encouraged to express their views and opinions, both because ownership of ideas promotes learning and because it prepares them to take stands and express personal opinions later in life. However, students also need to learn that individual freedoms have limits; for example, these freedoms may not impinge on the rights of others. By encouraging the open exchange of ideas, while reminding students of their responsibilities to one another, teachers can create classrooms that become democratic models. This is a worthwhile ideal.

Permissible Search and Seizure

The Fourth Amendment to the Constitution protects U.S. citizens from unlawful searches and seizures, and warrants are normally required before a person or that person's property can be searched. How do these protections apply to students? Again, educators face dilemmas. We don't want to run our schools like prisons or teach students that personal privacy is not a right. However, as drug and alcohol use and violence on school campuses increase, many school leaders feel compelled to conduct searches of students and their property or even use entryway metal detectors to maintain the safety of the schools. Where do the courts draw the line on the issue?

Student freedom from unlawful search and seizure became an issue when a teacher discovered two girls smoking cigarettes in a restroom. When questioned by

School officials may search student lockers if they have probable cause to believe they contain something illegal or dangerous.

the vice principal, one student admitted smoking and the other (T.L.O.) denied the charge. The vice principal opened T.L.O.'s purse and found rolling papers in addition to cigarettes, which prompted him to empty the purse. Inside were marijuana, a pipe, empty plastic bags, a number of dollar bills, and a list titled "People who owe me money." (*New Jersey v. T.L.O.,* 1985). T.L.O. confessed that she had been selling marijuana at school and was sentenced to a year's probation by the juvenile court.

T.L.O. appealed the ruling, claiming that she was the victim of an illegal search. The U.S. Supreme Court reviewed the evidence and upheld both the verdict and the legality of the search, concluding that school searches are legal if they are targeted at a problem. Schools must have probable cause to conduct the search; that is, they must have a reasonable suspicion that the student being searched deserves the treatment (Zirkel, 2001/2002).

In addition to probable cause, the nature of the search is important. Does it involve passing through a metal detector or opening a school bag, or is it more intrusive? The courts have consistently upheld the legality of metal detectors at school entrances, asserting that such searches are nonintrusive (Zirkel, 1999). However, in one case a high school student was strip-searched for drugs after a police dog mistakenly identified her as carrying drugs. (Authorities later found that the dog was drawn to the young girl because she had been playing earlier that day with her dog, which was in heat.) The school district was required to pay damages to the girl's family (*Doe v. Renfrow,* 1980). While condoning searches for probable cause, the courts remain sensitive to the rights of students (Ehlenberger, 2001/2002). School lockers, however, are considered school property and may be searched if reasonable cause (such as suspicion of drug or weapon possession) exists.

The use of urine tests to detect drug use illustrates how legal issues can become convoluted. In one case, the Supreme Court held that random drug testing for student athletes was legal, arguing that the safety of students and the importance of a drug-free school environment outweighed the privacy rights of student athletes who were participating voluntarily (Zirkel, 2001/2002). A later case involved an Indiana youth suspended for fighting (Zirkel, 1999). To be readmitted after a 5-day suspension, the school required a urine test for drugs. In this case the courts ruled in favor of the student, defending the boy's right to privacy.

Students' Records and Privacy

Students' records—grades, standardized test scores, teacher comments, and letters of recommendation—can determine whether or not students are admitted to special programs and colleges of their choice. They also influence students' abilities to get jobs. What legal safeguards guide the creation and use of these potentially life- and career-influencing records?

In 1974 Congress passed the *Family Educational Rights and Privacy Act (FERPA)* as an amendment to the Elementary and Secondary Education Act of 1965. Also called the **Buckley Amendment,** FERPA is *a federal act that makes school records open and accessible to students and parents.* Under this act schools must do the following:

1. Inform parents of their rights regarding their child's records
2. Provide parents access to their child's records
3. Maintain procedures that allow parents to challenge and possibly amend information that they believe is inaccurate
4. Protect parents from disclosure of confidential information to third parties without their consent

The law doesn't guarantee access to all student records, however. Teachers may jot down notes during a busy school day, such as reminders about a student's behavior that will help the teacher decide whether to refer the child for special education testing. These notes cannot be made public without the teacher's consent. Also, a teacher's letter of recommendation may remain confidential if students waive their rights to access. To protect teachers in these situations, the Buckley Amendment excludes teachers' private notes, grade books, or correspondence with administrators.

A recent court case further defined the types of information protected by the Buckley Amendment (Walsh, 2002d). A mother in Oklahoma objected to the practice of having her children's papers graded by other students and the results called out in class. She claimed this violated her children's rights to privacy, and a federal circuit court agreed. However, in a unanimous decision, the U.S. Supreme Court overturned the lower court's decision. The Supreme Court concluded that the term *education records* did not cover student homework or classroom work.

CW

Increasing Understanding 9.11

You are a high school teacher and receive a letter from a prospective employer asking you to provide a recommendation for one of your former students. You are also asked to fill out a form with information about the student's grade point average. What are the legal aspects of this request?

Administrators and teachers have mixed feelings about the Buckley Amendment because of the extra effort and paperwork required to put these procedural safeguards into place, and because of potential encroachments into teachers' private records. However, the law has improved parents' access to information as they try to make sound decisions about their children, and it has made school officials more sensitive to the importance of confidentiality for students' and parents' needs for information.

Corporal Punishment

In one Pennsylvania elementary school, a 36-year-old, 6-foot-tall, 210-pound school principal paddled a 45-pound first-grade boy four different times during a school day for a total of 60 to 70 swats. After the incident the boy needed psychological counseling, cried frequently, and had nightmares and trouble sleeping. (*Commonwealth of Pennsylvania v. Douglass,* 1991)

The Fayette County Board of Education in Tennessee specified in 1994 that any paddles used to discipline students must be

- Not less than ⅜ inch or more than ½ inch thick
- Free of splinters
- Constructed of quality white ash
- Three inches wide (except the handle) and not more than 15 inches long for grades K–5
- Three and a half inches wide (except the handle) and not more than 18 inches long for grades 6–12

Students can receive a maximum of three swats with these district-approved paddles. (Johnston, 1994)

Corporal punishment is highly controversial, both because of the legal issues involved and because using physical punishment as a disciplinary tool is questionable. In a 1977 landmark case the U.S. Supreme Court ruled that corporal punishment in schools is not a violation of the Eighth Amendment to the Constitution (which prohibits cruel and unusual punishment). The Court further ruled that states may authorize corporal punishment without prior hearing and without the prior permission of parents (*Ingraham v. Wright,* 1977). As of 2004, it was prohibited in 28 states and the District of Columbia, which means the door is left open for the use of corporal punishment in the remaining 22 states (Center for Effective Discipline, n.d.). So where does that leave prospective teachers?

CW

Increasing Understanding 9.12

How would these guidelines apply to the Pennsylvania principal who paddled a first grader?

In the states where corporal punishment is permitted, legal guidelines suggest teachers may use corporal punishment under the following conditions:

- The punishment is intended to correct misbehavior.
- Administering the punishment doesn't involve anger or malice.
- The punishment is neither cruel nor excessive and doesn't result in lasting injury.

Teachers considering this disciplinary option should also ask themselves several questions:

- Is this the best way to teach students about inappropriate behavior?
- Would other options be more effective in encouraging students to consider their behaviors and the effects of those behaviors on others?
- What does corporal punishment teach children about the use of force to solve problems?

Behavioral psychologists have this to say about corporal punishment:

> There should never be a need to use physical punishment with a regular classroom population. If there are severe behavior problems that cannot be treated by other response-weakening techniques in conjunction with positive reinforcement, the classroom structure and the teaching procedures should be carefully examined. (Jenson, Sloane, & Young, 1988, pp. 110–111)

Their point is a good one; corporal punishment should be avoided in all but the most extreme conditions.

Students' Rights in Disciplinary Actions

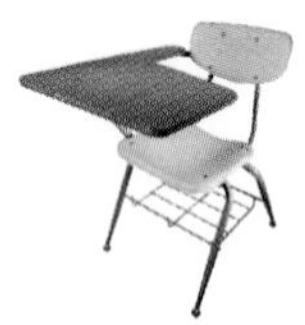

Case STUDY Jessie Tynes, a sixth-grade teacher, turned around just in time to see Billy punch Jared.

"Billy, what did I tell you about keeping your hands to yourself?" the teacher demanded. "This school and my classroom have no room for this kind of nonsense! You're out of this class until I meet with your parents. Come with me to the principal's office where you'll sit until we can solve this problem of keeping your hands to yourself."

Sean, a high school junior, was walking to his locker when someone reached in from behind to knock his books on the floor. When he turned around, he saw Dave standing behind him with a smirk on his face. Losing his temper, Sean pushed Dave. A scuffle began, but it was broken up by Mr. Higgins, the vice principal. Both students received 10-day suspensions from school.

CW

Increasing Understanding 9.13

What amendment to the Constitution guarantees students due process? (Hint: Under what circumstances are teachers guaranteed due process?)

How are the problems similar? How are they different? What legal guidelines assist educators as they try to deal fairly and effectively with school discipline problems? Both incidents involve infractions of school rules, but they differ in the severity of the problem and resulting actions. These differences are important when the courts consider *due process*, a central issue with respect to students' rights.

Students have a right to an education, and the courts specify that limiting this right can occur only when due process is followed. However, the courts also acknowledge the rights of schools to discipline students in the day-to-day running of schools.

Suspending Billy from class, for example, would be considered an internal affair best resolved by his teacher, parents, and himself. Unless a suspension lasts longer than 10 days or results in expulsion from school, teachers and administrators are generally free to discipline as they see fit, assuming the punishment is fair and administered equitably.

Actions that lead to out-of-school suspensions, such as the incident between Sean and Dave, entry on a student's record, or permanent expulsion require more formalized safeguards. These include the following:

1. A written notice specifying charges and the time and place of a fair, impartial hearing
2. A description of the procedures to be used, including the nature of evidence and names of witnesses
3. The right of students to legal counsel and to cross-examine and present their own evidence
4. A written or taped record of the proceedings as well as the findings and recommendations
5. The right of appeal

As we see from this list, the procedures involved in long-term (longer than 10 days) suspensions and expulsions are quite detailed and formal (Zirkel, 2001/2002). Whether due process means that students have a right to a lawyer during suspension proceedings remains unclear, however. A current court case in North Carolina involving this issue could set a national precedent (Bowman, 2003). Due process rights exist to safeguard students' rights to an education, an economic necessity in today's modern world. They also consume time and energy, so suspensions are generally used only as a last resort.

Students with AIDS

AIDS (acquired immune deficiency syndrome) became a major health and legal issue in the schools in the 1980s. Previously thought to be limited to sexually active gay men and drug users who shared hypodermic needles, AIDS entered the school-age population through contaminated blood transfusions.

Battle lines were quickly drawn. Concerned parents worried that the AIDS virus would be spread in school through either casual contact or the sometimes rough-and-tumble world of children on playgrounds. Parents of children with AIDS wanted their children to have access to as normal an education as possible. The courts were soon drawn into the fray.

A landmark and precedent-setting case occurred in St. Petersburg, Florida, in 1987 and involved 7-year-old Randy Ray, a hemophiliac infected with the AIDS virus through a blood transfusion. Because of his condition and fears about possible spread

Exploring Diversity

AFFIRMATIVE ACTION

Affirmative action, *a collection of policies and procedures designed to overcome past racial, ethnic, gender, and disability discrimination,* was one outcome of the civil rights movement of the 1960s. Affirmative action was based on the belief that merely outlawing discrimination was not enough; to correct past discriminatory practices, society should take steps that would ensure racial and gender equity and balance in all aspects of society, including schools. Currently, advocates of some forms of affirmative action emphasize the educational benefits of racial diversity for all students.

The legal basis for affirmative action comes from at least three sources. The Fourteenth Amendment to the Constitution guarantees equal protection under the law. Titles VI and VII of the Civil Rights Act of 1964 specifically prohibit discrimination in federally assisted educational programs with respect to race, color, religion, sex, or national origin. The Americans with Disabilitities Act of 1990 extends similar protection to persons with disabilities.

Affirmative action affects schools in two important areas: hiring policies for teachers and admission policies for students. In an attempt to remedy past discriminatory hiring practices, a number of school districts were required under affirmative action guidelines to hire more minority teachers. The courts have generally upheld this practice if affirmative action is deemed necessary to reverse past discriminatory practices (Fischer et al., 2003). However, if discrimination was not seen as a problem in past instances, preferential hiring practices for minorities on criteria other than merit or qualifications are discouraged. For example, because of declining enrollments, a school district in New Jersey was forced to reduce the teaching staff in the business department of a high school by one teacher. Two teachers, one White and one African American, had equal seniority and were considered to be of equal quality. The school board decided to retain the African American, using affirmative action as a rationale. The White teacher sued, claiming she was being discriminated against, and the courts agreed, arguing that minorities

of the disease, school officials refused to allow Randy and his two brothers, who also were infected, to attend school. His parents first reacted by moving elsewhere, but when that failed to open school doors, they moved back to St. Petersburg and sued the school district.

A U.S. district court ruled that the boys should be allowed to attend school with special safeguards, including special attention to the potential hazards of blood spills (*Ray v. School District of DeSoto County,* 1987). Subsequent cases involving other students with HIV/AIDS have been similarly resolved, with courts holding that these children are protected by the Individuals with Disabilities Act of 1991 as well as Section 504 of the Rehabilitation Act of 1973, laws that prohibit discrimination against individuals with disabilities. Central to the courts' decisions has been the potential negative effects of exclusion on the social and emotional well-being of the child. The courts have been clear in rejecting exclusion as the automatic solution to the problem of dealing with HIV-infected students and instead have required schools to address the specific risk factors involved in each case.

had not been underrepresented in the district's teaching force in the past (*Taxman v. Board of Education of Township of Piscataway,* 1996). Subsequently, higher federal courts ruled in her favor, deciding that for affirmative action to be legal there must be a logical basis for its use (Fischer et al., 2003).

Affirmative action affects K–12 students in two ways (Walsh, 2002a). A number of districts nationwide attempt to achieve racially balanced schools through voluntary transfers across schools. In these cases a student from a poor-performing school would have the option to transfer to a better school elsewhere in the district. In addition, magnet schools, designed to provide diversity by attracting talented students, use race as one selection criteria.

Affirmative action cases have resulted in charges of reverse discrimination, with critics alleging that minorities and women have been given unfair preferential treatment in hiring and admission decisions. One such claim was made in 1974 by Alan Bakke, a White student denied admission to medical school. Bakke sued the school because minority candidates with grades and test scores lower than his had been admitted. The case reached the U.S. Supreme Court, which ruled in a 5–4 vote that Bakke should be admitted. However, in making its decision, the Court did not rule out other forms of race-conscious admission procedures (*Regents of the University of California v. Bakke,* 1978). Recently, the Supreme Court heard an affirmative action case involving the University of Michigan. In a close 5–4 vote, the Court upheld the practice of considering race in admissions decisions (Walsh, 2003a). The benefits of a diverse student body were central to the Court's decision. Experts predict that this decision will influence not only colleges and universities but also future efforts to achieve racial balance in K–12 schools.

The issue of affirmative action is likely to remain controversial in the future. Toward the end of the 1990s, voters in California and Washington supported legislation eliminating preferential admission policies in higher education (Dworkin, 1998). In addition, court cases have raised questions about the legality of racial quotas for magnet schools (Dowling-Sendor, 1999). Legal experts in this area conclude, "Whether affirmative action will be mended by government and supported by voters is a question that is likely to continue to challenge schools and colleges during the coming decade" (Fischer et al., 1999, p. 480).

AFFIRMATIVE ACTION

This ABC News video examines the issues around the recent U.S. Supreme Court decision on affirmative action policies at the University of Michigan. The video features a short clip of President George W. Bush calling the University of Michigan policy a quota system and shows the president of the University of Michigan defending the school's policies.

Think About This

1. What are the arguments for and against affirmative action policies in admissions?
2. How is a point-based formula system different from a quota system?
3. What are some educational benefits that might result from a diverse student body?

To answer these questions online and receive immediate feedback, go to the Companion Website at www.prenhall.com/kauchak, *then to this chapter's* Video Perspectives *module.*

Decision Making

Defining Yourself as a Professional

This text is designed to help you answer the question, "What kind of teacher do I want to become?" We hope that, after studying this chapter, you will see the benefit of answering, "a knowledgeable teacher." Knowledge about the legal rights and responsibilities of teachers and students can be essential to your effective functioning as a professional.

The growing tendency to settle problems in court is a societal trend in our country. As one legal expert observed, "Americans are a litigious people" (Fischer et al., 1999, p. vii). We seek lawyers rather than talk, sue rather than compromise. The United States has more lawyers per capita than any other country in the world. Teachers, fearful of this trend, are increasingly seeking protection through professional liability insurance (Portner, 2000b).

How should you, as a professional, respond to this litigious climate? A simplistic response would be to embrace the confrontational approach in solving educational disputes. But this "my lawyer's tougher than your lawyer" approach to problem solving is inadequate for at least two reasons. First, it creates adversarial relationships within the profession. Second, and more importantly, it emphasizes standards of professional behavior that are minimal rather than ideal. Instead of looking to courts and lawyers for professional guidance, teachers should try to improve and enforce their professional code of ethics to make it a guiding light in legally and morally confusing times.

But where does this leave individual teachers who can be vulnerable to legal challenges? Teachers need to become "legally literate" with respect to their rights and responsibilities as professional educators (Fischer et al., 2003). Knowing their rights provides them with the authority to do what they know is right and just; knowing their responsibilities better enables them to effectively serve their students.

Becoming legally literate has another professional benefit: It will improve your teaching. Teachers who understand rights guaranteed by the Constitution can help students understand how these rights apply to them and their lives in and out of classrooms (Raskin, 2001/2002; Torney-Purta, 2001/2002). Also, teachers who understand issues involving freedom of speech, freedom of religion, freedom from unreasonable search and seizure, and due process are more likely to behave democratically in their classrooms than uninformed teachers.

Summary

Laws, Ethics, and Teacher Professionalism

Laws and ethical codes provide guidelines as teachers make professional decisions. Laws specify what teachers must and can do. Codes of ethics provide guidelines for what teachers should do as conscientious and caring professionals.

The U.S. Legal System

The U.S. legal system is a complex web of interconnected bodies. At the federal level the U.S. Constitution provides broad guidelines for legal issues, and Congress passes laws that impact education. However, most of the direct legal responsibility for running schools belongs to states and local school districts.

Teachers' Rights and Responsibilities

Teachers have rights and responsibilities as professional educators. Licensure provides them with the right to teach; a teaching contract specifies the legal conditions for employment. Most new teachers are hired on probationary status. Once granted tenure, teachers cannot be dismissed without due process.

Teachers' academic freedom is guaranteed by the First Amendment to the Constitution. However, in deciding upon issues of academic freedom, the courts examine the educational relevance of the content or method involved and the age of students.

Copyright laws, designed to protect the property rights of authors, provide restrictions on teachers' use of others' original materials. New questions about fair use are being raised by the increased use of videotape and material presented on the Internet.

Liability poses unique challenges to teachers. The courts hold that teachers act *in loco parentis,* and when they fail to protect the children under their charge, they can be sued for negligence. When deciding on issues of liability, the courts take into account the age and developmental level of students as well as the kinds of risks involved in an activity.

Teachers' private lives are not as private as some would wish. Teachers are expected to be role models to students, so what they do in their hours away from school is often scrutinized and, if illegal, can result in dismissal.

Religion and the Law

Religion provides a legal battleground in the schools. Organized prayer is banned in schools, but the courts have approved religious clubs and organizations and private expressions of student religious beliefs. Although the courts disapprove of religious advocacy, teaching about religion is legal when it can be justified educationally.

Students' Rights and Responsibilities

Many of the same issues of rights involving freedom of speech and due process that affect teachers also pertain to students. In addition, students are protected from unreasonable search and seizure by the U.S. Constitution, and their education records are protected by federal legislation called the Buckley Amendment.

Important Concepts

academic freedom (p. 319)
affirmative action (p. 338)
Buckley Amendment (p. 335)
copyright laws (p. 320)
establishment clause (p. 327)
fair use guidelines (p. 321)
free exercise clause (p. 327)
in loco parentis (p. 322)
licensure (p. 317)
negligence (p. 322)
notoriety (p. 324)
professional ethics (p. 313)
reduction in force (p. 319)
teaching contract (p. 318)
tenure (p. 318)

Developing as a Professional

Praxis Practice

Read the case study, and answer the questions that follow.

"Hi, Kyle. What are you working on?" Jan Trefino asked, as she wheeled the borrowed overhead projector into her neighbor's classroom.

"Oh, just trying to plan for next week. You know, try to stay a day or two ahead of the students. How did it work?"

"Great! Thanks a lot. It was a real life-saver. I had all these transparencies and. . . . While I have you here, can I ask you a question? Since you're a veteran, you seem to know everything."

"Yeah, right. Teaching for 4 years will do that to you," Kyle said, laughing. "What's the question?"

"Well, the unit coming up is on the labor movement in the U.S., and I'd like to connect it with some of the controversies we've been reading about in the local papers. I'd like to talk about the unionization of the migrant farm workers, but I'm a little nervous about getting into hot water. Any advice?"

"I'd say go for it. Students need to see how abstract ideas from the past relate to their everyday lives," Kyle responded. "Let me tell you about something that happened to me in my English class. We were reading a short story about a young runaway girl who was in trouble. The story hinted at, but didn't say explicitly, that she might be pregnant. So as we were discussing the story, I mentioned that there were agencies around like adoption agencies and Planned Parenthood to help people in that situation."

"Yikes, you're brave. Any fallout?"

"Not yet, though I may have overstepped my bounds when one student started preaching about morality and religion. I cut him off, saying, 'We can't talk about religion in school.' He gave me a funny look but didn't say anything more."

"So, you think it's okay to bring in clippings from the local newspaper about the union controversy?" Jan asked.

"Sure, if it's in the newspaper, why couldn't you?"

1. What professional legal issue were Jan and Kyle wrestling with, and what legal safeguards influence this issue?
2. How did the two teachers differ in terms of work experience, and how might this influence their curricular decisions?
3. Comment on Kyle's statement, "We can't talk about religion in school," from a legal perspective.

4. From a professional ethics perspective, what advice do you have for Jan about her discussion of local union controversies?

To receive feedback on your responses to the Praxis Practice exercises, go to the Companion Website at **www.prenhall.com/kauchak**, then to this chapter's *Praxis Practice* module.

Discussion Questions

1. What are the advantages and disadvantages of teacher tenure? What arguments might there be for a longer period of probation before granting a teacher tenure? A shorter period? Should teachers be reviewed periodically after tenure is granted?
2. What is the proper role of religion in the schools? In what areas of the curriculum should religion enter? Should teachers reveal their religious beliefs to students? What should a teacher do if a student shares his or her religious beliefs with the class?
3. Touching can be a powerful way of expressing caring or concern. Should teachers touch their students? How and under what circumstances? How might circumstances differ depending on the age and gender of students and the age and gender of the teacher?
4. What place should corporal punishment have in schools? How might the use of corporal punishment be influenced by the following factors: age of student, type of misbehavior, and age and gender of teacher?
5. Should teachers' private lives be placed under any more public examination than the lives of other professionals, such as doctors or lawyers? Why or why not?

Going into Schools

1. Obtain a teacher's contract from a local school district or teacher. What does it say about the following areas?
   a. Probationary period before tenure
   b. Tenure
   c. Extra teacher responsibilities
   d. Due process

   Compare your findings with information from the text.
2. Obtain a school's or district's policy handbook. What are the policies in the following areas?
   a. Student records and privacy
   b. Student freedom of speech
   c. Disciplinary guidelines and due process
   d. Student lockers and drug and alcohol searches

   Describe what you found in a paper, and discuss implications for you as a future teacher.
3. Interview a teacher about professional ethics.
   a. Does the teacher have a copy of either the NEA or AFT code of ethics? (If not, share the NEA Code of Ethics from Chapter 1.)

b. How helpful are these guidelines in professional decision making?
c. What changes would the teacher like to see made in these codes?

Reread the NEA Code of Ethics, and using the teacher's comments as a sounding board, decide how helpful this code of ethics would be for a beginning teacher.

4. Interview a teacher about the district's policy on reporting child abuse.
   a. Are the policy and procedures clear?
   b. Does the teacher know what his or her rights and responsibilities are in reporting child abuse?
   c. Has the teacher ever had to report child abuse, and if so, what was the outcome?

   In a paper, describe what your responsibilities would be in reporting child abuse. Also, list any unanswered questions you might have about the process.
5. Interview several middle or high school students to find out about their knowledge of legal issues. Ask them about their rights and responsibilities in the following areas:
   a. Freedom of speech
   b. Student records and privacy
   c. Search and seizure
   d. Student rights in disciplinary actions

   What do their responses tell you about their legal literacy? What could you do as a teacher to increase your level of legal literacy?

Virtual Field Experience

If you would like to participate in a Virtual Field Experience, go to the Companion Website at **www.prenhall.com/kauchak**, then to this chapter's *Field Experience* module.

Online Portfolio Activities

To complete these activities online, go to the Companion Website at **www.prenhall.com/kauchak**, then to this chapter's *Portfolio Activities* module.

Portfolio Activity 9.1

Assessing Your Knowledge of School Law

INTASC Principle 9: Commitment

Personal Journal Reflection

The purpose of this activity is to encourage you to assess your personal knowledge of legal issues facing the educational profession. To do this, review the Important Concepts found at the end of this chapter. How many of these can you define? Take the Self-Assessment Quiz for this chapter found on the Companion Website at **www.prenhall.com/kauchak**. What does your performance on these two measures tell you about areas that need additional study? Two excellent resources in this area are *Teachers and the Law* (Fischer, Schimmel, & Kelly, 2003) and *School Law* (LaMorte, 2002).

Portfolio Activity 9.2

School Law and Professional Ethics

INTASC Principle 10: Partnership

Sometimes professional ethics are backed by the law, but at other times they are not. The purpose of this activity is to acquaint you with connections between the NEA Code of Ethics and legal issues. Reexamine Principle I (Commitment to the Student) in the NEA Code of Ethics in light of the content of this chapter. Note places where the professional ethics overlap with legal issues.

Portfolio Activity 9.3

Deepening Your Knowledge of Legal Issues

INTASC Principle 9: Commitment

The purpose of this activity is to encourage you to deepen your understanding of one aspect of school law. Choose a topic from this chapter, and research it further. (*Teachers and the Law* by Fischer et al., 2003, is an excellent source.) In a short paper, describe the issue and implications it might have for you as a teacher.

Part 4

Teaching

Chapter 10
The School Curriculum

Chapter 11
Instruction in American Classrooms

Chapter 12
Technology in America's Schools

Chapter 10

The School Curriculum

In your work as a teacher, you'll continually be faced with two questions: "What am I teaching?" and "Why am I teaching that?" These questions are so fundamental that we almost forget that a great deal of thought, decision making, and sometimes controversy goes into answering them. The answers are important because they determine the school curriculum—what we expect our students to learn.

Our purpose in this chapter is to examine the K–12 curriculum and help you understand your role in shaping it as we try to answer the following questions:

- How does philosophy influence the curriculum?
- How do states and local districts attempt to control the curriculum?
- What is the relationship between textbooks and the curriculum?
- How do professional organizations influence the curriculum?
- What kinds of controversies exist in the curriculum?

This logo appears throughout the chapter to indicate where case studies are integrated with chapter content.

Case STUDY Suzanne Brush, a second-grade teacher at Webster Elementary School, had her students involved in a unit on graphing. After getting the students settled down for math, she began, "I'm planning a party for our class. While I was doing that, a question came to my mind that I thought maybe you could help me solve today. I need to know how I can figure out the class's favorite kind of jelly bean. How could we find out? If you can help me out, raise your hand."

Several students offered suggestions, and after considerable discussion, the class finally settled on giving each student several jelly beans and having him or her choose a favorite.

"It just so happens," Suzanne smiled, as they decided on the idea, "that I did bring in some jelly beans today, and you'll be able to taste these jelly beans and vote for your favorite flavor."

She then gave each student a Baggie with seven different-flavored jelly beans in it.

"Okay," she started when everyone was done tasting. "Right now I need your help. . . . Raise your hand, please, if you can tell me what we can do now that we have this information. How can we organize it so that we can look at it as a whole group? Jacinta?"

"See how many people like the same one, and see how many people like other ones," Jacinta responded.

"Okay, can you add to that? . . . Josh?"

"You can write their names down and see how many . . . like black," Josh answered uncertainly.

"That was right in line with what Jacinta said," Suzanne smiled and nodded. "Here's what we're going to do. We have an empty graph up in the front of the room," she continued, moving to the front and displaying the outline of a graph that appeared as follows:

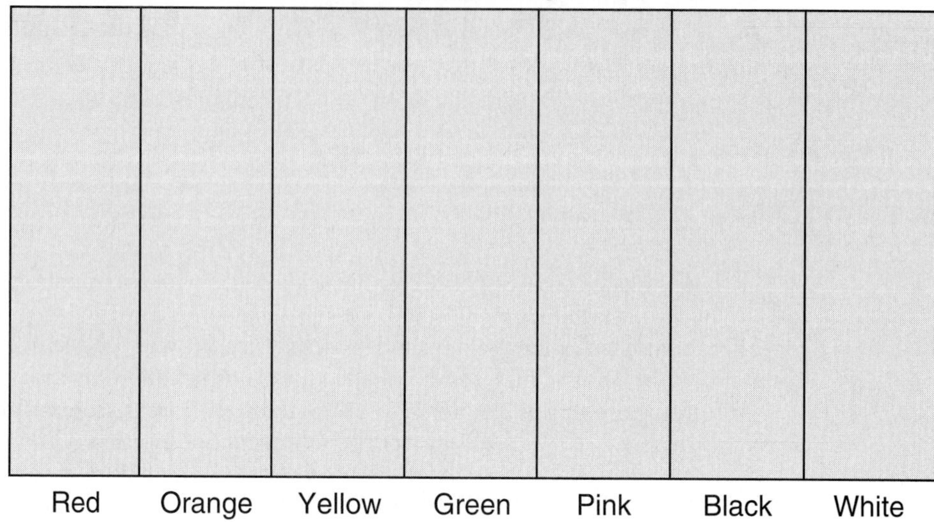

"Yes, Justin," she nodded in response to his raised hand.

"See which ones like red, get the people that like red and write it down; get all the colors like yellow, green, orange, black, yellow, white," he suggested haltingly, as Suzanne carefully monitored the attention of the rest of the students.

"That's a great idea. We're going to do that," Suzanne responded.

She explained that she had some colored cardboard pieces that matched the colors of the jelly beans for the graph. She directed students to come to the front of the room and paste the colored pieces that represented their favorite jelly beans on the graph. When the students were done, the graph appeared as follows:

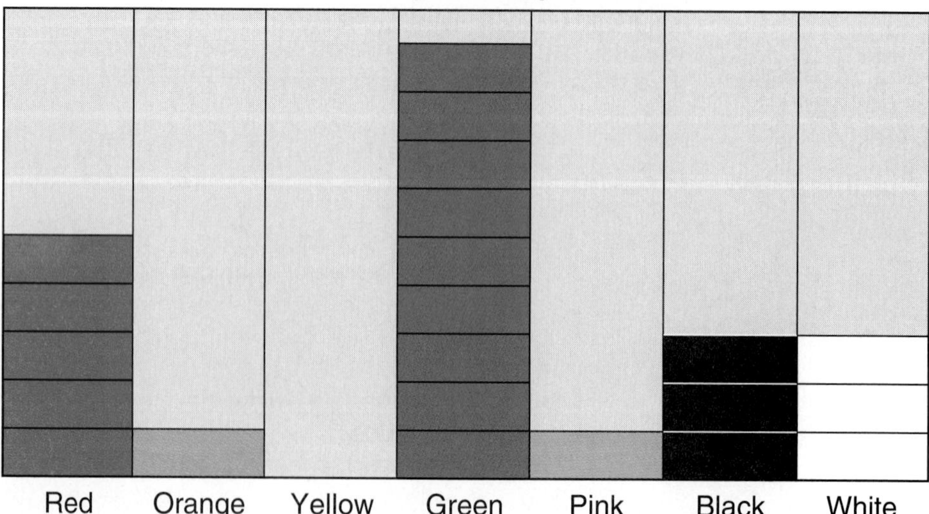

"I need your attention back up here, please," she continued. "We collected the information and organized the information up here on the graph. Now we need to look at and analyze the information. I need you to tell me what we know by looking at this graph. . . . Candice, what do we know?" she asked, walking toward the middle of the room.

"People like green," Candice answered.

"Candice said most people like the green jelly beans . . . Candice, how many people like green?"

". . . Nine."

"Nine people like green. . . . And how did you find that out? Can you go up there and show us how you read the graph?"

Candice went up to the graph and moved her hand up from the bottom, counting the green pieces as she went.

"What else do we know by just looking at the graph? . . . Justin?"

"There are three people that like black and three people that like white."

"Three people like black and three people like white," Suzanne repeated, pointing to the black and white columns on the graph. "Let's let Stacey add some more to that."

"No one liked yellow," Stacey answered.

"Nobody picked yellow," Suzanne repeated.

"Okay, what else do we know from looking at the bar graph? . . . Andrew?"

"One took orange."

"Only one person picked orange," Suzanne repeated.

"And one person picked pink. . . . Okay, now I'm going to ask you a different kind of question. . . . How many more people liked green than red?" she asked, changing the direction of the questioning. "How many more people liked the green jelly beans than the red? Look up at the graph. Try to find the information, set up the problem, and then we'll see what you come out with. You have to have a problem set up on your paper."

Suzanne watched as the students looked at the graph and began setting up the problem. She commented, "Quite a few hands, and a few people are still thinking," as she moved across the room. She stopped briefly to offer Carlos some help, continued watching the students as they finished, and then said, "I'm looking for a volunteer to share an answer with us. . . . Dominique? How many more people liked the green jelly beans than the red ones?"

"Nine plus 5 is 14," Dominique answered.

"Dominique says 9 plus 5 is 14. Let's test it out," Suzanne said, asking Dominique to go up to the graph and show the class how she arrived at her answer.

As Dominique went to the front of the room, Suzanne said, "We want to know the difference. . . . How many more people liked green than red, and you say 14 people, . . . 14 more people liked green. Does that work?" Suzanne said, pointing at the graph.

Dominique looked at the graph for a moment, shrugged her shoulders, grinned sheepishly, and then said, "I mean 9 take away 5."

"She got up here and she changed her mind," Suzanne said with a smile to the rest of the class. "Tell them."

"Nine take away 5 is 4," Dominique said.

"Nine take away 5 is 4," Suzanne continued, "so how many more people liked green than red? . . . Carlos?"

"Four," Carlos responded.

"Four, good, four," Suzanne smiled warmly. "The key was you had to find the difference between the two numbers."

After several more similar problems, she said, "I have one more question, and then we'll switch gears a little bit. How many people participated in this voting? How many people took part or participated in this voting?"

Suzanne watched as students turned to the graph. "Matt? . . . How many people?" she said as she saw that most students were finished and several had their hands raised.

"Twenty-four," Matt answered.

"Twenty-four," Suzanne repeated. "How many people are in the room right now?"

"Uhmm, 24," he answered.

"Is that where you got your answer?" she asked, leaning over him and glancing at his paper. "What was the problem you set up?"

"How many people voted," he answered.

"Matt said 24. Did anyone get a different answer? So we'll compare. . . . I can't call on you if you're jumping up and down," she said as she walked among the students, who were waving their hands energetically.

"Roberto?"

"Twenty-two."

"How many people got 22 for their answer?"

A number of hands went up, and Suzanne asked, "How many people got a different number?" A few students raised their hands.

"How did you solve the problem?" she asked, motioning to Robert. "That's the most important thing."

"Nine plus 5 plus 3 plus 3 plus 1 plus 1 equals 22," he answered quickly.

"Where'd you get all those numbers?"

"There," he said, pointing to the graph.

"He went from the highest to the lowest, added the numbers, and the answer was 22. . . . Matt, why isn't it 24?" Suzanne asked, walking back toward him, smiling.

Matt didn't reply.

"Raise your hand if you didn't put a piece of cardboard up there," she directed to the class, and two students who didn't participate raised their hands. Suzanne explained why the answer wasn't 24.

As time for lunch neared, Suzanne said, "Raise your hand if you can tell me what you learned this morning in math."

"How to bar graph," Jenny responded.

"How to bar graph," Suzanne repeated. "More important, when we set up a problem, what do we have to do to solve the problem. . . . Timmy?"

"Add or subtract."

"Okay, but what do we have to decide *before* we add or subtract?"

"Which numbers to use."

"So, we have to collect the information, and then we have to organize it. We organized it by setting up a bar graph, something that we can look at and talk about and use to decide what we need to do with the information. Then we set up some problems, and we solved them. It's a nice way to look at information and make decisions about certain things," she said as she ended the lesson.

• • ● • •

What Is Curriculum?

To begin this section, let's look at Suzanne's lesson. She wanted her students to understand that information can be simplified and made more usable by representing it in a graph. She also had her students practice basic math skills and problem solving by asking questions such as "How many more people liked the green jelly beans than the red?" and then having the students create similar problems.

Suzanne's lesson reflects decisions about both curriculum and instruction. Let's see how they relate to each other.

The Relationship Between Curriculum and Instruction

Educational theorists offer a variety of definitions of *curriculum,* and no single one is generally accepted (Armstrong, 2003; Parkay & Hass, 2000). Some common ones include the following:

- The subject matter taught to students
- A course of study, or a systematic arrangement of courses
- The planned educational experiences offered by a school
- The experiences students have under the guidance of the school
- The process teachers go through in selecting and organizing learning experiences for their students

Also, definitions of *curriculum* and *instruction* often overlap, and in some cases the notion of curriculum appears to subsume instruction. We will avoid these issues and, as we have in previous chapters, simply define **curriculum** as *what teachers teach and what students learn.* **Instruction** is *the ways in which the curriculum is taught.*

The curriculum focuses on learning goals and the reasons the goals have been selected; instruction is the way teachers help students reach the goals. For example, Suzanne wanted her second graders to understand that graphs help us represent information; that goal indicated a curriculum decision. To reach the goal, she had her students sample a variety of jelly beans, pick their favorite flavors, and represent their preferences on a large graph; the method reflected a decision about instruction. As an alternative, she could have simply explained why graphs are valuable, given her students some information, and had them graph it. (We examine instruction in detail in Chapter 11.)

Increasing Understanding 10.1

Using the overhead projector, you display two short essays for your class. One effectively makes and defends an argument; the other does not. Your goal is to help students learn to make and defend an argument in writing. Identify the curriculum decision and the instructional decision you made. Describe an alternative instructional decision (a different way of reaching your goal).

To answer the Increasing Understanding questions online and receive immediate feedback, go to the Companion Website at www.prenhall.com/kauchak, then to this chapter's *Increasing Understanding* module. Type in your response, and then study the feedback.

Dimensions of the Curriculum

When we describe the curriculum as "what students learn," we are not just referring to the contents of each day's lesson. We are referring more broadly to *the content, skills, values, and attitudes students learn in school.* In fact, experts often describe the curriculum as having four dimensions or parts (Eisner, 1994):

- The explicit curriculum
- The implicit, or "hidden," curriculum
- The null curriculum
- Extracurriculum

Let's look at each of these.

The Explicit Curriculum The **explicit curriculum** is *the curriculum found in textbooks, curriculum guides, courses of study, and other formal educational experiences* (Vallance, 1995). Suzanne's lesson on graphing was part of the explicit curriculum. It *includes everything teachers are expected to teach, learners are expected to learn, and what schools are held accountable for.* The explicit curriculum at the elementary level is heavily influenced by language arts and math, as we'll see in the next section.

Curriculum in elementary schools. To begin this section, let's look again at Sharon's and Susie's schedules, which you first saw in Chapter 7. As you may recall from that chapter, Sharon is a first-grade teacher and Susie teaches third grade. Their schedules appear in Table 10.1.

Table 10.1 Schedules for Two Elementary School Teachers

Sharon's First-Grade Schedule		Susie's Third-Grade Schedule	
8:30 AM	School begins	8:30 AM	School begins
8:30–8:45	Morning announcements	8:30–9:15	Independent work (practice previous day's language arts and math)
8:45–10:30	Language arts (including reading and writing)	9:15–10:20	Language arts (including reading and writing)
10:30–11:20	Math	10:20–10:45	Snack/independent reading
11:20–11:50	Lunch	10:45–11:15	Physical education
11:50–12:20	Read story	11:15–12:15	Language arts/social studies/science
12:20–1:15	Center time (practice on language arts and math)	12:15–12:45	Lunch
1:15–1:45	Physical education	12:45–2:00	Math
1:45–2:30	Social studies/science	2:00–2.30	Spelling/catch up on material not covered earlier
2:30–2:45	Class meeting	2:30–2:45	Read story
2:45–3:00	Call buses/dismissal	2:45–3:00	Clean up/prepare for dismissal

We also saw in Chapter 7 that both teachers are responsible for all the content areas, such as language arts, math, and science, and the amount of time each teacher devotes to different content areas is a personal decision.

The way elementary schools are organized has an important influence on the curriculum. To see how, take another look at the schedules. Remember that we're now focusing on what is taught—the curriculum. What do you notice? Some similarities include the following:

CW

Increasing Understanding 10.2

How much time does each teacher devote to math? What do these allocations suggest about the relative importance of language arts compared to math?

- Both teachers strongly emphasize math and, especially, language arts. In a 6-hour instructional day (subtracting the time for lunch), Sharon devotes an hour and 45 minutes and Susie a minimum of an hour and 35 minutes to language arts (including spelling). Both teachers schedule additional time for reading stories.
- Science and social studies receive limited emphasis.
- Art and music don't appear in the schedules, and neither does computer instruction, in spite of today's emphasis on technology.

Both teachers reported that they have computers in their classrooms, however, and that their students take turns working with them. Art and music are handled by resource teachers who come into their classrooms on a rotating basis. Both also reported that science and social studies, when taught, are usually integrated with language arts; they are seldom taught independently (S. Mittelstadt, personal communication, January 22, 1999; S. Van Horn, personal communication, January 21, 1999). This is common in elementary classrooms.

If you observe in elementary classrooms, you're likely to encounter schedules that vary somewhat from those in Table 10.1. These variations are important because they reflect decisions individual teachers have made about the curriculum. The emphasis on language arts and math and de-emphasis on science, social studies, and the arts reflect curricular decisions that teachers make.

Curriculum in middle schools. In Chapter 7 you saw that middle schools are specifically designed to meet the needs of early adolescents, helping them make the often-

The elementary curriculum is heavily influenced by language arts and reading.

difficult transition from elementary to high schools. Students must move from the security of one classroom and one teacher to a school in which they travel from classroom to classroom to learn from several teachers. The rationale for this curricular organization is greater emphasis on content; students need experts in various content areas to challenge them. Unlike in elementary schools, the content areas are each allocated the same amount of time (the length of one class period).

The middle school curriculum also attempts to focus on real-life issues that personally concern middle school students, however, and they attempt to make connections among the different content areas (National Middle School Association, 1995). Let's look at some teachers attempting to help students make these connections.

Case STUDY Carrie Fisher is a seventh-grade social studies teacher in an urban middle school. She and her team members have a common planning period twice a week when the students go to P.E. During this planning period they touch base on the topics they're teaching and discuss the students they share in their classes. The students are heterogeneously grouped, and major learning differences occur in all of their classes.

To begin today's meeting, Carrie announces, "I'll be starting the Civil War in about 3 weeks. At the end of the unit, each group will have to make a report on some aspect of the war. Is there any way I can connect with what you're doing in the curriculum?"

"I could have them read Crane's *The Red Badge of Courage*. That's on the district's optional list and really does a good job of communicating the realities of the Civil War," Jim Heath, the language arts teacher, offers.

"That would be great," Carrie replies. "That's just what they need—something to help them understand that history is about real people. How about you, Jacinta? Any links to math?"

"Well, we're just starting to discuss different kinds of graphs. If you can give me some different kinds of data from the Civil War, I can use them to illustrate how different kinds of data fit with different kinds of graphs. Then they can include different kinds of graphs in their final reports."

As the meeting progresses, the discussion turns to common problems the teachers are having with students. They all agree that turning in homework is a major issue and talk about having students keep a personal notebook in which each student would write down assignments. They agree to follow up on this with their homeroom groups.

• • ● • •

These teachers were trying to make the curriculum meaningful for students by helping connect topics across disciplines and to real-world applications. Although these connections are valuable at any level, they are particularly emphasized in elementary and middle schools.

Curriculum in junior high and high schools. We also saw in Chapter 7 that the organization of junior high schools is similar to that of high schools—hence the name. This organization influences the curriculum. Whereas one team of teachers in middle schools often have the same group of students, as we saw with Carrie and her colleagues, no such coordination exists in the curriculum for junior high and high schools. The curriculum in junior high and high schools focuses on separate disciplines and becomes more specialized. Some say it also becomes more fragmented.

CW

Increasing Understanding 10.3

In a block schedule (see Chapter 2), classes might meet for 90–100 minutes a day for a half year. Identify at least two ways in which block scheduling might influence the curriculum.

Integrated curriculum. The emphasis on content in junior and senior high school has implications for students. A high school student might study algebra from 9:20 to 10:10, English from 10:15 to 11:05, and so on through the rest of the day. Critics argue that compartmentalizing the curriculum in this way detracts from learning, because teaching and learning bear little resemblance to the world outside of school. Instead, they argue, schools should offer an **integrated curriculum** in which *concepts and skills from various disciplines are combined and related* (Parkay & Hass, 2000). As we saw earlier, both Sharon and Susie integrated science and social studies topics with language arts, and different forms of integration occur informally in many elementary classrooms. For example, teachers might have students read about a science topic and then have them conduct an experiment or interview someone who has expertise in the area. As a culminating activity, they might have students write about the topic, thus integrating science with language arts.

In middle and secondary schools, some efforts have been made to formally integrate topics within a content area. For example, in middle schools students typically take general science in sixth grade, life science in seventh, and physical science in eighth. Some schools integrate these content areas by having students study related topics from earth, life, and physical science in each of the middle school years. For example, using energy as a focal point, students might study the sun as an energy source in earth science, food as a source of energy in life science, and nuclear power in physical science.

Not all educators believe that integrating the curriculum is a good idea, however. Those who do cite the following benefits:

- Integrating a curriculum increases the relevance of content by making connections among ideas explicit (Barab & Landa, 1997; Diem, 1996).
- Integrating a curriculum improves achievement (Furtado, 1997).
- Integrating a curriculum promotes collaborative planning, which increases communication among teachers (Haschak, 1992).

Curriculum integration, which attempts to connect separate content areas, is most popular at the elementary level.

Opponents of curriculum integration counter with the following arguments:

- Important concepts and the structure of a discipline are often lost in attempts to make linkages with other content areas (Carter, 1997).
- Integrating a curriculum is difficult for teachers, since teachers don't have a deep understanding of all the content areas that are to be integrated (Carter, 1997; Roth, 1994).
- Planning and instruction for integrating a curriculum are inordinately time-consuming (Brophy & Alleman, 1991; Beane, 1997).

Curriculum integration is most popular at the elementary level, where a single teacher can relate several topics, and at the middle school level, where teams of teachers periodically meet to interconnect content areas. It is least common at the high school level, where a disciplinary approach to the curriculum is entrenched. National standards driven by subject-matter areas, as well as increased emphasis on testing, are likely to hamper integrative efforts at all levels.

An important question is, "Is there evidence that curriculum integration increases learning?" At present, the answer is mixed, with some research finding positive results. One study at the high school level examined the effects of integrating geometry and art in a unit that culminated in constructing greeting cards that contained elements of both (Schramm, 1997). Comments from students attest to the motivational benefits of interconnected topics (Schramm, 1997, p. 7):

> "Geometry has become real to me, not just a subject in school."
>
> "I took geometry but had a hard time understanding. Now I see how the Pythagorean Theorem relates to a three dimensional work of art."

Another study found that elementary teachers who integrated reading with science or social studies produced greater reading comprehension in their students (Portner, 2000c). Experts explained the results by suggesting that the students were more motivated to read about interesting topics such as pirates and motorboats.

Other research, however, found either no learning benefits or negative results (Carter & Mason, 1997; Senftleber & Eggen, 1999). Advocates of curriculum integration counter this negative evidence by arguing that the measures presently available are inadequate, unable to assess the "subtle and difficult-to-measure improvements in student learning" (Vars, 1996, p. 151).

The Implicit Curriculum A second dimension of the school curriculum includes the unstated and sometimes unintended aspects of the curriculum. Also called the *hidden curriculum* (Jackson, 1990) or the *informal curriculum* (McCaslin & Good, 1996), the **implicit curriculum** consists of *the kinds of learnings children acquire from the nature and organization of the school and the attitudes and behaviors of their teachers* (Longstreet & Shane, 1993). It is reflected in the ways teachers present their content, the kinds of routines that are established, the general climate of the classroom, and the unstated values and priorities that shape the school day.

A great deal of learning takes place through the implicit curriculum, and it begins when children are very young.

Students, even those of so tender an age, learn early what it takes to "do school." They learn early what a teacher does in a classroom. They learn early how they must behave in order to get on. (Eisner, 2003, p. 648)

As an example of the implicit curriculum, let's look back at some of the dialogue between Suzanne and her second graders.

Suzanne: How many more people liked the green jelly beans than the red? Look up at the graph. Try to find the information, set up the problem, and then we'll see what you come out with. . . . (She stops briefly to offer Carlos some help.) I'm looking for a volunteer to share an answer with us. . . . Dominique?"

Dominique: Nine plus 5 is 14.

Suzanne: Dominique says 9 plus 5 is 14. Let's test it out. (She asks Dominique to go up to the graph and show the class how she arrived at her answer.) We want to know the difference. . . . How many more people liked green than red, and you say 14 people, . . . 14 more people liked green. Does that work?

Dominique: (Looking at the graph) I mean 9 take away 5.

Suzanne: She got up here and she changed her mind (smiling). Tell them.

Dominique: Nine take away 5 is 4.

Suzanne: Nine take away 5 is 4. So how many more people liked green than red? . . . Carlos?

Increasing Understanding 10.4

Look again at the case study of the middle school teachers planning for curriculum integration. What are some aspects of the implicit curriculum reflected in their planning?

We said earlier that curriculum is what students learn in school. What did Suzanne's students learn from this brief episode? They may have learned the following:

- Math is supposed to be more than simply memorizing basic facts.
- Making a mistake is a normal part of learning.
- Learning is much more than sitting quietly as a teacher talks.

These are powerful messages of the implicit curriculum.

Students learn from the implicit curriculum in many ways. For instance, expert teachers create orderly classrooms in which learners accept responsibility for their own behavior (Emmer, Evertson, & Worsham, 2003; Evertson et al., 2003), and the teachers invite all students to participate in lessons (Kerman, 1979; McDougall & Granby, 1996). In these classrooms students learn that the world is an orderly place and that

Increasing Understanding 10.5

Explain why it is important for teachers to be aware that the implicit curriculum exists. Provide an example to illustrate your answer.

they are responsible for keeping it so. They also learn that all students are welcome and expected to participate and learn. These messages reflect the implicit curriculum and are important parts of students' total learning experience.

Sometimes the implicit and explicit curriculum conflict. For example, research indicates that students who have independent and questioning minds, who are assertive, who challenge authority, and who insist on explanations are sometimes rejected by teachers (Kedar-Voivodas, 1983). This results in a clash between the explicit curriculum, which focuses on learning and mastery of content, and the implicit curriculum, which rewards docile students and conformity (Apple, 1995). What do students learn when they're expected to listen passively as teachers lecture, or if competition for grades is emphasized? They may learn that "playing the game" and "beating the system" are more important than hard work and mastery of content. These are not messages we want schools to send.

With awareness, teachers can help ensure that the implicit, or hidden, curriculum of their classrooms is consistent with the explicit curriculum. Making learning the focal point of your teaching, modeling your own interest in the topics you teach, respecting students and expecting them to respect you and each other, all communicate values and are part of the implicit curriculum. The learning that occurs through the implicit curriculum may be some of the most important that students experience in schools (Eisner, 1994).

The Null Curriculum The decisions schools and teachers make about what they do not teach may be as important as what they do teach (Eisner, 1994). *Topics left out of the course of study* are referred to as the **null curriculum.** Teachers don't have time to "cover" everything, so they choose the topics they consider most important or with which they feel most comfortable. For example, social studies teachers typically cover the events of the American Civil War, but they are less likely to carefully examine factors such as slavery and racism that converged to trigger the war. These important but controversial cause-and-effect events then become part of the null curriculum.

Teachers demonstrate their professionalism when they think carefully about the topics they choose to emphasize and those they choose to leave out. As with the implicit curriculum, important messages about learning are tacitly communicated through the null curriculum.

Increasing Understanding 10.6

A student participates in a high school jazz band. Under what conditions would this be part of the explicit curriculum? When would it be part of extracurriculum? Explain.

Extracurriculum A fourth component of the curriculum, the **extracurriculum,** consists of *learning experiences that extend beyond the core of students' formal studies.* Virtually everyone has a concept of extracurriculum; it includes clubs, sports, school plays, and other activities that don't earn academic credit.

Although outside the explicit curriculum, extracurricular activities provide valuable learning experiences. Research indicates that a well-developed extracurricular program is an integral part of an effective school. Students who participate in extracurricular activities tend to be more motivated and get higher grades than those who don't (Black, 2002; Coladarcci & Cobb, 1995); unfortunately, research shows that low-ability students, minority students, and students placed at-risk often don't participate in extracurricular activities, which increases feelings of alienation and not belonging in school (Barr & Parett, 2001; Manning & Baruth, 1995).

Sports can exert a powerful positive influence on students, especially members of cultural minorities. Research indicates that participation in sports can reduce behavior problems and increase positive attitudes toward school (Jordon & Brooks, 2000; Sokol-Katz & Braddock, 2000). A comprehensive study of the effects of participation in sports on women found that girls who engaged in sports had lower teen pregnancy rates, were less likely to be sexually active, and had fewer sexual partners (Sabo, Miller,

Extracurricular activities provide valuable learning opportunities for both students and teachers.

Farrell, Barnes, & Melnick, 1998). Experts concluded, "Sports might . . . help girls cut loose from the conventional form of femininity that encourages them to establish self-worth mainly in terms of sexuality and heterosexual appeal" (Sabo et al., 1998, p. 22).

Students' desire—or even willingness—to come to school, their need to be part of groups, and their beliefs in their ability to succeed can be strongly influenced by their participation in extracurricular activities such as sports. Educators wanting to help students develop in healthy ways in this sometimes confusing world might look more closely at extracurricular activities for answers. Experts recommend that schools take a more proactive role in recruiting students for extracurricular activities, such as by making them aware of the activities available (Black, 2002). This is especially important for students placed at-risk, minorities, and students with exceptionalities, groups that traditionally have been underrepresented in extracurricular activities.

Extracurricular activities also offer valuable opportunities for professional growth in beginning teachers. Sponsoring clubs and coaching teams can provide you with extra pay, as well as opportunities to interact with your fellow teachers in different and personal ways. In addition, working with students in these activities can be emotionally rewarding and can provide you with insights into students' personalities and lives. Both of your authors coached sports and sponsored clubs while teaching in public schools and found the experience time-consuming but rewarding. We were able to get to know students in ways not possible in the regular classroom.

One controversy surrounding extracurricular activities is the policy of requiring passing grades in academic subjects to participate (Camerino, 2003). Critics of no-pass/no-play policies claim they penalize groups of students who may benefit from participation in extracurricular activities the most. Advocates claim that extracurricular activities are a privilege, not a right, and that requiring good grades serves as a motivator for students. Given the research on the positive benefits of extracurricular activities, no-pass/no-play policies, while well-intended, appear counterproductive.

Forces That Influence the Curriculum

To this point we've examined the curriculum as it commonly exists. But how does it come to be that way? Why do we see the emphasis on language arts and math in many elementary school schedules? Why are music and art de-emphasized? Answers to questions such as these can be found by examining the different forces that influence the curriculum. They are outlined in Figure 10.1 and discussed in this section.

The Curriculum and the Professional Teacher

One reason you're taking this course is to better understand your essential role in promoting student learning. In Chapter 1 we said that professionals are people who use their knowledge and understanding to make decisions in complex and often ill-defined

Figure 10.1 Forces Infuencing Curriculum

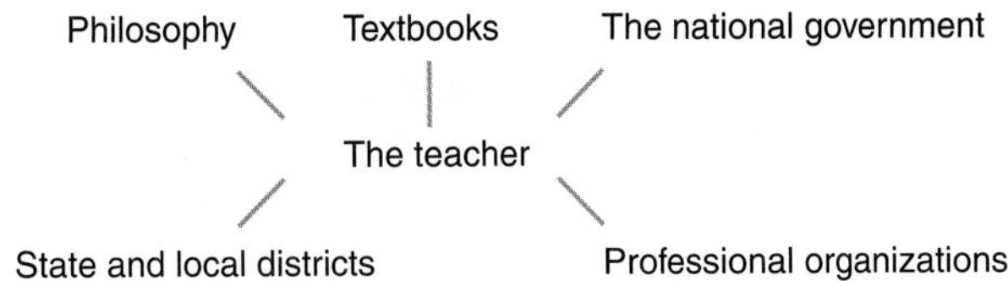

situations. Nowhere will professionalism be more important than in making curriculum decisions, and this is the reason the teacher is at the center of Figure 10.1.

Although a number of factors influence what is taught and learned, you, the teacher, are at the center of the process, and each of the elements of professionalism discussed in Chapter 1 comes into play. For instance, professionals frequently make curriculum decisions on their own (autonomy), and these decisions are based on professional knowledge and reflections from their past experiences. They're made with benefits to students as the primary goal, which is an essential aspect of professional ethics.

We see these elements of professionalism illustrated in Suzanne's, Sharon's, and Susie's work. Suzanne, for example, emphasized graphing and problem solving as part of her math curriculum and made a special effort to link the content to students' experiences with a hands-on activity. Because she believes that her students benefit from additional experiences with language, Susie allocates an hour and 5 minutes to language arts in the morning and sometimes teaches additional language arts from 11:15 to 12:15. Sharon teaches math in the morning, rather than the afternoon, because she believes that her first graders tend to be drowsy and less attentive after lunch.

These decisions are made by the teachers. No one told Suzanne how much emphasis to place on graphing and problem solving in her math class. She could have deemphasized them or even ignored them completely. Also, if Susie chooses to teach science on Monday from 11:15 to 12:15 and additional language arts on Tuesday during the same time, it is her decision, based on her understanding of her students' needs, the content, and her goals. These are professional decisions that only teachers can make.

Middle and secondary teachers have only slightly less autonomy than elementary teachers have. For example, a teacher in beginning algebra might choose to spend a great deal of time on basic skills, such as solving problems like $x + 2x + 3x = 24$, or she might choose to emphasize word problems such as the following:

Greg has some coins in his pocket, Sally has twice as many as Greg, and Juanita has three times as many as Greg. They have 24 coins altogether. How many does each student have?

Again, these are professional decisions based on understanding and knowledge—understanding what students need and how they learn and knowing how to represent a topic so it makes sense to students. One geography teacher might focus on the influence of geography on culture, whereas another might emphasize climate and physical features, such as mountains, rivers, and plains. Similar curricular decisions are made in all the content areas every day.

Teachers are essentially "alone" as professionals when they shut their classroom doors. Closing the door is symbolic, representing teachers' professional control over what is taught in their classrooms and how it is taught. But external forces, some subtle, others not so subtle, influence teachers' curricular decisions. We examine them in the following sections as we consider:

- The philosophical foundations of the curriculum
- The influence of textbooks on the curriculum
- The role of standards and standardized testing in curriculum decisions
- The impact of the federal government on the school curriculum

Philosophical Foundations: Sources of Curricula

We said earlier that the curriculum reflects learning goals and the reasons the goals have been selected. Because time doesn't allow equal emphasis on all goals, decisions have to be made about priorities. For instance, of the following, which would you consider to be most important?

Increasing Understanding 10.7

Teachers who feel strongly that basic skills are a crucial part of the curriculum are basing their belief most nearly on what educational philosophy? Explain.

- To thoroughly understand traditional content, such as important concepts and ideas from literature, science, history, and advanced mathematics
- To develop basic skills, such as the ability to read fluently, write effectively, and complete mathematical tasks
- To develop workplace skills, such as the ability to work with others and solve problems
- To develop self-esteem and the motivation to be involved in learning for its own sake

Answers to this question vary. Some educators suggest that the last goal is most important, arguing that intrinsically motivated people will adapt and acquire the skills needed to function effectively in a rapidly changing world. The development of the individual is preeminent in their view. Others favor the third goal, suggesting that society needs people who can solve problems and function well in groups. Still others advocate the first or second goal, asserting that academic skills, knowledge, and understanding are the keys to expertise and the ability to solve today's complex problems.

As we think back to Chapter 6, we see that these arguments are grounded in different philosophical positions, which reflect varying degrees of emphasis on the needs of individuals, our society, or the academic disciplines. Each of these positions has both strengths and weaknesses, as outlined in Table 10.2.

Many of today's curriculum controversies are rooted in these different philosophical positions. For example, the recent reform movement has resulted from widespread complaints about young people entering the workforce without the basic skills needed to function effectively in today's society (Hirsch, 2001). Reformers are making an essentialist argument, and we see this essentialist position reflected in Sharon's and Susie's work with their students. Their schedules reflect an emphasis on language arts, reading, and math, which are all basic skills.

Increasing Understanding 10.8

The emphasis on children's needs is most nearly based on which educational philosophy? Explain.

Although an emphasis on basic skills is currently prominent, the needs of individuals occupy an important place in the curriculum as well. An emphasis on the development of self-esteem has led to lowered standards and decreased achievement, according to critics (Pintrich & Schunk, 2002), but advocates counter that a major goal of schools should be to give students self-confidence about their ability to learn. Students can't learn if they dislike themselves and the content they're learning, advocates assert.

As a teacher, you will need to think about the students you are teaching, the content, and the time and resources that are available. Based on your understanding of these factors, you will then develop your own philosophy about the curriculum. This

Table 10.2 Philosophical Foundations of Curricula

Basis for Curriculum	Dominant Educational Philosophy	Advantages	Disadvantages
Needs of individuals	Progressivism	• Concern for individuals is placed at the heart of curriculum development. • Learner motivation is promoted.	• Efforts to respond to the special needs of each individual are virtually impossible. • Students may not be the best judges of their long-range needs, opting for shallow learning experiences.
Needs of society	Progressivism	• Students learn to integrate information from a variety of sources. • Curriculum is relevant, contributing to learner motivation.	• Society's needs change rapidly, often making curriculum obsolete. • Learners may be steered into career choices too early, limiting long-range opportunities.
Academic disciplines	Essentialism Perennialism	• Research indicates that expertise and problem-solving ability depend on knowledge (Bruning, Shraw, Norby & Ronning, 2004). • Schools and teachers are being held accountable, and accountability depends on discipline-based tests.	• Academic disciplines tend to artificially "compartmentalize" what students learn. • Students complain that traditional subjects are irrelevant.

is not an easy task, but every teacher faces these decisions. Consciously recognizing the task ahead is an important first step in the long professional journey of creating a productive and defensible curriculum for your students.

Textbooks

Increasing Understanding 10.9

How are educational philosophies reflected in textbooks? For example, what would you expect to see in a math textbook based on essentialism? a math textbook based on progressivism? Explain in each case.

You're a beginning teacher, and you're thinking about what you will teach during the next week. Where will you turn for help? If you're typical, you will reach for a textbook, the book you'll be using for the content area you're teaching (Zahorik, 1991).

For better or worse, textbooks are a fact of teaching life. Research indicates that teachers depend heavily on them; in one study of grades K–8, texts in some form were involved in instruction 95 percent of the time and influenced 90 percent of homework assignments (Venezky, 1992). In some of your education classes in college, you may be encouraged to set textbooks aside or at least not depend heavily on them. If your behavior is consistent with patterns identified by research, you're unlikely to do so (Zahorik, 1991). Some experts believe that textbooks are the most powerful influence on all curriculum decisions (Morrison, 1993).

Despite questions about quality, most teachers rely heavily on the use of textbooks.

Textbooks can be valuable resources, and we don't advocate that you abandon them. The following are some reasons to use them selectively and strategically:

- *Student needs.* The topics presented in textbooks may not be consistent with the specific needs of your students, school, or district. Following a textbook too closely then fails to meet these needs as effectively as possible.
- *Scope.* To appeal to a wide market, textbook publishers include a huge number of topics, more than teachers can possibly teach in the time available. Curriculum experts conclude that there is often twice as much material in texts and curriculum guides than is feasible for students to learn. They recommend that teachers select the most important concepts and skills to emphasize and concentrate on the quality of understanding rather than on the quantity of information presented (Marzano, 2003; Rutherford & Algren, 1990).
- *Quality.* Textbooks are sometimes poorly written, lack adequate examples, or even contain errors of fact. One study of history textbooks found, "Content is thinner and thinner, and what there is, is increasingly deformed by . . . politics" (Sewall, 2000), and an analysis of middle school science texts concluded, "It's a credit to science teachers that their students are learning anything at all" (A. Bradley, 1999c, p. 5). Similar problems have been found in other subject areas (Manzo, 2000a). Following some textbooks too closely can lead to shallow understanding or even faulty ideas that detract from learning.

On the positive side, researchers have found that innovative textbooks and other curriculum materials can be catalysts for change, encouraging teachers to rethink what and how they teach (Pittman & Frykholm, 2002).

To access up-to-date information about textbook quality, go to the Companion Website at **www.prenhall.com/kauchak,** then to this chapter's *Web Links* module.

What does this information mean for you as a teacher? At the start of this section of the chapter, we said that nowhere in teaching is professionalism more important than in making curriculum decisions. This is particularly true regarding textbooks. It's easy to allow textbooks to make professional decisions for you; this is what many teachers do when they teach the next chapter simply because it's there.

Textbooks can be a valuable resource, and they will certainly influence your curriculum decisions. However, you should not be afraid to de-emphasize, or even eliminate, topics and chapters in the text and include other topics that aren't in it. Curriculum decision making such as this requires understanding, effort, and energy.

Teachers report that the process of personal curriculum construction can be one of the most creative and satisfying aspects of teaching (Clandinin & Connelly, 1996).

To analyze a case study examining questions about using textbooks as a guide in making curriculum decisions, go to the Companion Website at **www.prenhall.com/kauchak**, then to this chapter's *Reflect on This* module.

Standards and Standardized Testing

A great deal has been written about Americans and American students lacking knowledge about the world. In surveys, for example, 60 percent of adult Americans didn't know the name of the president who ordered the dropping of the atomic bomb, only 42 percent of college seniors could place the Civil War in the correct half century, and 43 percent were unable to find England on a map (Bertman, 2000). A more recent survey didn't reveal much better map skills: Only about 15 percent of 18- to 24-year-olds could locate Afghanistan, Iraq, and Israel (Paxson, 2003). These examples focus on history and geography, but even greater concerns have been raised in math, science, and writing. The result has been a move toward **standards-based education,** *the process of focusing curricula and instruction on predetermined standards.* **Standards** are *statements specifying what students should know and what skills they should have upon completing an area of study.* An important component of standards-based education is the development of valid and reliable assessment systems that can be used to ascertain whether students have attained the standards (Armstrong, 2003). Standards are prescribed primarily by professional organizations and states and local districts, but they are also influenced by the federal government. Let's look at some of these attempts to influence the curriculum through standards.

Professional Organization Standards Professional organizations exist in virtually every teaching area. Math teachers, for example, might join the National Council of Teachers of Mathematics (NCTM), or teachers of students with exceptionalities might join the Council for Exceptional Children. Among other services, the organizations hold national conferences and produce a variety of publications. (A list of professional organizations, their Web site addresses, and brief mission statements appears in Table 13.5 in Chapter 13.)

Professional organizations also produce standards, and these standards will influence your curriculum. The following standard for middle school math students was created by NCTM. The standard is followed by *performance expectations,* which further specify what learners should be able to do.

• • • • •

Number and Operations Standard for Grades 6–8

Instructional programs from pre-kindergarten through grade 12 should enable all students to compute fluently and make reasonable estimates:

In grades 6–8 all students should:

- work flexibly with fractions, decimals, and percents to solve problems;
- compare and order fractions, decimals, and percents efficiently and find their approximate locations on a number line;
- develop meaning for percents greater than 100 and less than 1. (National Council of Teachers of Mathematics, 2000, p. 214)

• • • • •

To clarify curricular expectations, NCTM also provides assessment examples. For instance, the council suggests the following to assess students' ability to "work flexibly with fractions":

. . ● . .

a. If ▬▬▬▬▬ is ¾, draw the fraction strip for ½, for ⅔, for ⅚, and for 3/2. Be prepared to justify your answers.

b. ◄——+——+——► (1, 1½)

Using the points you are given on the number line above, locate ½, 2½, and ¼. Be prepared to justify your answer. (National Council of Teachers of Mathematics, 2000, p. 214)

. . ● . .

Knowing what students are expected to do helps teachers make professional decisions about what they should teach.

As another example, the National Council for the Social Studies (1994) presents 10 unifying themes that form the framework for their standards. The themes include culture; people, places, and environments; and civic ideals and practices. For the culture theme, examples of performance expectations at the early, middle, and high school levels, respectively, ask learners to do the following (National Council for the Social Studies, 1994):

- Give examples of how experiences may be interpreted differently by people from diverse cultural perspectives and frames of reference.
- Explain how information and experiences may be interpreted by people from diverse cultural perspectives and frames of reference.
- Predict how data and experiences may be interpreted by people from diverse cultural perspectives and frames of reference.

We can see how the performance expectations build on each other as students progress through the grades. Additional expectations exist for the culture theme, and each of the other themes has its own set of performance expectations as well.

Unfortunately, professional organizations representing content areas, such as math, science, and social studies, don't always speak with a single voice, so examining the curriculum standards generated by different groups can sometimes be confusing. Science is an example. The National Research Council (1996) published the *National Science Education Standards,* and the American Association for the Advancement of Science (1989) also published a list of recommendations. Both lists of standards are designed to achieve the goal of scientific literacy for all students by the time they leave school, but the lists differ in fundamental ways, such as emphasis on scientific literacy for all versus a deep understanding of science by a few. Teachers are often left to sort through these issues by themselves.

CW

Increasing Understanding 10.10

Look again at what is receiving increased emphasis in science. What educational philosophy is best reflected in this increased emphasis? Explain.

The goals of professional organizations don't always appear as standards and performance expectations. The National Research Council (1996), for instance, describes science goals in terms of "changes in emphasis." Examples of these appear in Table 10.3.

State and District Standards States also publish standards to influence teachers' curriculum decisions in different content areas. The following are some examples of standards in effect in 2003–2004:

. . ● . .

Science:

In Science, students in Missouri public schools will acquire a solid foundation which includes knowledge of

1. properties and principles of matter and energy
2. properties and principles of force and motion

3. characteristics and interactions of living organisms
4. changes in ecosystems and interactions of organisms with their environments
5. processes (such as plate movement, water cycle, air flow) and interactions of earth's biosphere, atmosphere, lithosphere and hydrosphere
6. composition and structure of the universe and the motions of the objects within it
7. processes of scientific inquiry (such as formulating and testing hypotheses)
8. impact of science, technology and human activity on resources and the environment (Missouri Department of Education, 1996)

. . • . .

Reading:
Goal: Determine meanings of words using contextual and structural clues, illustrations, and other reading strategies.

Students will

- use context clues to choose the correct meaning for identified words in the reading passage.
- use knowledge of commonly used prefixes and suffixes to help define words in context.
- use knowledge of contractions and possessives to help determine the meaning of words in the passage.
- use illustrations such as pictures, charts, graphs, or diagrams to determine the meaning of words in the passage. (Oregon Public Education Network, 2003)

. . • . .

Social Studies:
Grade Eight World History to 1000 A.D.

The standards for the eighth grade enable students to explore the historical development of people, places, and patterns of life from ancient times until about 1000 A.D. Students study the origins of much of our heritage using texts, maps, pictures, stories, diagrams, charts, chronological skills, inquiry/research skills, and technology skills.

8.1 The student will describe early physical and cultural development of mankind from the Paleolithic Era to the revolution of agriculture, with emphasis on

- the impact of geography on hunter-gatherer societies;
- characteristics of hunter-gatherer societies;
- toolmaking and use of fire;
- technological and social advancements that gave rise to stable communities; and
- how archeological discoveries are changing our knowledge of early peoples. (Board of Education, the Commonwealth of Virginia, 1995)

. . • . .

As you can see, these standards are stated in general terms. Not until they are translated into specific learning activities or test items do teachers or students have a clear idea of what should be learned or how it will be measured. This is another example of why teacher knowledge and decision making is so essential.

Table 10.3 Examples of Changes in Emphasis in Science

Area	Increased Emphasis	Decreased Emphasis
Facts and concepts	Understanding concepts	Knowing facts and information
Curriculum	Selecting and adapting curriculum	Rigidly following curriculum
Content coverage	Studying fewer topics in depth	Covering many topics superficially
Communication	Discussion and communication between teacher and students and students with each other	Answering factual questions presented by the teacher
Teaching practices	Guiding students in active inquiry	Presenting knowledge through lecture, books, and demonstrations

Source: National Research Council (1996).

The standards movement is widespread; virtually all states have specified standards for at least some of the content areas, and students as well as teachers are being held accountable for meeting these standards. The No Child Left Behind Act, described in Chapter 1, requires all states to create standards for what every child should know and be able to do for different subjects. Standards for math and reading must be developed immediately and standards for science must be developed by the 2005–2006 school year. Joan Baratz-Snowden, spokesperson for the American Federation of Teachers, summarized this trend, "It is a new day. Standards-based education is significantly different, and we have to prepare teachers to be successful in it" (Blair, 2000).

Curriculum guides. Every state publishes curriculum guides to assist teachers in helping their students meet prescribed standards. The organization of curriculum guides varies from state to state, but they generally include standards, learning activities, and student performance expectations that are sequenced by grade level. In addition, districts will sometimes publish their own curriculum guides to augment those published by the state.

CW

Increasing Understanding 10.11

You are required by your principal to follow state curriculum guides. You find some factual errors in one of the sections. As a professional teacher, what should you do? Explain.

These curriculum guides are one of the first things that teachers pick up as they plan, and teachers are often pressured by their principals to follow them closely (Cuban, 1996). We offer the same recommendations and cautions with these guides as we did with textbooks. Use them thoughtfully and selectively to create a curriculum that makes sense to you and your students. You will find, however, that it may be difficult to resist the pressures to follow curriculum guides because of the powerful influence of standardized testing (Kohn, 2000).

Standardized testing. Standardized testing also exerts a powerful influence on the curriculum. In virtually all states, standards correspond to standardized tests that measure the extent to which the standards are being met. As you saw in Chapter 1, whether or not students will be promoted from one grade to another, or even graduate from high school, often depends on their ability to achieve passing scores on these tests. Because the stakes are very high for these students, the term ***high-stakes tests*** is commonly used. These tests also become high-stakes instruments for districts, schools, and teachers, whose performance is measured by them.

Standardized testing unquestionably exerts a great deal of influence on teachers' curricular decisions. One elementary teacher, reassigned to a different grade level, described how test content affected her decisions about what to teach:

• • ● • •

When I came up to fifth grade, I really didn't know everything that would be covered in the fifth grade, so one of the teachers said, "Well, this skill will be on the achievement test, and you'll find this on the achievement test, and you'll find this on the test." And I know to teach my children survival skills that I had to teach those. Let's just face it, that's just the way it is. You know, I tell them, "This may be on the achievement test and this is something that I really want to stick." (D. Brown, 1991, pp. 102–103)

• • ● • •

As we saw earlier in the chapter, reading, writing, and math are strongly emphasized in the elementary curriculum. They are also the content areas for which students are most commonly held accountable; they are the most frequently tested. "What gets tested, gets taught" is a common maxim in education (Cuban, 1996).

Testing, a central component of current reform efforts, exerts a powerful influence on curriculum, or what is taught.

With the passage of No Child Left Behind, all states have adopted statewide testing systems. It is highly likely that the curriculum in your school will be influenced by standardized tests developed or adopted at the state or local level. As a beginning teacher, you need to be aware of the different kinds of tests your students will be required to take. Armed with this information, you can make wise professional decisions about what curriculum is best for your students.

Graduation requirements. In addition to standards and standardized testing, states and districts influence the curriculum through graduation requirements. In Chapter 6 we saw that the influential report *A Nation at Risk* (National Commission on Excellence in Education, 1983) called for more rigorous graduation requirements as one way to achieve higher academic standards. In addition, low national averages on the SAT and ACT have been blamed on students not taking enough core classes in English and math (Cavanagh, 2002). Many districts have responded by increasing the number of academic courses required for graduation (Olson, 2003b). Many states now require 4 years of English and 3 years of math in high school, with similar increases in science and social studies. Although some educators decry the overemphasis on certain "basic" subjects at the expense of others like art and music, the trend is likely to continue.

Increasing Understanding 10.12

To what educational philosophy—perennialism, progressivism, essentialism, or postmodernism—is the message of *A Nation at Risk* most closely related? Explain.

The Federal Government

As we saw in Chapter 5, the framers of the U.S. Constitution granted control of education to the states, rather than the federal government. However, the federal government has a long and rich history of involvement in education, and this role has increased rather than decreased over time. One of its most recent and far-reaching efforts is the No Child Left Behind Act of 2001, which we have discussed in several chapters. One expert described this legislation as "the most significant change in federal regulation of public schools in three decades" (Hardy, 2002, p. 201).

Teaching in an Era of Reform

THE MATH CURRICULUM REFORM ISSUE

One area of the curriculum that has undergone many changes in the past decade is the mathematics curriculum. As educators have debated over the best ways to teach math, professional organizations and states have altered their standards.

Table 10.4 lists several recommendations presented in the *Curriculum and Evaluation Standards for School Mathematics,* published by the National Council of Teachers of Mathematics in 1989. NCTM recommended, for example, that schools de-emphasize "memorizing rules and algorithms" and "memorizing procedures." Instead, they should strongly emphasize learning activities that teach students the ideas behind the rules and algorithms, such as open-ended problem solving, discussion of concepts, and experimentation with different ways of reaching a mathematical solution.

When the standards were published, critics immediately reacted to these changes, raising the following questions:

- Do the techniques suggested by the standards adequately teach students basic math concepts and facts?
- Can the traditional emphasis on arithmetical and algebraic paper-and-pencil skills be reduced with no detrimental effects on important student learning?
- Can individual students effectively learn mathematics if they often investigate mathematical ideas and problems cooperatively with classmates (another recommendation of the NCTM standards)?

Over time, research spurred by the critics' concerns uncovered evidence that instruction based on NCTM's 1989 standards was resulting in students with "content light" understandings of mathematics (Hoff, 2003a). In recent years the pendulum has slowly shifted back toward more emphasis on fundamental skills. The issue of how best to teach mathematics remains under debate, however.

The Issue

The crux of the debate revolves around two questions: "Are curricula that emphasize conceptual understanding the best way to teach mathematics? Or should schools continue the traditional approach of teaching the rudimentary skills of the discipline before expecting students to apply them in real-life situations?" (Hoff, 2003a, p. 28).

Table 10.4 Examples of Changes in Emphasis in Mathematics

Area	Increased Emphasis	Decreased Emphasis
Problem solving	• Pursuing open-ended problems	• Practicing routine problems
Communication	• Discussing mathematical ideas	• Doing worksheets
Operations and computation	• Developing operation sense • Using estimation in problem solving and emphasizing sensibility of answers	• Memorizing rules and algorithms • Memorizing procedures
Algebra	• Using a variety of methods to solve equations	• Memorizing procedures and drilling on equation solving
Teaching practices	• Actively involving students • Facilitating learning	• Having students passively listen to explanations • Dispensing information

Source: National Council of Teachers of Mathematics (1989).

Supporters of the curriculum reforms make two primary arguments. First, they assert, the traditional math curriculum isn't working; American students consistently score lower than their counterparts from other countries in international comparisons (Hoff, 2003a). Second, the reformed curricula are consistent with the latest learning theory and research. For instance, reformed curricula emphasize understanding in depth instead of memorization, students actively involved in learning activities instead of passively listening to teachers, and teachers guiding learning instead of merely lecturing. Research has consistently confirmed that each of these factors increases learning (Bruning et al., 2004).

Recent standards reforms in all content areas emphasize student understanding through their active involvement in learning activities.

Critics counter that reformed curricula fail to adequately teach basic skills, such as math facts (e.g., $9 \times 8 = 72$) and concepts (e.g., equivalent fractions). Critics also report that the pendulum shift back toward more emphasis on skills is evidence that the reforms haven't succeeded. For example, in a 2000 revision of the 1989 standards, NCTM asked for an increased emphasis on basic skills and noted, "Developing fluency requires a balance and connection between conceptual understanding and computational proficiency" (p. 34). The 2000 revision, in fact, reversed some of the standards that were published in 1989. It can take school districts several years to evaluate and respond to the latest research and curriculum recommendations, however, and many schools today use math curricula that came out of the older reform effort.

Critics further assert that American education is a study in failed curriculum reform (Labaree, 1999; Pogrow, 1996).

> It might be said that Americans are always fixing their schools. Each decade another fad emerges. . . . Schools are usually asked to adopt these fads as single ideas laid on top of old structures. Such ideas are poorly assimilated and quickly rejected. . . . This creates a sense within schools that whatever the innovation, "this too will pass." (Darling-Hammond, 1997, p. 22).

School veterans often simply ignore reforms and go about their business (Ozmon & Craver, 2003), and many teachers believe that the reforms that do occur aren't actually needed or beneficial (Hirsch, 1996; Public Agenda, 1994).

You Take a Position

Now it's your turn to take a position on the issue. State in writing whether you believe that math instruction like that proposed by the NCTM in 1989 is likely to increase student learning, and provide a two-page rationale for your position.

CW *For additional references and resources, go to the Companion Website at* **www.prenhall.com/kauchak**, *then to this chapter's* Teaching in an Era of Reform *module. You can respond online or submit your response to your instructor.*

THE MATH CURRICULUM IN ELEMENTARY SCHOOLS

Having examined the relationship between the curriculum and instruction, the explicit and implicit curriculum, and the forces that influence the curriculum, you now have the chance to examine the actual lesson with Suzanne Brush and her second graders which was our chapter's opening case study.

To complete this activity, do the following:

- Go to the DVD, and view the video episode titled "Math Curriculum in Elementary Schools."
- Answer the questions you'll find on the DVD.

To answer the questions online and receive immediate feedback, go to the Companion Website at **www.prenhall.com/kauchak**, *then to this chapter's* Classroom Windows *module.*

The federal government's efforts to influence school curricula dramatically increased in the 1950s when people began to see education as a major vehicle to accomplish national goals. Table 10.5 outlines some of the major pieces of federal legislation that have impacted not only the curriculum but also many other aspects of how schools are operated.

As we can see from Table 10.5, federal legislation has led to significant changes in U.S. classrooms. For example, when you begin your teaching career, you will almost

Table 10.5 The Federal Government's Influence on the Curriculum

Act	Date	Impact on Curriculum
National Defense Education Act	1958	Made math, science, and foreign language high curriculum priorities.
Economic Opportunity Act	1964	Increased emphasis on vocational training and teaching marketable skills.
Civil Rights Act	1964	Prohibited discrimination on the basis of race, color, or national origin. Intended to provide all students with equal access to the curriculum.
Elementary and Secondary Education Act	1965	Created Title I, designed to help disadvantaged children acquire basic skills.
Bilingual Education Act	1968	Provided for teaching the curriculum in students' native languages as they gradually learned English.
Title IX	1972	Increased girls' participation in physical education and sports.
Individuals with Disabilities Education Act (IDEA)	1975	Increased participation of learners with exceptionalities in the regular curriculum.
Environmental Education Act	1991	Stimulated the modern environmental education movement.
Goals 2000: Educate America Act	1994	Established goals to be met by American education by the year 2000.
The No Child Left Behind Act	2001	Requires states to establish standards for what learners should know and be able to do in different subjects and holds them accountable for student performance on tests linked to these standards.

certainly have some students with exceptionalities in your classes; examples include students who have difficulty in reading and children with emotional disabilities. Their participation in your classroom is mandated by the Individuals with Disabilities Education Act (IDEA), legislation passed in 1975 requiring that all students have access to the regular curriculum. The National Defense Education Act (passed in 1958) resulted in much greater emphasis on math, science, and foreign languages, particularly in high schools. Although this emphasis has varied somewhat over the years, well-qualified math, science, and foreign language teachers continue to be in high demand.

Curriculum Controversies

In your work as a teacher, you will encounter controversies. Many of them will be related to what is taught (or not taught)—that is, the curriculum. We examine some of these controversies in this section as we consider the following:

- A national curriculum
- Social issues in the curriculum
- Diversity: cultural minorities and women in the curriculum

A National Curriculum

In our study of Chapter 5, we saw that in the late 1700s, the federal government declined to take a central role in the operation of schools and instead passed the Tenth Amendment, which put curriculum decisions in the hands of the states. The principle of state control of curricula has been in place since that time.

Today, this principle is being questioned by some prominent voices who advocate a national curriculum. Some arguments for a national curriculum include the following:

- Students in countries such as Germany and Japan, which have national standards and national exams, have higher achievement than U.S. students.
- A national curriculum would provide stability and coherence. The population in the United States is highly mobile: 20 percent of Americans relocate every year, and some inner-city schools have a 50 percent turnover rate during the school year (Hirsch, 1996). Teachers working with new students often can't tell what they have or haven't already studied.
- Standards vary significantly from state to state; some states have much lower standards and levels of achievement than do others. A national curriculum would create uniform standards for all.

Opponents of a national curriculum also make compelling arguments. Some are wary of a large federal bureaucracy, which would also weaken local control and accountability. Others believe that a national curriculum would be unresponsive to individual diversity and needs and create more difficulties for disadvantaged students.

One response to these opposing views is for the federal government to recommend, but not require, exemplary textbooks. For example, several years ago the U.S. Department of Education published a list of promising and exemplary math texts, most based on National Council of Teachers of Mathematics standards (Viadero, 1999a). Even this approach has drawn criticism. One critic, a conservative math professor, commented, "This is an abomination. It [the math curriculum] has no business being debated by the federal government." (Viadero, 1999a, p. 14). The same type of effort to influence the curriculum is also occurring in the area of reading, although federal efforts in this area focus more on methods than textbook selection (Manzo, 2004). Defenders of federal leadership with respect to curricular recommendations compare it to *Consumer Reports*, noting that this publication serves an educational function and that not everyone who reads it is forced to buy the same product.

As you begin your career, you will probably see increased federal influence in the form of goals and standards. The recently enacted No Child Left Behind Act politically sidestepped this controversial issue by mandating standards but leaving the content of these standards up to states. However, there currently is a push at the federal level to define the curriculum in response to "research-based findings." Critics of this approach question whether research findings are being selectively chosen and whether this approach will result in a national curriculum that ignores opposing viewpoints and eliminates competing programs (Yatvin, 2003). Richard Allington, a nationally recognized expert in the area of reading, commented, "They [federal officials] can play all the semantic games they want, but state education officials are being coerced to buy particular tests and particular reading programs" (Manzo & Hoff, 2003, p. 11). The controversy over federal influences on the curriculum is likely to continue.

Social Issues in the Curriculum

Think back to your experiences in high school. Did you take a course called "Family Life," "Life Management," "Health Education," or something similar? Many students did and still do. These courses often deal with controversial topics, including sex education and moral development.

Sex Education Sex education is controversial for at least two reasons. First, some people insist that it shouldn't be part of the school curriculum, believing that it is the sole or primary responsibility of families or churches. They contend that sex is inextricably connected with personal, moral, and religious values, and the proper place for sex education is the home, where parents can embed it in a larger moral framework.

Proponents of sex education counter with these statistics you first encountered in Chapter 4 (National Campaign to Prevent Teen Pregnancy, 2003):

- The United States has the highest rate of teenage pregnancy in the Western industrialized world.
- Thirty-five percent of young women become pregnant at least once before the age of 20—about 850,000 a year.
- Eight in 10 of these teenage pregnancies are unintended, and 79 percent are to unmarried teens.

If parents and churches are responsible for sex education, they're doing a poor job, proponents contend. They further argue that schools have both a right and a responsibility to ensure that all students have access to information about their bodies and their developing sexuality. Courts have upheld school districts' rights to offer sex education courses (Fischer et al., 2003). Parents who object are free to remove their children from attendance.

The second controversial issue is the content of sex education courses. Some argue that the content should focus strictly on the biology of sex and reproduction—what some call a "plumbing approach." Others suggest that this is ineffective, and personal responsibility and moral development should be included.

Sex education, while controversial, has become a common curriculum component in many school districts.

A national study found that 69 percent of public school districts have districtwide policies in place to teach sex education. The study also found the following about the districts that have sex education policies (Landry, Kaeser, & Richards, 1999):

- Fourteen percent have a comprehensive policy that treats abstinence as one option for adolescents in a broader sex education program.
- Fifty-one percent teach abstinence as the preferred option for adolescents, but also permit discussion about contraception as an effective means of protecting against unintended pregnancy and disease (an abstinence-plus policy).
- Thirty-five percent (or 23 percent of all U.S. school districts) teach abstinence as the only option outside of marriage, with discussion of contraception either prohibited entirely or permitted only to emphasize its shortcomings (an abstinence-only policy). In other words, one school district in three (who have sex education policies in place) forbids dissemination of any positive information about contraception, regardless of whether their students are sexually active or at risk of pregnancy or disease.

How does the public feel? Ninety-three percent of surveyed Americans said they favor sex education and believe that young people should be given information to protect themselves from unplanned pregnancies and sexually transmitted diseases (Sexuality Information and Education Council of the United States and Advocates for Youth, 1999). In another recent survey, 94 percent of parents said they want schools to address real-life issues, such as pressure to have sex and the emotional consequences of becoming sexually active (T. Hoff, 2002).

In a review of different sex education programs, the U.S. Surgeon General concluded that "given that one-half of adolescents in the United States are already sexually active and at risk of unintended pregnancy and STD/HIV infection, it also seems clear that adolescents need accurate information about contraceptive methods so that they can reduce those risks" (cited in T. Hoff, 2002, p. 61). Congress, however, has committed more than a half billion dollars to abstinence-only programs and zero dollars to comprehensive sex education programs that include information on contraception and protection. It appears that the actions of Congress are at odds with the views of most Americans as well as the U.S. Surgeon General. David Landry, a nationally recognized expert in this area, observed, "Students aren't receiving accurate, balanced information about how to protect themselves from unplanned pregnancy or disease" (Coles, 1999a, p. 13). This is unfortunate, as the statistics regarding teen pregnancy at the beginning of this section reveal a real student need.

Moral and Character Education The proper place of values and moral education in the curriculum is also controversial. Although most educators agree that this type of education is needed, they disagree about the form it should take.

As you learned in previous chapters, one position, called **character education,** *suggests that moral values and positive character traits, such as honesty and citizenship, should be emphasized, taught, and rewarded.* Proponents of character education believe that right and wrong do exist and that parents and schools have a responsibility to teach students to recognize the difference. For example, the state of Georgia passed a law requiring character education programs to focus on 27 character traits including patriotism, respect for others, courtesy, and compassion (Jacobson, 1999). Instruction in character education emphasizes the study of values, practicing these values both in school and elsewhere, and rewarding displays of these values.

Moral education, by contrast, is more value-free, *emphasizing instead the development of students' moral reasoning.* Moral education uses moral dilemmas and classroom discussions to teach problem solving and to bring about changes in the way learners think about moral issues.

Critics of character education argue that it indoctrinates rather than educates (Kohn, 1997); critics of moral education assert that it has a relativistic view of morals, with no right or wrong answers (Wynne, 1997). The strength of character education is its willingness to identify and promote core values, such as honesty, caring, and respect for others. Few would argue that these values are inappropriate. Further, research indicates that character education programs are effective for developing both students' social skills and their academic abilities (Viadero, 2003a). However, emphasizing student thinking and decision making is important as well, and this is the focus of the moral education perspective.

For either moral or character education to work, there must be some public consensus about what values are important for students to learn. Does such consensus exist? Polls suggest that it does (Rose & Gallup, 2000). When asked whether the following values should be taught in public schools, the following percentages of a national sample replied affirmatively: honesty (97 percent), democracy (93 percent), acceptance of people of different races and ethnic backgrounds (93 percent), and caring for friends and family members (90 percent). Fewer people supported the idea of teaching acceptance of people with different sexual orientations, specifically homosexuals or bisexuals (55 percent), and acceptance of the right of a woman to choose an abortion (48 percent). Research indicates, however, that these less-popular issues receive little or no emphasis in the curriculum (Thornton, 2003).

In considering which values to promote in their classrooms, teachers should be aware of public attitudes toward these values. This doesn't mean that teachers should avoid discussing controversial topics or values; instead, it suggests that they should be

Service learning attempts to teach values by actively involving students in helping projects.

aware of current public views. Students often have many of the same values and beliefs as their parents. Building upon these beliefs makes sense both pedagogically as well as politically (Eggen & Kauchak, 2004; Ormrod, 2003).

Service learning. **Service learning** is *an approach to character education that combines service to the community with content learning objectives with the intent that the activity change both the recipient and the provider of the service* (National Service-Learning Clearing House, 2001). For example, if students remove trash from an urban streambed, they are providing a service to the community as volunteers. When they share the results with residents of the neighborhood and make suggestions for reducing pollution, they are attempting to change the recipients of the service (the people in the neighborhood). At the same time, the students are learning about water quality and laboratory analysis, developing an understanding of pollution issues, and learning to present science issues to the public. In this way, the providers of the service (the students) are also changed. Thus, service learning intentionally combines *service* and *learning*.

Service-learning programs can be divided into two main categories: those that have social change as a goal and those that have charity as a goal (Kahne & Westheimer, 1996). Examples of service-learning programs that focus on social change include environmental education projects designed to encourage people to recycle and voter education projects aimed at getting people out to vote. Charity-oriented projects include delivering food to shut-ins and doing volunteer work in hospitals.

The popularity of service-learning programs is growing. Between 1984 and 1997, the number of K–12 students involved in service-learning programs rose from 900,000 to more than 12.6 million, while the proportion of high school students participating in service learning grew from 2 percent to 25 percent during the same time period (Campus Compact, 2001; Fiske, 2001).

An important policy question is whether to make service learning voluntary or required. The state of Maryland requires 75 hours of service before high school graduation. A number of districts in California, Washington, Pennsylvania, and North Carolina have similar requirements (Fischer et al., 1999). Not all parents support the service-learning requirements, however, and some have legally challenged schools that have mandatory service-learning courses. Courts have upheld the legality of these courses, noting that they promote habits of good citizenship and introduce students to the idea of social responsibility. Involvement in service-learning activities is also seen by some as a means to promote greater involvement of young people in our political system (T. Martin & Richardson, 2003), and service learning is particularly emphasized in the social studies curriculum (E. Bloom, 2003).

Evolution Versus Creationism The issue of whether to teach creationism, evolution, or both is a controversy that has existed for scores of years. **Creationism** is, in essence, *the theory that the universe was created by God as described in the Bible,* whereas **evolution** is *the theory suggesting that all living things have changed in response to environmental conditions through a process of natural selection.* You may recall from our

Exploring Diversity

MINORITIES AND WOMEN IN THE CURRICULUM

The curriculum in U.S. schools has been criticized because it has, according to critics, failed to adequately represent the contributions of women and cultural minorities. These criticisms continue to the present (Sincero & Woyshner, 2003). For example, until as recently as the 1960s and 1970s, the majority of the works included in junior high and high school literature books were written by White males, such as William Shakespeare, Mark Twain, and Robert Frost, with only a few additional contributions by White women.

Recognition of the historical contributions of minorities was similarly lacking. For example, Dr. Charles Drew (1904–1950), an African American, developed the procedure for separating plasma from whole blood. This was an enormous contribution that unquestionably saved many soldiers' lives in World War II. Dr. Charles Norman (b. 1930), another African American, was the first person to implant an artificial heart in a human. Until recently, most history books ignored contributions such as these.

In response to critics, as well as shifts in our society, this has changed. For example, a postage stamp was issued in Drew's honor in 1981, and science fiction writer Isaac Asimov, a friend of Norman's, based his novel *Fantastic Voyage* on work done in Norman's laboratory. History texts have been expanded to include the contributions of women and minorities. Literature books, too, have changed. Many now include works written by members of various cultural minority groups, such as Maya Angelou, Sandra Cisneros, Gary Soto, and Toni Cade Bambara (Probst, Anderson, Brinnin, Leggett, & Irvin, 1997).

The issue is controversial, with some critics charging that cultural minorities remain underrepresented in the curriculum (Wong-Fillmore & Meyer, 1996). Content focusing primarily on the contributions of men of northern European descent—often derisively described as a "Eurocentric" curriculum—is perceived as out of balance and irrelevant to minorities. Because more than a third of our schoolchildren are minorities and this percentage is increasing, the curriculum should be further broadened to better re-

discussion of religion and the curriculum in Chapter 9 that the controversy first surfaced in 1925, when a biology teacher named John Scopes challenged a Tennessee law that made it illegal to teach any theory that denied the Divine Creation of humanity as taught in the Bible in any public school. What become known as the "Scopes Monkey Trial" ended after 11 contentious days, with Scopes being fined $100 for a violation of the law he challenged. The decision was later overturned by the Tennessee Supreme Court on a technicality.

CW

Increasing Understanding 10.13

What principle is grounded in the First Amendment? What implications has this principle had for education?

The controversy has continued since that time. During the 1980s, religious fundamentalists won court rulings requiring that equal emphasis be placed on both creationism and evolution, but the equal-treatment laws were later ruled a violation of the First Amendment by the U.S. Supreme Court.

The controversy emerged again in Tennessee in 1996 when lawmakers stuck down legislation that would have allowed districts to dismiss teachers who taught evolution as a fact. More recently, the Texas House of Representatives passed a bill that would restore the State Board of Education's authority to reject textbooks for any reason, a

flect minority members' contributions and presence in our society, critics argue. In addition, they assert, some time-honored literature, such as Mark Twain's *The Adventures of Huckleberry Finn*, portrays characters in ways that promote racial stereotypes and prejudice.

Some critics argue further that entire curricula should be oriented to specific ethnic groups. For instance, to help African American students understand and appreciate their cultural heritage, proponents of an "Afrocentric" curriculum advocate focusing on the achievements of African cultures, particularly ancient Egypt. Students who study the contributions of people with ethnicity similar to their own will make gains in self-esteem, motivation, and learning, they contend. Afrocentric curricula are currently being experimented with in a number of inner-city school districts (Toch, 1998).

These positions have critics of their own, however. Some educators and social commentators question the accuracy and balance of the content and whether the emphasis on differences leads to racial and ethnic separatism (Coughlin, 1996; Ravitch, 1990). They also argue that schools have already gone too far in emphasizing cultural differences, resulting in the reduction or elimination of studies that focus on some of the great contributions of literature, such as the works of Shakespeare. Further, they maintain, we are all Americans, and an overemphasis on diversity has resulted in the failure of students to develop a common cultural heritage and shared national identity (Hirsch, 1987; Schlesinger, 1992).

The role of women in the curriculum is also controversial. For example, many feminist groups contend that women continue to be both underrepresented and misrepresented in the curriculum, arguing that students read too many books and materials that portray men as doctors, lawyers, and engineers, and women as nurses, teachers, and secretaries. When this occurs, they assert, girls are sent messages about what are and are not appropriate careers for them (American Association of University Women, 1992).

However, a strong and systematic national effort has been made to address the needs of girls and women in today's schools (Riordan, 2004). Some people contend that the emphasis on girls' needs has gone too far. This is the argument made in *The War Against Boys*, the provocative book written by Christine Hoff Sommers (2000) that we discussed in Chapter 3.

The debate continues, and the controversy is likely to remain in the future.

power which had been restricted in recent years by other legislation. Evolution has been strongly attacked by creationists, and because of the size of its educational system, Texas exerts considerable influence over textbook publishers who want to compete in its market. Local observers expect the return of pressure to modify biology texts to include discussion of creationism if the state board regains absolute control over textbook contents (Meikle, 2003). Legislation aimed at the censorship of science textbooks has also occurred in other states. This leads us to the more general topic of censorship.

Censorship What do the following books have in common?

Of Mice and Men by John Steinbeck
The Diary of a Young Girl by Anne Frank
The Adventures of Huckleberry Finn by Mark Twain
To Kill a Mockingbird by Harper Lee
Leaves of Grass by Walt Whitman

All of these works have, at various times, been targeted to be banned from the public school curriculum (People for the American Way, 1991). The language arts area has often served as a battleground for curriculum controversy due to the issue of censorship. **Censorship** is *the practice of prohibiting the use of objectionable materials, such as certain books used in libraries or in academic classes.*

The controversial nature of censorship can be seen in a battle that took place in Kanawha County in West Virginia. In the mid-1970s, parents objected to certain books that were being used in language arts classes, including *The Diary of a Young Girl* as well as works by John Steinbeck and Mark Twain (Manzo, 2000b). Emotions reached crisis level quickly, resulting in death threats to teachers, pipe bombs, and a school boycott. The Ku Klux Klan and John Birch Society got involved, and several local ministers were convicted for their roles in school bombings. Censorship scars are evident even today in Kanawha County; recently, district officials who felt censorship pressures ordered health teachers to avoid teaching about the excretory and reproductive systems of the human body. Can you imagine a student asking his health teacher about how the kidneys work and the teacher replying, "We can't talk about that in this class"?

Attempts have also been made to censor textbooks because of material someone deems unfit for the classroom. For example, a fourth-grade history text used in Utah contained the following passage:

> People often hurt the land. Automobiles and factories pollute the air. People and factories sometimes dump trash and harmful chemicals into lakes and rivers. These kill birds and fish and make the water unsafe for people. Companies cut down forests. They build roads, dams, and cities. They put oil wells and telephone lines on the land. We need these things, but sometimes they look ugly and destroy nature. (Egan, 1997, p. B1)

The passage seems innocuous, but one critic contended, "This book is a blatant attempt by the federal government and environmentalists to try to 'brainwash' our young students into believing their ancestors were petty opportunists having no conscience about the lands for which they had stewardship" (Egan, 1997, B3). When textbooks become political footballs, their content becomes watered down and their quality diminishes, because text writers aim for "the middle of the road" at the expense of accuracy or making a point (Manzo, 2003c). This is a problem you'll encounter as you attempt to use textbooks to help students learn.

Censorship also raises questions with conflicting answers about other important issues in education. One is parents' control over their children's education. Shouldn't parents have a say in the books their children read? A second, related, conflicting question involves professional autonomy. Shouldn't teachers be free to select books that professional judgment tells them are important, if not essential, to student development and learning? In considering these opposing views, the courts have usually decided against censorship of books, ruling that schools and teachers have a right to expose students to different ideas and points of view through literature (Fischer et al., 1999).

To get additional information about censorship and banned books, go to the Companion Website at **www.prenhall.com/kauchak** then to this chapter's *Web Links* module.

Decision Making

Defining Yourself as a Professional

A theme throughout this text is the need for teachers to define themselves through the professional decisions they make. Nowhere is this more important than in the area of curricula, where teachers make decisions every day. For example, you may choose to allow textbooks to make your curriculum decisions for you, deciding to teach a topic because it is the one that appears next in the textbook. Or you may choose to base curriculum decisions on a carefully considered philosophy. Beginning now to consider your beliefs about learners' needs and the kinds of curriculum that best meet these needs will equip you to make effective decisions later in your professional development.

You will also be forced to make decisions about the extent to which you allow the process of standardized testing to dictate the curriculum you provide to your students. Some teachers take the seemingly safe route, essentially "teaching to the test" and de-emphasizing other aspects of the curriculum. Others choose to make the skills the test measures a part of their curriculum, integrated with other content and skills that they believe are important for their students' growth. All beginning teachers will wrestle with this issue in some form or other as they begin their teaching careers.

You must also make decisions about aspects of the curriculum that are less obvious. For instance, what will you communicate through your implicit curriculum? Why will you choose to emphasize some topics, de-emphasize others, and ignore some completely? To what extent will you emphasize morals and values in your curriculum, and how will you communicate these values? These are decisions that a technician can avoid but that a professional consciously and deliberately makes.

The importance of knowledgeable and highly skilled teachers who are able and willing to make crucial curricular decisions is supported by research linking teacher quality and student achievement (Darling-Hammond, 1998). Students in high-achieving states, such as North Dakota, Minnesota, and Iowa, do as well as students in foreign countries with reputations for high achievement, such as Korea and Japan. Those states have rigorous requirements for teacher education and don't allow districts to hire unlicensed teachers. The opposite is true for the lowest achieving states (National Commission on Teaching and America's Future, 1996).

As we've emphasized in this chapter, you are ultimately the person who controls the curriculum in your classroom, and you will determine, to a large extent, what and how much your students learn: "If public education is to be made right, the work will be done quietly by teachers. These will be teachers who spend considerable time, not just teaching, but thinking about teaching—about how to become better and better at the work they know to be important" (Bunting, 2003, p. 41). Beginning now to make decisions about the kind of teacher you want to become will help ensure that your students have the benefit of a curriculum that best meets their needs as developing human beings.

Summary

What Is Curriculum?

While defined in a variety of ways, curriculum can be thought of as what teachers teach and students learn in schools. Instruction is the way the curriculum is taught. The explicit curriculum is the curriculum found in textbooks and other formal educational experiences; the implicit curriculum is reflected in the climate of the classroom along with its unstated values and priorities; and the null curriculum reflects what is not taught.

The explicit curriculum is sometimes integrated so that concepts and skills from different disciplines are combined. An integrated curriculum, although somewhat controversial, is common in elementary schools.

Extracurriculum includes learning experiences that extend beyond the core of students' formal studies. Participation in extracurricular activities is correlated with a number of positive outcomes, including achievement and attitudes toward school.

Forces That Influence the Curriculum

The teacher is the most powerful force influencing the curriculum. Ultimately it is the teacher who must decide what is taught and how it will be taught.

A teacher's philosophical orientation, available textbooks, federal mandates, state and local district guidelines, and reform movements sponsored by national committees and professional organizations all influence a teacher's curriculum decisions.

Curriculum Controversies

Whether or not the United States should have a national curriculum is a controversial issue facing education. Proponents cite the mobility of the population and the achievement of students in other countries with national curricula; opponents fear a large federal bureaucracy, reduction of local accountability, and a decrease in the positive aspects of our cultural diversity.

Sex education, education in morals and values, creationism versus evolution, censorship, and the underrepresentation of women and minorities in the curriculum remain controversial issues. These issues are likely to remain unresolved in the near future.

Important Concepts

censorship (p. 380)
character education (p. 376)
creationism (p. 377)
curriculum (p. 353)
evolution (p. 377)
explicit curriculum (p. 353)
extracurriculum (p. 359)
implicit curriculum (p. 358)
instruction (p. 353)
integrated curriculum (p. 356)
moral education (p. 376)
null curriculum (p. 359)
service learning (p. 377)
standards (p. 365)
standards-based education (p. 365)

Developing as a Professional

Praxis Practice

Read the case study, and answer the questions that follow.

David Hendricks, an earth science teacher, was preparing a unit on the solar system. "The kids need to be able to think about this kind of stuff," he thought to himself. He assembled a large model to illustrate the planets in their orbital planes and their relative distances from the sun. He also prepared an outline of a matrix that had room for information about the planets' sizes, forces of gravity compared to the Earth's, periods of rotation and revolution, and other physical characteristics. On Monday he introduced the unit, and had the students work in groups of three to gather information about individual planets from books, computer files, and the Internet. The groups got to select the planet they wanted and had to negotiate if more than one group wanted the same planet. The students spent the rest of the day and Tuesday gathering information about the planets and putting it into the matrix.

On Wednesday and Thursday David led a discussion during which he raised a number of questions, such as why Pluto's orbit is different from the orbits of the other planets, why Saturn's gravity is about the same as the Earth's when its diameter is so much larger, and why Mercury is so hot on one side and so cold on the other. During the discussion he commented that learning to think about relationships such as these was the most interesting part of studying the solar system. On Friday he gave the students a quiz that covered the topics in the unit.

Steve Grant, another earth science teacher, was also working on a unit on the solar system. After checking with the text he was using, he prepared a series of lessons on important facts about the solar system. The students were told to read the next chapter in their books, and he spent the first day of the unit identifying the parts of the solar system and the names of the planets. He listed the planets on the board in order and pointed out that Mercury, Venus, Earth, and Mars were quite small and close to the sun, so they were called the inner planets, and that the others were called the outer planets. He also told students that Venus was called the Earth's twin because its size was about the same as the Earth's. He then showed the students a transparency that pictured the inner and outer planets.

On Tuesday Steve reviewed the information he had presented on Monday and said, "Remember when we listed the names of the planets on the board, I said that we needed to know all of them in order. This is important. Look back in your notes if you're not sure."

He then presented information about asteroids and comets, pointing out that Halley's comet is the most famous. He explained that Pluto is the smallest planet and is farthest away from the sun, and that many scientists believe that its origin is unlike that of the other planets.

Steve continued presenting information about the planets on Wednesday and Thursday. For example, he told students that Venus is very hot because of its thick cloud cover, that Saturn is essentially a large ball of gas, and that Mercury is very hot on one side but cold on the other because it rotates very slowly on its axis. On Friday, he gave the students a quiz that covered the information he presented.

1. Describe differences between David's explicit curriculum and Steve's explicit curriculum. Explain how these differences relate to teacher autonomy.
2. Describe differences in the implicit curriculum for these two teachers.
3. What forces do you think influenced the curriculum decisions made by each of the teachers?
4. Explain how David's and Steve's curriculum decisions influenced their instruction.

To receive feedback on your responses to the Praxis Practice exercises, go to the Companion Website at **www.prenhall.com/kauchak**, then to this chapter's *Praxis Practice* module.

Discussion Questions

1. Which has the greater influence on students' learning, the curriculum or instruction? Why do you think so?
2. Think back to your own experience in schools and then consider what you've read in this chapter. Which has changed more over time, the curriculum or instruction? Why do you think so?
3. Some critics argue that the implicit curriculum has more impact on students' overall education than does the explicit curriculum. Do you agree or disagree with this argument? Defend your position with a concrete example.
4. During financial crises, some schools have reduced their extracurricular offerings. To what extent does this detract from students' overall education? Defend your position with a concrete example.
5. Which of the factors that influence the curriculum do you believe will most influence your teaching? Why do you think so?

Video Discussion Questions

The following discussion questions refer to video segments found on the Companion Website. To answer these questions online, view the accompanying video, and receive immediate feedback to your answers, go to the Companion Website at **www.prenhall.com/kauchak**, then to this chapter's *Video Discussion* module.

1. Theodore Sizer is the director of the Coalition for Effective Schools, which attempts to reform high schools. In his view, what is the most important thing that schools can do to prepare students for college? Where in the curriculum would we find this emphasis, and how could teachers integrate it into their teaching?
2. Theodore Sizer also recommends a standard, focused curriculum for all students. How could a standard, focused curriculum be used to encourage student critical thinking? What are the advantages and disadvantages of this approach to curriculum?

Classroom Observation Guide

Before You Begin: The purpose of this observation activity is to help you understand how teachers use textbooks in their curricula. After observing the different ways that textbooks are used in the classroom, talk to the teacher to gain insights into professional practice.

1. Observe a classroom over the course of a day or for an extended period of time.
   a. How many of the lessons integrally involve textbooks in the instruction? How do teachers integrate them into their instruction?
   b. How do students use the textbooks (for example, as workbooks, sources of information, reference works)?
   c. Does the teacher use any supplementary books such as workbooks or in-class reference sources?
   d. Do all students have a textbook? Are they expected to bring them to class? Do they take them home at night?
   e. How recent are the textbooks? Are they in good condition?

   Interview the teacher, and ask how the use of textbooks could be improved to increase learning in the classroom. Summarize your findings in a paper that describes your plans for textbook use in your classroom.

Going into Schools

1. Obtain a copy of a teacher's lesson plans for a week. Based on the teacher's plans, what is being emphasized? What is being de-emphasized? What do these lesson plans tell you about the teacher's explicit and implicit curriculum?
2. Examine the teacher's textbook (or textbooks). To what extent do the teacher's lesson plans appear to depend on the textbook(s)? What other resources are the basis for the teacher's plans?
3. Interview a teacher about different forces that shape his or her curriculum.
   a. Ask why he or she emphasizes and de-emphasizes certain aspects of the curriculum.
   b. How much does the teacher depend on textbooks to determine what to teach? How much do curriculum guides influence what is taught? How much does testing influence what is taught?
   c. Ask the teacher to describe the school's extracurricular program. Find out who participates and why. (For example, do low-SES students and minorities participate as much as other students?) How important does the teacher think the extracurricular program is? Why?
   d. Ask the teacher to describe his or her impression of current curriculum reforms. Do they influence what and how he or she teaches? Ask for specific examples. If reforms have little influence, ask the teacher to explain why.

   Compare the forces that shape this teacher's curriculum to forces described in this chapter.
4. Interview a teacher to determine her views of controversial topics in the curriculum.
   a. *Sex education.* Should the schools teach sex education, or should it be the responsibility of parents and churches? Why?
   b. *Morals and values education.* Should schools teach morals and values? Is so, how should they be taught?

c. *The underrepresentation of minorities and women in the curriculum.* Does the teacher believe minorities and women are underrepresented? If so, how can the problem be solved?

How does the teacher find out about whether and how these topics should be taught? To what extent are curricular decisions based on personal choice, and to what extent are they based on guidance or restrictions from external sources? Consider the teacher's responses and their implications for you as a teacher who will be faced with similar curricular decisions.

5. Observe in a classroom (for an extended period of time, if possible) to see how the implicit curriculum is reflected in classroom management.
   a. What rules and procedures guide student behavior? How are they explained or defended?
   b. When the teacher corrects or reprimands a student, what explanation or rationale is given?
   c. How does the teacher motivate students? What reasons are given for learning different things?
   d. How does the teacher treat students? How do students treat each other?

   Based on your observations, what implicit curriculum is being promoted in the classroom? Defend your conclusions with examples taken directly from your observations.

Virtual Field Experience

If you would like to participate in a Virtual Field Experience, go to the Companion Website at **www.prenhall.com/kauchak**, then to this chapter's *Field Experience* module.

Online Portfolio Activities

To complete these activities online, go to the Companion Website at **www.prenhall.com/kauchak**, then to this chapter's *Portfolio Activities* module.

Portfolio Activity 10.1

Planning for Instruction

INTASC Principle 9: Commitment

Personal Journal Reflection

The purpose of this activity is to encourage you to think about the topics you will plan to teach. Write a two-page description of your philosophy of curriculum, or what is important for students to learn in your class. In it, explain specifically how it is consistent with the description of your overall philosophy of education (which you described in Portfolio Activity 6.1).

Portfolio Activity 10.2

Making Decisions About the Curriculum

INTASC Principle 7: Planning

The purpose of this activity is to acquaint you with resources, such as textbooks, that will influence your curricular decisions. Locate a textbook for an area in which you will teach. (If you're a middle school science major, for example, you might select a seventh grade life science book. If you're an elementary major, you can select from a variety of texts.)

Photocopy the table of contents from the book. Then identify several topics from the table that you would delete if you were using the book. Also, identify several topics you might emphasize or add. Defend your additions and deletions, and also explain how these changes are consistent with your curriculum philosophy.

Portfolio Activity 10.3

Using Curriculum Guides to Plan Decisions

INTASC Principle 8: Assessment

The purpose of this activity is to acquaint you with curriculum guides as a planning resource. Analyze either a state or district curriculum guide in one area of the curriculum (or compare two levels).

a. How recent is the curriculum guide?
b. Who constructed it?
c. How is it organized (for example, chronologically, developmentally, topically, and so on)?
d. How do the topics covered compare with a text for this area?
e. How many objectives are listed for a particular course of study?
f. How many objectives per week are implicitly suggested? Is it a realistic number?
g. What types of learning (for example, memorization versus higher-level thinking) are targeted?

How helpful would this curriculum guide be for you as a first year teacher?

Chapter 11

Instruction in American Classrooms

The reason you're taking this and other courses in your teacher preparation program is to help you understand American schools, how they attempt to promote student learning, and what teachers can do to contribute to that process. Over the past 25 years a continually expanding body of research has provided educators with a great deal of information about the relationships between teaching and learning. In this chapter we describe this research as we try to answer the following questions:

- How do effective teachers plan for instruction?
- What kinds of personal characteristics do effective teachers possess?
- What kinds of instructional strategies do effective teachers use?
- How do effective teachers manage their classrooms to create productive learning environments?
- How do effective teachers assess their students?
- On what theories of learning do effective teachers base their instruction?

Let's begin by looking at a teacher's thinking as she plans for her next week's math instruction.

This logo appears throughout the chapter to indicate where case studies are integrated with course content.

Case STUDY

"What are you doing?" Jim Barton asked his wife, Shirley, as he saw her hard at work on a Saturday afternoon cutting and drawing on cardboard pieces.

"Working on a unit on equivalent fractions and adding fractions with unlike denominators. . . . What do you think?" she said, grinning at him. "Do they look like pizzas and cakes?" she asked and held up the pieces of cardboard.

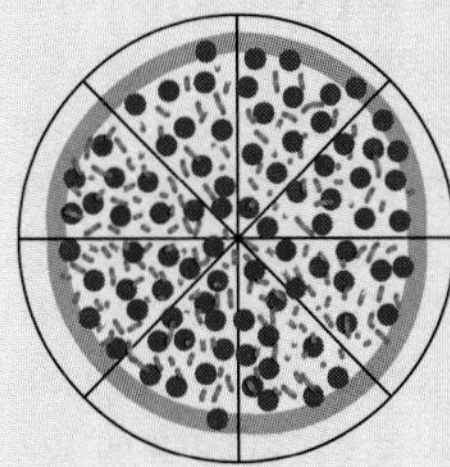
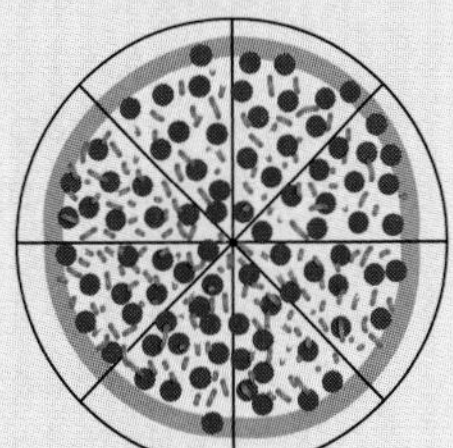

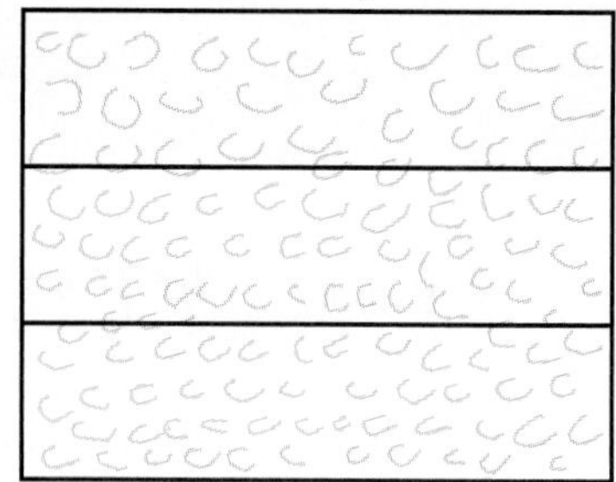

"They really do," he answered with a smile.

"My students didn't score as well as I would have liked on the fractions part of the Stanford Achievement Test last year, and I promised myself they were going to do better this year."

"But you said the students aren't as sharp this year."

"That doesn't matter. I'm pushing them harder. I think I can do a better job than I did last year," Shirley replied. "They're going to be so good at finding equivalent fractions and adding fractions with unlike denominators that they'll be able to do the problems in their sleep."

"You never lose your enthusiasm, do you?" Jim asked. He smiled as he turned to walk out of the room and mumbled something about thinking that teachers who taught for 11 years were supposed to burn out.

"Okay," Shirley thought to herself as Jim was leaving, "I'll use the pizzas for review, and then I'll use the cakes to help them understand equivalent fractions."

She then prepared a worksheet with more drawings that the students would complete for additional practice on finding equivalent fractions. "If they do okay on the worksheet, I'll give them a quiz at the end of the week that will cover both equivalent fractions and adding fractions with unlike denominators," she murmured. "I think I'm ready."

• • ● • •

We'll begin to analyze Shirley's teaching by examining her thinking as she planned her lessons for the next week. Shirley's thinking illustrates an essential element of instruction that has been thoroughly researched. Let's take a look at this research.

Looking in Classrooms to Define Effective Teaching

Classrooms are logical places to look for answers to questions about good teaching. To explain why students in some teachers' classrooms appeared to be learning much more than students in other classrooms, researchers in the 1970s and 1980s decided to look more closely at what was happening in classrooms. They interviewed a great many teachers and analyzed literally thousands of hours of teaching, focusing on both effective teachers (teachers of higher-than-expected achievers) and less effective teachers (teachers of lower-than-expected achievers). The research revealed important differences in the teachers' thinking as they planned their lessons, teachers' personal characteristics, their teaching strategies, the ways they managed their classrooms, and their assessment techniques (Good & Brophy, 2003; Shuell, 1996). This research is important because it identified links between teacher actions and student learning in real-world classroom settings. Studies that replicate these results are ongoing (e.g., D. Hoff, 2003c; Manzo, 2003b).

The dimensions on which effective and less effective teachers differ are outlined in Figure 11.1. Let's analyze these differences in more detail.

Figure 11.1 Dimensions on Which Effective and Less Effective Teachers Differ

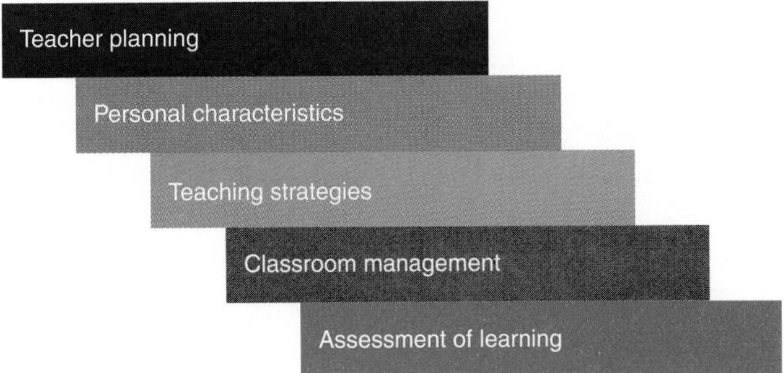

CW

Increasing Understanding 11.1

Research indicates that when they plan, beginning teachers write much more on paper than do veterans (Zahorik, 1991). Does this suggest that beginning teachers plan more effectively than do veterans? Explain.

To answer this question online and receive immediate feedback, go to the Companion Website at www.prenhall.com/kauchak, then to this chapter's *Increasing Understanding* module. Type in your response, and then study the feedback.

Planning and the Professional Teacher

Throughout this book we have emphasized that professional teachers are skilled in making a great many decisions, and these decisions result from reflection and are based on specialized knowledge. We see these characteristics in Shirley's thinking as she planned her unit on fractions.

Shirley reflected on her work from the previous year, concluded that she could have done a better job, and thought about different ideas for improvement. She then made several decisions intended to increase her students' learning. They included the following:

- Decisions about her goals for the unit
- Decisions about how to represent the content so that it made sense to the students
- Decisions about homework
- Decisions about assessment

Each of Shirley's decisions was based on a thorough understanding of the content she was teaching, as well as an understanding of her students and how they learn.

Goals and Teachers' Thinking When effective teachers plan, they think carefully about their **goals,** *what they want students to understand or be able to do when they complete a lesson.* For instance, Shirley was very clear about her goals; she wanted her students to be able to find equivalent fractions and to be able to add fractions with unlike denominators. Precise thinking about goals is essential, because each of a teacher's other planning decisions depends on having specified clear goals. For instance, Shirley's goals guided her thinking as she made decisions about her examples, her worksheet, and her assessment. Without clear goals, these decisions wouldn't have been possible. Less effective teachers don't think as carefully about what they want their students to learn, and as a result, their other planning decisions, as well as their teaching, are not as effective in promoting student learning (Borko & Putnam, 1996; Eggen, 1998).

Let's look at Shirley's first goal in a bit more detail. She wanted students to be able to find equivalent fractions. We can infer that Shirley had other, related goals for students, such as knowing what the term *equivalent fraction* means and being able to identify pairs of fractions that are equivalent and pairs that are not.

To help teachers in creating instructional goals, researchers have developed a system to classify different kinds of goals (L. Anderson & Krathwohl, 2001). A revision

Figure 11.2 A Taxonomy for Learning, Teaching, and Assessing

	The Cognitive Process Dimension					
The Knowledge Dimension	1. Remember	2. Understand	3. Apply	4. Analyze	5. Evaluate	6. Create
A. Factual knowledge						
B. Conceptual knowledge						
C. Procedural knowledge						
D. Metacognitive knowledge						

Source: From Lorin W. Anderson & David R. Krathwohl, *A Taxonomy for Learning, Teaching and Assessing: A Revision of Bloom's Objectives.* Copyright 2001. Published by Allyn and Bacon, Boston, Ma. Copyright 2001 by Pearson Education. Reprinted by permission of the publisher.

of the famous "Bloom's Taxonomy" that was first published in 1956 (B. Bloom, Englehart, Furst, Hill, & Krathwohl, 1956), the new system uses a matrix with 24 cells that represent the intersection of four types of knowledge with six cognitive processes (see Figure 11.2). The revised taxonomy reflects the dramatic increase in understanding of teaching and learning since the middle of the twentieth century when the original taxonomy was created, as well as the influence of cognitive learning theory on education (L. Anderson & Krathwohl, 2001). (We examine cognitive learning theory later in the chapter.)

Increasing Understanding 11.2

Classify the goal "to know what the term *equivalent fraction* means" into one of the cells of the taxonomy.

Teachers use the taxonomy to think about and clarify their instructional goals. For instance, one of Shirley's goals was for students to be able to find equivalent fractions. The goal involves applying a procedure, so it would be placed in the cell where *procedural knowledge* intersects with the cognitive process *apply.* In order to identify pairs of fractions that are equivalent, students would need to understand the concept *equivalent fractions.* That goal would be placed in the cell where *conceptual knowledge* intersects with the cognitive process *understand.* Using the taxonomy during planning allows teachers to see what types of knowledge and cognitive processes they are emphasizing in their teaching.

The taxonomy reminds us that teaching and learning are complex processes with many possible outcomes. It also reminds us that we want our students to do much more than "remember" "factual knowledge." Unfortunately, a great deal of schooling focuses as much on this most basic type of goal as it does on the other 23 combined. Moving to the other forms of knowledge and more advanced cognitive processes is even more important in the twenty-first century, as student thinking, decision making, and problem solving are increasingly emphasized.

Instructional Alignment and Teacher Thinking **Instructional alignment** refers to *the consistency among goals, learning activities, practice, seatwork, homework, and assessments.* Effective teachers think about the relationships between their goals and

Careful planning helps teachers define their goals and make sure that instructional activities are aligned with these goals.

learning activities, and they carefully design learning activities to be consistent with the goals. Let's look at Shirley's thinking again. She wanted her students to be able to find equivalent fractions. So, she created examples of equivalent fractions that would help students understand both what equivalent fractions are and how to find them. Her learning activity—having students work with different forms of equivalent fractions—was consistent with her goal. She also created a worksheet that would give students practice in finding equivalent fractions and planned an assessment (the quiz) that would measure the extent to which students had reached her goal. Shirley planned so that each component—goal, examples (to be used in her learning activity), practice, and assessment—was consistent with every other component. These relationships are illustrated in Figure 11.3.

Figure 11.3 Instructional Alignment

As another example, let's examine the following description of a lesson with eighth-grade physical science students.

Case STUDY Ray Adams began his lesson by saying that he wanted his students to understand heat transfer. He began by conducting a demonstration in which he attached a piece of wax 2 inches from the end of a copper wire, an aluminum wire, and a steel wire. He then simultaneously heated the end of each wire with candles and had the students make observations. Seeing that the wax fell off the copper wire first, the students discussed their findings and concluded that the heat traveled the most rapidly along the copper wire.

Ray then displayed a list of the following vocabulary words on the overhead:

conductor	insulator	conduction
convection	radiation	heat
temperature	energy	matter

For homework, he told the students to look up the terms in their books and write the definition of each. The next day he gave a quiz in which the students had to match the terms and their definitions.

• • ● • •

Let's look at Ray's lesson. He stated that his objective was for students to understand heat transfer, and his learning activity—the demonstration and discussion—illustrated differences in the ability of different metals to transfer heat. However, his homework assignment and his quiz focused on the definitions of vocabulary words; they were only vaguely related to his objective and learning activity. This is a case of instruction that is out of alignment.

Why was Ray's lesson out of alignment? Most likely, Ray hadn't thought carefully or clearly about his goal; he didn't decide precisely what he wanted his students to understand about heat transfer, and as a result, he was unable to make effective decisions about his practice (homework) and assessment. This lack of careful thinking and planning detracts from learning.

Although effective teachers have thought carefully about their choice of goals, they are also able to adapt if they see that their students have misconceptions that interfere with learning. For instance, a teacher involving her students in a lesson on heat found that they believed that coats and sweaters *caused* heat, which explained for them why we stay warmer in a coat than in a light sweater. Because of these misconceptions, the teacher rethought her goals, changed the direction of the lesson, and had her students put thermometers in coats and sweaters to see which one "caused" more heat. When students found no differences, they were more prepared to accept the idea that clothing traps rather than causes or generates heat (Watson & Konicek, 1990).

Personal Characteristics

Think about some of the best teachers you've had. What is the first thing that comes to mind? If you're typical, you believe that these teachers cared about you as a person, were committed to your learning, and were enthusiastic about the topics they taught.

Effective teachers tend to have several personal characteristics that provide a foundation for their interactions with students. In this section we examine their attributes in four areas:

- Personal teaching efficacy
- Caring

- Modeling and enthusiasm
- Expectations

Personal Teaching Efficacy To introduce this section, let's look back to Shirley's brief conversation with her husband, Jim.

> *Shirley:* My students didn't score as well as I would have liked on the fractions part of the Stanford Achievement Test last year, and I promised myself they were going to do better this year.
>
> *Jim:* But you said the students aren't as sharp this year.
>
> *Shirley:* That doesn't matter. I'm pushing them harder. I think I can do a better job than I did last year. They're going to be so good at finding equivalent fractions and adding fractions with unlike denominators that they'll be able to do the problems in their sleep.
>
> *Jim:* You never lose your enthusiasm, do you?

Shirley's comments illustrate a characteristic called **personal teaching efficacy,** a concept we introduced in our discussion of effective schools in Chapter 7 and defined as *a teacher's belief that he or she can promote learning in all students regardless of their backgrounds* (Bruning et al., 2004). Shirley's comments "I think I can do a better job than I did last year" and "They're going to be so good at finding equivalent fractions" reflect her belief in her ability to help all her students learn and her decision to take responsibility for the success or failure of her own instruction. This is characteristic of teachers with high personal teaching efficacy (Lee, 2000).

When students aren't learning as much as they could, high-efficacy teachers don't blame it on lack of intelligence, poor home environments, uncooperative administrators, or some other external cause. Instead, they redouble their efforts, convinced they can increase student learning. They create classroom climates in which students feel safe and free to express their thinking without fear of embarrassment or ridicule. They emphasize praise rather than criticism, persevere with low achievers, and maximize the time available for instruction. Low-efficacy teachers, in contrast, are less student-centered, spend less time on learning activities, "give up" on low achievers, and are more critical when students fail (Kagan, 1992). High-efficacy teachers also adopt new curriculum materials and change strategies more readily than do low-efficacy teachers. Not surprisingly, students taught by high-efficacy teachers learn more than those taught by low-efficacy teachers (Tschannen-Moran, Woolfolk-Hoy, & Hoy, 1998).

CW

Increasing Understanding 11.3

Explain why low-efficacy teachers are likely to spend less time on learning activities than high-efficacy teachers.

Caring You've made an appointment to meet an instructor about some problems you're having in his class, and he shows up 15 minutes late with a mumbled, "I've been so terribly busy lately." As he talks with you, he keeps glancing at his watch, giving you the impression he wants to be somewhere else. In contrast, when you meet with another instructor, he is in his office at the agreed-upon time, and he spends as much time with you as you need. How do you feel in each situation?

These simple incidents relate to **caring,** *a teacher's ability to empathize with and invest in the protection and development of young people* (Chaskin & Rauner, 1995). We all want to be cared about, and advertisers capitalize on that fact with slogans such as "We care about you after the sale" and "Shop with the people who care."

CW

Increasing Understanding 11.4

The single most important indicator of caring is a teacher's willingness to devote time to a student. Use this indicator to explain why you are likely to react badly when an instructor arrives 15 minutes late to an appointment.

We saw in Chapter 2 that "caring professional" is one of the many roles of a teacher, and caring is essential for effective teaching. Students can tell when teachers care, all parents want their children to be with caring teachers, and even university students value instructors who genuinely care about them and their learning. A growing body of research documents the importance of caring for both student achievement and learner motivation (Bosworth, 1995; Stipek, 2002). Caring teachers are

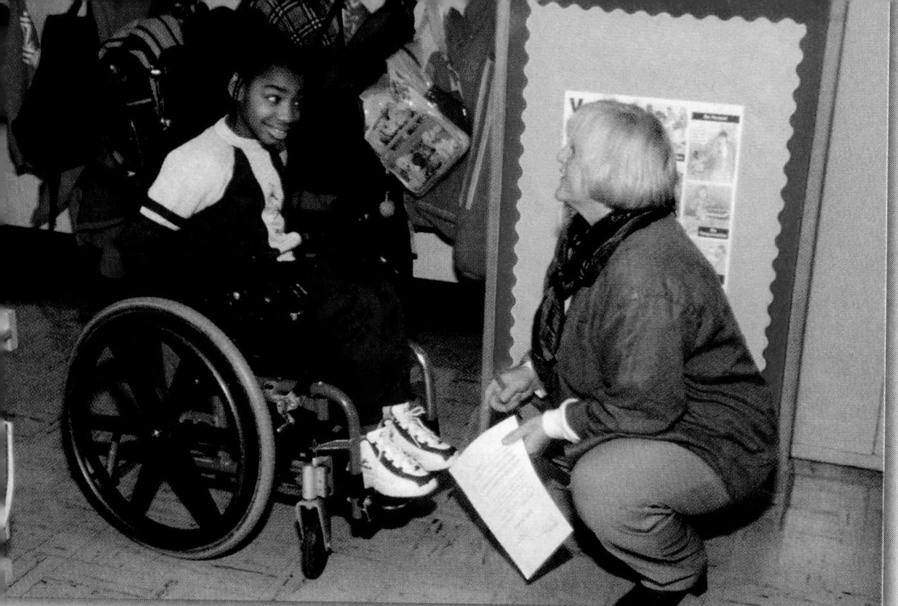

Caring, an essential component of effective teaching, connects teachers with students on a human level.

committed to their students' learning and developing competence. They attempt to do their very best for the people under their charge (Noddings, 1995).

Modeling and Enthusiasm We often hear that "actions speak louder than words," and this statement is especially true for teachers. Teachers are powerful role models for students, and the way they act influences both learning and motivation (Bandura, 1989). **Modeling** means *exhibiting behavior that is observed and imitated by others.* Like all people, students have a tendency to imitate behaviors they observe in others. So, to be a good role model, you should behave in ways you would like your students to imitate. For instance, if you want your students to be courteous and respectful to you and each other, you will treat them with courtesy and respect. If you want them to be diligent and conscientious in their studies, you will demonstrate that you also prepare thoroughly and work hard at your teaching.

Teachers model enthusiasm or lack of it. Suppose one of your instructors said, "I know this stuff is boring, but we have to learn it" or "This isn't my favorite topic either." How would you feel? Almost certainly, your interest in the topic would decrease. In contrast, think again about Jim's comment to Shirley, "You never lose your enthusiasm, do you?" Assuming Shirley displays this enthusiasm in front of her students, she is modeling her interest in the content she is teaching.

Teachers demonstrate enthusiasm most effectively by modeling their own genuine interest in the topics they're teaching (Good & Brophy, 2003). You can make even the most mundane topic more palatable to students if you can show this. Teachers who present information enthusiastically increase both student achievement and learners' beliefs about their ability to understand the topics they're studying (Perry, 1985; Perry, Magnusson, Parsonson, & Dickens, 1986).

Teacher Expectations To begin this section, let's analyze two short interactions between a teacher and her students.

Mrs. Vaughn: What kind of triangle is this? . . . Lisa?

Lisa: I . . . don't know.

Mrs. Vaughn: Sure you do. What do you notice about the lengths of these three sides?

Lisa: They're . . . equal. It's an equilateral triangle.

Now compare what you've just read with the following:

Mrs. Vaughn: What kind of triangle is this? . . . Jessica?

Jessica: I . . . I don't know.

Mrs. Vaughn: Can you help her out, Gena?

The difference between the way Mrs. Vaughn communicated with Lisa and the way she communicated with Jessica may not seem particularly important, but it is. Her comments to Lisa suggest that she *expected* Lisa to be able to answer, but she didn't have the same expectations for Jessica. A single incident may not be significant, but if Mrs. Vaughn's interactions with the two girls represent a pattern, differences in achievement can result (Good & Brophy, 2003).

Research indicates that teachers who have high expectations for students treat them differently than those for whom they have low expectations. Students for whom teachers have high expectations receive different treatment in the following areas:

- *Emotional support.* When teachers have high expectations for students, they interact with them more, and the interactions are more positive.
- *Teacher effort.* Teachers give them clearer and more thorough explanations and require more complete and accurate answers.
- *Questioning.* Teachers call on them more often, give them more time to answer, and prompt them more.
- *Feedback.* Teachers give them more praise and less criticism, and they provide more complete and thorough feedback.

Students are sensitive to these differences, and children as young as first grade are aware of differential treatment (Stipek, 2002). In one study, researchers concluded, "After ten seconds of seeing and/or hearing a teacher, even very young students (third grade) could detect whether the teacher talked about or to an excellent or a weak student and could determine the extent to which that student was loved by the teacher" (Babad, Bernieri, & Rosenthal, 1991, p. 230). This is both amazing and disquieting; it places a heavy burden on teachers to communicate caring and high expectations to all students.

Expectations can be self-fulfilling. When we treat students as if they can't learn, they don't try as hard. The reduced effort results in less learning, and a downward spiral begins (R. Weinstein, 1998). Unfortunately, teachers often can't control their actions because they don't realize they hold different expectations for their students. As they become aware of these possibilities, however, and with effort, they can learn to treat all students as equally as possible. We examine specific strategies to promote equitable treatment in the next section of the chapter.

Teaching Strategies

To begin this section, let's return to Shirley's work. We join her on Monday morning just before math, which she schedules each day from 10:00 to 11:00.

Case STUDY As Shirley walked up and down the aisles, she put sheets of paper on each student's desk as the students finished a writing assignment in language arts.

"Quickly turn in your writing, and get out your math books," she directed. The students stopped their writing and passed the papers forward, each putting his or her paper on top of the stack. Shirley put the papers into a folder, and at 10:01 she pulled out her cardboard "pizzas." "Let's see what we remember about adding fractions. How many pieces of the first pizza did we eat? . . . Dean?" she asked as she displayed the pizzas, which now had some pieces covered with colored paper.

"Three."

"And how about this pizza? How many pieces did we eat? . . . Kathy?"

"Two."

She then wrote $3/8 + 2/8$ on the board and, pointing to these numbers, asked, "Why did I write $3/8$ here and $2/8$ there? . . . Omar?"

"You have . . . 8 pieces altogether . . . and you ate 3 of them," Omar responded hesitantly.

"Good," Shirley smiled. "And what about the second one? How many pieces of that pizza did we eat? . . . Selina?"

"Two."

"So what fraction of a total pizza did we eat altogether? . . . Gabriel?" she asked as she walked down the aisle.

"Five . . . eighths of a pizza?" Gabriel responded after thinking for a few seconds.

As soon as Shirley walked past him, Kevin stuck his foot across the aisle, tapping Alison on the leg with his shoe while he watched Shirley's back. "Stop it, Kevin," Alison muttered, swiping at him with her hand.

Shirley turned, came back up the aisle, and continued, "Good, Gabriel," and standing next to Kevin, asked, "Why is it $\frac{5}{8}$? . . . Kevin?" she looked directly at Kevin.

". . ."

"How many pieces altogether in each pizza?"

"Eight," Kevin answered.

"Good, . . . and how many did we eat, altogether?"

"Five."

"Yes," she smiled at Kevin, "so we ate $\frac{5}{8}$ of a pizza."

Shirley then wrote $\frac{3}{7} + \frac{4}{7} = ?$ and $\frac{1}{12} + \frac{5}{12} = ?$ on the board and had the students solve and explain the problems. During the discussion she moved over to Sondra, who had been whispering and passing notes to Sherill across the aisle, and said quietly, "Move up here," nodding to a desk at the front of the room.

"What did I do?" Sondra protested.

"When we talked about our rules at the beginning of the year, we agreed that it was important to listen when other people are talking," Shirley whispered to her.

Tapping her knuckle on the chalkboard, Shirley said, "Now, let's think once more about these problems (referring to the solved problems from the previous discussions). What is similar about them?"

". . . They all have the same number of pieces," Karen noted.

"Explain what you mean," Shirley probed.

". . . Like 8 and 8, 7 and 7, and 12 and 12."

"Good!" Shirley emphasized. "In each of these problems, the two fractions have the same denominator. . . . Be sure to keep that in mind as we continue our study of fractions.

"Now, we're going to shift gears because I've got another, different kind of problem," Shirley continued, pulling out the two cardboard "cakes."

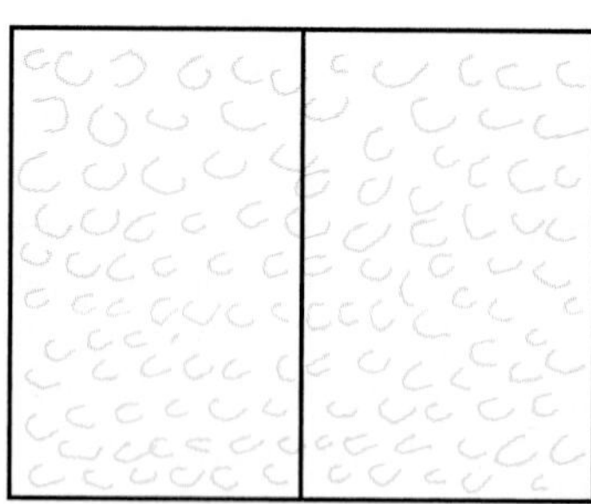

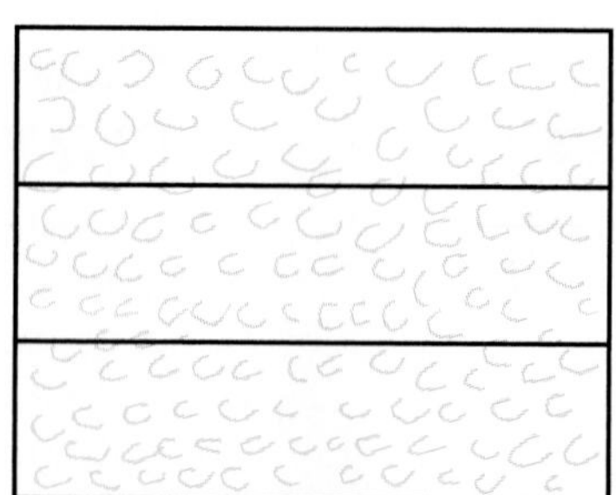

"Now we have cakes instead of pizza, . . . and I'm still hungry, so I eat this piece," she said, pointing to a third. "Then I go sort of wild and eat this piece too," she added, pointing to one of the halves. "How much cake have I eaten?"

"A third of one and a half of the other," Tenisha volunteered.

"Makes sense, . . . but is that more than a whole cake, a whole cake, or part of a cake?"

". . . I think less," Adam offered.

"How do you think we could find out for sure?" Shirley wondered. She paused and then said, "To help us, take two of the sheets of paper that I put on your desks, and carefully fold them like our cakes here."

The students quickly began, and Shirley helped some of them who had trouble folding their papers into thirds.

"Now we have two whole cakes. Let's think about our problem again. If we eat a third of one and a half of the other one, how much have we eaten altogether? . . . How can we figure that out?"

". . . Let's lay one on top of the other," Jan suggested, after thinking for several seconds.

"Good idea. . . . Go ahead and try it."

"It's less than a whole cake," Tanya offered after peering carefully at the papers.

"How much less?"

The students offered a few uncertain suggestions, and Shirley then asked, "Let's think about the work we've been doing. What did we just review?" She pointed at the chalkboard.

"Adding up the pizzas," Juan offered.

"And what do we know about them?"

". . . They weren't like the cakes," Bryan added.

"In what way?" Shirley asked with a quizzical shrug.

"They had the same-size parts, and these are different," he said and pointed to the cakes.

"Maybe we need to cut them different so they're the same," Enrico suggested.

"Good idea, Enrico. . . . Let me make a suggestion about how we can get them to be the same, using Enrico's idea. . . . Go ahead and shade one part of each of your papers, so you have a third shaded on this one and a half shaded on the other one," Shirley said, pointing to the papers.

She continued, "How much cake do we have here? . . . Tim?"

"A third."

"Fine," Shirley smiled. "Now, let's all fold our cakes this way." She folded the three-piece cake in half vertically as she watched the students. "How many pieces do I have altogether now? . . . Karen?"

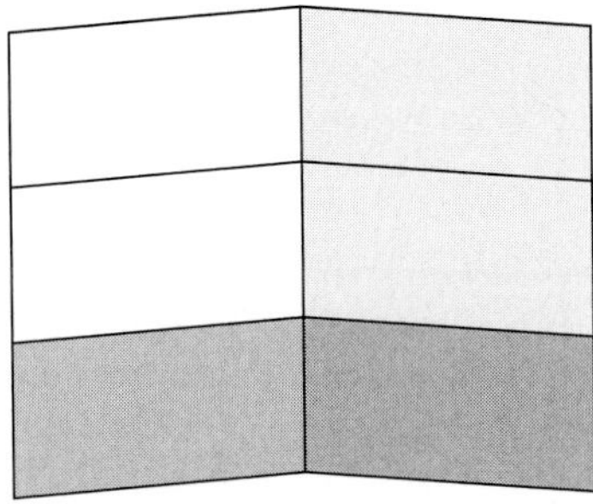

". . . It looks like six," she responded.

"Yes. Good, Karen. I saw you actually counting them," Shirley noted and then counted the six squares again out loud. "So what portion is now shaded? . . . Jon?"

"Two sixths."

"Excellent, Jon!" She moved to the chalkboard and wrote $\frac{1}{3} = \frac{2}{6}$.

"Now how do we know that the $\frac{1}{3}$ and $\frac{2}{6}$ are equal?"

"It's the same amount of cake," Dan shrugged.

Shirley continued by having the students divide the two-piece cake in thirds, horizontally, so it appeared as follows:

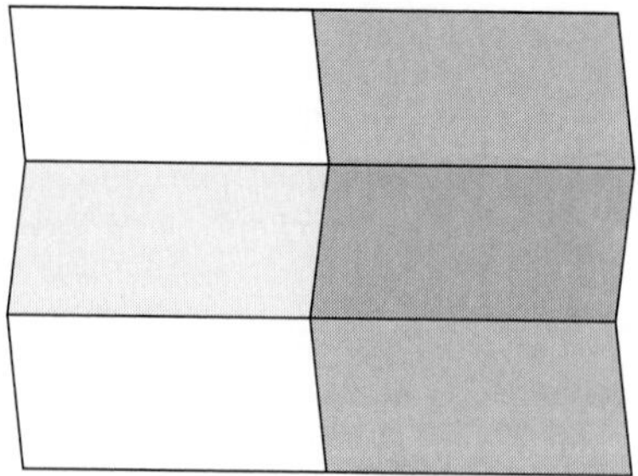

"What do we see here?"

". . . They both have the same number of pieces," Lorraine noted.

"And all the pieces are the same size," Crystal added.

"Ooh, ooh, I know!" Adam said excitedly. "We've eaten $\frac{5}{6}$ of the cake."

"That's an interesting thought, Adam. Would you explain that for us please?"

"It's like the pizza. We have two pieces there, and three pieces there, so it's $\frac{5}{6}$ of the pizza, . . . uh cake."

"Let's think about what we did," Shirley continued. "What was our problem?"

". . . We were trying to figure out how much cake we ate," Lakesha offered.

"Why was that a problem?"

"The pieces weren't the same size."

"So what did we do about it? . . . Karen?"

"We fixed them so they were the same size."

"And exactly how did we do that? . . . Bryan?"

"We made the $\frac{1}{3}$ of a cake into $\frac{2}{6}$, and we made the $\frac{1}{2}$ of a cake into $\frac{3}{6}$, and then we could just add them up."

Shirley then gave the students the problem $\frac{1}{3} + \frac{1}{4}$ and had them fold two additional sheets of paper to demonstrate that $\frac{1}{3} = \frac{4}{12}$ and $\frac{1}{4} = \frac{3}{12}$, so they could get an answer of $\frac{7}{12}$.

As the discussion was winding down, Shirley announced, "Tomorrow, I'll show you a way to make the parts equal a little more quickly. Then we won't have to work as hard as we did with the problems today."

Finally, seeing it was 10:59, Shirley said, "It's nearly time for our break. As soon as you've cleaned up around your desks, we'll go."

• • ● • •

In addition to differences in the thinking and the personal characteristics of effective and less effective teachers, research has also identified important differences in the way they teach. Differences in teaching strategies are evident in the following areas:

- The way teachers organize their classrooms
- How they communicate with students
- Their questioning skills
- The way they present their subject matter
- The kind of feedback they provide

Classroom Organization Let's look back at Shirley's lesson. She scheduled math from 10:00 to 11:00, and she made the transition from language arts to math in 3 minutes. She continued the lesson until 10:59; so, of a possible 60 minutes of time al-

Table 11.1 Teacher Actions That Promote Organization

Teacher Action	Example
Starting on time	Shirley's students had their math books out and were waiting at 10:01.
Making smooth transitions	Shirley made the transition from language arts to math in 3 minutes.
Preparing materials in advance	Shirley had her cardboard pizzas and cakes easily accessible.
Establishing routines	At Shirley's signal, the students put their paper on the top of the stack without being told specifically to do so.

located to math, she used 58 minutes for instruction. In addition, she had her cardboard pizzas and cakes placed where she could easily access them, and she distributed the sheets of paper on the students' desks as they turned in their papers. Further, Shirley had taught her students time-saving routines; for instance, they placed their papers on the top of the stacks as they were passed forward, without being reminded to do so.

These examples illustrate **classroom organization,** *the set of teacher actions that maximizes the amount of time available for instruction.* Some of these actions, along with examples, are outlined in Table 11.1.

Less effective teachers often aren't well organized. They spend more time in transitions from one activity to another, so they often fail to start lessons when they're scheduled; they spend valuable class time accessing materials; and their routines are not well established. The result is fewer minutes available for instruction and, ultimately, less learning.

Communication The link between effective teacher communication, student achievement, and student satisfaction with instruction is well established (Cruickshank, 1985; S. Snyder et al., 1991). Research also indicates that the way teachers interact with students influences their motivation and attitudes toward school (Pintrich & Schunk, 2002). Effective and less effective teachers exhibit differences in four areas related to communication:

- Language clarity
- Thematic lessons
- Transition signals
- Emphasis

Language clarity is *a clearness of language that results from eliminating vague terms (such as* perhaps, maybe, might, and so on, *and* usually*).* When teachers use these terms in their explanations and responses to students' questions, students are left uncertain about the topics they're studying, and this uncertainty can detract from learning (Shuell, 1996). For example, suppose you ask, "What do high-efficacy teachers do that promotes learning?" One instructor responds, "Usually, they use their time somewhat better and so on." Another responds, "They believe they can increase learning, and one of their characteristics is the effective use of time." The first response is muddled and uncertain, whereas the second is clear and precise.

Increasing Understanding 11.5

Could a lesson be thematic if the teacher interjected unplanned or unrelated content or topics during instruction? Explain.

Teachers who are effective communicators create lessons that are thematic. A **thematic lesson** is *a lesson in which all parts of a teacher's instruction are related, so that the lesson leads to a specific point.* If the point of the lesson isn't clear, if it is sequenced inappropriately, or if incidental information is interjected without indicating how it relates to the topic, the lesson becomes disconnected and less meaningful for students. Effective teachers keep their lessons on track, minimizing time on matters unrelated to the topic (Coker, Lorentz, & Coker, 1980; L. Smith & Cotten, 1980).

Effective teachers also use transition signals to connect different parts of their lesson. **Transition signals** are *verbal statements within a lesson that indicate one idea is ending and another is beginning.* For example, an American government teacher might signal a transition by saying, "We've been talking about the Senate, which is one house of Congress. Now we'll turn to the House of Representatives." Because not all students are mentally at the same place, a transition signal alerts them that the lesson is making a conceptual shift—a move to a new topic—and allows them to adjust and prepare for it. Shirley signaled a transition when she said, "Now, we're going to shift gears because I've got another, different kind of problem," as she pulled out her cardboard cakes.

Not all information in a lesson is equally important; teachers who are effective communicators use **emphasis,** *verbal and vocal cues and repetition used to alert students to important information in a lesson* (Jetton & Alexander, 1997). Shirley, for example, used emphasis when she said, "In each of these problems, the two fractions have the same denominator. . . . Be sure to keep that in mind as we continue our study of fractions." When teachers say "This is very important," or "Listen carefully now," they're using verbal emphasis. Teachers can also give vocal cues—by enunciating certain words or speaking more loudly, for instance—to draw attention to what they're saying.

Repeating a point—redundancy—is also a form of emphasis. For instance, the question "What did we say earlier that these problems had in common?" reminds students of an important feature in the problems and helps them link new to past information. Redundancy is particularly effective when reviewing abstract rules, principles, and concepts that are hard to learn (Shuell, 1996).

One characteristic of teachers that affects all aspects of communication is their knowledge of content. When teachers' own understanding of the topics they teach is uncertain, communication suffers. They use more vague terms in their questions and explanations, their lessons are less thematic, and they fail to emphasize the most important points in the lesson. When teachers recognize their grasp of a topic is uncertain, they should spend extra time studying and preparing (Carlsen, 1987; Cruickshank, 1985).

Teacher Questioning In the last 20 years a major shift in classrooms has occurred. In the past, teachers explained topics and students were expected to listen quietly and then work independently at their desks. Expert teachers knew, however, that learners are naturally active and that the best way to increase understanding is to design learning activities in which students are as involved as possible. One of the most effective ways of involving students is through *questioning.*

Questioning can be an exhilarating experience for both you and your students. Being able to ask effective questions is the most important ability teachers have for guiding student learning (M. Wang et al., 1993). A teacher skilled in questioning can determine how much students already know about a topic, encourage learners to rethink their ideas, help students form relationships, involve shy or reticent students, recapture students' attention, promote success, and enhance self-esteem. Becoming skilled in questioning is difficult, but with effort and experience, teachers can and do become expert at it (Kerman, 1979; Rowe, 1986).

With respect to questioning, effective and less effective teachers differ in four areas:

- Frequency
- Equitable distribution
- Wait-time
- Prompting

Frequency. **Questioning frequency** is *the number of times a teacher asks a question during a given period of instructional time.* Effective teachers ask many more questions than do less effective teachers, and Shirley's lesson illustrates this point. Instead of relying on explaining and telling as her strategy, Shirley developed her entire lesson with questioning. Students involved in question-and-answer sessions are more attentive than those who listen passively to teacher explanations, and as a result, achievement increases (Morine-Dershimer, 1985; Pratton & Hales, 1986).

Equitable distribution. Who should teachers call on during a lesson? To begin to answer this question, let's look again at some dialogue from Shirley's lesson.

> *Shirley:* Let's see what we remember about adding fractions. How many pieces of the first pizza did we eat? . . . Dean? (as she displayed the cardboard pizzas)
>
> *Dean:* Three.
>
> *Shirley:* And how about this pizza? How many pieces did we eat? . . . Kathy?
>
> *Kathy:* Two.
>
> *Shirley:* Why did I write $\frac{3}{8}$ here and $\frac{2}{8}$ there? . . . Omar? (as she pointed to the fractions she had written on the board)
>
> *Omar:* You have . . . 8 pieces altogether . . . and you ate 3 of them.
>
> *Shirley:* Good. And what about the second one? How many pieces of that pizza did we eat? . . . Selina?
>
> *Selina:* Two.
>
> *Shirley:* So what fraction of a total pizza did we eat altogether? . . . Gabriel?

Here we see that Shirley directed each of her questions to a different student, and in each case, she addressed the student by name. This pattern illustrates **equitable distribution,** *the practice of calling on all students—both volunteers and nonvolunteers—as equally as possible.* This practice sends an important message to students. By treating students equally, the teacher is saying, "I don't care whether you're a boy or girl, minority or nonminority, high achiever or low achiever, I want you in my classroom, and I want you actively involved. I believe you're capable of learning, and I will do whatever it takes to ensure that you're successful." When a teacher practices equitable distribution, students believe that the teacher expects them to participate and learn. Perhaps even more importantly, because the teacher is making this effort, students believe the teacher is genuinely committed to their learning.

CW

Increasing Understanding 11.6

Describe what might happen if a student in a classroom was rarely called on.

Equitable distribution is a powerful tool for promoting both achievement and student motivation (Stipek, 2002). In classrooms where it is practiced, student achievement rises, classroom management problems decrease, and attendance rates go up (Good & Brophy, 2003; Kerman, 1979). Equitable distribution also works at the college level; students who expect to be called on prepare more fully for class, retain more information, and have greater confidence in what they learn (McDougall & Granby, 1996).

Less effective teachers spend more time lecturing and explaining than do effective teachers, and when they do question, they either allow only volunteers to answer, or they call on the highest achievers in their classes (Good & Brophy, 2003). This communicates that they have lower expectations for nonparticipants, and it also communicates that the teacher cares less about these students (Stipek, 2002).

Wait-time. Look again at the dialogue between Shirley and her students. In each case, after asking a question, Shirley paused briefly and gave the students a few seconds to think before she called on someone. This *period of silence after a question is asked* is called **wait-time.** Giving students a few seconds to think about their answers makes sense, but in most classrooms—regardless of grade or ability levels—wait-times are very short, often one second or less (Rowe, 1986). Increasing wait-time to about 3 to 5 seconds positively influences learning in at least three ways (Rowe, 1986; Tobin, 1987):

- The length and quality of student responses improve.
- Failures to respond are reduced.
- Student participation in general, as well as participation from minority students, improves.

Prompting. Let's look at some additional dialogue from Shirley's lesson.

Shirley: Why is it [the fraction of the pizza they ate] $\frac{5}{8}$? . . . Kevin?

Kevin: . . .

Shirley: How many pieces altogether in each pizza?

Kevin: Eight.

Shirley: Good, . . . and how many did we eat, altogether?

Kevin: Five.

Kevin was initially unable to answer correctly, so Shirley provided him with a **prompt,** *a teacher question or directive that elicits a student response after the student*

Questioning provides opportunities for the teacher to assess learning and motivate students by actively involving them in learning activities.

has failed to answer or has given an incorrect or incomplete answer. The importance of prompting is well documented by research (Shuell, 1996). As with equitable distribution, it communicates that the teacher believes the student is capable and that he or she expects the student to answer.

Less effective teachers, instead of prompting, tend to turn the question to another student, asking, for instance, "Can someone help Kevin out here?" This communicates that the teacher doesn't believe Kevin is capable of answering and doesn't expect him to do so. This is not a message we want to send students.

Presentation of Subject Matter Teachers use a variety of teaching strategies when they present subject matter, and these vary in their ability to promote learning. Describing and explaining the topics is the most common method teachers use to help learners understand them (Cuban, 1984; Goodlad, 1984). However, research indicates that simply explaining or telling isn't the most effective way of helping students learn (Bransford et al., 2000; Brenner et al., 1997). In contrast, the following two interrelated strategies can significantly increase learning:

- Use of examples
- High levels of interaction

Use of examples. Let's think again about how Shirley conducted her lesson. She used cardboard pizzas to illustrate the addition of fractions with like denominators, and she used cardboard cakes and folded sheets of paper to illustrate equivalent fractions and the addition of fractions with unlike denominators. Each was an **example,** *a specific real-world instance of an object or event.* Because they link abstract ideas to concrete information, examples help students develop their understanding.

In another lesson, a science teacher might have students compress cotton balls in a clear cup as an example of the concept *density*. By seeing that the compressed cotton is more compact (dense), students experience a real-world instance of the concept. The science teacher might also drop an ice cube into a cup of water and another into a cup of alcohol. The ice floats on the water but sinks in the alcohol, demonstrating that the ice is less dense than the water but more dense than the alcohol. In language arts, teachers can use actual student writing samples to provide examples of good organization, grammar, and punctuation. In social studies, the teacher might prepare descriptions, such as the following, as examples of the concept *culture:*

. . • . .

Pedro is a boy living in a small Mexican village. Every day he rises early, for he must walk the 2 miles to his school. He has breakfast of beans and tortillas made from ground corn, then leaves the house to begin his trek. He likes the walk because he can wave to his papa as he toils in the cornfields that provide the food and income for the family.

When Pedro comes home from school, he often plays soccer with his friends in the village. After dinner his family either plays music or reads, as they don't have electricity. But this evening his mother must go to a meeting of the town council, whose members are trying to raise money for a new addition to the school. No decisions can be made without the approval of the council.

. . • . .

Chu is a young girl living in a fishing village in Japan. Chu is up early and helps her mother with breakfast for her younger brothers and sisters. Chu loves the rice smothered in fish sauce that she often eats in the morning.

Chu skips out the door, bowing to her father as she goes. He is preparing tools to take to the docks, where he will meet his partner for their daily fishing expedition. He has been a fisherman for 30 years. Chu comes home from school, finishes her work, and then goes down the street to play ping pong with the rest of the neighborhood boys and girls. She is the best player in the area. Before bed Chu listens to stories of the old days told by her grandmother, who lives with them.

• • ● • •

Each example describes foods, recreation, the way the people make a living, and aspects of home life. These are all characteristics of the concept *culture.* Unlike an abstract definition, the examples provide students with concrete information about what culture is and how it influences lives.

The importance of high-quality examples in teaching can't be overstated. Effective teachers illustrate topics in ways that are understandable to students, whereas less effective teachers tend to rely on verbal explanations (Cassady, 1999; Spiro, Feltovich, Jacobson, & Coulson, 1992).

High levels of interaction. High-quality examples, alone, don't ensure learning. Students may either miss important characteristics illustrated in the examples, or they may not perceive the information in the examples correctly. To prevent this problem, effective teachers use high levels of interaction, as Shirley did, to guide learning. This interaction actively involves students and allows teachers to diagnose and correct student misconceptions, connect the lesson to earlier lessons, and bring the lesson to closure. The use of high-quality examples and high levels of interaction are two of the most important teaching strategies for promoting learning.

Feedback Have you ever been in a class where you had to wait until the midterm exam to find out how you were doing? Have you handed in assignments and had to wait weeks before they were scored and returned? In both instances you were left uncertain about your learning progress because of the absence of feedback. **Feedback** is *information about current performance that can be used to increase future learning.* Feedback should be immediate, specific, and provide corrective information about the extent to which students' understanding of a topic is valid.

One of the most effective ways of providing feedback is through our interactions with learners. For instance, let's consider the concept *density* again. Students commonly equate density with weight, concluding that heavy objects are more dense than light objects. When they do, they must be provided with feedback that helps them eliminate this misconception. As an example, let's look at a class where the teacher had students compress cotton in the cup as an example of density.

Teacher: What can we conclude about the cotton now? (after being compressed)

Student: It's heavier.

Teacher: How does the total amount of cotton we have now compare to the amount before we compressed it?

Student: It's . . . the same.

Teacher: So, if the amount is the same, how does the weight now compare to the weight before?

Student: Must be . . . the same.

Teacher: What is different?

Student: The . . . amount of space it takes up. It's squished down.

Teacher: Yes, good. The weight is the same. The density has changed.

This kind of interactive feedback is essential for learning. Merely explaining that the weight is the same is much less effective, because students passively listen to the explanation instead of actively wrestling with their own understanding.

Classroom Management

To begin this section let's revisit part of Shirley's lesson. We rejoin her as she is finishing her review of adding fractions with like denominators.

Case STUDY "So what fraction of a total pizza did we eat altogether? . . . Gabriel?" she asked as she walked down the aisle.

"Five . . . eighths of a pizza?" Gabriel responded after thinking for a few seconds.

As soon as Shirley walked past him, Kevin stuck his foot across the aisle, tapping Alison on the leg with his shoe while he watched Shirley's back. "Stop it, Kevin," Alison muttered, swiping at him with her hand.

Shirley turned, came back up the aisle, and continued, "Good, Gabriel," and standing next to Kevin, asked, "Why is it 5/8? . . . Kevin?" She looked directly at Kevin.

". . ."

"How many pieces altogether in each pizza?"

"Eight," Kevin answered.

"Good, . . . and how many did we eat, altogether?"

"Five."

"Yes," she smiled at Kevin, "so we ate 5/8 of a pizza."

Shirley then wrote 3/7 + 4/7 = ? and 1/2 + 5/12 = ? on the board and had students solve and explain the problems. During the discussion she moved over to Sondra, who had been whispering and passing notes to Sherill across the aisle, and said quietly, "Move up here," nodding to a desk at the front of the room.

"What did I do?" Sondra protested.

"When we talked about our rules at the beginning of the year, we agreed that it was important to listen when other people are talking," Shirley whispered to her.

Tapping her knuckle on the chalkboard, Shirley said, "Now, let's think once more about these problems (referring to the solved problems from the previous discussions). What is similar about them?"

• • ● • •

From the 1960s until the present, national Gallup polls have identified classroom management as one of the most challenging problems teachers face. Seventy-six percent of those polled in 2002 said discipline was a very or somewhat serious problem in U.S. schools (Rose & Gallup, 2002). It's the primary concern of beginning teachers (Rose & Gallup, 1999), and Shirley's experience illustrates why. She had carefully planned her lesson and was conducting it effectively, but she still had to respond to Kevin's and Sondra's disruptions. These kinds of incidents are common occurrences in most classrooms and can seriously disrupt learning.

Disruptive students are also an important source of stress for both beginning and veteran teachers (Abel & Sewell, 1999). Nearly half of the teachers who leave the profession during the first 3 years do so because of discipline problems (Curwin, 1992), and difficulty with classroom management is a primary reason teachers leave urban classrooms (Weiner, 2002).

Classroom management has also been a major concern of policy makers, parents, and the public at large, particularly in the wake of highly publicized incidents of school violence (Elam & Rose, 1995). Although incidents of school violence arouse fear and concern in both parents and students, they are rare; it is the difficult job of establishing and maintaining orderly, learning-focused classrooms that teachers grapple with daily.

Classroom management is *the process of creating and maintaining orderly classrooms.* The importance of classroom management to effectively run classrooms is clear.

Table 11.2 The Obedience and Responsibility Models of Management

	Obedience Model	Responsibility Model
Goal	Teach students to follow orders.	Teach students to make responsible choices.
Organizing Principle	Obey authority.	Learn from actions and decisions.
Teacher Actions	Punish and reward.	Explain and apply logical consequences.
Student Outcomes	Students learn obedience and conformity.	Students internalize the reasons for rules and learn to self-regulate.

Source: Curwin and Mendler (1988b).

One group of researchers concluded, "Effective classroom management has been shown to increase student engagement, decrease disruptive behaviors, and enhance use of instructional time, all of which results in improved student achievement" (Wang et al., 1993, p. 262). Effective management is one of the key characteristics of an effective school (Purkey & Smith, 1983), and an orderly classroom increases students' motivation to learn (Radd, 1998).

Teachers should have two goals when they plan for and implement classroom management. The first is to create environments that promote the most learning possible (Morine-Dershimer & Reeve, 1994), and the second is to help students learn to manage and direct their own learning (McCaslin & Good, 1992).

CW

Increasing Understanding 11.7

Review the episode from Shirley's classroom presented at the beginning of this section. Does Shirley have an obedience or a responsibility approach to management? Cite specific evidence from the episode to support your answer.

In attempting to teach students to manage their own learning, the difference between an obedience orientation and a responsibility orientation is important (Curwin & Mendler, 1988a). An **obedience model of management** is *an approach to classroom management in which teachers teach students to follow rules and obey authority through the use of reward and punishment.* A **responsibility model of management,** by contrast, is *an approach in which teachers teach students to make responsible choices by explaining reasons for rules and applying logical consequences for misbehavior.* Teachers who take the obedience approach may maintain control of their classroom, but those who take the responsibility approach are more likely to help their students learn self-management. Differences between these orientations are outlined in Table 11.2.

The key to teaching responsibility is to help students understand the consequences of their actions. Let's see how one teacher does this.

Case STUDY Allen, a rambunctious sixth grader, was running down the hall toward the lunchroom. As he rounded the corner, he bumped into Alyssia, causing her to drop her books.

"Oops," he replied, continuing his race to the lunchroom.

"Hold it, Allen," said Doug Ramsay, who was monitoring the hall. "Go back and help her pick up her books and apologize."

"Aww."

"Go on," Doug said firmly.

Allen walked back to Alyssia, helped her pick up her books, mumbled an apology, and then returned. As he approached, Doug again stopped him.

"Now, why did I make you do that?" Doug asked.

"Cuz we're not supposed to run."

"Sure," Doug said pleasantly, "but more important, if people are running in the halls, somebody might get hurt, and we don't want that to happen. . . . Remember that you're responsible for your actions. Think about not wanting to hurt yourself or anybody else, and the next time you'll walk whether a teacher is here or not. . . . Now, go on to lunch." (Eggen & Kauchak, 2004, p. 448)

• • ● • •

By emphasizing logical consequences, Doug helped Allen understand his behavior and its effect on other people. Research indicates that children who understand the effects of their actions on others become more altruistic and are more likely to take actions to make up for their misbehavior (Berk, 2004).

Classroom management is a challenge, but research offers some guidelines in the following areas:

- Using effective instructional strategies
- Preventing problems through planning
- Intervening effectively

Let's consider them.

Using Effective Instructional Strategies Often overlooked in discussions of management and discipline is the role of effective instruction. Research indicates that it is virtually impossible to maintain an orderly classroom in the absence of good teaching and vice versa (W. Doyle, 1986).

Shirley's lesson was effective from both a management and instructional perspective for at least three reasons. First, she was well organized. She had well-established routines, she taught the students to make quick and smooth transitions from one learning activity to another, and she had her examples ready and waiting. Disruptions are most likely to occur during transitions and noninstructional times, such as when roll is being taken or papers are being turned in. Second, Shirley used high-quality examples in her teaching. They helped attract and maintain students' attention, and they included all the information the students needed to understand the topic. Third, the students were actively involved in the lesson. When students are involved, and they know they're likely to be called on, their attention increases, and the likelihood of inappropriate behavior decreases.

Preventing Problems Through Planning In some classrooms, management is nearly invisible. The atmosphere is calm but not rigid, physical movement around the classroom and interaction within lessons are comfortable, and students work quietly. Teachers give few directions that focus on behavior, they reprimand students infrequently, and the reprimands rarely intrude on learning. This was the case in Shirley's lesson. She stopped Kevin's and Sondra's disruptions without interrupting the flow of the lesson.

Obviously, some classes are tougher to manage than others, but an orderly classroom is possible in most instances. It doesn't happen by accident, however. It requires careful planning, and beginning teachers often underestimate the amount of time and energy it takes (C. Weinstein, Woolfolk, Dittmeier, & Shankar, 1994).

The cornerstone of effective management is a clearly understood and consistently monitored set of rules and procedures that prevents management problems before they occur (Emmer et al., 2003; Evertson et al., 2003). Prevention is essential; experts estimate that it is 80 percent of an effective management system (Freiberg, 1999).

In planning rules and procedures, teachers must consider both the characteristics of their students and the physical environment of their classrooms. For example, first graders are compliant and eager to please their teachers, but they also have short attention spans and tire easily (Evertson et al., 2003). In comparison, middle schoolers may attempt to test their independence, and they're sometimes rebellious and capricious. They need rules clearly stated and administered (Emmer et al., 2003). If you're preparing to be a first-grade teacher, you will make different management planning decisions than if you're preparing to be a middle school teacher.

As you consider the physical environment, you need to think about arranging desks and other furniture so that students can move freely when completing routine activities, such as lining up for breaks, sharpening pencils, or turning in work. All students must be able to easily see the board and screen, and the room should be arranged to avoid distractions from outside.

Preparing rules and procedures. Having considered your students' characteristics and your physical environment, you are ready to plan procedures and rules for your classroom. **Procedures** are *management routines students follow in their daily learning activities,* such as how they turn in papers, sharpen pencils, and make transitions from one activity to another. For instance, Shirley's students had been taught to turn in their papers from the ends of the rows, with each student putting his or her paper on the top of the stack as it moved forward. This allowed Shirley to collect the stacks from the students in the front. A similar procedure could be used to return papers to students. Seemingly minor procedures such as these help create a sense of order for students, and they save teachers both time and energy.

Effective teachers commonly create procedures related to the following:

- Entering and leaving the classroom
- Handing in and distributing papers
- Accessing materials such as scissors and paper
- Participating in class (e.g., when to raise hands)
- Making trips to the bathroom

After planning and teaching students about procedures, expert teachers have students practice procedures until they become routines students follow automatically (Borko & Putnam, 1996).

Rules (such as "Listen when someone else is talking") are *statements that provide standards for acceptable classroom behavior*, and research confirms their value in creating productive learning environments (Emmer et al., 2003; Evertson et al., 2003). When consistently enforced, clear, reasonable rules not only can reduce behavior problems that interfere with learning but also can promote a feeling of pride and responsibility in the school community. Perhaps surprisingly, students also see the enforcement of rules as evidence of caring: "Students also say that they want teachers to articulate and enforce clear standards of behavior. They view this not just as part of the teacher's job but as evidence that the teacher cares about them" (Brophy, 1998, p. 23).

Some examples of rules at different grade levels are found in Table 11.3. Note that some types of rules occur at all the levels, such as rules about students staying in their seats and waiting for permission to speak. Other rules are specific to a grade level and reflect the developmental characteristics of students at that level.

Some guidelines for preparing rules include the following:

- State rules positively.
- Emphasize rationales for rules.
- Minimize the number of rules.
- Monitor rules throughout the school year.

Table 11.3 Examples of Classroom Rules

First-Grade Teacher	Seventh-Grade Teacher	Tenth-Grade Teacher
• We raise our hands before speaking. • We leave our seats only when given permission by the teacher. • We stand politely in line at all times. • We keep our hands to ourselves. • We listen when someone else is talking.	• Be in your seat and quiet when the bell rings. • Follow directions the first time they're given • Bring covered textbooks, notebook, pen, pencils, and planner to class every day. • Raise your hand for permission to speak or leave your seat. • Keep hands, feet, and objects to yourself. • Leave class only when dismissed by the teacher. • Do all grooming outside of class.	• Be in your seat before the bell rings. • Stay in your seat at all times. • Bring all materials daily. This includes your book, notebook, pen/pencil, and paper. • Give your full attention to others in discussions, and wait your turn to speak. • Leave when I dismiss you, not when the bell rings.

Source: Eggen, P., & Kauchak, D. (2004). *Educational psychology: Windows on classrooms.* Upper Saddle River, NJ: Merrill/Prentice Hall, p. 433.

Each of these guidelines is intended to help students understand rules and the reasons for them, and understanding helps students begin to accept responsibility for their own behavior. Stating rules positively communicates desirable expectations for students, and keeping the number small helps prevent students from breaking rules simply because they forget. Providing rationales for rules is perhaps the most essential guideline. Students are much more likely to accept responsibility for their own behavior and obey rules when they understand the reasons for them. Finally, in spite of teachers' best efforts during planning and the initial teaching of rules, students will need periodic reminders throughout the year.

Intervening Effectively Even when teachers have planned carefully, disruptions inevitably occur, as we saw in Shirley's lesson. She planned her lesson, presented high-quality examples, and actively involved her students. Nevertheless, Kevin and Sondra were off task.

Dealing with off-task or potentially disruptive behavior requires immediate and judicious decision making. If a misbehavior is brief and minor, such as a student asking another student a quick question, it often can be ignored. However, if the behavior has the potential to disrupt the learning activity, you must intervene. Some guidelines can help when intervention is necessary:

- Intervene immediately.
- Direct the intervention at the correct students.
- Use the least intrusive intervention.

Let's see how Shirley implemented these guidelines. First, after concluding that Kevin's and Sondra's behaviors could distract others and potentially detract from learning, she intervened immediately. Because Kevin tapping Alison on the foot was more disruptive than Sondra's whispering, she responded to him first. Second, she targeted the correct students. She recognized that Alison's muttering was a response to

Classroom management, when done right, not only maintains an orderly learning environment but also teaches students about their rights and responsibilities in relation to others.

Kevin tapping her, so she said nothing to Alison; instead, she quickly moved to where Kevin was seated to address his behavior. Third, she used the least intrusive intervention possible. She stopped Kevin's misbehavior by looking him in the eye and calling on him, and she briefly whispered her direction to Sondra and reminded her of an agreed-upon classroom rule. Her actions simultaneously stopped the misbehaviors without disrupting the flow of her lesson.

During the episode Shirley demonstrated a concept called **withitness,** *a teacher's awareness of what is going on in all parts of the classroom at all times and the communication of this awareness to students both verbally and nonverbally* (Kounin, 1970). As you may recall from Chapter 2, withit teachers seem to have eyes in the backs of their heads, and they use this awareness to monitor and direct student behavior. For instance, had Shirley admonished Alison for her muttering, she would have "caught the wrong one," and in doing so subtly communicated that she didn't know what was going on in her classroom.

Keeping a lesson moving while simultaneously intervening requires sophisticated skills, but expert teachers do it virtually without thinking. This is a professional ideal toward which you should strive. In some cases, it may be necessary to use a more intrusive intervention, such as applying a consequence or even removing the student from the classroom if the disruption is severe. With effective instruction and careful planning, most disruptions can be handled as Shirley handled hers.

Handling Serious Management Problems: Violence and Aggression Earlier in the section we said that violent incidents at school are rare. As part of schoolwide safety programs (see Chapter 5), most schools have created prevention programs, taken security measures, and established detailed procedures to protect students and teachers from violent acts like those that make national headlines. The violent and aggressive acts teachers are more likely to encounter involve verbal aggression and physical fights between students. These situations don't happen often, but teachers do need to be prepared for them.

When a student is acting out verbally, the goal is to keep the problem from escalating. Directing the student in a calm and unemotional voice often helps. When students become physical, teachers should take immediate action and follow three steps: (1) Stop the incident (if possible), (2) protect the victim, and (3) get help. For instance, if students are fighting, a loud noise, such as shouting, clapping, or slamming a chair against the floor will often surprise the students enough so they'll stop. At that point, you can begin to talk to them, check to see if anyone is hurt, and then take the students to the main office, where you can get help. If your interventions don't stop the fight, you should immediately rush an uninvolved student to the office for help. Unless you're sure that you can separate the students without danger to yourself, or them, attempting to do so is unwise.

You are legally required to intervene in the case of a fight. If you ignore a fight, even on the playground, parents can sue for negligence on the grounds that you failed to protect a student from injury. However, the law doesn't say that you're required to physically break up the fight; immediately reporting it to administrators is an acceptable form of intervention.

Breaking up a fight, of course, is only a short-term solution. Whenever students are aggressive or violent, experts recommend involving parents and other school personnel (Brophy, 1996; Moles, 1992). Research indicates that a large majority of parents (88%) want to be notified immediately if school problems occur (L. Harris et al., 1987). In addition, school counselors, school psychologists, social workers, and principals have all been trained to deal with these problems and can provide advice and assistance. Experienced teachers can also provide a wealth of information about how they've handled similar problems. No teacher should face persistent or serious problems of violence or aggression alone. Further, excellent programs are available to teach conflict resolution and to help troubled students. If they can get the help they need when teachers and adults first suspect a problem, many incidents can be prevented.

To analyze a case study examining issues involved in classroom management, go to the Companion Website at **www.prenhall.com/kauchak**, then to this chapter's *Reflect on This* module.

Assessment

How do teachers know if their instruction is effective? To answer this question, let's return once more to Shirley's thinking and her work with her students. She wanted her students to understand equivalent fractions, and she wanted them to be able to add fractions with unlike denominators. She prepared examples and conducted a learning activity to help her students reach her goals. But how does Shirley know if students have reached the goals?

The final dimension on which effective and less effective teachers differ is **assessment,** *the process of gathering information and making conclusions about student learning*. Effective teachers ensure that assessment is not something tacked on at the end of instruction; they make it an integral and crucial part of the entire teaching–learning process (Bransford et al., 2000).

Let's look at some items that Shirley used to assess her students' learning.

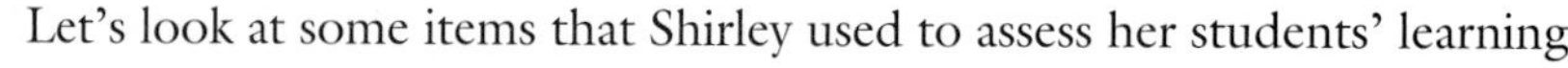

Part I.

Look at the drawings of pairs of fractions below. Circle the pairs that are equivalent, and explain why they are equivalent in each case.

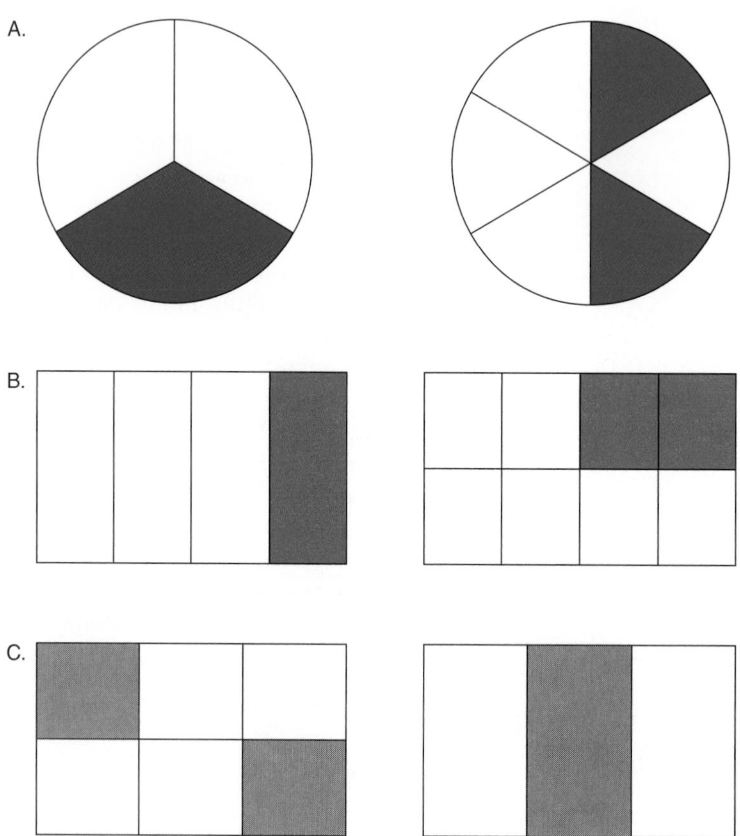

Part II.

Add the following fractions.

$\frac{1}{5} + \frac{2}{5} =$ ________ $\frac{2}{7} + \frac{4}{7} =$ ________

$\frac{1}{3} + \frac{1}{2} =$ ________ $\frac{3}{4} + \frac{1}{8} =$ ________

Part III.

Jeremy and Kenisha were sharing two pizzas. Both pizzas were the same size. Jeremy's pizza was cut into 8 equal parts, but Kenisha's was cut into 4 parts. Jeremy ate 2 pieces of his pizza and 1 piece of Kenisha's pizza. Kenisha ate 1 piece of each. What fraction of a whole pizza did Jeremy eat? What fraction of a whole pizza did Kenisha eat? Show your work in each case.

Earlier in the chapter we introduced the concept of *instructional alignment,* or the consistency among goals, learning activities, practice, and assessments. Now we see why instructional alignment is so important. If assessments are not aligned with goals, teachers cannot determine whether or not the goals have been met. This leaves them without the information they need to make decisions about their next set of learning activities.

Research supports the crucial role of assessment in learning (Bransford et al., 2000; Walberg, 2003).

· · • · ·

Weekly or even more frequent classroom tests provide teachers with information useful in planning their lessons. . . . Frequent tests encourage students to be prepared for classes. Even in themselves, tests can be a powerful source of learning: Regular essays and feedback, for example, help students not only comprehend subject matter but become better writers. (Walberg, 2003, p. 42)

· · • · ·

Feedback from teachers is an essential part of the assessment process; students need to know if their efforts at learning were successful. Their motivation during assessment is high—when they miss items, they want to understand why. In fact, students often learn more from assessments and feedback than they do from any other part of instruction.

Assessment, and the grading that accompanies it, can be challenging for first-year teachers, as the following comments illustrate:

· · • · ·

Of all the paperwork, grading is the nitty-gritty of teaching for me. Students take their grade as the bottom line of your class. It is the end-all and be-all of the class. To me, a grade for a class is, or at least should be, a combination of ability, attitude, and effort. Put bluntly: How do you nail a kid who really tried with an F? Or how do you reward a lazy, snotty punk with an A? (K. Ryan, 1992, p. 4)

· · • · ·

I try not to [play favorites even though I have them]—I don't like S.'s personality . . . I do like J.'s, isn't it unfair? . . . you want to be easier on someone you like. Or harder on someone you don't. (Bullough, 1989, p. 64)

· · • · ·

Even after the teacher quoted above had worked through some of her problems and had developed a grading system she was happy with, she still considered this aspect of instruction challenging:

· · • · ·

Grading is still kind of a problem for me. I wouldn't mind taking a class on grading. I think grading could be hit much better in college. (Bullough, 1989, p. 66)

· · • · ·

As you progress through your teacher education program, you'll learn how to assess students in different ways. As we said earlier, effective teachers understand that assessments must be aligned with the goals of instruction. When traditional paper-and-pencil tests aren't the best way to measure skills and understanding, teachers turn to alternative assessments.

Changing Views of Assessment: Alternative Assessments Think about your experiences as a student and also about some of the tests you've taken. If your experiences are typical, many were multiple-choice, true–false, or fill-in-the-blank tests. These traditional formats—particularly multiple-choice—have been the mainstay of both classroom assessments and standardized intelligence and achievement tests. However, in recent

Alternative assessments provide opportunities for students to demonstrate their knowledge in active, realistic ways.

years, they've been increasingly criticized as being artificial and removed from the realities of both learning and life (Paris, 1998; Reckase, 1997). Critics instead encourage the use of **alternative assessments,** *assessments that directly measure student performance through "real-life" tasks* (Wiggins, 1996/97; Worthen, 1993).

Some examples of alternative assessments include the following:

- Writing an essay or letter to the editor of the school newspaper
- Determining the best deals by comparing sales offers in different newspaper advertisements
- Designing menus for a week's worth of balanced meals
- Designing and conducting an experiment to see which brand of aspirin is likely to be most effective
- Creating an original piece of watercolor art
- Giving a speech in support of one side of a controversial topic

Teachers using alternative assessments examine not only the products—such as the essay, menu, or piece of art—but also students' thinking as they create the products. For example, the teacher might interview students to examine their thinking as they design an experiment, organize an essay, or create a work of art. The interview provides the teacher with insights into how the student approached the task and exposes misconceptions students might have.

The idea of alternative assessment isn't new. Oral exams, exhibits of artwork, proficiency testing in language, and hands-on assessments in vocational areas, such as word processing, have been used for years. In recent years, however, concerns about traditional testing, primarily in multiple-choice formats, and poor student performance have led to more widespread interest in alternative assessment.

Alternative assessments commonly occur in two forms. In a **performance assessment,** *learners are asked to demonstrate their competence in a lifelike situation.* Applying first aid, writing an essay, or giving a speech are all examples of performance assessments because they ask students to demonstrate their knowledge in realistic, lifelike situations.

In **portfolio assessment,** *teachers evaluate collections of student work using pre-set criteria.* More than half the teachers in the United States currently use portfolios to assess student achievement in some area of learning (Viadero, 1999b), and research shows that use of student portfolios can help teachers become more reflective about their instructional effectiveness (Ellsworth, 2002). You were introduced to portfolios in Chapter 1, portfolio activities are found at the end of each chapter in this book, and a discussion of how to construct a professional portfolio appears in Appendix A.

CW

Increasing Understanding 11.8

A geography teacher assesses her students' understanding of longitude and latitude by having them identify the longitudes and latitudes of several cities around the world. Is this a traditional or an alternative assessment? Explain.

One unique feature of portfolio assessment is the active involvement of students in selecting and evaluating portfolio content. In a language arts class, for example, students might select different pieces that they have written over the course of a year. These writing samples then provide personal and concrete evidence of writing progress for parents, the teacher, and the students themselves. (As you develop your professional portfolio during your teacher preparation experience, you'll see similar evidence of growth in your teaching expertise.)

Using Our Understanding of Learning to Define Effective Teaching

In the first section of the chapter, we learned about effective instruction by studying teachers—their planning, their personal characteristics, and the ways in which they involve students, present topics, and assess students' understanding. We saw that some teachers are more effective at applying these variables than others, and as a result, their students have higher achievement.

We can also learn about effective instruction by studying students. How do students learn? How can we use our understanding of learning to teach more effectively? The answers to these questions provide professionals with important knowledge about learners and learning that they can use to promote achievement in the classroom.

Psychology, and particularly educational psychology, attempts to explain how we learn and develop. We examine this body of knowledge in this section.

Behaviorism

Behaviorism, a *theory of learning that focuses on specific and observable behaviors and the factors that influence those behaviors,* dominated education for the first half of the twentieth century. From a behaviorist perspective, **learning** is *a change in observable behavior that occurs as a result of experience.* Behaviors are learned through reinforcement and punishment.

Let's see how these principles might work in a classroom. For example, suppose a teacher is teaching spelling. In practice sessions, she asks, "How do you spell *Tennessee*?" When a student responds "T-e-n-n-e-s-s-e-e," the teacher smiles, nods, or says "Right!" The smile, nod, or comment reinforces the student; consequently, the response is strengthened. When a student responds T-e-n-e-s-s-e," for instance, the teacher says "Not quite" or "You'd better check your list," decreasing the likelihood that the student will use the incorrect spelling a second time. The responses (behaviors) are specific, and the teacher can observe (hear) them.

The goal of instruction, according to behaviorism, is to increase the number, or strength, of correct student responses. Learning is assessed by observing changes in behavior, such as seeing that Robert at first couldn't spell Tennessee, began spelling it correctly in the practice sessions, and now consistently spells it correctly in assignments and assessments.

When using behaviorism as a guide for planning and conducting instruction, the teacher designs learning activities that require students to produce specific, observable responses to questions and exercises. Then, during lessons, the teacher reinforces desired responses, as we saw in the correct spelling of *Tennessee*, and punishes undesired ones.

Let's look now at a teacher using behaviorism to structure his instruction.

Case STUDY

Jeff Lageman, an eighth-grade English teacher at Longview Middle School, was working with his students on pronoun cases.

"All right, listen everyone," Jeff began. "Today we're going to begin a study of pronoun cases. . . . Everybody turn to page 484 in your text.

"Using pronoun cases correctly is important," he continued, "because we want to be able to use good English when we write, and this is one area where people get mixed up. . . . So, when we're finished with our study here, you'll all be able to use pronouns correctly in your writing."

He then displayed the following on the overhead:

> Pronouns use the nominative case when they're subjects and predicate nominatives.
>
> Pronouns use the objective case when they're direct objects, indirect objects, or objects of prepositions.

"Let's review briefly," Jeff continued. "Give me a sentence that has both a direct and indirect object in it. . . . Anyone?"

"Mr. Lageman gives us too much homework," Leon offered, to the laughter of the class.

Jeff smiled and wrote the sentence on the chalkboard.

Behaviorism emphasizes the learning of discrete items of information through practice and reinforcement.

"Okay, Leon. Good sentence, even though it's incorrect. I don't give you *enough* work. . . . What's the subject in the sentence?"

". . . "

"Go ahead, Leon."

"Ahh, . . . *Mr. Lageman.*"

"Yes, good. *Mr. Lageman* is the subject," Jeff replied as he underlined *Mr. Lageman* in the sentence and wrote *Subject* above it.

"Now, what's the direct object? . . . Joanne?"

". . . *Homework.*"

"All right, good. And what's the indirect object? . . . Anya?"

". . . *Us.*"

"Excellent, everybody."

Jeff continued by reviewing predicate nominatives and objects of prepositions.

"Now let's look at a few examples of pronouns up here on the overhead," he said as he displayed 10 sentences. The following are the first four:

1. Did you get the card from Kelly and (I, me)?
2. Will Antonio and (she, her) run the concession stand?
3. They treat (whoever, whomever) they hire very well.
4. I looked for someone (who, whom) could give me directions to the theater.

"Okay, look at the first one. Which is correct? . . . Omar?"

". . . *Me.*"

"Good, Omar. How about the second one? . . . Lonnie?"

". . . *Her.*"

"Not quite, Lonnie. This one is a little tricky, but it's the nominative case. *She* is part of the subject. That's what makes it nominative case."

Jeff then pointed at the overhead and asked, "How about the third one. . . . Cheny?"

". . . I don't know. . . . *whomever*, I guess."

"Excellent, Cheny. Indeed, that's correct."

Jeff continued with the rest of the sentences and then assigned a page of similar exercises from the students' textbook as homework.

On Tuesday, Wednesday, and Thursday, Jeff covered pronoun-antecedent agreement (pronouns must agree with their antecedents in gender and number) and the use of indefinite pronouns—*anybody, either, each, one, someone*—as antecedents for personal pronouns. He then had the students work examples as he had done before.

On Friday Jeff gave a test composed of 30 sentences: 10 of the sentences dealt with case, 10 more with antecedents, and the final 10 with indefinite pronouns.

The following are some items from the test:

For each of the items below, mark A on your answer sheet if the pronoun case is correct in the sentence, and mark B if it is incorrect. If it is incorrect, supply the correct pronoun.

1. Be careful *who* you tell.
2. Will Renee and *I* be in the outfield?
3. My brother and *me* like water skiing.

• • ● • •

Let's look at Jeff's lesson to see how it is based on behaviorism. To elicit observable responses, Jeff displayed exercises such as this one:

1. Did you get the card from Kelly and (I, me)?

Increasing Understanding 11.9

Give an example of punishment in Jeff's interaction with his students. Explain why it is an example of punishment.

He then asked, "Okay, look at the first one. Which is correct? . . . Omar?" Omar responded "*Me*," and Jeff reinforced him by saying, "Good, Omar." Jeff designed the learning activity so that students could give specific, observable responses that he could reinforce if correct, as he did with Omar.

Being able to provide specific, observable responses is desirable for some forms of fact learning. For example, a learner must respond "Fifty four" quickly and effortlessly when asked "What is six times nine?" Behaviorists often view memorization of facts as a foundation or prerequisite for more complex behaviors. For example, knowing multiplication tables helps in solving word problems and being able to pronounce words quickly and efficiently helps students comprehend when they read (Bruning et al., 2004; Mayer, 2002).

Increasing Understanding 11.10

Reflection is the process of asking ourselves questions, such as "What am I doing in my class?" and "Why am I doing that?" If Jeff had been a reflective teacher, would he have conducted his lesson as he did? Explain.

For many other learning goals, however, behaviorism isn't a satisfactory basis for guiding instruction. For instance, being able to write effectively was Jeff's goal for his students, as indicated by his comment, "Using pronoun cases correctly is important, because we want to be able to use good English when we write. . . . So, when we're finished with our study here, you'll all be able to use pronouns correctly in your writing." Writing, however, is a complex process that includes planning, putting ideas on paper, and revising until the ideas are clearly communicated (Hayes, 1996). Being able to provide specific, observable responses to exercises involving grammar rules is unlikely to dramatically improve writing ability (Mayer, 1999; Kellogg, 1994). Instead, students learn to write by planning, translating their plans into drafts, obtaining feedback, and revising. The more they practice and think about their writing, the better their writing becomes.

A problem with behaviorism is that it treats learners as if they're passive recipients of reinforcers and punishers. However, anyone who has taught knows that students can be dynamos of energy, wanting to move and talk and share their opinions. Behaviorism also asserts that behavioral changes occur only in response to reinforcement and punishment; it ignores any other causes of change. In addition, behaviorism reduces the teacher's role to simply dispensing rewards and punishers. Teaching is much more than that. An alternate, cognitive view of learning attempts to address these issues.

Cognitive Views of Learning

To begin this section, let's look at some ideas students have about a variety of topics.

- Large objects are more dense than small objects.
- The larger the number in the denominator, the larger the fraction.
- The phases of the moon are caused by clouds.

Obviously, teachers didn't teach these ideas, and students certainly weren't reinforced for expressing them. Instead, students created, or "constructed," them on their own. As researchers began to systematically examine students' thinking in cases like these, they arrived at an inescapable conclusion: *Learners don't passively respond to the environment; they actively seek to make sense of it.* Researchers' efforts led to what is called the "cognitive revolution," which began about the middle of the twentieth century and continues to this day.

The cognitive revolution led to a view of learning dramatically different from the behaviorist perspective. From a cognitive perspective, **learning** is *a change in a person's mental representations of the world that may or may not result in an immediate change in behavior.* The idea that learners are mentally active is at the core of cognitive learning theory, and it has important implications for teaching. Specifically, teachers need to design learning activities that actively engage learners in making sense of

Table 11.4 Comparison of Behaviorist and Cognitive Views of Learning and Teaching

	View of Learning	View of Learners	Role of the Teacher
Behaviorist	Increase in number of desirable responses resulting from reinforcement	Passive recipients of stimuli (reinforcers and punishers) from the environment	Present reinforcers to increase desirable behaviors and present punishers to decrease undesirable behaviors
Cognitive	Developing understanding by searching for patterns in the world	Constructors of knowledge through actively processing information from the environment	Guide learners in their efforts to make sense of the world

the content being taught. The teacher's role changes from dispenser of reinforcers to a guide who helps students as they construct knowledge. Table 11.4 summarizes differences between behaviorist and cognitive views of learning.

Let's see what these differences look like in classrooms.

Case STUDY Leslie Nelson, another English teacher at Longview Middle School, was also working on pronoun cases with her students

She began by saying, "We're making progress on the editorial section of the school newspaper we've been working on. I read the essays you turned in on Friday, and your writing is getting better and better, but we have some things to work on today that will improve them even more."

Leslie displayed two passages side by side on the overhead projector. The passage on the left appeared as follows:

> Katrina and Simone were talking. "Did you get that information *from Kelly and me*?" Simone asked.
>
> "No, I didn't," Katrina responded. "What was it about?"
>
> "Kelly wanted to know if it's okay *that Molly and she* run the concession stand on Friday night at the game."
>
> "Sure, that's fine with me," Katrina responded. "The teachers treat *whoever works* there very well, so everything will be fine. By the way, *to whom* do I give the list of people *who are working* that night."

The passage on the right looked like this:

> Katrina and Simone were talking. "Did you get that information *from Kelly and I*?" Simone asked.
>
> "No, I didn't," Katrina responded. "What was it about?"
>
> "Kelly wanted to know if it's okay *that Molly and her* run the concession stand on Friday night at the game."
>
> "Sure, that's fine with me," Katrina responded. "The teachers treat *whomever works* there very well, so everything will be fine. By the way, *to who* do I give the list of people *whom are working* that night."

Leslie gave her students a few moments to read the passages and then said, "Get together with your partner, and see if you can figure out how these passages are similar and different. You've got 2 minutes." Two minutes later she called the class back together and continued. "Look at the parts of the paragraphs that are italicized. . . . Let's start with the first paragraph in each passage. What do you notice? . . . Devon."

After a couple seconds, Devon offered, "*Me* over there (pointing to the left) and *I* over there (pointing to the right)."

"Okay," Leslie nodded, "What else? . . . Tonya?"

"Both . . . have *Kelly*."

"Okay, good. What else? . . . Carlos?"

"*From*."

"What do you mean, *from*?"

"Both have *from* in the . . . different kind of letters."

"All right, good observations everyone. . . . Now, look at the paragraph on the left again. What part of speech is the word *from*? . . . Andrew?"

". . . A preposition, I think."

"Yes, excellent, Andrew. It is a preposition. . . . So let's take a look at this," she said while taking the passages off the overhead and displaying the following:

> Pronouns use the nominative case when they're subjects and predicate nominatives.
>
> Pronouns use the objective case when they're direct objects, indirect objects, or objects of prepositions.

Leslie gave the students a few seconds to read the rules and then continued, "I'd like you to work with your partner again and decide, based on these rules, which of the two versions up here is correct. Again, I'll give you 2 minutes."

She again displayed the passages and, when the 2 minutes were up, said, "So, which do you believe is correct, . . . 'from Kelly and me' or 'from Kelly and I'? . . . Jon?"

"I . . . think it should be 'from Kelly and I.'"

Cognitive views of learning emphasize social interaction and the active involvement of learners in hands-on activities.

"And why do you think so?"

". . . It sounds better, I think."

"Listen to this and tell us which one sounds better: 'Kelly and me got some soft drinks,' or 'Kelly and I got some soft drinks.'"

". . . 'Kelly and I.'"

"Must be 'from Kelly and me,'" Calvin volunteered.

"Why do you think so?"

"Well, they're . . . not the subject, and *I* was used when it was the subject, . . . so, it must be *me*."

"Hmm, class, think about this. . . . 'Kelly and I' is what part of the sentence? . . . April?"

"The . . . subject."

"Yes, good. Indeed it is. So, . . . let's go back to the other example. Which is correct?"

Leslie continued the discussion until 20 minutes were left in the period. The students were instructed to begin revising their essays in light of the information they had learned that day and to turn them in the next day. On Tuesday and Wednesday, Leslie discussed two additional paragraphs, and on Thursday she returned the students' writing assignments and completed the discussion of pronouns, their antecedents, and indefinite pronouns.

On Friday Leslie assigned an additional paragraph to be written as a quiz. The students had to embed at least two examples each of pronoun cases, pronouns and antecedents, and indefinite pronouns in the paragraphs. In addition, she had students read each others' essays, checking for the content they'd just been studying.

• • ● • •

LEARNING ABOUT BALANCE BEAMS IN FOURTH GRADE

Having examined the thinking and classroom conduct of effective teachers, as well as differences between behaviorist and cognitive views of learning, you now have the chance to view a video of a classroom lesson that illustrates some of these characteristics.

The episode involves a fourth-grade class focusing on the principle of beam balances. The principle states that a beam will balance if the weight times the distance on one side of the fulcrum is equal the weight times the distance on the opposite side of the fulcrum. The class is organized into groups of four, and the groups experiment with beam balances in their attempts to understand the principle. The group work is followed by a whole-class discussion during which the principle is further illustrated and explained. The lesson is followed by an interview with a group of four students that further examines their understanding of the principle.

To complete this activity, do the following:

- Go to the DVD, and view the video episode titled "Learning About Balance Beams in Fourth Grade."
- Answer the questions you'll find on the DVD.

CW *To answer the questions online and receive immediate feedback, go to the Companion Website at* **www.prenhall.com/kauchak**, *then to this chapter's* Classroom Windows *module.*

Teaching in an Era of Reform

THE TEACHER-CENTERED VERSUS LEARNER-CENTERED ISSUE

In Chapter 10 we saw that overemphasis on memorization and drill-and-practice activities resulted in the math reforms emphasized in the 1989 *Curriculum and Evaluation Standards for School Mathematics.* Critics suggested that this emphasis left students with inadequate basic skills and called for a new wave of reform, reflected in revised standards from the National Council of Teachers of Mathematics in 2000. This is an example of broad trends in curriculum reform; reforms occur, criticisms of the reforms begin, and counter-reforms are then offered. A similar trend can be seen in reforms supporting either teacher-centered or learner-centered instruction.

Historically, classroom instruction has been **teacher-centered instruction,** *in which teachers carefully specify goals, present the content to be learned, and actively direct learning activities* (Shuell, 1996). For example, a teacher might want her students to solve algebraic equations, such as $4a + 6b = 24$ and $5a - 6b = 3$, for the values of a and b. Using a teacher-centered approach, teachers model and explain the solution to the problem and then have students practice, first with guidance, and then independently. A lecture, in which teachers systematically present carefully organized information, is another example.

Criticisms of teacher-centered instruction led to a wave of reform, resulting in **learner-centered instruction,** *in which teachers guide learners toward an understanding of the topics they study, rather than explaining content to them.* Prominent professional publications that illustrate this emphasis include *How Students Learn: Reforming Our Schools Through Learner-Centered Education*, published by the American Psychological Association in 1998, and *The Right to Learn*, which was written by well-known Columbia University educator Linda Darling-Hammond and published in 1997.

Discovery learning, *a teaching strategy in which the teacher identifies a content goal, arranges information so that patterns can be found, and guides students to the goal*, and **cooperative learning,** *a teaching strategy that consists of students working together in groups small enough so that everyone can participate in a clearly assigned task* (E. Cohen, 1994), are prominent examples of learner-centered approaches to instruction. Leslie Nelson used aspects of both in her lesson. She displayed the paragraphs on the overhead so that students could "figure out how these passages are similar and different," and she had students work with partners. Working together capitalized on cooperative learning, and looking for similarities and differences is characteristic of discovery learning.

The Issue

Critics of teacher-centered instruction argue that it is based on behaviorist views of learning and emphasizes teacher actions rather than student understanding (Marshall, 1992; Stoddart, Connell, Stofflett, & Peck, 1993). The following episode, in which a teacher is attempting to help her third graders understand place value, illustrates this criticism.

The teacher, based on the directions given in the teacher's manual, begins by putting 45 tally marks on the chalkboard and circles four groups of 10.

Teacher: How many groups of 10 do we have there, boys and girls?

Children: 4.

Teacher: We have 4 groups of 10, and how many left over?

Children: 5.

Teacher: We had 4 tens and how many left over?

Beth: 4 tens.

Sarah: 5.

Teacher: 5. Now, can anybody tell me what number that could be? We have 4 tens and 5 ones. What is that number? Ann?

Ann: (Remains silent)

Teacher: If we have 4 tens and 5 ones, what is that number?

Ann: 9.

Teacher: Look at how many we have there (points to the 4 groups of ten) and 5 ones. If we have 4 tens and 5 ones we have? (slight pause) 45.

Children: 45.

Teacher: Very good. (Wood, Cobb, & Yackel, 1992, p. 180)

As the dialogue suggests, Ann and probably many others didn't understand place value, but the teacher did little to increase their understanding. Once students gave the desired response, they were reinforced with "Very good" and the lesson moved on.

Critics also point to research indicating that student verbalization or overt performance at the expense of understanding occurs in many classrooms (Goodlad, 1984; Stodolsky, 1988), and they further note that teacher-centered approaches, such as lecture and explanation, are the most common strategies (Cuban, 1984, 1996). Critics contend that "the most effective learning takes place when students . . . play an active role in making sense of ideas" (Kohn, 1999, p. 43).

Critics of learner-centered instruction argue that the approach is one more example of widespread "dumbing down" of the curriculum, that learning basic skills is abandoned in favor of fuzzy thinking, and self-esteem is emphasized instead of understanding (Battista, 1999; Schoen, Fey, Hirsch, & Coxford, 1999). They defend teacher-centered instruction by asserting that the lack of understanding so prominent in classrooms is not the result of teacher-centered instruction per se; it is with teachers' inability to implement it effectively. When teacher-centered instruction is done effectively, they argue, none of these criticisms is valid (Rosenshine, 1997). They contend that some criticisms of teacher-centered instruction are made on political grounds, teacher-centered instruction not being "politically . . . or romantically correct" (Rosenshine, 1997, p. 2). Because of these criticisms, a pendulum shift back in the direction of teacher-centered instruction is occurring (M. Stein & Carnine, 1999).

You Take a Position

Now it's your turn to take a position on the issue. State in writing whether you favor learner-centered instruction or teacher-centered instruction, and provide a two-page rationale for your position.

For additional references and resources, go to the Companion Website at **www.prenhall.com/kauchak**, *then to this chapter's* Teaching in an Era of Reform *module. You can respond online or submit your response to your instructor.*

Exploring Diversity

THE ACHIEVEMENT GAP AND EFFECTIVE TEACHING

In Chapter 7 we saw that a widening gap exists between the achievement of cultural minorities, particularly African American and Hispanic students, and the achievement of their White and Asian peers (D. Hoff, 2000b). We also saw in Chapter 7 that reducing class size is one promising aspect of school organization that can help close the gap. The research has much more to say about narrowing the achievement gap, particularly in the area of effective instruction. For example, schools in which the achievement gap is narrowing share the following characteristics (Barth, et al., 1999; Haycock, 1998; Viadero, 2000b):

- A vision established by the school leadership that all students can and will learn
- Specific and demanding goals
- Teaching that actively involves students
- Regular and thorough assessment of student progress

These characteristics are consistent with both the research on effective schools that you studied in Chapter 7 and the effective-teaching research and cognitive views of learning discussed earlier in the chapter. A vision that all students can learn relates to *teaching efficacy*, specific and demanding goals are consistent with effective planning and high expectations, and the active involvement of learners is supported by cognitive learning theory. Finally, regular and thorough assessment provides both teachers and learners with feedback about learning progress.

Sound instruction isn't enough, however. One study of inner-city minority high school students found that many effective practices were being implemented (Miller, Leinhardt, & Zigmond, 1988). The schools were adapting at every level, from school policies to classroom instruction, and this adaptation kept students in school. Nevertheless, researchers also found these problems:

Let's compare Leslie's lesson to Jeff's. Their goals were the same; they wanted their students to correctly apply the rules for nominative and objective cases in their writing. Their approaches were very different, however. Jeff focused on isolated items of information, such as the sentence "Did you get the card from Kelly and (I, me)?" Leslie made her examples more realistic by embedding them in the context of paragraphs; in other words, they were like information we find in books, newspapers, and magazines. Second, instead of reinforcing and punishing specific responses, Leslie led a discussion of the rules, why they made sense, and how they were used. Her approach emphasized a deep and thorough understanding of the rules. Her instruction was more sophisticated and demanding than Jeff's, but it was also likely to result in more student learning. Her teaching was guided by cognitive views of learning; his was based on behaviorism.

- Lowered expectations for students
- Lack of emphasis on higher-level thinking and problem solving and increased use of low-level worksheets
- Student apathy and boredom

In essence, increased efforts to provide instructional structure and support had resulted in a remedial program that lacked intellectual rigor and excitement.

Programs that address these problems while trying to narrow the minority achievement gap have these common features:

- High expectations
- Highly structured classroom environments
- A focus on higher-order thinking
- A focus on the development of learning strategies

Each of these components is integrated into the regular curriculum so that students can see their usefulness in different content areas (Marzano, 2003; Means & Knapp, 1991). Research suggests that teachers and schools can and do make a difference in student learning. Narrowing the achievement gap obviously isn't easy, and daunting problems remain. The task isn't impossible, however. With sustained effort, that gap can be narrowed.

Effective programs for minority students combine challenge with high expectations for success.

CW

Increasing Understanding 11.11

Assess Leslie's teaching in terms of the effective teaching characteristics in Figure 11.1.

Research supports instruction grounded in cognitive views of learning (Eggen & Kauchak, 2004; Ormrod, 2003). For example, an international study that compared instruction in the United States and six other countries found that instruction emphasizing understanding and the conceptual underpinnings of topics resulted in students learning more and scoring higher on standardized tests (D. Hoff, 2003e). In recognition of these findings, many school systems are now initiating instructional reforms grounded in cognitive views of learning (Viadero, 2003b). These reforms acknowledge that learners construct their own understanding, they emphasize the importance of student activity and dialogue in learning, and they are centered strongly on assessment.

Decision Making

Defining Yourself as a Professional

There are a number of decisions with respect to instruction that you'll make as you prepare to be a teacher and move into your own classroom. Before you can make decisions about instruction, however, you'll need to have already made decisions about learning goals. Learning goals and instruction go hand in hand. For example, if acquiring knowledge is your primary goal for students, then lecturing and having students read from textbooks can be acceptable strategies. (We would contend, however, that even in this case more effective strategies are available. See Kauchak & Eggen [2003] and Eggen & Kauchak [2001] for some alternatives.) On the other hand, if your goal is to teach students to solve problems, think critically, or learn to work in groups, then you need to choose more sophisticated instructional approaches that require a higher level of teacher knowledge and expertise.

Instructional alignment, a concept introduced earlier in the chapter, requires a match between instruction and goals. Higher-level processes, such as *applying, analyzing, evaluating*, and *creating*, found in the taxonomy presented in Figure 11.2, require expertise beyond simply explaining and having students read texts. Similarly, helping students learn information at the conceptual, procedural, and metacognitive levels requires sophisticated and demanding instructional strategies that actively involve students in the construction of knowledge.

Beginning teachers must make similar critical decisions about classroom management. Faced with the daunting task of maintaining order in a class of 25 to 30 students, beginning teachers sometimes revert to authoritarian strategies emphasizing, "Do as I say, or else . . . " (V. Richardson & Placier, 2001). Taking this approach sacrifices long-term development of student responsibility for the sake of immediate compliance. Ultimately, we want students to monitor and regulate their own behavior.

Meeting valuable instructional and classroom management goals requires a high level of teacher expertise. For example, when using questioning that involves students and guides their learning, teachers must decide, on the spot, what question to ask and who to call on, while at the same time watching other students to be sure they're paying attention. This is very sophisticated instruction. So is being able to prompt students if they're unable to answer, but not spend so much time with a single student that others "drift off." Similarly, knowing when to intervene with a simple "Mary turn around"—versus a more prolonged discussion about the importance of listening when others are speaking—also requires sophisticated decision making.

To join the ranks of instruction experts, you must be intelligent, hard-working, sensitive, and caring. In addition, you must be knowledgeable about instruction and management options and their effects on the students you teach. Acquiring this knowledge and expertise is very challenging, but it is the essence of being a professional.

Summary

Looking in Classrooms to Define Effective Teaching

Effective teachers teach differently than less effective teachers. They believe they are capable of helping all students learn, they are caring and enthusiastic, and they have high expectations for their students. They actively involve students in learning through questioning, provide detailed feedback about learning progress, create orderly and learning-focused environments, and use assessment as a mechanism to further increase learning.

Using Our Understanding of Learning to Define Effective Teaching

Behaviorists view learning as a change in specific, observable student behaviors and see learners as passively responding to their environments. In the past, teaching was based on this behaviorist view of learning.

About the middle of the twentieth century, views of learning began to change, and learners were seen as actively attempting to make sense of their experiences. Learners' background knowledge, interaction between the teacher and students, and the quality of examples and representations that teachers use are now considered essential in helping learners construct their own understanding of the topics they study.

Important Concepts

alternative assessments (p. 416)
assessment (p. 413)
behaviorism (p. 417)
caring (p. 395)
classroom management (p. 407)
classroom organization (p. 401)
cooperative learning (p. 424)
discovery learning (p. 424)
emphasis (p. 402)
equitable distribution (p. 403)
example (p. 405)
feedback (p. 406)
goals (p. 391)
instructional alignment (p. 392)
language clarity (p. 401)
learner-centered instruction (p. 424)
learning (behaviorist) (p. 417)
learning (cognitive) (p. 420)
modeling (p. 396)
obedience model of management (p. 408)
performance assessment (p. 416)
personal teaching efficacy (p. 395)
portfolio assessment (p. 417)
procedures (p. 410)
prompt (p. 404)
questioning frequency (p. 403)
responsibility model of management (p. 408)
rules (p. 410)
teacher-centered instruction (p. 424)
thematic lesson (p. 402)
transition signals (p. 402)
wait-time (p. 404)
withitness (p. 412)

Developing as a Professional

Praxis Practice

Read the following case study, and answer the questions that follow.

Diane Smith, a fifth-grade teacher at Oneida Elementary, was beginning a language arts lesson on comparative and superlative adjectives. She wanted her students to understand and to be able to use comparative and superlative adjectives correctly in their writing.

She began by having two of her students hold their pencils up, so everyone could see.

Diane: Candice and Daniel, hold your pencils up high, so everyone can see. What do you notice about the pencils? . . . Mary?

Mary: Candice's is red and Daniel's is blue.

Diane: OK, what else? . . . Sheila?

Sheila: You write with them.

Diane: Indeed you do! What else, Kevin?

Kevin: Candice's is longer.

Diane: That's true. Does everyone see that? Hold them up again.

Candice and Daniel held their pencils up again, and Diane moved to the chalkboard and wrote:

Candice has a long pencil. *Candice has a longer pencil than does Daniel.*

Diane: Now, let's look at Matt and Aaron. What do you notice about their hair? . . . Maddie?

Maddie: Matt's is longer than Aaron's.

Diane: Good, Maddie. What else? What about the color? Nicholas?

Nicholas: Aaron's is brown and Matt's is blond.

Diane: Okay, good, Nicholas. So which one has darker hair?

The Class: Aaron!!

Diane: Okay, everyone. I understand your eagerness, and I think it's good. . . . Just as a reminder, what is one of our most important rules in here? . . . Todd?

Todd: We wait until you call on us before we answer.

Diane: Okay, excellent, everyone. You've all done very well with this. We just need a little reminder now and then. . . . Now, let's see where we are. What did we say about Aaron's and Matt's hair? . . . Vicki?

Vicki: Aaron's was darker.

Diane: Good!

Diane wrote three more sentences on the board, as follows:

Candice has a long pencil	*Candice has a longer pencil than does Daniel.*
Aaron has brown hair.	*Aaron has darker hair than does Matt.*
Matt has blond hair.	

Diane: Now let's look at the adjectives in the sentences on the left compared to the adjectives in the sentences on the right. How do they compare? Heather?

Heather: The adjectives in the sentences on the right have an 'er' on the end of them.

Diane guided students to the conclusion that comparative adjectives have an "er" on the end of them and then repeated the process for superlative adjectives. Next, she gave the students an assignment in which they were to write a paragraph that included at least two examples of comparative adjectives and two examples of superlative adjectives. The students completed their paragraphs by the end of their language arts time. At the end of the week, Diane gave a quiz in which the students had to identify examples of comparative and superlative adjectives embedded in a written paragraph and also had to write a paragraph of their own that included examples of each. (Adapted from Eggen & Kauchak, 2004, p. 164)

1. Was Diane's instruction aligned? Explain why or why not.
2. Was Diane's instruction teacher-centered or was it learner-centered? Explain.
3. Assess Diane's questioning. Support your assessment with information taken directly from the case study.
4. Did Diane base her instruction primarily on behaviorism or on cognitive views of learning? Explain.

To receive feedback on your responses to the Praxis Practice exercises, go to the Companion Website at **www.prenhall.com/kauchak**, then to this chapter's *Praxis Practice* module.

Discussion Questions

1. Why is the practice of calling on volunteers to answer a question so prevalent? What are its advantages? What are its disadvantages?
2. Almost any teacher would agree that it is important to be a good model. Given that belief, why do you suppose some teachers don't model the behaviors they expect their students to imitate?
3. Many teachers lecture instead of guiding their students to their goals using questioning. Why do you think this is the case?
4. Why is the obedience model of management so popular in many schools? What are the advantages and disadvantages of this model?
5. What do you see as the future of alternative assessment? Will it continue to be emphasized, or will its popularity among reformists decline in favor of more traditional testing? Why do you think so?

Classroom Observation Guide

Before You Begin: The purpose of these observation activities is to provide you with some classroom examples of teachers' instruction. Observe a lesson at a grade level or in a content area in which you plan to teach. Begin your observation as soon as the class is scheduled to begin. (For example, if an elementary teacher schedules math to begin at 11:00 am, begin your observation at this time.) Describe the teacher's classroom and lesson with respect to the following:

1. How much time does the teacher spend on noninstructional activities, such as taking roll, passing out papers, and gathering materials to be used in the lesson, before beginning her instruction?
2. How does the teacher conduct his or her instruction? Does instruction rely primarily on lecturing and explaining, or are students guided to the goal with questioning?
3. How much time does the teacher spend directly instructing the class, and how much time do students spend completing seatwork?
4. How often does the teacher reprimand students for misbehavior? Is the reprimand brief and even tempered, or is the reprimand harsh and angry?
5. How often does the teacher praise students for desirable behavior or good answers to questions? Count the number of times students receive praises.

On the basis of these observations, decide whether the instruction is based more on a behaviorist or a cognitive view of learning and teaching. Explain your conclusion.

Going into Schools

1. Interview a teacher about the use of questioning strategies to promote learning. To guide your interview, you might want to ask the following questions:
   a. Do you believe it is important to ask a lot of questions in class? Why or why not?
   b. How do you decide who to call on?
   c. What do you do if a student is unable to respond?
   d. What is the biggest problem you face in using questioning in your classroom?

   Compare the teacher's responses to the content of this chapter.
2. Interview a teacher about student diversity. Ask what he or she does through instructional strategies and classroom management strategies to accommodate students' background differences.
3. Obtain a copy of a test a teacher has used in reading, language arts, math, science, and social studies (if you're in an elementary school), or get a copy of a test for one of the courses the teacher teaches (if you're in a middle or secondary school). After examining the test, answer the following questions:
   a. What format is used (e.g., multiple-choice, true–false, matching, etc.)?
   b. At what level are the items written? Do they require mere recall of information, or do they require the students to apply understanding to new situations?
4. Talk with the teacher about his or her goals for the content being assessed. Were the goals and the assessment aligned; that is, did the assessment measure important goals of instruction?
5. Interview the teacher about assessment practices. The following questions might be used in the interview.
   a. What does "alternative" or "performance" assessment mean to you?
   b. Do you use alternative assessments in your teaching? If so, how do you use them?

c. Do you use portfolios? If so, how do you use them?
d. Ask to examine the contents of a portfolio. Ask: How do you decide what will be included and what will be left out?

On the basis of the interview, determine one advantage and one disadvantage of alternative assessment formats.

Virtual Field Experience

If you would like to participate in a Virtual Field Experience, go to the Companion Website at **www.prenhall.com/kauchak**, then to this chapter's *Field Experience* module.

Online Portfolio Activities

To complete these activities online, go to the Companion Website at **www.prenhall.com/kauchak**, then to this chapter's *Portfolio Activities* module.

Portfolio Activity 11.1

Effective Instruction

INTASC Principle 9: Commitment

Personal Journal Reflection

The purpose of this activity is to encourage you to think about and develop your own personal theory of effective teaching. Think about two of your most effective teachers. List specific things these teachers did that made them effective. Now think about two of the least effective teachers you've encountered and list specific things these teachers did that hampered their effectiveness. Analyze the lists for differences. What kinds of things from the lists could you use in your own teaching to become more effective? What kinds of things should you avoid?

Portfolio Activity 11.2

Planning for Instruction

INTASC Principle 7: Planning

The purpose of this activity is to help you think about reasons for teaching topics and the role of planning in effective instruction. Think about topics that you are likely to teach. Identify a topic you believe is very important and a second topic you find less important. Explain why the first is more important. Then write three specific goals related to the more important topic.

Portfolio Activity 11.3

Designing Instruction

INTASC Principle 1: Knowledge of Subject

The purpose of this activity is to assist you in thinking about instructional alignment and ways that teachers can link goals to teaching strategies. Describe how you would help students from a variety of backgrounds reach the goals you specified in Portfolio Activity 11.2. Be specific in your description, and explain how you would accommodate background differences in your students.

Chapter 12

Technology in American Schools

Technology is changing education in the United States in many ways. In Chapter 1 we said that one of this book's goals was to help you decide what kind of teacher you want to become. How you plan to use technology is one decision you'll have to make in this process. This decision is important, because it can affect how much your students learn as well as how hard you will have to work. Technology has the potential to make you, as a teacher, both more effective and more efficient.

Technology use is also tied to teacher professionalism. Technology can make teachers better instructors, but only if teachers understand technology and how it can influence learning. One of our goals in this chapter is to provide you with a technology knowledge base that will assist you in making professional decisions about your teaching.

In this chapter we present an overview of technology and its uses in schools as we try to answer the following questions:

- What is technology?
- How can technology increase learning in our schools?
- What different types of technology are available to teachers as they attempt to help students learn?
- What obstacles are there to greater technology use in our schools?

To begin, let's look at two teachers using technology in their classrooms.

This logo appears throughout the chapter to indicate where case studies are integrated with chapter content.

Case STUDY

Latisha Evans, a first-year teacher at Henderson Middle School, ran into one of her colleagues and friends, Carl DeGroot, in the hallway.

"You sure look excited," Carl said with a smile. "What's happening?"

"Wow," Latisha responded, gesturing for emphasis. "They got it today; they really got it. . . . I've been trying to get my language arts classes to understand what we mean by *internal conflict*, and it seemed to be just too abstract for them. . . . Plus, they would only half pay attention when I would explain it. . . . So I wrote up a few little vignettes, like 'Kelly didn't know what to do. She was looking forward to the class trip, but if she went she wouldn't be able to try out for city soccer league.' Then, I put them together with a PowerPoint presentation and included some pictures of people with pensive looks on their faces and that kind of thing. . . . Neat animation tricks to make each example appear on the screen and then follow it with the pictures. . . . It was the best I've ever done. Using PowerPoint to get their attention really made a difference."

• • • • •

Peter Adamson, a 5-year veteran at the same school, is highly regarded by the principal, his students, and their parents. As we enter Peter's classroom, it appears chaotic, and we wonder how anyone could consider him a "good" teacher. One group of five students is working on a 4-by-8-foot sheet of heavy paper to be used in a presentation to their classmates. Two other groups of four students are working on different displays, and the seven computers in his room are all being used by pairs of students searching the Internet. The noise level is quite high, giving the impression that there is no order. As we walk around the room, we notice that each group of students is working intently. Peter explains that he had the students organize themselves into pairs—with one group of three, since he has 27 students—and each pair selected one of the original 13 colonies. Their task was to create a company like the Hudson Bay Trading Company for each colony. Pairs could team up and work on two related colonies together if they chose to do so, as indicated by the group of five and the two groups of four.

Peter explains that he wanted to try something different in this unit on American history. Instead of simply presenting information to students and discussing it, he continues, he presented students with a problem—creating a company that could use the resources of the particular colony or colonies. The students went to work searching for information that would help them solve the problem. They were using the classroom's computers to gather information, and they had to collaborate in making decisions about how to present the information to their classmates. Their presentation had to include a description of how their investors could make a profit using the resources of the colony.

• • ● • •

What Is Technology?

We tend to think of technology as a recent innovation in American education, and we usually link technology to computers. In fact, technology is much broader and has been used in teaching about as long as schools have existed. For example, teachers in our country's first schools had children use individual slate boards to practice their "letters and numbers." As the multi-age, one-room school evolved into schools organized by grade levels, the chalkboard became an essential tool for communicating with larger groups of students. These are rudimentary forms of technology.

The invention of electricity revolutionized instruction by allowing teachers to use radio, television, filmstrips, films, and overhead projectors (Trotter, 1999b). Technology further evolved, and now teachers routinely use videotapes, many can play DVDs, virtually all have at least one computer in their classrooms, and some even have video projection equipment, such as Latisha used to give her slide presentation. These are all forms of technology.

But how is this increasingly powerful resource most effectively utilized? Will it make your job as a teacher simpler and more efficient or more complex and demanding? Before we begin answering these questions, let's consider the most basic question: What is technology?

Contrasting Views of Technology

In the past 50 years, experts have defined educational technology in two distinct ways: as hardware and as a process (Gentry, 1995; Seels & Richey, 1994). Those holding a hardware view see technology as primarily "gadgets, instruments, machines, devices . . . [and] computers" (Muffoletto, 1994, p. 25). They believe technology can increase learning by providing tools to support and amplify the teacher's message (Lumsdaine,

The hardware view of technology emphasizes its capability to present information in a clear and organized manner.

Increasing Understanding 12.1

Describe the teacher's role and the students' role during technology use when the teacher has a hardware view. Describe the roles when the teacher has a process view. How might you incorporate these two views in your own classroom? What benefits would you expect to gain from either approach?

To answer the Increasing Understanding questions online and receive immediate feedback, go to the Companion Website at **www.prenhall.com/kauchak**, then to this chapter's *Increasing Understanding* module. Type in your response, and then study the feedback.

1964). Whether their tools have been chalkboards, filmstrips, or computers, teachers throughout most of America's history have thought of technology as a handy accessory to instruction. Latisha's use of a PowerPoint presentation reflects this view of technology.

Over time, experts began to recommend a more comprehensive, process-oriented view of technology. Rather than a classroom accessory, technology is something that can be integrated into various aspects of teaching and learning; for example, it can be used by teachers to improve the effectiveness of instructional strategies and increase student motivation, and it can be used by students as both a communication and a learning tool (Gentry, 1995). A process perspective asks teachers to think broadly about how technology can be utilized more systematically in the classroom. Peter's incorporation of technological and other learning resources into his history instruction illustrates a more process-oriented view of technology.

Hardware and process views of technology are grounded in different theories of learning and teaching. The hardware view is based on a behaviorism-oriented, transmission view of teaching. It assumes that the teacher is in control of the learning activity and that technology improves learning by enhancing the transmission of the information to be learned. In contrast, the process view of technology is based on cognitive and constructivist views (discussed in Chapter 11) that consider students active participants in the learning process. The process perspective encourages students to analyze information, construct knowledge, and learn to use technological tools as aids to learning.

Experts now think of **instructional technology** as "*a combination of the processes and tools involved in addressing educational needs and problems*" (Roblyer, 2003, p. 6). Peter emphasized the process aspects of technology by presenting his students with a problem and helping them as they tried to solve it; his students used the computers as tools as they worked toward their solutions. Remembering that technology is a combination of tools and processes, let's turn now to some of its instructional uses.

Technology Use in the Classroom

Unquestionably, we live in a technological world. There is so much cell phone usage, for example, that some states now ban use of the phones when people are driving, and cell phones ringing in restaurants has become an etiquette issue. Most homes have computers, and the majority of those have Internet access. Sending e-mails halfway around the world has become nearly routine. Similarly, technology is increasingly affecting the way teaching and learning occur. In this section we examine some of these applications, which are outlined in Figure 12.1.

Using Technology to Support Instruction

One of the most common uses of technology is to support instruction. Let's look at an example.

Case STUDY Fifth-grade teacher Sandy Hutton was presenting a unit on the circulatory system and wanted her students to understand the functions of the heart and how blood pressure influences it. Searching the Internet, she found some photographs of a real heart on the Web site for the National Institutes of Health. She used the photos in a PowerPoint presentation on the heart, showing its parts and the way it works with the lungs and other parts of the body.

On a CD-ROM accompanying the class science textbook, Sandy also found a model that illustrated how the heart is like a bicycle pump with valves opening and closing. She shared the model with her class by using her computer to project it on a screen, and she brought in an old bicycle pump to illustrate how valves open and close to create pressure. With the help of the school nurse, she was able to find several sphygmomanometers (devices for measuring blood pressure), which students then used to measure their blood pressure during different types of activities. She asked the students to search for patterns in their measurements and to organize their information into charts on their computers. Finally, they shared their results with the class.

• • ● • •

Figure 12.1 Classroom Applications of Technology

- Using technology to support instruction
- Using technology to deliver instruction
- Capitalizing on technology to teach problem solving and higher-level thinking skills
- Word processing: using technology to teach writing
- Employing technology to support learners with disabilities
- Using the Internet as an instructional tool

Sandy used technology to support her instruction in several ways:

- Her PowerPoint presentation helped her students see the parts and function of the heart in a way that was more real and effective than would have been possible with the textbook alone.
- The CD-ROM provided a graphic image of the heart actually working.
- The bicycle pump acted as a concrete metaphor for the heart's function; it helped students understand the pumping function of the heart.
- The use of the sphygmomanometers allowed students to feel the cuff tightening around their arms, feel the pulse of their blood, and see a digital readout of their own blood pressures.

Technology helped Sandy's students translate abstract ideas, such as blood pressure and the functions of the heart, into concrete experiences.

Sandy also used technology as a learning tool. She gave her students the blood pressure equipment and asked them to work in small groups to find patterns in the ways different activities affected their blood pressures. They used computers to organize information into charts, which they then shared with the class. In addition to learning the functions of the heart and about blood pressure, her students were also learning how to design and conduct experiments, use a computer to organize information, and work productively in small groups. Technology provided a vehicle for students to reach these goals by directly involving them in their investigations.

To be effective, technology should be integrated across the curriculum (Roblyer, 2003). This helps students see its significance in different aspects of their lives and allows teachers to utilize technology more efficiently. Some ways to integrate technology into different content areas are outlined in Table 12.1.

As you can see in Table 12.1, technology can be used to support instruction in a variety of ways. Technology can be used as a source of information, as well as a supplement to the teacher's instruction. It can be used to directly support teachers' instruction or as

Table 12.1 Integrating Technology into Different Content Areas

Content Area	Application
Reading/language arts	• Software programs to develop basic reading skills • Word processing to teach writing skills • Internet search engines to develop basic research skills
Math	• Tutorial and drill-and-practice software to develop math facts • Graphing calculators to illustrate abstract or hard to visualize relationships • Software to illustrate and explore geometry concepts
Science	• Simulations to illustrate complex relationships • Data-gathering instruments to conduct experiments in and out of the lab • Internet links to access information and communicate with other scientists
Social studies	• Simulations to explore distant places and times • Online archives to access many years of social science research • Spreadsheets and databases to organize information

an alternative to teacher-centered instruction. In the next section we examine different ways that technology can be used to actually deliver instruction.

To analyze a case study examining issues involved in using technology to support instruction, go to the Companion Website at **www.prenhall.com/kauchak**, then to this chapter's *Reflect on This* module.

Using Technology to Deliver Instruction

Computers and the software used with them have become powerful tools for delivering instruction. When educators recognized that computers and other forms of technology could perform tasks quickly and systematically, they began to search for ways to use these innovations to imitate and improve on the functions of human teachers (Roblyer, 2003). For instance, students often use worksheets and flashcards to practice basic skills, such as word recognition and phonetic analysis in reading and addition and multiplication facts in math. Could computers be used to provide an improved form of practice, educators wondered? This question led to the development of **software**—*programs written in a computer language*—specifically designed to deliver instruction. We examine two general types of instructional software in this section: drill-and-practice and tutorials.

Drill-and-Practice As a student you may have used flashcards to help you memorize math facts like 6 × 9 = 54, foreign language vocabulary, important dates in history, or the definitions of new concepts in science. A friend or relative showed you a card, you gave the answer, the other person let you know if the answer was correct, and you turned to the next card. On many occasions your partner probably grew tired of the activity, and you ended up studying on your own. A computer-based drill-and-practice program is similar to the flashcards you used, but the computer never gets tired or impatient; it keeps presenting card after card as long as you give an answer, even if you repeatedly respond 48 for 6 × 9 = ?.

Students can use drill-and-practice programs on their own; the teacher doesn't have to be directly involved. However, they don't substitute for a teacher's expertise, and developers of these programs assume that students have had previous instruction related to the facts or concepts. For example, when students first learn about multiplication, the teacher helps them understand that 6 × 9 is 6 sets of 9 items, or 9 sets of 6 items. The teacher presents many concrete examples to illustrate the abstract concept (multiplication). Drill-and-practice programs are used after instruction to help students practice until the skill becomes automatic—that is, until they know the facts essentially without having to think about them.

Some drill-and-practice software programs use a "game" format to increase student motivation. For example, rather than just typing in the correct response to 6 × 9 = ?, students might aim a laser blaster at an alien emblazoned with the correct answer.

The best drill-and-practice programs are adaptive, which means they match the demands of the task to a student's ability. For example, in a program designed to improve knowledge of multiplication facts, an adaptive program would begin by pretesting to determine what multiplication facts the student already knows. Problems are

Computers can be used to provide drill-and-practice, perform tutorials, and present simulations and problems to students.

presented to the student to ensure a high success rate. When the student fails to answer, or answers incorrectly, the program prompts by providing the answer and then retests that fact. More difficult problems are introduced only when the student has reached a certain skill level. Because the ultimate goal is for students to be able to recall math facts automatically, the amount of time given to answer is often shortened as students become more proficient. This also increases motivation by challenging students to become quicker in their responses.

What are the benefits of drill-and-practice programs? First, they provide practice with effective feedback, informing students immediately of what they've mastered and where they need more work. Research supports the effectiveness of this process (Archer, 1998). Second, they are often motivating for students turned off by paper-and-pencil exercises (Roblyer, 2003). Third, they save teachers' time, since teachers don't have to present the information and score students' responses.

Researchers caution, however, that more time on computers does not necessarily equal more learning (Roblyer, 2003). More important are the quality of the learning experiences and the extent to which they are linked to the teacher's goals.

Tutorials In contrast with drill-and-practice software, which focuses on mastery of isolated facts, a **tutorial** is a *software program that delivers an entire integrated instructional sequence similar to a teacher's instruction on the topic.* For example, a tutorial on calculating depreciation might be used in a high school accounting class. The program might first present and explain the formula "annual depreciation = cost/expected life" and then ask, "If an electric pasta machine costs $400 and is expected to last 4 years, what is the annual depreciation?" In response to the correct answer ($100), the computer would say, "Good," and go on to the next problem or concept. A student who typed $400 might be told, "Sorry, but you're probably not ready to work for H & R Block. $400 is the cost. To find annual depreciation, divide this figure by the expected life (4 years). Please type the correct answer."

Let's look at another application.

Case STUDY Lisa Hoover, a first-grade teacher, has created a number of learning centers in her classroom where her students can work independently. Students can earn "classroom money" for good behavior and finishing assignments and can use the money to purchase prizes from the class store. The students who work in the store as clerks must first complete several of the math units, with the last one focusing on giving change. Lisa's students have widely varying backgrounds, and she believes that they shouldn't complete the giving-change unit until they're ready. As a result, she has students who want to take the unit at various times during the fall semester. In the past, they often had to wait or she had to drop some other activity to teach them the rules for calculating and counting change. Recently, Lisa took a technology course in which she learned to use a software program called HyperStudio. She used the program to design an interactive multimedia lesson—an elaborate tutorial—on giving change. The tutorial includes pictures of various coins and presents a number of scenarios that provide students with practice in giving change. Now students can complete the unit anytime they have access to one of the computers in the classroom. In addition, Lisa designed the tutorial so that it would give students virtually unlimited numbers of problems and continual help until they mastered the information. Lisa noticed that students easily got used to the process and were happy about having access to the instruction immediately.

• • • • •

Tutorials can consist of simple sequences of text and graphics, as in the accounting program, or they can be more elaborate programs involving **hypermedia,** *a computer-based system of information representation in which data in various formats—text, graphics, audio, or video—are stored in interlinked nodes.* Lisa's tutorial on making change allowed students to interact with different forms of money on the screen, making change and receiving feedback from the computer. As another example, a hypermedia product on the solar system might include descriptive text, such as information on Saturn's rings, an animation of the planets in motion, and a video clip showing the launch of a recent spacecraft. To link to some parts of the program, students might click on an **icon,** *a picture on a computer screen that acts as a symbol for some action or item.* To view the video, for example, they might click on a small picture of a videocassette. This type of program is interactive because students can view various parts of the presentation in any sequence they wish.

CW

Increasing Understanding 12.2

Based on the definition of *hypermedia*, identify one important difference between hypermedia and a multimedia program such as PowerPoint.

The technology in effective tutorials has several valuable features that make the instruction within them flexible, adaptive, and efficient. For example, Lisa's interactive lesson was available anytime; the students didn't have to wait until Lisa had free time to teach them. Second, it was adaptive and individualized, providing each student with the right amount of practice needed to master the content. Before she prepared her tutorial, Lisa worked with students individually, but she was frequently interrupted and often unable to tutor students when they were ready to work on the unit. She had previously used printed worksheets, but the instruction was inefficient because Lisa had to interrupt what she was doing to assess and monitor the task in order to provide immediate feedback. In addition, hypermedia are generally more motivating for students than worksheets.

CW

Increasing Understanding 12.3

Was the tutorial Lisa developed to teach her students to make change aimed at rote memorization tasks or higher-level thinking? Explain.

The effectiveness of tutorials depends on the quality of interactions between the technology and the learner. Tasks can range from asking for simple, factual information, such as "What color was the ball that Billy found?" to higher-level questions such as "Who do you think lost the ball?" and "What should Billy do with the lost ball?"

Tutorials have been criticized for focusing too much on memorized information instead of challenging students to think and apply understanding (Newby, Stepich, Lehman, & Russell, 2000; Roblyer, 2003). Although this doesn't have to be the case, finding high-quality software and hypermedia materials is an obstacle facing teachers who want to integrate tutorials into their classrooms. We discuss this problem later in the chapter.

Capitalizing on Technology to Teach Problem Solving and Higher-Level Thinking Skills

Knowing facts and demonstrating basic skills are an important part of the school curriculum, and many experts consider facts and basic skills to be the building blocks of learning (Bruning et al., 2004). But other important kinds of learning also exist. Students need to learn how to find patterns in factual information and use these patterns to solve problems. Technology provides effective tools to help reach these goals.

Simulations Simulations teach higher-order thinking skills by bringing the real world into the classroom. A **simulation** (or *microworld*) *is a program, either in software or Web-based form, that models a real or imaginary system in order to help learners understand that system.* Let's look at an example.

Case STUDY Ninth-grade social studies students file into their classroom and log on to one of six workstations. They discuss what they are finding, as they unearth an archaeological site in ancient Greece. They have been working on this computer-based archaeology simulation for about 3 weeks, and teams of students are responsible for excavating different quadrants of the site. They "dig up" pottery shards, fragments of weapons, pieces of masonry, and bits of ancient texts. They then try to identify each artifact and fit it into an emerging picture of the site as a whole. As they try to make sense of their findings, the students visit local museums; consult reference works on Greek history, art, and architecture; and ask other teachers in the school to help translate texts. Their teachers have purposefully included ambiguous evidence in the site so that some teams find data suggesting the site was a temple, whereas others find artifacts more nearly suggesting it was a battlefield. The teams present their latest findings to the rest of the class in weekly meetings, and a spirited debate follows as the amateur archaeologists struggle to reconcile inconsistencies in the data. On this day, students take turns at the computer, graphing their findings on large wall charts, calling across the room to ask if anyone has a spearhead to compare with one just found, and arguing about whose final interpretation of the site will best explain the bulk of the evidence. (Adapted from Brunner & Tally, 1999)

• • ● • •

As opposed to textbooks and lectures, simulations have the advantage of involving students in complex, realistic learning tasks that are usually unavailable in classrooms. Simulations become virtual field trips that allow students to see and do things otherwise beyond the confines of their classroom walls. Simulations also provide benefits to teachers; as students are immersed in a simulation, teachers can work with different groups, asking questions and facilitating learning.

Simulations also provide safety along with realism. One simulated driver's education course, for example, has students use a driving simulator to experience a near accident designed to help them learn to drive defensively (and avoid the wrath of their driving instructors) (Trotter, 2003). The simulator can provide students with risky scenarios such as driving in rain, in fog, or at night. The learning is particularly valuable because the simulation is both realistic and safe.

As another example, students can use computer software to simulate a frog dissection, rather than cut up an actual frog. Although the simulation has the disadvantage of not allowing students the experience of working with a real frog, it has at least three advantages: It is less expensive, since it can be used over and over; it is more flexible, because the frog can be "reassembled"; and the simulation avoids sacrificing a frog for science (Roblyer, 2003).

One of the most popular social studies simulations, Oregon Trail (and subsequent versions), allows students to travel like the original Oregon Trail pioneers from Independence, Missouri, to Oregon's Willamette Valley (Forcier, 1999). Students shop for supplies with a given budget before they start and make decisions along the way about the pace of travel, food supplies, and health problems. As students proceed, they interact with Native Americans and other settlers, gaining valuable historical information. A networked version of the program allows a number of users to interact simultaneously during their journeys.

CW

Increasing Understanding 12.4

Recall Lisa's tutorial program to teach her students how to make change. How might she adapt her work to make it more realistic by reformatting it into a simulation?

Other simulations give students a sense of what it would be like to walk on the moon or see how personnel work together in a hospital emergency room. As the quality of software improves, representations will become more sophisticated and simulations more interactive, further increasing learner motivation and understanding.

Problem Solving Computer software can also be used to teach students to solve problems. When we teach problem solving, we want students to get the right answer *and* become better at figuring out how to solve future problems. Creating real-world problems that aren't cut and dried is one difficulty in teaching problem solving in traditional classroom settings. Problems in textbooks are usually well defined and routine; that is, the information needed to solve a problem (and only that information) is included, and even the procedure for finding the solution (such as using subtraction in a math problem) is often suggested by where the problem is presented (in a chapter on subtraction, for example) (Cognition and Technology Group at Vanderbilt, 1997).

Unlike textbook problems, the problems people typically face in the real world are often ill-defined and unlikely to have routine solutions. Technology can help learners acquire experience with more realistic problems. Here is an example.

Jasper has just purchased a new boat and is planning to drive it home. The boat consumes 5 gallons of fuel per hour and travels at 8 mph. The gas tank holds 12 gallons of gas. The boat is currently located at mile marker 156. Jasper's home dock is at mile marker 132. There are two gas stations on the way home. One is at mile marker 140.3 and the other is at mile marker 133. They charge \$1.109 and \$1.25 per gallon, respectively. They don't take credit cards. Jasper started the day with \$20. He bought 5 gallons of gas at \$1.25 per gallon (not including a discount of 4 cents per gallon for paying cash) and paid \$8.25 for repairs to his boat. It's 2:35. Sundown is at 7:52. Can Jasper make it home before sunset without running out of fuel? (S. Williams, Bareiss, & Reiser, 1996, p. 2)

This problem is a condensed episode taken from a videodisc-based, problem-solving series called The New Adventures of Jasper Woodbury (Cognition and Technology Group at Vanderbilt, 1997). The series consists of 12 episodes that each begin with a 15–20 minute video. The video illustrates a challenge, like the one above, to the characters in the episode. Researchers designed these video-based episodes to be complex and open-ended in an effort to teach skills better matched to actual applications (Williams et al., 1996).

The problems in each episode are purposefully left ill-defined to give students practice in identifying the problem (e.g., What am I supposed to find out?) and separating relevant from irrelevant information (e.g., Is the cost of gas important?). They also get experience in breaking the problem down into subgoals, such as finding out how much money Jasper has left for the trip home. As students solve these problems, they work in teams over several class periods (ranging from a few days to more than a week). Students share their ideas, receive feedback to refine their thinking, and present their solutions to the class. These learning activities provide additional opportunities to analyze strengths and weaknesses of different solution strategies as well as opportunities to work together with other students in solving problems.

Research indicates that middle school students using the Jasper series are more successful than students in traditional programs in solving additional mathematics word problems such as these, and they also become better at planning for problem solving and generating subgoals. They also understand basic math concepts as well as traditional students and have more positive attitudes toward math (Cognition and Technology Group at Vanderbilt, 1992). One teacher commented:

"The kids would go home so excited [the parents would say] 'I've got to find out about this Jasper. It is all my kids would talk about. . . .'" Teachers also felt the results were long lasting. "If you have any way of getting to (my) kids in high school, you'll find that they remember those four Jasper episodes. They may not remember anything else that we did that year but they'll remember . . . those episodes because it did hit them and it did make an impact on them this year." (Cognition and Technology Group at Vanderbilt, 1992, p. 308)

Simulations such as these are very demanding, however, and require a great deal of sophisticated support from the teacher to be effective. Teachers must plan carefully and monitor students closely to prevent students from getting frustrated and wasting time.

Databases and Spreadsheets

Case STUDY Angela Travers was teaching sixth-grade science in a suburban middle school. She divided the class into teams of four to five students. For the first unit, the teams measured a number of trees in the school's immediate neighborhood. They took notes on the appearance of the bark and the shape of the leaves. They then put the information into a database and classified the trees into one of several categories. Later, the students used their database to find answers to questions. They identified which type of tree was most common, which trees were the largest, and the approximate age of each tree, for instance.

Databases and spreadsheets are other forms of technology that can be used to teach higher-order thinking skills. A **database program** is *a computer program that allows users to store, organize, and manipulate information, including both text and numerical data* (Roblyer, 2003). The user can then sort and find specific information in the database. Angela used a database program to help her students organize information about trees. Earlier in the chapter you saw how Sandy Hutton taught information about the heart; she used a database to help organize information relating exercise and blood pressure. If you have ever used a library catalog (either an old card catalog or an electronic catalog), you have used a form of database.

As another example, a teacher working on a unit involving factors that influence economic growth might have students develop a database containing information on several countries: population and population density, gross national product, defense budget, literacy rate, and personal income. Once the database is constructed, learners can compare the countries and form conclusions about their economies and potential for growth. Commercial programs such as AppleWorks or Microsoft Office are available to assist teachers as they integrate databases into their instruction.

A **spreadsheet program** is *a computer program that organizes and manipulates numerical data.* Just as word processing software is somewhat comparable to a typewriter, spreadsheets can be compared to calculators. Spreadsheets were first used for accounting purposes but have evolved into sophisticated math tools. For example, Angela's students put the diameter of each of the trees in their database into a spreadsheet and determined the average diameter of the trees by using a formula in the spreadsheet program. They could also try to determine if there is a relationship between the diameter and height of a tree by graphing their data. Finally, they could include digital photographs and use a word processing application to write a report and present their findings.

In solving problems such as these, students are gaining experience with word processing, e-mail, the Internet, spreadsheets, databases, and presentation software—technologies that many students' parents are using in their work every day. Gaining experience with software and its uses in the real world is an important additional benefit to using each of these forms of technology.

Database and spreadsheet programs provide opportunities for students to learn how to analyze, organize, and present information.

Word Processing: Using Technology to Teach Writing

Using word processing to teach writing is probably the most widespread use of educational technology. Do you remember your first letter-writing assignment?

• • ● • •

Your teacher emphasized that a draft copy was to be done in pencil, so you could erase your mistakes and write in corrections. When you were given approval to make a final copy, you took out a nice, clean sheet of white notebook paper and a new ball point pen. Using your best handwriting to copy the letter, you had the date, address, greeting, and first paragraph looking great when Bobby "accidently" bumped your arm. Your pen slashed across the letter, ruining it. After yelling at Bobby, you pulled out another clean sheet of notebook paper and began again.

[It] looked great! Then your teacher reminded you to proofread your letter before turning it in. You thought it was a waste of time, but you did it anyway. To your dismay, you realized you had left out a complete sentence, so that the last paragraph did not make any sense. You reluctantly pulled out yet another clean sheet of notebook paper. All of the elation was gone. In fact, writing had become something that you did not like anymore. (Morrison, Lowther, & DeMuelle, 1999, p. 123)

• • ● • •

For many of us, memories like these are all too familiar. Fortunately, technology, in the form of word processing, is making writing and learning to write easier, more efficient, and more fun. Word processing has the potential to improve student writing in the following ways (B. Alexander et al., 1997; Owston & Wideman, 1997):

- Increasing the legibility of text
- Increasing the amount of text available for viewing at one time
- Making it easier to enter, revise, and edit text

- Allowing students to store and combine ideas
- Facilitating the development of communities of writers by using e-mail to provide feedback on written products

Increasing Understanding 12.5

Based on the information in this section, explain why word processing can result in more positive attitudes toward writing.

In addition, the Internet can provide a valuable reference source for new information.

Research indicates that students who use word processing write more, revise their products more thoroughly, make fewer grammatical and punctuation errors, and have more positive attitudes toward writing (Bangert-Drowns, 1993; Roblyer, 2003). However, word processing alone won't teach writing. Teachers still play an essential role in setting goals, guiding students, and providing feedback. Word processing is a tool; it isn't a panacea.

Using the Internet as an Instructional Tool

Individual computers provide a number of instructional options, but these applications remain isolated without some mechanism for sharing information across distances. The **Internet** is *a complex web of interconnections among computers that allows tens of millions of people to communicate and share information worldwide.*

The Internet was established in 1969 by the Department of Defense to facilitate communication among researchers in 30 different locations around the country (Roblyer, 2003). In the 1980s the National Science Foundation funded a similar high-speed connection network to allow researchers in different universities to exchange information. The advantages of the Internet in terms of cost and the ability to send and access large amounts of information quickly became apparent, and its use has skyrocketed.

In today's world, anyone who isn't at least somewhat familiar with the Internet has been living in a cave. The Internet has literally become a part of our daily lives; we communicate with friends and colleagues on the Internet and even use it to shop for items such as clothes, music, and plane tickets on the World Wide Web (part of the Internet). Government agencies, businesses, schools, and many individuals have their own **Web sites,** *locations on the World Wide Web identified with a uniform resource locator (URL).* A **URL** is *a series of letters and/or symbols that acts as an address for a site on the Internet.* For example, some interesting Web sites include The Internet Movie Database, which contains information about virtually every movie ever made; the ESPN Sports Page, which provides up-to-the minute sports results; the Cable News Network (CNN); the Doonesbury comic strip; and Sleepnet, which provides help for insomniacs.

The Internet addresses for these Web sites can be found in this chapter's *Web Links* module on the Companion Website at **www.prenhall.com/kauchak**.

Even this very small sample gives some idea of the variety of information available on the Internet and helps us understand the comment, "You can find anything on the Internet." One of the challenges facing teachers wanting to use the Internet as an information source, however, is what experts call "link rot," the tendency of Web sites to become antiquated or dysfunctional over time (Trotter, 2002b). Nevertheless, the Internet can be a powerful teaching tool by providing access to multiple sources of information and allowing links to other learners.

The Internet as a source of information is widely known. Students use it to gather information for school reports and projects, and teachers use the information they find to plan lessons (Robin, 1999). However, the Internet's potential to influence communication, social development, and problem solving isn't as commonly examined. We discuss these uses in the next section.

Exploring Diversity

EMPLOYING TECHNOLOGY TO SUPPORT LEARNERS WITH DISABILITIES

Jaleena is partially sighted, with a visual acuity of less than 20/80, even with corrective lenses. Despite this disability, she is doing well in her fourth-grade class. Tera Banks, her teacher, placed her in the front of the room so that she could better see the chalkboard and overhead and has assigned students to work with her on her projects. Using a magnifying device, Jaleena is able to read most written material, but the computer has been giving her special problems. The small text size on many Web sites and in the site addresses has made it very difficult for her to learn to use the computer as an information source.

Tera contacts the special education consultant in her district and is able to get a monitor that magnifies content several times. She knows it is working when she sees Jaleena quietly working alone at her computer on the report due next Friday.

As we've said throughout this chapter, technology is changing the ways we teach and the ways students learn. **Assistive technology,** *adaptive tools that support students with disabilities in their learning activities and daily life tasks,* is having a particularly important impact on students with exceptionalities. These assistive tools are required by federal law, under the Individuals with Disabilities Education Act (IDEA), when students need help in order to access or benefit from special education services (Heward, 2003). These adaptive tools include motorized chairs, remote control devices that turn machines on and off with the nod of the head or other muscle action, and machines that amplify sights and sounds.

Probably the most widespread contribution of assistive technology has been in the area of computer adaptations. For example, some students, such as those who are blind or who have severe physical impairments, cannot interact with a standard computer without adaptations. These adaptations include both input and output devices (Lewis & Doorlag, 1999).

To use computers effectively, students must be able to input their words and ideas. This can be difficult if not impossible for those with visual or other physical disabilities that don't allow standard keyboarding. Keyboards that are larger and easier to see, that have the letters arranged alphabetically to make them easier to find, that use pictures for nonreaders, or that feature Braille are adaptations that accommodate these disabilities.

Additional adaptations completely bypass the keyboard. For example, speech/voice recognition software can translate speech into text on the computer screen, eliminating the need for keyboard inputting (Newby et al., 2000). These systems can be invaluable for students with physical disabilities that affect hand and finger movement. Other adaptations use switches activated by a body movement, such as a

The Internet as a Communication Tool **E-mail (electronic mail)** is *a system that allows a message to be sent via telecommunication from one person to one or more other people.* It has revolutionized communication by allowing people to quickly and efficiently communicate with others almost anywhere in the world. The user can also attach a computer file—containing pictures, a text document, a database, or a spreadsheet, for example—and transmit it along with the e-mail message. With the click of a mouse, an individual can effortlessly send family photos to friends in Germany, Japan, or Kenya.

When students and teachers want to interact with groups of people through the Internet, they can turn to chat rooms. A **chat room** is *a site on the Internet where many people can simultaneously communicate in real time.* For example, when one user in a chat room types comments, they are immediately seen by everyone in the "room."

head nod, to interact with the computer. Touch screens allow students to go directly to the monitor to indicate their responses.

Output devices include monitors and printers. Adaptations to the standard computer monitor either bypass visual displays or increase their size. Size enhancement can be accomplished by using a special large-screen monitor, such as the one Jaleena used, or by using a magnification device with a standard monitor. For students who are blind, speech synthesizers can translate electronic text into spoken words. In addition, special printers can convert regular text into Braille and Braille into regular text.

In addition to alternative input and output devices, many other tools are available for students with exceptionalities. For example, software programs can be used to help students with learning disabilities learn to read and write (MacArthus, Ferretti, Okolo, & Cavalier, 2001). Reading programs help teach students phonetic skills, and other programs simplify word processing demands in writing (Vaughn, Bos, & Schumm, 2000). AlphaSmart, one widely used program, helps developing writers by providing spell-checking and word-prediction software (Fine, 2002). When a student hesitates to finish a word, the computer, based on the first few letters, then either completes the word or offers a menu of suggestions. Advocates claim it frees students to concentrate on ideas and text organization.

These technologies are important because they prevent disabilities from becoming handicaps and obstacles to learning. Their importance to students with exceptionalities is likely to increase as technology becomes a more integral part of classroom instruction.

Assistive technology provides adaptive tools to help students with exceptionalities learn.

CW

Increasing Understanding 12.6

How could assistive technology be combined with other forms of instructional technologies?

Chat rooms are considered the most interactive of all the written communication options; in essence, they are online discussion groups. **A bulletin board** is *an electronic message center for a given topic.* It functions just like a physical bulletin board; it's a place where messages can be posted and stored. Students can read the comments of others and then leave their own messages.

A bulletin board, message board, and chat room for students using this text can be found on the Companion Website at **www.prenhall.com/kauchak**.

Because the Internet efficiently connects students to others all over the world and allows them to share views and perspectives, it can promote learning as well as social growth. This kind of access is impossible to obtain in any other way.

CW

Increasing Understanding 12.7

What is one advantage of a chat room over a bulletin board? One disadvantage?

Increasing Understanding 12.8

"Flaming"—the practice of sending emotional and often derogatory e-mails—has become a communication problem. Using the information in this section, explain why flaming has become more common.

Advantages and disadvantages of Internet communication. As with any educational tool, Internet communication has both advantages and disadvantages (Jehng, 1997; D. Johnson & Johnson, 1996). For example, Internet interactions are more equitable than face-to-face communication, since extraneous factors such as attractiveness, prestige, and material possessions are eliminated. In addition, communicating on the Internet gives students time to think, reflect, and connect ideas, so their thoughts and arguments are often more complete (Marttunen & Laurinen, 2001).

However, Internet communication uses only one channel—the written word—which doesn't help students learn to read nonverbal social cues, such as facial expressions and eye contact, or vocal signals, such as emphasis and intonation. This is a problem for two reasons. First, communications research suggests a large part (perhaps as much as 90%) of a message's credibility is communicated through nonverbal channels (Mehrabian & Ferris, 1967). It is often more difficult for people to understand each others' messages in the absence of nonverbal cues. Second, because Internet communication doesn't give students experience in learning to read social cues, writers may be out of touch with their audiences and may feel a greater sense of anonymity. This can be helpful when it encourages students to disagree or to express opinions, but it can also lead students to show insensitivity and treat others like objects instead of people.

In addition, some experts caution that the amount of time students spend on computers can impair social development by limiting the number of face-to-face interactions they have (Kuh & Vesper, 1999). However, other research suggests that children who are active online are no less likely to spend time reading, playing outside, or interacting with their families (Trotter, 2000), and they are less likely to spend large amounts of time watching television (UCLA Center for Communication Policy, 2001).

Use of the Internet in Problem-Based Learning The Internet can also be a useful tool for developing students' problem-solving skills through problem-based learning. **Problem-based learning** is *an instructional strategy that uses a problem and the data gathered in attempts to solve it as the focal point of a lesson* (Eggen & Kauchak, 2004). Problem-based learning is more open-ended than problem solving, which typically results in convergent answers. The Internet can facilitate problem-based learning by serving as a source of information and a way to share information across sites. For example, in one fifth-grade classroom, students interviewed each other about their pets and then used the Internet to share their data with other students around the country. One class wrote back to another, "We would like to know more about your pet bear . . . Where does the bear stay? How much does the bear eat in a week?" (Julyan, 1989, p. 33). In another classroom students gathered data about water quality in their area and shared it with students in other states (Bradsher & Hagan, 1995).

As another example of problem-based learning, a Web-based simulation project asks high school social studies students to act as diplomats and policy makers to grapple with solutions to real international problems (Rottier, 1995). Students from all over the world dialogue and negotiate about possible solutions to problems related to world health, human rights, and the spread of nuclear weapons. Projects like these use text, graphics, videos, and simulations as conversational props to support exchanges between students (Pea et al., 1999). When students use the Internet in this way, they not only develop problem-solving abilities. They also learn how to use technology to obtain and organize information, and they develop their cooperation skills.

The popularity of the Internet in problem-based learning is due to two important capabilities (Roblyer, 2003). First, students using the Internet can access large amounts of information through the millions of Web sites that currently exist, and second, they can communicate with other research teams working at different sites to either share data or collaborate in problem solving. Internet linkages allow students to transcend

Technology allows teachers to bridge long distances in bringing instruction to students.

the physical boundaries of their classroom to access resources around the world.

Distance Education Technologies When most people think of instruction, they imagine a teacher standing in front of a room of students. **Distance education,** a *catch-all term used to describe organized instructional programs in which teachers and learners, though physically separated, are connected through technology,* is changing that view (Newby et al., 2000). Distance education can be valuable in meeting student needs in at least three situations. First, it can offer students in rural communities courses in specialized areas, such as advanced physics or Japanese, for which a local teacher is unavailable. Second, it can provide instruction for nontraditional students, such as adults who can't attend classes during the day or those who are homebound, and third, it can deliver a class to students over a broad geographic area where driving to a central location is not possible. Students enrolled in online courses appreciate the increased flexibility that allows them to pursue an education while caring for families and maintaining busy careers (L. Cooper, 2001).

The earliest efforts at distance education were correspondence courses where students read books, answered questions, and received feedback from instructors through the mail. Currently, distance education includes a number of options:

- Video broadcasting allows learners to watch instructional programs on television. For example, in one program students across the country viewed Gettysburg battlefields, heard profiles of individual soldiers, and were directed to Web sites where they could find additional information for study (Furlan, 2000).
- Videoconferencing allows learners and teachers from various sites to ask and answer questions over great distances.
- Computer conferencing systems give students and teachers the opportunity to interact via the Internet. Like bulletin boards and chat rooms, these interactions can be synchronous.

Research suggests that the type of distance learning employed is not as important as the quality and organization of the course and the availability of the instructor for answering questions and providing feedback (Roblyer, 2003).

The greatest interest in distance education has been in higher and postsecondary education; about 60 percent of American colleges and universities presently offer some type of distance learning program, and these numbers are growing (Roblyer, 2003). The U.S. Army has made plans to spend $453 million over a 5-year period to create an online university capable of teaching as many as 80,000 soldier–students at locations all around the world (Trotter, 2001a).

Virtual K–12 school programs are also appearing around the country, providing alternatives to standard attendance at school. Currently 19 states have statewide virtual schools, and 14 states allow for the creation of cyber charter schools (Ansell & Park, 2003). Although most common at the high school level, virtual courses are also appearing in elementary and middle schools (Galley, 2003). Most popular with homeschooled students, virtual courses also provide students in rural areas with access to education and students in all areas with courses in hard-to-teach areas such as advanced mathematics or some languages. Critics warn against relying too heavily on this technology and argue that the lack of social interaction results in less learning and decreased social development (Maeroff, 2003). Jane Healy, a technology expert in this area cautions, "If you let your child be educated by a machine, don't be surprised if what comes out isn't totally human" (Galley, 2003, p. 12).

Teacher Support Applications

So far we have emphasized the use of technology as a tool to support student learning. It can also assist teachers by making their work in four major areas simpler and more efficient:

- Preparing instructional materials
- Assessing student learning
- Maintaining student records
- Communicating with parents

Preparing Instructional Materials

Increasingly teachers are being asked to help learners understand complex ideas that are often abstract and difficult to understand (Eggen & Kauchak, 2004). Technology provides one tool that teachers can use to make these ideas accessible to students. For example, at the beginning of the chapter we saw that Latisha Evans created vignettes to illustrate the concept *internal conflict.* She used a word processing program to create and store the examples. If, in using the examples, she finds that one is confusing, she can easily modify it to make it more effective. Revising learning materials is simple with the support of technology but labor-intensive without it.

Teachers can also create databases that can be used in learning activities, as you saw earlier in an example about an activity involving factors that influence economic development. In that example, the students gathered the information to be included in the database, but teachers may choose to create the databases themselves and have the students analyze them. Spreadsheets can be used in a similar way.

Assessing Student Learning

Assessing student learning is one of the most important tasks teachers face. Research confirms that frequent and thorough assessments increase learning (Brookhart, 1997; Dochy & McDowell, 1997; Tuckman, 1998), but creating these assessments can be quite demanding on teachers' time and energies. Technology, and particularly computers, can serve four time-saving assessment functions. They are summarized in Table 12.2 and discussed in the paragraphs that follow and in the subsequent section on maintaining student records (Newby et al., 2000).

Planning and Constructing Tests The word processing capabilities of computers provide teachers with an effective tool for writing, storing, and revising individual test items and then constructing tests from the items. In addition, a number of commercially prepared software programs can assist in this process. These programs can be used to

- Develop a test file or item bank of multiple-choice, true–false, matching, and short-answer items that can be stored in the system
- Organize items within a file by topic, chapter, objective, or difficulty
- Select items from the created file bank randomly, selectively, or by categories to generate multiple versions of a test

Table 12.2 Assessment Functions Supported by Computers

Function	Examples
Planning and constructing tests	Preparing objectives Writing, editing, and storing items Compiling items into tests Printing tests
Administering tests	Administering tests online Providing immediate corrective feedback Analyzing results
Scoring and interpreting tests	Scoring tests Summarizing results Analyzing items
Maintaining student records	Recording results Developing class summaries Reporting results to students Preparing grade reports

- Modify items and integrate them into the total test
- Produce student-ready copies and an answer key

These software test generators have at least three advantages over basic word processing. First, they produce a standard layout; the teacher doesn't have to worry about spacing or format. Second, they automatically produce alternate forms, which can be helpful for creating makeup tests and preventing cheating. Third, they can be used with commercially prepared test banks that come with textbooks to customize assessments.

Administering Tests Computer software now exists that allows teachers to construct and administer tests online (Roblyer, 2003). This is useful in some situations where students must be absent from school when the test is given or in individualized programs where students progress at their own rate. These programs can also give students immediate feedback about right and wrong answers, and they can provide the teacher with updated information about the test performance of individual students and the performance of the class as a whole.

Experts believe that online testing will play a major role in states' new accountability programs (Edwards, 2003). Currently, 12 states and the District of Columbia have either a computerized exam or pilot project under way to evaluate the effectiveness of computer-based testing. The almost immediate feedback provided to both teachers and students is an important strength of these systems. Experts also predict that online technologies will become increasingly important in providing preparation and practice for these high-stakes tests (Borja, 2003).

Scoring and Interpreting Tests Technology can also assist in the process of scoring tests and reporting results, saving time for the teacher and providing students with more immediate and informative feedback. For example, a high school teacher with five sections of 30 students and a 40-item exam faces the daunting task of grading 6,000 ($5 \times 30 \times 40$) individual items! Scoring and analyzing test data, converting scores to grades, and recording the grades can be enormously time-consuming without the help of technology.

There are a number of software programs available to machine-score tests (e.g., QuickSCORE). These programs can perform the following functions:

- Score objective tests and provide descriptive statistics, such as test mean, median, mode, range, and standard deviation
- Generate a list of items showing difficulty level, the percentage of students who selected each response, the percentage of students who didn't respond to an item, and the correlation of each item with the total test
- Sort student responses by score, grade/age, or gender

Maintaining Student Records

Record keeping is another time-consuming teacher task that technology can assist with. One teacher commented,

I keep my grades in an electronic gradebook. By entering my grades into an electronic gradebook as I grade papers, I always know how my students are progressing and exactly where my students stand in relation to each other. It does take a little time to enter the grades, but it makes my job easier during reporting periods. All I have to do is open my disk and record my students' grades on the grade sheet. (Morrison et al., 1999, p. 355)

In addition to saving teacher time and energy, these programs are accurate (assuming the original data are accurately entered) and fast, which allows teachers to generate grades at the end of a marking period with just a few keystrokes. In addition, records are available at any time, providing students with ongoing feedback. Some programs can even print student reports in a language other than English, such as Spanish (Forcier, 1999).

Schools are also using technology to keep attendance records (M. Jennings, 2000). When students come into school, they slide their identification cards into a device similar to those used by credit card machines. In addition to keeping daily attendance, the machines are effective for helping schools identify unwelcome outside visitors and students who cut classes during the day.

Communicating with Parents

We saw in Chapter 2 that helping parents become involved in their children's education is an important teacher role. Communication is an essential step in that process, and technology can help make home–school links more effective.

The busy schedules of parents and teachers are obstacles to home–school communication. Voice mail and e-mail can help overcome these obstacles by creating communication channels between parents who work and teachers who are busy with students all day (Cameron & Lee, 1997). For instance, parents (and students) can e-mail teachers to monitor students' learning progress, checking current grades and getting information about missed assignments.

Schools also provide other communication options. A growing number of teachers create or use established Web sites to present current class topics and post assignments, and schools set up electronic hotlines to keep parents informed about current events, schedule changes, lunch menus, and bus schedules. However, research indicates that many parents still prefer more traditional information sources such as newsletters and open houses (Langdon, 1999). This may be because some households don't have Internet service and because people have an instinctive desire for the face-to-face contact they experience at open houses.

One innovation uses the Internet to provide parents with real-time images of their children at school (Kleiman, 2001). An increasing number of preschool and day-care programs are installing cameras and Internet systems that allow parents to log on to secure-access Web sites where they can monitor their children during the day.

Instructional Issues in the Use of Technology

In earlier sections we looked at process and hardware views of technology and examined some of the most common applications of technology in schools. But, as with any innovation or reform, controversies exist. In this section we examine the following instructional issues teachers face as they attempt to use technology in their classrooms:

- Instructional goals for the use of technology
- Quality of available software
- Curricular issues
- Plagiarism and cheating

We also discuss Internet censorship in our Teaching in an Era of Reform feature.

Instructional Goals for the Use of Technology

Why use technology in your classroom? Let's walk down the hallway of a typical elementary school to try to answer this question.

• • • • •

Chris Carter is working with her first graders on basic word processing skills in an attempt to get them ready to use computers on creative writing assignments.

Down the hall several of Jim Henderson's fourth graders are working in the back of the classroom at a program called Math Blaster. After answering a certain number of questions correctly, the program rewards them with an arcade-like game.

Maria Robles's sixth graders are working on projects in teams, using the Internet to gather information on pollution problems in their state and other parts of the country. They also correspond with students in other states who are working on similar projects to share information.

• • • • •

These teachers obviously had very different instructional goals. Your goals should influence the ways you use technology. Although it can perform a wide variety of tasks, technology that isn't linked to clear and important goals is questionable and potentially counterproductive.

The International Society for Technology in Education (ISTE) lists the following six technology goals for students (ISTE, 2000):

- To become proficient in basic operations and concepts (e.g., word processing and printing)
- To understand the social and ethical issues involved in the use of technology (e.g., computer hacking and plagiarism)
- To use technology as a productivity tool (e.g., creating an online literary magazine)
- To use technology as a communication tool (e.g., interacting with peers across the country)

- To use technology as a research tool (e.g., using Internet search engines to locate information on a specific topic)
- To use technology for problem solving and decision making (e.g., using technology to find the best price for an airline ticket)

To help teachers integrate these goals into their teaching, ISTE has produced a detailed guide containing lesson plans linked to appropriate technologies.

To link to the ISTE publication, go to the Companion Website at **www.prenhall.com/kauchak**, then to this chapter's *Web Links* module.

Increasing Understanding 12.9

What kind of school computer configuration—in-class computers or a computer lab—is most compatible with the goal of computer literacy? Why isn't this configuration compatible with other ISTE goals?

Note that only one of the ISTE goals is targeted at **computer literacy,** *a basic understanding of how to use computers.* When schools were first introduced to computer technology, computer literacy was a primary goal. Now, as more and more students come to school with computer skills, the emphasis has shifted to more complex goals.

Despite the shift in emphasis, teachers must be aware of their students' computer backgrounds and skills. Students can't use computers as learning tools if they don't have basic computer skills. For example, word processing can be effective for teaching writing but only if students have basic keyboarding skills and the ability to cut, move, paste, and edit text.

Quality of Available Software

Quality is an important issue in technology, because it affects how easy it is to use and how much students learn. Existing educational software is generally well rated by teachers, but at least two factors influence its quality (Trotter, 1999a; Zehr, 1999a). First, the market economy drives software production. Companies create software to make money, and quality is often less important than profit. Second, much software is based on antiquated views of learning, which led to a proliferation of "drill and kill" programs that are little more than electronic flashcards.

Curricular Issues

With respect to technology, two curricular issues exist: (1) the alignment of software with learning objectives and (2) pressures to "cover" the curriculum.

Increasing Understanding 12.10

What can teachers do to ensure a match between software and either district curricula or tests?

Alignment Problems Effective instruction requires that learning objectives and instruction are aligned, or consistent with each other (Porter, 2002). For example, if a teacher wants her students to develop their writing skills, but she spends much of her time having the students punctuate specific sentences, her instruction is out of alignment. Technology tools must also be matched with objectives. Suppose that, after a search of catalogs and Web sites, a teacher finds an appealing (and perhaps high-quality) software program. If the learning activities on the program don't align with district curriculum guides, mandated tests, or the teacher's specific learning objectives, use of the program amounts to a waste of time and money on "bells and whistles" (Trotter, 1999a). In one national teacher survey, the match between software and state/district curricula was rated C or lower by more than 59 percent of teachers, and the match with state/district tests received a C or lower by more than 39 percent of the same teachers (Trotter, 1999b). This problem is not unique to software; textbook series also are often out of synch with state and district goals and standardized tests (Porter, 2002). When this mismatch occurs, students may be spending valuable time learning content that is not aligned with curricular goals, a major instructional problem in this age of reform and accountability.

Time Constraints Pressure to cover the curriculum—to teach technology—is a second issue. Schools and classrooms are busy places, and teachers struggle to "get it all in." Teachers often feel that integrating technology into an already crowded curriculum is difficult. Many of the better quality software programs are problem-based (like the Jasper series described earlier in the chapter) and do take more time. When faced with the pressures of accountability-driven tests, teachers have trouble implementing advice from learning experts suggesting that "slower and deeper is better than faster and broader" (Ormrod, 2003). Larry Cuban, a respected educational historian, noted, "The current frenzy for testing and accountability is so extreme that the idea of squeezing something else (like technology) into the core curriculum . . . is highly unlikely" (Zehr, 2000c, p. 18). Effectively integrating technology requires careful planning and a significant measure of teacher creativity.

Good teaching requires extensive planning time, something U.S. teachers don't have (Darling-Hammond, 1997). During school hours the average teacher in the United States has between a half hour and an hour each day to grade papers, plan lessons, assemble learning materials, consult with colleagues, and communicate with students and parents. (This is considerably less than in most other industrialized countries.) Teachers feel rushed to complete basic tasks such as planning and organizing materials for the next lesson; locating, experimenting with, and integrating technology into the curriculum creates an additional planning burden. To properly integrate technology into the classroom, teachers require a minimum of preparation time (Cuban, 1999), and ease of use and amount of preparation time are two reasons teachers commonly give for not using technology more than they presently do (Trotter, 1999a).

Plagiarism and Cheating

The easy access to information, and even complete papers, on the Internet has become a temptation for students and a problem for teachers. Students are downloading papers or sections of papers and handing them in as their own. In addition to ethical problems, this practice robs students of experiences in analyzing, organizing, and expressing their own ideas.

Suggestions for addressing this problem range from instructional approaches to high-tech solutions that analyze student work and compare it to databases containing hundreds of thousands of papers. Instructionally, the place to start is an honest discussion with students about the problems involved in plagiarism. Plagiarism can also be reduced by closely working with students from the initial draft stages to the final product. If all else fails, teachers may wish to try online services that detect copying and wholesale borrowing of intact passages.

For information on companies that provide plagiarism detection services, go to the Companion Website at **www.prenhall.com/kauchak**, then to this chapter's *Web Links* module.

Access Issues in the Use of Technology

One of the most important issues in the use of technology is easy to understand: the simple matter of access. If teachers and students don't have access to technology, they can't use it to increase learning.

One survey of educational technology use across the country found that as of 2001, the vast majority—99 percent—of public schools had Internet access (Flanigan, 2003). Another study found that the ratio of students per Internet-connected computer changed from 6.8 students per computer in 2001 to 5.6 pupils in 2002 (Ansell & Park, 2003). So, in a class of 30 students, the "average" teacher will have something

Teaching in an Era of Reform

THE INTERNET CENSORSHIP ISSUE

The Internet can be a powerful learning tool, but students' ability to access online information at the click of a button also raises concerns about the kinds of materials available to children. Internet-filtering software can be used to block out entire lists of Web pages in specific, predetermined categories or to limit access to sites that contain certain words. For example, the state of Tennessee uses a filter to prevent students from accessing pornography, hate speech, violent material, chat rooms, MTV, games, or World Wide Web sites about cheating in school (Furlan, 1999).

The Issue

Several controversies surround the practice of Internet filtering. The first is the whole issue of censorship and free speech that we encountered in Chapter 9 under the topic of school law. Free speech advocates contend such filtering is unconstitutional, violating students' rights to free speech and access to information. Critics counter that Internet filtering is no different from selecting curriculum content and textbooks for students based on fundamental principles of good teaching.

This comparison with school books illustrates how difficult and complex Internet filtering can be. Textbook selection is centralized and consequently much easier; school districts and schools are given lists of textbook series that a state curriculum committee finds acceptable. Educators have much less ability to control students' access to the Internet. In trying to filter out objectionable content, schools are aiming at a moving target, since new Web sites appear daily. The Tennessee statewide system mentioned earlier controls access to 100,000 computers used by 900,000 students. The system needs to be updated every night and has blocked access to 7 million Web pages.

A second controversy surrounding Internet filtering is the level at which it should occur. Some argue for federal legislation, claiming this is a national problem; others argue for state or district control, pointing out that local agencies are in a better position to determine the needs of school children. Local control, however, could mean thousands of districts would be performing essentially the same function. There are no easy answers with this issue. In 2000 the U.S. Congress passed the Children's Internet Protection Act, which requires that all schools and libraries that receive federal funds for Internet connection install pornography filters in their systems (Trotter, 2001d). However, these restrictions

like five Internet-connected computers available. This is a significant improvement from one Internet-connected computer per 20 students in 1998.

Nevertheless, when asked to identify major barriers to effective use of technology, 71 percent of teachers and 66 percent of principals targeted "insufficient number of computers" (Jerald & Orlofsky, 1999). Another national teacher survey also identified insufficient computers as the major obstacle to greater software and Web site utilization (Trotter, 1999b).

CW

Increasing Understanding 12.11

Is the problem of Internet access more serious at some K–12 levels than others? in some content areas than others? Explain.

Efforts to achieve the tech boosters' ideal—one computer for every student—have focused on variations of the standard desktop personal computer. Laptop computers allow students to take computers home and to libraries with them. Handheld computers, miniature versions of regular computers that cost between $250 and $500, also provide flexibility, but screen and keyboard limitations pose problems (Trotter, 2001c). Experts also worry about annual maintenance and upgrade costs.

apply only to pornography and don't deal with other objectionable content, such as violence, or games, which the Tennessee state filter screens.

New teachers should determine the Internet access procedures at the school where they teach before allowing their students to go online. Guidelines should clearly specify teacher responsibilities, and new teachers should seek guidance from administrators or more experienced peers if questions remain. The whole area of Internet access will, in all likelihood, continue to grow in importance as more classrooms use the Internet to access data.

Internet filters can prevent students from accessing pornography, violent material, or games.

You Take a Position

Now it's your turn to take a position on the issue. State in writing whether you favor or oppose the use of Internet filtering in schools, and provide a two-page rationale for your position. If you favor, at what level should this filtering take place?

For additional references and resources, go to the Companion Website at **www.prenhall.com/kauchak**, *then to this chapter's* Teaching in an Era of Reform *module. You can respond online or submit your response to your instructor.*

CW

Another factor affecting access is where computers are situated in a school. Overall, 43 percent of school computers are found in labs, and 48 percent are found in classrooms (the remainder are used by teachers, administrators, and school secretaries). At the elementary level, computers are much more likely to be found in classrooms, whereas computer labs are more typical at the middle school level. For example, 84 percent of all fourth graders had computers available in classrooms, compared to 47 percent of eighth graders; 91 percent of eighth graders had computers available in computer labs compared to 79 percent of fourth graders (U.S. Department of Education, 1998a).

The question of whether to place computers in labs or classrooms is a complex one (Roblyer, 2003). Labs typically have a person available to help with questions and troubleshoot equipment problems, but students have to leave their classrooms, and lab time is limited. Computer labs allow the teacher to present basic computer

TECHNOLOGY IN CLASSROOMS

Having examined different ways that technology can be used to enhance learning in the classroom, you now have the chance to view a video of a teacher using technology in a variety of ways to reinforce her students' developing understanding of graphing.

In one segment, students call different pizza restaurants to find the price of pizza and then graph their results. In another, students watch a video clip of students racing through alternate routes on an obstacle course. They are then asked to time and graph the runners' results. In another, students use computers to graph the results of a student survey on students' soft drink preferences.

To complete this activity, do the following:

- Go to the DVD, and view the video episode titled "Technology in Classrooms."
- Answer the questions you'll find on the DVD.

CW *To answer the questions online and receive immediate feedback, go to the Companion Website at* **www.prenhall.com/kauchak**, *then to this chapter's* Classroom Windows *module.*

CW

Increasing Understanding 12.12

Would you predict that more school computers in the future will be found in labs or classrooms? Why? How does your answer relate to process and hardware views of technology?

literacy skills in a whole-class format, and clustered computers provide opportunities for students to individually practice skills and receive feedback. Classroom workstations provide ready access and convenient use, but the numbers are typically limited, and there is no immediate assistance to either teachers or students if problems arise. The placement of computers in your school will have a major influence on the ways you will use them in your instruction.

Computer labs allow schools to cluster computers in one location to teach basic computer literacy skills.

Cost of Technology

Cost is a major factor influencing technology use and accessibility in schools. As anyone who has tried to buy a computer has discovered, technology is expensive. In the 2001–2002 school year, the United States spent $5.6 billion on education technology (McCabe & Skinner, 2003)

The problem doesn't end with the purchase of the computer itself. Experts attempting to describe the overall costs involved with technology use the concept *total cost of ownership* (Soulé, 2000), which includes costs associated with software, maintenance and repairs, system linkages, technical support, and training. Districts hard-pressed by the public to increase the use of technology in their schools often rush out to buy computers but fail to consider the support needed to make the technology effective and efficient. U.S. school districts spend more than 50 percent of their budgets on hardware, software, and supplies, allocating only 27 percent to networking, Internet service, and staff development, a figure much less than in industry (Jerald & Orlofsky, 1999).

Federal Support The federal government has responded to the problem of technology funding through the Telecommunications Act of 1996, which provided a fund of $2 billion per year for districts to help provide equal access and "universal service." These funds can be used to provide electronic networking, access to the Internet, high-speed data lines, and pay for telephone charges linked to technology use.

Equity Issues in Access to Technology

One current reform calls for greater access to, and use of, technology. Reformers suggest that technology can be the great equalizer, minimizing learning gaps between the rich and poor, minority and nonminority, and male and female students. Let's see how this reform effort is progressing.

We saw in Chapter 8 that great disparities in educational funding exist between "rich" and "poor" school districts. These disparities result in differences in teachers' salaries, the kinds of buildings and classrooms teachers work in, as well as the kinds of resources available to promote learning. They also impact students' access to technology, suggesting a growing "digital divide," between these different groups (Light, 2001; National Telecommunications and Information Administration, 1999).

Ethnicity and Technology Access As we see in Table 12.3, the percentage of people who own computers and use the Internet at home varies by ethnicity. For example, in 2002, 83 percent of households with school-age children had a computer in the home, but only 71 percent of African American and 69 percent of Hispanic households had them (Corporation for Public Broadcasting, 2003). Disparities in Internet use were

Table 12.3 Ethnicity and Technology Access

	Ownership of Computer	Internet Use at Home
Caucasian	87%	49%
African American	71%	29%
Hispanic	69%	33%

Source: Corporation for Public Broadcasting (2003).

Issues of computer access have raised questions about technology's ability to act as a great equalizer.

even greater, with 49 percent of Caucasian students using the Internet at home versus 29 percent and 33 percent for African American and Hispanic students, respectively. The differences in home use are especially troubling because research shows that education is the primary use for home computers (53% of students), outdistancing e-mail (32%) and games (12%) (Trotter, 2000).

CW

Increasing Understanding 12.13

Access to computers, both at school and at home, increases as income increases (see Table 12.4). Predict whether the access disparities between high- and low-income households will increase or decrease in the future.

Income and Technology Access Household income also leads to disparities in technology access. As we see in Table 12.4, there are considerable differences in access to both computers and the Internet for students from low- and high-income families. For example, in 2002, 65 percent of low-income families reported owning computers versus 98 percent of high-income families (Corporation for Public Broadcasting, 2003). When asked about the ability to access the Internet from any location (home, school, or library), 55 percent of low-income students reported access versus 77 percent of high-income students. The biggest difference between the groups was seen in online home use of computers; less than half as many low-income as high-income students

Table 12.4 Household Income and Technology Access

Household Income	Ownership of Computer	Online Use at Home	Access to Internet from Any Location
Low Income	65%	29%	55%
Middle Income	85%	49%	62%
High Income	98%	66%	77%

Source: Corporation for Public Broadcasting (2003).

said they used the Internet at home. The cost of buying, installing, and maintaining computers has been identified as the main reason for this disparity (U.S. Department of Commerce, 1998). When students are expected to work on computers at home to complete assignments, access can be a serious problem.

The quality of available computers is also important because it influences the kinds of software that can be used, as well as access to the Internet. Schools serving high percentages of cultural minorities and schools located in communities with high poverty rates tend to have older, lower-quality computers without CD-ROM capabilities or high-speed processors (Bracey, 1999a).

Access to the Internet also requires infrastructure and wiring, which are also influenced by school financial resources. School financial resources, in turn, correspond to the percentage of economically disadvantaged students in a school. Although virtually all U.S. public schools (99%) had access to the Internet in 2001, there were income-related disparities in terms of classroom access to the Internet (Ansell & Park, 2003). Nationwide, 87 percent of classrooms had Internet service, but this figure fell to 79 percent for high-poverty schools. To remedy this problem, the Federal Communication Commission's E-rate program has spent $1.5 billion in additional funds to make technology available to schools serving students eligible for federal school lunch programs and schools with high numbers of parents with incomes below the poverty level (Charp, 2001).

For additional information on the problem of Internet access, go to the Companion Website at **www.prenhall.com/kauchak**, then to this chapter's *Web Links* module. Find the "Digital Divide" heading.

Gender Divides Gender also influences computer access and use. Research over the past decade has revealed that girls are not taking advantage of computer technologies at the same rate or in the same ways as boys. They are less likely to participate in computer clubs, use computer software, and take technology-related courses (Hale, 1998). In *Tech-Savvy: Educating Girls in the New Computer Age*, the American Association of University Women (AAUW) reported the following about one large school district:

> [N]early all (94 percent) of the students in "artificial intelligence" classes were male, as were a large majority (77 percent) of the students in business-computer programming classes. Information systems and desktop publishing classes are less skewed, with 54 percent male and 46 percent female enrollment, respectively. The only class where males do not predominate is word processing. (AAUW Education Foundation on Technology, Gender, and Teacher Education, 2000, p. 46)

As we noted in Chapter 3, at the high school level only 11 percent of students taking the College Board advanced placement test in computer science in 2001 were women. (Stabiner, 2003). This "digital divide" persists when girls enter the work world. The AAUW reported that only 20 percent of information technology professionals are women (AAUW Education Foundation, 2000).

Interestingly, one large survey found that about the same percentage of girls and boys use the Internet, but they use it for different purposes (National School Boards Foundation, 2000). The girls were using the Internet for education and schoolwork and to chat with others (through e-mail or online), whereas the boys were going online for games and entertainment. A number of researchers have suggested girls' participation in computer activities would rise if products and courses were designed with their interests and learning styles in mind and educators addressed larger issues related to gender roles (AAUW Education Foundation, 2000; Margolis & Fisher, 2003).

These differences in computer access and use are troubling for several reasons. Research suggests that the number and quality of computers influences teachers' use of technology. When obstacles are too great, teachers tend not to use it, which deprives their students of valuable learning opportunities (Collis, Peters, & Pals, 2001). From a student perspective, these statistics raise the question of whether all students are being provided with equal opportunities to learn. In the long term, access to computers can influence the kinds of career options available to students. Students are less likely to pursue high-tech careers in areas such as science and engineering if they have inadequate technology backgrounds or have not been introduced to ways that technology is used in these areas. According to one estimate, "by 2010, one in every four new jobs will . . . involve the use, design, application, or maintenance of computers" (AAUW Education Foundation, 2000, 56). The challenge for educators is to prepare all students to compete in such an environment.

Equity Issues: Proposed Solutions

There is no doubt that unequal access to technology influences the educational experiences of low-income students, minorities, and women. But the question of what to do about the problem is perplexing. Money alone can't solve the problem, as evidenced by the problems of computer accessibility in homes and women not pursuing careers in technology-related fields. The level at which funding should occur is also an issue. Some advocate increased federal spending, claiming the problem is a national one. Others advocate increased funding at the state or local level, but recent budget shortfalls and cuts make this unlikely.

Knowledge and awareness of the problem will certainly help. The public needs to be made aware of these inequities and public support for solutions marshaled. In addition, teachers and administrators need to work on this problem at the school and classroom levels.

Decision Making

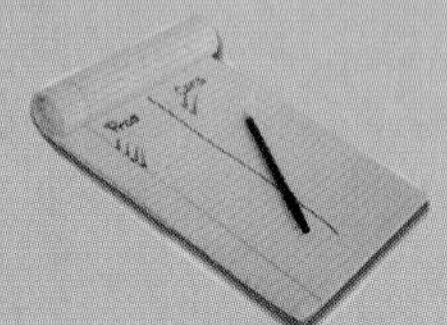

Defining Yourself as a Professional

As we've seen, technology is changing not only the way we teach but also the ways students learn. It is also changing your role as a teacher, the challenges you'll encounter as you begin your new career, and your professional development as you progress from novice to expert. This chapter raises a number of questions you'll need to consider as you decide what kind of teacher you want to become.

One of the first is how you will prepare yourself to use technology in your teaching. Forty states and the District of Columbia currently require teachers to have formal training in technology (Ansell & Park, 2003). You may take a specific course in technology, or it will be integrated into several of the courses in your certification program. Each option has advantages and disadvantages. A stand-alone course can focus exclusively on technology but may not provide as many applications in different content areas. Technology components integrated into various methods courses are often strong on specific applications but may not provide a "big picture" of technology uses across content areas.

The kind of support you will receive once you're on the job is a second consideration. The most common source of support in the 1999–2000 school year was a full-time teacher who was also the technology coordinator (21% of schools surveyed), followed by a district-level coordinator (17%), full-time school-level coordinator (16%), and library media specialist (14%) (Ansell & Park, 2003). Technical assistance is essential, as research indicates that the more training and help teachers receive, the more likely they are to use technology in their teaching and the more likely they are to use it to promote problem solving and higher-level thinking (Archer, 1998; Collis et al., 2001). The kind of technology support available to you as a beginning teacher may be an important factor to consider when weighing options for your first job.

Unfortunately, staff development receives little funding. The major part (66%) of districts' technology budget goes to hardware, 20 percent goes to software, and only 14 percent is allocated to staff development (Ansell & Park, 2003). In industry the rule of thumb is that companies should spend one third of their technology budget on training and support (Gursky, 1999). By this standard, the allocation to teacher development in technology is clearly inadequate.

In addition, although access to technology has increased rapidly in recent years, the percentage of schools with full-time technology coordinators has increased slowly, and schools in poorer districts are less likely to have such support. One study found that the Chicago Public School System had only six computer technicians—each responsible for 93 schools (Gursky, 1999)!

One of the questions you'll want to ask as you interview for a teaching position is what kind of expectations the school has for your use of technology and what support you can expect. This is important, because only 42 percent of new teachers reported being very well or well prepared to use technology in their classrooms (Ansell & Park, 2003). Once you land a job, you should contact the technology support person in your school or district to identify available resources and find out how to get help when you need it. This help will be a major factor in your use of technology as you begin your career (Strudler, McKinney, Jones, & Quinn, 1999).

As your professional skills develop, your ability to use technology will also improve. Novice teachers tend to use technology either as an end in itself or as a reward to students for completing other instructional tasks (Zehr, 1999a). As teachers progress, they use technology to support the existing curriculum and instruction. Finally, at the highest level experts use technology as a tool to change and improve their teaching by involving students in real-world, challenging tasks. As a beginning teacher, you will want to experiment with using technology, but it is likely to take several years before you're able to use it to transform your teaching. An individualized self-administered assessment, found in Portfolio Activity 12.1, is a tool that can assist you in this area of professional growth.

Summary

What Is Technology?

One view of technology looks at it in terms of hardware, such as computers, whereas another, more recent view sees technology as an integrative process that completely transforms instruction. Most experts see instructional technology as a combination of the processes and tools needed to address educational needs.

Technology Use in the Classroom

Technology has many different uses in the classroom. Most involve drill-and-practice software or tutorials, which provide entire instructional sequences. Technology can also be used to teach higher-level thinking skills through simulations, which bring realistic slices of the world into classrooms, and problem-solving activites, which capture aspects of real-world situations for instructional purposes. Database and spreadsheet programs, which assist students in organizing and analyzing data, can also become powerful tools to teach higher-level thinking skills.

The word processing capabilities of computers have revolutionized the teaching of writing by allowing students to edit and revise their works in progress. Assistive technology provides students who have exceptionalities with tools to function successfully in the classroom.

The Internet can help both teachers and students in the teaching–learning process. It provides a ready source of information and allows students to communicate with others around the world who are involved in similar research ventures. It has also provided educational opportunities through various forms of distance learning.

Teacher Support Applications

Technology can help teachers prepare instructional materials, design and administer tests, maintain student records, and communicate with parents. A number of commercial software programs provide assistance in these areas.

Instructional Issues in the Use of Technology

Teachers' use of technology is affected by a number of instructional issues. Experts have identified six major goals for technology use; only one of these targets computer literacy. When using technology, clear goals are essential; technology should match teacher and district goals and relate to existing assessment systems. As teachers attempt to integrate technology into their instruction, they are often faced with curricular pressures and preparation time constraints. The easy access to information on the Internet also exacerbates cheating and plagiarism problems. In addition, the whole issue of Internet access places the teacher directly in the middle of censorship and student protection issues.

Access Issues in the Use of Technology

Access issues also challenge teachers as they attempt to use technology in their teaching. Foremost among these are how many computers are available and how they are organized and distributed in schools. Computer labs are designed to teach computer literacy skills but are not optimal for integrating technology into instruction. Funding, availability, and accessibility also influence the ways teachers use technology in their teaching.

Research shows that different ethic groups do not have the same access to computers and the Internet. Household income and school finances influence access, both in terms of number and quality of computers, as well as Internet availability. Gender also plays an important role in computer access and use, and females are underrepresented in technology courses and computer-related professions.

Important Concepts

assistive technology (p. 448)
bulletin board (p. 449)
chat room (p. 448)
computer literacy (p. 456)
database program (p. 445)
distance education (p. 451)
e-mail (electronic mail) (p. 448)
hypermedia (p. 442)
icon (p. 442)
instructional technology (p. 437)
Internet (p. 447)
problem-based learning (p. 450)
simulation (p. 443)
software (p. 440)
spreadsheet program (p. 446)
tutorial (p. 441)
URL (uniform resource locator) (p. 447)
Web sites (p. 447)

Developing as a Professional

Praxis Practice

Read the case study, and answer the questions that follow.

Maria Villenas, a middle-school health teacher in an inner-city school, sat at her desk during her planning period.

"How can I make this unit on nutrition come alive for my students?" she thought as she gazed at the mound of planning materials on her desk. "I know last year's lecture almost put them and me to sleep."

"I know," she thought. "They love thinking about themselves and finding out how they're similar and different from their friends. I'll have them keep a food journal for a week, and then we'll see if we can organize the class's eating habits into a chart or graph. That should give them practice in using the computer to organize information as well as with working in groups. Hmm, I'll need to check the district's curriculum guidelines for nutrition to make sure I'm still covering all the bases."

With these thoughts in mind, Maria prepared the following lesson plan.

LESSON PLAN

Topic: Food and Nutrition

Goals

1. Students should understand the role of calories in their diet.
2. Students should understand the Food Guide Pyramid and apply it to their diets.
3. Students should be able to analyze diets in terms of calories and the major food groups.

Procedures

1. Introduce concept of calories. Have students read section in text on calories. Students will complete worksheet in small groups. Discuss as a whole-group activity.
2. Display food pyramid transparency. Explain differences between carbohydrates, proteins, and fats. Illustrate with common foods. Use Think–Pair–Share to categorize additional foods. Check categorization in whole group.
3. Introduce journaling assignment. Take first 5 minutes of class each day to allow time for students to edit and answer questions.

Follow-up

1. Check on availability of software to do spreadsheets.
2. Explain and demonstrate how to use computer to analyze and graph data.

3. Form research groups to analyze data. Make sure equal numbers of high-ability and low-ability students and boys and girls are in each group. Assign rotating roles so boys and high-ability students don't do everything.
4. Make sure research groups have plenty of research time to complete assignments, as many students don't have computers at home to work on.
5. Plan for group presentations.

Assessment

1. Test on basic concepts (check last year's and update).
2. Group presentation.

"Whew," Maria sighed. "This is going to be a lot of work, and it'll take time, but it should be a fun learning experience—for them and me."

1. Did Maria's lesson plan reflect a hardware or process view of technology use? Explain.
2. Did Maria's lesson focus more on problem solving or problem-based learning? Explain.
3. Which of the following instructional issues did Maria wrestle with as she planned her lesson: instructional goals, quality of software, curricular match with instructional goals, curricular pressures, preparation time constraints, plagiarism and cheating, and Internet access?
4. How did Maria address equity issues in her planning?

To receive feedback on your responses to the Praxis Practice exercises, go to the Companion Website at **www.prenhall.com/kauchak**, then to this chapter's *Praxis Practice* module.

Discussion Questions

1. Which view of technology—hardware or process—is more prevalent in the schools? Why is this the case? What could be done to improve the balance?
2. In what areas of the curriculum is it most useful to use technology to deliver instruction? In what areas is it least useful? Why?
3. What are the relative advantages and disadvantages of using drill-and-practice software and tutorials versus teacher-led instruction? In what areas and at what levels are these forms of technology most effective?
4. Should Internet filtering occur at the national or local level? What are the advantages and disadvantages of each approach?
5. What can teachers do to overcome the digital divide in their own classrooms? What can they do at the school or district level?
6. What is the biggest obstacle to more effective technology use in schools? What can beginning teachers realistically do to address this problem?

Classroom Observation Guide

Before You Begin: The purpose of these observation activities is to provide you with insights into the different ways that teachers use technology in their classrooms. As you observe teachers as they use technology, talk with them about the promises and pitfalls of technology from their perspective.

1. Observe two classrooms that have computers. How are the computers used? Are they used for instruction? If so, are they for remediation, new learning, rewards, or enrichment? Describe the uses in a paper, and make suggestions for alternate or improved ways to utilize technology in the classroom.
2. Observe a teacher and students in a classroom with computers and also in a lab with computers. How does the teacher's role change in the two environments? Are the goals and activities different? Describe these differences in a summary that examines advantages and disadvantages of each configuration.

Going into Schools

1. Interview a teacher about his or her use of technology to support instruction. Ask about the following applications:
   a. Preparing instructional materials
   b. Assessing student learning
   c. Maintaining student records
   d. Communicating with parents

   What suggestions does the teacher have for making these applications more effective? Summarize your findings in a paper that describes how you will use technology to support your teaching.
2. Visit a school and make an inventory of the various types of media production aids and equipment available for use in the classroom (e.g., cameras, videotape equipment, lettering equipment, computer graphics, etc.). (These are typically found in a centralized teacher prep room.) How could these tools be used to enhance your instruction? Describe at least three concrete ways that you could use different forms of technology in your teaching.
3. Interview a teacher about the district's Internet-filtering policy. Ask to see the policy. Is the policy effective and easy to implement? Are there any gray areas? Are parents active in shaping the policy? What are parents' and administrators' major concerns? Describe these practices and how filtering policies will influence your teaching.
4. Interview a teacher about the technology support available at his or her school. Is a support person available on site? How easy is it to access help? What professional development activities are available to increase technology skills? Describe these opportunities in a paper.

Virtual Field Experience

If you would like to participate in a Virtual Field Experience, go to the Companion Website at **www.prenhall.com/kauchak**, then to this chapter's *Field Experience* module.

Online Portfolio Activities

To complete these activities online, go to the the Companion Website at **www.prenhall.com/kauchak**, then to this chapter's *Portfolio Activities* module.

Portfolio Activity 12.1

Technology and You

INTASC Principle 9: Commitment

Personal Journal Reflection

The purpose of this activity is to help you analyze your own strengths and weaknesses in the area of technology. Begin by completing the assessment in Figure 12.2.

Figure 12.2 Technology Self-Assessment

Technology	Proficiency Level		
	Proficient	Somewhat Proficient	Not Proficient
1. Computer Operation a. Start and shut down computer systems and peripherals. b. Identify and use icons, windows, menus.			
2. Word Processing/Introductory Desktop Publishing a. Enter and edit text. b. Cut, copy, and paste text.			
3. Spreadsheets a. Interpret and communicate information in an existing spreadsheet. b. Enter data into an existing spreadsheet.			
4. Databases a. Interpret and communicate information in an existing data base. b. Add and delete records.			
5. Internet a. Send, receive, and forward e-mail messages. b. Attach files to e-mails c. Use a file server. d. Share files with others on a network. e. Use Internet search engines for information retrieval.			
6. Media Integration a. Set up and operate video media. b. Connect video output devices and other presentation systems to computers and video sources for large-screen display.			
7. CD-ROMs/videodiscs/digital video disks (DVD)			
8. Scanners			
9. Faxes			
10. Digital cameras			
11. Video cameras			

Source: Adapted from Colorado Department of Education (1999). *Colorado technology competency guidelines for classroom teachers and school library media specialists.* Adapted by permission. To read the full text, please go to www.cde.state.co.us/edtech/download/tgui.pdf.

How comfortable are you with each of the various forms of technology in the figure? How much do you use technology in your own learning? What can you do to make yourself more effective at utilizing technology in your teaching?

Portfolio Activity 12.2

Technology and Curriculum

INTASC Principle 7: Planning

The purpose of this activity is to acquaint you with technology resources in the content area(s) in which you'll be teaching. Decide on a content area (your major or minor if you're leaning toward the secondary level or one of the content areas taught in the elementary schools) and locate the teacher's edition of a textbook in that area. What technological tools are available to you in teaching the course? What kinds of hardware and software are needed to use these? What kinds of skills would be required of you to use these? Describe your findings in a paper.

Portfolio Activity 12.3

Technology and Instruction

INTASC Principle 4: Strategies

The purpose of this activity is to acquaint you with instructional technology resources described online. Locate a Web site in a content area in which you may teach. Two resources for locating this website are the September 2000 issue of *Instructor* magazine, which contains 44 "top sites for teachers" and Provenzo and Gotthoffer's (2000) *Quick Guide to the Internet for Education.* After exploring the Web site, describe the instructional resources discussed on the site in a two-page paper.

Portfolio Activity 12.4

Technology and Assessment

INTASC Principle 8: Assessment

The purpose of this activity is to familiarize you with the technology resources available in the area of assessment. Research how technology can be used to make assessment more efficient and effective. Two excellent sources are *Integrating Educational Technology into Teaching* (Roblyer, 2003) and *Instructional Technology and Teaching and Learning* (Newby et al., 2000). After reading about the resources available, write a two-page paper describing specifically how technology can help you personally in the assessment process.

Part 5

Careers

Chapter 13
Developing as a Professional

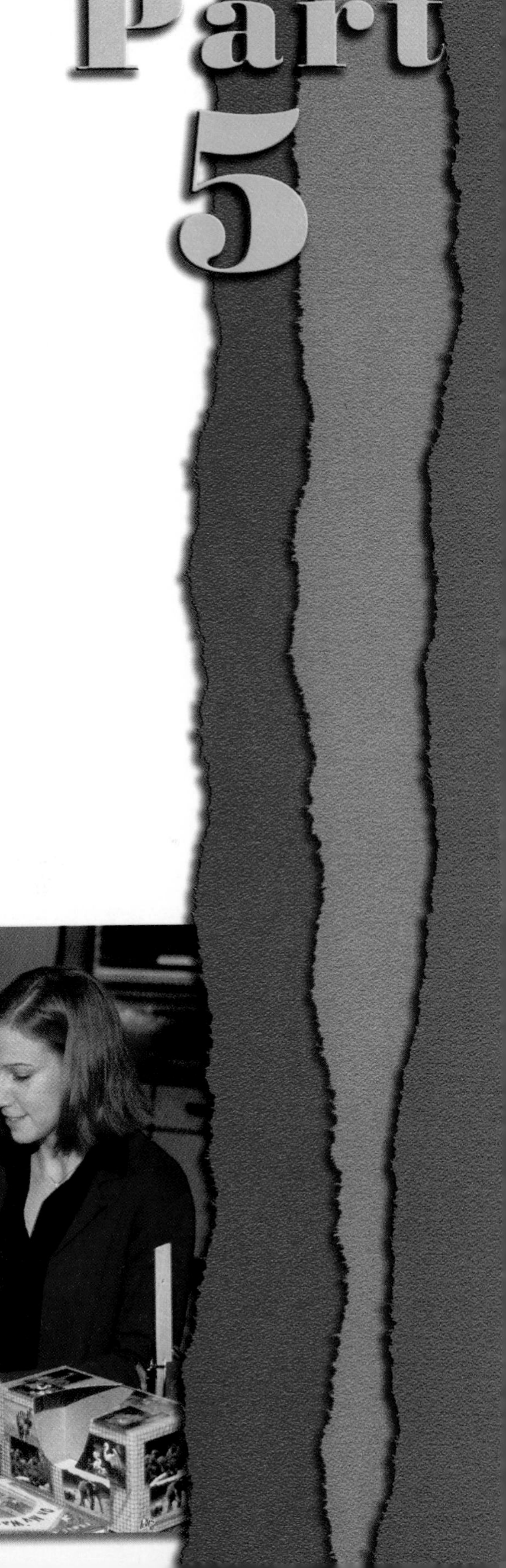

Chapter 13

Developing as a Professional

You're now reading the last chapter of this text, so on the surface it appears your study is coming to a close. On the contrary, it's really just beginning. Our goal in writing this book has been to provide you with information that will help you take the first steps toward becoming a competent and confident professional. The path is long and demanding, but with effort you can become an expert teacher.

In this chapter we hope to take some of the surprises out of your first years of teaching and help you begin the transition from thinking like a student, who wants to succeed in university courses, to thinking like a teacher, who can make professional decisions in complex situations. To help you in this process, we try to answer the following questions:

- Who are beginning teachers, and what happens during their first years of teaching?
- What do beginning teachers believe, and how do these beliefs influence their actions?
- What kinds of knowledge must teachers possess, and how does this knowledge influence their teaching?
- How are teachers licensed, and what efforts are being made to increase teacher professionalism?
- What can preservice teachers do to make themselves marketable, and how can they secure their first job?
- How can preservice teachers prepare for their first year of teaching?

This logo appears throughout the chapter to indicate where case studies are integrated with chapter content.

Case STUDY

My first faculty meeting. Very interesting. Mrs. Zellner (the principal) seems really nice. She went on and on about what a great job the teachers did last year and how test scores were way up compared to the year before. She also extended a special welcome to those of us who are new.

Speaking of new teachers, there sure are a lot of us. I wonder if they're all as scared as I am. I'm not sure what I would have done if Mrs. Landsdorp (the teacher in the room next door) hadn't taken me under her wing. She made me feel a lot better about starting in an inner-city school. So many of the kids come from low-income homes, and English isn't the first language for a lot of them. She said that some of the teachers tend to "write them off" and assume that they can't learn, but that isn't true at all. In fact, a lot of them are quite bright. They just need help and support. She's wonderful. She's sort of gruff, but Andrea (a new friend and second-year teacher) say's she's a softy underneath, and she really loves the kids.

I can't believe how much there is to do—IEPs, progress reports, CPR training, responsibility to look for signs of abuse. When do I teach? I hope I can cut it. (Shelley, a new third-grade teacher, reflecting on her first faculty meeting)

When you finish your program, and if you choose to teach, you'll join the growing ranks of beginning teachers. Let's see what this beginning teacher population looks like.

Characteristics of Beginning Teachers

You're a beginning teacher. Who are your colleagues? What does the future hold for you? How do you feel about teaching and the people who are now in the profession? We consider these questions in this section as we examine the following:

- The beginning teacher population
- The first years of teaching
- The beliefs of preservice and beginning teachers

The Beginning Teacher Population

At the beginning of the twenty-first century, nearly 3.1 million people were teaching in public K–12 schools in this country, and another 400,000 were teaching in private schools (National Center for Education Statistics, 2001). Many of these teachers are now in the twilight of their careers and will be retiring within the next several years. The coming years will also see increased immigration into our country, growing school populations, and a greater demand for smaller classes. These conditions have led researchers and policy makers to predict that school districts will need to hire about 200,000 teachers a year over the next decade, for a total of more than 2 million new teachers (Fideler & Haselkorn, 1999).

As we've moved into the new millennium, concerns about the looming teacher shortage have been so prominent that the October 2, 2000, front cover of *Newsweek* asked "Who Will Teach Our Kids?" and the magazine made "Teachers Wanted" its feature article. In the next few years the teaching profession is going to see many more people like Shelley, the teacher we heard from at the start of this chapter.

How do the Shelleys of the profession compare to the existing teaching force? As you may recall from Chapter 3, they are more likely to be female (79% versus 74% for the total teaching force), White (91% compared to 87%), and younger (28 years old as opposed to 43) (Darling-Hammond & Sclan, 1996). New teachers who studied education after earning other college degrees (a small but growing group) tend to be older—about 30—and are more likely to be male than teachers who attended teacher education programs as undergraduates (A. Bradley, 1999c).

The First Years of Teaching

A significant number of beginning teachers drop out in the first few years on the job (U.S. Department of Education, 1998d). The statistics on teacher attrition, also presented in Chapter 3, bear repeating. About 6 percent of all public school teachers leave the profession each year, but the number of new teachers who leave after their first year is much higher—about 15 percent. In addition, another 15 percent leave after their second year, and still another 10 percent after their third (Croasmun et al., 1999). (More than 10 percent of all private school teachers leave each year, with low salaries in private schools a commonly cited reason [Croasmun et al., 1999].)

The following comments help explain why some beginning teachers leave the profession:

Case STUDY Wow! Was I naive. I was tired of sitting in classes, and I wanted so badly to be finished and get out into the "real world." What I never realized was just how cushy being a student was. If I was a little tired or didn't study enough, I would just coast through class. Now, no coasting. You have to be ready every minute of every day. I've never been so tired in my life. You're in front of kids all day, and then you go home and work all night to get ready for the next day. They have us filling out reports, doing surveys, and everything other than teaching, so I don't get a chance to plan during the day. I can't even make a phone call unless it's during my lunch break or planning period.

And then there's my fourth period. They come in from lunch just wired. It takes me half the period to get them settled down, and that's on a good day.

Sometimes I just need someone to talk to, but we're all so busy. Everybody thinks they're an expert on teaching, because they've been a student. They don't have a clue. Let them try it for 2 days, and they'd be singing a different tune. (Antonio, a first-year high school English teacher)

CW

Increasing Understanding 13.1

Of the problems listed here, which can teachers best control? What might they do to lessen the other problems?

To answer the Increasing Understanding questions online and receive immediate feedback, go to the Companion Website at **www.prenhall.com/kauchak**, then to this chapter's *Increasing Understanding* module. Type in your response and then study the feedback.

Paperwork demands, a difficult class, and not having someone to talk to are examples of the following problems cited by new teachers:

- Working conditions that require teachers to spend too much time on nonteaching duties and offer them too little time for planning and no time for themselves
- Unruly students and a disorderly teaching environment
- Loneliness and alienation (Darling-Hammond, 2003; S. Johnson & Birkeland, 2003)

It probably is difficult to believe now, but separation from the support of your professors and other students can also be very stressful in the first year of teaching (Bullough, 1989).

The stress of the first year is lessened, however, when teachers have someone to turn to for help, as Shelley did ("I'm not sure what I would have done if Mrs. Landsdorp

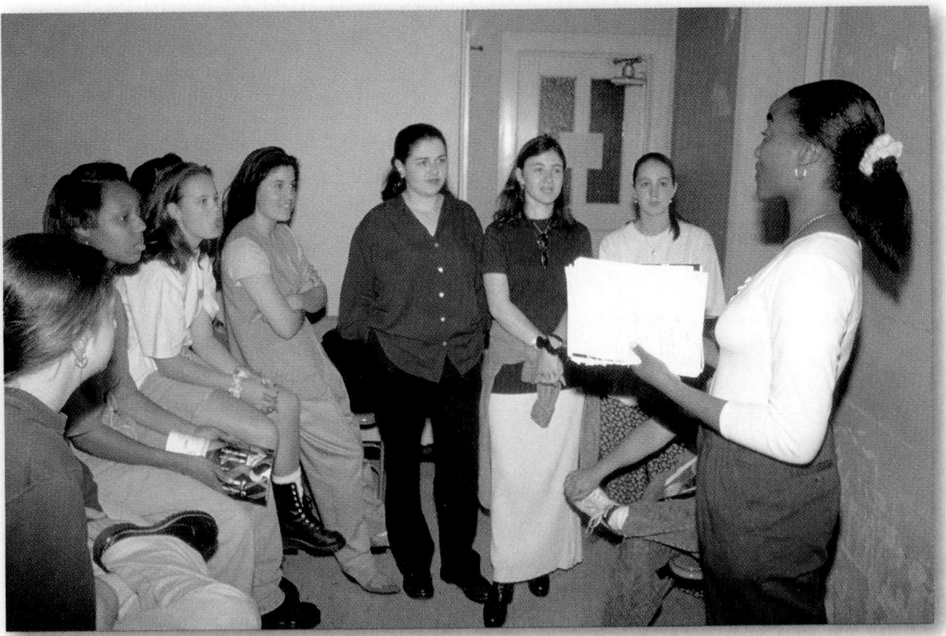

Beginning teachers face many challenges, but these challenges can lead to personal and professional rewards.

hadn't taken me under her wing"). Beginning teachers without mentors and support are nearly twice as likely to leave as those with structured programs designed to help them make the transition from the university to the K–12 classroom (Moskowitz & Stephens, 1997).

The first year also offers much to look forward to.

Case STUDY My first lesson with the kids. Chris (her supervising teacher) said I was on my own, sink or swim. I hardly slept last night, but today I feel like celebrating. The kids were so into it. I brought my Styrofoam ball and had the kids compare the latitude and longitude lines I had drawn on it and then look at the globe. I thought the first period was supposed to be Chris's lowest, but they did the best. He was impressed.

Now I understand the stuff Dr. Martinez (one of her professors) stressed so much when he was always after us to use concrete examples and question, question, question. I know I have a lot to learn. I thought I could just explain everything to them, but they got confused and drifted off so fast I couldn't believe it. As soon as I started asking questions about the lines on the Styrofoam ball, though, they perked right up. I think I can do this. It was actually a heady experience. (Sheila, an intern in a seventh-grade geography class)

• • ● • •

In Chapter 1 we talked about rewards in teaching, and Sheila experienced some of those rewards. It is, indeed, a heady experience to see students understand something new, knowing that you're the cause of that understanding.

Sheila's comments also illustrate beliefs typical of preservice and beginning teachers. These beliefs often affect beginning teachers' professional growth. Let's examine them.

Beliefs of Preservice and Beginning Teachers

The course for which this book is used is likely one of the first you'll take in your teacher preparation program. One of the goals of the course is to help you begin the process of learning to teach.

Teachers' beliefs have a strong influence on their teaching and the process of learning to teach (Borko & Putnam, 1996). Our goal in this section is to help you become aware of your beliefs and to help you understand how they can help or hinder your professional growth as a teacher. To begin, please respond to the short survey that follows.

Preservice Beliefs Survey

Using the scale to guide your responses, circle the number that best represents your beliefs.

5 = Strongly agree
4 = Agree
3 = Agree and disagree
2 = Disagree
1 = Strongly disagree

1. When I begin teaching, I will be a better teacher than most of the teachers now in the field.	1	2	3	4	5
2. As I gain experience in teaching, I expect to become more confident in my ability to help children learn.	1	2	3	4	5
3. The most effective teachers are those best able to clearly explain the content they teach to their students.	1	2	3	4	5

4. I will learn about most of the important aspects of teaching when I get into a classroom. 1 2 3 4 5
5. If I thoroughly understand the content I'm teaching, I'll be able to figure out a way of getting it across to students. 1 2 3 4 5

If you either agreed or strongly agreed with each of the statements, your beliefs are consistent with those generally held by other students in teacher preparation programs. Let's see what research tells us about these beliefs.

Increasing Understanding 13.2

What concept is illustrated by teachers believing they are capable of helping all students learn and achieve? What do teachers who take responsibility for the success or failure of their instruction do differently than teachers who blame failure on students' lack of intelligence or home environments?

Item 1: *When I begin teaching, I will be a better teacher than most of the teachers now in the field.* Preservice teachers are optimistic and idealistic: "Prospective teachers report being confident and self-assured in their teaching ability," but they "may be unrealistically optimistic about their future teaching performance" (Borko & Putnam, 1996, p. 678). The danger occurs when the realities of classrooms shock beginning teachers, who then feel as though "nobody prepared me for this" (Feiman-Nemser, 2001). Optimism wanes, they may question their career choice, and, as we saw earlier, about one in six quits after the first year.

Item 2: *As I gain experience in teaching, I expect to become more confident in my ability to help children learn.* As with Item 1, most preservice teachers expect to become increasingly confident in their ability to help children learn. However, the opposite often occurs. As they gain experience, some tend to become less democratic in their work with students and less confident that teachers can overcome the limitations of home environments and family background (Woolfolk & Hoy, 1990). As we saw in both Chapters 7 and 11, teachers' confidence in their ability to influence learning is essential (Lee, 2000). We emphasize this point so that you might avoid the trap that snares many beginning teachers.

Item 3: *The most effective teachers are those best able to clearly explain the content they teach to their students.* Many preservice teachers believe that teaching is essentially a process of "telling" or explaining content to students, probably because most of their own teachers simply lectured (van den Berg, 2002; J. Wang & Odell, 2002).

As Sheila quickly discovered, teaching is much more complex than simply explaining. Research indicates that explaining, by itself, is often ineffective for helping students understand topics in depth (Bransford et al., 2000; Greeno, Collins, & Resnick, 1996). The video episode you saw in Chapter 11 further illustrates the problem with explaining. (If you didn't see the video episode, you can go to Chapter 11's *Classroom Windows* module on the Companion Website and read the written transcript.) In that lesson Suzie, one of the students in the small group, was provided with at least three clear and accurate solutions to the problem of making the beam balance—Molly's in the group, Mavrin's at the board, and the teacher's. In spite of these explanations, she continued to ignore the position of the tiles and retained her belief that the beam would balance if the number of tiles on each side of the fulcrum was the same. She began to understand the principle only when she was directly involved in a question-and-answer session during an interview after the lesson.

Item 4: *I will learn about most of the important aspects of teaching when I get into a classroom.* This is another commonly held belief of preservice teachers. Many preservice teachers believe that experience is the only way they can learn to teach, and they also believe that their teacher education classes are little more than hoops they must jump through before getting into their own classrooms (Grant, Richard, & Parkay, 1996). The belief in the central importance of experience in learning to teach is also shared by others both inside and outside the profession (Gross, 1999; Neisler, 2000).

Experience in classrooms *is* essential in learning to teach, but it isn't sufficient by itself. In many cases, experience results in using the same procedures and techniques

Current views of learning replace telling as an instructional strategy with interactive dialogue between teachers and students.

CW

Increasing Understanding 13.3

Offer two reasons why students who go through traditional teacher preparation programs are more successful and more satisfied in their work than those who experience less formal preservice education.

year after year, even when they're ineffective (Putnam, Heaton, Prawat, & Remillard, 1992). Research also consistently indicates that students who go through traditional teacher preparation programs (such as the one you're in) are more successful and satisfied in their work than those who experience less formal preservice education (Darling-Hammond, 2000, 2003). Research and theory, combined with experience, help beginning teachers understand the classrooms and students they'll encounter. This is one of the reasons you're studying this book.

Item 5: ***If I thoroughly understand the content I'm teaching, I'll be able to figure out a way of getting it across to students.*** One of the most pervasive myths in teaching is that knowledge of subject matter is all that is necessary to teach it effectively. Knowledge of content is essential, of course, but learning to teach requires a great deal of additional knowledge—knowledge you'll acquire in your teacher preparation program.

Knowledge and Learning to Teach

Case STUDY My kids were off the wall. They wouldn't pay attention, some were disruptive, and those that weren't had their heads down on the desk. I tried enforcing the rules and communicating that I meant business, but it wasn't working.

Linda (a veteran and colleague) saved me. I'm not sure I would have made it through this year if it hadn't been for her. She changed my thinking completely. I was so scared to get the kids involved in lessons, because I was afraid I wouldn't be able to control them, but she said it's just the opposite—kids want to be involved and they want to answer questions, and if the lesson is any good, they're actually less likely to misbehave. When they act like they don't want to answer questions, it's because they're afraid they won't be able to. "Everyone wants to feel smart" she would say with a laugh. "Plus," she'd continue, "the more active they are in trying to learn the topic, the more likely they are to truly understand it."

Now, I mostly think about what examples I can use to best illustrate the topics I'm teaching and what I can do to get the kids involved. Wow, what a difference. (Paula, first-year eighth-grade science teacher)

• • ● • •

Let's look again at Paula's comments. She said, "She [Linda] changed my *thinking* completely," and "Now, what I mostly *think* about. . . . " Paula's growth as a teacher is reflected in the differences in the way she *thinks*.

The Development of Expertise

During the last quarter of the twentieth century, researchers began to examine how the thinking of **experts,** *people who are highly experienced, knowledgeable, and skilled in a field,* compared with the thinking of **novices,** *people who are unskilled, inexperienced, and lack knowledge* in the same field. The fields they studied varied widely, ranging across areas as diverse as chess, physics, anesthesiology, and teaching.

The researchers found important differences in the thinking of experts and novices (Bruning et al., 1999; Glaser & Chi, 1988):

- Experts search for significant patterns and relationships in events and experiences, whereas novices see events superficially and in isolated pieces.
- Experts plan carefully, with important goals in mind, whereas novices plan haphazardly.
- Experts are aware of their own thinking and actions and the effects these have on others, whereas novices tend to be unaware.

Let's see how these characteristics influence the way people think about teaching. Read the following case study, and respond to the question that appears at the end. This is an abbreviated transcript of an actual fifth-grade lesson that was videotaped and shown to teachers at different stages of their professional development.

Case STUDY Judith Thomson, a fifth-grade teacher, was in the second day of a unit on the Civil War in social studies. On the first day, which was abbreviated because of an extra long language arts activity, she briefly introduced the unit by writing the following vocabulary words on the board and quickly providing a verbal description of each.

amendment	indivisible	KKK
Free State	Underground Railroad	Reconstruction
sectionalism	abolitionists	Appomattox
secede	Grant	blockade
Lincoln	Lee	Davis
Emancipation Proclamation		

"There are vocabulary words on the board," she began today, pointing to her written list. "You were introduced to them yesterday. We have talked a little bit about the meanings.

"When this lesson is over," she went on, "this is what I hope you'll understand: the geography of the war. And I want you to have an understanding of the dynamics of the war—why it was fought, how it was fought, and why it ended the way it did."

Judith pulled down a small map of the United States in 1850 and started talking about sectionalism. She briefly discussed the fact that there were factories in the North but farms in the South, and she asked the students to imagine that they were slaves and how they might have felt. The students were very attentive throughout the discussion, and a number of hands were raised in attempts to answer each question Judith asked.

Judith then turned the discussion to abolitionists.

"So we have a group of people in the North and in the South who want to free the slaves. They want slavery to end; these people are called abolitionists."

After a brief discussion of the desire to end slavery by abolitionists in the North, Judith discussed Abraham Lincoln, the beginning of the war, the respective advantages of the North and the South, and some information about the reconstruction of the South. The students remained attentive and well-behaved throughout the lesson.

"I'm going to give you an assignment to complete during the remainder of this time period," she said as she wrapped up the activity. "Here are the vocabulary words that we have touched on," she said, referring again to her list on the board. "I'd like for you to develop from your notes, and from listening, an essay about the war as you understand it, using all of these words."

As their time for social studies came to a close, Judith stopped the students' writing.

"I would like for you to look at this word," she instructed, writing the word *indivisible* in large letters at the center of the board. "Tonight I'd like for you to go home and think about the Pledge of Allegiance as you know it. You might want to write it out. And I'd like to have you write two or three paragraphs about what you understand this word means since we've talked about the Civil War. . . . Indivisible. Use a dictionary. Talk to parents. That's your homework assignment."

After school, Judith began scanning the essays the students had written.

"My word," she said to herself after looking at several of the papers. "They must not have listened at all."

Several of the papers included only one or two of the vocabulary words, and other essays were vague and rambling pieces of information about the Civil War that hadn't been covered in class.

"Of course," she thought to herself, "several of these kids have poor backgrounds."

• • ● • •

Question: If you were to rate the quality of Judith's lesson using a scale of 5 = excellent, 4 = very good, 3 = good, 2 = fair and 1 = poor, what rating would you give and why? Think about that question for a moment before you read further.

If you gave Judith a high rating, your thinking would be consistent with the thinking of other preservice teachers, who, in one research study, cited concrete factors, such as the fact that the students were orderly, as reasons for their ratings. In contrast, veteran teachers gave the teacher low ratings, noting that her goals, learning activity, and assignments didn't relate to one another (D. Harris & Eggen, 1993). In addition, veterans made comments like the following:

> "How in the world could fifth graders learn from that? She used abstract words and didn't illustrate them with examples."
>
> "Her lesson was all over the place. Students wouldn't be able to follow her."

The veterans—the experts—focused primarily on student learning, which is more subtle and elusive than more concrete and obvious things such as management and smooth performance.

These results mirror a more general pattern in teachers' development (Feiman-Nemser, 2001; van den Berg, 2002). Beginning teachers are preoccupied with management; they worry about their ability to maintain order in a classroom of 25 to 30 or more students. As they develop, their thinking centers on their own actions, such as whether or not their questioning is effective and their explanations are clear. Finally, as their expertise advances, their focus shifts to the students' learning. Ultimately, all beginning teachers will reach a point at which their main concern is how much their students are learning and growing.

How do teachers become experts? They acquire both content knowledge and knowledge about their chosen field—teaching—and they combine this knowledge with a great deal of experience. Acquiring knowledge about teaching is the reason you're taking this course and the others that are part of your teacher preparation program. Let's look at this knowledge in more detail.

Four Kinds of Knowledge

As we've seen throughout this book, professionals possess a great deal of knowledge about their chosen field of study. Specialized knowledge is an element of professionalism (see Figure 13.1), and research indicates that expert teachers possess at least four different kinds of knowledge (Borko & Putnam, 1996):

- Knowledge of content
- Pedagogical content knowledge
- General pedagogical knowledge
- Knowledge of learners and learning

Let's look at these different kinds of knowledge and see how they can affect your growth as a teacher.

Knowledge of Content We can't teach what we don't understand. This simple statement is self-evident, and it is well documented by research examining the relationships between what teachers know and how they teach (Borko & Putnam, 1996; Shuell, 1996). To effectively teach about the American Revolution, for example, a social studies teacher must know not only basic facts about the war but also how the war relates to other aspects of history, such as the French and Indian War, the colonies' relationship with England before the revolution, and the characteristics of the

Figure 13.1 Professionalism Requires a Specialized Body of Knowledge

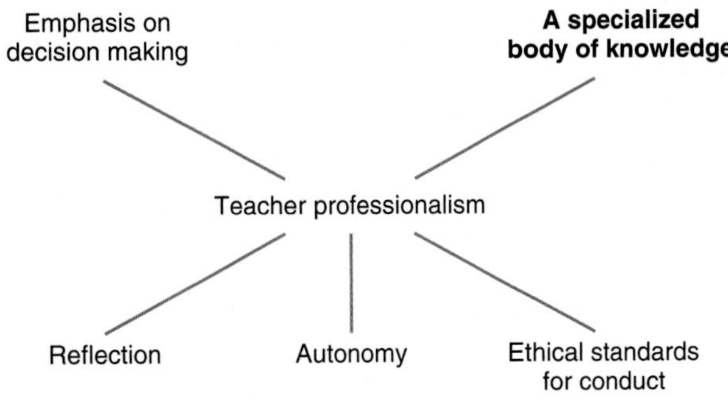

Pedagogical content knowledge allows teachers to illustrate difficult-to-learn concepts with concrete examples.

colonies. The same is true for any topic in any content area.

Pedagogical Content Knowledge

Pedagogical content knowledge is *an understanding of ways to represent topics so that they're comprehensible to others and an understanding of what makes topics easy or difficult to learn* (Borko & Putnam, 1996; Shulman, 1986). Pedagogical content knowledge depends on an understanding of a particular topic, such as understanding the factors leading to the American Revolution, but it goes beyond this understanding to knowing how to illustrate and explain these factors so they make sense to students.

Teachers who possess pedagogical content knowledge recognize when topics are hard to understand and illustrate these difficult-to-teach ideas with concrete experiences that make them meaningful. For example:

- In Chapter 1 David Jackson illustrated the principle of *inertia* for his eighth-grade science students with examples about seatbelts in cars, the spin cycle of a clothes washer, and a dog shaking itself off when it came out of a pond.
- In Chapter 10 Suzanne Brush helped her second graders understand graphing by using a bar graph to represent their favorite jelly bean flavors.
- In Chapter 11 Leslie Nelson used written paragraphs displayed on an overhead to illustrate pronoun cases for her students.

Paula (the teacher with the "off the wall" students) had begun to appreciate the importance of pedagogical content knowledge when she commented, "Now, I mostly think about what examples I can use to best illustrate the topics I'm teaching."

These teachers undoubtedly had a thorough understanding of content, but it was not sufficient in helping their students understand the topics they were studying. Majoring in math, for example, doesn't ensure that a teacher will be able to create examples that will help students understand why multiplying two numbers sometimes results in a smaller number ($\frac{1}{4} \times \frac{1}{3} = \frac{1}{12}$, for instance), nor does majoring in history ensure that a teacher will think of using a student "crusade" to have extracurricular activities governed by a student council as a metaphor for the real Crusades. The ability to create or choose effective examples requires both a clear understanding of content together with pedagogical content knowledge. If either is lacking, teachers commonly paraphrase information in learners' textbooks or have students memorize steps, such as procedures for graphing equations, that don't make sense to them.

Increasing Understanding 13.4

Describe the pedagogical content knowledge that Sheila (the teaching intern in the case on p. 478) demonstrated in her lesson on longitude and latitude. Be specific in your response.

Developing pedagogical content knowledge is one of the most challenging aspects of learning to teach. You can begin to acquire that knowledge by looking for ways of illustrating topics as you complete your teacher preparation program. Indeed, if you are to become an expert teacher, you'll continue to search for new illustrations throughout your career.

General Pedagogical Knowledge Knowledge of content and pedagogical content knowledge are "domain specific"; that is, they focus on knowledge of a particular topic or content area, such as multiplying fractions or the Crusades. In comparison, **general pedagogical knowledge** is *a general understanding of instruction and management that transcends individual topics or subject-matter areas* (Borko & Putnam, 1996).

Increasing Understanding 13.5

Explain why questioning is such an essential teaching skill. Explain specifically how questioning and knowledge of learners and learning are related.

Instruction is at the heart of teaching. Expert teachers understand different ways of involving students in learning activities, techniques for checking their understanding, and strategies for keeping lessons running smoothly. Questioning is perhaps the most important aspect of general pedagogical knowledge. Regardless of the content or topic, expert teachers ask questions that get students to think, engage all students as equally as possible (McDougall & Granby, 1996), give them time to think about their responses, and provide prompts and cues when they're unable to answer (Shuell, 1996). Expert teachers are also able to provide students with feedback about their understanding of a topic, identifying areas that need additional work.

Regardless of the content area or topic being taught, expert teachers also know how to create classroom environments that are orderly and focused on learning; they need to understand the components of classroom management (Emmer et al., 2003; Evertson et al., 2003). Understanding how to keep 25 to 30 or more students actively engaged and working together in learning activities requires that teachers know how to plan, implement, and monitor rules and procedures, organize groups, deliver meaningful lessons, and respond to misbehavior.

Knowledge of Learners and Learning Lastly, in addition to the other forms of professional knowledge, expert teachers possess **knowledge of learners and learning**—*an understanding of students and how they learn*. Knowledge of learners and learning is "arguably the most important knowledge a teacher can have" (Borko & Putnam, 1996, p. 675).

Linda, Paula's colleague, demonstrated an understanding of learners and learning. She pointed out that kids *want* to be involved and want to answer questions, and if they act like they don't want to answer, it's because they're afraid they won't be able to. Linda also understood that "the more active [students] are in trying to learn the topic, the more likely they are to truly understand it." By sharing this knowledge with Paula, Linda helped her understand what she could concretely do to help her students learn; as Paula explained, "Now, I mostly think about . . . what I can do to get the kids involved. Wow, what a difference."

Each type of knowledge—knowledge of content, pedagogical content knowledge, general pedagogical knowledge, and knowledge of learners and learning—is essential for acquiring teaching expertise and will influence your thinking as you develop as a professional. As you plan, for example, you will *think* about ways to actively involve your students, because you realize they will be less motivated (knowledge of learners) and less likely to understand (knowledge of learning) than if you lecture and allow them to sit passively through your lessons. You will also *think* about ways to illustrate your topics (pedagogical content knowledge), because you know that the illustrations are the basis for the students' developing understanding (again, knowledge of learning).

Teachers are unlikely to acquire all the knowledge needed to be effective from experience alone. The knowledge you acquire from your teacher preparation program, however, will complement your experiences in schools and start you on your way to becoming an expert teacher.

DEMONSTRATING KNOWLEDGE IN CLASSROOMS

Having examined the kinds of knowledge that expert teachers possess, you now have the chance to see this knowledge displayed in a video of four teaching segments with students at different ages.

In the first segment Jenny Newhall, a kindergarten teacher, explores the properties of air with her students. In the second, Richard Nelms, a seventh-grade teacher, illustrates the concept of symmetry for his students. The third segment shows chemistry teacher Didi Johnson as she attempts to help her students understand Charles's law of gases. In the final segment De Vonne Lampkin, a fifth-grade teacher, uses real and live examples to teach students the characteristics of arthropods.

To complete this activity, do the following:

- Go to the DVD, and view the video episode titled "Demonstrating Knowledge in Classrooms".
- Answer the questions you'll find on the DVD.

To answer these questions online and receive immediate feedback, go to the Companion Website at **www.prenhall.com/kauchak**, *then to this chapter's* Classroom Windows *module.*

Into the Real World

You've seen the different kinds of knowledge and thinking that are needed to become an expert. In addition to this knowledge, some formal processes are required to allow you to work in the real world. All professionals—physicians, lawyers, and engineers, as well as teachers—must be "licensed" in order to work in their occupations.

Traditional Licensure

In Chapter 9 we saw that K–12 teachers are required by law (in all 50 states plus the District of Columbia) to be licensed by a state department of education before they can teach in public schools. **Licensure** is *the process by which a state evaluates the credentials of prospective teachers to ensure that they have achieved satisfactory levels of teaching competence and are morally fit to work with youth.* By awarding a license, the state certifies that a teacher is competent in subject-area content, teaching skills, and the ability to manage classrooms.

You're likely taking this course in a traditional licensure program through which you'll earn a bachelor's degree. The program consists of a general education component that includes courses in history, English, math, and science, as well as education courses designed to help you develop your professional knowledge—the pedagogical content knowledge, general pedagogical knowledge, and knowledge of learners and learning discussed earlier. If you're a secondary major, you are also required to accumulate a specified number of course hours in the subject area (e.g., math) in which you plan to teach (30 states have this requirement) (Wayne & Youngs, 2003).

Increasingly, as you learned in Chapter 1, teachers are also being asked to pass competency tests that measure their basic skills in reading, writing, and mathematics (34 states had this requirement in 2001); their background in an academic area such as chemistry or English (30 states required this); and their understanding of learning

During the process of licensure, teachers are increasingly being asked to demonstrate their competence through tests and on-the-job performance.

and teaching (25 states required this) (Wayne & Youngs, 2003). The Praxis Series, which consists of all three of these types of components, is currently being used in 35 states (Educational Testing Service, 2001).

The specific requirements for licensure vary from state to state, and the student advising office in your college or university can help you access them. If you're planning to move to another state, your education library may have books that describe the licensure requirements for all the states. If it doesn't, you can write or call the state certification office directly. The addresses and phone numbers of these offices can be found in Appendix B at the end of this book.

Finding a Job

To this point we have discussed factors influencing your growth as a professional—factors that will make you more effective once you get a teaching position. But when and how do you get started in the process of finding a job? The answer to when is *now*. We address the question of how in this section as we consider the following:

- Making yourself marketable
- Developing a professional reputation
- Identifying where jobs exist
- Building a portfolio and résumé
- Creating a credentials file
- Interviewing effectively
- Assessing prospective schools

Making Yourself Marketable The most effective way to make yourself marketable is to acquire as much professional knowledge and experience as possible. The knowledge component will be addressed in the courses you take in the future; your professional experiences will complement this knowledge by applying it in varied

Teaching in an Era of Reform

THE ALTERNATIVE LICENSURE ISSUE

To meet the demand for more teachers, many states are developing alternative routes to licensure. Currently 45 states have alternative-route programs, and more than 75 percent of college or university teacher education programs run or collaborate with them. About a third of the teachers hired each year are licensed in this way (Blair, 2003).

A person seeking alternative licensure must hold a bachelor's degree in the content area to be taught, such as math or English; pass a licensure test; complete a brief, intensive teacher training experience; and complete a supervised teaching internship.

The Issue

Proponents of alternative licensure make several arguments supporting this teacher preparation route (Dill & Stafford-Johnson, 2002). Most alternative licensure candidates are older than students in undergraduate education programs, so they've had more life experiences. They have already earned bachelor's degrees, so they are more focused on learning to teach than are undergraduates who must combine classes in their content areas with courses in professional education. Also, alternative programs are shorter and tend to attract members of cultural minorities and talented and experienced people in areas of critical need, such as math and science (Blair, 2003). Proponents also argue that students in these programs are more academically talented than students in traditional programs (Croasmun et al., 1999).

Critics, however, point to the limited training in pedagogy that alternative licensure candidates receive (such as acquiring the pedagogical content knowledge, general pedagogical knowledge, and knowledge of learners and learning that we discussed earlier). This results in instruction that is not responsive to students' needs, they argue (Darling-Hammond et al., 2001;

contexts. Some suggestions for potential professional experiences are included in Table 13.1. If you pursue any of the experiences described, you can write about them in your portfolio and include them in the résumé you construct to summarize your qualifications.

Developing a Professional Reputation

Case STUDY I really wish someone had reminded me of these things sooner. When I started, like a lot of others, I didn't take it all too seriously. I'd blow class off now and then, and I didn't always get there on time. I actually did study, but I guess not as hard as I should have.

When I asked Dr. Laslow for a letter of recommendation, he refused. Actually, he said he didn't know me well enough to write a good one. I couldn't believe it. He was nice about it, but he wouldn't write one, advising me to find someone who knew me better and was more familiar with my work. And a couple others were sort of lukewarm. Now it's too late. My record is a little spotty and I feel bad about it now, but I can't go back. I used to wonder why Brad and Kelly always seemed to get all the breaks. Now I get it. (Jeremy, a recent graduate without a job)

• • ● • •

Darling-Hammond, Chung, & Frelow, 2002). Further, the intensive mentoring and supervision during the first few months of full-time teaching that is supposed to compensate for the new teachers' lack of formal coursework often doesn't exist (Ansell & McCabe, 2003). Consequently, the first year of teaching becomes a sink-or-swim situation, with many teachers (and their students) failing (Darling-Hammond et al., 2001, 2002).

Finally, critics cite statistics indicating that the 2-year dropout rate for alternative licensure candidates is more than three times greater than the national average for new teachers (Darling-Hammond, 2000). This statistic may be skewed, however, because alternative licensure teachers are disproportionately assigned to the most demanding teaching situations, such as inner-city schools with high numbers of cultural minorities from low-income households (Blair, 2003; National Commission on Teaching and America's Future, 1996). It is paradoxical that the students who need experienced teachers the most are often least likely to have them (Archer, 2003; Blair, 2003).

Conclusive assessments of alternative licensure are difficult to make because there is so much variation among different states' programs. High-quality alternative licensure programs are both time-consuming and costly (Olson, 2000b). Research examining the performance of students taught by teachers from alternative licensure programs is also mixed. Some data suggest students fare as well as those taught by traditionally prepared teachers; however, most data do not (Darling-Hammond et al., 2001; Laczko-Kerr & Berliner, 2003).

You Take a Position

Now it's your turn to take a position on the issue. State in writing whether you do or do not support alternative licensure, and provide a two-page rationale for your position.

CW

For additional references and resources, go to the Companion Website at **www.prenhall. com/kauchak**, *then to this chapter's* Teaching in an Era of Reform *module. You can respond online or submit your response to your instructor.*

Do you know people who seem to get a lot of breaks? Do you get your share? Do your instructors know you, and do they respect and value your work? Students who get breaks do so for a reason. They attend all their classes, turn their work in on time, and attempt to learn as much as possible from their experiences. The quality of their work is consistently high. In other words, they behave professionally. Just as teachers in the field demonstrate professional behaviors, students do as well. Professors value conscientiousness, and students like Jeremy bother them. It's easy to understand why Brad and Kelly got breaks while Jeremy didn't.

What can you do to develop a professional reputation? Here are some suggestions:

- Attend all classes, and be on time. If you must miss, see your professor in advance or explain afterwards.
- Turn in required assignments on time, and follow the established guidelines or criteria.
- Study conscientiously, and try to learn as much as possible in all your classes.
- Participate in class. Offer comments and ask questions. You will enjoy your classes more and also learn more from them.
- Extend your classroom behavior to your life. Take every opportunity to learn something new. For example, travel, especially to other countries, provides opportunities

Table 13.1 Making Yourself Marketable

Suggested Experience	Example	Professional Benefits
Develop a minor area of study in a high-need area.	If you're a French major, consider a minor in Spanish. If you're a biology major, consider a minor in chemistry.	You'll have more versatility in the jobs you apply for.
Join professional organizations.	Join your university's chapter of the National Education Association or a student chapter of another professional organization. (Professional organizations are listed on the Companion Website and in Table 13.5.)	You'll stay up-to-date on issues in your field and expand your network of professional contacts.
Tutor a child.	Become a reading tutor at a local school. Most schools welcome volunteer tutors and may also share your name with parents interested in a private tutor.	You'll gain direct experience working with children and may earn some extra money.
Seek leadership positions.	Run for a student government office.	Leadership experience on a résumé tells potential employers that you have effective human relations skills and the desire to be a lifelong learner.
Do volunteer work.	Spend a few hours each weekend helping out at the local food pantry.	Volunteer work can be enriching, and it indicates your desire to contribute to society.
Become an aide.	Ask your local school district about job openings for part-time classroom aides.	Working as an aide will give you valuable classroom experience and a part-time job.

to learn about other cultures and the ways they approach education. Trips like this also make valuable entries on your résumé.

- Set being the best student you can be as your goal.

If you sincerely attempt to learn and grow, your professional reputation will take care of itself. But you must take time to think about it *now*.

Identifying Where Jobs Exist Your ultimate goal is to locate a teaching position that will allow you to utilize your skills and develop as a professional, but such a position may not be easy to find. Several factors influence teacher supply and demand.

Geography is one factor. As you can see from Table 13.2, student growth patterns vary by both geographic area and grade level. The greatest student enrollment increases in elementary education will occur in the West; in secondary education, large increases are expected in the West, South, and Northeast. These regions will have the greatest demand for teachers.

Within geographic areas, specific locations also influence teacher supply and demand. Job opportunities are much greater in rural and inner-city schools than they are in the suburbs, and these districts employ a number of recruiting strategies to attract competent new teachers, such as offering signing bonuses, financial help for professional development courses, and even housing incentives (Archer, 2003; Keller, 2003). Shelley, the teacher in the vignette that introduced the chapter, experienced these patterns:

Table 13.2 Projected Changes in Public School Student Enrollment by Grade Level and Geographic Area (1998–2008)

	Grades K–8	Grades 9–12
Northeast	−3.8%	+11.9%
Midwest	−4.1%	+1.5%
South	+3.2%	+16.3%
West	+10.8%	+28.6%

Source: National Center for Education Statistics (1998b).

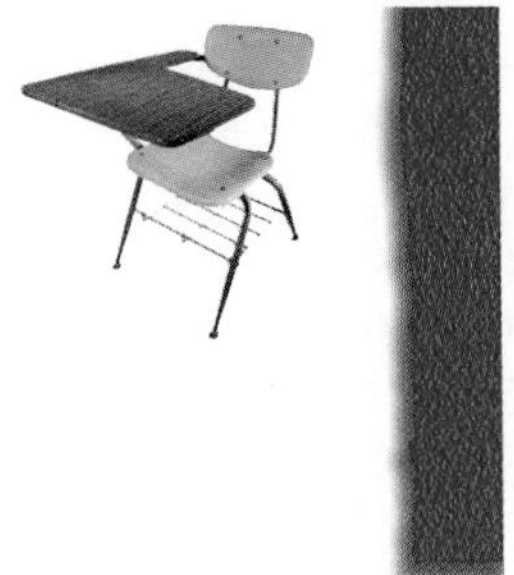

Case STUDY At first I looked for jobs in two suburban schools, but there were no openings. However, I received offers from three different inner-city schools. I was a little hesitant at first because I had read about the challenges of working in urban settings, especially for first-year teachers. But one of the assistant principals was great. She talked to me about the job, what it entailed, and the kind of help I'd receive in a structured induction program at that school. I was paired with a wonderful mentor, and I'm having a challenging but great year. I love these kids and think I'm going to make it. (Shelley, a first-year third-grade teacher)

• • ● • •

Increasing Understanding 13.6

Explain the job patterns described in the text. Why, for example, are more jobs available in the inner city than in the suburbs? Why are more jobs available in math than in English?

The specific teaching position you seek will also affect your chances of finding a job. Areas such as audiology, speech pathology, English language learning (including bilingual education and English as a second language), foreign languages (especially Spanish), special education, technology, math, physics, and chemistry need teachers more than others like English or history (Darling-Hammond, Berry, Haselkorn, & Fideler, 1999; Keller, 2003).

What implications do these job patterns have for you? First, if you haven't already decided on a major, don't select one based on job availability alone. To be effective, you must want to teach in the area you select. Don't major in chemistry, for example, if you dislike chemistry. However, if you want to teach chemistry, you now know that there is a high probability of getting a job in the area. Second, try to become knowledgeable about where teaching jobs exist. The career placement center at your college or university can help you. You'll increase your chances of finding a job if you're flexible about where you'll teach. Your first teaching position may not be in an ideal location, but you can use it to gain experience and as a stepping stone to other positions.

Building a Portfolio and Résumé

Case STUDY The interview was going okay, but I was uneasy. The principal I was interviewing with was cordial, but she certainly wasn't enthusiastic. "I've had it," I thought to myself. She even quit asking me questions after about 20 minutes. I really wanted the job too.

As I was about to leave, I happened to mention, "Would you like to see my portfolio?" She looked at it for a couple minutes, and then she started asking some probing questions. When she stuck my CD-ROM in her computer and saw me teaching, she really lit up. I got the job! (Greg, a recent graduate and new teacher)

• • ● • •

Portfolios provide a concrete way for beginning teachers to display their developing knowledge and skills.

You were introduced to professional portfolios in Chapter 1 and have completed portfolio entries throughout your study of this book. In doing so, you have been acquiring experience that will help you organize your portfolio so that it gives the best possible impression of your work and potential. Specific guidelines for creating your portfolio are found in Appendix A, at the at the end of this text.

The first item that appears in your portfolio should be a résumé summarizing your strengths and accomplishments as a teacher. A **résumé** is *a document that provides an overview of an individual's job qualifications and work experience.* It typically is the first thing a prospective employer sees and should make a clear and persuasive statement about your qualifications as a teacher (Moffatt & Moffatt, 2000).

The organization and contents of a résumé can vary, but clarity and simplicity should be guiding principles. People reading your résumé want to be able to easily find personal information, such as your address and phone number, as well as information about your education, work experience, and interests. They'll expect you to list references or be willing to provide them later. Some people suggest including a description of the type of position you seek and your educational philosophy, whereas others feel that this information detracts from the simplicity and clarity of the résumé. The office of career planning and placement at your college or university will be able to help you in preparing a résumé. A sample is shown in Figure 13.2.

CW

Increasing Understanding 13.7

Explain how a portfolio and a résumé are different. Be specific in your explanation. What is the purpose of each?

Creating a Credentials File Your college or university will have a placement center designed to help graduates find jobs. An essential service of this center, in addition to providing information about job openings, is to serve as a repository for your credentials file. A **credentials file** is *a collection of important documents teachers need to submit when they apply for teaching positions.* It typically includes background information about you, your résumé, type of position sought, courses taken, performance evaluations by your internship cooperating teacher and college or university supervisor, and letters of recommendation (usually three or more). When you apply for a job, you notify the placement center, which then sends your credentials file to the prospective employer. If, after reviewing this file, the district feels there is a potential match, you'll be contacted for an interview.

Interviewing Effectively We've emphasized professionalism throughout this book and particularly in this chapter. One area in which professional behavior is essential is the interview. This is the setting that almost certainly will determine whether or not you get a job. Some guidelines for interviewing effectively are outlined in Table 13.3.

What are some things schools look for in new teachers during an interview? Research suggests the following (Moffatt & Moffatt, 2000):

- A sincere interest in making a difference in students' lives
- A variety of life experiences that can contribute to the classroom
- The ability to work with others
- Adaptability and the ability to work under demanding circumstances

Figure 13.2 A Sample Résumé

Your name
Your address
Your phone number
Your e-mail address

Education (most recent first)

Year:	Degree (for example, B.S. in Education) Name of college or university Major Minor(s)
Year:	Previous college or university coursework
Year:	High School

Teaching Experience (most recent first)

Dates:	Substitute teaching Name of school
Dates:	Internship Name of school
Dates:	Field experience Name of school

Work Experience (most recent first)

Dates:	Employer, job title Responsibilities

Extracurricular Activities and Interests

Organizations to which you belong (highlight leadership positions)
Volunteer work (dates)
Hobbies

Honors and Awards

Scholarships, grants, honor societies

References

You might write "available on request," or you may include names and addresses. (If names and addresses are included, be sure that you have first obtained permission from the individuals listed.)

If you are *genuinely* interested in working with young people, and if you've been conscientious in your teacher preparation program, the interview will largely take care of itself. Nothing communicates more effectively than a sincere desire to do the job for which you're interviewing.

Additional preparation can increase the positive impression you make, however. For example, how would you respond to the following questions, all of which are frequently asked in teacher interviews?

- Why do you want to teach?
- Why do you want to work in this school?
- What is your philosophy of education?
- How would you motivate unmotivated learners?

Table 13.3 Guidelines for Interviewing Effectively

Guideline	Rationale
Be on time.	Nothing creates a worse impression than being late for an interview.
Dress appropriately.	Wear an outfit appropriate for an interview, and be well-groomed. Shorts, jeans, and T-shirts are inappropriate, as is an eyebrow ring. You have the right to dress and groom yourself in any way you choose, but if you are serious about getting a job, you won't demonstrate your freedom of expression during a job interview.
Speak clearly, and use standard English and grammar.	Clear language is correlated with effective teaching, and your verbal ability creates an impression of professional ability.
Sit comfortably and calmly.	Fidgeting or worse—glancing at your watch—suggests that you're either nervous or you'd rather be somewhere else.
Communicate empathy for children and a desire to work with them.	Communicating an understanding of learning, learner development, and instruction demonstrates that you have a professional knowledge base.

- How would you handle classroom management?
- How would you organize a unit on a topic in your area?
- How would you involve parents or caregivers to help your students learn?

The more specific and concrete you can be in responding to each of the questions, the more positive your impression will be. For instance, here is a specific response to the question about teaching philosophy:

Interviews provide opportunities for teaching candidates to explain their qualifications as well as find out about the positions they're applying for.

. . ● . .

"I believe that all children can learn, and I would try my best to make that happen by ensuring that all students are involved in the lessons I teach. Research suggests that active involvement is essential for learning. I would get them involved by calling on each of them as often as possible and using groupwork when it is appropriate."

. . ● . .

CW

Increasing Understanding 13.8

What will determine how able you are to provide a clear and concrete response to an interviewer's question? (Hint: Think back to the second major topic of the chapter.)

The answer communicates that you're clear about what you would try to do and why. Also, citing research suggests that you are knowledgeable about research linking teacher actions to student learning, and such knowledge is something school districts value (Strong & Hindman, 2003). In contrast, a vague response, such as "I am a humanistic and learner-centered teacher," leaves the interviewer with the impression that you're saying words you learned in a class and is much less persuasive.

The more you think about the questions frequently asked of teachers, the better prepared for the interview you'll be. If you are prepared, you will also be more at ease during the interview.

Assessing Prospective Schools The interview process is a two-way street. Not only are you being interviewed, but you are also interviewing the school. You want a job, but you also want to determine if the school is the kind of place in which you want to work. As we've said throughout this text, when you interview, you should ask questions of the principal and other people you would work with. Doing so helps you learn about the position and communicates that you are thoughtful and serious about the job.

Some factors to consider when evaluating a school as a potential workplace include the following:

- *Commitment and leadership of the principal.* The principal's leadership abilities and style set the tone for the school (S. Johnson & Birkeland, 2003; Ubben et al., 2001). Does the principal demonstrate caring for students and support for teachers? The answers to these questions are highly inferential, but you can look for evidence in the principal's manner and comments.
- *School mission.* Does the principal communicate a clear mission for the school? If you have a chance to talk to other teachers, ask them if the teachers feel like they're a team, all working for the benefit of students.
- *School climate.* Does the emotional climate of the school seem positive? How do office personnel treat students? Do the support staff, such as custodians and cafeteria workers, feel like part of the team? Do school employees communicate a positive and upbeat attitude?
- *The physical plant.* Are student work products such as art and woodshop projects displayed in cases and on the walls? Do signs and notices suggest that the school is a positive environment for learning? Are the classrooms, halls, and restrooms generally clean and free of debris and graffiti?
- *The behavior of students.* Are students generally orderly and polite to one another and to the teachers? Do they seem happy to be at school?
- *Community support.* Do people in the community value education and support the district's schools? How are parents involved in their children's education, and do they support school functions?
- *An induction program for teachers.* Does the school have a beginning support system (such as a mentoring program) for first-year teachers? First-year teachers who participate in formal mentoring programs are more likely to succeed and stay in

Exploring Diversity

THE COMPETITION FOR MINORITY TEACHERS

In Chapter 2 we saw that nearly a third of school-age children in the United States are members of cultural minorities, compared to only 10 percent of the teaching force (National Education Association, 2003). In recent years the proportion of African American teachers has declined and that of Latino teachers has increased only slightly. At the same time, the percentage of K–12 students who are members of minority groups is increasing sharply. Projections indicate that at some time between 2030 and 2040, more than half of the nation's students will be members of cultural minorities.

Concern over these changing demographics has resulted in greater efforts to recruit minority teachers. As we discussed in Chapter 2, although no evidence suggests that nonminority teachers cannot work effectively with minority students, many educators believe that minority teachers bring valuable and unique perspectives to the classroom (Archer, 2000a). Students need role models who share their cultural backgrounds, and such role models may more effectively motivate students (Pintrich & Schunk, 2000). To attract minority candidates to teaching, recruiters in various states have developed scholarships and loan-forgiveness programs and specifically sought out bright high school and college students as well as adults interested in career changes. Alternative licensure programs often interest older career changers and are one promising avenue for bringing minorities into the profession.

The recruitment programs are not perfect. One broad issue is that recruitment strategies sometimes

teaching than those who don't (Darling-Hammond, 2003; Edwards & Chronister, 2000). We examine induction and mentoring programs in more detail later in the chapter.

These questions are difficult to answer in one visit to the school, but they are important. The working conditions in schools vary dramatically, and they can be the difference between a positive, rewarding first year of teaching and one that makes you reconsider your decision to be a teacher (S. Johnson & Birkeland, 2003). Poor working conditions are one of the most common reasons cited by beginning teachers for leaving the profession (Edwards & Chronister, 2000; J. Park, 2003). In addition, the support of parents and the community is important because it makes a huge difference in the attitudes, behaviors, and work habits of students (Marzano, 2003).

Reflect on This

To analyze a case study examining issues involved in interviewing for a job, go to the Companion Website at **www.prenhall.com/kauchak**, then to this chapter's *Reflect on This* module.

conflict with the current reform toward raising academic standards for teachers. Whereas recruiters are looking for new ways to find teachers, reformers are calling for more traditional forms of evaluating potential educators, such as standardized testing. This practice has a history of negatively and disproportionately affecting minorities.

Alternative licensure has had advantages and disadvantages. It has been quite successful in attracting minorities to teaching. Nearly half of the candidates who went through California's alternative program in 1998–1999 were members of minority groups, for example, as were 41 percent of those who went through the Texas program in 1998 (National Center for Education Information, 2000). On the other hand, as we saw earlier in the chapter, a much higher percentage of teachers who go through alternative licensure programs leave teaching than do those who complete traditional programs.

There is some room for optimism in this area. The enrollment of African American students in colleges of education increased from 6 percent to 9 percent in the 1990s, suggesting that the downward trend in the number of African American teachers might be reversing (Archer, 2000a). However, this increase only slows the diversity gap and doesn't address a larger issue: the ability of K–12 schools to produce enough minority students who can then go on to become teachers. Surveys indicate that African American, Native American, and Hispanic college graduates are more likely to become teachers than are White graduates. Unfortunately, students in these groups are less likely to succeed in and ultimately graduate from high school (Archer, 2000a). Leaders suggest that a nation wanting the teaching force to more nearly reflect the composition of society must first focus its educational efforts on today's elementary and secondary students.

Succeeding in Your First Year of Teaching

As with interviews, your first teaching job is probably 2 or more years away. However, again, now is the time to start learning to think like a teacher when you have the luxury of time for learning and growth.

Although the idea is unsettling, you will experience many uncertainties during your first year of teaching (Imbeau & McGee, 2001). To a certain extent, however, you can anticipate and prepare for them. One way is to be well informed. Learn as much as you can about as many aspects of teaching as possible. A second is to ask questions; teachers, in general, are cooperative, and veteran teachers will be willing to answer your questions and give advice.

In addition, you can anticipate some specific areas of concern that are likely to emerge during your first year and begin to think about them now. They include the following:

- Time
- Classroom management
- Induction and mentoring experiences
- Teacher evaluation

Let's look at them.

Time

One of your first experiences as a beginning teacher will be lack of time. You'll feel as though you don't have a second to yourself. As first-year teacher Antonio said earlier in the chapter, "I've never been so tired in my life. You're in front of kids all day, and then you go home and work all night to get ready for the next day." Shelley, another first-year teacher, also noted, "I can't believe how much there is to do—IEPs, progress reports, CPR training, responsibility to look for signs of abuse. When do I teach?"

Although a perfect solution to the problem of inadequate time doesn't exist, one key is *organization.* A large body of research, dating back to the 1970s, indicates that effective teachers are very organized (S. Bennett, 1978; Rutter et al., 1979). The students in one of our classes described a first-year teacher they had visited: "His desk is a mess. Books and papers piled everywhere. He can't find anything there." If he can't find "anything" there, you can bet that he wastes precious time looking for lesson plans and student papers. If you frequently or even occasionally lament that "I must get organized," now is a good time to start changing your habits. Having your instructional materials stored and readily accessible, creating procedures for everyday tasks (such as turning in, scoring, and returning papers), and establishing policies for absences and making up missed work are all essential for saving time.

Classroom Management

Classroom management is consistently identified as one of the most pressing problems teachers face. Seventy-six percent of the respondents in a 2002 poll said discipline was a very or somewhat serious problem in U.S. schools (Rose & Gallup, 2002), it is the primary concern of beginning teachers (Kellough, 1999; Rose & Gallup, 1999), and new teachers often feel ill-equipped to deal with management (Kher-Durlabhji, Lacina-Gifford, Jackson, Guillory, & Yandell, 1997).

The guidelines for effective management you studied in Chapter 11 can help you be as prepared as possible for dealing with management issues. In addition, two other strategies can help you with management issues. Let's look at them.

Careful planning and effective instruction can help prevent many management problems.

Many of the problems encountered by beginning teachers can be avoided through thorough professional preparation and careful planning.

Get to Know Your Students Getting to know your students is crucial. It communicates that you care about them as people, which is essential for effective teaching. Commit yourself to knowing all your students' first names within the first week of school.

Again, watch your professors and teachers out in the field. See how they use students' names in their instruction. You will notice a striking difference between teachers who know and address students by name and teachers who do not.

Use Effective Instructional Strategies You might wonder why we're discussing "effective instructional strategies" when the issue is classroom management. The answer is simple; as you saw in Chapter 11, it is virtually impossible to maintain classroom order in the absence of effective instruction (Good & Brophy, 2003). If you're not teaching effectively, the likelihood of having classroom management problems increases dramatically.

The active involvement of students in learning activities is one of the most important aspects of effective instruction. Students who are actively involved in learning are much less likely to misbehave than those who are sitting passively or who don't understand the topic. A guiding principle for your instruction should be this: *All students want to learn and want to participate.* It may not seem like it at times, but students who act as though they don't care or don't want to learn are more likely to be demonstrating fear that they can't learn. Look for models of effective instruction in the schools you visit, and seize opportunities to practice involving students in learning activities; particularly practice your questioning. Again, these experiences will help reduce some of the uncertainty of your first job.

Following guidelines for classroom management, knowing your students, and teaching effectively won't solve all of your management problems, but they will make a big difference—so big a difference that they can largely determine the success of both your internship and your first year of teaching.

Induction and Mentoring Programs

Case STUDY Steve has been very supportive. He's the person I go to when I want a straight answer about what's *really* going on in the school and the district. He's also been very helpful in giving suggestions about how to deal with difficult parents and how I should handle myself in situations where I'm uncertain. He hasn't helped me a whole lot with nitty-gritty stuff, like planning lessons or watching me teach, but that's not his fault. He has a full teaching load too, so he really doesn't have time. I guess what it really amounts to is, he's been a real source of emotional support, and this year is going better than I could have hoped for. (Nicole, a first-year teacher talking about her mentor)

The transition to teaching is rarely as smooth as Nicole experienced. Teachers are sometimes hired at the last moment, left isolated in their classrooms, and given little help—a true example of the sink-or-swim attitude toward those newly hired. Consequently, attrition rates among new teachers are five times higher than among experienced teachers (Archer, 2003; Moskowitz & Stephens, 1997).

To help solve this problem, increasing emphasis is being placed on induction and mentoring programs. **Induction programs** are *professional experiences for beginning teachers that provide systematic and sustained assistance to ease the transition into teaching.* Induction programs may include structured staff development activities (such as workshops focusing on problems commonly experienced by first-year teachers), procedures for providing first-year teachers with crucial information, and mentors (Feiman-Nemser, 2001). **Mentors** are *experienced teachers who provide guidance and support for beginning teachers.* Ideally, mentors provide not only emotional support, as Nicole reported, but also technical support in planning and conducting lessons and assessing student learning. Induction and mentoring programs can reduce first-year attrition by almost one third (Ingersoll & Smith, 2003)

Successful induction programs have the following characteristics (U.S. Department of Education, 1998d):

- Special attention is given to teachers in the beginning years of their career to help them link their performance to state and district standards.
- Mentors for beginning teachers are compensated for their work and are given opportunities for their own professional growth through classes that help them become effective mentors.
- Teachers receive assistance and support with everyday problems and are encouraged to develop a reflective professional attitude.
- Universities and schools collaborate to create clinical learning environments for beginning teachers. These relationships provide professional development for both K–12 teachers and university faculty.

Research on well-designed mentoring programs is promising. By providing professional support during the first year of teaching, these programs substantially increase the retention rates for beginning teachers (Ingersoll & Smith, 2003; J. Wang & Odell, 2002). The best mentoring programs are structured and include classroom observations and feedback (Giebelhaus & Bendixen-Noe, 2001). Effective programs produced teachers who were better at organizing and managing instruction, and their students were better behaved and more engaged during lessons (Evertson & Smithey, 2000).

Many beginning teachers, however, do not participate in anything more than perfunctory school orientations, and most of the mentoring programs that do exist have the characteristics Nicole described—they provide emotional support but little specific help in the process of learning to teach (Olson, 2003a). As we said earlier in the chapter, the existence of an effective mentoring program is one of the factors you should consider when looking for your first job.

Teacher Evaluation

As you saw in Chapter 1, teacher testing and accountability are facts of professional life, and you likely will be required to pass competency tests before you're licensed. You will also be evaluated during your first years of teaching. Teacher evaluation has two primary purposes: formative and summative (Ubben et al., 2001). **Formative evaluation** is *the process of gathering information and providing feedback that teachers can use to improve their practice.* **Summative evaluation** is *the process of gathering information about a teacher's competence, often for the purpose of making administrative* *decisions about retention and promotion.* You will likely encounter both in your first years of teaching.

Evaluation processes vary among states and districts, so you should check to see how your state and district handle evaluation during your first years of teaching. We'll examine two approaches here: research-based evaluation and standards-based evaluation. These approaches are not mutually exclusive, as standards are often grounded in learning theory and research.

Research-Based Evaluation Research-based evaluation systems utilize structured observations to focus on essential teaching skills identified by research. Florida was the first state to implement a research-based teacher evaluation system, the Florida Performance Measurement System (FPMS) (Florida Department of Education, 2002). Beginning teachers in Florida are evaluated in six different domains:

- Planning
- Classroom management
- Instructional organization and development
- Presentation of subject matter
- Verbal and nonverbal communication
- Assessment

For example, in the domain of classroom management, research indicates that effective teachers establish classroom routines, use instructional strategies that produce high levels of student involvement, and quickly identify sources of disruption (Emmer et al., 2003; Evertson et al., 2003). The observation instrument used to evaluate these skills asks the observer to

- Assess whether or not routines are in place and used effectively
- Count the number of students who are off-task or inattentive
- Decide whether the teacher correctly identifies sources of misbehavior and deals with them quickly

Observers use the same process to evaluate skills in other domains.

Observations can serve both summative and formative functions. From a summative perspective, they give supervisors the information they need to ensure that all teachers, including beginning ones, are competent. From a teacher development perspective, they provide valuable feedback that teachers can use to improve their teaching (Giebelhaus & Bendixen-Noe, 2001).

Standards-Based Evaluation Standards-based evaluation systems use broad categories of teacher skills and competencies as targets or standards for teacher performance. For example, North Carolina bases its beginning teacher evaluation system on the INTASC principles introduced in Chapter 1 (see Table 1.3). During their second year of teaching, provisionally licenced teachers compile, with the help of mentors, portfolios of lesson plans, videotapes, student artifacts, and reflections that address areas such as planning, assessment, and communication skills (Lashley, 2001). These portfolios are then evaluated by trained experts.

If the beginning teacher passes the portfolio evaluation, he or she is recommended for permanent licensure. If unsuccessful, the candidate has a third year to improve and revise the portfolio. Portfolio-based teacher evaluation systems are likely to become more prominent in the future. This is another reason for you to learn how to develop an effective portfolio.

Career-Long Professional Development

To this point we have discussed finding your first job and how to be successful in your first year of teaching. Now is also the time to begin thinking about your career 3 to 5 or more years down the road, because long-term professional goals can guide you during your teacher preparation program. In this section we examine three aspects of career-long professional development:

- Becoming a teacher–leader
- Attaining certification: the National Board for Professional Teaching Standards
- Becoming involved in professional organizations

Becoming a Teacher–Leader

As you've seen throughout this book, reform has important implications for teachers. Expectations for teachers have risen significantly since the beginning of the 1990s, and teachers' roles are also changing. For example, teachers now have much more input into decisions about teacher preparation, certification, and staff development than they had in the past. This has thrust teachers into new leadership roles, and the term *teacher–leader* has become part of the language of educational reform.

Teachers can develop leadership skills in a number of ways. Some examples include the following:

- Serving on school-level or districtwide curriculum committees
- Helping establish school-level or districtwide policies on issues such as grading, dress codes, and attendance policies
- Writing grant proposals for student- or teacher-development projects
- Proposing and facilitating staff development projects
- Arranging school-business partnerships
- Initiating and facilitating school-to-work activities
- Conducting action research

Because of its emphasis on research and the development of professional knowledge and its potential for developing teachers as professionals, we examine action research in more detail next.

Designing and Conducting Action Research Understanding and critically examining others' research is one way for teachers to increase their professional knowledge. Another is for teachers to conduct research in their own classrooms. **Action research** is *a form of applied research designed to answer a specific school- or classroom-related question* (Gall, Gall, & Borg, 2003; Wiersma, 2000). Action research can be conducted by teachers, school administrators, or other education professionals, and it can include descriptive, correlational, or experimental methods. Conducting action research projects (and sharing the results with others) is one effective way to promote career-long professional development, because it helps teachers understand research and the link between research and improved classroom practice (Sagor, 2000). The primary intent in action research is to improve practice within a specific classroom or school (McMillan, 2000).

Four steps guide teachers as they plan and conduct action research studies (B. Johnson & Christensen, 2000):

1. Identify a problem.
2. Plan and conduct a research study.

3. Implement the findings.
4. Use the results to generate additional research.

Let's see how Tyra Forcine, an eighth-grade English teacher, attempted to implement these steps in her classroom.

***Case* STUDY** Tyra and a group of her colleagues were discussing the problems they were having with homework. Kim Brown complained that her students often "blew off assignments," and Bill McClendon said he had so much trouble getting his students to do homework that he stopped assigning it.

"I've heard teachers say that homework doesn't help that much in terms of learning, anyway," Selena Cross added.

"That doesn't make sense to me," Tyra countered, shaking her head. "It has to help. The more kids work on something, the better they have to get at it."

Tyra consistently gave her students homework and checked to see if they had done it, but because of the conversation, she decided to take a more systematic look at its effects. She couldn't find a satisfactory answer on the Internet or in any of her college textbooks, so she decided to find out for herself.

Tyra began her study at the start of the third grading period. She collected homework every day and gave the students 2 points for having done it fully, 1 point for partial completion, and 0 points for minimal effort or not turning it in. Each day she discussed some the most troublesome items on the homework. On Fridays she quizzed students on the content covered Monday through Thursday, and she also gave a midterm test and a final exam. She then tried to see if a relationship existed between students' homework averages and their performance on the quizzes and tests.

At the end of the grading period, each student had a homework score, a quiz average, and an average on the two tests. Tyra called the district office to ask for help in summarizing the information, and together they found a positive but fairly low correlation between homework and test averages.

"Why isn't the correlation higher?" she wondered in another lounge conversation.

"Well," Kim responded. "You're only giving the kids a 2, 1, or 0 on the homework—you're still not actually grading it. So I suspect that some of the kids are simply doing the work to finish it, and they aren't really thinking about it."

"On the other hand," Bill acknowledged, "homework and tests are correlated, so maybe I'd better rethink my stand on no homework. . . . Maybe I'll change what I do next grading period."

"Good points," Tyra responded. "I'm going to keep on giving homework, but I think I need to change what I'm doing too. . . . It's going to be a ton of work, but I'm going to do two things. . . . I'm going to repeat my study next grading period to see if I get similar results, and then, starting in the fall, I'm going to redesign my homework, so it's easier to grade. I'll grade every assignment, and we'll see if the correlation goes up."

"Great idea," Kim nodded. "If the kids see how important it is for their learning, maybe they'll take their homework more seriously, and some of the not-doing-it problem will also get better. . . . I'm going to look at that in the fall." (Adapted from Eggen & Kauchak, 2004, p. 18)

• • ● • •

Let's see how Tyra attempted to apply the four steps in her classroom. First, she identified a problem: To what extent does homework contribute to my students' performance on quizzes and tests? This personalized approach increases teachers'

Figure 13.3 Conducting Action Research Enhances Professionalism

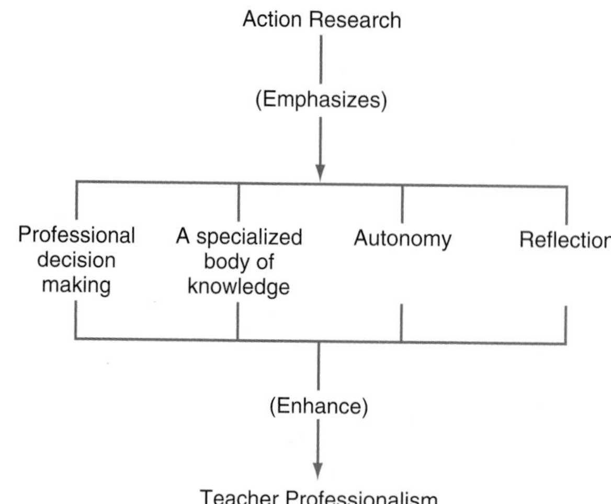

motivation, because it answers questions that are important to them (Mills, 2002; Quiocho & Ulanoff, 2002).

Second, she systematically designed and conducted her study, and third, Tyra and her colleagues were able to implement the results of her project immediately. Bill, for example, planned to give homework during the next grading period.

Finally, like most research, her project led to further studies. Tyra planned another study to see if scoring the homework more carefully would increase the correlation between homework and tests, and Kim planned to investigate the question of whether or not more careful scoring would lead to students more conscientiously doing their homework.

In addition to answering questions about real classroom issues, conducting action research increases teachers' feelings of professionalism. Contributing to a body of knowledge and making decisions based on reflection helps teachers grow both personally and professionally (Bransford et al., 2000). Engaging in action research projects also contributes to teachers' perceptions of their own autonomy. These factors are outlined in Figure 13.3.

The results of well-designed studies can often be presented at professional conferences and published in professional journals. This allows the knowledge gained to be made public and integrated with other research, two important steps in the development of a professional body of knowledge (J. Hiebert, Gallimore, & Stigler, 2002).

Attaining Certification: The National Board for Professional Teaching Standards

Earlier we saw that licensure is the process states use to ensure that teachers meet professional standards. In comparison, **certification** is *special recognition by a professional organization indicating that an individual has met certain requirements specified by the organization.*

To receive certification from the National Board for Professional Teaching Standards, teachers must demonstrate their expertise through exams and classroom performance.

One important form of certification is offered by the *National Board for Professional Teaching Standards (NBPTS)*. Created in 1987 as an outgrowth of the Carnegie Forum report, *A Nation Prepared: Teachers for the 21st Century* (Carnegie Forum on Education and the Economy, 1986), the board is composed mostly of K–12 teachers but also includes union and business leaders and university faculty (NBPTS, 1995). NBPTS seeks to strengthen teaching as a profession and raise the quality of education by recognizing the contributions of exemplary teachers, compensate them financially, give them increased responsibility, and increase their role in decision making (Harrison, 2003; Serafini, 2002).

National Board certification is based on standards that grew out of the report *What Teachers Should Know and Be Able to Do,* a policy statement from the National Board. The professional standards contained in this report were summarized into five core propositions about what professional educators should know and be able to do. These propositions and descriptions of how they play out in practice are outlined in Table 13.4.

National Board certification has five important features:

- It is designed for experienced teachers. Applicants must have graduated from an accredited college or university and must have taught at least 3 years.
- Applying for National Board certification is strictly voluntary and independent of any state's licensure. It is intended to indicate a high level of skill and professionalism.
- Acquiring National Board certification requires that teachers pass a set of exams in their area of specialty, such as math, science, early childhood, or physical education and health.
- Additional evidence, such as videotapes of teaching and a personal portfolio, are used in the assessment process.
- The primary control of the NBPTS is in the hands of practicing teachers, which increases the professionalism of teaching.

Table 13.4 Propositions of the National Board for Professional Teaching Standards

Proposition	Description
1. Teachers are committed to students and their learning.	• Accomplished teachers believe that all students can learn, and they treat students equitably. • Accomplished teachers understand how students develop, and they use accepted learning theory as the basis for their teaching. • Accomplished teachers are aware of the influence of context and culture on behavior, and they foster students' self-esteem, motivation, and character.
2. Teachers know the subjects they teach and how to teach those subjects to students.	• Accomplished teachers have a rich understanding of the subject(s) they teach, and they appreciate how knowledge in their subject is linked to other disciplines and applied to real-world settings. • Accomplished teachers know how to make subject matter understandable to students, and they are able to modify their instruction when difficulties arise. • Accomplished teachers demonstrate critical and analytic capacities in their teaching, and they develop those capacities in their students.
3. Teachers are responsible for managing and monitoring student learning.	• Accomplished teachers capture and sustain the interest of their students and use their time effectively. • Accomplished teachers are able to use a variety of effective instructional techniques, and they use the techniques appropriately. • Accomplished teachers can use multiple methods to assess the progress of students, and they effectively communicate this progress to parents.
4. Teachers think systematically about their practice and learn from experience.	• Accomplished teachers are models for intellectual curiosity, and they display virtues—honesty, fairness, and respect for diversity—that they seek to inspire in their students. • Accomplished teachers use their understanding of students, learning, and instruction to make principled judgments about sound practice, and they are lifelong learners. • Accomplished teachers critically examine their practice, and they seek continual professional growth.
5. Teachers are members of learning communities.	• Accomplished teachers contribute to the effectiveness of the school, and they work collaboratively with their colleagues. • Accomplished teachers evaluate school progress, and they utilize community resources. • Accomplished teachers work collaboratively with parents, and they involve parents in school activities.

Source: Reprinted with permission from the National Board for Professional Teaching Standards. *What Teachers Should Know and Be Able to Do*, 1994.

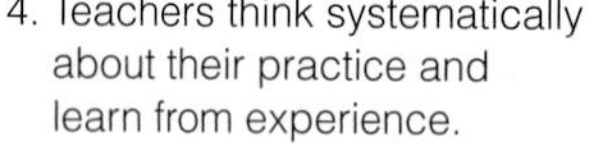

Increasing Understanding 13.9

Identify an example of *pedagogical content knowledge, general pedagogical knowledge,* and *knowledge of learners and learning* in the descriptions of the propositions. Include information directly from the descriptions in your response.

Certification by the NBPTS is for veterans, so you may be wondering why we are providing information about it to preservice teachers early in their programs. There are three reasons. First, one of the themes of this book has been professionalism, and the NBPTS is a national effort to professionalize teaching. The propositions in Table 13.4 emphasize the pedagogical content knowledge, general pedagogical knowledge, and knowledge of learners and learning discussed earlier in the chapter. The NBPTS recognizes that increasing professionalism requires teachers who are both highly knowledgeable and skilled in their areas of specialization.

Second, National Board certification is an excellent long-term career goal for which there is also a financial incentive. As of 2003, an estimated $316 million had been spent on this venture at the national level, and 39 states and nearly 200 school districts had spent millions of additional dollars to reward teachers who successfully completed the process (Lustick, 2002; Thirunarayanan, 2004). For example, the state of Florida appropriated $69 million during 2003–2004 to provide board-certified teachers and mentors for future ones with a 10 percent salary raise (Thirunarayanan, 2004). In addition, in 2003–2004 the state of Washington rewarded board-certified teachers with a $3,500 bonus (Margolis, 2004). As of 2004, there were 32,134 board-certified teachers, and this number is likely to increase (Thirunarayanan, 2004).

Increasing Understanding 13.10

Identify at least three similarities between the INTASC principles (Table 1.3) and the NBPTS propositions (Table 13.4). Take information directly from the tables in identifying the similarities.

Finally, evidence indicates that National Board certification makes a difference in teacher quality. In a study comparing teachers who had successfully completed the process to those who had attempted but failed to achieve certification, the nationally certified teachers scored higher on nearly all measures of teaching expertise. The study involved at least 75 hours of observation of each teacher, along with interviews and samples of student work (Blair, 2000). Another study found that the certification process encouraged teachers to become more reflective about their work and their relationships with other professionals (Lustick, 2002). National Board certification is well worth pursuing, and we encourage you to keep it in mind as you begin your career.

To learn more about NBPTS, go to the Companion Website at **www.prenhall.com/kauchak**, then to this chapter's *Web Links* module.

Becoming Involved in Professional Organizations

Teacher leadership and professional growth are also facilitated through the activities of a number of professional organizations. The organizations support a variety of activities, such as the following, designed to improve teaching and schools:

- Producing professional publications that provide up-to-date research and information on trends in the profession
- Providing professional development activities for teachers
- Holding yearly conferences that present theory and research about recent professional advances
- Providing resources where teachers can find answers to questions about professional issues and problems
- Providing politicians and policy makers with information about important issues facing education

Table 13.5 includes a list of prominent professional organizations, their Web site addresses, and descriptions of their missions or goals. We recommend that you join at least one professional organization as an integral part of your professional growth. Many organizations have student memberships that allow you to become involved while still in school.

Table 13.5 Professional Organizations for Educators

Organization and Web Address	Organization Mission or Goal
American Council on the Teaching of Foreign Languages **http://www.actfl.org**	To promote and foster the study of languages and cultures as an integral component of American education and society
Association for Supervision and Curriculum Development **http://www.ascd.org**	To enhance all aspects of effective teaching and learning, including professional development, educational leadership, and capacity building
Council for Exceptional Children **http://www.cec.sped.org**	To improve educational outcomes for individuals with exceptionalities, students with disabilities, and/or the gifted
International Reading Association **http://www.reading.org**	To promote high levels of literacy for all by improving reading instruction, disseminating research and information about reading, and encouraging the lifetime reading habit
Music Teachers National Association **http://www.mtna.org/flash.html**	To advance the value of music study and music making to society and to support the professionalism of music teachers
National Art Education Association **http://www.naea-reston.org**	To promote art education through professional development, service, advancement of knowledge, and leadership
National Science Teachers Association **http://www.nsta.org**	To promote excellence and innovation in science teaching and learning for all
National Council for the Social Studies **http://www.ncss.org**	To provide leadership, service, and support for all social studies educators
National Council of Teachers of English **http://www.ncte.org**	To promote the development of literacy, the use of language to construct personal and public worlds and to achieve full participation in society, through the learning and teaching of English and the related arts and sciences of language
National Council of Teachers of Mathematics **http://www.nctm.org**	To provide broad national leadership in matters related to mathematics education
National Association for Bilingual Education **http://www.nabe.org**	To recognize, promote, and publicize bilingual education
Phi Delta Kappa **http://www.pdkintl.org**	To promote quality education as essential to the development and maintenance of a democratic way of life by providing innovative programs, relevant research, visionary leadership, and dedicated service
Teachers of English to Speakers of Other Languages **http://www.tesol.org**	To improve the teaching of English as a second language by promoting research, disseminating information, developing guidelines and promoting certification, and serving as a clearinghouse for the field

Decision Making

Defining Yourself as a Professional

This chapter has raised a number of questions to consider as you make decisions about what type of teacher preparation program to pursue, how to use your teacher preparation program to make yourself marketable, and what type of teaching position to seek. We consider the implications of these issues for you in this section.

The first question you will need to consider—if you haven't already—is whether to pursue your education in a traditional or alternative teacher education program. In considering alternative teacher education programs, you should carefully analyze the kinds of courses you would take and the quality of support you would receive during clinical experiences and the first years of teaching. Alternative programs vary greatly in the extent to which they adequately prepare beginning teachers for the classroom (Blair, 2003; Darling-Hammond et al., 2002). The most successful graduates of alternative programs are older, more experienced and confident students who can fill in any missing gaps in alternative programs.

A second decision you will need to make is how to best use your teacher education program to grow and develop as a professional. This chapter was a transitional one, helping you to start thinking about the change from student to teacher, and from consumer to user. Throughout the chapter we have emphasized the need for you to be proactive in seeking out education-related experiences. School districts near colleges and universities typically offer a variety of ways for students to become involved, such as by tutoring students and leading afterschool programs. Most opportunities are for volunteers, but some pay a small salary. These experiences can be invaluable, not only in terms of professional growth but also as a way to establish yourself as a competent, dependable future teacher.

A third decision to start thinking about is the nature of your first teaching job. The trend is clear: Large numbers of future teaching positions will be found in challenging urban and rural schools (Olson, 2003a). What can you do to prepare yourself for these opportunities? We've already talked about actively seeking out firsthand experiences in these settings. You can also focus additional coursework in related, high-need areas. Coursework in multicultural education, English language learning, and special education will help you prepare for the challenges of diversity as well as make you more marketable.

Currently you're preparing for one of the most challenging and rewarding professions in the world—teaching—and when you complete your program, you'll begin some of the most important work that exists. We hope that your study of this book has helped launch you on your way.

Summary

Characteristics of Beginning Teachers

The teaching population is aging, and the number of beginning teachers is likely to increase significantly in the next 10 years. The population will become increasingly White, female, and younger than the existing population. A greater number of people are entering teaching after they've earned bachelor's degrees than in the past.

Beginning teachers drop out during their first year at over twice the attrition rate for teachers in general, and significant numbers also leave after their second and third years.

Preservice and beginning teachers tend to be optimistic about their abilities, but their optimism wanes as they get more experience. They tend to believe that the essence of teaching is "explaining" and that most of what they learn about teaching will come to them once they get into classrooms.

Knowledge and Learning to Teach

As the desire for teacher professionalism increases, more emphasis is placed on what teachers know and how they think. Expert teachers know the content of the subjects they teach; they are able to represent the content in ways that are understandable to learners (they have pedagogical content knowledge); they have general pedagogical knowledge, such as knowing how to manage classrooms and instruct effectively; and they know how students learn and develop and what motivates learners.

Into the Real World

The majority of teachers are licensed in traditional programs, which are designed and implemented by colleges and universities in different states. In alternative licensure programs, people who have bachelor's degrees in areas other than education complete a short, intensive training program with a clinical component.

The more quickly students in preservice programs begin to develop a professional portfolio, gathering experiences that make them marketable and building their professional reputation, the better equipped they will be to find a job when they graduate.

Succeeding in Your First Year of Teaching

Lack of time and classroom management are the most common problems beginning teachers face. Getting organized, becoming well-informed, and developing effective instructional skills are the most effective ways teachers have of preparing for both their internship and their first year of teaching.

Evaluation is also a part of a beginning teacher's experience. Formative evaluation is designed to provide helpful feedback to teachers; summative evaluation is designed to ensure adequate performance by teachers. Teacher evaluation based on research and standards-based evaluation are two approaches commonly used throughout the United States.

Career-Long Professional Development

Teachers are being thrust into more and more leadership roles as calls for professionalism increase. Teachers can demonstrate leadership in a variety of ways, such as by serving on district- and state-level committees, writing grants, designing and facilitating staff development activities, and conducting action research, research designed to address an immediate school-level problem.

The National Board for Professional Teaching Standards (NBPTS), in an attempt to professionalize teaching, has established rigorous standards and assessments for teachers who have completed at least 3 years of successful service. Substantive financial rewards exist in most states for teachers who have successfully completed National Board certification.

Professional organizations provide a variety of services for teachers throughout their careers.

Important Concepts

action research (p. 502)
certification (p. 504)
credentials file (p. 492)
experts (p. 481)
formative evaluation (p. 500)
general pedagogical knowledge (p. 485)
induction programs (p. 500)
knowledge of learners and learning (p. 485)
licensure (p. 486)
mentors (p. 500)
novices (p. 481)
pedagogical content knowledge (p. 484)
résumé (p. 492)
summative evaluation (p. 500)

Developing as a Professional

Praxis Practice

Look again at Judith Thomson's lesson on page 481. Rate Judith's demonstration of each of four forms of domain-specific knowledge in teaching: knowledge of content, pedagogical content knowledge, general pedagogical knowledge, and knowledge of learners and learning. Use the following scale:

5 = Displays the knowledge characteristic of an expert
4 = Displays a high degree of knowledge
3 = Displays an adequate degree of knowledge
2 = Displays minimal knowledge
1 = Displays virtually no knowledge

Provide a rationale for each of your ratings.

To receive feedback on your responses to the Praxis Practice exercises, go to the Companion Website at **www.prenhall.com/kauchak**, then to this chapter's *Praxis Practice* module.

Discussion Questions

1. What can preservice teachers do to decrease the likelihood that they will leave the profession? What can school leaders do?
2. The National Board for Professional Teaching Standards is attempting to increase the professionalism of teaching. How successful is it likely to be? Explain your thinking.
3. Some critics suggest that teaching isn't a profession because it doesn't have a body of knowledge on which to base its decisions. How would you respond to these critics?
4. It was suggested in the chapter that you attempt to establish a professional reputation by being conscientious in your classes. What are some other ways students can develop a professional reputation?
5. Several suggestions for making yourself marketable were offered in the chapter. Is it reasonable to expect that preservice teachers involve themselves in these activities? Explain your thinking.
6. What are some professional qualities beginning teachers should look for in a mentor? What are some personal qualities?

Going into Schools

1. Interview a teacher about developing as a professional. Ask him or her the following questions:
   a. Do you believe that understanding content or understanding how to communicate content to students is more important in teaching?
   b. Do you believe if you understand the content you're teaching well enough that you'll be able to get it across to students? Why?
   c. Are you more or less confident in your ability to get kids to learn than you were as a beginning teacher?
   d. Do you believe that explaining topics clearly or asking good questions is more effective for getting students to understand the topics you're teaching?
   e. What were the most important problems you faced during your first year of teaching?
   f. What suggestions would you offer prospective teachers to help them best prepare for their first year of teaching?
2. Interview a new teacher about their job-seeking experiences.
   a. Ask to see the teacher's résumé. How does it compare to the one in Figure 13.2?
   b. Did the teacher use a portfolio when looking for a job? If so, what did it include? How well did it work? What would the teacher have done differently?
   c. How valuable are the guidelines for making yourself marketable found in Table 13.1?
   d. How well did the teacher's interview(s) go? What questions were asked? What advice would the teacher give you regarding the guidelines for interviewing found in Table 13.3?
3. Interview a teacher familiar with NBPTS certification. Ask the following questions:
   a. Does the basic idea behind NBPTS certification have value? What are its basic strengths and weaknesses?
   b. Share the propositions behind NBPTS certification found in Table 13.4. Which are more valuable? Should any be added?
   c. Discuss the evaluation procedures for selecting teachers. Are these adequate? Should any additional be added?
4. Interview a school administrator. Ask how many teachers in the school are licensed through traditional means. How many are licensed through an alternative process? Ask whether the traditional or alternative process seems to be more effective. Why?
5. Interview a school administrator involved in hiring new teachers. Ask the following questions:
   a. What personal characteristics—such as attitudes and personality traits—do you look for in a new teacher?
   b. What kinds of knowledge (such as knowledge of content, learning, or learner development) do you look for in beginning teachers?
   c. How important is personal appearance and manner in an interview? What suggestions do you have in this regard?
   d. How important is a prospective teacher's use of standard English and grammar in an interview?
   e. Do you like to see a professional portfolio when you interview a prospective teacher? If so, what do you look for?

Virtual Field Experience

If you would like to participate in a Virtual Field Experience, go to the Companion Website at **www.prenhall.com/kauchak**, then to this chapter's *Field Experience* module.

Online Portfolio Activities

To complete these activities online, go to the Companion Website at **www.prenhall.com/kauchak**, then to this chapter's *Portfolio Activities* module.

Portfolio Activity 13.1

Preparing a Résumé

INTASC Principle 9: Commitment

Personal Journal Reflection

The purpose of this activity is to establish a beginning point in your development as a teacher and to provide you with the opportunity to reflect on your growth as a professional. Using Figure 13.1 as a model, prepare a résumé describing your education, experience, interests, and honors at this point in your life. Identify areas in which you should acquire additional education and experiences to make yourself marketable as a teacher.

Portfolio Activity 13.2

Motivating Learners

INTASC Principle 5: Motivation and Management

The purpose of this activity is to encourage you to begin thinking about learners and learner motivation. Describe a simple way of introducing a lesson in your content area or grade level that would capture students' attention and bring them into the lesson. Why would it be effective, and what does this tell you about learners? Which of the four kinds of knowledge discussed in the chapter are you demonstrating by developing this motivational strategy?

Portfolio Activity 13.3

Professional Organizations

INTASC Principle 9: Commitment

The purpose of this activity is to acquaint you with some of the resources that professional organizations provide. From Table 13.5, select an organization that interests you. Locate the organization's Web site, and explore the different services described there. Find out what it costs to join and what the membership benefits are. Report your findings in a one- or two-page summary.

Appendix A

Guidelines for Beginning a Professional Portfolio

Preparing a professional portfolio typically involves five steps (Martin, 1999).

Step 1. *Specify a goal.* For example, you're probably taking this course because you've either decided that you want to teach, or you're at least considering teaching. Finding a satisfying job would be a likely goal.

Step 2. *Determine how both past and future experiences relate to the goal.* You might choose to tutor a student with a reading problem, for example, to get professional experience that will make you more marketable.

Step 3. *Collect items that provide evidence of your developing knowledge and skill.* In addition to your résumé, which is always included in a portfolio, you might consider the following types of entries typically found in a teaching portfolio:

- Unit and lesson plans
- Samples of your work as a student
- Philosophy of education paper
- Description of your management system, including rules and procedures
- Grading policies
- Videotapes of you interacting with students (a clip of you working with the student you are tutoring, for example)
- Transcripts

The Portfolio Activities you completed throughout this text were meant to get you thinking about several of these components. In fact, any number of the activity products would make excellent entries for your portfolio. Other suggestions for portfolio components can be found in Bullock and Hawk (2001).

As you gather and create items, you should date each potential entry. The dates will help you later when you are organizing your portfolio.

Step 4. *Decide what items among your collection best illustrate your knowledge and skills.* A prospective employer is unlikely to view a bulky collection or series of videotapes, so you need to be selective; a videotaped lesson is likely a better entry than is a clip from a tutoring session.

Although you want to be selective, we suggest that you err on the side of including too much in your portfolio at first. If you think you might use an item, include it now. You can always remove an item, but you usually can't recover something that's been discarded.

Step 5. *Determine how to best present the items to the person or people connected to your goal.* You may be presenting your portfolio to the personnel director of a school district in which you want to teach, for example.

You will want to organize your portfolio to make it accessible to an evaluator. The portfolio should open with a title page, followed by a table of contents. The most impressive entries should precede those less significant. Work samples and evidence of performance, such as video clips, should always be displayed more prominently than, say, testimonial letters, which an evaluator often disregards. A chronological arrangement would provide viewers with some idea of your progress during the program.

To help you organize, put yourself in the evaluator's shoes. Remember, the evaluator knows little about you, and your portfolio is a way of introducing yourself. You're trying to convince a prospective employer that you're knowledgeable and skilled. Let communication and ease of access be your guide for arranging the information in your portfolio. If the portfolio is well organized, it will create a positive impression; the opposite will occur if it is disorganized.

As we move further into the information age, many more preservice teachers are developing electronic portfolios (Kilbane & Milman, 2003). They include everything a paper-based product includes, but they do it more efficiently. For example, one CD-ROM disk can hold the equivalent of 300,000 text pages. Typed documents can be scanned into word processing files and stored on floppy disks or CD-ROMs, and video can be digitized and also stored on CD-ROMs. This saves both time and energy. Evaluators who want to view a video episode in a paper-based portfolio must find a VCR, review the tape, and put it back into the correct portfolio container. In contrast, video footage in an electronic portfolio can be augmented with text and graphics and accessed with the click of a mouse.

To create an electronic portfolio, a person must have the proper computer equipment and software and be skilled in their use. If these are obstacles for you, you can certainly create a traditional portfolio. However, you will also want to hone your computer skills and educate yourself about electronic portfolios. With the expansion of technology into more and more areas of teaching, it is likely that paper-based portfolios will eventually become obsolete.

Regardless of whether your portfolio is paper-based or electronic, it should provide your prospective employer with an overview of your experience and qualifications and offer an inviting snapshot of you as a developing professional in the field of teaching. A detailed discussion of professional portfolios is found in Bullock and Hawk (2001) and Campbell, Cignetti, Melenyzer, Nettles, & Wyman (2003).

Appendix B

Directory of State Teacher-Certification Offices

Alabama
Department of Education
Division of Instructional Service
5108 Gordon Persons Building
50 North Ripley Street
Montgomery, AL 36130-2101
334-229-4271
www.alsde.edu/html/home.asp

Alaska
Department of Education
Teacher Education and Certification
Goldbelt Building
801 West 10th Street, Suite 200
Juneau, AK 99801-1894
907-465-2831
www.educ.state.ak.us/teachercertification

Arizona
Department of Education
Teacher Certification Unit
1535 West Jefferson
Phoenix, AZ 85007
602-542-4367
www.ade.state.az.us/certification

Arkansas
Department of Education
Teacher Education and Licensure
#4 State Capitol Mall, Rooms 106B/107B
Little Rock, AR 72201
501-682-4342
www.arkedu.state.ar.us/teachers/index.html

California
Commission on Teacher Credentialing
1812 9th Street
Sacramento, CA 95814-7000
916-445-0184
www.ctc.ca.gov or **www.calteach.com**

Colorado
Department of Education
Educator Licensing, Room 105
201 East Colfax Avenue
Denver, CO 80203-1704
303-866-6628
www.cde.state.co.us/index_license.htm

Connecticut
State Department of Education
Bureau of Certification and Professional Development
P.O. Box 2219
Hartford, CT 06145
860-566-5201
www.state.ct.us/sde/dtl/cert/index.htm

Delaware
State Department of Education
Office of Certification
Townsend Building, P.O. Box 1402
Dover, DE 19903-1402
302-739-4686
www.doe.state.de.us/information/certification.shtml

District of Columbia

Teacher Education and Certification Branch
Logan Administration Building
215 G Street, N.E., Room 101A
Washington, DC 20002
202-442-5377
www.k12.dc.us/dcps/home.html

Florida

Department of Education
Bureau of Teacher Certification
Florida Education Center
325 West Gaines Street, Room 203
Tallahassee, FL 32399-0400
904-488-5724
www.firn.edu/doe/edcert/home0022.htm

Georgia

Professional Standards Commission
1454 Twin Towers East
Atlanta, GA 30334
404-657-9000
www.gapsc.com/TeacherCertification.asp

Hawaii

State Department of Education
Office of Personnel Services
P.O. Box 2360
Honolulu, HI 96804
800-305-5104
www.htsb.org

Idaho

Department of Education
Teacher Certification and Professional Standards
P.O. Box 83720
Boise, ID 83720-0027
208-332-6884
www.sde.state.id.us/certification

Illinois

State Teacher Certification Board
Division of Professional Preparation
100 North First Street
Springfield, IL 62777-0001
217-782-2805
www.isbe.net/teachers.htm

Indiana

Professional Standards Board
251 East Ohio Street, Suite 201
Indianapolis, IN 46204-2133
317-232-9010
www.state.in.us/psb/

Iowa

Board of Educational Examiners
Teacher Licensure
Grimes State Office Building
East 14th and Grand
Des Moines, IA 50319-0146
515-281-3245
www.state.ia.us/boee

Kansas

State Department of Education
Certification and Teacher Education
120 South East 10th Avenue
Topeka, KS 66612-1182
913-296-2288
www.ksbe.state.ks.us/Welcome.html

Kentucky

Office of Teacher Education and Certification
1024 Capital Center Drive
Frankfort, KY 40601
502-573-4606
www.kyepsb.net/Cert/default.html

Louisiana

State Department of Education
Bureau of Higher Education, Teacher Certification, and Continuing Education
626 North 4th Street
P.O. Box 94064
Baton Rouge, LA 70804-9064
504-342-3490
www.louisianaschools.net/lde/tsac/home.html

Maine

Department of Education
Certification Office
23 State House Station
Augusta, ME 04333-0023
207-287-5944
www.usm.maine.edu/coe/etep/certify.htm

Maryland

State Department of Education
Division of Certification and Accreditation
200 West Baltimore Street
Baltimore, MD 21201
410-767-0412
http://certification.msde.state.md.us

Massachusetts

Department of Education
Certification and Professional Development Coordination
350 Main Street
P.O. Box 9140
Malden, MA 02148-5023
781-388-3300
www.doe.mass.edu/educators/e_license.html

Michigan

Department of Education
Office of Professional Preparation and Certification Services
608 West Allegan, 3rd Floor
Lansing, MI 48933
517-335-0406
www.michigan.gov/mde

Minnesota

State Department of Children, Families, and Learning
Personnel Licensing
610 Capitol Square Building
550 Cedar Street
St. Paul, MN 55101-2273
612-296-2046
http://education.state.mn.us/html/intro_licensure.htm

Mississippi

State Department of Education
Office of Educator Licensure
Central High School Building
359 North West Street
P.O. Box 771
Jackson, MS 39205-0771
601-359-3483
www.mde.k12ms.us/license

Missouri

Department of Elementary and Secondary Education
Teacher Certification Office
205 Jefferson Street
P.O. Box 480
Jefferson City, MO 65102-0480
573-751-0051
http://dese.mo.gov/divteachqual/teachcert

Montana

Office of Public Instruction
Teacher Education and Certification
1227 11th Avenue East, Room 210
Box 202501
Helena, MT 59620-2501
406-444-3150
www.opi.state.mt.us/Cert

Nebraska

Department of Education
Teacher Education and Certification
301 Centennial Mall South, Box 94987
Lincoln, NE 68509-4987
402-471-0739
www.nde.state.ne.us/TCERT/TCERT.html

Nevada

Department of Education
Licensure Division
700 East 5th Street
Carson City, NV 89701
702-687-9141
www.nde.state.nv.us/licensure

New Hampshire

State Department of Education
Bureau of Credentialing
101 Pleasant Street
Concord, NH 03301-3860
603-271-2407
www.ed.state.nh.us/Certification/teacher.htm

New Jersey

Department of Education
Office of Professional Development and Licensing
Riverview Executive Plaza, Building 100, Rte. 29
Trenton, NJ 08625-0500
609-292-2045
www.state.nj.us/njded/educators/license

New Mexico

State Department of Education
Professional Licensure Unit
Education Building
Santa Fe, NM 87501-2786
505-827-6587
www.sde.state.nm.us/div/ais/lic

New York

State Education Department
Office of Teaching
Cultural Education Center, Room 5A47
Nelson A. Rockefeller Empire State Plaza
Albany, NY 12230
518-474-3901
www.highered.nysed.gov/tcert

North Carolina

Department for Public Instruction
Licensure Section
301 North Wilmington Street
Raleigh, NC 27601-2825
919-733-4125
www.ncpublicschools.org/employment.html

North Dakota

Department of Public Instruction
Educational Standards and Practices Board
600 East Boulevard Avenue
Bismarck, ND 58505-0540
701-328-2264
www.state.nd.us/espb

Ohio

Department of Education
Division of Professional Development and Licensure
65 South Front Street, Room 412
Columbus, OH 43215-4183
614-466-3593
www.ode.state.oh.us/Teaching-Profession/default.asp

Oklahoma

State Department of Education
Professional Standards Section
Hodge Education Building
2500 North Lincoln Boulevard, Room 212
Oklahoma City, OK 73105-4599
405-521-3337
www.sde.state.ok.us/pro/tcert/profstd.html

Oregon

Teacher Standards and Practices Commission
Public Service Building, Suite 105
255 Capitol Street, N.E.
Salem, OR 97310
503-378-3586
www.tspc.state.or.us

Pennsylvania

State Department of Education
Bureau of Teacher Preparation and Certification
333 Market Street, 3rd Floor
Harrisburg, PA 17126-0333
717-787-3356
www.teaching.state.pa.us/teaching/site/default.asp?g-0

Puerto Rico

Department of Education
Certification Office
P.O. Box 190759
San Juan, PR 00919-0759
787-754-0060

Rhode Island

Department of Education
Office of Teacher Preparation, Certification, and Professional Development
Shepard Building
255 Westminster Street
Providence, RI 02903
401-222-2675
www.ridoe.net/teacher_cert/Default.htm

St. Croix District

Department of Education
Educational Personnel Services
2133 Hospital Street
St. Croix, VI 00820
340-773-1095

St. Thomas/St. John District

Department of Education
Personnel Services
44-46 Kongens Gade
St. Thomas, VI 00802
340-774-0100
www.usvi.org/education

South Carolina

State Department of Education
Office of Organizational Development
Teacher Certification Section
Rutledge Building, Room 702
Columbia, SC 29201
803-734-8466
www.scteachers.org/cert/index.cfm

South Dakota

Division of Education and Cultural Affairs
Office of Policy and Accountability
Kneip Building, 700 Governors Drive
Pierre, SD 57501-2291
605-773-3553
www.state.sd.us/deca/OPA/index.htm

Tennessee

State Department of Education
Teacher Licensing and Certification
Andrew Johnson Tower, 5th Floor
710 James Robertson Parkway
Nashville, TN 37243-0375
615-532-4880
www.state.tn.us/education/lic_home.htm

Texas

State Board of Educator Certification
1001 Trinity Street
Austin, TX 78701-2603
888-863-5880
www.sbec.state.tx.us/SBECOnline

United States Department of Defense

Dependent Schools
Certification Unit
4040 N. Fairfax Drive
Arlington, VA 22203-1634
703-696-3081, ext. 133
www.odedodea.edu/pers/percu

Utah

State Office of Education
Certification and Personnel Development
250 East 500 South
Salt Lake City, UT 84111
801-538-7741
www.usoe.k12.ut.us/cert

Vermont

State Department of Education
Licensing and Professional Standards
120 State Street
Montpelier, VT 05620
802-828-2445
www.state.vt.us/educ/new/html/maincert.html

Virginia

Department of Education
James Monroe Building
P.O. Box 2120
Richmond, VA 23218-2120
804-371-2522
www.pen.k12.va.us/VDOE/newvdoe/teached.html

Washington

Superintendent of Public Instruction
Professional Education and Certification Office
Old Capitol Building
600 South Washington Street
P.O. Box 47200
Olympia, WA 98504-7200
360-753-6773
www.k12.wa.us/certification

West Virginia

Department of Education
Office of Professional Preparation
1900 Kanawha Boulevard East
Building #6, Room B-252
Charleston, WV 25305-0330
304-558-7010
http://wvde.state.wv.us/certification

Wisconsin

Department of Public Instruction
Teacher Education and Licensing Teams
125 South Webster Street, P.O. Box 7841
Madison, WI 53707-7841
608-266-1879
www.dpi.state.wi.us/dpi/dlsis/tel/index.html

Wyoming

Professional Teaching Standards Board
Hathaway Building, 2nd Floor
2300 Capital Avenue
Cheyenne, WY 82002
307-777-6248
www.k12.wy.us/ptsb/certification.htm

References

AAUW Education Foundation Commission on Technology, Gender, and Teacher Education. (2000). *Tech-savvy: Educating girls in the new computer age.* Washington, DC: Author.

Abedi, J. (1999, Spring). CRESST report points to test accommodations for English Language Learning students. *The CRESST Line,* 6–7.

Abel, M., & Sewell, J. (1999). Stress and burnout in rural and urban secondary school teachers. *Journal of Educational Research, 92,* 287–294.

Abington School District v. Schempp, 374 U.S. 203 (1963).

Abowitz, K. (2000). A pragmatist revisioning of resistance theory. *American Educational Research Journal, 39,* 877–907.

Adams, D. (1995). *Education for extinction: American Indians in the boarding school experience, 1875–1928.* Lawrence: University Press of Kansas.

Adler, M. (1982). *The Paideia proposal: An educational manifesto.* New York: Macmillan.

Adler, M. (1998). *The Paideia proposal: An educational manifesto.* New York: Simon & Schuster.

Airasian, P. (2000). *Classroom assessment* (4th ed.). New York: McGraw-Hill.

Alexander, B., Crowley, J., Lundin, D., Murdy, V., Palmer, S., & Rabkin, E. (1997, September). E-Comp: A few words about teaching writing with computers. *T.H.E. Journal, 25,* 66–67.

Alexander, K., & Alexander, M. D. (2001). *American public school law.* Belmont, CA: Wadsworth.

Alexander, K., Entwisle, D., & Kabbani, N. (1999). Grade retention, social promotion and "third way" alternatives. Paper presented at the National Invitational Conference for Early Childhood Learning: Programs for a New Age, Alexandria, VA.

Alexander, L., & Riley, R. (2002). A compass in the storm. *Education Week, 22*(6), 36–37, 48.

Alexander, P., & Murphy P. (1998). The research base for APA's learner-centered psychological principles. In N. Lambert & B. McCombs (Eds.), *How students learn: Reforming schools through learner-centered education* (pp. 25–60). Washington, DC: American Psychological Association.

Allen, R. (2002). Big schools: The way we are. *Educational Leadership, 59*(5), 36–41.

Allison, C. (1995). *Present and past: Essays for teachers in the history of education.* New York: Peter Lang.

Altermatt, E., Jovanovic, J., & Perry, M. (1998). Bias or responsivity? Sex and achievement-level effects on teachers' classroom questioning practices. *Journal of Educational Psychology, 90,* 516–527.

American Association for the Advancement of Science. (1989). *Project 2061: Science for all Americans.* Washington, DC: Author.

American Association of University Women. (1992). *How schools shortchange girls.* Annapolis Junction, MD: Author.

American Association of University Women. (1993). *Hostile hallways: The AAUW survey on sexual harassment in America's schools.* New York: Louis Harris & Associates.

American Association of University Women. (1998). *Gender gaps: Where schools still fail our children.* Annapolis Junction, MD: Author.

American Council of Trustees and Alumni. (2000). *Losing America's memory: Historical illiteracy in the 21st century.* Washington, DC: Author.

American Federation of Teachers. (2002). Salary picture a mixed bag. *American Teacher, 87*(1), 3.

American Federation of Teachers. (2003a). *Survey and analysis of teacher salary trends 2002.* Retrieved February 2004 from http://www.aft.org/research/survey02/SalarySurvey02.pdf

American Federation of Teachers. (2003b). *Voucher home page.* Retrieved February 2004 from http://www.aft.org/research/vouchers

Amrein, A., & Berliner, D. (2003). The effects of high-stakes testing on student motivation and learning. *Educational Leadership, 60*(5), 32–38.

Anderson, G., Jimerson, S., & Whipple, A. (2002). *Student's ratings of stressful experiences at home and school: Loss of a parent and grade retention as superlative stressors.* Manuscript prepared for publication, available from authors at the University of California, Santa Barbara.

Anderson, J. (1988). *The education of Blacks in the South.* Chapel Hill: University of North Carolina Press.

Anderson, L., & Krathwohl, D. (Eds.). (2001). *A taxonomy for learning, teaching, and assessing: A revision of Bloom's taxonomy of educational objectives.* New York: Addison Wesley Longman.

Annie E. Casey Foundation. (2001). *Kids count data book 2001.* Baltimore: Annie E. Casey Foundation.

Ansell, S., & McCabe, M. (2003). Off target. *Education Week, 22*(17), 57–58.

Ansell, S., & Park, J. (2003). Tracking tech trends. *Education Week, 22*(35), 43–49.

Apple, M. (1995). *Education and power* (2nd ed.). New York: Rutledge.

Archer, J. (1998). The link to higher scores. *Education Week, 28*(5), 10–14, 18–21.

Archer, J. (2000a). Competition fierce for minority teachers. *Education Week, 19*(18), 32–33.

Archer, J. (2000b). Teachers warned against teaching contracts. *Education Week, 20*(15), 30.

Archer, J. (2003). Increasing the odds. *Education Week, 22*(17), 52–56.

Arias, M., & Casanova, U. (Eds.). (1993). Bilingual education: Politics, practice, and research. *Ninety-second yearbook of the National Society for the Study of Education, Part 2.* Chicago: University of Chicago Press.

Armstrong, D. (2003). *Curriculum today.* Upper Saddle River, NJ: Merrill/Prentice Hall.

Arnold, M. (1998). Three kinds of equity. *American School Board Journal, 85*(5), 34–36.

Associated Press. (2000, December 29). Texas legislative panel calls for charter schools moratorium. *Boston Globe,* p. A13.

Astor, R., Meyer, H., & Pitner, R. (2001). Elementary and middle-school students' perceptions of violence-prone school subcontexts. *The Elementary School Journal, 101,* 511–528.

Ayers, W., Dohrn, B., & Ayers, R. (Eds.). (2001). *Zero tolerance: Resisting the drive for punishment in our schools.* New York: The New Press.

Babad, E., Bernieri, F., & Rosenthal, R. (1991). Students as judges of teachers' verbal and nonverbal behavior. *American Educational Research Journal, 28,* 211–234.

Bailey, W. (1997). *Educational leadership for the 21st century: Organizing schools.* Lancaster, PA: Technomic.

Ball, D. (1992, Summer). Magical hopes: Manipulatives and the reform of math education. *American Educator,* 28–33.

Bandura, A. (1989). Social cognitive theory. In R. Vasta (Ed.), *Annals of child development* (Vol. 6, pp. 1–60). Greenwich, CT: JAI Press.

Bangert-Drowns, R. (1993). The word processor as an instructional tool: A meta-analysis of word processing in writing instruction. *Review of Educational Research, 63,* 69–93.

Banks, J. (2001). *Cultural diversity and education.* Boston: Allyn & Bacon.

Banks, J. (2002). *An introduction to multicultural education* (3rd ed.). Boston: Allyn & Bacon.

Banks, J. (2003). *Teaching strategies for ethnic studies* (7th ed.). Boston: Allyn & Bacon.

Barab, S., & Landa, A. (1997). Designing effective interdisciplinary anchors. *Educational Leadership, 54,* 52–55.

Barone, M. (2000). In plain English: Bilingual education flunks out of schools in California. *U.S. News & World Report, 128*(21), 37.

Barr, R., & Parrett, W. (2001). *Hope fulfilled for at-risk youth.* Boston: Allyn & Bacon.

Barth, P., Haycock, K., Jackson, H., Mora, K., Ruiz, P., Robinson, S., & Wilkins, A. (Eds.). (1999). *Dispelling the myth: High poverty schools exceeding expectations.* Washington, DC: The Education Trust.

Battista, M. (1999). The mathematical miseducation of America's youth: Ignoring research and scientific study in education. *Phi Delta Kappan, 80,* 425–433.

Beane, J. (1997). *Curriculum integration: Designing the core of democratic education.* New York: Teachers College Press.

Bebeau, M., Rest, J., & Narvaez, D. (1999). Beyond the promise: A perspective on research in moral education. *Educational Researcher, 28*(4), 18–26.

Behuniak, P. (2002). Consumer-referenced testing. *Phi Delta Kappan, 84,* 199–206.

Benard, B. (1993). Fostering resilience in kids. *Educational Leadership, 51*(3), 44–48.

Benard, B. (1994). *Fostering resilience in urban schools.* San Francisco: Far West Laboratory.

Bender, W., & McLaughlin, P. (1997). Violence in the classroom. *Intervention in School and Clinic, 32*(4), 196–198.

Bennett, C. (1999). *Comprehensive multicultural education: Theory and practice* (4th ed.). Boston: Allyn & Bacon.

Bennett, S. (1978). Recent research on teaching: A dream, a belief, and a model. *British Journal of Educational Psychology, 48,* 27–147.

Benninga, J., & Wynne, E. (1998). Keeping in character: A time-tested solution. *Phi Delta Kappan, 79,* 439–448.

Berg, J. H. (2003). *Improving the quality of teaching through national Board certification theory and practice.* Norwood, MA: Christopher-Gordon.

Berk, L. (2003). *Child development* (6th ed.). Boston: Allyn & Bacon.

Berk, L. (2004). *Development through the lifespan* (3rd ed.). Boston: Allyn & Bacon.

Berliner, D. (1992, February). *Educational reform in an era of disinformation.* Paper presented at a meeting of the American Association of Colleges in Teacher Education, San Antonio, TX.

Berliner, D. (1994). Expertise: The wonder of exemplary performances. In J. Mangieri, & C. Collins (Eds.), *Creating powerful thinking in teachers and students* (pp. 161–186). Fort Worth, TX: Harcourt Brace.

Berliner, D. (2000). A personal response to those who bash education. *Journal of Teacher Education, 51,* 358–371.

Bertman, S. (2000). *Cultural amnesia: America's future and the crisis of memory.* Westport, CT: Praeger.

Bethel School District No. 403 v. Fraser, 106 S. Ct. 3159 (1986).

Biddle, B., & Berliner, D. (2002). Unequal school: Funding in the United States. *Education Leadership, 59*(8), 48–59.

Billings, L., & Fitzgerald, J. (2002). Dialogic discussion and the Paideia Seminar. *American Educational Research Journal, 39,* 907–942.

Bishop, J. (1995). The power of external standards. *American Educator, 19,* 10–14, 17–18, 42–43.

Bishop, J. (1998). The effect of curriculum-based external exit systems on student achievement. *Journal of Economic Education, 29,* 171–182.

Black, S. (1996). The pull of magnets. *American School Board Journal, 183*(9), 35.

Black, S. (2002). The well-rounded student. *American School Board Journal, 189*(6), 33–35.

Blair, J. (2000). AFT urges new tests, expanded training for teachers. *Education Week, 19*(32), 11.

Blair, J. (2001). Teacher performance-pay plan modified in Cincinnati. *Education Week, 21*(3), 3.

Blair, J. (2003). Skirting tradition. *Education Week, 22*(17), 35–38.

Bloom, B., Englehart, M., Furst, E., Hill, W., & Krathwohl, O. (1956). *Taxonomy of educational objectives: The classification of educational goals: Handbook 1. The cognitive domain.* White Plains, NY: Longman.

Bloom, E. (2003). Service learning and social studies: A natural fit. *Middle Level Learning, 17,* M4–M7.

Board of Education of the Westside Community School v. Mergens, 496 U.S. 226 (1990).

Board of Education, the Commonwealth of Virginia. (1995). *History and social science standards of learning for Virginia Public Schools.* Richmond, VA: Author. Retrieved February 2004 from http://www.pen.k12.va.us/go/Sols/history.html#GradeEight

Bond, H. (1934). *The education of the Negro in the American social order.* New York: Prentice Hall.

Borja, R. (2002). Study: Urban school chiefs' tenure is 4.6 years. *Education Week, 21*(21), 5.

Borja, R. (2003). Prepping for the big test. *Education Week, 22*(35), 23–26.

Borko, H., & Putnam, R. (1996). Learning to teach. In D. Berliner, & R. Calfee (Eds.), *Handbook of educational psychology* (pp. 673–708). New York: Simon & Schuster Macmillan.

Borman, G. (2002/2003). How can Title I improve achievement? *Educational Leadership, 60*(4), 49, 53.

Bostic, J., Rustuccia, C., & Schlozman, S. (2001). The shrink in the classroom: The suicidal student. *Educational Leadership, 59*(2), 81–82.

Bosworth, K. (1995). Caring for others and being cared for: Students talk about caring in school. *Phi Delta Kappan, 76,* 686–693.

Boulton, M. (1996). Lunchtime supervisors' attitudes towards playful fighting, and ability to differentiate between playful and aggressive fighting: An intervention study. *British Journal of Educational Psychology, 66,* 367–381.

Bowman, D. (2000a). Arizona poised to revisit graduation exam. *Education Week, 20*(13), 16, 18.

Bowman, D. (2000b). Charters, vouchers earning mixed report card. *Education Week, 19*(34), 1, 19–21.

Bowman, D. (2000c). White House proposes goals for improving Hispanic education. *Education Week, 19*(41), 9.

Bowman, D. (2002). Researchers see promising signs in DARE's new drug ed. program. *Education Week, 22*(11), 6–7.

Bowman, D. (2003). N.C. court to mull right to a lawyer in discipline cases. *Education Week, 22*(18), 1, 12.

Boyer, E. (1995). *The basic school: A community for learning.* Princeton, NJ: The Carnegie Foundation for the Advancement of Teaching.

Bracey, G. (1999a). Research: The growing divide. *Phi Delta Kappan, 81,* 90.

Bracey, G. (1999b). Top-heavy. *Phi Delta Kappan, 80,* 472–473.

Bracey, G. (2002). The 12th Bracey report on the condition of public education. *Phi Delta Kappan, 84,* 135–150.

Bracey, G. (2003a). Investing in preschool. *American School Board Journal, 90*(1), 32–35.

Bracey, G. (2003b). Not all alike. *Phi Delta Kappan, 84,* 717–718.

Braddock, J. (1990). Tracking the middle grades: National patterns of grouping for instruction. *Phi Delta Kappan, 71,* 445–449.

Bradley, A. (1998). Muddle in the middle. *Education Week, 17*(31), 38–42.

Bradley, A. (1999a). Confronting a tough issue: Teacher tenure. *Education Week, 18*(17), 48–52.

Bradley, A. (1999b). Pool of aspiring teachers is growing older. *Education Week, 19*(7), 3.

Bradley, A. (1999c). Science group finds middle school textbooks inadequate. *Education Week, 19*(6), 5.

Bradley, A. (2000a). Chicago makes deal with feds to hire foreign teachers. *Education Week, 19*(19), 17.

Bradley, A. (2000b). L.A. proposes linking teacher pay to tests. *Education Week, 19*(28), 3.

Bradley, A. (2000c). Massachusetts to test teachers in school with low math scores. *Education Week, 19*(21), 19.

Bradley, D., & Switlick, D. (1997). The past and future of special education. In D. Bradley, M. King-Sears, & D. Tessier-Switlick (Eds.), *Teaching students in inclusive settings* (pp. 1–20). Boston: Allyn & Bacon.

Bradley v. Pittsburgh Board of Education, 913 F.2d 1064 (3d Cir. 1990).

Bradsher, M., & Hagan, L. (1995). The kids network: Student-scientists pool resources. *Educational Leadership, 53*(2), 38–43.

Bransford, J., Brown, A., & Cocking, R. (Eds.). (2000). *How people learn: Brain, mind, experience, and school.* Washington, DC: National Academy Press.

Brenner, M., Mayer, R., Moseley, B., Brar, T., Durán, R., Reed, B., & Webb, D. (1997). Learning by understanding: The role of multiple representations in learning algebra. *American Education Research Journal, 34*(4), 663–689.

Brimley, V., & Garfield, R. (2002). *Financing education* (8th ed.). Boston: Allyn & Bacon.

Brint, S. (1998). *Schools and societies.* Thousand Oaks, CA: Pine Forge Press.

Brody, N. (1992). *Intelligence* (2nd ed.). San Diego, CA: Academic Press.

Bronfenbrenner, U. (1999). Is early intervention effective? Some studies of early education in familial and extra-familial settings. In A. Montague (Ed.), *Race and IQ* (pp. 343–378). New York: Oxford University Press.

Brookhart, S. (1997). A theoretical framework for the role of classroom assessment in motivating student effort and achievement. *Applied Measurement in Education, 10*(2), 161–180.

Brophy, J. (1996). *Teaching problem students.* New York: Guilford Press.

Brophy, J. (1998). *Motivating students to learn.* Boston: McGraw-Hill.

Brophy, J., & Alleman, J. (1991). A caveat: Curriculum integration isn't always a good idea. *Educational Leadership, 49,* 66.

Brouillette, L. (2000, April). *What is behind all that rhetoric? A case study of the creation of a charter school.* Paper presented at the annual meeting of the American Educational Research Association, New Orleans, LA.

Brown, A., & Campione, J. (1986). Psychological theory and the study of learning disabilities. *American Psychologist, 41,* 1059–1068.

Brown, D. (1991). *The effects of state-mandated testing on elementary classroom instruction.* Unpublished doctoral dissertation. Knoxville: University of Tennessee–Knoxville.

Brown, D. (2002, April). *How do urban teachers' professed classroom management strategies reflect culturally responsive teaching?* Paper presented at the annual meeting of the American Educational Research Association, New Orleans, LA.

Brown, H. (2003). Charter schools found lacking resources. *Education Week, 22*(31), 30.

Brown v. Bathhe, 416 F. Supp. 1194 (D. Neb. 1976).

Brown v. Board of Education of Topeka, 347 U.S. 483 (1954).

Brown v. Board of Education of Topeka, 349 U.S. 294 (1955) (Brown II).

Bruning, R., Schraw, G., Norby, M., & Ronning, R. (2004). *Cognitive psychology and instruction* (4th ed.). Upper Saddle River, NJ: Merrill/Prentice Hall.

Bruning, R., Schraw, G., & Ronning, R. (1999). *Cognitive psychology and instruction* (3rd ed.). Upper Saddle River, NJ: Prentice Hall.

Brunner, C., & Tally, W. (1999). *The new media literacy handbook: An educator's guide to bringing new media into the classroom.* New York: Anchor Books.

Brunsma, D., & Rockquemoro, K. (1999). Effects of student uniforms on attendance, behavior problems, substance abuse and academic achievement. *Journal of Educational Research, 92,* 53–62.

Bryant, A., & Zimmerman, M. (2002). Examining the effects of academic beliefs and behaviors on changes in substance use among urban adolescents. *Journal of Educational Psychology, 94,* 621–637.

Bullock, A., & Hawk, P. (2001) *Developing a teaching portfolio: A guide for preservice and practicing teachers.* Upper Saddle River, NJ: Merrill/Prentice-Hall.

Bullough, R., Jr. (1989). *First-year teacher: A case study.* New York: Teachers College Press.

Bullough, R., Jr. (1999, April). *In praise of children at-risk: Life on the other side of the teacher's desk.* Paper presented at the annual meeting of the American Educational Research Association, Montreal, Canada.

Bullough, R., Jr. (2001). *Uncertain lives: Children of promise, teachers of hope.* New York: Teachers College Press.

Bullough, R., Jr., & Baughman, K. (1997). *"First-year teacher" eight years later: An inquiry into teacher development.* New York: Teachers College Press.

Bunting, C. (2003). Quiet transformations: Good teachers are the key to everything. *Education Week, 22*(30), 41.

Bushweller, K. (1998). Probing the roots and prevention of youth violence. *American School Board Journal, 85*(12), A8–A12.

Button, H., & Provenzo, E. (1989). *History of education in American culture.* New York: Holt, Rinehart & Winston.

Butts, R. (1978). *Public education in the United States.* New York: Holt, Rinehart & Winston.

Butts, R., & Cremin, L. (1953). *A history of education in American culture.* New York: Holt, Rinehart & Winston.

Cahupe, P., & Howley, C. (1992). *Indian nations at risk.* Charleston, WV: Clearinghouse on Rural Education and Small Schools.

Calderhead, J. (1996). Teachers: Beliefs and knowledge. In D. Berliner & R. Calfee (Eds.), *Handbook of educational psychology* (pp. 709–725). New York: Macmillan.

Callahan, C. (2001). Beyond the gifted stereotype. *Educational Leadership, 59*(3), 42–46.

Calsyn, C., Gonzales, P., & Frase. (1999). *Highlights from TIMSS.* Washington, DC: National Center for Educational Statistics.

Camerino, C. (2003). Pay to play? *Education Week, 22*(23), 32, 34.

Cameron, C., & Lee, K. (1997). Bridging the gap between home and school with voice-mail technology. *Journal of Educational Research, 90,* 182–190.

Campbell, D. (2000). *Choosing democracy: A practical guide to multicultural education* (2nd ed.). Upper Saddle River, NJ: Merrill/Prentice Hall.

Campbell, D., Cignetti, P., Melenyzer, B., Nettles, D., & Wyman, R. (2003). *How to develop a professional portfolio: A manual for teachers* (3rd ed.). Boston: Allyn & Bacon.

Campbell, F., & Raney, C. (1995). Cognitive and school outcomes for high-risk African-American students at middle adolescence: Positive effects of early intervention. *American Educational Research Journal, 32,* 742–772.

Campbell, J., & Beaudry, J. (1998). Gender gap linked to differential socialization for high achieving senior mathematics students. *Journal of Educational Research, 91,* 140–147.

Campbell, P., & Clewell, B. (1999). Science, math, and girls. *Education Week, 19*(2), 50–53.

Campus Compact. (2001). *Annual service statistics 2000.* Providence, RI: Brown University.

Caplan, N., Choy, M., & Whitmore, J. (1992). Indochinese refugee families and academic achievement. *Scientific American, 266*(2), 36–42.

Carkci, M. (1998, November 8). A classroom challenge I just had to take. *Washington Post,* p. C3.

Carlsen, W. (1987, April). *Why do you ask? The effects of science teacher subject-matter knowledge on teacher questioning and classroom discourse.* Paper presented at the annual meeting of the American Educational Research Association, Washington, DC.

Carnegie Forum on Education and the Economy. (1986). *A nation prepared: Teachers for the 21st century.* Washington, DC: Author. (ERIC Document Reproduction Service No. ED268120)

Carr, N. (2003). The toughest job in America. Education vital signs [Supplement.]. *American School Board Journal, 190*(2), 14–19.

Carter, C. (1997). Integrated middle school humanities: A process analysis. *Teacher Education Quarterly, 24*(3), 55–73.

Carter, C., & Mason, D. (1997, March). *Cognitive effects of integrated curriculum.* Paper presented at the annual meeting of the American Educational Research Association, Chicago.

Casey, J., Andreson, K., Yelverton, B., & Wedeen, L. (2002). A status report on charter schools in New Mexico. *Phi Delta Kappan, 83,* 518–524.

Cassady, J. (1999, April). *The effects of examples as elaboration in text on memory and learning.* Paper presented at the annual meeting of the American Educational Research Association, Montreal, Canada.

Cavanagh, S. (2002). Officials tie entrance-score dips to curriculum. *Education Week, 22*(1), 5.

Ceci, S., & Williams, W. (1997). Schooling, intelligence, and income. *American Psychologist, 53,* 185–204.

Center for Effective Discipline. (n.d.). *Delaware legislature bans school paddling 4-1-03.* Retrieved February 2004 from http://www.stophitting.com/news

Center on Addiction and Substance Abuse. (2001). *Malignant neglect: Substance abuse and America's schools.* New York: Columbia University.

Centers for Disease Control and Prevention. (1996). *HIV/AIDS surveillance report.* Atlanta, GA: Author.

Chalk v. U.S. District Court Cent. Dist. of California, 840 F.2d. 701 (9th Cir. 1988).

Chance, P. (1997). Speaking of differences. *Phi Delta Kappan, 78,* 506–507.

Charp, S. (2001). Bridging the digital divide. *T.H.E. Journal, 29*(10), 10–12.

Chaskin, R., & Rauner, D. (1995). Youth and caring: An introduction. *Phi Delta Kappan, 76,* 667–674.

Chekley, K. (1997). The first seven . . . and the eighth: A conversation with Howard Gardner. *Educational Leadership, 55*(1), 8–13.

Child Care Bureau. (1997). *Out-of-school time: School-age care.* Washington, DC: U.S. Department of Health and Human Services.

Children's Defense Fund. (1999). *The state of America's children yearbook 1999.* Washington, DC: Author.

Children's Defense Fund. (2001). Children in the states 2001. Washington, DC: Author.

Christie, I. (2003). States ain't misbehavin' but the work is hard! *Phi Delta Kappan, 84,* 565–566.

Clandinin, J., & Connelly, M. (1996). Teacher as curriculum maker. In P. Jackson, (Ed.), *Handbook of research on curriculum* (pp. 363–401). New York: Macmillan.

Clark, S., & Clark, D. (1993). Middle level school reform: The rhetoric and the reality. *The Elementary School Journal, 93,* 447–460.

Clinton, W. (1998). State of the Union address (January 1, 1999). Washington, DC: U.S. Government Printing Office.

Clinton, W. (1999). State of the Union address (January 1, 2000). Washington, DC: U.S. Government Printing Office.

Cognition and Technology Group at Vanderbilt. (1992). The Jasper Series as an example of anchored instruction: Theory, program description, and assessment data. *Educational Psychologist, 27,* 291–315.

Cognition and Technology Group at Vanderbilt. (1997). *The Jasper Project: Lessons in curriculum, instruction, assessment, and professional development.* Mahwah, NJ: Erlbaum.

Cohen, D. (1993). Perry preschool graduates show dramatic new social gains at 27. *Education Week, 12*(28), 1, 16–17.

Cohen, E. (1994). Restructuring the classroom: Conditions for productive small groups. *Review of Educational Research, 64,* 1–35.

Coker, H., Lorentz, C., & Coker, J. (1980, April). *Teacher behavior and student outcomes in the Georgia study.* Paper presented at the annual meeting of the American Educational Research Association, Boston.

Coladarcci, T., & Cobb, C. (1995, April). *The effects of school size and extracurricular participation on 12th grade academic achievement and self-esteem.* Paper presented at the annual meeting of the American Educational Research Association, San Francisco.

Coles, A. (1997). Poll finds growing support for school choice. *Education Week, 17*(1), 14.

Coles, A. (1999a). Surveys examine sex education programs. *Education Week, 19*(6), 13.

Coles, A. (1999b). Teenage drug use continues to slide. *Education Week, 19*(10), 100.

Coles, A. (2000). Drug use more prevalent among rural teenagers, study warns. *Education Week, 19*(21), 8.

Colley, A. (2002). What can principals do about new teacher attrition? *Principal, 81*(4), 22–24.

Collis, B., Peters, O., & Pals, N. (2001). A model for predicting the educational use of information and communication technologies. *Instructional Science, 29,* 95–125.

Colorado Department of Education. (1999). *Colorado technology competency guidelines for classroom teachers and school library media specialists.* Retrieved February 2004 from http://www.cde.state.co.us/edtech/download/tgui.pdf

Comer, J. (1994, April). *A brief history and summary of the school development program.* Paper presented at the annual meeting of the American Educational Research Association, San Francisco.

Comer, J., Haynes, N., Joyner, E., & Ben-Avie, M. (1996). *Rallying the whole village: The Comer process for reforming education.* New York: Teachers College Press.

Commonwealth of Pennsylvania v. Douglass, 588 A.2d 53 (Pa. Super. Ct. 1991).

Compayre, G. (1888). *History of pedagogy* (W. Payne, Trans.). Boston: Heath.

Conant, J. (1959). *The American high school.* New York: McGraw-Hill.

Conger, R., Conger, K., Elder, G., Lorenz, F., Simons, R., & Whitbeck, L. (1992). A family process model of economic hardship and adjustment of early adolescent boys. *Child Development, 63,* 526–541.

Cooper, D., & Snell, J. (2003). Bullying—not just a kid thing. *Educational Leadership, 60*(6), 22–25.

Cooper, H., Nye, B., Charlton, K., Lindsey, J., & Greathouse, S. (1996). The effects of summer vacation on achievement test scores: A narrative and meta-analytic review. *Review of Educational Research, 66,* 227–268.

Cooper, H., Valentine, J., Charlton, K., & Melson, A. (2003). The effects of modified school calendars on student achievement and on school and community attitudes. *Review of Educational Research, 73,* 1–52.

Cooper, L. (2001). A comparison of online and traditional computer applications classes. *T.H.E. Journal, 28*(8), 52–58.

Cooperman, S. (2003). A new order of things. *Education Week, 22*(38), 30, 32.

Corbett, D., & Wilson, B. (2002). What urban students say about good teaching. *Educational Leadership, 60*(1), 18–22.

Corey, G., Corey, M., & Callahan, P. (1993). *Issues and ethics in the helping professions.* Pacific Grove, CA: Brooks/Cole.

Cornelius, L. (2002, April). *Legal implications of school violence.* Paper presented at the annual meeting of the American Educational Research Association, New Orleans, LA.

Corporation for Public Broadcasting. (2003). *Connected to the future: A report on children's Internet use from the Corporation for Public Broadcasting.* Retrieved February 2004 from http://www.cpb.org/Ed/resources/connected

Coughlin, E. (1996, February 16). Not out of Africa. *Chronicle of Higher Education,* A6–A7.

Council of Chief State School Officers. (2003). *Chief state school officers method of selection.* Retrieved February 2004 from http://www.ccsso.org/chief_state_school_officers/method_of_selection/index.cfm

Craig, W., Pepler, D., & Atlas, R. (2000). Observations of bullying in the playground and in the classroom. *School Psychology International, 21,* 22–36.

Cremin, L. (1970). *American education: The colonial experience, 1607–1783.* New York: Harper & Row.

Crick, N., & Grotpeter, J. (1995). Relational aggression, gender, and social-psychological adjustment. *Child Development, 66,* 710–722.

Croasmun, J., Hampton, D., & Herrmann, S. (1999). *Teacher attrition: Is time running out?* Retrieved February 2004 from the University of North Carolina, Horizon Web site: http://horizon.unc.edu/projects/issues/papers/Hampton.asp

Cruickshank, D. (1985). Applying research on teacher clarity. *Journal of Teacher Education, 35,* 44–48.

Cruickshank, D. (1987). *Reflective teaching: The preparation of students of teaching.* Reston, VA: Association of Teacher Educators.

Cuban, L. (1984). *How teachers taught: Constancy and change in American classrooms: 1890–1980.* White Plains, NY: Longman.

Cuban, L. (1996). Curriculum stability and change. In P. Jackson (Ed.), *Handbook of research on curriculum* (pp. 216–247). New York: Macmillan.

Cuban, L. (1999). The technology puzzle. *Education Week, 19*(43), 47, 68.

Cunningham, W., & Cordeiro, P. (2000). *Education administration.* Boston: Allyn & Bacon.

Curry, L. (1990). A critique of research on learning styles. *Educational Leadership, 48*(2), 50–52, 54–56.

Curwin, R. (1992). *Rediscovering hope: Our greatest teaching strategy.* Bloomington, IN: National Education Service.

Curwin, R., & Mendler, A. (1988a). *Discipline with dignity.* Alexandria, VA: Association for Supervision and Curriculum Development.

Curwin, R., & Mendler, A. (1988b). Packaged discipline programs: Let the buyer beware. *Educational Leadership, 46*(2), 68–71.

Curwin, R., & Mendler, A. (1999). Zero tolerance for zero tolerance. *Phi Delta Kappan, 81,* 119–120.

Cypher, T., & Willower, D. (1984). The work behavior of secondary school teachers. *Journal of Research and Development in Education, 18,* 19–20.

Dai, D., Moon, S., & Feldhusen, J. (1998). Achievement motivation and gifted students: A social cognitive perspective. *Educational Psychologist, 33,* 45–63.

Darling-Hammond, L. (1996). *What matters most: Teaching for America's future.* Washington, DC: National Commission on Teaching and America's Future.

Darling-Hammond, L. (1997). *The right to learn.* San Francisco: Jossey-Bass.

Darling-Hammond, L. (2000). How teacher education matters. *Journal of Teacher Education, 51,* 166–173.

Darling-Hammond, L. (2001). The challenge of staffing our schools. *Educational Leadership, 58*(8), 12–17.

Darling-Hammond, L. (2003). Keeping good teachers. *Educational Leadership, 60*(8), 7–13.

Darling-Hammond, L., Berry, B., Haselkorn, D., & Fideler, E. (1999). Teacher recruitment, selection, and induction: Policy influences on the supply and quality of teachers. In L. Darling-Hammond & G. Sykes (Eds.), *Teaching as the learning profession: Handbook of policy and practice.* San Francisco: Jossey-Bass.

Darling-Hammond, L., Berry, B., & Thoreson, A. (2001). Does teacher certification matter? Evaluating the evidence. *Educational Evaluation and Policy Analysis, 23,* 57–77.

Darling-Hammond, L., Chung, R., & Frelow, F. (2002). Variation in teacher preparation: How well do different pathways prepare teachers to teach? *Journal of Teacher Education, 53,* 286–302.

Darling-Hammond, L., & Sclan, E. (1996). Who teachers are and why: Dilemmas of building a profession for twenty-first century schools. In J. Sikula (Ed.), *Handbook of research on teacher education* (2nd ed., pp. 67–101). New York: Macmillan.

Datnow, A., Hubbard, L., & Conchas, G. (2001). How context mediates policy: The implementation of single gender public schooling in California. *Teachers College Record, 103,* 184–206.

Davenport, E., Davison, M., Kuang, H., Ding, S., Kim, S., & Kwak, N. (1998). High school mathematics course-taking by gender and ethnicity. *American Educational Research Journal, 35,* 497–514.

Davis, G., & Rimm, S. (1998). *Education of the gifted and talented* (4th ed.). Upper Saddle River, NJ: Prentice Hall.

Davis, M. (2003). Title IX panel deadlocks on critical change. *Education Week, 22*(21), 24–25.

Dawson, P. (1999). A primer on student grade retention: What the research says. *Communiqué, 26,* 28–30.

Delaware Department of Education. (1996). *The Delaware professional teaching standards.* Dover, DE: Author.

Delgado-Gaitan, C. (1992). School matters in the Mexican American home: Socializing children to education. *American Educational Research Journal, 29,* 495–516.

deMarrais, K., & LeCompte, M. (1999). *The way schools work* (3rd ed.). New York: Longman.

DeMeulenaere, E. (2001, April). *Constructing reinventions: Black and Latino students negotiating the transformation of their academic identities and school performance.* Paper presented at the annual meeting of the American Educational Research Association, Seattle, WA.

Deneen, C. (2002, April). *Masculinities and complexities: Men who teach below the high school level.* Paper presented at the annual meeting of the American Educational Research Association, New Orleans, LA.

Dewey, J. (1902). *The child and the curriculum.* Chicago: University of Chicago Press.

Dewey, J. (1906). *Democracy and education.* New York: Macmillan.

Dewey, J. (1923). *The school and society.* Chicago: University of Chicago Press.

Dewey, J. (1938). *Experience and education.* New York: Macmillan.

Diamond, J. (1999). *Guns, germs and steel: The fates of human societies.* New York: Norton.

Dickinson, G., Holifield, M., Holifield, G., & Creer, D. (2000). Elementary magnet school students' interracial interaction choices. *Journal of Educational Research, 93,* 391–394.

Diem, R. (1996). Using social studies as the catalyst for curriculum integration: The experience of a secondary school. *Social Education, 60,* 95–98.

Dill, V., & Stafford-Johnson, D. (2002). A different road. *American School Board Journal, 189*(11), 44–46.

Dillon, D. (1989). Showing them that I want them to learn and that I care about who they are: A microethnography of the social organization of a secondary low-track English reading classroom. *American Educational Research Journal, 26,* 227–259.

Dochy, F., & McDowell, L. (1997). Introduction: Assessment as a tool for learning. *Studies in Educational Evaluation, 23,* 279–298.

Doe v. Renfrow, 635 F.2d 582 (7th Cir. 1980).

Dowling-Sendor, B. (1999). Struggling with set-asides. *American School Board Journal, 186*(4), 20, 22, 63.

Doyle, D. (1997). Education and character. *Phi Delta Kappan, 78,* 440–443.

Doyle, D. (1999). De facto national standards. *Education Week, 18*(42), 36, 56.

Doyle, W. (1986). Classroom organization and management. In M. Wittrock (Ed.), *Handbook of research on teaching* (3rd ed., pp. 392–431). New York: Macmillan.

Drajem, L. (2002, April). *Life stories: Successful White women teachers of ethnically and racially diverse students.* Paper presented at the annual meeting of the American Educational Research Association, New Orleans, LA.

Dulude-Lay, C. (2000). *The confounding effect of the dimensions of classroom life on the narratives of student teachers.* Unpublished manuscript, University of Utah, Salt Lake City.

Dunn, R., & Dunn, K. (1992a). *Teaching elementary students through their individual learning styles: Practical approaches for grades 3–6.* Boston: Allyn & Bacon.

Dunn, R., & Dunn, K. (1992b). *Teaching secondary students through their individual learning styles: Practical approaches for grades 7–12.* Boston: Allyn & Bacon.

Dworkin, R. (1998, October 23). Affirming affirmative action. *New York Times Review of Books,* pp. 91–102.

Easton, L. (2002). Lessons from learners. *Educational Leadership, 60*(1), 64–68.

Echevarria, J., & Graves, A. (2002). *Sheltered content instruction* (2nd ed.). Boston: Allyn & Bacon.

Economic Policy Institute. (2002). *Inequality at the starting gate: Social background differences in achievement as children begin school.* Washington, DC: Author.

Educational Excellence for All Children Act of 1999. (1999). *Education Week, 18*(39), 28–54.

Educational Testing Service. (1999). *Principles of Learning and Teaching test bulletin.* Princeton, NJ: Author.

Educational Testing Service. (2001). *Principles of Learning and Teaching study guide.* Princeton, NJ: Author.

Edwards, V. (2003). Techs answer to testing. *Education Week, 22*(35), 8, 10.

Edwards, V., & Chronister, G. (2000). Who should teach? The states decide. *Education Week, 19*(18), 8–9.

Egan, D. (1997, September 26). Critics claim history textbook is trying to "brainwash" kids. *Salt Lake Tribune,* pp. B1, B3.

Eggen, P. (1998, April). *A comparison of inner-city middle school teachers' classroom practices and their expressed beliefs about learning and effective instruction.* Paper presented at the annual meeting of the American Educational Research Association, San Diego, CA.

Eggen, P., & Kauchak, D. (2001). *Strategies for teachers* (4th ed.). Boston: Allyn & Bacon.

Eggen, P., & Kauchak, D. (2004). *Educational psychology: Windows on classrooms* (6th ed.). Upper Saddle River, NJ: Merrill/Prentice Hall.

Ehlenberger, K. (2001/2002). The right to search students. *Educational Leadership, 59*(4), 31–35.

Eisenberg, N., & Fabes, R. A. (1998). Prosocial development. In N. Eisenberg (Ed.), *Handbook of child psychology: Vol. 3. Social, emotional, and personality development* (5th ed., pp. 701–778). New York: Wiley.

Eisner, E. (1994). *The educational imagination: On the design and evaluation of school programs* (3rd ed.). New York: Macmillan.

Eisner, E. (2003). Questionable assumptions about schooling. *Phi Delta Kappan, 84,* 648–657.

Elam, S., & Rose, L. (1995). The 27th annual Phi Delta Kappa/Gallup Poll of the public's attitudes toward the public schools. *Phi Delta Kappan, 77,* 41–49.

Ellis, S., Dowdy, B., Graham, P., & Jones, R. (1992, April). *Parental support of planning skills in the context of homework and family demands.* Paper presented at the annual meeting of the American Educational Research Association, San Francisco.

Ellsworth, J. (2002). Using student portfolios to increase reflective practice among elementary teachers. *Journal of Teacher Education, 64,* 342–356.

Emmer, E., Evertson, C., & Worsham, M. (2003). *Classroom management for secondary teachers* (6th ed.). Boston: Allyn & Bacon.

Engle v. Vitale, 370 U.S. 421 (1962).

Epstein, J., Sanders, M., Simon, B., Salinas, K., Jansorn, N., & Van Voorhis, F. (2002). *School, family, and community partnerships: Your handbook for action.* Thousand Oaks, CA: Corwin Press.

Evertson, C., Emmer, E., & Worsham, M. (2003). *Classroom management for elementary teachers* (6th ed.). Boston: Allyn & Bacon.

Evertson, C., & Smithey, M. (2000). Mentoring effects on proteges' classroom practice: An experimental field study. *Journal of Educational Research, 93,* 294–304.

Fagen v. Summers, 498 P.2d 1227 (Wyo. 1972).

Fairchild, R. (2003, November). *What if summer learning loss were an education policy priority?* Paper presented at the Association for Public Policy Analysis and Management Research Conference, Washington, DC.

Falk, B. (2002). Standards-based reforms: Problems and possibilities. *Phi Delta Kappan, 60,* 612–617.

Federal Interagency Forum on Child and Family Statistics. (2001). *America's children: Key national indicators of well-being 2001.* Washington, DC: U.S. Government Printing Office.

Federation of Tax Administrators. (n.d.). *2002 State tax collection by source.* Retrieved February 2004 from http://www.taxadmin.org/fta/rate/02taxdis.html

Feiman-Nemser, S. (2001). From preparation to practice: Designing a continuum to strengthen and sustain teaching. *Teachers College Record, 103,* 1013–1055.

Feingold, A. (1995). Gender differences in personality: A meta-analysis. *Psychological Bulletin, 116,* 429–456.

Feldhusen, J. (1998). Programs and service at the elementary level. In J. VanTassel-Baska (Ed.), *Excellence in educating gifted and talented learners* (3rd ed., pp. 211–223). Denver, CO: Love.

Ferguson, J. (2002). Vouchers—an illusion of choice. *American School Board Journal, 189*(1), 42–45, 51.

Feuerstein, A. (2000). School characteristics and parent involvement: Influences on participation in children's schools. *Journal of Educational Research, 94,* 29–41.

Fideler, E., & Haselkorn, D. (1999). *Learning the ropes: Urban teacher induction programs and practices in the United States.* Belmont, MA: Recruiting New Teachers.

Fine, L. (2002). Writing takes a digital turn for special-needs students. *Education Week, 21*(20), 8.

Finn, J. (2002). Small classes in American schools: Research, practice, and politics. *Phi Delta Kappan, 83,* 551–560.

Finn, K., Willert, H., & Marable, M. (2003). Substance use in schools. *Educational Leadership, 60*(6), 80–85.

First Amendment Center. (1999). *The Bible and public schools: A First Amendment guide.* Nashville, TN: Author. Retrieved February 2004 from http://www.freedomforum.org/publications/first/BibleAndPublicSchools/bibleguide_reprint.pdf

Fischer, L., Schimmel, D., & Kelly, C. (1999). *Teachers and the law* (5th ed.) New York: Longman.

Fischer, L., Schimmel, D., & Kelly, C. (2003). *Teachers and the law* (6th ed.). New York: Longman.

Fiske, E. (2001). *Learning in deed: The power of service-learning for American schools.* Battle Creek, MI: W. K. Kellogg Foundation.

Fiske, E., & Ladd, H. (2000). A distant laboratory. *Education Week, 19*(56), 38.

Flanagan, A., & Grissmer, D. (2002). The role of federal resources in closing the achievement gap. In J. Chubb & T. Loveless (Eds.), *Bridging the achievement gap* (pp. 199–226). Washington, DC: Brookings Institute Press.

Flanigan, R. (2003). A challenging year for schools. Education Vital Signs [Supplement]. *American School Board Journal, 190*(2), 21–25.

Fleischfresser v. Directors of School District No. 200, 15 F.3d 680 (7th Cir. 1994).

Florida Department of Education. (2002). *Knowledge base of the Florida Performance Measurement System.* Tallahassee, FL: Author.

Forcier, R. (1999). *The computer as an educational tool: Productivity and problem solving* (2nd ed.). Upper Saddle River, NJ: Merrill/Prentice Hall.

Foster, M. (1992). Sociolinguistics and the African-American community: Implications for literacy. *Theory into Practice, 31,* 303–311.

Frank, M., & Walker-Moffat, W. (2001, April). *Evaluation of urban after-school programs: Effective methodologies for a diverse and political environment.* Paper presented at the annual meeting of the American Educational Research Association, Seattle, WA.

Frankenberg, E., & Lee, C. (2003). *Charter schools and race: A lost opportunity for integrated education.* Retrieved February 2004 from Harvard University, Civil Rights Project Web site: http://www.civilrightsproject.harvard.edu/research/deseg/Charter_Schools03.pdf

Franklin, W. (1997, March). *African-American youth at promise.* Paper presented at the annual meeting of the American Educational Research Association, Chicago.

Freese, S. (1999, April). *The relationship between teacher caring and student engagement in academic high school classes.* Paper presented at the annual meeting of the American Educational Research Association, Montreal, Canada.

Freiberg, J. (1999). Consistency management and cooperative discipline. In J. Freiberg (Ed.), *Beyond behaviorism: Changing the classroom management paradigm* (pp. 75–97). Boston: Allyn & Bacon.

Furlan, C. (1999). States tackle Internet-filter rules for schools. *Education Week, 17*(43), 22, 28.

Furlan, C. (2000). Satellite broadcasts seek to enliven study of history. *Education Week, 19*(26), 8.

Furtado, L. (1997, November). *Interdisciplinary curriculum.* Paper presented at the annual meeting of the California Educational Research Association, Santa Barbara, CA.

Gall, M., Gall, J., & Borg, W. (2003). *Educational research: An introduction* (7th ed.). Boston: Allyn & Bacon.

Gallagher, H. A. (2002, April). *The relationship between measures of teacher quality and student achievement: The case of Vaughn Elementary.* Paper presented at the annual meeting of the American Educational Research Association, New Orleans, LA.

Galley, M. (1999). New school curriculum seeks to combat anti-gay bias. *Education Week, 19*(10), 6.

Galley, M. (2000a). Male preschool teachers face skepticism but earn acceptance. *Education Week, 19*(20), 1, 10.

Galley, M. (2000b). Report charts growth in special education. *Education Week, 19*(32), 35.

Galley, M. (2002). Bullying policies slow to reach schools. *Education Week, 22*(15), 1, 17.

Galley, M. (2003). Despite concerns, online elementary schools grow. *Education Week, 22*(16), 1, 12.

Gardner, H. (1983). *Frames of mind: The theory of multiple intelligences.* New York: Basic Books.

Gardner, H. (1999). The understanding pathway. *Educational Leadership, 57*(3), 12–17.

Gardner, H., & Hatch, T. (1989). Multiple intelligences go to school. *Educational Researcher, 18*(8), 4–10.

Gay, B. (1997). Educational equality for students of color. In J. Banks & C. Banks (Eds.), *Multicultural education: Issues and perspectives* (3rd ed., pp. 195–228). Boston: Allyn & Bacon.

Gaziel, H. (1997). Impact of school culture on effectiveness of secondary schools with disadvantaged students. *Journal of Educational Research, 90,* 310–318.

Gehring, J. (1999a). Displays entangle Ten Commandments, First Amendment. *Education Week, 19*(15), 7.

Gehring, J. (1999b). Groups endorse guidelines on using the Bible in instruction. *Education Week, 19*(12), 7.

Gehring, J. (2000a). Massachusetts teachers blast state tests in new TV ads. *Education Week, 20*(12), 1, 22.

Gehring, J. (2000b). Schools' Bible courses "taught wrong" report says. *Education Week, 19*(19), 10.

Gehring, J. (2002a). Benefit of Illinois credit misses needy, study says. *Education Week, 22*(8), 11.

Gehring, J. (2002b). Vouchers battles head to state capitols. *Education Week, 21*(42), 1, 24, 25.

Geiger, K. (1993). A safe haven for children. *Education Week, 12*(24), 15.

Gentry, C. (1995). Educational technology: A question of meaning. In G. Anglin (Ed.), *Instructional technology: Past, present, and future* (2nd ed., pp. 1–10). Englewood, CO: Libraries Unlimited.

Gewertz, C. (2000a). Levy to stay in N.Y.C., Ackerman quits D.C., *Education Week, 19*(37), 3.

Gewertz, C. (2000b). More districts add summer coursework. *Education Week, 19*(30), 1, 12.

Gewertz, C. (2000c). Wisconsin study finds benefits in classes of 15 or fewer students. *Education Week, 19*(31), 10.

Gewertz, C. (2002). Edison buffeted by probe, loss of contracts. *Education Week, 22*(1), 3.

Gewertz, C. (2003a). Study: No academic gains from vouchers for Black student. *Education Week, 22*(30), 13.

Gewertz, C. (2003b). Vallas calls for cuts to private companies. *Education Week, 22*(29), 3.

Gibsen, R. (1998, July 3). Growth, diversity alter face of religion in U.S. *Salt Lake Tribune,* pp. A1, A10.

Gibson, P. (1989). Gay male and lesbian youth suicide. In M. Feinleib (Ed.), *Report of the secretary's task force on youth suicide* (pp. 3–142). Washington, DC: U.S. Department of Health and Human Services.

Giebelhaus, C., & Bendixen-Noe, M. (2001, April). *Mentoring: Enhancing the professional development of beginning teachers.* Paper presented at the annual meeting of the American Educational Research Association, Seattle, WA.

Gilman, D., & Kiger, S. (2003). Should we try to keep class sizes small? *Educational Leadership, 60*(7), 80–85.

Ginsberg, M., & Murphy, D. (2002). How walkthroughs open doors. *Educational Leadership, 59*(8), 34–36.

Gladden, J. E. (2003). Where have all the reading groups gone? *Education Week, 22*(36), 33.

Gladney, L., & Greene, B. (1997, March). *Descriptions of motivation among African American high school students for their favorite and least favorite classes.* Paper presented at the annual meeting of the American Educational Research Association, Chicago.

Glaser, R., & Chi, M. (1988). Overview. In M. Chi, R. Glaser, & M. Farr (Eds.), *The nature of expertise* (pp. xv–xxviii). Hillsdale, NJ: Erlbaum.

Goddard, R., Hoy, W., & Hoy, A. (2000). Collective teacher efficacy: Its meaning, measure, and impact on student achievement. *American Educational Research Journal, 37,* 479–507.

Goldhaber, D. (1999). School choice: An examination of the empirical evidence on achievement, parental decision making and equity. *Educational Researcher, 28*(9), 16–25.

Goldhaber, D., & Hyde, E. (2002). What do we know (and need to know) about the impact of school choice reforms on disadvantaged students? *Harvard Educational Review, 72,* 157–173.

Goldstein, L. (2002). Election results boost special ed. vouchers. *Education Week, 22*(14), 21, 24.

Gollnick, D., & Chinn, P. (2002). *Multicultural education in a pluralistic society* (6th ed.). Upper Saddle River, NJ: Merrill/Prentice Hall.

Good, T., & Brophy, J. (1986). School effects. In M. Wittrock (Ed.), *Third handbook of research on teaching* (pp. 570–604). New York: Macmillan.

Good, T., & Brophy, J. (2003). *Looking in classrooms* (9th ed.). New York: HarperCollins.

Good, T., & Marshall, S. (1984). Do students learn more in heterogeneous or homogeneous groups? In P. Peterson, L. Wilkinson, & M. Hallinan (Eds.), *The social context of instruction: Group organization and group process* (pp. 15–38). San Diego, CA: Academic Press.

Goodenow, C. (1993). Classroom belonging among early adolescent students: Relationships to motivation and achievement. *Journal of Early Adolescence, 13,* 21–43.

Goodlad, J. (1984). *A place called school.* New York: McGraw-Hill.

Gordon, J. (1993). *Why did you select teaching as a career? Teachers of color tell their stories* (Tech. Rep. No. 143). Washington, DC: Western Washington University. (ERIC Document Reproduction Service No. ED363653)

Gorman, J., & Balter, L. (1997). Culturally sensitive parent education: A critical review of quantitative research. *Review of Educational Research, 67,* 339–369.

Gould, P. (2003). Scheduling choice: Is that all there is? *Education Week, 22*(34), 34–35.

Gracenin, D. (1993). On their own terms. *The Executive Educator, 15*(10), 31–34.

Grant, P., Richard, K., & Parkay, F. (1996, April). *Using video cases to promote reflection among preservice teachers: A qualitative inquiry.* Paper presented at the annual meeting of the American Educational Research Association, New York.

Greene, J. (2000). Why school choice can promote integration. *Education Week, 19*(31), 52, 72.

Greenfield, P. (1994). Independence and interdependence as developmental scripts: Implications for theory, research, and practice. In P. Greenfield, & R. Cocking (Eds.), *Cross-cultural roots of minority child development.* Hillsdale, NJ: Erlbaum.

Greenleaf, C. (1995, March). *You feel like you belong: Student perspectives on becoming a community of learners.* Paper presented at the annual meeting of the American Educational Research Association, San Francisco.

Greeno, J., Collins, A., & Resnick, L. (1996). Cognition and learning. In D. Berliner & R. Calfee (Eds.), *Handbook of Educational Psychology* (pp. 15–46). New York: Macmillan.

Gresham, A., Hess, F., Maranto, R., & Milliman, S. (2000). Desert bloom: Arizona's free market in education. *Phi Delta Kappan, 81,* 751–757.

Griffith, J. (2002). A multilevel analysis of the relation of school learning and social environments to minority achievement in public elementary schools. *The Elementary School Journal, 102,* 349–366.

Gross, M. (1999). *The conspiracy of ignorance: The failure of American public schools.* New York: HarperCollins.

Grove, K. (2002). The invisible role of the central office. *Educational Leadership,* 59(8), 45–47.

Gruhn, W., & Douglass, H. (1971). *The modern junior high school* (3rd ed.). New York: Ronald Press.

Grunbaum J., Kann, L., Kinchen, S., Williams, B., Ross, J., Lowry, R., & Kolbe, L. (2002). Youth risk behavior surveillance—United States, 2001. *MMWR, 51*(SS–4), 1–64.

Gunderson, L., & Siegel, L. (2001). The evils of the use of IQ tests to define learning disabilities in first- and second-language learners. *Reading Teacher, 55*(1), 48–55.

Gursky, D. (1999). Wired . . . but not plugged in? *American Teacher, 84*(2), 10, 19.

Gutiérrez, K., Asato, J., Pacheco, M., Moll, L., Olson, K., Horng, E., Ruiz, R., García, E., & McCarty, T. (2002). "Sounding American": The consequences of new reforms on English language learners. *Reading Research Quarterly, 37,* 328–343.

Gutiérrez, R. (2002). Beyond essentialism: The complexity in teaching mathematics to Latino students. *American Educational Research Journal, 39,* 1047–1088.

Haberman, M. (1995). *Star teachers of children of poverty.* West Lafayette, IN: Kappa Delta Pi.

Hale, E. (1998, February). Cyber gap costs women at work. *Gannett News Service* in *Salt Lake Tribune,* pp. A1, A4.

Hallahan, D., & Kauffman, J. (2003). *Exceptional learners: Introduction to special education* (9th ed.). Needham Heights, MA: Allyn & Bacon.

Hallinan, M. (1984). Summary and implications. In P. Peterson, L. Wilkinson, & M. Hallinan (Eds.), *The social context of instruction: Group organization and group processes* (pp. 229–240). San Diego, CA: Academic Press.

Halpern, D., & LaMay, M. (2000). The smarter sex: A critical review of sex differences in intelligence. *Educational Psychology Review, 12*(2), 229–245.

Hamm, J., & Coleman, H. (1997, March). *Adolescent strategies for coping with cultural diversity: Variability and youth outcomes.* Paper presented at the annual meeting of the American Educational Research Association, Chicago.

Hanushek, E. (1996). A more complete picture of school resource policies. *Review of Educational Research, 66,* 397–410.

Hardman, M., Drew, C., & Egan, W. (2002). *Human exceptionality* (7th ed.). Needham Heights, MA: Allyn & Bacon.

Hardy, L. (2002). A new federal role. *American School Board Journal, 189*(9), 20–24.

Harp, L. (1993). Advocates of year-round schooling shift focus to educational advantages. *Education Week, 12*(24), 1, 17.

Harris, D., & Eggen, P. (1993, April). *The impact of experience on conceptions of expertise: A comparison of the thinking of veteran, first-year, and preservice teachers.* Paper presented at the annual meeting of the American Educational Research Association, Atlanta, GA.

Harris, L., Kagay, M., & Ross, J. (1987). *The Metropolitan Life survey of the American teacher: Strengthening links between home and school.* New York: Louis Harris & Associates.

Harris, S., & Lowery, S. (2002). A view from the classroom. *Educational Leadership, 59*(8), 64–65.

Harry, B. (1992). An ethnographic study of cross-cultural communication with Puerto Rican American families in the special education system. *American Educational Research Journal, 29,* 471–488.

Hartnett, P., & Gelman, R. (1998). Early understandings of numbers: Paths or barriers to the construction of new understandings? *Learning and Instruction, 8,* 341–374.

Haschak, J. (1992). It happens in the huddle. In J. Lounsbury (Ed.), *Connecting the curriculum through interdisciplinary instruction.* Columbus, OH: National Middle School Association. (ERIC Document Reproduction Service No. ED362262)

Hauser, R. (1999). What if we ended social promotion? *Education Week, 18*(7), 37, 64.

Haycock, K. (1998). Good teaching matters . . . a lot. *Thinking K–16, 3*(2). Washington, DC: The Education Trust.

Hayes, J. (1996). A new framework for understanding cognition and affect in writing. In C. Levy & S. Ransdell (Eds.), *The science of writing* (pp. 1–28). Mahwah, NJ: Erlbaum.

Hazelwood School District v. Kuhlmeier, 484 U.S. 260 (1988).

Heath, S. (1982). Questioning at home and at school: A comparative study. In G. Spindler (Ed.), *Doing the ethnography of schooling*. New York: Holt, Rinehart & Winston.

Heath, S. (1989). Oral and literate traditions among Black Americans living in poverty. *American Psychologist, 44,* 367–373.

Hendrie, C. (1999). Harvard study finds increase in segregation. *Education Week, 18*(41), 6.

Hendrie, C. (2002a). New scrutiny for sponsors of charters. *Education Week, 22*(12), 1, 18.

Hendrie, C. (2002b). Number of charter schools up 14 percent, report says. *Education Week, 22*(5), 4.

Hendrie, C. (2003a). California charter-funding fight hits home. *Education Week, 22*(18), 18–19.

Hendrie, C. (2003b). States target sexual abuse by educators. *Education Week, 22*(33), 1, 16–18.

Herman, P. (1999). *An educator's guide to school-wide reform.* Washington, DC: American Institute for Research.

Herrnstein, R., & Murray, C. (1994). *The bell curve.* New York: Free Press.

Heward, W. (2003). *Exceptional children* (6th ed.). Upper Saddle River, NJ: Merrill/Prentice Hall.

Hiebert, E., & Raphael, T. (1996). Psychological perspectives on literacy and extensions to educational practice. In D. Berliner & R. Calfee (Eds.), *Handbook of educational psychology* (pp. 550–602). New York: Macmillan.

Hiebert, J., Gallimore, R., & Stigler, J. (2002). A knowledge base for the teaching profession: What would it look like and how can we get one? *Educational Researcher, 31*(5), 3–15.

Hillocks, G., Jr. (1999). *Ways of thinking, ways of teaching.* New York: Teachers College Press.

Hirsch, E. (1987). *Cultural literacy: What every American needs to know.* Boston: Houghton-Mifflin.

Hirsch, E. (Ed.). (1994). *What your third grader needs to know: Fundamentals of a good third-grade education.* New York: Delta.

Hirsch, E. (Ed.). (1995). *What your 6th grader needs to know: Fundamentals of a good sixth-grade education.* New York: Delta.

Hirsch, E. (1996). *The schools we need and why we don't have them.* New York: Doubleday.

Hirsch, E. (2000). The tests we need and why we don't quite have them. *Education Week, 19*(21), 40–41, 64.

Hirsch, E. (2001). Seeking breadth and depth in the curriculum. *Educational Leadership, 59*(2), 22–25.

Hodgkinson, H. (2001). Demographics of diversity. *Principal, 82*(2), 15–18.

Hodgkinson, H. (2002). Elementary schools must prepare for a large but uneven influx of children who defy racial and ethnic stereotyping. *Principal, 82*(2), 15–18.

Hoff, D. (1998). On Capital Hill, Congress picks up bilingual education debate. *Education Week, 17*(37), 20.

Hoff, D. (2000a). Conservative group seeks to end state NAEP program. *Education Week, 19*(29), 29.

Hoff, D. (2000b). Gap widens between Black and White students on NAEP. *Education Week, 20*(1), 6–7.

Hoff, D. (2000c). Massachusetts to put math teachers to the test. *Education Week, 19*(38), 16, 18.

Hoff, D. (2003a). Adding it all up. *Education Week, 22*(23), 28–31.

Hoff, D. (2003b). KERA: In midlife crisis or golden years? *Education Week, 23*(2), 18, 21.

Hoff, D. (2003c). Math education panel issues long-range plan for action. *Education Week, 22*(33), 11.

Hoff, D. (2003d). Science-lab safety upgraded after mishaps. *Education Week, 22*(33), 20–21.

Hoff, D. (2003e). Taped lessons offer insights into teaching. *Education Week, 22*(29), 1, 24.

Hoff, T. (2002). A fresh approach to sex education. *American School Board Journal, 189*(11), 60–61, 66.

Hoffman, M. (1998, June). Upstarts: Staking out a share of public school gold. *Inc.,* 25–27.

Holland, H. (1997). KERA: A tale of one teacher. *Phi Delta Kappan, 79,* 264–271.

Holloway, J. (2001). Grouping students for increased achievement. *Educational Leadership, 59*(3), 84–85.

Holloway, J. (2001/2002). Research Link: The dilemma of zero tolerance. *Educational Leadership, 59*(4), 84–85.

Holloway, J. (2002/2003). Research Link: Addressing the needs of homeless students. *Educational Leadership, 60*(4), 89–90.

Hoover-Dempsey, K., Bassler, O., & Burow, R. (1995). Parents' reported involvement in students' homework: Strategies and practices. *The Elementary School Journal, 95,* 435–449.

Hoover-Dempsey, K., & Sandler, H. (1997). Why do parents become involved in their children's education? *Review of Educational Research, 67,* 3–42.

Hunsader, P. (2002). Why boys fail—and what we can do about it. *Principal, 82*(2), 52–54.

Hussar, W., & Gerald, D. (2001). *Projections of educaton statistics to 2011.* Washington, DC: National Center for Education Statistics.

Hvitfeldt, C. (1986). Traditional culture, perceptual style, and learning: The classroom behavior of Hmong adults. *Adult Education Quarterly, 36*(2), 65–77.

Illig, D. (1996). *Reducing class size: A review of the literature and options for consideration.* Sacramento, CA: California Research Bureau.

Imbeau, M., & McGee, C. (2001, April). *Informing professional practice: A study of six first-year teachers.* Paper presented at the annual meeting of the American Educational Research Association, Seattle, WA.

Ingersoll, R. (1997). *The status of teaching as a profession: 1990–1991.* Washington DC: U.S. Department of Education.

Ingersoll, R., & Smith, T. (2003). The wrong solution to the teacher shortage. *Educational Leadership, 60*(8), 30–33.

Ingraham v. Wright, 430 U.S. 651 (1977).

Institute for Families in Society. (1997). *Program to combat bullying in schools.* Columbia: University of South Carolina.

International Society for Technology in Education. (2000). *National educational technology standards for students.* Eugene, OR: Author.

Interstate New Teacher Assessment and Support Consortium. (1993). *Model standards for beginning teacher licensing and development: A resource for state dialogues.* Washington, DC: Council of Chief State School Officers.

Jackson, P. (1968). *Life in classrooms.* New York: Holt, Rinehart & Winston.

Jackson, P. (1990). *Life in classrooms* (2nd ed.). New York: Teachers College Press.

Jacobsen, D. (2003). *Philosophy in classroom teaching: Bridging the gap* (2nd ed.). Upper Saddle River, NJ: Prentice Hall.

Jacobsen, D., Eggen, P., & Kauchak, D. (2002). *Methods for teaching* (6th ed.). Upper Saddle River, NJ: Merrill/Prentice Hall.

Jacobson, L. (1999). A kinder, gentler student body. *Education Week, 18*(42), 1, 22–23.

Jacobson, L. (2000). Huge middle school has big job in feeling smaller to its students. *Education Week, 19*(35), 1, 16–17.

Jacoby, R., & Glauberman, N. (Eds.). (1995). *The bell curve debate: History, documents, opinions.* New York: Random House.

Jamar, I. (1994). *Fall testing: Are some students differentially disadvantaged?* Pittsburgh, PA: University of Pittsburgh Learning Research and Development Center.

Jehng, J. (1997). The psycho-social processes and cognitive effects of peer-based collaborative interactions with computers. *Journal of Educational Computing Research, 17*(1), 19–46.

Jencks, C., & Phillips, M. (Eds.). (1998). *The Black–White test score gap.* Washington, DC: Brookings Institution Press.

Jennings, J. (2000). Title I—a success. *Education Week, 19*(20), 30.

Jennings, J. (2002). Knocking on your door. *American School Board Journal, 189*(9), 25–27.

Jennings, M. (2000). Attendance technology easing record-keeping burden. *Education Week, 19*(35), 7.

Jenson, W., Sloane, H., & Young, K. (1988). *Applied behavior analysis in education.* Upper Saddle River, NJ: Prentice Hall.

Jerald, C., & Orlofsky, G. (1999). Raising the bar on school technology. *Education Week, 19*(4), 58–62.

Jetton, T., & Alexander, P. (1997). Instructional importance: What teachers value and what students learn. *Reading Research Quarterly, 32,* 290–308.

Jimerson, S. (2001). Meta-analysis of grade retention research: Implications for practice in the 21st century. *School Psychology Review, 30,* 420–437.

Jimerson, S., Anderson, G., & Whipple, A. (2002). Winning the battle and losing the war: Examining the relation between grade retention and dropping out of high school. *Psychology in the Schools, 39,* 441–457.

Jimerson, S., Ferguson, P., Whipple, A., Anderson, G., & Dalton, M. (2002). Exploring the association between grade retention and dropout: A longitudinal study examining social-emotional, behavioral, and achievement characteristics of retained students. *The California School Psychologist, 7,* 51–62.

Johnson, B., & Christensen, L. (2000). *Educational research: Quantitative and qualitative approaches.* Boston: Allyn & Bacon.

Johnson, D., & Johnson, R. (1996). Cooperation and the use of technology. In D. Jonassen (Ed.), *Handbook of research for educational communications and technology* (pp. 1017–1042). New York: Macmillan.

Johnson, J., Livingston, M., Schartz, R., & Slate, J. (2000). What makes a good elementary school? A critical examination. *Journal of Educational Research, 93,* 399–349.

Johnson, L., Bachman, J., & O'Malley, P. (2001). *Monitoring the future: Questionnaire responses from the nation's high school seniors, 1997.* Ann Arbor, MI: Institute for Social Research.

Johnson, S., & Birkeland, S. (2002, April). *Pursuing a "sense of success": New teachers explain their career decisions.* Paper presented at the annual meeting of the American Educational Research Association, New Orleans, LA.

Johnson, S., & Birkeland, S. (2003). The schools that teachers choose. *Educational Leadership, 60*(8), 20–24.

Johnson, V. (1994, Winter). Parent centers send clear message. *Equity and Choice,* 42–44.

Johnston, R. (1994). Policy details who paddles students and with what. *Education Week, 14*(11), 17–18.

Johnston, R. (1998). Report finds no easy solution for disparities in school funding. *Education Week, 17*(41), 16.

Johnston, R. (2000a). As the U.S. Hispanic population soars, raising performance becomes vital. *Education Week, 19*(27), 18–19.

Johnston, R. (2000b). Bumper summer school crop yields mixed test results. *Education Week, 20*(1), 10.

Johnston, R. (2000c). Dallas names former state chief as superintendent. *Education Week, 20*(7), 3.

Johnston, R. (2000d). Federal data highlight disparities in discipline. *Education Week, 19*(41), 3.

Johnston, R. (2000e). N.C. district to integrate by income. *Education Week, 19*(3), 1, 19.

Johnston, R., & Viadero, D. (2000). Unmet promise: Raising minority achievement. *Education Week, 19*(27), 1, 18–23.

Jordan, W. (2001, April). *At-risk students during the first year of high school: Navigating treacherous waters.* Paper presented at the annual meeting of the American Educational Research Association, Seattle, WA.

Jordan, W., & Brooks, W. (2000). *Mending the safety net: A preliminary analysis of the twilight school.* Paper presented at the annual meeting of the American Educational Research Association, New Orleans, LA.

Julyan, C. (1989). National Geographic Kids Network: Real science in the elementary classroom. *Classroom Computer Learning, 10*(2), 30–41.

Kaestle, C. (1983). *Pillars of the republic: Common schools and American society, 1780–1860.* New York: Hill & Wang.

Kagan, D. (1992). Implications of research on teacher beliefs. *Educational Psychologist, 27,* 65–90.

Kahlenberg, R. (1999). Economic school desegregation. *Education Week, 18(29),* 31, 52.

Kahlenberg, R. (2000). *Economic school integration* (IDEA Brief No. 2). Washington, DC: The Century Foundation.

Kahlenberg, R. (2002). Beyond *Brown*: The new wave of desegregation litigation. *Educational Leadership, 59*(4), 13–19.

Kahne, J., & Westheimer, J. (1996). In the service of what? The politics of service learning. *Phi Delta Kappan, 77,* 593–599.

Kamerman, S., & Kahn, A. (1995). *Starting right.* New York: Oxford University Press.

Kann, L., Warren, W., Collins, J., Ross, J., Collins, B., & Kalbe, L. (1993). Results from the national school-based 1991 Youth Risk Behavior Survey and progress toward achieving related health objectives for the nation. *Public Health Reports, 108*(Suppl. 1), 47–55.

Karweit, N. (1989). Time and learning: A review. In R. Slavin (Ed.), *School and classroom organization.* Hillsdale, NJ: Erlbaum.

Kauchak, D., & Burbank, M. (2000). *Case studies of minority teacher development.* Paper presented at the annual meeting of the American Educational Research Association, New Orleans, LA.

Kaufman, P., Alt, M., & Chapman, C. (2001). *Dropout rates in the United States: 2000.* Washington, DC: National Center for Education Statistics. Retrieved February 2004 from http://nces.ed.gov/pubs2002/droppub_2001

Kaufman, P., Chen, X., Choy, S., Chandler, K., Chapman, C., Rand, M., & Ringel, C. (1999). Indicators of school crime and safety, 1998. *Educational Statistics Quarterly, 1*(1), 42–45.

Kedar-Voivodas, G. (1983). The impact of elementary children's school roles and sex roles on teacher attitudes: An interactional analysis. *Review of Educational Research, 20,* 417.

Keller, B. (2002). Report urges experimentation with teacher-pay schemes. *Education Week, 21*(39), 11.

Keller, B. (2003). Hiring headway. *Education Week, 22*(17), 43–44.

Keller, B., & Coles, A. (1999). Kansas evolution controversy gives rise to national debate. *Education Week, 19*(1), 1, 24–25.

Kellogg, R. (1994). *The psychology of writing.* New York: Oxford Press.

Kellough, R. (1999). *Surviving your first year of teaching: Guidelines for success.* Upper Saddle River, NJ: Merrill/Prentice Hall.

Kelly, E. (1998). *Legal basics: A handbook for educators.* Bloomington, IN: Phi Delta Kappan.

Kent, M., Pollard, K., Haaga, J., & Mather, M. (2001). *First glimpse from the 2000 U.S. Census.* Retrieved February 2004 from http://www.prb.org/AmeriStatTemplate.cfm

Kerman, S. (1979). Teacher expectations and student achievement. *Phi Delta Kappan, 60,* 716–718.

Kerr, M. (2000). Bullying: The hidden threat to a safe school. *Utah Special Educator, 21*(3), 9–10.

Kher-Durlabhji, N., Lacina-Gifford, L., Jackson, L., Guillory, R., & Yandell, S. (1997, March). *Preservice teachers' knowledge of effective classroom management strategies.* Paper presented at the annual meeting of the American Educational Research Association, Chicago.

Kilbane, C., & Milman, N. (2003). *The digital teaching portfolio handbook: A how-to guide for educators.* Boston: Allyn & Bacon.

King-Sears, M. (1997). Disability: Legalities and labels. In D. Bradley, M. King-Sears, & D. Tessier-Switlick (Eds.), *Inclusive settings: From theory to practice* (pp. 21–55). Boston: Allyn & Bacon.

Kirst, M. (1995). Recent research on intergovernmental relations in education policy. *Educational Researcher, 24*(9), 18–22.

Kleiman, C. (2001, October 30). Internet helps parents keep an eye on kids [Electronic version]. *Chicago Tribune.* Available from http://www.chicagotribune.com

Kochenberger-Stroeher, S. (1994). Sixteen kindergartners' gender-related views of careers. *The Elementary School Journal, 95,* 95–103.

Kogan, N. (1994). Cognitive styles. In R. Sternberg (Ed.), *Encyclopedia of human intelligence.* New York: Macmillan.

Kohn, A. (1997). How not to teach values. *Phi Delta Kappan, 78,* 429–439.

Kohn, A. (1999). Direct drilling. *Education Week, 18*(30), 43.

Kohn, A. (2000). Burnt at the high stakes. *Journal of Teacher Education, 51,* 315–327.

Konstantopoulos, S. (1997, March). *Hispanic–White differences in central tendency and proportions of high- and low-scoring individuals.* Paper presented at the annual meeting of the American Educational Research Association, Chicago.

Kounin, J. (1970). *Discipline and group management in classrooms.* New York: Holt, Rinehart & Winston.

Kozol, J. (1991). *Savage inequalities.* New York: Crown.

Kramer, L., & Colvin, C. (1991, April). *Rules, responsibilities, and respect: The school lives of marginal students.* Paper presented at the annual meeting of the American Educational Research Association, Chicago.

Kramer, R. (1991). *Ed school follies: The miseducation of America's teachers.* New York: Free Press.

Kramer-Schlosser, L. (1992). Teacher distance and student disengagement: School lives on the margin. *Journal of Teacher Education, 43,* 128–140.

Krashen, S. (1996). *Under attack: The case against bilingual education.* Culver City, CA: Language Education Associates.

Krueger, A., & Whitmore, D. (2002). Would smaller classes help close the Black–White achievement gap? In J. Chubb & T. Loveless (Eds.), *Bridging the achievement gap* (pp. 11–46). Washington, DC: Brookings Institute Press.

Kuh, D., & Vesper, N. (1999, April). *Do computers enhance or detract from student learning?* Paper presented at the annual meeting of the American Educational Research Association, Montreal, Canada.

Kunen, J. (1996, April 29). The end of integration. *Time,* 39–45.

Labaree, D. (1992). Power, knowledge, and the rationalization of teaching: A genealogy of the movement to professionalize teaching. *Harvard Educational Review, 62,* 123–154.

Labaree, D. (1999). The chronic failure of curriculum reform. *Education Week, 18*(36), 42–44.

Laczko-Kerr, I., & Berliner, D. (2003). In harm's way: How undercertified teachers hurt their students. *Educational Leadership, 60*(8), 34–39.

Ladson-Billings, G. (1994). *The dreamkeepers: Successful teachers of African-American children.* San Francisco: Jossey-Bass.

Lambert, N., & McCombs, B. (Eds.). (1998). *How students learn: Reforming schools through learner-centered education.* Washington, DC: American Psychological Association.

LaMorte, M. (2002). *School law* (7th ed.). Boston: Allyn & Bacon.

Land, D. (2002). Local school boards under review: Their role and effectiveness in relation to students' academic achievement. *Review of Educational Research, 72,* 229–278.

Land, R. (1997). Moving up to complex assessment systems: Proceedings from the 1996 CRESST Conference. *Evaluation Comment, 7*(1), 1–21.

Landry, D., Kaeser, L., & Richards, C. (1999). Abstinence promotion and the provision of information about contraception in public school district sexuality education policies. *Family Planning Perspectives, 31,* 280–286.

Langdon, C. (1999, April). The fifth Phi Delta Kappan poll of teachers' attitudes toward the public schools. *Phi Delta Kappan.* Retrieved February 2004 from http://www.pdkintl.org/kappan/klan9904.htm

Lashley, C. (2001, April). *Performance-based licensure: Developing support systems for beginning teachers.* Paper presented at the annual meeting of the American Educational Research Association, Seattle, WA.

Lau v. Nichols, 414 U.S. 563 (1974).

Leach, P. (1995). *Children first.* New York: Viking.

Lee, V. (2000). Using hierarchical linear modeling to study social contexts: The case of school effects. *Educational Psychologist, 35,* 125–141.

Lee, V., & Smith, J. (1999). Social support and achievement for young adolescents in Chicago: The role of school academic press. *American Educational Research Journal, 36,* 907–946.

Lee v. Weismann, 112 S. Ct. 29649 (1992).

Lewis, R., & Doorlag, D. (1999). *Teaching special students in general education classrooms.* Upper Saddle River, NJ: Merrill/Prentice Hall.

Light, J. (2001). Rethinking the digital divide. *Harvard Educational Review, 71,* 709–733.

Lind, M. (1995). *The next American nation.* New York: Free Press.

Linn, R. (2000). Assessments and accountability. *Educational Researcher, 29,* 4–14.

Lipka, J. (with G. Mohatt and the Ciulistet Group). (1998). *Transforming the culture of schools: Yup'ik Eskimo examples.* Mahwah, NJ: Erlbaum.

Longstreet, W., & Shane, H. (1993). *Curriculum for a new millennium.* Boston: Allyn & Bacon

López, G., & Scribner, J. (1999, April). *Discourses of involvement: A critical review of parent involvement research.* Paper presented at the annual meeting of the American Educational Research Association, Montreal, Canada.

Lortie, D. (1975). *Schoolteacher: A sociological study.* Chicago: University of Chicago Press.

Lou, Y., Abrami, P., & Spence, J. (2000). Effects of within-class grouping on student achievement: An exploratory model. *Journal of Educational Research, 94,* 101–112.

Louis, B., Subotnik, R., Breland, P., & Lewis, M. (2000). Establishing criteria for high ability versus selective admission to gifted programs: Implications for policy and practice. *Educational Psychology Review, 12,* 295–314.

Louis Harris & Associates. (1993). *The Metropolitan Life survey of the American teacher, 1993.* New York: Metropolitan Life Insurance Company.

Louis Harris & Associates. (1996). *The Metropolitan Life survey of the American teacher, 1996: Students voice their opinions on: Violence, social tension, and equality among teens, Part I.* New York: Metropolitan Life Insurance Company.

Louis Harris & Associates. (1999). *The Metropolitan Life survey of the American teacher, 1999: Violence in America's public schools—five years later.* New York: Metropolitan Life Insurance Company.

Lumsdaine, A. A. (1964). Educational technology: Issues and problems. In P. C. Lange (Ed.), *Programmed instruction: The sixty-sixth yearbook of the National Society for the Study of Education.* Chicago: University of Chicago Press.

Lustick, D. (2002, April). *National Board certification as professional development: A study that identifies a framework and findings of teachers learning to manage complexity, uncertainty, and community.* Paper presented at the annual meeting of the American Educational Research Association, New Orleans, LA.

Lynn, R. (2003, June 9). State fears teacher flight. *Salt Lake Tribune*, pp. D1–D2.

Ma, L. (1999). *Knowing and teaching elementary mathematics: Teachers' understanding of fundamental mathematics in China and the United States.* Hillsdale, NJ: Erlbaum.

Ma, X. (2001). Bullying and being bullied: To what extent are bullies also victims? *American Educational Research Journal, 38,* 351–370.

MacArthur, C., Ferreti, R., Okolo, C., & Cavalier, A. (2001). Technology applications for students with literacy problems: A critical review. *The Elementary School Journal, 101,* 273–302.

Macionis, J. (2003). *Sociology* (7th ed.). Upper Saddle River, NJ: Prentice Hall.

MacIver, D., & Epstein, J. (1993). Middle grades research: Not yet mature, but no longer a child. *The Elementary School Journal, 93,* 519–533.

Mael, F. (1998). Single-sex and coeducational schooling: Relationships to socioemotional and academic development. *Review of Educational Research, 68,* 101–129.

Maeroff, G. (2003). The virtual school house. *Education Week, 22*(24), 28, 40.

Mailloux v. Kiley, 323 F. Supp. 1387 (D. Mass 1971), 448 F.2d 1242 (lst Cir. 1971).

Manning, M., & Baruth, L. (1995). *Students at risk.* Boston: Allyn & Bacon.

Manzo, K. (2000a). Algebra textbooks come up short in Project 2061 review. *Education Week, 19*(34), 5.

Manzo, K. (2000b). Book binds. *Education Week, 19*(17), 29–33.

Manzo, K. (2003a). History invading social studies turf in schools. *Education Week, 22*(19), 1, 12.

Manzo, K. (2003b). Panel calls for writing revolution in schools. *Education Week, 22*(33), 10.

Manzo, K. (2003c). Upcoming Ravitch book confronts school textbook "language police." *Education Week, 22*(26), 9.

Manzo, K. (2004). Reading programs bear similarities across the states. *Education Week, 23*(21), 1, 13.

Manzo, K., & Hoff, D. (2003). Federal influence over curriculum exhibits growth. *Education Week, 22*(21), 1, 10–11.

Margolis, J. (2004). A response to "The National Board Hoax." *Teachers College Record.* Retrieved February 2004 from http://www.tcrecord.org/Collection.asp?CollectionID=72

Margolis, J., & Fisher, A. (2003). *Unlocking the clubhouse: Women in computing.* Cambridge, MA: MIT Press.

Marks, J. (1995). *Human biodiversity: Genes, race, and history.* New York: Aldine de Gruyter.

Marshall, H. (1992). Seeing, redefining, and supporting student learning. In H. Marshall (Ed.), *Redefining student learning: Roots of educational change* (pp. 1–32). Norwood, NJ: Ablex.

Martin, D. (1999). *The portfolio planner: Making professional portfolios work for you.* Upper Saddle River, NJ: Merrill/Prentice Hall.

Martin, T., & Richardson, S. (2003). Making citizens out of students: We cannot build abroad what we don't sustain at home. *Education Week, 22*(34), 35, 48.

Marttunen, M., & Laurinen, L. (2001). Learning of argumentation skills in networked and face-to-face environments. *Instructional Science, 29,* 127–153.

Marx, S. (2001, April). *A first year teacher working with children of color: An investigation into the meaning of "Trial by fire."* Paper presented at the annual meeting of the American Educational Research Association, Seattle, WA.

Marzano, R. (2003). *What works in schools.* Alexandria, VA: Association for Supervision and Curriculum Development.

Marzano, R., Kendall, J., & Gaddy, B. (1999). Deciding on "essential knowledge." *Education Week, 18*(32), 49, 68.

Maslow, A. (1968). *Toward a psychology of being* (2nd ed.). New York: Van Nostrand.

Maslow, A. (1970). *Motivation and personality* (2nd ed.). New York: Harper & Row.

Mathews. J. (1999, March 24). A home run for home schooling. *Washington Post,* p. A11.

Mathis, W. (2003). No Child Left Behind: Costs and benefits. *Phi Delta Kappan, 84,* 679–686.

Mayer, R. (1998). Cognitive theory for education: What teachers need to know. In N. Lambert & B. McCombs (Eds.), *How students learn: Reforming schools through learner-centered education* (pp. 353–377). Washington, DC: American Psychological Association.

Mayer, R. (1999). *The promise of educational psychology: Volume I. Learning in the content areas.* Upper Saddle River, NJ: Merrill/Prentice Hall.

Mayer, R. (2002). *The promise of educational psychology: Volume II. Teaching for meaningful learning.* Upper Saddle River, NJ: Merrill/Prentice Hall.

Mayes, C., & Ferrin, S. (2001). Spiritually committed public school teachers: Their beliefs and practices concerning religious expression in the classroom. *Religion and Education, 28*(1), 75–94.

McAdams, R. (1994). Mark, yen, buck, pound: Money talks. *American School Board Journal, 181*(7), 35–36.

McAllister, G., & Irvine, J. (2002). The role of empathy in teaching culturally diverse students: A qualitative study of teachers' beliefs. *Journal of Teacher Education, 53,* 433–443.

McCabe, M., & Skinner, R. (2003). *Analyzing the tech effect. Education Week, 22*(35), 50–52.

McCaslin, M., & Good, T. (1992). Compliant cognition: The misalliance of management and instructional goals in current school reform. *Educational Researcher, 21*(3), 4–17.

McCaslin, M., & Good, T. (1996). The informal curriculum. In D. Berliner, & R. Calfee (Eds.), *Handbook of educational psychology* (pp. 622–670). New York: Macmillan.

McCombs, B. (1998). Integrating metacognition, affect, and motivation in improving teacher education. In N. Lambert & B. McCombs (Eds.), *How students learn: Reforming schools through learner-centered education* (pp. 379–408). Washington, DC: American Psychological Association.

McCoy, A., & Reynolds, A. (1999). Grade retention and school performance: An extended investigation. *Journal of School Psychology, 37,* 273–298.

McCutcheon, G. (1982). How do elementary school teachers plan? The nature of planning and influences on it. In W. Doyle & T. Good (Eds.), *Focus on teaching* (pp. 260–279). Chicago: University of Chicago Press.

McDermott, J. (1994). Buddhism. *Encarta* [CD-ROM]. Bellevue, WA: Microsoft.

McDevitt, T., & Ormrod, J. (2002). *Child development and education.* Upper Saddle River, NJ: Merrill/Prentice Hall.

McDougall, D., & Granby, C. (1996). How expectations of questioning method affects undergraduates' preparation for class. *Journal of Experimental Education, 65,* 43–54.

McIntosh, J. (1996). *U.S.A. suicide: 1994 official final data.* Washington, DC: American Association of Suicidology.

McIntyre, D., Byrd, D., & Foxx, S. (1996). Field and laboratory experiences. In T. Sikula, & E. Guyton (Eds.), *Handbook of research on teacher education* (2nd ed., pp. 171–192). New York: Macmillan.

McLoyd, V. (1998). Socioeconomic disadvantages and child development. *American Psychologist, 53,* 185–204.

McMillan, J. (2000). *Educational research: Fundamentals for the consumer* (3rd ed.). New York: Longman.

McNeal, R. (1997). High school extracurricular activities: Closed structures and stratified patterns of participation. *Journal of Educational Research, 91,* 183–190.

Means, B., & Knapp, M. (1991). Introduction: Rethinking teaching for disadvantaged students. In B. Means, C. Chelemer, & M. Knapp (Eds.), *Teaching advanced skills to at-risk students* (pp. 1–27). San Francisco: Jossey-Bass.

Mehrabian, A., & Ferris, S. (1967). Inference of attitude from nonverbal behavior in two channels. *Journal of Consulting Psychology, 31,* 248–252.

Meier, D. (2002). Standardization versus standards. *Phi Delta Kappan, 84,* 190–198.

Meikle, E. (2003). *Textbook-related legislation moves forward.* Oakland, CA: National Center for Science Education. Retrieved February 2004 from http://www.ncseweb.org/resources/news/2003/TX/228_textbookrelated_legislation_m_5_14_2003.asp

Melnick, S., & Pullin, D. (2000). Can you take dictation? Prescribing teacher quality through testing. *Journal of Teacher Education, 51,* 262–275.

Merrow, J. (2002). The failure of Head Start. *Education Week, 22*(4), 38, 52.

Metropolitan Life Insurance Company. (1995). *The American teacher 1984–1995: Old problems, new challenges.* New York: Louis Harris & Associates.

Meyer, H., & Stein, N. (2002, April). *School policies on sexual harassment in an era of zero tolerance.* Paper presented at the annual meeting of the American Educational Research Association, New Orleans, LA.

Mickelson, R., & Heath, D. (1999, April). *The effects of segregation and tracking on African American high school seniors' academic achievement, occupational aspirations, and interracial social networks in Charlotte, North Carolina.* Paper presented at the annual meeting of the American Educational Research Association, Montreal, Canada.

Miller, S., Leinhardt, G., & Zigmond, N. (1988). Influencing engagement through accommodation: An ethnographic study of at-risk students. *American Educational Research Journal, 25,* 465–487.

Mills, G. (2002, April). *Teaching and learning action research.* Paper presented at the annual meeting of the American Educational Research Association, New Orleans, LA.

Missouri Department of Elementary and Secondary Education. (1996). *The Show Me standards: Science.* Jefferson City, MO: Author. Retrieved February 2004 from http://www.dese.state.mo.us/standards/science.html

Moffatt, C., & Moffatt, T. (2000). *How to get a teaching job.* Boston: Allyn & Bacon.

Moles, O. (1992, April). *Parental contacts about classroom behavior problems.* Paper presented at the annual meeting of the American Educational Research Association, San Francisco.

Molnar, A., Percy, S., Smith, P., & Zahorik, J. (1998). *1997–98 results of the Student Achievement Guarantee in Education (SAGE) program.* Milwaukee: University of Wisconsin–Milwaukee.

Molnar, A., & Reeves, J. (2001). Buy me! Buy me! *Educational Leadership, 59*(2), 74–79.

Molnar, A., Zahorik, J., Smith, P., Halback, A., & Ehrle, K. (2002). Wisconsin's SAGE program and achievement through small classes. In J. Chubb & T. Loveless (Eds.), *Bridging the achievement gap* (pp. 91–108). Washington, DC: Brookings Institute Press.

Morine-Dershimer, G. (1985). *Talking, listening, and learning in elementary classrooms.* New York: Longman.

Morine-Dershimer, G., & Reeve, P. (1994). Prospective teachers' images of management. *Action in Teacher Education, 16*(1), 29–40.

Morris v. Douglas County School District No. 9, 403 P.2d 775 (Or. 1965).

Morrison, G. (1993). *Contemporary curriculum K–8.* Boston: Allyn & Bacon.

Morrison, G., Lowther, D., & DeMuelle, L. (1999). *Integrating computer technology into the classroom.* Upper Saddle River, NJ: Merrill/Prentice Hall.

Morrison v. State Board of Education, 461 P.2d 375 (Cal. 1969).

Mortenson, T. (2001, March). *The condition of access: What the enrollment numbers say.* Paper presented at the annual conference of the Coalition of State University Aid Administrators, St. Augustine, FL. Posted on the Postsecondary Education Opportunity Web site: http:// www.postsecondary.org/archives/reports/COSUAAAF31801.pdf

Morton, E. (1988). *To touch the wind: An introduction to Native American philosophy and beliefs.* Dubuque, IA: Kendall/Hunt.

Moskowitz, J., & Stephens, M. (1997). *From students of teaching to teachers of students: Teacher induction around the Pacific Rim.* Washington, DC: Palavin Research Institute.

Mozert v. Hawkins County Public Schools, 827 F.2d 1058 (6th Cir. 1987), cert. denied, 108 S. Ct. 1029 (1988).

Muffoletto, R. (1994). Technology and restructuring education: Constructing a context. *Educational Technology, 34*(2), 24–28.

Mulrine, A. (2002, May 27). Risky business. *U.S. News & World Report,* 42–49.

Muñoz, M., & Portes, P. (2002, April). *Voices from the field: The perceptions of teachers and principals on the class size reduction program in a large urban school district.* Paper presented at the annual meeting of the American Educational Research Association, New Orleans, LA.

Murnane, R., & Tyler, J. (2000). The increasing role of the GED in American education. *Education Week, 19*(34), 48, 64.

Murray, F. (1986, May). *Necessity: The developmental component in reasoning.* Paper presented at the 16th annual meeting, Jean Piaget Society, Philadelphia.

Murray, K. (1994). Copyright and the educator. *Phi Delta Kappan, 75,* 552–555.

National Association for Year-Round Education. (2000). *Twenty-seventh reference directory of year-round education programs for the 2000–2001 school year.* San Diego, CA: Author.

National Association of Elementary School Principals. (2002). What you might not know about vouchers. *Education Week, 22*(1), 10.

National Association of State Boards of Education. (2004). *State education governance at-a-glance.* Retrieved February 2004 from http://www.nasbe.org/Educational_Issues/Governance/Governance_chart.pdf

National Board for Professional Teaching Standards. (1995). *An invitation to National Board certification.* Detroit: Author.

National Campaign to Prevent Teen Pregnancy. (2003). *Teen pregnancy—so what?* Retrieved December 2003 from http://www.teenpregnancy.org/whycare/sowhat.asp

National Center for Education Information. (2000). *Alternative teacher certification: A state by state analysis.* Washington, DC: Author.

National Center for Education Statistics. (1996). *Digest of educational statistics.* Washington, DC: U.S. Department of Education.

National Center for Education Statistics. (1997a). *America's teachers: Profile of a profession, 1993–1994.* Washington, DC: U.S. Department of Education.

National Center for Education Statistics. (1997b). *Characteristics of American Indian and Alaska native education.* Washington, DC: U.S. Department of Education.

National Center for Education Statistics. (1998a). *Digest of education statistics.* Washington, DC: U.S. Department of Education.

National Center for Education Statistics. (1998b). *Projection of education statistics to 2008.* Washington, DC: U.S. Department of Education.

National Center for Education Statistics. (2000a). *The condition of education.* Washington, DC: U.S. Department of Education.

National Center for Education Statistics. (2000b). *Digest of education statistics.* Washington DC: U.S. Department of Education, Office of Educational Research and Improvement.

National Center for Education Statistics. (2001). *Digest of education statistics.* Washington, DC: U.S. Department of Education.

National Center for Education Statistics. (2002). *Digest of education statistics.* Washington, DC: U.S. Department of Education.

National Commission on Excellence in Education. (1983). *A nation at risk: The imperative for educational reform.* Washington, DC: U.S. Government Printing Office.

National Commission on Teaching and America's Future (NCTAF). (1996). *What matters most: Teaching and America's future.* Author.

National Council for the Social Studies. (1994). *Expectations of excellence: Curriculum standards for the social studies.* Washington, DC: Author.

National Council of Teachers of Mathematics. (1989). *Curriculum and evaluation standards for school mathematics.* Reston, VA: Author.

National Council of Teachers of Mathematics. (2000). *Principles and standards for school mathematics.* Reston, VA: Author.

National Education Association. (1993). *Status of the American public school teacher.* Washington DC: Author.

National Education Association. (1995). *Focus on Hispanics.* Washington, DC: Author.

National Education Association. (1996). *Rankings of the states, 1995.* Washington, DC: Author.

National Education Association. (1997). *Status of the American public school teacher, 1995–1996.* Washington, DC: Author. Retrieved February 2004 from http://www.nea.org/neatoday/9709/status.html

National Education Association. (2002). *School vouchers: The emerging track record.* Washington, DC: Author.

National Education Association. (2003). *Status of the American public school teacher, 2000–2001.* Washington, DC: Author. Retrieved February 2004 from http://www.nea.org/edstats/images/status.pdf

National Joint Committee on Learning Disabilities. (1994). Learning disabilities: Issues on definition. A position paper of the National Joint Committee in Learning Disabilities. In *Collective perspectives on issues affecting learning disability: Position papers and statements.* Austin, TX: Pro-Ed.

National Middle School Association. (1995). *This we believe: Developmentally responsive middle level schools.* Columbus, OH: Author.

National Parent Teacher Association. (1998). *National standards for parent/family involvement programs.* Chicago: Author.

National Research Council. (1996). *National science education standards.* Washington, DC: National Academy Press.

National School Boards Association. (2000). Education vital signs: Leadership. *American School Board Journal, 187*(2), 32–37.

National School Boards Foundation. (2000). *Safe and smart: Research for children's use of the Internet.* Alexandria, VA: Author.

National Service-Learning Clearing House. (2001). *Service learning is . . .* Retrieved February 2004 from http://www.servicelearning.org/article/archive/35

National Telecommunications and Information Administration. (1999). *Falling through the Net: Defining the digital divide.* Retrieved February 2004 from http://www.ntia.doc.gov/ntiahome/fttn99/contents.html

Neill, M. (2003). High stakes, high risk. *American School Board Journal, 190*(2), 18–21.

Neisler, O. (2000). How does teacher education need to change to meet the needs of America's schools at the start of the 21st century? *Journal of Teacher Education, 51,* 248–255.

Nelson, C. (1999, April). *Litigation and the politics of equity: Testing the school finance process over time and across states.* Paper presented at the annual meeting of the American Educational Research Association, Montreal, Canada.

New Jersey v. T.L.O., 105 S. Ct. 733 (1985).

Newby, T., Stepich, D., Lehman, J., & Russell, J. (2000). *Instructional technology and teaching and learning* (2nd ed.). Upper Saddle River, NJ: Merrill/Prentice Hall.

Nieto, S. (1996). *Affirming diversity* (2nd ed.). New York: Longman.

Noblit, G., Rogers, D., & McCadden, B. (1995). In the meantime: The possibilities of caring. *Phi Delta Kappan, 76,* 680–685.

No Child Left Behind Act of 2001. Public Law 107–110 (8 January 2002). Washington, DC: U.S. Government Printing Office.

Noddings, N. (1992). *The challenge to care in schools: An alternate approach.* New York: Teachers College Press.

Noddings, N. (1995). Teaching themes of care. *Phi Delta Kappan, 76,* 675–679.

Noddings, N. (1999, April). *Competence and caring as central to teacher education.* Paper presented at the annual meeting of the American Educational Research Association, Montreal, Canada.

Nord, W., & Haynes, C. (1998). *Taking religion seriously across the curriculum.* Alexandria, VA: Association for Supervision and Curriculum Development.

Nussbaum, E. (2002). How introverts versus extroverts approach small-group argumentative discussions. *The Elementary School Journal, 102,* 183–198.

Nyberg, K., McMillin, J., O'Neill-Rood, N., & Florence, J. (1997). Ethnic differences in academic retracking: A four-year longitudinal study. *Journal of Educational Research, 91,* 33–41.

Nye, B., Hedges, L., & Konstantopoulos, S. (2001). Are effects of small classes cumulative? Evidence from a Tennessee experiment. *Journal of Educational Research, 94,* 336–341.

Nystrand, M., & Gamoran, A. (1989, March). *Instructional discourse and student engagement.* Paper presented at the annual meeting of the American Educational Research Association, San Francisco.

Oakes, J. (1985). *Keeping track: How schools structure inequality.* New Haven, CT: Yale University Press.

Oakes, J. (1992). Can tracking research inform practice? *Educational Researcher, 21*(4), 12–21.

Oakes, J. (1995). Matchmaking: The dynamics of high school teaching decisions. *American Educational Research Journal, 32,* 3–33.

Obidah, J., & Teel, K. (2001). *Because of the kids: Facing racial and cultural differences in schools.* New York: Teachers College Press.

O'Brien, V., Kopola, M., & Martinez-Pons, M. (1999). Mathematics self-efficacy, ethnic identity, gender, and career interests related to mathematics and science. *Journal of Educational Research, 92,* 231–235.

Odden, A. (2003). Leveraging teacher pay. *Education Week, 22*(43), 64.

Odden, A., & Clune, W. (1998). School finance systems: Aging structures in need of renovation. *Educational Evaluation and Policy Analyses, 20,* 158–177.

Odden, A., Monk, D., Nakib, Y., & Picus, L. (1995). The story of the education dollar: No academy awards and no fiscal smoking guns. *Phi Delta Kappan, 77,* 161–168.

Ogbu, J. (1987). Variability in minority school performance: A problem in search of an explanation. *Anthropology and Education Quarterly, 18,* 312–334.

Ogbu, J. (1999). Beyond language: Ebonics, proper English, and identity in a Black-American speech community. *American Educational Research Journal, 36,* 147–184.

Ogbu, J., & Simons, H. (1998). Voluntary and involuntary minorities: A cultural-ecological theory of school performance with some implications for education. *Anthropology & Education Quarterly, 29*(2), 155–188.

Olson, L. (1999a). A closer look: What makes a good report card. *Education Week, 18*(17), 29.

Olson, L. (1999b). Report cards for schools. *Education Week, 18*(17), 28–36.

Olson, L. (1999c). Shining a spotlight on results. *Education Week, 18*(17), 8–10.

Olson, L. (2000a). Finding and keeping competent teachers. *Education Week, 19*(18), 12–18.

Olson, L. (2000b). Taking a different road to teaching. *Education Week, 19*(18), 35.

Olson, L. (2003a). The great divide. *Education Week, 22*(17), 9–20.

Olson, L. (2003b). Quantity of coursework uses since 1983. *Education Week, 22*(32), 1, 14–17.

Oregon Public Education Network. (2003). *Oregon content standards: English.* Albany, OR: Author. Retrieved February 2004 from http://www.openc.k12.or.us/standards/docs/Englis01.rtf

Orfield, G., Frankenberg, E., & Lee, C. (2002/2003). The resurgence of school segregation. *Educational Leadership, 60*(4), 16–21.

Ormrod, J. (2003). *Educational psychology: Developing learners* (4th ed). Upper Saddle River, NJ: Merrill/Prentice Hall.

Osborne, J. (1996). Beyond constructivism. *Science Education, 80,* 53–81.

Owston, R., & Wideman, H. (1997). Word processors and children's writing in a high-computer-access setting. *Journal of Research on Computing in Education, 30*(2), 202–217.

Ozmon, H., & Craver, S. (2003). *Philosophical foundations of education* (7th ed.). Upper Saddle River, NJ: Merrill/Prentice Hall.

Palmer, P. (1998). *The courage to teach. Exploring the inner landscape of a teacher's life.* San Francisco: Jossey-Bass.

Paris, S. (1998). Why learner-centered assessment is better than high-stakes testing. In N. Lambert & B. McCombs (Eds.), *How students learn: Reforming schools through learner-centered education* (pp. 189–209). Washington, DC: American Psychological Association.

Park, C. (1997, March). *A comparative study of learning style preferences: Asian-American and Anglo students in secondary schools.* Paper presented at the annual meeting of the American Educational Research Association, Chicago.

Park, J. (2003). Deciding factors. *Education Week, 22*(17), 17–18.

Parkay, F., & Hass, G. (2000). *Curriculum planning: A contemporary approach* (7th ed.). Boston: Allyn & Bacon.

Patterson, F. (2001/2002). Teaching religious intolerance. *Rethinking Schools, 16*(2), 6, 7.

Paxson, R. (2003). Don't know much about history—never did. *Phi Delta Kappan, 85,* 265–273.

Pea, R., Tinker, R., Linn, M., Means, B., Bransford, J., Roschelle, J., Hsi, S., Brophy, S., & Songer, N. (1999). Toward a learning technologies knowledge network. *Educational Technology Research & Development, 47*(2),19–38.

Pedulla, J., Abrams, L., Madaus, G., Russell, M., Ramos, M., & Miao, J. (2003). *Perceived effects of state-mandated testing programs on teaching and learning: Findings from a national survey of teachers.* Boston: Boston College.

People for the American Way. (1991). *Attacks on the Freedom to Learn 1990–1991 Report.* Washington, DC: Author.

Peregoy, S., & Boyle, O. (2001). *Reading, writing, and learning in ESL* (3rd ed.). New York: Longman.

Perkins, D. (1995). *Outsmarting IQ.* New York: Free Press.

Perry, R. (1985). Instructor expressiveness: Implications for improving teaching. In J. Donald & A. Sullivan (Eds.), *Using research to improve teaching* (pp. 35–49). San Francisco: Jossey-Bass.

Perry, R., Magnusson, J., Parsonson, K., & Dickens, W. (1986). Perceived control in the college classroom: Limitations in instructor expressiveness due to noncontingent feedback and lecture content. *Journal of Educational Psychology, 78,* 96–107.

Peterson, K. (2000). *Teacher evaluation: A comprehensive guide to new directions and practices* (2nd ed.). Thousand Oaks, CA: Corwin Press.

Peterson, P. (1988). Teachers' and students' cognitional knowledge for classroom teaching and learning. *Educational Researcher, 17,* 5–14.

Petrill, S., & Wilkerson, B. (2000). Intelligence and achievement: A behavioral genetic perspective. *Educational Psychology Review, 12*(2), 185–199.

Petroska, J., Lindle, J., & Pankratz, R. (2000). *Executive summary: 2000 Review of research on the Kentucky Education Reform Act.* Retrieved December 2003 from http://www.kier.org/2000Research.html

Pew Hispanic Foundation. (2003). *Latinos in higher education: Many enroll, too few graduate.* Retrieved February 2004 from http://www.pewhispanic.org/site/docs/pdf/latinosinhighereducation-sept5-02.pdf

Phillips, K. (1990). *The politics of rich and poor.* New York: Random House.

Piaget, J. (1952). *Origins of intelligence in children.* New York: International Universities Press.

Piaget, J. (1970). *The science of education and the psychology of the child.* New York: Orion Press.

Pickering v. Board of Education, 225 N.E.2d. 1 (Ill. 1967), 391 U.S. 563 (1968).

Pintrich, P., & Schunk, D. (2002). *Motivation in education: Theory, research, and applications* (2nd ed.). Upper Saddle River, NJ: Merrill/Prentice Hall.

Pittman, M., & Frykholm, J. (2002). *Turning points: Curriculum materials as catalysts for change.* Paper presented at the annual meeting of the American Educational Research Association, Seattle, WA.

Pogrow, S. (1996). Reforming the wannabe reformers: Why education reforms almost always end up making things worse. *Phi Delta Kappan, 77,* 656–663.

Popham, W. (2003). The seductive lure of data. *Educational Leadership, 60*(5), 48–51.

Porter, A. (2002). Measuring the content of instruction: Uses in research and practice. *Educational Researcher, 31*(7), 3–14.

Portner, J. (1993). Prevention efforts in junior high found not to curb drug use in high school. *Education Week, 12*(40), 9.

Portner, J. (1999a). Florida's four-pronged attack on teen smoking pays off. *Education Week, 18(*41), 70.

Portner, J. (1999b). Schools ratchet up the rules on student clothing, threats. *Education Week 18*(35), 6–7.

Portner, J. (2000a). Complex set of ills spur rising teen suicide rate. *Education Week, 19*(31), 1, 22, 31.

Portner, J. (2000b). Fearful teachers buy insurance against liability. *Education Week, 19*(20), 1, 18.

Portner, J. (2000c). Maryland study finds benefits in "integrated instruction" method. *Education Week, 19*(37), 10.

Powell, R., McLaughlin, H., Savage, T., & Zehm, S. (2001). *Classroom management: Perspectives on the social curriculum.* Upper Saddle River, NJ: Merrill/Prentice Hall.

Pratton, J., & Hales, L. (1986). The effects of active participation on student learning. *Journal of Educational Research, 79,* 210–215.

Prawat, R. (1998). Current self-regulation views of learning and motivation viewed through a Deweyan lens: The problems with dualism. *American Educational Research Journal, 35,* 199–224.

Probst, R., Anderson, R., Brinnin, J., Leggett, J., & Irvin, J. (1997). *Elements of literature: Second course.* Austin, TX: Holt, Rinehart & Winston.

Proefriedt, W. (1999). Sorry, John. I'm not who you thought I was. *Education Week, XIX*(15), 28, 30.

Provenzo, E., & Gotthoffer, D. (2000). *Quick guide to the Internet for education.* Needham Heights, MA: Allyn & Bacon.

Public Agenda. (1994). *First things first: What Americans expect from the public schools.* New York: Author.

Public Agenda. (2000a). *Just waiting to be asked? A fresh look at attitudes on public engagement.* Available from http://www.publicagenda.org/research/research_reports_details.cfm?list=23

Public Agenda. (2000b). *A sense of calling: Who teaches and why.* Available from http://www.publicagenda.org/research/research_reports_details.cfm?list=28

Public Agenda. (2002). *Sizing things up: What parents, teachers and students think about large and small high schools.* Available from http://www.publicagenda.org/research/research_reports_details.cfm?list=21

Pulliam, J., & Van Patten, J. (1995). *History of education in America* (6th ed.). Upper Saddle River, NJ: Merrill/Prentice Hall.

Pulliam, J., & Van Patten, J. (1999). *History of education in America* (7th ed.) Upper Saddle River, NJ: Merrill/Prentice Hall.

Purkey, S., & Smith, M. (1983). Effective schools: A review. *The Elementary School Journal, 83,* 427–452.

Putnam, R., Heaton, R., Prawat, R., & Remillard, J. (1992). Teaching mathematics for understanding: Discussing case studies of four fifth-grade teachers. *The Elementary School Journal, 93,* 213–228.

Quiocho, A., & Ulanoff, S. (2002, April). *Teacher research in preservice teacher education: Asking burning questions.* Paper presented at the annual meeting of the American Educational Research Association, New Orleans, LA.

Radd, T. (1998). Developing an inviting classroom climate through a comprehensive behavior-management plan. *Journal of Invitational Theory and Practice, 5,* 19–30.

Rafferty, Y. (1995). The legal rights and educational problems of homeless children and youth. *Educational Evaluation and Policy Analysis, 17,* 39–61.

Raskin, J. (2001/2002). Bringing the high court to high school. *Educational Leadership, 59*(4), 51–55.

Raths, J., & Lynman, F. (2003). Summative evaluation of student teachers. *Journal of Teacher Education, 54,* 206–216.

Ravitch, D. (1983). *The troubled crusade: American education, 1945–1980.* New York: Basic Books.

Ravitch, D. (1990, October 24). Multiculturalism, yes, particularism, no. *Chronicle of Higher Education,* A44.

Ravitch, D. (2000). *Left back: A century of failed school reforms.* New York: Simon & Schuster.

Ray, B. (2003). *Facts on homeschooling.* Retrieved February 2004 from http://www.nheri.org/modules.php?name=Content&pa=showpage&pid=21

Ray v. School District of DeSoto County, 666 F. Supp. 1524 (M.D. Fla. 1987).

Reckase, M. (1997, March). *Constructs assessed by portfolios: How do they differ from those assessed by other educational tests?* Paper presented at the annual meeting of the National Educational Research Association, Chicago.

Reeves, J. (2004, January 30). Riley proposal would eliminate tenure panel [Electronic version]. *The Decatur Daily News.*

Regents of the University of California v. Bakke, 438 U.S. 265 (1978).

Reich, R. (1995, February). Class anxieties. *Harper's,* 4–5.

Reich, R. (2002). The civic perils of home schooling. *Educational Leadership, 59*(7), 56–59.

Reinhard, B. (1997). Ohio Supreme Court will allow Cleveland voucher program to begin its second year. *Education Week, 16*(41), 9.

Reinhard, B. (1998). Milwaukee choice program returns to Wisconsin Supreme Court. *Education Week, 17*(26), 2.

Reynolds, M. (Ed.). (1989). *Knowledge base for the beginning teacher.* New York: Pergamon Press.

Rich, D. (1987). *Teachers and parents: An adult-to-adult approach.* Washington, DC: National Education Association.

Richard, A. (1999). Pay soars for school chiefs in big districts. *Education Week, 19*(10), 1, 13.

Richard, A. (2000a). L.A. board taps Romer for top job. *Education Week, 19*(40), 1, 12–13.

Richard, A. (2000b). Studies cite lack of diversity in top position. *Education Week, 19*(25), 3.

Richard, A. (2002a). Florida lawmakers pave way for smaller classes. *Education Week, 22*(39), 16, 20.

Richard, A. (2002b). Florida sees surge in use of vouchers. *Education Week, 22*(1), 1, 34, 35.

Richard, A. (2003). Colorado voucher measure appears certain. *Education Week, 22*(29), 24, 30.

Richardson, J. (1995). Critics target state teacher tenure laws. *Education Week, 15*(4), 315–327.

Richardson, V., & Placier, P. (2001). Teacher change. In V. Richardson (Ed.), *Handbook of research on teaching* (4th ed., pp. 905–950). Washington, DC: American Educational Research Association.

Riordan, C. (1999). The silent gender gap. *Education Week, 19*(12), 46, 49.

Riordan, C. (2004). *Equality and achievement: An introduction to the sociology of education* (2nd ed.). Upper Saddle River, NJ: Prentice Hall.

Robelen, E. (2000). L.A. set to retain 4th and 8th graders based on state exam. *Education Week, 19*(37), 24.

Robelen, E. (2003). Ed. Dept. gets 6.3 percent increase for 2003. *Education Week, 22*(23), 24, 26.

Robin, B. (1999). Internet use in today's schools. *ATE Newsletter, 33*(1), 6.

Robinson, G. (1990). Synthesis of research on the effects of class size. *Educational Leadership, 47,* 80–88, 90.

Roblyer, M. (2003). *Integrating educational technology into teaching* (3rd ed.). Upper Saddle River, NJ: Merrill/ Prentice Hall.

Rodgers, C. (2002). Seeing student learning: Teacher change and the role of reflection. *Harvard Educational Review, 72,* 230–253.

Rogers, C. (1967). Learning to be free. In C. Rogers & B. Stevens (Eds.), *The problem of being human.* Lafayette, CA: Real People Press.

Rogers, D. (1991, April). *Conceptions of caring in a fourth-grade classroom.* Paper presented at the annual meeting of the American Educational Research Association, Chicago.

Rose, L., & Gallup, A. (1998). The 30th annual Phi Delta Kappa/Gallup Poll of the public's attitudes toward the public schools. *Phi Delta Kappan, 80,* 41–56.

Rose, L., & Gallup, A. (1999). The 31st annual Phi Delta Kappa/Gallup Poll of the public's attitudes toward the public schools. *Phi Delta Kappan, 81,* 42–56.

Rose, L., & Gallup, A. (2000). The 32nd annual Phi Delta Kappa/Gallup Poll of the public's attitudes toward the public schools. *Phi Delta Kappan, 82,* 41–58.

Rose, L., & Gallup, A. (2002). The 34th annual Phi Delta Kappa/ Gallup Poll of the public's attitudes toward the public schools. *Phi Delta Kappan, 84,* 41–46, 51–56.

Rosenshine, B. (1997, March). *The case for explicit, teacher-led, cognitive strategy instruction.* Paper presented at the annual meeting of the American Educational Research Association, Chicago.

Ross, S., Smith, L., Loks, L., & McNelie, M. (1994). Math and reading instruction in tracked first-grade classes. *The Elementary School Journal, 95,* 105–118.

Roth, K. (1994). Second thoughts about interdisciplinary studies. *American Educator, 18,* 44–48.

Rothman, R. (1997). KERA: A tale of one school. *Phi Delta Kappan, 79,* 272–275.

Rothstein, R. (1998). What does education cost? *American School Board Journal, 85*(9), 30–33.

Rottier, K. (1995). If kids ruled the world: Icons. *Educational Leadership, 53*(2), 51–53.

Rowan, B. (1994). Comparing teachers' work with work in other occupations: Notes on the professional status of teaching. *Educational Researcher, 23*(6), 4–17, 21.

Rowe, M. (1986). Wait-time: Slowing down may be a way of speeding up. *Journal of Teacher Education, 37,* 43–50.

Rutherford, F., & Algren, A. (1990). *Science for all Americans.* New York: Oxford University Press.

Rutter, M., Maughan, B., Mortimore, P., Ouston, J., & Smith, A. (1979). *Fifteen thousand hours: Secondary schools and their effects on children.* Cambridge, MA: Harvard University Press.

Ryan, K. (1992). *The roller coaster year: Essays by and for beginning teachers.* New York: HarperCollins.

Ryan, R., & Deci, E. (1998, April). *Intrinsic and extrinsic motivations: Classic definitions and new directions.* Paper presented at the annual meeting of the American Educational Research Association, San Diego, CA.

Sabo, D., Miller, K., Farrell, M., Barnes, G., & Melnick, M. (1998). The women's sports foundation report: Sport and teen pregnancy. *Volleyball, 26*(3), 20–23.

Sack, J. (1999). Riley says it's time to rethink high schools. *Education Week, 19*(3), 20.

Sack, J. (2000). IDEA opens doors, fans controversies. *Education Week, 20*(13), 1, 22–27.

Sack, J. (2002a). California restores money for school bonuses tied to testing. *Education Week, 22*(1), 24.

Sack, J. (2002b). Tennessee eyes next step toward lottery. *Education Week, 22*(12), 15, 17.

Sadker, M., Sadker, D., & Klein, S. (1991). The issue of gender in elementary and secondary education. In G. Grant (Ed.), *Review of research in education* (Vol. 17, pp. 269–334). Washington, DC: American Educational Research Association.

Sadker, M., Sadker, D., & Long, L. (1997). Gender and educational equality. In J. Banks, & C. Banks (Eds.), *Multicultural education: Issues and perspectives* (3rd ed., pp. 131–149). Boston: Allyn & Bacon.

Sagor, R. (2000). *Guiding school improvement with action research.* Alexandria, VA: Association for Staff and Curriculum Development.

Sanders, M., & Jordan, W. (1997, March). *Breaking barriers to student success.* Paper presented at the annual meeting of the American Educational Research Association, Chicago.

Sandham, J. (2000). Home sweet school. *Education Week, 19*(20), 24–29.

Sarason, S. (1993). *You are thinking of teaching? Opportunities, problems, realities.* San Francisco: Jossey-Bass.

Sarason, S. (1997). *How schools might be governed and why.* New York: Teachers College Press.

Sato, N., & McLaughlin, M. (1992). Context matters: Teaching in Japan and in the United States. *Phi Delta Kappan, 73,* 359–366.

Sautter, R. (1995). Standing up to violence. *Phi Delta Kappan, 76*(5), K1–K12.

Schiff, M., Duyme, M., Dumaret, A., & Tomkiewicz, S. (1982). How much could we boost scholastic achievement and IQ scores? A direct answer from a French adoption agency. *Cognition, 12,* 165–192.

Schlesinger, A. (1992). *The disuniting of America: Reflections on a multicultural society.* New York: Norton.

Schlozman, S. (2002a). The shrink in the classroom: Fighting school violence. *Educational Leadership, 60*(2), 89–90.

Schlozman, S. (2002b). The shrink in the classroom: Why "just say no" isn't enough. *Educational Leadership, 59*(7), 87–89.

Schnaiberg, L. (1999a). Arizona looks to its neighbor in crafting plan to take to voters. *Education Week, 18*(38), 9.

Schnaiberg, L. (1999b). Calif.'s year on the bilingual battleground. *Education Week, 18*(38), 1, 9, 10.

Schnaiberg, L. (2000). Charter schools: Choice, diversity may be at odds. *Education Week, 19*(35), 1, 18–20.

Schoen, H., Fey, J., Hirsch, C., & Coxford, A. (1999). Issues and options in the math wars. *Phi Delta Kappan, 80,* 444–453.

Schon, D. (1983). *The reflective practitioner: How professionals think in action.* New York: Basic Books.

School Board of Nassau County, Florida v. Arline, 480 U.S. 273 (1987).

School leaders focus on standards and achievement. (1998). Education vital signs [Supplement]. *American School Board Journal, 185*(12), A1–A30.

Schramm, S. (1997). *Related webs of meaning between the disciplines: Perceptions of secondary students who experienced an integrated curriculum.* Paper presented at the annual meeting of the American Educational Research Association, Chicago.

Schunk, D. (2000). *Learning theories: An educational perspective.* Upper Saddle River, NJ: Merrill/Prentice Hall.

Sears, J. (1991). Helping students understand and accept sexual diversity. *Educational Leadership, 49*(1), 54–56.

Sears, J. (1993). Responding to the sexual diversity of faculty and students: Sexual praxis and the critically reflective administrator. In C. Capper (Ed.), *Educational administration in a pluralistic society.* Albany, NY: SUNY Press.

Sebring, P., & Bryk, A. (2000). School leadership and the bottom line in Chicago. *Phi Delta Kappan, 81,* 440–443.

Seels, B., & Richey, R. (1994). *Instructional technology: The definition and domains of the field.* Washington, DC: Association for Educational Communications and Technology.

Senftleber, R., & Eggen, P. (1999, April). *A comparison of achievement and attitudes in a three-year integrated versus traditional middle-school science program.* Paper presented at the annual meeting of the American Educational Research Association, Montreal, Canada.

Serafini, F. (2002). Possibilities and challenges: The National Board for Professional Teaching Standards. *Journal of Teacher Education, 53,* 316–327.

Sergiovanni, T., Burlingame, M., Coombs, F., & Thurstone, P. (1999). *Educational governance and administration* (4th ed.). Boston: Allyn & Bacon.

Serrano v. Priest (1), 96 Cal. Rptr. 601, 487 P.2d 1241 (Calif. 1971).

Sewall, G. (2000). History 2000: Why the older textbooks may be better than the new. *Education Week, 19*(38), 36, 52.

Sexuality Information and Education Council of the United States and Advocates for Youth. (1999). *SIECUS/Advocates for Youth Survey of America's Views on Sexuality Education.* Washington, DC: Author.

Shakeshaft, C., Mandel, L., Johnson, Y., Sawyer, J., Hergenrother, M., & Barber, E. (1997). Boys call me cow. *Educational Leadership, 55*(2), 22–25.

Shaunessy, E. (2003, Summer). State policies regarding gifted education. *Gifted Child Today Magazine.* Retrieved February 2004 from http://www.findarticles.com/cf_dls/m0HRV/3_26/106290404/p1/article.jhtml

Shay, S., & Gomez, J. (2002, April). *Privatization in education: A growth curve analysis of achievement.* Paper presented at the annual meeting of the American Educational Research Association, New Orleans, LA.

Shea, D., Lubinski, D., & Benbow, C. (2001). Importance of assessing spatial ability in intellectually talented young adolescents: A 20-year longitudinal study. *Journal of Educational Psychology, 93,* 604–614.

Shelley, A. (2003). Vanishing heritage. *Education Week, 22*(38), 24–29.

Shepard, L. (2001). The role of classroom assessment in teaching and learning. In V. Richardson (Ed.), *Handbook of research on learning* (4th ed., pp. 1066–1101). Washington, DC: American Educational Research Association.

Shepard, L., & Smith, M. (1990). Synthesis of research on grade retention. *Educational Leadership, 47*(8), 84–88.

Shields, P., & Shaver, D. (1990, April). *The mismatch between the school and home cultures of academically at-risk students.* Paper presented at the annual meeting of the American Educational Research Association, Boston.

Shuell, T. (1996). Teaching and learning in a classroom context. In D. Berliner & R. Calfee (Eds.), *Handbook of educational psychology* (pp. 726–764). New York: Macmillan.

Shulman, L. (1986). Those who understand: Knowledge growth in teaching. *Educational Researcher, 15*(2), 4–14.

Shumow, L., & Harris, W. (1998, April). *Teachers' thinking about home-school relations in low-income urban communities.* Paper presented at the annual meeting of the American Educational Research Association, San Diego, CA.

Simpson, C. (2001/2002). Copyright 101. *Educational Leadership, 59*(4), 36–38.

Sincero, P., & Woyshner, C. (2003). Writing women into the curriculum. *Social Education, 67,* 218–225.

Skiba, R., & Peterson, R. (1999). The dark side of zero tolerance. *Phi Delta Kappan, 80,* 372–376, 381–382.

Skinner, E., & Belmont, M. (1993). Motivation in the classroom: Reciprocal effects of teacher behavior and student engagement across the school year. *Journal of Educational Psychology, 85,* 571–581.

Slavin, R., & Karweit, N. (1982). *School organizational vs. developmental effects on attendance among young adolescents.* Paper presented at the annual meeting of the American Psychological Association, Washington, DC.

Slavin, R., Karweit, N., & Madden, N. (Eds.). (1989). *Effective programs for students at risk.* Needham Heights, MA: Allyn & Bacon.

Slavin, R., Madden, N., Dolan, L., Wasik, B., Ross, S., Smith, L., & Dianda, M. (1996). Success for All: A summary of research. *Journal of Education for Students Placed at Risk, 1*(1), 41–76.

Smith, L., & Cotten, M. (1980). Effect of lesson vagueness and discontinuity on student achievement and attitude. *Journal of Educational Psychology, 72,* 670–675.

Smith v. Board of School Commissioners of Mobile County, 827 F.2d 684 (llth Cir. 1987).

Snyder, S., Bushur, L., Hoeksema, P., Olson, M., Clark, S., & Snyder, J. (1991, April). *The effect of instructional clarity and concept structure on students' achievement and perception.* Paper presented at the annual meeting of the American Educational Research Association, Chicago.

Snyder, T. (2002). Trends in education. *Principal, 81*(1), 44–45.

Snyderman, M., & Rothman, S. (1987). Survey of expert opinion on intelligence and aptitude testing. *American Psychologist, 42,* 137–144.

Sokol-Katz, J., & Braddock, J. (2000). *Interscholastic sport participation and school engagement: Do they deter dropouts?* Paper presented at the annual meeting of the American Educational Research Association, New Orleans, LA.

Sommers, C. (2000). *The war against boys: How misguided feminism is harming our young men.* New York: Simon & Schuster.

Sorensen, S., Brewer, D., Carroll, S., & Bryton, E. (1993). *Increasing Hispanic participation in higher education: A desirable investment.* Santa Monica, CA: Rand.

Soulé, H. (2000). Dumping old computers. *Education Week, 29*(36), 37, 40.

Spiro, R., Feltovich, P., Jacobson, M., & Coulson, R. (1992). Knowledge representation, content specification, and the development of skill in situation-specific knowledge assembly: Some constructivist issues as they relate to cognitive flexibility theory and hypertext. In T. Duffy & D. Jonassen (Eds.), *Constructivism and the technology of instruction: A conversation* (pp. 121–127). Hillsdale, NJ: Erlbaum.

Spring, J. (2001). *The American school, 1642–2000* (5th ed.). Boston: McGraw-Hill.

Stabiner, K. (2003, January 12). Where girls aren't [Electronic version]. *New York Times.* Available from http://www.nytimes.com

Stamouli, E. (2002, April). *Job satisfaction of teachers: A comparative study in Europe (Greece, Germany and Switzerland).* Paper presented at the annual meeting of the American Educational Research Association, New Orleans, LA.

Stark, C., & Berliner, D. (1994, April). *An experimental study of the ability of novice and experienced teachers to comprehend classroom interaction.* Paper presented at the annual meeting of the American Educational Research Association, New Orleans, LA.

State of the states: The nation in numbers. (2003). Education vital signs [Supplement]. *American School Board Journal, 190*(2), 26–32.

Stefkovich, J., & O'Brien, G. (2001, April). *The courts, school governance, and students' rights: A meta-analysis of educators' knowledge of Fourth Amendment law.* Paper presented at the annual meeting of the American Educational Research Association, Seattle, WA.

Stein, M., & Carnine, D. (1999). Designing and delivering effective mathematics instruction. In R. Stevens (Ed.), *Teaching in American schools* (pp. 245–270). Upper Saddle River, NJ: Merrill/Prentice Hall.

Stein, N. (2000). Sexual harassment in an era of zero tolerance. *Wellesley Center for Research on Women, 22*(1), 18–23.

Stepp, L. (1996, January 4). Cliques or gangs? *Washington Post,* p. C5.

Sternberg, R. (1986). *Intelligence applied: Understanding and increasing your intellectual skills.* San Diego, CA: Harcourt Brace Jovanovich.

Stevens, J., & Parkes, P. (2001, April). *A multilevel analysis of teacher satisfaction and retention.* Paper presented at the annual meeting of the American Educational Research Association, Seattle, WA.

Stevenson, H., Lee, S., & Stigler, J. (1986). Mathematics achievement of Chinese, Japanese, and American children. *Science, 231,* 693–699.

Stevens-Smith, R., & Remley, S. (1994). Drugs, AIDS, and teens: Intervention and the school counselor. *The School Counselor, 41,* 180–183.

Stigler, J., Gonzales, P., Kawanaka, T., Knoll, T., & Serrano, A. (1999). *The TIMSS videotape classroom study: Methods and findings from an exploratory research project on eighth-grade mathematics instruction in Germany, Japan, and the United States* (NCES 990074). Washington, DC: U.S. Department of Education, National Center for Education Statistics.

Stipek, D. (2002). *Motivation to learn: Integrating theory and practice* (4th ed.). Boston: Allyn & Bacon.

Stoddart, T., Connell, M., Stofflett, R., & Peck, D. (1993). Reconstructing elementary teacher candidates' understanding of mathematics and science content. *Teaching and Teacher Education, 9,* 229–241.

Stodolsky, S. (1988). *The subject matters: Classroom activity in math and social studies.* Chicago: University of Chicago Press.

Stone v. Graham, 449 U.S. 39 (1981).

Streitmatter, J. (1997). An exploratory study of risk-taking and attitudes in a girls-only middle school math class. *The Elementary School Journal, 98,* 15–26.

Strong, J., & Hindman, J. (2003). Hiring the best teachers. *Educational Leadership, 60*(8), 48–52.

Strudler, N., McKinney, M., Jones, P., & Quinn, L. (1999). First year teachers' use of technology: Preparation, expectations and realities. *Journal of Technology and Teacher Education, 7*(2), 112–129.

Swain, J., McEwin, C., & Irvin, J. (1998). Responsive middle level sports programs. *Middle School Journal, 30*(2), 72–74.

Takaki, R. (1993). *A different mirror: A history of multicultural education.* Boston: Allyn & Bacon.

Taxman v. Board of Education of Township of Piscataway, 91 F.3d 1547 (3rd Cir. 1996).

Taylor, B., Pressley, M., & Pearson, P. (2002). Research-supported characteristics of teachers and schools that promote reading achievement. In B. Taylor & D. Pearson (Eds.), *Teaching reading: Effective schools, accomplished teachers* (pp. 361–374). Mahwah, NJ: Erlbaum.

Tharp, R. (1989). Psychocultural variables and constants: Effects on teaching and learning in schools. *American Psychologist, 44*(2), 349–359.

Thirunarayanan, M. O. (2004). National Board certification for teachers: A billion dollar hoax. *Teachers College Record.* Retrieved February 2004 from http://www.tcrecord.org/Collection.asp?CollectionID=72

Thompson, G. (2000). The real deal on bilingual education: Former language-minority students discuss effective and ineffective instructional practices. *Education Horizons, 78*(2), 80–90.

Thompson, G. (2002). African American teens discuss their elementary teachers. *Educational Horizons, 80*(3), 147–152.

Thornton, S. (2003). Silence on gays and lesbians in social studies curriculum. *Social Education, 67,* 226–230.

Time to Learn. (1996). *Year-round schools may not be the answer.* San Antonio, TX: Author.

Tinker v. Des Moines Community School District, 393 U.S. 503 (1969).

Tishman, S., Perkins, D., & Jay, E. (1995). *The thinking classroom: Learning and teaching in a culture of thinking.* Needham Heights, MA: Allyn & Bacon.

Tobin, K. (1987). Role of wait-time in higher cognitive level learning. *Review of Educational Research, 57,* 69–95.

Toch, T. (1998, April 27). The new education bazaar. *U.S. News & World Report,* 35–46.

Tollefson, N. (2000). Classroom applications of cognitive theories of motivation. *Educational Psychology Review, 12,* 63–84.

Tomlinson, C., & Callahan, C. (2001, April). *Deciding to teach them all: Middle school teachers learning to teach for academic diversity.* Paper presented at the annual meeting of the American Educational Research Association, Seattle, WA.

Toppin, R., & Levine, L. (1992). *"Stranger in their presence": Being and becoming a teacher of color.* Paper presented at the annual meeting of the American Educational Research Association, San Francisco.

Torney-Purta, J. (2001/2002). What adolescents know about citizenship and democracy. *Educational Leadership, 59*(4), 45–50.

Triandis, H. (1995). *Individualism and collectivism.* Boulder, CO: Westview Press.

Trotter, A. (1999a). Preparing teachers for the digital age. *Education Week, 19*(4), 37–43.

Trotter, A. (1999b). Technology and its continual rise and fall. *Education Week, 18*(36), 30–31.

Trotter, A. (2000). Home computer used primarily for learning, families say in survey. *Education Week, 19*(30), 6.

Trotter, A. (2001a). Army's new cyber-school opens doors for online learners. *Education Week, 20*(16), 6.

Trotter, A. (2001b). Channel One drops cash-incentive plan aimed at teachers. *Education Week, 21*(2), 17.

Trotter, A. (2001c). Handheld computing: New best tech tool or just a fad? *Education Week, 21*(4), 8.

Trotter, A. (2001d). New law directs schools to install filtering devices. *Education Week, 20*(16), 32.

Trotter, A. (2002a). Tech firms land privatization role. *Education Week, 22*(4), 1, 11.

Trotter, A. (2002b). Too often, educators' online links lead to nowhere. *Education Week, 22*(14), 1, 15.

Trotter, A. (2003). Simulated driver's ed. takes virtual twists and turns. *Education Week, 22*(19), 8.

Tschannen-Moran, M., Woolfolk-Hoy, A., & Hoy, W. (1998). Teacher efficacy: Its meaning and measure. *Review of Educational Research, 68,* 202–248.

Tucker, M., & Codding, J. (1998). *Standards for our schools: How to set them, measure them and reach them.* San Francisco: Jossey-Bass.

Tuckman, B. (1998). Using tests as an incentive to motivate procrastinators to study. *Journal of Experimental Education, 66,* 141–147.

Turnbull, A., Shank, M., & Turnbull, R. (2002). *Exceptional lives: Special education in today's schools* (3rd ed.). Upper Saddle River, NJ: Merrill/Prentice Hall.

Tyack, P., & Cuban, L. (1995). *Tinkering toward Utopia.* Cambridge, MA: Harvard University Press.

Tyson, H. (1999). A load off the teachers' backs: Coordinated school health programs. *Phi Delta Kappan, 80*(5), K1–K8.

Ubben, G., Hughes, L., & Norris, C. (2001). *The principal* (4th ed.). Boston: Allyn & Bacon.

UCLA Center for Communication Policy. (2001). *Surveying the digital future: Year two.* Retrieved February 2004 from http://www.ccp.ucla.edu

U.S. Bureau of Census. (1990). *Statistical abstract of the United States* (110th ed.). Washington, DC: U.S. Government Printing Office.

U.S. Bureau of Census. (1996). *Statistical abstract of the United States* (116th ed.). Washington, DC: U.S. Government Printing Office.

U.S. Bureau of Census. (1997). *Poverty rate: Below the poverty line by race and ethnicity.* Washington, DC: Author.

U.S. Bureau of Census. (1998a). *Money, income in the United States: 1998* (Current Population Reports, P60–206). Washington, DC: U.S. Government Printing Office.

U.S. Bureau of Census. (1998b). *Statistical abstract of the United States* (118th ed.). Washington, DC: U.S. Department of Commerce.

U.S. Bureau of Census. (2000a). *Educational attainment in the United States: March 1999* (pp. 20–528). Washington, DC: U.S. Department of Commerce.

U.S. Bureau of Census. (2000b). *Statistical abstract of the United States* (120th ed.). Washington, DC: U.S. Government Printing Office.

U.S. Bureau of Census. (2002). *Poverty in the United States: 2000.* Washington, DC: U.S. Government Printing Office.

U.S. Bureau of Indian Affairs. (1974). Government schools for Indians (1881). In S. Cohen (Ed.), *Education in the United States: A documentary history* (Vol. 3, pp. 1734–1756). New York: Random House.

U.S. Department of Commerce. (1998). *Current population survey, 1997.* Washington, DC: U.S. Bureau of Census.

U.S. Department of Education. (1982). *Digest of education statistics.* Washington, DC: U.S. Government Printing Office.

U.S. Department of Education. (1993). *Schools and staffing survey, 1990–1991.* Washington, DC: National Center for Education Statistics.

U.S. Department of Education. (1995). *Digest of education statistics.* Washington, DC: U.S. Government Printing Office.

U.S. Department of Education. (1996a). *Digest of education statistics.* Washington, DC: U.S. Government Printing Office.

U.S. Department of Education. (1996b). *Youth indicators.* Washington, DC: National Center for Education Statistics.

U.S. Department of Education. (1998a). *Advanced telecommunications in U.S.: Public school survey.* Washington, DC: National Center for Education Statistics.

U.S. Department of Education. (1998b). *The baccalaureate and beyond.* Washington, DC: National Center for Education Statistics.

U.S. Department of Education. (1998c). *Indicators of school crime and safety.* Washington, DC: National Center for Education Statistics.

U.S. Department of Education. (1998d). *Promising practices: New ways to improve teacher quality.* Washington, DC: Author.

U.S. Department of Education. (1999a). *Digest of education statistics, 1998.* Washington, DC: U.S. Government Printing Office.

U.S. Department of Education. (1999b). *Statistics in brief: Revenues and expenditures for public elementary and secondary education: School year 1996–1997.* Washington, DC: National Center for Education Statistics.

U.S. Department of Education. (1999c). *Teachers' guide to religion in the public schools.* Washington, DC: Author.

U.S. Department of Education. (2000a). *Condition of education, 2000.* Washington, DC: U.S. Government Printing Office.

U.S. Department of Education. (2000b). *Digest of education statistics.* Washington, DC: Author.

U.S. Department of Education. (2000c). *Twenty-second annual report to Congress on the implementation of the Individuals with Disabilities Education Act.* Washington, DC: U.S. Government Printing Office.

U.S. Department of Education. (2001a). *Federal role in education.* Retrieved February 2004 from http://www.ed.gov/about/overview/fed/role.html?src=ln

U.S. Department of Education. (2001b). *The longitudinal evaluation of school change and performance (LESCP) in Title I schools: Final report.* Washington, DC: Author.

U.S. Department of Education. (2001c). *Schools and staffing survey, 1999–2000.* Washington DC: National Center for Education Statistics.

U.S. Department of Education. (2002a). *Education statistics quarterly, summer 2002.* Washington, DC: National Center for Education Statistics.

U.S. Department of Education. (2002b). *Twenty-fourth annual report to Congress on the implementation of the Individuals with Disabilities Education Act.* Washington, DC: U.S. Government Printing Office.

U.S. Department of Education. (2003). *Digest of education statistics, 2002.* Washington, DC: U.S. Government Printing Office.

U.S. Department of Health and Human Services. (1997). *Head Start program performance measures: Second progress report.* Washington, DC: Author.

U.S. Department of Health and Human Services. (1999). *Public health service centers for disease control and prevention (HIV/AIDS) surveillance report.* Washington, DC: U.S. Government Printing Office.

U.S. Department of Health and Human Services. (2003). *Child maltreatment 2001.* Washington, DC: U.S. Government Printing Office.

U.S. English, Inc. (2000). *States with official English laws.* Retrieved February 2004 from http://www.usenglish.org/inc/official/states.asp

U.S. Government Printing Office. (1975). *Historical statistics of the United States: Colonial times to 1970* (Vol. I). Washington, DC: Author.

U.S. Surgeon General. (2001, July 9). *U.S. Surgeon General's call to action to promote sexual health and responsible sexual behavior.* Retrieved February 2004 from http://www.surgeongeneral.gov/library/sexualhealth/call.htm

Vail, K. (2002). Same-sex schools. *American School Board Journal, 189*(11), 32–35.

Vallance, E. (1995). The public curriculum of orderly images. *Educational Researcher, 24,* 4–13.

van den Berg, R. (2002). Teachers' meanings regarding educational practice. *Review of Educational Research, 72,* 577–625.

Vander Ark, T. (2002). It's all about size. *American School Board Journal, 89*(20), 34–35.

Vander Ark, T. (2003). America's high school crisis: Policy reforms that will make a difference. *Education Week, 22*(29), 41, 52.

Vaugn, S., Bos, C., & Schumm, J. (2000). *Teaching exceptional, diverse, and at-risk students in the general education classroom.* Boston: Allyn & Bacon.

Vars, G. (1996). The effects of interdisciplinary curriculum and instruction. In P. Hlebowitsh & Wraga (Eds.), *Annual review of research for school leaders* (pp. 147–164). Reston, VA: National Association of Secondary School Principals.

Venezky, R. (1992). Textbooks in school and society. In P. Jackson (Ed.), *Handbook of research on curriculum* (pp. 436–464). New York: Macmillan.

Vergon, C. (2001). *The exclusion of students of color from elementary and secondary schools: A national dilemma and some research-based suggestions for its resolution.* Paper presented at the annual meeting of the American Educational Research Association, Seattle, WA.

Verstegen, D. (1994). The new wave of school finance litigation. *Phi Delta Kappan, 76,* 243–250.

Viadero, D. (1996). Middle school gains over 25 years chronicled. *Education Week 16*(8), 7.

Viadero, D. (1999a). Education Department is set to release its list of recommended math programs. *Education Week, 19*(6), 1, 14.

Viadero, D. (1999b). Study highlights benefits, shortcomings of magnet programs. *Education Week, 18*(39), 9.

Viadero, D. (1999c). Tennessee class-size study finds long-term benefits. *Education Week, 18*(34), 5.

Viadero, D. (2000a). High-stakes tests lead debate at researchers' gathering. *Education Week, 19*(34), 6.

Viadero, D. (2000b). Lags in minority achievement defy traditional explanations. *Education Week, 19*(28), 1, 18–19, 21.

Viadero, D. (2003a). Nice work: The growing research base for character education programs shows benefits for students' social—and academic—skills. *Education Week, 22*(33), 38–41.

Viadero, D. (2003b). R.I. district focuses on research-based "common language." *Education Week, 22*(29), 1, 20–21.

Viadero, D. (2003c). Staying power. *Education Week, 22*(39), 24–27.

Viadero, D. (2003d). Tormentors. *Education Week, 22*(18), 24–27.

Viadero, D. (2003e). Two studies highlight links between violence, bullying by students. *Education Week, 22*(36), 6.

Viadero, D., & Johnston, R. (2000). Lifting minority achievement: Complex answers. *Education Week, 19*(30), 1, 14–16.

Villegas, A. (1991). *Culturally responsive pedagogy for the 1990s and beyond.* Princeton, NJ: Educational Testing Service.

Vissing, Y., Schroepfer, D., & Bloise, F. (1994). Homeless students, heroic students. *Phi Delta Kappan, 75,* 535–539.

Voelkl, K., & Frone, M. (2000). Predictors of substance use at school among high school students. *Journal of Educational Psychology, 92,* 583–592.

Wadsworth, D. (2001). Why new teachers choose to teach. *Educational Leadership, 58*(8), 24–28.

Waggoner, D. (1995, November). Are current home speakers of non-English languages learning English? *Numbers and Needs, 5,* 1, 3.

Walberg, H. (2003). Accountability helps students at risk. *Education Week, 22*(33), 42, 44.

Walberg, H., & Niemiec, R. (1994). Is Chicago school reform working? *Phi Delta Kappan, 75,* 713–715.

Walsh, M. (1998a). Appeals court allows student-led graduation prayers. *Education Week, 17*(38), 7.

Walsh, M. (1998b). Green light for school vouchers? *Education Week, 18*(12), 1–19.

Walsh, M. (1998c). Judge defines church–state rules for Alabama. *Education Week, 17*(10), 1, 16.

Walsh, M. (1998d). Religious freedom amendment fails in house vote. *Education Week, 17*(39), 22.

Walsh, M. (1999). Appeals court tosses out ruling in Alabama religious-expression case. *Education Week, 18*(43), 1, 10.

Walsh, M. (2000a). Church–state rulings cut both ways. *Education Week, 19*(42), 1, 40–41.

Walsh, M. (2000b). Voucher initiatives defeated in Calif., Mich. *Education Week, 19*(11), 14, 18.

Walsh, M. (2002a). Admissions case could have impact on K–12 education. *Education Week, 20*(15), 1, 24.

Walsh, M. (2002b). Charting the new landscape of school choice. *Education Week, 21*(42), 1, 18–21.

Walsh, M. (2002c). Home school enrollment surge fuels "cottage" industry. *Education Week, 21*(39), 8.

Walsh, M. (2002d). Peer grading passes muster, justices agree. *Education Week, 21*(24), 1, 28, 29.

Walsh, M. (2003a). Justices give K–12 go-ahead to promote diversity. *Education Week, 22*(42), 1, 28, 30.

Walsh, M. (2003b). Private management of schools. *Education Week, 22*(29), 17.

Walsh, M. (2003c). Reports paint opposite pictures of Edison achievement. *Education Week, 22*(25), 5.

Walsh, M. (2003d). States say they're following prayer proviso. *Education Week, 22*(39), 21.

Wang, J., & Odell, S. (2002). Mentored learning to teach according to standards-based reform: A critical review. *Review of Educational Research, 72,* 481–546.

Wang, M., Haertel, G., & Walberg, H. (1993). Toward a knowledge base for school learning. *Review of Educational Research, 63,* 249–294.

Wang, M., Haertel, G., & Walberg, H. (1995, April). *Educational resilience: An emerging construct.* Paper presented at the annual meeting of the American Educational Research Association, San Francisco.

Washington, B. (1932). *Selected speeches of Booker T. Washington.* New York: Doubleday.

Wasserstein, P. (1995). What middle schoolers say about their schoolwork. *Educational Leadership, 53*(1), 41–43.

Watkins, W. (2001). *The White architects of Black education: Ideology and power in America, 1860–1954.*

Watson, B., & Konicek, R. (1990). Teaching for conceptual change: Confronting children's experience. *Phi Delta Kappan, 71,* 680–685.

Waxman, H., & Huang, S. (1996). Motivation and learning environment differences in inner-city middle school students. *Journal of Educational Research, 90,* 93–102.

Wayne, A., & Youngs, P. (2003). Teacher characteristics and student achievement gains: A review. *Review of Educational Research, 73,* 89–122.

Weaver, L., & Padron, Y. (1997, March). *Mainstream classroom teachers' observations of ESL teachers' instruction.* Paper presented at the annual meeting of the American Educational Research Association, Chicago.

Wechsler, D. (1991). The *Wechsler Intelligence Scale for Children–Third Edition (WISC–III).* San Antonio, TX: Psychological Corporation.

Weiner, L. (2002, April). *Why is classroom management so vexing to urban teachers? New directions in theory and research about classroom management in urban schools.* Paper presented at the annual meeting of the American Educational Research Association, New Orleans, LA.

Weinstein, C., Woolfolk, A., Dittmeier, L., & Shankar, U. (1994). Protector or prison guard? Using metaphors and media to explore student teachers' thinking about classroom management. *Action in Teacher Education, 16*(1), 41–54.

Weinstein, R. (1998). Promoting positive expectations in schooling. In N. Lambert & B. McCombs (Eds.), *How students learn: Reforming schools through learner-centered education* (pp. 81–111). Washington, DC: American Psychological Association.

Wenglinsky, Y. (1998). Finance equalization and within-school equity: The relationship between education spending and the social distribution of achievement. *Educational Evaluation and Policy Analyses, 20,* 269–283.

Wentzel, K. (1996). Social goals and social relationships as motivators of school adjustment. In J. Juvonen & K. Wentzel (Eds.), *Social motivation: Understanding children's school adjustment* (pp. 226–247). Cambridge, England: Cambridge University Press.

Wentzel, K. (1997). Student motivation in middle school: The role of perceived pedagogical caring. *Journal of Educational Psychology, 89,* 411–419.

West, E. (1972). *The Black American and education.* Columbus, OH: Merrill.

Whimbey, A. (1980). Students can learn to be better problem solvers. *Educational Leadership, 37,* 560–565.

White, K. (1999a). Girls' sports: "The best of times, the worst of times." *Education Week, 19*(7), 16–17.

White, K. (1999b). L.A. to ease requirements for promotion. *Education Week, 19*(16), 1, 17.

White, K., & Johnston, R. (1999). Summer school: Amid successes, concerns persist. *Education Week, 19*(3), 1, 8–9.

Wiersma, W. (2000). *Research methods in education: An introduction.* Needham Heights, MA: Allyn & Bacon.

Wiggins, G. (1996/1997). Practicing what we preach in designing authentic assessment. *Educational Leadership, 54*(4), 18–25.

Wildavsky, B. (1999, September 27). Achievement testing gets its day in court. *U.S. News & World Report,* 22–23.

Will KERA come to PA? (2003). *Education Advocate, 4*(3), 1–2. Retrieved February 2004 from http://www.ceopa.org/documents/Page1-4_001.pdf

Williams, A. (2002). Principals' salaries, 2001–2002. *Principal, 81*(5), 66–70.

Williams, J. (2003). Why great teachers stay. *Educational Leadership, 60*(8), 71–75.

Williams, S., Bareiss, R., & Reiser, B. (1996, April). *ASK Jasper: A multimedia publishing and performance support environment for design.* Paper presented at the annual meeting of the American Educational Research Association, New York.

Winograd, K. (1998). Rethinking theory after practice: Education professor as elementary teacher. *Journal of Teacher Education, 49,* 296–303.

Wolf, S., Borko, H., Elliott, R., & McIver, M. (2000). "That dog won't hunt": Exemplary school change efforts within the Kentucky reform. *American Educational Research Journal, 37,* 349–396.

Wong-Fillmore, L. (1992). When learning a second language means losing the first. *Education, 6*(2), 4–11.

Wong-Fillmore, L., & Meyer, L. (1996). The curriculum and linguistic minorities. In P. Jackson (Ed.), *Handbook of research on curriculum* (pp. 626–658). New York: Macmillan.

Wood, T., Cobb, P., & Yackel, E. (1992). Change in learning mathematics: Change in teaching mathematics. In H. Marshall (Ed.), *Redefining student learning: Roots of educational change* (pp. 177–205). Norwood, NJ: Ablex.

Woodward, T. (2002, June 20). *Edison's failing grade. Corporate Watch.* Retrieved February 2004 from http://www.corpwatch.org/issues/PID.jsp?articleid=2688

Woolfolk, A., & Hoy, W. (1990). Socialization of student teachers. *American Educational Research Journal, 27,* 279–300.

Worsnop, R. (1996). Year-round schools. *CQ Researcher, 6*(19), 433–456.

Worthen, B. (1993). Critical issues that will determine the future of alternative assessment. *Phi Delta Kappan, 74,* 444–454.

Wynne, E. (1997, March). *Moral education and character education: A comparison/contrast.* Paper presented at the annual meeting of the American Educational Research Association, Chicago.

Yatvin, J. (2003). I told you so! *Education Week, 22*(33), 44–45, 56.

Young, M., & Scribner, J. (1997, March). *The synergy of parental involvement and student engagement at the secondary level: relationships of consequence in Mexican-American communities.* Paper presented at the annual meeting of the American Educational Research Association, Chicago.

Zahorik, J. (1991). Teaching style and textbooks. *Teaching and Teacher Education, 7,* 185–196.

Zehr, M. (1999a). Moving teachers along a competency continuum. *Education Week, 19*(4), 41.

Zehr, M. (1999b). Texas exit exam under challenge in federal court. *Education Week, 19*(15), 1, 14–15.

Zehr, M. (2000a). Arizona curtails bilingual education. *Education Week, 20*(11), 1, 21.

Zehr, M. (2000b). Campaigns to curtail bilingual ed. advance in Colorado, Arizona. *Education Week, 19*(39), 19.

Zehr, M. (2000c). National standards on technology education released. *Education Week, 19*(31), 18.

Zehr, M. (2002a). Early bilingual programs found to boost test scores. *Education Week, 22*(1), 6.

Zehr, M. (2002b). Voters courted in two states on bilingual ed. *Education Week, 22*(2), 1, 22.

Zehr, M. (2003). No more vouchers for Florida Islamic school. *Education Week, 22*(43), 3.

Zeldin, A., & Pajares, F. (2000). Against the odds: Self-efficacy beliefs of women in mathematical, scientific, and technological careers. *American Educational Research Journal, 37,* 215–246.

Zhao, Y. (2002, August 5). Wave of pupils lacking English strains school [Electronic version]. *New York Times.* Available from http://www.nytimes.com

Zirkel, P. (1999). Urinalysis? *Phi Delta Kappan, 80,* 409–410.

Zirkel, P. (2001/2002). Decisions that have shaped U.S. education. *Educational Leadership, 59*(4), 6–12.

Zollars, N. (2000). Schools need rules when it comes to students with disabilities. *Education Week, 19*(25), 1, 46, 48.

Glossary

ability grouping The practice of placing students with similar aptitude and achievement histories together in an attempt to match instruction to the needs of different groups.

academic freedom The right of teachers to choose both content and teaching methods based on their professional judgment.

academy A type of secondary school developed during the 1700s that focused on the practical needs of colonial America as a growing nation. Math, navigation, astronomy, bookkeeping, logic, and rhetoric were all taught. Academies ultimately evolved into college-preparatory institutions.

acceleration An approach to gifted and talented education that keeps the curriculum the same but allows students to move through it more quickly.

accountability The process of requiring students to demonstrate that they have met specified standards or that they demonstrate understanding of the topics they study as measured by standardized tests, as well as holding educators at all levels responsible for students' performance.

action research A form of applied research designed to answer a specific school- or classroom-related question.

administrators Individuals responsible for the day-to-day operation of a school.

advanced placement classes Courses taken in high school that allow students to earn college credit.

affirmative action A collection of policies and procedures designed to overcome past racial, ethnic, gender, and disability discrimination.

alternating-day block schedule A type of secondary schedule in which classes are approximately 90–100 minutes long, students take a traditional number (5–6) of classes a semester, and classes meet every other day.

alternative assessments Assessments that directly measure student performance through "real-life" tasks.

assessment The process of gathering information and making conclusions about student learning.

assimilation A process of socializing people so that they adopt dominant social norms and patterns of behavior; an approach to multicultural education.

assistive technology Adaptive tools that support students with disabilities in their learning activities and daily life tasks.

autonomy The capacity to control one's own existence, identified as a basic need in people by researchers who study human motivation.

axiology A branch of philosophy that considers values and ethics.

behavior disorders Exceptionalities involving the display of serious and persistent age-inappropriate behaviors that result in social conflict, personal unhappiness, and school failure.

behaviorism A theory of learning that focuses on specific and observable behaviors and the factors that influence those behaviors.

between-class ability grouping A form of ability grouping that divides all students in a given grade into high, medium, and low groups with instruction adapted to the needs of each group.

block grants Federal monies provided to states and school districts with few restrictions for use.

block scheduling An alternate form of secondary scheduling that increases the length of classes, often doubling typical periods. Block scheduling aims to minimize disruptions caused by bells and transitions and to provide teachers with more flexibility and extended periods of time for instruction.

Buckley Amendment Another name for the Family Educational Rights and Privacy Act (FERPA), a federal act that makes school records open and accessible to parents.

bulletin board An electronic message center for a given topic that allows people to read the comments of others and leave their own messages.

caring A teacher's ability to empathize with and invest in the protection and development of young people.

categorical grants Federal monies targeted for specific groups and designated purposes.

censorship The practice of prohibiting the use of objectionable materials, such as certain books used in libraries or in academic classes.

certification Special recognition by a professional organization indicating that an individual has met certain requirements specified by the organization.

character education An approach to developing morality that suggests moral values and positive character traits, such as honesty and citizenship, should be emphasized, taught, and rewarded. Compare *moral education.*

charter schools Alternative schools that are independently operated but publicly funded and operated under a charter, or special contract.

chat room A site on the Internet where many people can simultaneously communicate in real time.

classroom management The process of creating and maintaining orderly classrooms.

classroom organization The set of teacher actions that maximizes the amount of time available for instruction.

common school movement A historical attempt in the 1800s to make education available to all children in the United States. The movement began with the goal of universal elementary education.

compensatory education programs Government attempts to create more equal educational opportunities for disadvantaged youth. For example, see *Head Start* and *Title I.*

comprehensive high school A secondary school that attempts to meet the needs of all students by housing them together and providing curricular options (such as vocational or college-preparatory programs) geared toward a variety of student ability levels and interests.

computer literacy A basic understanding of how to use computers.

cooperative learning A teaching strategy that consists of students working together in groups small enough so that everyone can participate in a clearly assigned task.

copyright laws Federal laws designed to protect the intellectual property of authors, which includes printed matter, videos, computer software, and various other types of original work.

creationism The theory that the universe was created by God as described in the Bible.

credentials file A collection of important documents teachers need to submit when they apply for teaching positions.

culturally responsive teaching Instruction that acknowledges and accommodates cultural diversity in classrooms.

culture The attitudes, values, customs, and behavior patterns that characterize a social group.

curriculum What teachers teach; also, the content, skills, values, and attitudes students learn in school.

database program A computer program that allows users to store, organize, and manipulate information, including both text and numerical data.

decision making Goal-oriented problem solving based on professional knowledge and the process of knowing when and why to implement different skills and strategies and how to adapt them when situations warrant.

development The physical changes in children as well as changes in the way they think and relate to their peers that result from maturation and experience.

developmental programs Educational programs designed to accommodate children's developmental differences by allowing children to acquire skills and abilities at their own pace through direct experiences.

discovery learning A teaching strategy in which the teacher identifies a content goal, arranges information so that patterns can be found, and guides students to the goal.

distance education A catch-all term used to describe organized instructional programs in which teachers and learners, though physically separated, are connected through technology.

early childhood education A catch-all term encompassing a range of educational programs for young children, including infant intervention and enrichment programs, nursery schools, public and private pre-kindergartens and kindergartens, and federally funded Head Start programs.

effective school A school in which learning for all students is maximized.

e-mail (electronic mail) A system that allows a message to be sent via telecommunication from one person to one or more other people.

emphasis Verbal and vocal cues and repetition used to alert students to important information in a lesson.

English as a second language (ESL) programs Pull-out programs in which students are provided with supplementary English instruction or modified instruction in content areas; also called *sheltered English programs.*

English classical school A free secondary school designed to meet the needs of boys not planning to attend college. The English Classical School of Boston, established in 1824, was the first such school.

enrichment An approach to gifted and talented education that provides richer and varied content through strategies that supplement usual grade-level work.

epistemology A branch of philosophy that examines questions of how we come to know what we know.

equitable distribution The practice of calling on all students—both volunteers and nonvolunteers—as equally as possible.

essentialism An educational philosophy suggesting that there is a critical core of information that all people should possess, so education should emphasize basic skills and academic subjects.

establishment clause First Amendment clause that prohibits the establishment of a national religion in the United States.

ethics See *professional ethics.*

ethnicity A person's ancestry; the way individuals identify themselves with the nation from which they or their ancestors came. Members of an ethnic group have a common identity defined by their history, language (although sometimes not spoken), customs, and traditions.

evolution The theory suggesting that all living things have changed in response to environmental conditions through a process of natural selection.

example A specific real-world instance of an object or event.

existentialism A traditional philosophy suggesting that humanity isn't part of an orderly universe, so individuals create their own existence in their own unique ways.

experts People who are highly experienced, knowledgeable, and skilled in a field.

explicit curriculum The curriculum found in textbooks, curriculum guides, courses of study, and other formal educational experiences; it includes everything teachers are expected to teach, what learners are expected to learn, and what schools are held accountable for.

extracurriculum The part of the curriculum that consists of learning experiences (such as sports and clubs) that extend beyond the core of students' formal studies.

extrinsic rewards Rewards that come from outside oneself; in teaching, they include job security, salaries, and summer vacations.

fair use guidelines Policies that specify limitations in the use of copyrighted materials for educational purposes.

Family Educational Rights and Privacy Act See *Buckley Amendment.*

feedback Information about current performance that can be used to increase future learning.

field dependence/independence A learning style difference indicating an individual's ability to identify relevant information in a complex and potentially confusing background. *Field-dependent* people see patterns as wholes; *field-independent* people are able to analyze complex patterns into their constituent parts.

formative evaluation The process of gathering information and providing feedback that teachers can use to improve their practice.

four-by-four block schedule A type of secondary schedule in which students take four classes a day of approximately 90–100 minutes for one semester. Courses that take a year in the traditional system are completed in one semester in the four-by-four plan.

free exercise clause First Amendment clause that prohibits the government from interfering with individuals' rights to hold religious beliefs and freely practice religion.

gender-role identity differences Expectations and beliefs about appropriate roles and behaviors of the two sexes.

general pedagogical knowledge A general understanding of instruction and management that transcends individual topics or subject-matter areas.

gifted and talented A designation given to students at the upper end of the ability continuum who need special services to reach their full potential.

goals What teachers want students to understand or be able to do when they complete a lesson.

grade retention The practice of having students repeat a grade if they don't meet certain criteria.

Head Start A federal compensatory education program designed to help 3- to 4-year-old disadvantaged children enter school ready to learn; also provides assistance to families of the children.

hidden curriculum See *implicit curriculum.*

high-collective-efficacy schools Schools in which most of the teachers are high in personal teaching efficacy. See *personal teaching efficacy.*

high-impact teachers Effective teachers for students placed at-risk who create caring, personal learning environments and assume responsibility for their students' progress.

high-stakes tests Assessments used to determine whether or not students will be promoted from one grade to another, graduate from high school, or have access to specific fields of study.

homeschooling An educational option in which parents educate their children at home.

hypermedia A computer-based system of information representation in which data in various formats—text, graphics, audio, or video—are stored in interlinked nodes.

icon A picture on a computer screen that acts as a symbol for some action or item.

idealism A traditional philosophy asserting that, because the physical world is constantly changing, ideas are the only reliable form of reality.

immersion programs Programs for English language learners in which students learn English by being "immersed" in classrooms where English is the only language spoken.

implicit curriculum The kinds of learning children acquire from the nature and organization of the school and the attitudes and behaviors of their teachers; also called the *hidden curriculum* or *informal curriculum.*

impulsive students In learning style theory, students who work quickly but make errors. Impulsive students perform better on activities requiring factual information. Compare *reflective students.*

inclusion A comprehensive approach to educating students with exceptionalities that advocates a total, systematic, and coordinated web of services.

induction programs Professional experiences for beginning teachers that provide systematic and sustained assistance to ease the transition into teaching.

informal curriculum See *implicit curriculum.*

in loco parentis Legal principle that requires teachers to use the same judgment and care as parents in protecting the children under their supervision.

instruction The ways in which the curriculum is taught.

instructional alignment The consistency among goals, learning activities, practice, seatwork, homework, and assessments.

instructional technology A combination of the processes and tools involved in addressing educational needs and problems, with an emphasis on applying the most current electronic tools.

integrated curriculum A curriculum in which concepts and skills from various disciplines are combined and related.

intelligence A construct that is commonly thought to comprise three dimensions: the capacity to acquire knowledge, the ability to think and reason in the abstract, and the ability to solve problems.

Internet A complex web of interconnections among computers that allows tens of millions of people to communicate and share information worldwide.

intrinsic rewards Rewards that come from within oneself and are personally satisfying for emotional or intellectual reasons.

junior high schools Schools created to provide a unique academic curriculum for early adolescent youth. The first junior high was created in 1909; today, these schools are increasingly being replaced by middle schools.

knowledge of learners and learning An understanding of students and how they learn.

language clarity Clearness of language that results from eliminating vague terms (such as *perhaps, maybe, might, and so on*, and *usually*).

latchkey children Children who go home to empty houses after school and who are left alone until parents arrive home from work.

Latin grammar school A type of college-preparatory school originally designed to help boys prepare for the ministry or, later, a career in law. The Boston Latin School, established in 1635, was the first such school in colonial America.

learner-centered instruction An approach to instruction in which teachers guide learners toward an understanding of the topics they study, rather than explaining content to them.

learning (behaviorist view) A change in observable behavior that occurs as a result of experience.

learning (cognitive view) A change in a person's mental representations of the world that may or may not result in an immediate change in behavior.

learning disabilities Exceptionalities that involve difficulties in acquiring and using listening, speaking, reading, writing, reasoning, or mathematical abilities.

learning style A preferred way of learning or processing information.

least restrictive environment (LRE) An environment that places students in as typical an educational setting as possible while still meeting their special academic, social, and physical needs. The right of a student with a disability to be placed in the LRE is mandated by the Individuals with Disabilities Education Act.

licensure The process by which a state evaluates the credentials of prospective teachers to ensure that they have achieved satisfactory levels of teaching competence and are morally fit to work with youth.

local school board A group of elected lay citizens responsible for setting policies that determine how a school district operates.

logic A branch of philosophy that examines the processes of deriving valid conclusions from basic principles.

looping The practice of keeping a teacher with one group of students for more than a year.

low-impact teachers Teachers who are ineffective for students placed at-risk because they are authoritarian, distancing themselves from students and placing primary responsibility for learning on them.

magnet schools Public schools originally developed to aid in the integration of White and minority students by providing innovative or specialized programs and accepting enrollment from students in all parts of a district.

mainstreaming The practice in special education of moving students with exceptionalities from segregated settings into regular education classrooms, often for selected activities only.

maintenance language programs Bilingual education programs in which the first language is maintained through reading and writing activities in the first language while English is introduced.

mental retardation An exceptionality that includes limitations in intellectual functioning, as indicated by difficulties in learning, and problems with adaptive skills, such as communication, self-care, and social ability.

mentors Experienced teachers who provide guidance and support for beginning teachers.

merit pay A supplement to a teacher's base salary to reward superior performance.

metacognition Students' awareness of the ways they learn most effectively and their ability to control these factors.

metaphysics A branch of philosophy that examines what we know; also called *ontology.*

microworld See *simulation.*

middle class A socioeconomic status category composed of managers, administrators, and white-collar workers who perform nonmanual work.

middle schools Schools, typically for grades 6–8, specifically designed to help students through the rapid social, emotional, and intellectual changes characteristic of early adolescence.

modeling Exhibiting behavior that is observed and imitated by others. Because of the tendency of people to imitate others, teachers should behave in ways they would like their students to imitate.

modified school calendars School calendars that eliminate long summer holidays without changing the total length of the school year.

moral education An approach to developing morality that emphasizes the development of students' moral reasoning but doesn't establish a preset list of values that learners should acquire. Compare *character education.*

multicultural education A catch-all term for a variety of strategies schools use to accommodate cultural differences and provide educational opportunities for all students.

multiple intelligences A theory of intelligence posited by Howard Gardner that suggests that overall intelligence is composed of eight relatively independent dimensions.

nature view of intelligence A view of intellectual development that asserts that intelligence is primarily determined by genetics.

negligence A teacher's or other school employee's failure to exercise sufficient care in protecting students from injury.

normal schools Two-year institutions developed in the early 1800s to prepare prospective elementary teachers. Normal schools were replaced by the present system of higher education in which teacher education is part of a larger college or university.

normative philosophy A description of the way something ought to be—for example, a description of the way educators ought to practice.

notoriety The extent to which a teacher's behavior becomes known and controversial.

novices People who are unskilled, inexperienced, and lack knowledge in a field.

null curriculum Topics left out of the course of study.

nurture view of intelligence A view of intellectual development that emphasizes the influence of the environment on intelligence.

obedience model of management An approach to classroom management in which teachers teach students to follow rules and obey authority through the use of reward and punishment. Compare *responsibility model of management.*

Old Deluder Satan Act A landmark piece of legislation, the Massachusetts Act of 1647, designed to create scripture-literate citizens who would thwart Satan's trickery.

ontology See *metaphysics.*

overlapping A teacher's ability to attend to more than one classroom activity at a time.

pedagogical content knowledge An understanding of ways to represent topics so they're comprehensible to others and an understanding of what makes topics easy or difficult to learn.

perennialism An educational philosophy suggesting that nature—including human nature—is constant, so education should focus on the classic intellectual pursuits that have endured throughout history.

performance assessment A form of alternative assessment in which learners are asked to demonstrate their competence in a lifelike situation.

personal teaching efficacy A teacher's belief that he or she can promote learning in all students regardless of their backgrounds.

philosophy A study of theories of knowledge, truth, existence, and good.

philosophy of education A type of philosophy that guides professional practice and provides a framework for thinking about educational issues.

portfolio A collection of materials representative of one's work, such as a professional portfolio or a student portfolio.

portfolio assessment A form of alternative assessment in which teachers evaluate collections of student work using preset criteria.

postmodernism An educational philosophy that contends that many of the institutions in our society, including schools, are used by those in power to control and marginalize those who lack power.

poverty thresholds Household income levels, determined by the federal government, that are meant to represent the lowest earnings needed to meet basic living needs. In 2001 the poverty level for a family of four was $18,267.

pragmatism A traditional philosophy that rejects the idea of absolute, unchanging truth, instead asserting that truth is what works.

principal The individual given the ultimate administrative responsibility for a school's operation.

problem-based learning An instructional strategy that uses a problem and the data gathered in attempts to solve it as the focal point of a lesson.

procedures Management routines students follow in their daily learning activities.

productive learning environment An environment that is orderly and focuses on learning.

professional ethics A set of moral standards for professional behavior.

professionalism Professional character, often seen as including these dimensions: a specialized body of knowledge, emphasis on decision making, reflection, autonomy, and ethical standards for conduct. Professionalism is a developing aspect of teaching.

professional portfolio A collection of work produced by a prospective teacher to document developing knowledge and skills.

progressive education An educational movement, which gained prominence during the early to mid-twentieth century, that advocates a child-centered curriculum that encourages individual problem solving. This educational philosophy is known as *progressivism.*

progressivism An educational philosophy emphasizing curricula that focus on real-world problem solving and individual development.

prompt A teacher question or directive that elicits a student response after the student has failed to answer or has given an incorrect or incomplete answer.

questioning frequency The number of times a teacher asks a question during a given period of instructional time.

realism A traditional philosophy asserting that the features of the universe exist whether or not a human being is there to perceive them.

reduction in force The elimination of teaching positions because of declining student enrollment or school funds; also called "riffing."

reflection The act of thinking about what you're doing. Engaging in reflection is one of the characteristics of a professional.

reflective practitioner A professional continually involved in the process of examining and evaluating the effectiveness of his or her own practice.

reflective students In learning style theory, students who analyze and deliberate before answering. Reflective students perform better on problem-solving activities. Compare *impulsive students.*

reforms Suggested changes in teaching and teacher preparation intended to increase the amount students learn.

resilient students Students placed at-risk who have been able to rise above adverse conditions to succeed in school and in other aspects of life.

responsibility model of management An approach to classroom management in which teachers teach students to make responsible choices by explaining reasons for rules and applying logical consequences for misbehavior. Compare *obedience model of management.*

résumé A document that provides an overview of an individual's job qualifications and work experience.

rules Statements that provide standards for acceptable classroom behavior.

school district An administrative unit within a state that is defined by geographical boundaries and is legally responsible for the public education of children within those boundaries.

separate but equal A policy of segregating minorities in education, transportation, housing, and other areas of public life if opportunities and facilities were considered equal to those of nonminorities. In education, the policy was evidenced by separate schools with different curricula, teaching methods, teachers, and resources.

service learning An approach to character education that combines service to the community with content learning objectives with the intent that the activity change both the recipient and the provider of the service.

sexual harassment Unwanted and unwelcome sexual behavior that interferes with another person's life.

sheltered English programs See *English as a second language (ESL) programs.*

simulation A program, either in software or Web-based form, that models a real or imaginary system in order to help learners understand that system; also called *microworld.*

single-gender classes and schools Classes and schools where boys and girls are segregated for part or all of the day.

site-based decision making A school management reform movement that attempts to place increased responsibility for governance at the individual school level.

social institution An organization with established structures and rules designed to promote certain goals.

socioeconomic status (SES) The combination of income, occupation, and level of education that describes a family or individual.

software Programs written in a computer language that tell the computer what to do. Educational software is used to deliver instruction.

special education Instruction designed to meet the unique needs of students with exceptionalities.

spreadsheet program A computer program that organizes and manipulates numerical data.

standards Statements specifying what students should know and what skills they should have upon completing an area of study.

standards-based education The process of focusing curricula and instruction on predetermined levels of performance on goals, or standards. See *standards.*

state board of education The legal governing body that exercises general control and supervision of the schools in a state.

state office of education The administrative branch of state government responsible for implementing education policy on a day-to-day basis.

state tuition tax-credit plans A variation on school voucher programs in which parents are given tax credits for money they spend on private-school tuition.

students placed at-risk Students in danger of failing to complete their education with the skills necessary to survive in modern society.

students with exceptionalities Learners who need special help and resources to reach their full potential.

summative evaluation The process of gathering information about a teacher's competence, often for the purpose of making administrative decisions about retention and promotion.

superintendent A school district's head administrative officer who, along with his or her staff, is responsible for implementing school board policy in the district's schools.

teacher-centered instruction An approach to instruction in which teachers carefully specify goals, present the content to be learned, and actively direct learning activities.

teaching contract A legal employment agreement between a teacher and a local school board.

technician A person who uses specific skills to complete well-defined tasks, such as an electrician wiring an outlet.

tenure A legal safeguard that provides job security by preventing teacher dismissal without cause.

thematic lesson A lesson in which all parts of a teacher's instruction are related, so that the lesson leads to a specific point.

theory A set of related principles that are based on observation and are used to explain additional observations.

Title I A federal compensatory education program that funds educational services for low-income students in elementary and secondary schools.

tracking A comprehensive form of ability grouping at the secondary level that places students in a series of different classes or curricula on the basis of ability and career goals.

transition programs Bilingual education programs in which students learn to read in their first language and are given supplementary instruction in English as a second language. Once English is mastered, students are placed in regular classrooms and the first language is discontinued.

transition signals Verbal statements within a lesson that indicate one idea is ending and another is beginning.

tutorial A software program that delivers an entire integrated instructional sequence similar to a teacher's instruction on the topic.

underclass A socioeconomic status category composed of people with low incomes who continually struggle with economic problems.

upper class A socioeconomic status category composed of highly educated (usually a college degree), highly paid (usually above $100,000) professionals that make up about 15 percent or less of the population.

URL (uniform resource locator) A series of letters and/or symbols that act as an address for a site on the Internet.

voucher A check or written document that parents can use to purchase educational services. Vouchers are designed to provide parents with greater school choice.

wait-time A period of silence after a question is asked that allows students a few seconds to think about their answers.

War on Poverty A general term for federal government programs designed to eradicate poverty during the 1960s.

Web sites Locations on the World Wide Web each identified with a uniform resource locator (URL).

within-class ability grouping A form of ability grouping that divides students within one classroom into high, medium, and low groups with instruction adapted to the needs of each group. Within-class grouping is used most commonly at the elementary level, particularly in reading and math.

withitness A teacher's awareness of what is going on in all parts of the classroom at all times and the communication of this awareness to students both verbally and nonverbally.

zero tolerance policies School discipline policies that call for students to receive automatic suspensions or expulsions as punishment for certain offenses, primarily those involving weapons, threats, or drugs.

Name Index

Subject Index